Lecture Notes in Computer Science   **10469**

Commenced Publication in 1973
Founding and Former Series Editors:
Gerhard Goos, Juris Hartmanis, and Jan van Leeuwen

Formal Methods

Subline of Lectures Notes in Computer Science

More information about this series at http://www.springer.com/series/7407

Alessandro Cimatti · Marjan Sirjani (Eds.)

Software Engineering and Formal Methods

15th International Conference, SEFM 2017
Trento, Italy, September 4–8, 2017
Proceedings

Springer

Editors
Alessandro Cimatti ⓘ
University of Trento
Trento
Italy

Marjan Sirjani ⓘ
Mälardalen University
Västerås
Sweden

ISSN 0302-9743   ISSN 1611-3349 (electronic)
Lecture Notes in Computer Science
ISBN 978-3-319-66196-4   ISBN 978-3-319-66197-1 (eBook)
DOI 10.1007/978-3-319-66197-1

Library of Congress Control Number: 2017949511

LNCS Sublibrary: SL1 – Theoretical Computer Science and General Issues

Printed on acid-free paper

This Springer imprint is published by Springer Nature
The registered company is Springer International Publishing AG
The registered company address is: Gewerbestrasse 11, 6330 Cham, Switzerland

Preface

This volume contains the papers presented at SEFM 2017, the 15th International Conference on Software Engineering and Formal Methods, held on September 4–8 in Trento, Italy. SEFM 2017 was organized and hosted by the Fondazione Bruno Kessler (FBK), Trento, Italy.

The SEFM conference aims to bring together leading researchers and practitioners from academia, industry and government, to advance the state of the art in formal methods, to facilitate their uptake in the software industry, and to encourage their integration within practical software engineering methods and tools. The topics of interest for submission included the following aspects of software engineering and formal methods:

- New frontiers in software architecture: self-adaptive, service-oriented, and cloud computing systems; component-based, object-based, and multi-agent systems; real-time, hybrid, and embedded systems; reconfigurable systems
- Software verification and testing: model checking and theorem proving; verification and validation; probabilistic verification and synthesis; testing
- Software development methods: requirement analysis, modeling, specification, and design; light-weight and scalable formal methods
- Application and technology transfer: case studies, best practices, and experience reports; tool integration
- Security and safety: security and mobility; safety-critical, fault-tolerant, and secure systems; software certification
- Design principles: domain-specific languages, type theory, abstraction, and refinement

SEFM 2017 hosted six workshops:

- FAACS – Formal Approaches for Advanced Computing Systems
- MSE – Microservices: Science and Engineering
- POTENTIAL – Technology Transfer in Software Engineering and Formal Methods
- DataMod – From Data to Models and Back
- CoSim-CPS – Formal Co-Simulation of Cyber-Physical Systems
- FOCLASA – Foundations of Coordination Languages and Self-Adaptive Systems

SEFM 2017 solicited full research papers describing original research results, case studies and tools, and short papers on new ideas and work-in-progress, describing new approaches, techniques and/or tools that are not fully validated yet. We received 102 submissions (88 full and 14 short) from 36 different countries. Each submission was reviewed by at least four Program Committee members. We accepted 22 regular papers, with an acceptance rate of 25%. We also accepted 6 short papers on new ideas and work-in-progress. The program also included three remarkable invited talks:

- Marsha Chechik, from the University of Toronto, Canada, presented "Software Safety and Security, Assurance Cases and Model Management".
- Jeff Kramer, from Imperial College London, UK, presented "The Challenge of Change".
- Alberto Sangiovanni-Vincentelli, from the University of California, Berkeley, USA, presented "A Formal Contract-Based Design Methodology for Cyber-Physical Systems".

Our first words of thanks go to the Program Committee members and to the external reviewers, who carried out thorough and careful reviews and enabled the assembly of this high-quality work. We thank the authors for their submissions, and for their collaboration in further improving their papers. A special word of thanks goes to our invited speakers, Marsha Chechick, Jeff Kramer and Alberto Sangiovanni-Vincentelli, for accepting our invitation and for their very stimulating contributions. We also thank the workshop chairs, Antonio Cerone and Marco Roveri, and the organizers of the workshops: Paolo Arcaini, Marina Mongiello, Elvinia Riccobene and Patrizia Scandurra (FAACS); Marcello M. Bersani, Antonio Bucchiarone, Luca Ferrucci, Manuel Mazzara, Fabrizio Montesi and Nicola Dragoni (MSE); Roberto Confalonieri and Andrea Janes (POTENTIAL); Paolo Milazzo, Vashti Galpin and Andre Teixeira (DataMod); Cinzia Bernardeschi, Paolo Masci and Peter Gorm Larsen (CoSim-CPS); Carlos Canal and Gwen Salaün (FOCLASA). Many thanks to Alberto Griggio (publicity chair) and Gianni Zampedri (web master). A special word of thanks goes to Annalisa Armani and to all the other members of the Ufficio Eventi of FBK, who largely contributed to the success of this event. We also thank the developers and maintainers of the EasyChair conference management system, which was of great help in handling paper submission, reviewing, discussion, and the assembly of the proceedings. Finally, we are most grateful to Hossein Hojjat, who provided invaluable help in the preparation of the conference proceedings.

July 2017

Alessandro Cimatti
Marjan Sirjani

Organization

Program Committee

Wolfgang Ahrendt	Chalmers University of Technology, Sweden
Farhad Arbab	CWI and Leiden University, Netherlands
Luis Barbosa	Universidade do Minho, Portugal
Antonia Bertolino	ISTI-CNR, Italy
Dirk Beyer	LMU Munich, Germany
Jonathan Bowen	London South Bank University, UK
Mario Bravetti	University of Bologna, Italy
Ana Cavalcanti	University of York, UK
Alessandro Cimatti	FBK, Italy
Paul Curzon	Queen Mary University of London, UK
Hung Dang Van	UET, Vietnam National University, Hanoi
Jim Davies	University of Oxford, UK
Rocco De Nicola	IMT - School for Advanced Studies Lucca, Italy
Patricia Derler	National Instruments, USA
John Derrick	Unversity of Sheffield, UK
Anke Dittmar	University of Rostock, Germany
George Eleftherakis	The University of Sheffield International Faculty, CITY College, Greece
José Luiz Fiadeiro	Royal Holloway, University of London, UK
Wan Fokkink	Vrije Universiteit Amsterdam, Netherlands
Adrian Francalanza	University of Malta, Malta
Hubert Garavel	Inria Rhône-Alpes/CONVECS, France
Dimitra Giannakopoulou	NASA Ames, USA
Stefania Gnesi	ISTA-CNR, Italy
Klaus Havelund	Jet Propulsion Laboratory, California Institute of Technology, USA
Rob Hierons	Brunel University London, UK
Hossein Hojjat	Rochester Institute of Technology, USA
Michaela Huhn	Ostfalia, Germany
Einar Broch Johnsen	University of Oslo, Norway
Gabriel Juhas	Slovak University of Technology, Bratislava, Slovakia
Jens Knoop	TU Wien, Austria
Paddy Krishnan	Oracle, Australia
Eva Kühn	TU Wien, Austria
Kung-Kiu Lau	The University of Manchester, UK
Sergio Mover	University of Colorado Boulder, USA
Viet Yen Nguyen	Hypefactors, Denmark
Fernando Orejas	UPC, Barcelona, Spain

Corina Pasareanu	CMU/NASA Ames Research Center, USA
Marinella Petrocchi	IIT-CNR, Italy
Anna Philippou	University of Cyprus, Cyprus
Sanjiva Prasad	Indian Institute of Technology, India
Geguang Pu	East China Normal University, China
Leila Ribeiro	UFRGS, Federal University of Rio Grande do Sul, Brazil
Bernhard Rumpe	RWTH Aachen University, Germany
Gwen Salaün	Grenoble INP - Inria - LIG, France
Augusto Sampaio	Federal University of Pernambuco, Brazil
Vesna Sesum-Cavic	TU Wien, Austria
Marjan Sirjani	Malardalen University, Sweden
Graeme Smith	University of Queensland, Australia
Bernhard Steffen	University of Dortmund, Germany
Markus Stumptner	University of South Australia, Australia
Francesco Tiezzi	Università di Camerino, Italy
Danny Weyns	Linnaeus University, Sweden

Additional Reviewers

Achilleos, Antonis	Dokter, Kasper
Adam, Kai	Dongol, Brijesh
Attard, Duncan	Eikermann, Robert
Åman Pohjola, Johannes	Ertl, M. Anton
Banach, Richard	Fazzolari, Michela
Barbon, Gianluca	Fedyukovich, Grigory
Basile, Davide	Fornari, Fabrizio
Bertram, Vincent	Friedberger, Karlheinz
Blanchette, Jasmin Christian	Grech, Neville
Bliudze, Simon	Green, Ryan
Bolognesi, Tommaso	Greifenberg, Timo
Bride, Hadrien	Grossmann, Georg
Bubel, Richard	Guo, Jian
Butting, Arvid	Howar, Falk
Carvalho, Gustavo	Inverso, Omar
Cassar, Ian	Jebali, Fatma
Chen, Yuting	K.R., Raghavendra
Chimento, Jesus Mauricio	Kappé, Tobias
Colvin, Robert	Kautz, Oliver
Cooper, Gregory	Kourtis, Georgios
Crass, Stefan	Krall, Andreas
Cresci, Stefano	Kusmenko, Evgeny
Dangl, Matthias	Lang, Frédéric
De Angelis, Francesco	Lazovik, Alexander
Del Vigna, Fabio	Lemberger, Thomas
Din, Crystal Chang	Li, Jianwen

Loreti, Michele
Lu, Yi
Luiz Leite Jr., Fabio
Madeira, Alexandre
Maggi, Alessandro
Margheri, Andrea
Marsso, Lina
Martins, Francisco
Matteucci, Ilaria
Mauro, Jacopo
Mavridou, Anastasia
Mayer, Wolfgang
Mazzanti, Franco
Messinger, Anita
Miao, Weikai
Morichetta, Andrea
Mota, Alexandre
Muzi, Chiara
Nelson, Tim
Olesen, Mads Chr.
Oliveira, Marcel Vinicius Medeiros
Owens, Scott
Ozeer, Umar
Pinisetty, Srinivas
Planer, Martin
Polini, Andrea
Proenca, Jose
Pun, Ka I
Puntigam, Franz
Pérez, Jorge A.
Qiang, Wang

Raco, Deni
Radschek, Sophie Therese
Razavi, Joseph
Re, Barbara
Riely, James
Robillard, Simon
Rossi, Lorenzo
Rossi, Matteo
Rüthing, Oliver
Saracino, Andrea
Saraiva, João
Schlatte, Rudolf
Schoepe, Daniel
Seceleanu, Cristina
Selway, Matt
Serwe, Wendelin
Tapia Tarifa, Silvia Lizeth
Tesei, Luca
Tognazzi, Stefano
Trivedi, Ashutosh
Tutu, Ionut
Vandin, Andrea
von Wenckstern, Michael
Vorobyov, Kostyantyn
Voß, Jan-Niklas
Weber, Jean-Francois
Wehrheim, Heike
Welch, James
Wendler, Philipp
Winter, Kirsten

Invited Talks

The Challenge of Change

Jeff Kramer

Department of Computing, Imperial College London, London, UK
j.kramer@imperial.ac.uk

Abstract. One of the grand challenges of our time is the provision of self-managing adaptive systems. In the extreme, these are required to handle unexpected and unplanned changes that occur at run-time. These unexpected changes can be in any or all of the following: the environment in which the system operates, the capabilities of the system, or in the requirements and goals that the system should achieve. Although ad hoc techniques can be used for specific circumstances, what we need are rigorous, comprehensive, and pragmatic approaches to deal with the challenges that operational run-time change presents. Formal models, appropriate for the aspects of concern, are essential to support dynamic (semi-) automatic reasoning about change. Furthermore, these models need to be available at runtime and should themselves be amenable to modification. These models@runtime are needed for aspects such as domain modelling and model revision, software configuration and reconfiguration, requirements goals and goal revision and planning and plan revision. The foundation necessary to support these models@runtime is a sound software architecture. This talk will elaborate on this vision and propose a software architecture to support run-time change and adaptation.

Software Safety and Security, Assurance Cases and Model Management

Marsha Chechik

Department of Computer Science, University of Toronto,
Toronto, ON, M5S2E4, Canada
chechik@cs.toronto.edu

Abstract. From financial services platforms to social networks to vehicle control, software has come to mediate many activities of daily life. Governing bodies and standards organizations have responded to this trend by creating regulations and standards to address issues such as safety, security and privacy. In this environment, the compliance of software development to standards and regulations has emerged as a key requirement; yet, software compliance is a costly and complex goal to achieve. For example, one estimate of the cost of compliance in the US to the Sarbanes-Oxley Act (SOX) is $8B per year [1]. Regulatory compliance creates software development complexity in various ways. An organization may have to comply with multiple standards due to multiple jurisdictions or to address different aspects of the software, and these may overlap and conflict with each other. Evidence of compliance must be collected, managed and linked to an *assurance case* that contains the claims and arguments for compliance. When software evolves, compliance must be reassessed, which can delay the release of changes. Finally, maintaining families of related software products (product lines) multiplies the effort even further.

Standards, development artifacts and compliance evidence can all be expressed as *models*. The field of Model Management [2] has emerged to address another software development complexity problem – the proliferation of software models in model-driven software development [3]. Model management focuses on a high-level view in which entire models and their relationships (i.e., mappings between models) can be manipulated using specialized operators to achieve useful outcomes.

In this talk, we look at the connection between compliance and modeling to reduce compliance complexity and cost, as well as to facilitate reuse and evolution, with a special focus on automotive software development [4, 5].

Acknowledgements

Joint work with Sahar Kokaly, Rick Salay, Tom Maibaum, Mark Lawford, Alessio DiSandro, Nick Fung.

References

1. Carney, W.J.: The costs of being public after sarbanes-oxley: the irony of going private. Emory LJ **55**, 141 (2006)
2. Bernstein, P.A.: Applying model management to classical meta data problems. In: Proceedings of the CIDR 2003, vol. 2003, pp. 209–220 (2003)
3. Beydeda, S., Book, M., Gruhn, V., et al.: Model-Driven Software Development. vol. 15, Springer, Heidelberg (2005)
4. Kokaly, S., Salay, R., Chechik, M., Lawford, M., Maibaum, T.: Safety case impact assessment in automotive software systems: an improved model-based approach. In: Proceedings of the SafeComp 2017 (2017)
5. Kokaly, S., Salay, R., Cassano, V., Maibaum, T., Chechik, M.: A model management approach for assurance case reuse due to system evolution. In: Proceedings of the MoDELS 2016, pp.196–206 (2016)

A Formal Contract-Based Design Methodology for CyberPhysical Systems

Alberto Sangiovanni-Vincentelli

Department of Electrical Engineering and Computer Sciences,
University of California, Berkeley
alberto@berkeley.edu

Abstract. In cyber-physical systems (CPS) computing, networking and control (typically regarded as the "cyber" part of the system) are tightly intertwined with mechanical, electrical, thermal, chemical or biological processes (the "physical" part). The increasing sophistication and heterogeneity of these systems requires radical changes in the way sense-and-control platforms are designed to regulate them. In this presentation, I introduce a design methodology whereby platform-based design is combined with assume-guarantee contracts to formalize the design process and enable realization of CPS architectures and control software in a hierarchical and compositional manner.

Contents

Information Flow Tracking for Linux Handling Concurrent System Calls and Shared Memory

Laurent Georget[1]([⊠]), Mathieu Jaume[2], Guillaume Piolle[1], Frédéric Tronel[1], and Valérie Viet Triem Tong[1]

[1] EPC CIDRE CentraleSupelec/Inria/CNRS/Université de Rennes 1, Rennes, France
`laurent.georget@irisa.fr`
[2] Sorbonne Universités, UPMC, CNRS, LIP6 UMR 7606, Paris, France

Abstract. Information flow control can be used at the Operating System level to enforce restrictions on the diffusion of security-sensitive data. In Linux, information flow trackers are often implemented as Linux Security Modules. They can fail to monitor some indirect flows when flows occur concurrently and affect the same containers of information. Furthermore, they are not able to monitor the flows due to file mappings in memory and shared memory between processes. We first present two attacks to evade state-of-the-art LSM-based trackers. We then describe an approach, formally proved with Coq [12] to perform information flow tracking able to cope with concurrency and in-memory flows. We demonstrate its implementability and usefulness in Rfblare, a race condition-free version of the flow tracking done by KBlare [4].

Keywords: Information flow tracking · Linux · LSM

1 Introduction

Information Flow Control (IFC) at the Operating System (OS) scale is a security mechanism preventing leaks or improper manipulation of information stored in the system. At the OS level, flows are the actions of the processes causing the copy of data from a container of information to another. Containers are OS-level abstractions such as processes, files, message queues, network sockets, etc. The security status of each container is given by a security label, called a *taint*, initially set by a security officer. The taint of a container encodes the history of the flows that have altered its content. Consider the situation presented here:

The process *cp* copies a *file*, that the process *wc* reads to output the number of lines in it. *file* is originally tainted with ⋆, *cp* with †, *wc* with •. IFC maintains the knowledge of past flows in the system through *taint propagation*. When a flow occurs, the taint of the destination is updated with the taint of the source, in order to record the flow in the system. Assuming flows are performed from

A. Cimatti and M. Sirjani (Eds.): SEFM 2017, LNCS 10469, pp. 1–16, 2017.
DOI: 10.1007/978-3-319-66197-1_1

left to right in the example, we see that the taint from the *file* is propagated to *cp* and then to the *copy* and *wc*, and eventually to */dev/stdout*. The focus of this article is on three IFC systems developed for the generic Linux kernel: KBlare [4], Laminar [9,11], and the Android Linux kernel: Weir [8].

The implementations of Laminar, KBlare, and Weir are based on the Linux Security Modules (LSM) framework. This framework provides (1) extra security fields in Linux's internal data structures and (2) a set of callbacks, called LSM *hooks*, positioned in the code of system calls. Security mechanisms can register functions on these hooks to be executed just before security-sensitive operations are made, to enforce security decisions. The crucial property we expect from these systems is that they are able to correctly track all flows in the system. If malware could escape them, the confidentiality and integrity of user data would no longer be guaranteed.

However, the LSM framework has been conceived primarily for access control, and not for IFC [14] so it is not obvious that it is also appropriate for this purpose. In a previous work [3], we have developed an approach to verify that LSM hooks were available in each system call generating an information flow, so that an information flow tracker could monitor all of them. This is a necessary condition to implement a correct information flow tracker. This approach led to the identification of some shortcomings in the placement of LSM hooks and the addition of a few hooks. This necessary condition is nevertheless not a *sufficient* one. Indeed, detecting each individual direct flow is not equivalent to detecting *all* flows. Flows occurring concurrently in the system and involving a common information container may cause *indirect* flows (i.e. compositions of individually detected flows) to be undetected. This is because the sequence ⟨detection of the flow by the tracker (a function registered in a LSM hook); actual occurrence of the flow (another function called later in the same system call)⟩ is not atomic, and thus taint propagation is subject to *race conditions*.

Information flow trackers also have to cope with the existence of *continuous flows*, which are started by one system call and stopped by another. A typical example of these flows is caused by shared memory segments. When a process shares a memory segment with another one, they can freely communicate through it. No system call is required for a process to read and write its own memory, and thus, the trackers cannot see these individual flows. Therefore, they have to make the overapproximation that the flow is occurring "continuously" between the system call setting the shared memory up and the system call shutting it down. Even if a security mechanism could tolerate missing some flows, the hassle of handling race conditions is justified by the existence of these *continuous flows*, which cannot be monitored otherwise. Comments in the source code of Blare and Laminar stress the importance of the issue and the lack of a straightforward solution. In this article, we propose a solution to handle concurrency between system calls as well as continuous flows. To the best of our knowledge, our approach is the first to propose a provably correct way to do so.

We propose three contributions in this article, described in Sects. 2, 3 and 4. The paper is organized as follows.

In Sect. 2, we detail two ways of evading Laminar, KBlare, and Weir by exploiting a race condition between a read and a write operations and by exploiting indirect continuous flows between files mapped in memory.

In Sect. 3, we describe formally the mechanism of taint propagation common to the three tools as well as the concrete flows of information between containers. We describe how considering flows as operations spanning over some time instead of atomic ones allow us to propose a new way of propagating taints that takes into account all possible flows in the system. We prove two properties on our result: (1) the overapproximation of flows we compute is sound, no flow can be missed; (2) the overapproximation is the smallest one in our model, i.e. any smaller overapproximation would be unsound because there would exist a way to perform an indirect flow missed by the algorithm. We have proved the correctness of our algorithm in our model with the Coq proof assistant [12].

In Sect. 4, we describe Rfblare, a new taint propagation mechanism for KBlare, implementing our solution from the previous point. We show that it correctly handles the attacks developed in the first point and encurs little overhead. This work describes precisely how the LSM framework can be modified to allow the implementation of correct flow tracking, independently from any particular semantics for the labels or any flow policy model.

We revise related works in Sect. 5 and conclude in Sect. 6. Due to space limitations, we give in this article an overview of our main results. Our complete implementation, tests, as well as the proofs of our formal results are available online on the project's website: https://blare-ids.org/rfblare.

2 Evading Existing Information Flow Trackers

2.1 Exploiting a Race Condition to Copy a File Without Its Taint

KBlare, Laminar and Weir use the `file_permission` LSM hook when a process reads from or writes to a file to perform the taint propagation. There is a risk of race conditions even on uniprocessor systems because the process is allowed to sleep and yield the CPU between the time the LSM hook is triggered and the time the function that actually performs the flow is called. This can be exploited to copy a file without its taint. Consider this example:

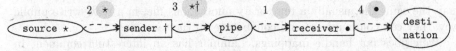

The dashed lines represent the observations of flows by the tracker (made in the order given by the numbering for the sake of this example) and the plain lines the actual flows in the system (done from left to right). The content from the *source* file is propagated to the *destination* via processes *sender* and *receiver* and the pipe. Nevertheless, since *receiver* has started reading from the pipe before *sender* has written to it, the taint is not propagated properly.

This attack works reliably and effectively on KBlare as a simple one-liner: `mkfifo pipe; cat < pipe > destination& cat < source > pipe`. On Weir, it is more difficult because processes benefit from a stricter isolation by default. To perform the attack, we have developed two toy applications. One offers a text box in which the user can write a message. When clicking on a send button, the process allocates a new security tag from the Weir tag manager and then copy this message to a pipe whose name is known by both applications. The other application has a text area and a receive button. Clicking on the latter copies the message from the pipe to the text area. We install both applications with the same user id so that they can share a folder, and we create the pipe inside. We observe that if the user clicks on send before clicking on receive, the logs from Weir show that the taint is correctly propagated to the *receiver*. However, clicking on receive first triggers the race condition. The apparent result is the same (the text appears in the *receiver*'s text area) but the logs show that the taint from the *sender* only reaches the *pipe* and not the *receiver*.

On Laminar, this attack is not possible because the developers put the entire system call in a critical section to prevent race conditions between concurrent reads and writes. However, this solution is not entirely satisfactory. First of all, it incurs sacrificing parallelism on very common system calls from the family of read and write. Reading a file from a high-latency filesystem (e.g. a network-backed filesystem) might block all other reads and writes for a long time. Secondly, many existing applications rely on the semantics that reading from an empty pipe blocks until it is written to. This is not possible if operations cannot interleave. Laminar does not care about this since it mandates that all pipes are open in non-blocking mode to avoid a covert channel but KBlare and Weir are committed not to require any porting of existing applications.

2.2 Making a Flow in Memory

Ordinarily, to read from and write to a file, a process uses system calls from the read and write family but this is not the only way. There exists a system call, mmap, which can make a file (or better said, the pages of cache memory buffering the file's content) appear as part of the process's memory space. When a file is mapped in its memory, a process can read from it and write to it (provided that the mapping has the read–write permissions) without system calls, by usual memory manipulations. Another system call, munmap, unmaps a file. The same mechanism is used to share memory segments between processes. If two processes map the same file, usually a temporary anonymous file, in a read–write public way, they can communicate and collaborate on the same data.

Weir does not handle mappings. Laminar has an interesting comment in its source code stating: "XXX: Should do something about mmaped files." [10, security/difc.c, l. 944] which suggests that the problem is known to the developers and considered important enough but is not trivially solvable. KBlare supports propagating taints between the file and the memory space of the process when the former is mapped. It also claims to handle shared memory segments by maintaining a list of attached shared memory segments for each process. When propagating taints from or to this process, the shared memory segments participate in the propagation [4]. The implementation is incomplete however and even the design is somewhat flawed. If processes A and B share memory, as well as processes B and C, we must consider that processes A and C share memory, although they do so indirectly. KBlare fails to handle that "transitivity".

We can reuse the attack from the previous section by replacing the reading by *sender* from *source* by a read-only mapping, the writing by *receiver* to *destination* by a read-write mapping and finally, the *pipe* by a shared memory segment between *receiver* and *sender*. We could not test it on KBlare, Laminar and Weir directly because of the lack of implementation on these platforms but a toy implementation of KBlare's described propagation [4] shows the problem: depending on the order in which the mappings and the shared memory are set up, taints are not propagated from *source* to *destination* in all cases, although the content from *source* is copied to *destination*.

These two attacks show that the trackers' observations are inconsistent with the actual flows altering the containers. A sound tracker needs at least to compute an overapproximation of the actual flows. To solve this problem, we propose in the following section a formal model of the propagation done by the trackers, what a perfect propagation would be and a way to compute a correct overapproximation of this perfect propagation in practice.

3   A New Algorithm for Taint Propagation

We propose a formal model of information flows between containers as well as a formal description of taint propagation in order to describe the shortcomings of current trackers and prove the correctness of our taint propagation.

3.1   Tags, Information Flows and Executions

A container is anything in the system that can carry data (usually originating from a user). Files, network sockets, pipes are examples of containers. We write $\mathcal{C}$ for the set of containers of information. Contrarily to most approaches, we do not consider processes or threads as containers of information *per se*. Instead, we consider that the *memory space* of each process is a container (i.e. a flow from/to a process is a flow from/to its memory). This distinction is useful since in Linux systems, it is possible to create distinct processes sharing their entire memory space, and thus the data they store and produce.

To record the origin of the information stored in any container, a tracker attaches a security label, also called a taint, to all of them. In our model, a taint is a set of *tags*. In the example above, we have chosen the set $\{\star, \dagger, \bullet\}$ as tags whereas actual implementations generally use a predefined range of integers. Without loss of generality, we consider that each container $c \in \mathcal{C}$ is initially associated to a unique tag written t^c. Intuitively, a tag represents a primary source of information in the system. Let $\mathcal{T} = \uplus_{c \in \mathcal{C}} \{t^c\}$ be the set of all tags. During the lifetime of the system, as information gets exchanged between containers, the tracker's task is to reflect these changes in the set of tags associated to the containers. This is the taint propagation.

Definition 1 (Configuration, Taint). *A configuration $\theta : \mathcal{C} \to \wp(\mathcal{T})$ maps each container to its set of tags. $\theta(c) = \{t^{c_1}, \ldots, t^{c_n}\}$ is called the* taint *of c and indicates that c contains information originating from containers $c_1, \ldots, c_n$.*

We write Θ for the set of configurations and θ_{init} for the initial configuration such that $\forall c \in \mathcal{C}$ $\theta_{init}(c) = \{t^c\}$. A configuration is an abstraction of the state of the containers, it represents an overapproximation of the sources of information contributing to the current content of a container. This state evolves upon occurrence of specific events relative to information flows. An information flow is the copy of (a portion of) the content of a container, called the *source* of the flow, into another, called the *destination*. We consider that an information flow is not an atomic operation. Instead, we consider that a flow is successively *enabled, executed* and *disabled*. The execution of the flow (i.e. the copy of information) may happen only after it is enabled, and before it is disabled. It may happen once, several times, or even not at all. Several different flows from a container c_1 to a container c_2 may occur during the lifetime of the system, and may even overlap. In order to distinguish them, we introduce the set $\mathcal{F}$ of flow identifiers (typically, we choose $\mathcal{F} = \mathbb{N}$ so that each flow is uniquely identified by a ever-increasing counter).

Definition 2 (Event). *Let $c_1, c_2 \in \mathcal{C}$ and $f \in \mathcal{F}$. We define the relation $c_1 \to_f c_2$ which is to be understood as a flow called f from c_1 to c_2. An event $e \in \mathcal{E}$ is either a pair $(f, (c_1, c_2))$ where $c_1 \xrightarrow{enable}_f c_2$ or $c_1 \xrightarrow{disable}_f c_2$, or a pair $(f, (c_1, c_2))$ where $c_1 \xrightarrow{exec}_f c_2$. We call the first set $\mathcal{O}$ and the second one $\mathcal{X}$. These relations have the following intuitive meaning:*

$c_1 \xrightarrow{enable}_f c_2$ *means that the flow named f from c_1 to c_2 is enabled*

$c_1 \xrightarrow{exec}_f c_2$ *means that the flow named f from c_1 to c_2 is executed*

$c_1 \xrightarrow{disable}_f c_2$ *means that the flow named f from c_1 to c_2 is disabled*

In other words, $\mathcal{O}$ contains the events enabling and disabling flows whereas $\mathcal{X}$ contains the events corresponding to actual flow executions.

We write $\mathbf{E} \subseteq \mathcal{E}^+$ for the set of executions, defined as non-empty sequences of events. We write $e[i]$ for the i-th event of an execution $e \in \mathbf{E}$, $\lg(e)$ the length of e and $e[:n]$ (resp. $e[n:]$) the prefix $(e[1], \ldots, e[n])$ of length n of e (resp. the suffix $(e[n], \ldots, e[\lg(e)])$ of length $\lg(e) - n + 1$ of e). Executions in $\mathbf{E}$ satisfy two conditions of causality: a flow is always enabled before being executed or disabled, and cannot be executed after it is disabled:

$$\forall i \ e[i] = c_1 \xrightarrow{disable}_f c_2 \vee e[i] = c_1 \xrightarrow{exec}_f c_2 \Rightarrow \tag{1}$$
$$\left(\exists j < i \ e[j] = c_1 \xrightarrow{enable}_f c_2 \wedge \left(\forall k \ j < k < i \Rightarrow (e[k] \neq c_1 \xrightarrow{disable}_f c_2) \right) \right)$$

We suppose that only events in $\mathcal{O}$ are observable by the tracker and that it cannot react on events in $\mathcal{X}$. This models the fact that a tracker cannot perform taint propagation all the time during the execution of a system call but only when the execution reaches a LSM hook. We write $\mathbf{O}$ the set of observable executions, containing only events in $\mathcal{O}$, and $\mathbf{X}$ the set of concrete executions, containing only events in $\mathcal{X}$. Observable executions are the sequences of events observed by the tracker whereas concrete executions describe the executions of flows, i.e. how the content of containers actually changes over time. Given $e \in \mathbf{E}$, we write $e_{\mathcal{O}} \in \mathbf{O}$ (resp. $e_{\mathcal{X}} \in \mathbf{X}$) the observable execution (resp. the concrete execution) obtained by removing the unobservable events (resp. the observable events) from e. We define a compatibility relation between observable and concrete executions.

Definition 3 (Compatibility). *An observable execution ω is compatible with a concrete execution x iff they are projections from an execution in $\mathbf{E}$. Formally, $\forall x \in \mathbf{X} \; \forall \omega \in \mathbf{O}$, we write $\omega \vdash x$ iff $\exists e \in \mathbf{E} \; (\omega = e_{\mathcal{O}} \wedge x = e_{\mathcal{X}})$.*

Example 1. We consider the first attack presented in Sect. 2 and illustrate it on the figure below. We abbreviate the name of the containers in the rest of this article: *src* is the source, *se* the sender, *p* the pipe, *r* the receiver and *d* the destination. The x column represents the concrete execution of flows between the containers of information. The ω column is the sequence of enabling and disabling events seen by the tracker. These two executions are compatible because there exists an execution e which is a linearization of both, respecting the causality conditions expressed by (1).

Event		e	ω	x
$p \xrightarrow{enable}_{f_1} r$		$e[1]$	$\omega[1]$	—
$src \xrightarrow{enable}_{f_2} se$		$e[2]$	$\omega[2]$	—
$src \xrightarrow{exec}_{f_2} se$		$e[3]$	—	$x[1]$
$src \xrightarrow{disable}_{f_2} se$		$e[4]$	$\omega[3]$	—
$se \xrightarrow{enable}_{f_3} p$		$e[5]$	$\omega[4]$	—
$se \xrightarrow{exec}_{f_3} p$		$e[6]$	—	$x[2]$
$p \xrightarrow{exec}_{f_1} r$		$e[7]$	—	$x[3]$
$p \xrightarrow{disable}_{f_1} r$		$e[8]$	$\omega[5]$	—
$se \xrightarrow{disable}_{f_3} p$		$e[9]$	$\omega[6]$	—
$r \xrightarrow{enable}_{f_4} d$		$e[10]$	$\omega[7]$	—
$r \xrightarrow{exec}_{f_4} d$		$e[11]$	—	$x[4]$
$r \xrightarrow{disable}_{f_4} d$		$e[12]$	$\omega[8]$	—

Left-side flow groupings: f_1 (pipe → receiver), f_2 (source → sender), f_3 (sender → pipe), f_4 (receiver → destination).

3.2 Flow-Based Interpretations of Executions

A tracker is said to be *sound* if it does not miss any flow. However, a given observable execution can correspond to several concrete executions, when several flows are enabled at the same time. Thus, a tracker cannot track flows with an absolute precision. Thus, a sound tracker can only provide an overapproximation of the taints considering the flows generated by all the compatible concrete executions. Actually, in the example, due to the synchronous nature of the pipe, there is only one possible execution order between the reading and the writing because reading from the pipe blocks until some content has been written to it.

We chose a pipe because it makes triggering the race condition trivial but we could replace the pipe by a regular file in the example, in which case the order of execution would not be constrained.

Ideal Tag Propagation. We define a transition relation $\hookrightarrow \subseteq \Theta \times \mathcal{X} \times \Theta$ describing how the information flows influence the content of containers.[1]

$$\forall \theta, \theta' \in \Theta \; \forall c_1 \xrightarrow{exec}_f c_2 \in \mathbf{X} \; \theta \xleftarrow{c_1 \xrightarrow{exec}_f c_2} \theta' \leftrightarrow \theta' = \theta[c_2 \leftarrow \theta(c_2) \cup \theta(c_1)]$$

For $x \in \mathbf{X}$ we write $\theta_0 \xleftarrow{x[:n]} \theta_n$ when $\theta_0 \xleftarrow{x[1]} \theta_1 \xleftarrow{x[2]} \cdots \theta_{n-1} \xleftarrow{x[n]} \theta_n$. This relation is the way an ideal tracker would propagate tags if it could observe the execution of the flows themselves instead of the enabling and disabling events. Table 1a details the tag propagation represented by this relation according to the concrete execution x from Example 1.

Tag Propagation by LSM-based Trackers. Formally, the computation done by LSM-based trackers such as Laminar, KBlare, and Weir can be described by a transition relation $\rightarrow \subseteq \Theta \times \mathcal{O} \times \Theta$ defined as follows:

$$\theta \xrightarrow{c_1 \xrightarrow{enable}_f c_2} \theta[c_2 \leftarrow \theta(c_2) \cup \theta(c_1)] \qquad \theta \xrightarrow{c_1 \xrightarrow{disable}_f c_2} \theta$$

Considering again Example 1, Table 1b describes the computation done from ω. This taint propagation is not sound: it can miss indirect flows. For example, in the concrete execution x compatible with ω, there is an indirect flow from *source* to *destination* ($t^{src} = \bigstar \in \theta(d) = \{t^d = \blacktriangle, t^r = \odot, t^p = \square, t^{se} = \blacksquare, t^{src} = \bigstar\}$ in the computation made by $\hookrightarrow$), but this is not the case in the computation made by $\rightarrow$.

This model describes straightforwardly "floating labels" systems such as Blare and Weir, in which a flow automatically updates the label of the destination container with the label of the source to show the dissemination of the tagged data. It also describes correctly, although this is less intuitive, the behavior of systems such as Laminar in which labels must be changed explicitly by the process. In both cases, the race condition is the same and has the same effect. In Blare and Weir, the flow occurs but the label of the destination is not updated accordingly. If this flow is illegal, then the violation of the security policy is not detected. In Laminar, even if the flow is illegal, which means that the destination label does not dominate the source one, no alert is raised and it occurs anyway. In our model, the labels only represent the knowledge the tracking system has about past flows in the system, and is not tied to any specific policy semantics.

---

[1] $f[x \leftarrow a]$ is the function such that $f[x \leftarrow a](y) = \begin{cases} a & \text{if } x = y \\ f(y) & \text{otherwise.} \end{cases}$

Computation of the Smallest Correct Overapproximation. Given an observable execution ω, we define $Enabled_\omega \subseteq \mathcal{C} \times \mathcal{C}$ as the set of flows that have been enabled during ω and not disabled (yet) at the end of ω. $Enabled_\omega^*$ stands for the reflexive and transitive closure of relation $Enabled_\omega$.

$$(c_1, c_2) \in Enabled_\omega \Leftrightarrow \exists i \; \omega[i] = c_1 \xrightarrow{enable}_f c_2 \wedge \forall j > i \; \omega[j] \neq c_1 \xrightarrow{disable}_f c_2$$

An overapproximation, written $Flows_\omega \subseteq \mathcal{C} \times \mathcal{C}$, of flows that can be generated by some concrete execution compatible with a given observable execution $\omega \in \mathbf{O}$ can be computed as follows.[2]

$$Flows_\omega = \begin{cases} Enabled_\omega^* & \text{if } \lg(\omega) = 1 \\ Flows_{\omega[:k]} \cdot Enabled_\omega^* & \text{if } \lg(\omega) = k + 1 \end{cases}$$

For example, if the flow (A, B) has happened in the past, and the flow (B, C) gets enabled, then the composition (A, C) is a new flow in the system. This would not be the case if the flow (B, C) were anterior to (A, B). Considering Example 1, Table 1c illustrates how $Flows_\omega$ is computed. As we can see, $Flows_\omega$ is not necessarily a transitive relation. Proposition 1 below ensures the soundness of the tag propagation mechanism, as illustrated in Table 1d. Proposition 2 ensures that it is impossible to compute a better overapproximation in our model.

Proposition 1 (Soundness). *Flows generated by a concrete execution compatible with an observable execution ω belong to $Flows_\omega$.*

$$\forall e \in \mathbf{E} \; \forall \theta \in \Theta \; \theta_{init} \xrightarrow{ex} \theta \Rightarrow \forall c \in \mathcal{C} \; \theta(c) \subseteq \bigcup_{(c',c) \in Flows_{e_{\mathbf{O}}}} \theta_{init}(c')$$

Proof (Sketch). By induction on $\lg(e)$. It suffices to show that if a concrete execution exists, then, by the causality conditions, there necessarily exists a sequence of observable events that have enabled the flows executed in the concrete execution. $Flows_\omega$ contains these flows by construction.

Proposition 2 (Smallest overapproximation/Completeness). *All flows in $Flows_\omega$ are generated by at least one concrete execution compatible with the observable execution ω.*

$$\forall \omega \in \mathbf{O} \; \forall c, c' \in \mathcal{C}$$
$$(c, c') \in Flows_\omega \Rightarrow \exists x \in \mathbf{X} \left(\omega \vdash x \wedge \forall \theta \in \Theta \; \theta_{init} \xrightarrow{x} \theta \Rightarrow \theta_{init}(c) \subseteq \theta(c') \right)$$

Proof (Sketch). By induction on $\lg(\omega)$. Suppose that $(c, c') \in Flows_{\omega[:n]}$ is the flow $(c = c_1, c_2), (c_2, c_3), \ldots, (c_{m-1}, c_m = c')$. Then by definition, there exists $i \leq m$ such that $(c_1, c_i) \in Flows_{\omega[:n-1]}$ and $(c_i, c_m) \in Enabled_{\omega[:n]}^*$. By the induction hypothesis, there exists $x \vdash \omega[:n-1]$ which propagates tags from c_1 to c_i. Concatenating x with the executions of the flows $(c_i, c_{i+1}), \ldots, (c_{m-1}, c_m)$ (which are enabled and not disabled yet in $\omega[:n]$) in this order yields a concrete execution $x' \vdash \omega[:n]$ propagating tags from $c = c_1$ to $c_m = c'$ via c_i.

---

[2] Given two relations $R_1 \subseteq E \times F$ and $R_2 \subseteq F \times G$, the relation $R_1 \cdot R_2 \subseteq E \times G$ is defined by $(x, y) \in R_1 . R_2$ iff there exists $z \in F$ such that $(x, z) \in R_1$ and $(z, y) \in R_2$.

Table 1. Flow-based interpretations of executions. For the sake of legibility, we note: $t^{src} = \bigstar$, $t^{se} = \blacksquare$, $t^p = \square$, $t^r = \odot$, $t^d = \blacktriangle$

(a) Computation of $\theta_{init} \xrightarrow{x[:n]} \theta$ (Ideal propagation)

n	$x[n]$	$\theta(src)$	$\theta(se)$	$\theta(p)$	$\theta(r)$	$\theta(d)$
1	$src \xrightarrow{exec}_{f_1} se$	$\bigstar$	$\blacksquare, \bigstar$	$\square$	$\odot$	$\blacktriangle$
2	$se \xrightarrow{exec}_{f_2} p$	$\bigstar$	$\blacksquare, \bigstar$	$\square, \blacksquare, \bigstar$	$\odot$	$\blacktriangle$
3	$p \xrightarrow{exec}_{f_3} r$	$\bigstar$	$\blacksquare, \bigstar$	$\square, \blacksquare, \bigstar$	$\odot, \square, \blacksquare, \bigstar$	$\blacktriangle$
4	$r \xrightarrow{exec}_{f_4} d$	$\bigstar$	$\blacksquare, \bigstar$	$\square, \blacksquare, \bigstar$	$\odot, \square, \blacksquare, \bigstar$	$\blacktriangle, \odot, \square, \blacksquare, \bigstar$

(b) Computation of $\theta_{init} \xrightarrow{\omega[:n]} \theta$ (LSM-based trackers)

n	$\omega[n]$	$\theta(src)$	$\theta(se)$	$\theta(p)$	$\theta(r)$	$\theta(d)$
1	$p \xrightarrow{enable}_{f_1} r$	$\bigstar$	$\blacksquare$	$\square$	$\odot, \square$	$\blacktriangle$
2	$src \xrightarrow{enable}_{f_2} se$	$\bigstar$	$\blacksquare, \bigstar$	$\square$	$\odot, \square$	$\blacktriangle$
4	$se \xrightarrow{enable}_{f_3} p$	$\bigstar$	$\blacksquare, \bigstar$	$\square, \blacksquare, \bigstar$	$\odot, \square$	$\blacktriangle$
7	$r \xrightarrow{enable}_{f_4} d$	$\bigstar$	$\blacksquare, \bigstar$	$\square, \blacksquare, \bigstar$	$\odot, \square$	$\blacktriangle, \odot, \square$

(c) $Enabled_{\omega[:n]}$, $Enabled^*_{\omega[:n]}$ and $Flows_{\omega[:n]}$

n	$Enabled_{\omega[:n]}$	$Enabled^*_{\omega[:n]}$	$Flows_{\omega[:n]}$
0		$(src,src), (se,se), (p,p),$ $(r,r), (d,d)$	$(src,src), (se,se), (p,p), (r,r), (d,d)$
1	(p,r)	$(src,src), (se,se), (p,p),$ $(r,r), (d,d), (p,r)$	$(src,src), (se,se), (p,p), (r,r), (d,d),$ (p,r)
		...	
7	(r,d)	$(src,src), (se,se), (p,p),$ $(r,r), (d,d), (r,d)$	$(src,src), (se,se), (p,p), (r,r), (d,d),$ $(p,r), (p,d), (src,se), (src,p), (src,r),$ $(src,d), (se,p), (se,r), (se,d)$

(d) Computation of $\bigcup\limits_{(c_1,c_2)\in Flows_{\omega[:n]}} \theta_{init}(c_1)$ (Rfblare's Overapproximation)

n	$\omega[n]$	$\theta(src)$	$\theta(se)$	$\theta(p)$	$\theta(r)$	$\theta(d)$
1	$p \xrightarrow{enable}_{f_1} r$	$\bigstar$	$\blacksquare$	$\square$	$\odot, \square$	$\blacktriangle$
2	$src \xrightarrow{enable}_{f_2} se$	$\bigstar$	$\blacksquare, \bigstar$	$\square$	$\odot, \square$	$\blacktriangle$
3	$src \xrightarrow{disable}_{f_2} se$	$\bigstar$	$\blacksquare, \bigstar$	$\square$	$\odot, \square$	$\blacktriangle$
4	$se \xrightarrow{enable}_{f_3} p$	$\bigstar$	$\blacksquare, \bigstar$	$\square, \blacksquare, \bigstar$	$\odot, \square, \blacksquare, \bigstar$	$\blacktriangle$
5	$p \xrightarrow{disable}_{f_1} r$	$\bigstar$	$\blacksquare, \bigstar$	$\square, \blacksquare, \bigstar$	$\odot, \square, \blacksquare, \bigstar$	$\blacktriangle$
6	$se \xrightarrow{disable}_{f_3} p$	$\bigstar$	$\blacksquare, \bigstar$	$\square, \blacksquare, \bigstar$	$\odot, \square, \blacksquare, \bigstar$	$\blacktriangle$
7	$r \xrightarrow{enable}_{f_4} d$	$\bigstar$	$\blacksquare, \bigstar$	$\square, \blacksquare, \bigstar$	$\odot, \square, \blacksquare, \bigstar$	$\blacktriangle, \odot, \square, \blacksquare, \bigstar$
8	$r \xrightarrow{disable}_{f_4} d$	$\bigstar$	$\blacksquare, \bigstar$	$\square, \blacksquare, \bigstar$	$\odot, \square, \blacksquare, \bigstar$	$\blacktriangle, \odot, \square, \blacksquare, \bigstar$

4   Implementation and Experiments

We have implemented our taint propagation algorithm as Rfblare, the *race-free KBlare*, into the version 4.7 of the vanilla Linux kernel. We have not contributed to the policy enforcement part of KBlare and do not discuss it here. Rfblare covers the flows listed in Table 2. Consistently with the formal description of our algorithm, we use one LSM hook as an enabling event and another one as a disabling event for each flow. We have leveraged the expertise from our previous work on LSM [3] to map our model onto the LSM framework. Some flows cannot possibly enter in a race condition with others and require no disabling hook. For example, the execve system call is used to run a new program, causing a flow from the executable file to the memory of the process. However, this flow cannot race with any flow to the file, because it is forbidden both to write into a file being executed and to execute a file being written to. In the case of fork, no race condition occurs with the new process since it has not started yet, and race conditions with the parent process are irrelevant since the mm_dup_security hook is actually called *after* the copy of the parent process's memory is finished (i.e. after the flow has taken place). mq_timedsend and msgsnd are in the same situation. When a message is to be sent to a message queue, it is first copied to a buffer in the kernel, then checked by the LSM module before it can be registered to the queue. This order of actions prevents the calling process from tampering with the message being checked. Since the kernel already avoids the data race condition on the message, using our algorithm would be redundant.

We have added two LSM hooks as disabling events: syscall_before_return for discrete flows and ptrace_unlink for process_vm_readv (discrete flow) and ptrace (continuous flow). ptrace lets one process attach to another and monitor its execution. It is used by debuggers. We consider it a continuous flow because it opens many ways for the tracer process to exchange data with the tracee, in overt or covert ways. We have placed the syscall_before_return hook before the normal return of the system calls generating the flows. The case of mmap and mprotect is special. We need not track the unmapping of files because the kernel already does so. More precisely, for any file, we can query the kernel for the list of processes' memory spaces it is mapped into, and for any memory space, we can similarly know which files are mapped into. Therefore, when computing the taint propagation for a flow to a file or a memory space, we use this knowledge maintained by the kernel to take into account the continuous flow caused by the mapping. We still need the enabling hooks nonetheless to perform the taint propagation between the file and the memory space as soon as the file is mapped. If the mapping is read-only, the flow is from the file to the memory space, otherwise, it is bidirectional. mprotect can be used to change a read-only mapping to a read-write one, so we need to monitor it.

We have tested the attacks presented in Sect. 2. In the case of the *Stealthily Copying a File*, the sequence of events is of course still the same but Rfblare reacts correctly to it. The flow from the pipe to the receiver is *enabled* when the receiver goes through the *file_permission* hook. The flow remains enabled as the process is blocked for the pipe to be written to. On the sender side, the flow from

Table 2. Flows monitored by Rfblare

System call family	Flow	Enabling event	Disabling event
Discrete flows			
read	File→memory	file_permission[a]	before_return[b]
write	Memory→file	file_permission[a]	before_return[b]
recv	Socket→memory	socket_recvmsg[a]	before_return[b]
send	Memory→socket	socket_sendmsg[a]	before_return[b]
process_vm_readv	Memory→memory	ptrace_access_check[a]	ptrace_unlink[b]
migrate_pages	Memory→memory	task_movememory[a]	before_return[b]
move_pages	Memory→memory	task_movememory[a]	before_return[b]
msgrcv	Message queue → memory	mq_store_msg[a]	before_return[b]
msgsnd	Memory → message queue	msg_msg_alloc_security[a]	—[c]
mq_timedreceive	Message queue → memory	mq_store_msg[a]	before_return[b]
mq_timedsend	Memory → message queue	msg_msg_alloc_security[a]	—[c]
clone/fork	Memory→memory	mm_dup_security[b]	—[c]
execve	File→memory	bprm_set_creds/ bprm_committing_creds[a]	—[c]
kill	Memory→memory	task_kill[a]	before_return[b]
Continuous flows			
mmap	File↔memory	mmap_file[a]	—[d]
mprotect	File↔memory	file_mprotect[a]	—[d]
ptrace	Memory↔memory	ptrace_access_check[a]	ptrace_unlink[b]
ptrace	Memory↔memory	ptrace_traceme[a]	ptrace_unlink[b]

[a] LSM hook already present in the LSM framework.
[b] LSM hook added by us.
[c] No LSM hook needed because this operation cannot race with any other.
[d] No LSM hook needed because we query the kernel for the active mappings.

the source file to the sender is enabled (the source's tags are propagated to the sender), and then disabled immediately after. Then, when the sender process writes to the pipe, the flow from the sender to the pipe is enabled and the tags from the sender (which includes tags from the source file) are propagated to the pipe. Since the flow from the pipe to the receiver is still enabled, the tags are also propagated to the receiver. Finally, when the receiver restarts, the actual reading is performed, the flow from the pipe to the receiver is disabled and the read system call finishes. The receiver then writes to the destination file, and thus propagates its taint to it. The content of the destination file is correctly reflected by its taint, despite the flows involving the pipe having occurred in the reverse order with respect to the corresponding passages through the *file_ permission*

Table 3. Linux compilation micro-benchmark results. Times are given as an average over thirty runs, with the 95% confidence interval. Ratios are the fraction of each system time over the reference system time and the 0-tags system time, respectively.

Number of tags	User time (s)	System time (s) and ratios		Elapsed time (s)
(Reference)	1180 ± 10.8	82.95 ± 0.75	1.000 0.981	170.8 ± 1.7
0	1174 ± 8.4	84.56 ± 0.46	1.019 1.000	170.1 ± 1.3
400	1175 ± 10.3	84.66 ± 0.55	1.021 1.001	170.8 ± 1.5
800	1175 ± 10.6	84.82 ± 0.57	1.022 1.003	170.1 ± 1.5
1200	1173 ± 10.2	84.90 ± 0.58	1.023 1.004	170.9 ± 1.5
1600	1169 ± 10.2	86.43 ± 1.43	1.042 1.022	171.3 ± 1.8
2000	1168 ± 9.5	86.92 ± 1.58	1.048 1.027	170.6 ± 1.8

hook. For the second attack with memory-mapped files and shared memories, we have used a similar setup. The sender and the receiver map respectively the source and destination file, and the pipe is replaced by a shared memory segment. We observe again the correct behavior: whichever mapping is done last (either one of the file, or the shared memory), the tags of the source file are propagated to all containers linked by the enabled continuous flows.

Measuring the overhead caused by Rfblare is critical to ensure its practicality. Our testcase is a compilation of the Linux kernel, version 4.7, on a machine with Rfblare. We place a unique tag on a varying number of source files to study the impact of the number of tags to propagate on the performance on the kernel. We believe compilation to be an appropriate benchmark because it is reproducible reliably and involves numerous flows to and from files as well as the spawning of numerous processes. Furthermore, it is relatively easy to verify the correct propagation because we put a unique tag on each source file and we can check by other means what files are supposed to participate to the compilation of each intermediary and final output of the compiler. Our results are presented in Table 3. We measure the time taken by the compilation depending on the number of tagged source files. As a reference, we have taken the time on a similar system without Rfblare. Tests are run thirty times each, on a virtual machine with 16 Gb of RAM, and 8 × 3.2 Ghz CPUs. The user time is the cumulated time spent by all threads outside the kernel. Logically, it shows no significant variation. The system time is the cumulated time spent in the kernel doing system calls, including taint propagation. Overall, on the Rfblare-equipped system, there is an increase of about 2 to 5% of the system time. This is small, especially if we consider the wall clock time spent during the compilation (column "elapsed time") which shows no significant variation.

5   Related Work

IFC has been an active topic of research and prototyping for a long time. It can be applied in programming languages or at the OS level, we only discuss the latter case here. Along with the various implementations, formal descriptions have been proposed, following the seminal work of Denning [2]. Denning showed that information flow policies could be described as lattices of security labels. This works helped reasoning about the respective expressiveness and objectives of the different kinds of policies. However, Denning only describes *access control* policies. The difference between access control and information flow control is explicited by Jaume et al. [5]: IFC bases its security decisions based on the history of flows in the system (maintained with taint propagation) whereas access control does not maintain this knowledge. The practical consequence is that thanks to this knowledge, IFC allows more policies while maintaining the guarantee that no illegal flow can occur. For example, it is possible to let a process read a secret file or communicate with an unauthorized process, but not both. Access control can either allow both (which is a security hazard) or deny both (which is overly restrictive). However, despite the extensive literature on the models of labels (for example: [13,15]) and on the properties enforceable with IFC, like non-interference [6], there is little formal work on taint propagation itself. However, implementing IFC in Linux systems raises practical difficulties, mainly due to concurrency and arcane corner cases in both the design and the implementation of the Linux kernel. Flume [7] is an IFC system implemented as an execution monitor in userspace, able to track the flows done by an individual process. It uses a LSM module to propagate taints to and from files. This is different from our solution, implemented entirely in-kernel which tracks flows in the entire system. Flowx [1] is a LSM module enforcing non-interference in an entire Linux system. Its implementation covers all IPCs present in Linux systems, including shared memory. However, it does not perform IFC according to our definition but rather access control since it does not maintain a knowledge of the flows in the system. Instead, it dynamically instantiates copies of existing containers of information with appropriate labels of security, each time an illegal access is asked for. We have already discussed the case of KBlare [4], Laminar [11] and Weir [8], which have a similar design. The main differences are the target (Android for Weir, all Linux systems for Laminar and KBlare), the model of label (inherited from Flume [7] for Laminar and Weir, radically different for KBlare) and the use of floating labels (KBlare and Weir) versus explicit changes (Laminar). They claim to cover a different range of overt and covert channels of information, Laminar putting a special focus on covert channels while KBlare disregarding them completely.

6   Conclusion

Information flow trackers are powerful tools to maintain a history of how data is disseminated and used in an operating system. This knowledge is necessary to enforce strong information flow policies or analyze malware activity. In Linux, most trackers are implemented using the Linux Security Modules framework, which provides hooks trackers can use to monitor the system calls making information flow. However, being able to monitor individual flows is not a guarantee of being able to correctly trace them all. We have shown that information flows generated by concurrent system calls can cause trackers to miss indirect information flows because of race conditions. To handle this issue, we have modeled information trackers as being able to monitor not the execution of flows themselves, but rather the events that enable and disable the flow. With this model as a basis, we have designed and proved an algorithm to compute the smallest overapproximation of the flow tracking in a given execution, considering all sequences of flow executions compatible with the events observable in this execution. The solution we propose has the very practical consequence that it makes possible to track continuous flows, including continuous flows caused by memory mappings and shared memory segments, which were not fully handled before. We have implemented our approach in Rfblare, available at https://blare-ids.org/rfblare.

References

1. Cristiá, M., Mata, P.E.: Runtime enforcement of noninterference by duplicating processes and their memories. In: Workshop de Seguridad Informática WSEGI, vol. 2009 (2009)
2. Denning, D.E.: A lattice model of secure information flow. Commun. ACM **19**(5), 236–243 (1976)
3. Georget, L., Jaume, M., Piolle, G., Tronel, F., Viet Triem Tong, V.: Verifying the reliability of operating system-level information flow control systems in Linux. In: FormaliSE: FME Workshop on Formal Methods in Software Engineering. IEEE, Buenos Aires, May 2017
4. Hauser, C.: Détection d'intrusion dans les systémes distribués par propagation de teinte au niveau noyau. Ph.D. thesis, University of Rennes 1, France., June 2013
5. Jaume, M., Andriatsimandefitra, R., Tong, V.V.T., Mé, L.: Secure states *versus* secure executions. In: Bagchi, A., Ray, I. (eds.) ICISS 2013. LNCS, vol. 8303, pp. 148–162. Springer, Heidelberg (2013). doi:10.1007/978-3-642-45204-8_11
6. Krohn, M., Tromer, E.: Noninterference for a practical DIFC-based operating system. In: IEEE Symposium on Security and Privacy, pp. 61–76. IEEE Computer Society, Washington, DC (2009)
7. Krohn, M., Yip, A., Brodsky, M., Cliffer, N., Kaashoek, M.F., Kohler, E., Morris, R.: Information flow control for standard OS abstractions. In: ACM SIGOPS Symposium on Operating Systems Principles, pp. 321–334. ACM, Stevenson, October 2007
8. Nadkarni, A., Andow, B., Enck, W., Jha, S.: Practical DIFC enforcement on Android. In: 25th USENIX Security Symposium, USENIX Security 2016, pp. 1119–1136. USENIX Association, Austin, August 2016
9. Porter, D.E., Bond, M.D., Roy, I., Mckinley, K.S., Witchel, E.: Practical fine-grained information flow control using laminar. ACM Trans. Program. Lang. Syst. **37**(1), 1–51 (2014)
10. Roy, I., Porter, D.: Laminar, August 2014. https://sourceforge.net/p/jikesrvm/research-archive/26
11. Roy, I., Porter, D.E., Bond, M.D., McKinley, K.S., Witchel, E.: Laminar: practical fine-grained decentralized information flow control. In: Proceedings of the 30th ACM SIGPLAN Conference on Programming Language Design and Implementation, pp. 63–74. ACM, Dublin, June 2009

12. The Coq Development Team: The Coq Proof Assistant Reference Manual. Technical report, Inria, December 2016
13. VanDeBogart, S., Efstathopoulos, P., Kohler, E., Krohn, M., Frey, C., Ziegler, D., Kaashoek, F., Morris, R., Maziéres, D.: Labels and event processes in the asbestos operating system. ACM Trans. Comput. Syst. **25**(4), December 2007. Article No. 11. https://dl.acm.org/citation.cfm?id=1314302
14. Wright, C., Cowan, C., Smalley, S., Morris, J., Kroah-Hartman, G.: Linux security modules: general security support for the Linux kernel. In: USENIX Security Symposium, pp. 17–31. USENIX Association, San Francisco (2002)
15. Zimmermann, J., Mé, L., Bidan, C.: Experimenting with a policy-based HIDS based on an information flow control model. In: Proceedings of the Annual Computer Security Applications Conference (ACSAC), December 2003

Focused Certification of an Industrial Compilation and Static Verification Toolchain

Zhi Zhang[1]([⊠]), Robby[1], John Hatcliff[1], Yannick Moy[2],
and Pierre Courtieu[3]

[1] Kansas State University, Manhattan, Kansas, USA
{zhangzhi,robby,hatcliff}@ksu.edu
[2] AdaCore, Paris, France
moy@adacore.com
[3] Conservatoire National des Arts et Métiers, Paris, France
pierre.courtieu@cnam.fr

Abstract. SPARK 2014 is a subset of the Ada 2012 programming language that is supported by the GNAT compilation toolchain and multiple open source static analysis and verification tools. These tools can be used to verify that a SPARK 2014 program does not raise language-defined run-time exceptions and that it complies with formal specifications expressed as subprogram contracts. The results of analyses at source code level are valid for the final executable only if it can be shown that compilation/verification tools comply with a common deterministic programming language semantics.

In this paper, we present: (a) a mechanized formal semantics for a large subset of SPARK 2014, (b) an architecture for creating certified/certifying analysis and verification tools for SPARK, and (c) tools and mechanized proofs that instantiate that architecture to demonstrate that SPARK-relevant Ada run-time checks inserted by the GNAT compiler are correct; this includes mechanized proofs of correctness for abstract interpretation-based static analyses that are used to certify correctness of GNAT run-time check optimizations.

A by-product of this work is a substantial amount of open source infrastructure that others in academia and industry can use to develop mechanized semantics, and mechanically verified correctness proofs for analyzers/verifiers for realistic programming languages.

1 Introduction

SPARK is a subset of the Ada programming language targeted at safety- and security-critical applications. It builds on the strengths of Ada for creating highly reliable and long-lived software. SPARK restrictions ensure that the behavior of a SPARK program is unambiguously defined and simple enough that formal verification tools can automatically check the conformance of a program

---

This material is based upon work supported by the US Air Force Office of Scientific Research (AFOSR) under contract FA9550-09-1-0138.

A. Cimatti and M. Sirjani (Eds.): SEFM 2017, LNCS 10469, pp. 17–34, 2017.
DOI: 10.1007/978-3-319-66197-1_2

to its software-contract-based specification. The SPARK language and toolset for formal verification have been applied over many years to on-board aircraft systems, control systems, cryptographic systems, and rail systems [1,15]. The latest version – SPARK 2014 [12], builds on the new specification features added in Ada 2012 [2]. One consequence of the new specification foundation is that SPARK contracts are no longer phrased in Ada comments understood only by the SPARK tools, but the formal specifications are phrased in Ada 2012 meta-data constructs that can be understood by a much wider class of tools (including the GNAT compiler) and they have an execution semantics. The definition of the SPARK 2014 language subset is motivated by the simplicity and feasibility of formal analysis and the need for an unambiguous semantics.

Static analysis tools are available that provide flow analysis, symbolic execution and proof of SPARK programs. The industrial tool GNATprove[1] co-developed by Altran and AdaCore performs flow analysis to check correct access to data in the program (correct access to global variables as specified in data and information flow contracts and correct access to initialized data) and uses deductive methods to demonstrate that the program is free from run-time errors and that the specified contracts are correctly implemented. The academic tool Bakar Kiasan [3] developed by Kansas State University allows executing symbolically a SPARK program with or without contracts, to detect possible run-time errors and contract violations, and in some cases also prove that no such errors can occur.

Motivations: A major reason for using SPARK for developing critical software is the ability to prove statically that no language specified run-time errors, such as arithmetic overflow, buffer overflow and division-by-zero, can occur.[2] Besides the additional confidence in the software that this result brings, it can be used in some certification domains to lower the verification effort in some other areas like testing. For example, the most recent version DO-178C of the avionics certification standard allow using both tests or proofs as acceptable verification methods [13]. It is also commonly used as an argument to justify the suppression of run-time checks in the final executable, typically for increasing execution speed.

The absence of run-time errors can be guaranteed only relative to the correctness of the compiler and analyzers used. Although correctness is not proved for tools used in practice on typical industrial projects, there is a special process known as tool qualification in safety-critical industry which aims at giving sufficient confidence that the tools behave correctly [9].

A critical element for the qualification of both the GNAT compiler (the most widely used Ada compiler) and the GNATprove analyzer, both developed by AdaCore, is that they correctly interpret the semantics of SPARK with respect

---

[1] http://www.adacore.com/sparkpro.

[2] *Language-specified* run-time errors that are relevant for all programs in the language can be contrasted with *application-specific* run-time errors that correspond to violations of a program's application-specific requirements. Our work addresses the former notion.

to the placement of run-time checks. The compiler works by producing first a semantically analyzed abstract syntax tree (AST) of the program, decorated with flags that indicate positions in the AST where run-time checks should be inserted. This AST is then expanded into a lower level representation with explicit run-time checking code. The input of GNATprove is based on the same AST used for compilation (using the same compilation *front-end*), decorated with the same flags that, in this case, indicate where absence of a particular run-time error should be proved. Because the compiler and the analyzer share the code that inserts decorations in the AST, this code is much less likely to miss checks, and some effort has been invested in optimizing out useless checks.

Hence, the compiler and analyzers all share the AST produced by the front-end, with decorations indicating where run-time checks should be inserted. However, we have discovered various situations where decorations were missing, which ultimately led to a correction of the GNAT front-end. The last such occasion was the implementation of a Tetris game in SPARK for a demo at a customer gathering[3]: after proving that the program was free of run-time errors, the first test on the actual board stopped unexpectedly due to a range check failing during execution. There was indeed a possible check failure in the code (later corrected) on a new attribute recently introduced in SPARK, which was not detected during proof because the corresponding decoration was not set by GNAT.

Thus, it is of critical importance to be able to guarantee that all check decorations are set on the AST produced by the front-end, as defined in SPARK 2014 language reference semantics. That is, instead of assuming that GNAT correctly decorates AST with the required run-time checks, this paper presents our work to ensure that is indeed the case.

Contributions: To address the issues described above, and to enable a long-term research program investigating the use of mechanized semantics and proofs for SPARK 2014[4], we have developed multiple proof infrastructure components in the Coq proof assistant. We have created *certified*[5] SPARK run-time check generators with a small trust-base footprint that can be used to substantiate the correctness of the industrial SPARK 2014 toolchain. Our contributions include:

- The formalization of the language (dynamic/evaluation) semantics for a core subset of the SPARK 2014 language using the Coq proof assistant [20] (Sect. 2.1). The core language subset includes scalar subtypes and derived types, array types, record types, procedure calls, and locally defined subprograms; a large class of programs can be desugared to this core subset, thus, enabling evaluations on realistic SPARK systems to some extent.

---

[3] http://blog.adacore.com/tetris-in-spark-on-arm-cortex-m4.

[4] By "mechanized", we mean the construction of formal definitions (of semantics, translations, analysis, etc.) and formal proofs of associated properties in a proof assistant that enables correctness to be checked automatically by the proof assistant.

[5] Certified here means that there are formal mathematical artifacts (such as machine-checked proofs) that serve as rigorous evidence that an implementation is consistent with its specification [5].

The formal semantics specification represents our trust-base (along with Coq, which itself has been highly-regarded as a proof system that has a smaller trust-base compared to others); the specification is trustable because, for example, it has been manually inspected by leading experts in SPARK/Ada both in industry and academia. Hence, it can be considered as *the* reference SPARK 2014 formal semantics.

- An implementation of a certified run-time check generator for the core language (Sect. 2.2); that is, the implementation is proved to be *consistent* with the reference semantics with respect to the class of errors that can arise in the language subset (such as overflow checks, range checks, array index checks and division by zero checks). The consistency guarantees that if language-defined run-time checks generated by the certified implementation do not fail, a program cannot "go wrong" according to the SPARK formal semantics. The generated checks by the implementation represents the baseline as the most conservative run-time check set (i.e., a larger set is unnecessary and could even be problematic).
- An implementation of a certified run-time check optimizer (Sect. 2.3). The optimization is needed because the GNAT frontend employs various optimizations to reduce the set of run-time checks that it generates for run-time efficiency sake. The certified optimizer uses an abstract interpretation-based [7] interval analysis; it generates a smaller set of run-time checks compared to the ones produced by the GNAT frontend, while still being consistent.
- An implementation of a conformance checker as a back-end of the GNAT front-end (including, e.g., a SPARK program translator to fully resolved SPARK ASTs in Coq) that automates evaluations of the GNAT frontend against the certified run-time check generators (Sect. 2.4). This essentially turns the industrial GNAT frontend into a certifying[6] tool with respect to introduction of run-time error check decorations. This increases the confidence in the GNAT compiler back-end that embeds run-time assertion checking when it emits machine code for testing, as well as in the GNATprove verifier that uses the run-time check decorations to determine what verification conditions to generate.
- The evaluation of the GNAT front-end against both the certified run-time check generators (Sect. 2.4). We evaluated that: (1) the set of run-time check decorations inserted by the GNAT front-end is in fact a subset of the decorations generated by the unoptimized run-time check generator, while (2) it is a superset of the decorations generated by the optimized run-time check generator. In addition to confirming the correctness of the GNAT front-end run-time check decoration generator, the evaluation exposed some subtle differences in the run-time checks generated by the GNAT frontend, as well as exposing further optimizations that can be done by the frontend while still preserving its correctness property.

---

[6] Certifying here means that the tool generates evidence testifying that it is in fact consistent with its specification for a particular use of the tool.

While our research work includes making an industrial impact on SPARK run-time error checking, the significant investments reflected in our contributions (e.g., over 25,000 lines of Coq proofs and reusable AST, translations, and semantics infrastructure), enable much broader research and engineering. All of the Coq artifacts and associated tools created in this work are publicly available under an EPL open source license[7]. The formalized SPARK semantics and certified run-time check generators can be leveraged to develop certified/certifying program analyzers (e.g., a contract verifier) and translators (e.g., a SPARK to CompCert [19] intermediate representation translator to benefit from CompCert's certified translation toolchain down to machine-code level). In general, our approach of using both unoptimized and optimized certified run-time check generators to turn an untrusted (industrial) implementation into a certifying tool can be adopted to other programming languages/development tools for critical systems that ensure absence of run-time errors.

2   Technical Approach

Figure 1 gives an architectural overview of our approach; the subsequent subsections describe each of the components. Due to space constraints, we only highlight some limited language features sufficient to illustrate our approach (see the publicly available artifacts for the complete definitions).

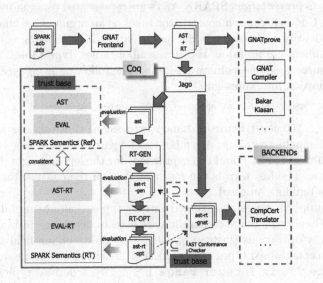

Fig. 1. Architectural overview

[7] http://santoslab.org/pub/TR/SAnToS-TR2016-03-11/.

2.1   Core SPARK 2014 Mechanized Semantics

As stated previously, one main component of our approach is a formal language reference semantics of core SPARK 2014 mechanized using Coq [20]; Coq allows for specifying, implementing, and proving programming language related properties. We chose Coq due to the fact that it has a relatively small core which has been vetted by many experts in the programming language community (small trust-base).

The core language includes features typically found in imperative languages such as arrays, records, and procedure calls, as well as SPARK-specific structures, such as nested procedures and subtypes. One major difference between SPARK and other programming languages (e.g., C) is that verification for absence of run-time errors is required by the semantics of the language itself. Thus, the constraints associated with the required run-time checks are specified within the operational semantics rules for the language; that is, as the rules are used to "evaluate" the program, the semantics of the run-time checks are enforced at appropriate points in the program, and the evaluation will terminate with a run-time error message as soon as one of its run-time checks fails.

The formalization includes: (a) a SPARK AST representation (symbols and types are fully resolved), and (b) a rule-based "big step" operational semantics for SPARK (including state/value representations, expression evaluation, and statement execution).

SPARK AST Representation: SPARK ASTs are represented using inductive type definitions in Coq, where each constructor takes as an argument a number used to uniquely identify and reference the particular AST node being constructed. The AST numbers are useful as keys for symbol tables, type tables, and mappings from source code line/column positions. The following is an excerpt of the inductive definition for expressions

```
Inductive exp: Type :=  | BinOp: astnum→ binOp→ exp→ exp→ exp | ...
```

where `BinOp` is the constructor for binary expressions that takes as arguments a unique AST number `astnum`, a symbol for the particular operator being used (*e.g.*, `Add`, `Sub`, `Mul`, *etc.*.), and the expressions for the left and right arguments to the operator. The last `exp` is the resulting type of the constructor (*i.e.*, the constructor is building an `exp`).

SPARK supports range constrained integer types that are useful as array index types; that is, the range constraints are used to determine in-bounds/out-of-bounds array operations (instead of using a special `.length` field such as in Java). Range constrained types can be declared by either a subtype declaration (e.g., **subtype** T10 **is** Integer **range** 1 .. 10), a derived type definition (e.g., **type** U10 **is new** Integer **range** 1 .. 10), or an integer type definition (e.g., **type** W10 **is range** 1 .. 10); they semantically differ in that the last two introduce a new type, while the first one does not; the differences have to be taken into account in the formalization. This illustrates the non-trivial number of language features that one has to cover when formalizing a real programming language that can be directly leveraged for developing high-integrity industrial tools.

State/Value: Due to the semantics enforcing the run-time checks, evaluating either an expression or a statement may produce an error state when the run-time check fails (otherwise a value or a state is produced, respectively). The following definition defines a generic return type `Ret`:

```
Inductive Ret (A: Type): Type :=  | OK: A→ Ret A | RTE: errorType→ Ret A.
```

Type parameter A is either the value/state type, and `errorType` is the run-time error state type (e.g., division by zero, overflow, out of range).

Expression Semantics: The mechanized big-step operational semantics definition consists of an inductively defined type with constructors corresponding to the individual "rules" of the semantics. Intuitively, each constructor takes as arguments: (a) Coq objects representing operational semantics derivations corresponding to evaluation of expression/statement sub-components, and (b) Coq objects representing derivations establishing that some necessary "side conditions" hold. Each expression rule relates a symbol table, the current state, and the expression to be evaluated, to a return value. The expression rules are complicated by the fact that sub-expression evaluation can produce an error state, as follows.

```
Inductive evalExp: symTab→ state→ exp→ Ret value→ Prop :=
| EvalBinOpE1_RTE: ∀ st s e1 msg n op e2,    (* e1 returns error *)
   evalExp st s e1 (RTE msg)→ evalExp st s (BinOp n op e1 e2) (RTE msg)
| EvalBinOpE2_RTE: ∀ st s e1 v1 e2 msg n op, (* e2 returns error *)
   evalExp st s e1 (OK v1)→ evalExp st s e2 (RTE msg)→
     evalExp st s (BinOp n op e1 e2) (RTE msg)
| EvalBinOp: ∀ st s e1 v1 e2 v2 op v n,       (* no error from e1 & e2 *)
   evalExp st s e1 (OK v1)→ evalExp st s e2 (OK v2)→ evalBinOp op v1 v2 v→
     evalExp st s (BinOp n op e1 e2) v
...
Inductive evalBinOp: binOp→ value→ value→ Ret value→Prop :=
| CheckBinops: ∀ op v1 v2 v v', (* binop results in overflow *)
   op = Add∨ op = Sub∨ op = Mul→ Denotational.binOp op v1 v2 = Some (Int v)→
     overflowCheck v v'→  evalBinOp op v1 v2 v'
| CheckDivRTE: ∀ v1 v2,          (* check for div by zero *)
   divCheck v1 v2 (RTE DivByZero)→ evalBinOp Div (Int v1) (Int v2) (RTE DivByZero)
| CheckDiv: ∀ v1 v2 v v',        (* no div by zero, check result overflow *)
   divCheck v1 v2 (OK (Int v))→ overflowCheck v v'→
     evalBinOp Div (Int v1) (Int v2) v'   ...
```

`EvalBinOpE1_RTE` specifies the evaluation of a binary expression (e1 op e2) where the evaluation of e1 produces an error state (similarly, `EvalBinOpE2_RTE` for when e2 fails). `EvalBinOp` specifies the situation where evaluations of both e1 and e2 produce operand values, which are then evaluated using `evalBinOp`; `evalBinOp` incorporates various run-time checks such as division by zero and overflow/underflow by using `divCheck` and `overflowCheck`; `divCheck` produces a value if the second operand is non-zero (otherwise, it produces the error state `RTE DivByZero`), and `overflowCheck` produces a value if the given value fits within the (platform) integer type value range (otherwise, it produces `RTE Overflow`). Run-time checks for other language features such as array indexing are specified in the same spirit as the above.

Statement Semantics: Range checks are enforced during statement executions of, for example, assignments and procedure calls. We describe the intuition behind statement semantic rules using examples instead of verbosely listing the Coq specifications.

For an assignment, a range check is enforced for its right hand side expression if the left hand side expression's type is a range constrained type. For example,

```
subtype MyInt is Integer range 1 .. 10;   X: MyInt;   ...;   X := X + 1;
```

That is, X is a variable of type MyInt, which is defined as a subtype of Integer ranging from 1 to 10. The assignment increments X by 1, as follows. First, X + 1 is evaluated; if it returns a value (instead of an error state), the value is checked against the range of MyInt before updating X.

For a procedure call, range checks are required for both input arguments and output parameters if the types of input parameters and output arguments are range constrained types because input arguments are assigned to the procedure input parameters, and output parameters are assigned to the output arguments.

In general, there are three categories of run-time checks in the core SPARK subset: (1) overflow (including underflow) run-time checks (for integer arithmetic operations), (2) division by zero run-time checks (for modulus and division operations), and (3) range run-time checks (for integer variable assignments, array assignments, array accesses, and procedure calls).

Evaluation: We designed the semantics rules including the specification of run-time checks by referring to the SPARK [21] and Ada [17] reference manuals. The rules were subsequently inspected and refined by various experts including SPARK/Ada designers and developers. We then proved that our SPARK mechanized semantics enjoys a form of type safety (Sect. 2.3), which guarantees, to some extent, its internal consistency.

2.2 Certified Run-Time Check Generator

Given a SPARK program, the GNAT compiler front-end builds the program fully-resolved (symbol/type) AST decorated with flags that indicate the position and nature of the run-time checks to be performed. When down-stream tools process the ASTs, they interpret/transform the decorations. For example, a later phase of the GNAT compiler replaces each decoration with an assertion AST representing code that implements the corresponding run-time check. In contrast, the Why3 [22]-based GNATprove verification tool uses the decorations to generate verification conditions. Both tools assume that the run-time check decorations inserted by the GNAT compiler front-end are correct.

To formally capture the notion of decorating ASTs with run-time check information, we implemented in Coq a run-time check decoration generator (RT-GEN in Fig. 1) whose consistency with the mechanized SPARK reference semantics was established via a Coq proof. Hence, the correctness of RT-GEN is *certified*. To achieve this, a different set of operational semantic rules is needed (called EVAL-RT) – one that "evaluates" an AST with run-time check decorations and only enforces the checking semantics where a decoration occurs. Then, one can prove that, for any program and for any program initial state, EVAL-RT supplied with run-time check decorations generated by RT-GEN produces *exactly the same* state as EVAL (*i.e.*, the SPARK reference semantics).

EVAL-RT: is a modified EVAL that accepts AST-RT where run-time check decorations are represented as tree attributes. For example, AST-RT expression is defined as follows.

```
Inductive expRT: Type :=
| BinOpRT: astnum→ binOp→ expRT→ expRT→ interiorChecks→ exteriorChecks→ expRT
...
```

The difference from AST is that two additional fields interior/exterior Checks are introduced; interiorChecks are intended for run-time checks associated with the binary operator (e.g., addition requires overflowCheck), while exteriorChecks are checks associated with expression's context (e.g., if the expression is used for array indexing, then it should be range-checked against the array size). Once AST-RT is defined, one can then define EVAL-RT that accepts AST-RT and enforces the explicitly listed run-time checks (e.g., in interiorChecks and exteriorChecks), as illustrated below.

```
Inductive evalExpRT: symTabRT→ state→ expRT→ Ret value→ Prop :=
| EvalBinOpRT: ∀ st s e1 v1 e2 v2 ins op v n exs,
    evalExpRT st s e1 (OK v1)→ evalExpRT st s e2 (OK v2)→ (* no error on e1, e2 *)
    evalBinOpRTS ins op v1 v2 v→                           (* process RT checks *)
    evalExpRT st s (BinOpRT n op e1 e2 ins exs) v
...
```

evalBinOpRTS iterates over the run-time check decorations to enforce the interior- Checks for a binary expression. The binary operation is performed if none of the run-time checks produces an error state; otherwise, it returns the error state. (Note that enforcement of exteriorChecks is not presented above as it involves arrays, which is not presented due to space constraint.)

RT-GEN: translates AST to AST-RT. In developing RT-GEN, we first specified its behavior declaratively as a Coq inductively defined relation (e.g., toExpRT below) between AST to AST-RT (with the symbol table as an auxiliary component). Then, we implemented the translation as a Coq function (e.g., toExpRTImpl).

```
Inductive toExpRT: symTab→ exp→ expRT→ Prop :=
| ToBinOpO: ∀ st op e1 e1RT e2 e2RT n, (* insert overflow checks on op result *)
    op = Add ∨ op = Sub ∨ op = Mul → toExpRT st e1 e1RT → toExpRT st e2 e2RT →
    toExpRT st (BinOp n op e1 e2) (BinOpRT n op e1RT e2RT [OverflowCheck] nil)
| ToBinOpDO: ∀ st e1 e1RT e2 e2RT n,   (* Div: div by 0 + overflow *)
    toExpRT st e1 e1RT → toExpRT st e2 e2RT →
    toExpRT st (BinOp n Div e1 e2)
            (BinOpRT n Div e1RT e2RT [DivCheck, OverflowCheck] nil)
...
Function toExpRTImpl(st:symTab)(e:exp): expRT :=...
```

As can be observed, ToBinOpO specifies that RT-GEN should generate (interior) Overf- lowCheck for addition, subtraction, or multiplication, and both DivCheck and Overfl- owCheck for division; toExpRT is implemented by toExpRTImpl using Coq's programming language features (like ML's) which is extractable to OCaml to produce an executable.

Evaluation: To certify RT-GEN, we proved that its specification is consistent (*sound* and *complete*) with respect to the SPARK mechanized semantics. For example, for expressions, we proved the following consistency lemma:

```
Lemma toExpRTConsistent: ∀ e eRT st stRT s v,
  toExpRT st e eRT→toSymTabRT st stRT→(evalExpRT stRT s eRT v ↔ evalExp st s e v).
```

where `toSymTabRT` transforms `symTab` to `symTabRT`, which, among other things, maps procedure names to their AST-RT. We then proved that the RT-GEN implementation is consistent with respect to its specification, for example:

```
Lemma toExpRTImplConsistent: ∀ e eRT st, toExpRTImpl st e = eRT ↔ toExpRT st e eRT.
```

Therefore, the implementation is transitively consistent with respect to the SPARK semantics (by transitivity of implication →/↔).

2.3   Certified Run-Time Check Optimizer

While RT-GEN generates a sufficient set of run-time checks, some of them may not be necessary. In fact, the GNAT front-end uses optimization techniques to reduce the set of run-time checks that it generates; in practice, we expect the set generated by GNAT to be a subset of the RT-GEN generated set (we confirmed through experiments that this is indeed the case in Sect. 2.4). The question is then whether GNAT's optimizations are (certifiably) sound. Our approach to answer this is to have a certified optimizer (RT-OPT) that reduces the run-time checks generated by RT-GEN. It is widely known that, in general, an optimizer cannot actually ever be optimal (due to the halting problem). Thus, the best we can hope for is to have RT-OPT reduce to the same (or even better, i.e., smaller) set as GNAT's (a smaller set implies that GNAT can be improved further); Sect. 2.4 confirms that this is indeed the case through validation.

RT-OPT: transforms AST-RT to another AST-RT by removing some run-time checks whose corresponding verification conditions (VCs) can be discharged; RT-OPT discharges the VCs by employing a (certified) abstract interpretation [7] analysis with interval numeric domain (Sect. 2.4 shows that RT-OPT is on par or better than GNAT's runtime-check optimizations). Similar to RT-GEN, we first specified RT-OPT as inductively defined relation and then implemented it as a function. For expressions, RT-OPT produces AST-RT along with the expression's interval domain (if any) as follows:

```
Inductive optExp: symTabRT→ expRT→ (expRT * interval)→ Prop = ...
Function optExpImpl(st:symTabRT) (e:expRT): option(expRT * interval) = ...
```

where `optExp` is typeset in Fig. 2 for readability. One invariant of RT-OPT is that integer expression optimization should produce an interval that fits within the compilation target platform-specific two's complement integer range, which makes up the default interval $[INT_{MIN}, INT_{MAX}]$. Γ holds the abstract interpretation context such as symbol table, etc. For notational convenience, `interiorChecks` and `exteriorChecks` are not explicitly shown; *EraseOverflowCheck* and *EraseDivCheck* remove overflow and division `interiorChecks`, respectively.

$$\dfrac{n \in [INT_{MIN}, INT_{MAX}]}{\Gamma \vdash optExp(n) = (EraseOverflowCheck(n),\ [n, n])}\ \text{INT1}\qquad \dfrac{n \notin [INT_{MIN},\ INT_{MAX}]}{\Gamma \vdash optExp(n) = (n,\ [INT_{MIN},\ INT_{MAX}])}\ \text{INT2}$$

$$\dfrac{\Gamma \vdash optExp(e_i) = (e_i',[v_i, w_i]),\ i \in \{1,2\}\quad v = v_1 + v_2\quad w = w_1 + w_2\quad \{v, w\} \subseteq [INT_{MIN}, INT_{MAX}]}{\Gamma \vdash optExp(e_1 + e_2) = (EraseOverflowCheck(e_1' + e_2'),\ [v, w])}\ \text{ADD1}$$

$$\dfrac{\Gamma \vdash optExp(e_i) = (e_i',[v_i, w_i]),\ i \in \{1,2\}\quad v = v_1 + v_2\quad w = w_1 + w_2\quad \{v, w\} \not\subseteq [INT_{MIN}, INT_{MAX}]}{\Gamma \vdash optExp(e_1 + e_2) = (e_1' + e_2',\ [max(v, INT_{MIN}),\ min(w, INT_{MAX})])}\ \text{ADD2}$$

$$\dfrac{\Gamma \vdash optExp(e_i) = (e_i',\ [v_i, w_i]),\ i \in \{1,2\}\quad 0 \notin [v_2, w_2]\quad INT_{MIN} \notin [v_1, w_1] \vee -1 \notin [v_2, w_2]}{\Gamma \vdash optExp(e_1/e_2) = (EraseOverflowCheck(EraseDivCheck(e_1'/e_2')),\ divInterval(v_1, w_1, v_2, w_2))}\ \text{DIV1}$$

$$\dfrac{\Gamma \vdash optExp(e_i) = (e_i',\ [v_i, w_i]),\ i \in \{1,2\}\quad 0 \notin [v_2, w_2]\quad INT_{MIN} \in [v_1, w_1] \wedge -1 \in [v_2, w_2]}{\Gamma \vdash optExp(e_1/e_2) = (EraseDivCheck(e_1'/e_2'),\ divInterval(v_1, w_1, v_2, w_2))}\ \text{DIV2}$$

$$\dfrac{\Gamma \vdash optExp(e_i) = (e_i',\ [v_i, w_i]),\ i \in \{1,2\}\quad 0 \in [v_2, w_2]\quad INT_{MIN} \notin [v_1, w_1] \vee -1 \notin [v_2, w_2]}{\Gamma \vdash optExp(e_1/e_2) = (EraseOverflowCheck(e_1'/e_2'),\ divInterval(v_1, w_1, v_2, w_2))}\ \text{DIV3}$$

$$\dfrac{\Gamma \vdash optExp(e_i) = (e_i',\ [v_i, w_i]),\ i \in \{1,2\}\quad 0 \in [v_2, w_2]\quad INT_{MIN} \in [v_1, w_1] \wedge -1 \in [v_2, w_2]}{\Gamma \vdash optExp(e_1/e_2) = (e_1'/e_2',\ divInterval(v_1, w_1, v_2, w_2))}\ \text{DIV4}$$

$$\dfrac{\Gamma(x) = \tau_{INT}\qquad [\![\tau_{INT}]\!] = [\tau_{MIN}, \tau_{MAX}]}{\Gamma \vdash optExp(x) = (x,\ [max(\tau_{MIN}, INT_{MIN}),\ min(\tau_{MAX}, INT_{MAX})])}\ \text{VARINT}$$

$$divInterval\ (v_1, w_1, v_2, w_2) = \begin{cases} [w_1/v_2, min(v_1/w_2, INT_{MAX})], & \text{if } w_2 < 0 \wedge w_1 < 0\quad(1) \\ [w_1/w_2, v_1/v_2], & \text{if } w_2 < 0 \wedge v_1 > 0\quad(2) \\ [w_1/w_2, min(v_1/w_2, INT_{MAX})], & \text{if } w_2 < 0 \wedge p_1\quad(3) \\ [v_1/v_2, w_1/w_2], & \text{if } v_2 > 0 \wedge w_1 < 0\quad(4) \\ [v_1/w_2, w_1/v_2], & \text{if } v_2 > 0 \wedge v_1 > 0\quad(5) \\ [v_1/v_2, w_1/v_2], & \text{if } v_2 > 0 \wedge p_1\quad(6) \\ [v_1, min(|v_1|, INT_{MAX})], & \text{if } p_2 \wedge w_1 < 0\quad(7) \\ [-w_1, w_1], & \text{if } p_2 \wedge v_1 > 0\quad(8) \\ [-max(|v_1|, |w_1|), min(max(|v_1|, |w_1|), INT_{MAX})], & \text{if } p_1 \wedge p_2\quad(9) \end{cases}$$

where $p_i = \neg(w_i < 0 \vee v_i > 0),\quad i \in \{1, 2\}$

Fig. 2. RT-OPT specification for expression (excerpts)

The INT1 rule in Fig. 2 optimizes away the overflow check in the case of an integer literal AST-RT n where n is within the platform's integer range; a single-value interval $[n, n]$ is returned along with the optimized AST-RT (i.e., the tight single-value interval allows for concrete interpretation). On the other hand, INT2 specifies the case where the overflow check is kept whenever n is outside the range, thus, the default interval is returned (in this case, an error message can be generated to notify the developer). ADD1 and ADD2 first try to optimize the two operands and compute the expression interval bounds (i.e., $[u, v]$). ADD1 specifies the case where the bounds are within the platform's integer range, hence, the overflow check associated the binary operation can be safely removed; otherwise, ADD2 specifies that run-time checks are preserved, and the resulting interval is the platform's integer range.

For division, four cases (DIV1-4) specify the different situations where division by zero and/or operation overflow (i.e., when dividing INT_{MIN} by -1) could occur; in all the cases, the resulting interval is specified by *divInterval* that does case analysis on the positivity/negativity of the interval operands. For example,

(5) specifies the case where both of the operand intervals $[v_1, w_1]$ and $[v_2, w_2]$ are positive (i.e., the low bounds v_1 and v_2 are positive); in this case, the resulting interval is $[v_1/w_2, w_1/v_2]$ where its low bound v_1/w_2 is computed by dividing the smallest value of the first operand's interval with the largest value of the second operand's interval, and its high bound w_1/v_2 is computed by dividing the largest value of the first operand's interval with the smallest value of the second operand's interval. The *divInterval* specification illustrates a slice of the RT-OPT's complexity for computing tight intervals in order to optimize away many run-time checks; rest assured however that they are proven to be correct in Coq.

Lastly, the VARINT rule specifies that an integer variable reference's interval is its integer type range intersected by the platform's integer range (i.e., leveraging the RT-OPT invariant that all computed integer values are always checked for overflows).

Well-Typed State: VARINT assumes that it can use the variable's integer type range for the variable reference's interval. This holds if all values in the state are well-typed. To discharge this assumption, we first specified the meaning for a state to be well-typed:

```
Inductive wellTypedState: symTabRT→ state→ Prop:=
| WellTypedState: ∀ stRT s,
   (∀ x v, fetch x s = Some v→ ∃ t, lookup stRT x = Some t ∧ wellTypedValue t v)→
wellTypedState stRT s.
```

then proved that EVAL-RT specification (hence, by virtue of consistency transitivity, EVAL specification) preserve state well-typed-ness, for example, for EVAL-RT statement semantics that may incur state changes, we proved the following preservation lemma:

```
Lemma wellTypedStatePreservation: ∀ s s' stmt stRT,
  wellTypedState stRT s→ evalStmtRT stRT s stmt s'→ wellTypedState stRT s'.
```

Evaluation: To certify RT-OPT, we proceeded similarly to RT-GEN certification (albeit much more complex to prove); that is, we proved that RT-OPT specification is consistent with respect to the RT-GEN specification described in Sect. 2.2, and that RT-OPT implementation is consistent with respect to its specification. Therefore, the implementation is transitively consistent with respect to the SPARK mechanized semantics.

2.4   Certifying GNAT RT Check Generator

Now that we have RT-GEN and RT-OPT, we can implement a conformance checker that can establish that, for a SPARK 2014 program p, the run-time check decoration insertion of the GNAT front-end for p conforms to the mechanized SPARK 2014 reference semantics. Specifically, for program p, the GNAT front-end generates a fully resolved AST with run-time check decorations, and we developed a tool called Jago that takes the GNAT AST and produces: (1) a Coq object of type AST (ast), where the GNAT run-time decorations are erased, and (2) a Coq object of type AST-RT (ast-rt-gnat), where the GNAT run-time decorations are preserved (Jago also applies some program transformations to desugar language constructs that lie outside of the language subset to fall within the language subset). Then, applying RT-GEN on ast produces ast-rt-gen, and applying RT-OPT on ast-rt-gen produces ast-rt-opt, both of which are of type AST-RT.

To automate the actual AST conformance check, we implemented a tool in Coq – $\subseteq$, that given two objects of type AST-RT, it determines whether the set of run-time checks in the first object is a subset of the second's. Thus, GNAT run-time decoration insertion on program p is conformant to the SPARK 2014 reference semantics if ast-rt-opt $\subseteq$ ast-rt-gnat $\subseteq$ ast-rt-gen. This toolchain essentially turns the GNAT front-end into a certifying run-time check decoration generator; that is, for a given program p, it generates evidence of "conformity to SPARK 2014 reference semantics for p's run-time check decorations" that is automatically machine-checked by certified tools.

Note that this does not guarantee that the actual binary run-time check assertion code for p subsequently generated by the GNAT compiler back-end is correct; it simply means that decorations indicating what assertions should be produced is correct. This, alone has significant value because, for example, it goes a long way toward establishing the correspondence between GNAT and GNATprove's (as well as any other SPARK backend tools') treatment of run-time checks. Moreover, since there are only three categories of run-time checks relevant for this language subset, since each of these categories can be represented by a simple code pattern involving a few numerical comparisons, since the pattern itself can be easily inspected and tested, and since the generation of binary code for the pattern is reasonable straightforward and can also be easily tested, one might argue that establishing the correctness of the decorations is one of the most important steps in establishing trust in the overall end-to-end production of the executable run-time checks.

3   Evaluation: Certifying GNAT

We evaluated GNAT according to the methodology described in Sect. 2.4 on a collection of programs. Table 1 presents the experiment data for various program units (packages/procedures) from the test programs. The first two SPARK programs come from the Ada Conformity Assessment Test Suite (ACATS) [16] that all Ada compilers must pass. SPARKSkein is an implementation of the Skein hash algorithm in SPARK, which was proved free of run-time errors [4]. Tetris is the motivating example described in Sect. 1, which is implemented partly in SPARK and partly in Ada (we only checked the SPARK part). All other examples are representative code from AdaCore, Altran and our own designed benchmark covering the core language subset. For each unit, **LoC** gives the line number of code. **Base**, **GNAT** and **Opt** give the number of run-time checks in ast-rt-gen, ast-rt-gnat and ast-rt-opt respectively, and **Diff** represents the number of run-time checks in **GNAT** that differs from the ones in **Opt**. Dash ("–") means "none"; a negative number $-n$ in **Diff** means that **Opt** removes n more run-time checks than **GNAT**; and, a positive number $+m$ means **Opt** has m

Table 1. Experiment data (excerpts)

Unit	LoC	Base				GNAT				Opt				Diff			
		D	O	R	T	D	O	R	T	D	O	R	T	D	O	R	T
ACATS_c53007a	143	–	16	–	16	–	14	–	14	–	14	–	14	–	–	–	–
ACATS_c55c02b	74	–	2	5	7	–	2	–	2	–	2	–	2	–	–	–	–
array_record_package	54	1	11	2	14	1	11	2	14	1	11	2	14	–	–	–	–
array_subtype_index	12	–	1	1	2	–	1	–	1	–	1	1	2	–	–	+1	+1
arrayrecord	43	1	9	2	12	1	9	–	10	1	9	–	10	–	–	–	–
assign_subtype_var	10	–	1	1	2	–	1	–	1	–	1	1	2	–	–	+1	+1
binary_search	40	1	6	12	19	1	–	4	5	–	–	4	4	–1	–	–	–1
bounded_in_out	17	–	1	4	5	–	–	3	3	–	–	4	4	–	–	+1	+1
dependence_test_suite_01	164	–	2	–	2	–	2	–	2	–	2	–	2	–	–	–	–
dependence_test_suite_02	249	–	15	–	15	–	15	–	15	–	15	–	15	–	–	–	–
division_by_non_zero	12	1	2	1	4	1	–	–	1	–	–	–	–	–1	–	–	–1
faultintegrator	25	–	2	–	2	–	2	–	2	–	2	–	2	–	–	–	–
gcd	18	1	3	–	4	1	3	–	4	1	3	–	4	–	–	–	–
linear_div	21	–	3	–	3	–	3	–	3	–	3	–	3	–	–	–	–
modulus	24	1	2	3	6	1	1	–	2	–	1	–	1	–1	–	–	–1
odd	14	1	2	–	3	1	1	–	2	–	1	–	1	–1	–	–	–1
p_simple_call	36	–	5	–	5	–	5	–	5	–	5	–	5	–	–	–	–
prime	21	1	2	–	3	1	2	–	3	1	2	–	3	–	–	–	–
quantifiertest	14	–	1	2	3	–	1	–	1	–	1	–	1	–	–	–	–
SPARKSkein	646	7	94	246	347	7	58	29	94	–	52	25	77	–7	–6	–4	–17
sort	43	–	5	6	11	–	5	6	11	–	5	6	11	–	–	–	–
Tetris	373	–	29	58	87	–	–	25	25	–	–	25	25	–	–	–	–
the_stack	42	–	4	6	10	–	–	6	6	–	–	6	6	–	–	–	–
the_stack_praxis	35	–	2	4	6	–	–	4	4	–	–	4	4	–	–	–	–
two_way_sort	49	–	4	17	21	–	–	4	4	–	–	4	4	–	–	–	–

more number of run-time checks than **GNAT** "somehow". Sub-column **D** gives the number of division by zero run-time checks; **O** and **R** give the number of overflow run-time checks and range run-time checks; and, **T** is the total number of run-time checks (i.e., **D+O+R**). RT-GEN and RT-OPT run fast (within seconds) and the data are omitted here due to space constraints.

As can be observed from Table 1, the GNAT frontend is a solid tool for run-time check generation/verification as most of its generated run-time checks match the certified RT-OPT. This is reasonable because our formalization captures the most commonly used run-time checks in SPARK and GNAT is quite mature after many years of effort to improve it, as well as the effort to improve the GNATprove toolchain by AdaCore and Altran (which drives some of the improvements in GNAT). However, RT-OPT edges out GNAT in some cases, especially for SPARKSkein. One reason is that GNAT does not take any advanced optimizations, for the division/modulus binary operator, it does not optimize even with constant; for example, GNAT generates division by zero check for the expression (R + 1) **mod** 3 while RT-OPT optimized it away. For SPARKSkein, consider a procedure call Inject_Key(R * 2), (for procedure declaration Inject_Key(X: **in** U32)), R is a variable of type U32, and U32 is a subtype of Integer with range 0..INT_MAX; an overflow check for R * 2 is enough to guarantee the absence of both overflow and range error, while GNAT keeps both overflow check and range check for such cases. There are other cases showing that RT-OPT is better than GNAT's optimizations.

In our initial evaluation (shown in the experiment table), GNAT produces fewer run-time checks than RT-OPT; these inconsistencies turned out to be benign because they are due to differences in how GNAT (vs RT-OPT) reports the need for checks and in how it assumes down-stream translation will interpret decorations for run-time checks. Once observed, the inconsistencies are rectified by slightly modifying $\subseteq$ to match GNAT's conventions, thus, resulting in a fully automatic approach to justify correctness of GNAT run-time check decorations. For completeness sake, we document the inconsistencies that we found (and fixed) here. In procedure array_subtype_index, there is an assignment A(0):=0, where the index type of A is a subtype of integer with range 1..10; thus, accessing A with the index 0 is out of its required range, so it will cause a range error. GNAT gives a compile time *warning* as specified in Ada reference manual without generating a range check; on the other hand, RT-OPT keeps this check (a similar issue exists for assign_subtype_var). Another difference is due to a single run-time check decoration in the GNAT AST that can lead downstream translation steps to introduce run-time checking code that implements multiple checks, e.g., a single GNAT run-time check AST decoration for an argument (both in and out) is interpreted as giving rise to code for two checks for both passing in argument and passing out return value.

Lessons Learned: The fact that RT-OPT is better in some cases illustrates that, despite its maturity, GNAT can still be improved further, e.g., by adopting the optimization specified and implemented in RT-OPT; that is, the RT-OPT specification can be used as a reference for implementing further optimizations in GNAT, and once implemented, they can then be checked for conformance against the RT-OPT implementation. Furthermore, in the case where new optimizations are added to GNAT that goes beyond RT-OPT as presented here, those new optimizations can be added to RT-OPT in order to: (a) mechanically verify that they are correct, and (b) further keep GNAT as a certifying run-time check generator.

Our research work demonstrates the feasibility of engineering an approach and corresponding tools with mechanized correctness proofs that leverage recent advancements and maturity of various formal method techniques and tools to make a direct impact in significantly increasing confidence in industrial tools; in our case, the industrial tools are used to develop critical systems that require the utmost level of integrity, thus, warranting such effort. From a business perspective, we believe it is desirable as it adds to the value proposition – the trustworthiness of GNAT compiler and associated SPARK 2014 is increased. Furthermore, we believe that the approach can eventually help in tool qualification processes typically done in certifications and regulatory reviews associated with standards (e.g., DO-178C in avionics) that increasingly recognize the value of formal methods and an official tool qualification process.

Threats To Internal Validity: Our approach is predicated on the assumption that practitioners are willing to trust the approach's trust-base, which includes Coq and the SPARK formal language semantics presented in Sect. 2.1. In addition, our current implementation uses: (a) the parser, symbol resolver, and type checker of GNAT itself, and (b) Jago to build program representations in Coq; both are not certified tools. Ideally, a certified frontend can be developed to address this issue; this certified frontend is orthogonal and out of the scope of the work presented here, and they can be addressed in the future. Moreover, the ⊆ tool that compares AST-RT objects is manually inspected instead of certified (it is small – 172 LoC, and its functionality is very simple); regardless, it should be considered as part of the trust-base at this point of time.

Threats To External Validity: One must also consider the extent to which the results presented for the given test suite would extend to SPARK 2014 programs in general. For this objective, program size and execution time are not really issues – the cost of insertion of run-time checks is in general linear in the number of AST nodes. The interval analysis needed for optimization does add some additional complexity, but not enough to significantly impact performance. On the other hand, a principle concern is that our test suite provides appropriate coverage of all the different types of run-time checks specified in the SPARK 2014 language reference manual. In addition, our language subset needs to be expanded to eventually cover the full-programming language (in fact, this work represents our third iteration based on the initial work [6]).

4 Related Work

The idea of a certifying approach that generates evidence that can be machine-checked goes back to proof-carrying code (PCC) [14] for memory safety. Since then, recent advancements and maturity in interactive theorem proving has enabled one to implement certified systems directly inside a theorem prover with what widely acknowledged as a relatively small trust-base footprint. One prominent work is the CompCert project [11], which demonstrates that one can now feasibly develop a certified optimizing compiler in Coq that guarantees the machine code it produces is behaviorally equivalent to its C source code. To provide such guarantee, it starts with formalizing a large subset of the C programming language – Clight [18], which is then used for proving program behavior preservation throughout its compilation pipeline. The main difference to our semantics work is that SPARK requires run-time checks as part of its semantics, which complicated our formalization effort (as described in Sect. 2.1).

In contrast to CompCert where the certified compiler is developed in Coq, the GNAT compiler is not developed in Coq. In fact, there are often a number of goals driving the development of language tools – performance, scalability, reusability, maintainability, etc. Many, if not most, of these often conflict with the goal of verifiability (and thus "mechanized" verifiability). In addition, it is hard to imagine verifying tools with a lot of legacy software (such as GNAT). Thus, there are strong forces against developing a certified language tool, and in situations like these creating a certifying tool can be an appropriate strategy when high-assurance is needed.

Some advantages of the certifying approach are that: (1) it can be adopted by existing/untrusted (high-performing) tools, and (2) it is much easier and a lot less costly to develop. One main advantage of the certified approach is that its correctness evidence (proof) is for all uses (runs) of the tool, while the certifying one is specific to a particular use; this specificity is sufficient and in line with typical tool qualification processes where tools are qualified for the particular use on the software being regulatorily certified for standard compliance [9].

The closest work on run-time checks to ours is Verasco [10] – a certified run-time check analyzer for C, whose design was inspired by Astrée [8]. RT-OPT employs a simpler abstract numerical domain compared to Verasco; thus, it can potentially discharge more verification conditions associated with run-time checks. This presents opportunities for RT-OPT future improvements. On the other hand, the soundness of Verasco was proven, but not its completeness. Because SPARK (unlike C) includes implicit run-time checks that must be accounted for in the semantics, completeness guarantees that all run-time checks are as prescribed by (traceable to) the reference semantics.

5   Conclusions and Future Work

In this paper, we have illustrated how the formal semantics of SPARK can be used in a mechanized proof infrastructure to check that ASTs produced by the GNAT compiler frontend having correctly incorporated decorations for run-time checks. This included developing an optimizer with mechanized proofs of correctness that achieves run-time check placement optimizations equal to or better than GNAT. The effectiveness of the approach was demonstrated using programs from AdaCore test suites.

Our next step is to build a mechanically proved translation from SPARK into CompCert's Clight, which would then provide a verified compiler for SPARK 2014 to the target languages supported by CompCert. In addition, the Jago translator also enables one to develop in Coq an integrated verification environment that includes the ability to use Coq to mechanically verify that a SPARK program conforms to its formally specified contracts. In situations where very high confidence is needed, this type of infrastructure could be used directly by verification engineers, or it could enable existing automated tools like Kiasan [3] or GNATprove [13] to emit Coq proofs establishing that their verification results for a particular program are correct.

References

1. Barnes, J.: SPARK: The Proven Approach to High Integrity Software. Altran Praxis (2012)
2. Barnes, J.: Ada 2012 Rationale - The Language, The Standard Libraries, Lecture Notes in Computer Science, vol. 8338. Springer, Heidelberg (2013)

3. Belt, J., Hatcliff, J., Robby, Chalin, P., Hardin, D., Deng, X.: Bakar kiasan: flexible contract checking for critical systems using symbolic execution. In: Bobaru, M., Havelund, K., Holzmann, G.J., Joshi, R. (eds.) NFM 2011. LNCS, vol. 6617, pp. 58–72. Springer, Heidelberg (2011). doi:10.1007/978-3-642-20398-5_6
4. Chapman, R., Botcazou, E., Wallenburg, A.: SPARKSkein: a formal and fast reference implementation of skein. In: Simao, A., Morgan, C. (eds.) SBMF 2011. LNCS, vol. 7021, pp. 16–27. Springer, Heidelberg (2011). doi:10.1007/978-3-642-25032-3_2
5. Chlipala, A.: Certified Programming with Dependent Types - A Pragmatic Introduction to the Coq Proof Assistant. MIT Press, Cambridge (2013)
6. Courtieu, P., Aponte, M., Crolard, T., Zhang, Z., Robby, Belt, J., Hatcliff, J., Guitton, J., Jennings, T.: Towards the formalization of SPARK 2014 semantics with explicit run-time checks using coq. In: HILT, pp. 21–22 (2013)
7. Cousot, P., Cousot, R.: Abstract interpretation: a unified lattice model for static analysis of programs by construction or approximation of fixpoints. In: POPL, pp. 238–252 (1977)
8. Cousot, P., Cousot, R., Feret, J., Mauborgne, L., Miné, A., Monniaux, D., Rival, X.: The astreé analyzer. In: ESOP, pp. 21–30 (2005)
9. Hatcliff, J., Wassyng, A., Kelly, T., Comar, C., Jones, P.L.: Certifiably safe software-dependent systems: challenges and directions. In: FOSE, pp. 182–200 (2014)
10. Jourdan, J., Laporte, V., Blazy, S., Leroy, X., Pichardie, D.: A formally-verified C static analyzer. In: POPL, pp. 247–259 (2015)
11. Leroy, X.: Formal verification of a realistic compiler. Commun. ACM **52**(7), 107–115 (2009)
12. McCormick, J.W., Chapin, P.C.: Building High Integrity Applications with SPARK. Cambridge University Press, Cambridge (2015)
13. Moy, Y., Ledinot, E., Delseny, H., Wiels, V., Monate, B.: Testing or formal verification: DO-178C alternatives and industrial experience. IEEE Software, pp. 50–56 (2013)
14. Necula, G.C.: Proof-carrying code. In: POPL, pp. 106–119 (1997)
15. O'Neill, I.: SPARK - a language and tool-set for high-integrity software development. In: Industrial Use of Formal Methods: Formal Verification. Wiley (2012)
16. Ada conformity assessment test suite (ACATS). http://www.ada-auth.org/acats.html
17. Ada reference manual. http://www.ada-auth.org/standards/ada12.html
18. Clight. http://compcert.inria.fr/doc/html/Clight.html
19. Compcert-c. http://compcert.inria.fr/compcert-C.html
20. The Coq proof assistant. http://coq.inria.fr
21. SPARK 2014 reference manual. http://docs.adacore.com/spark2014-docs/html/lrm/
22. Why3 - where programs meet provers. http://why3.lri.fr/

A Complete Generative Label Model for Lattice-Based Access Control Models

N.V. Narendra Kumar and R.K. Shyamasundar[(✉)]

Department of Computer Science and Engineering,
Indian Institute of Technology Bombay, Mumbai 400076, India
naren.nelabhotla@gmail.com, shyamasundar@gmail.com

Abstract. Lattice-based access control models (LBAC) initiated by Bell-LaPadula (BLP)/Biba models, and consolidated by Denning have played a vital role in building secure systems via Information Flow Control (IFC). IFC systems typically label data and track labels, while allowing users to exercise appropriate access privileges. This is defined through a finite set of security classes over a lattice. Recently, IFC has also been playing a crucial role in formally establishing the security of operating systems/programs. Towards such a goal, researchers often use assertions to keep track of the flow of information from one subject/object to another object/subject. Specifying and realizing these assertions will be greatly benefitted, if the underlying labels of objects/subjects can be interpreted in terms of access permissions/rights of subjects/objects as well as subjects/objects that have influenced them; these would lead to automatic generation of proof obligations/assertions. Thus, if one can arrive at a label model for LBAC that satisfies properties like (i) intuitive and expressive labels, (ii) completeness w.r.t. Denning's lattice model, and (iii) efficient computations on labels, then building/certifying secure systems using LBAC will be greatly benefitted.

In this paper, we arrive at such a semantic generative model (that tracks readers/writers of objects/subjects) for the Denning's lattice model, and establish a strong correspondence between syntactic label policies and semantically labelled policies. Such a correspondence leads to the derivation of the recently proposed Readers-Writers Flow Model (RWFM). It may be noted that RWFM [11] also deals with declassification rules which is not discussed here as it is not relevant here. The relationship, further establishes that the RWFM label model provides an application-independent concrete generative label model that is sound and complete wrt Denning's Model. We define the semantics of information flow in this label model, and argue that reading and writing induce possibly different pre-orders on the set of subjects. Hence, the subject relations become explicit, making it possible to derive relations from the labels. We further define a notion of information dominance on subjects and show that the notion of principal hierarchy can be naturally defined that is consistent with the IFC model; this perhaps overcomes the adverse impact on the flow policy that is often experienced during the classical approach of defining the hierarchy orthogonally. This enables us

N.V. Narendra Kumar — Currently at IDRBT, Hyderabad 500057, India.

© Springer International Publishing AG 2017
A. Cimatti and M. Sirjani (Eds.): SEFM 2017, LNCS 10469, pp. 35–53, 2017.
DOI: 10.1007/978-3-319-66197-1_3

to realize Role-Based Access Control (RBAC) structurally and enforce information flow security. Further, we demonstrate how the underlying label model succinctly subsumes various lattice-based control models like BLP, Biba, RBAC, Chinese wall model, etc.

Keywords: MAC · DAC · LBAC · RBAC · Chinese wall

1 Introduction

The ability to control the release and propagation of information lies at the heart of systems security. Standard access control models [2,6–8] control the release of information but do not provide the means for controlling its subsequent propagation. Lattice model of secure information flow proposed by Denning [5] provides support for controlling information propagation by assigning security levels to objects and subjects, and allowing information flow from a level to a higher or equal level only.

The lattice model is a simple policy that is compositional, which makes it possible to specify and verify end-to-end security guarantees. The lattice model of secure information flow together with DAC succinctly captures well known security models like the Bell-LaPadula model for secrecy/confidentiality [1], Biba's model for integrity [9], the Chinese-Wall security policy [3] etc.

The main objective of this paper is to first derive a semantic label model that has the following characteristics (i) expressive and intuitive labels, (ii) complete with respect to Denning's lattice model, and (iii) efficient label computations. Using such a label model, we then derive the recently proposed RWFM model [11,14] and thus establish the expressivity of the label structure of RWFM. Having established a strong correspondence between the Denning's lattice flow model and RWFM, we show how security (confidentiality/integrity) policies in multi-level secure (MLS) systems could be specified naturally in such a label structure. Further, we capture various prominent security models such as Bell-LaPadula model for secrecy/confidentiality [1], Biba's model for integrity [9], the Chinese-Wall security policy [3] etc., succinctly in the RWFM model. Furthermore, we arrive at the notion of information dominance in RWFM and through such a notion, we relate the model with RBAC and show how information flow control can also be established in RBAC through RWFM models. The crux of novelty of our work lies in the derivation of a generative concrete label model through which information flows in systems can be analyzed in an application independent manner.

Rest of the paper is organized as follows: Sect. 2 provides an overview of the Denning's lattice model, and a description of an algorithm for extracting semantic labels from Denning's model is presented in Sect. 3. Derivation of the basic RWFM, its transitions and its characteristic properties are presented in Sect. 4. Section 5 shows how to encode common security policies in RWFM. This is followed by a comparison of RWFM with RBAC in Sect. 6 followed by conclusions in Sect. 7.

2   Overview of Denning's Lattice Model

In this section, we introduce Denning's lattice model [5] of secure information flow, which is derived from security classes and is justified by the semantics of information flow. The salient feature of this model is that it encompasses several well known models like the Bell-LaPadula model for secrecy/confidentiality [1], Biba's integrity model [9], the Chinese-wall security policy [3] etc.

Denning's information flow model (DFM) is defined by the 5-tuple $DFM = (S, O, SC, \leqslant, \oplus)$, where (i) S is a set of *subjects/principals* (active agents responsible for information flow), (ii) O is a set of *objects* (information containers), (iii) SC is a set of *security classes*, (iv) $\leqslant$ is a binary relation on the security classes that specifies *permissible information flows*. $sc_1 \leqslant sc_2$ means that information in security class sc_1 is permitted to flow into security class sc_2, and (v) $\oplus$ is the *class-combining binary operator* (associative and commutative) that specifies, for any pair of operand classes, the class in which the result of any binary function on values from the operand classes belongs.

Example 1: An example of security classes in DFM could be $SC = \{l_1, l_2\}$, with $l_1 < l_2$ as the ordering. This means that information at security class l_1 is allowed to flow to security class l_2, but not vice-versa.

A pictorial representation of this lattice along with more example lattices is given in Fig. 1.

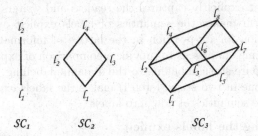

Fig. 1. Hasse diagrams of some example information flow lattices

The pictorial representations are to be interpreted as follows: if there is an upward path from class l to l', then information is allowed to flow from class l to l'. For example, in SC_1, information is allowed to flow from class l_1 to l_2 but not vice-versa. Similarly, in SC_2, information is allowed to flow from l_2 to l_4 but not to l_1 or l_3. In SC_3, information is allowed to flow from l_3 to l_4, l_7 and l_8 but to no others.   □

Subjects (S) and objects (O) are bound to security classes (SC) (either statically or dynamically depending on the application) by a labelling function, $\lambda : S \cup O \rightarrow SC$, that defines the *information-flow policy*. Note that, when a subject s reads an object o, information flows from o to s and this is permissible only if $\lambda(o) \leqslant \lambda(s)$. Similarly, when a subject s writes to an object o, information flows from s to o and this is permissible only if $\lambda(s) \leqslant \lambda(o)$.

Example 2: Consider the security lattice SC_1 given in Example 1. Let $S = \{s_1, s_2\}$ and $O = \{o_1, o_2\}$.

An example information-flow policy is given by $\lambda_1(s_1) = \lambda_1(o_1) = l_1$ and $\lambda_1(s_2) = \lambda_1(o_2) = l_2$. According to λ_1, s_1 can read o_1, because $\lambda_1(o_1) \leqslant \lambda_1(s_1)$ is satisfied by λ_1. Similarly, it is easy to verify that λ_1 permits s_1 to write o_1 and o_2 (because $\lambda_1(s_1) = l_1 \leqslant \lambda_1(o_2) = l_2$) but not read o_2; and s_2 can read and write o_2 and can read but not write to o_1.

Another information-flow policy could be defined by $\lambda_2(o_1) = l_1$ and $\lambda_2(s_1) = \lambda_2(s_2) = \lambda_2(o_2) = l_2$. If policy λ_2 is enforced, then both s_1 and s_2 are allowed to read and write o_2 and read but not write to o_1.   □

A system enforcing Denning's flow model DFM is *secure* iff execution of any sequence of operations of the system cannot give rise to a flow that violates the permissible information flow relation. Further, the natural conditions required of information flow force the structure $(SC, \leqslant)$ to be a lattice with $\oplus$ as the least upper bound operator.

3   Recasting Denning's Model via Semantic Labels

In this section, we recast the Denning's label model and formally arrive at a new label structure that explicitly captures the readers and writers of information. Such a label system makes the semantics of labels explicit and immediately provides an intuition for its position in the lattice of information-flow policy. Further, the recasting enables us to provide a comparison of expressive power of systems from the pure static labelling to the dynamic labelling.

Recasting is done in two steps: (step i) makes the labels explicit, and (step ii) incorporates the semantics of flow into labels.

STEP (i): Making the labels explicit
Consider Denning's flow model $DFM = (S, O, SC, \leqslant, \oplus)$. Unfortunately, from an application designer's perspective the labels in DFM do not provide any intuition about the flow policy. Our objective is to make the labels more intuitive while not losing the generality of the model.

Consider an element $sc \in SC$. From the perspective of sc, the only flows possible as per DFM are the following:

- for an element $sc' \in SC$ such that $sc \leqslant sc'$ information is allowed to flow from sc to sc'.
  Define $sc^\uparrow \triangleq \{sc' \in SC \mid sc \leqslant sc'\}$.
- for an element $sc' \in SC$ such that $sc' \leqslant sc$ information is allowed to flow from sc' to sc.
  Define $sc^\downarrow \triangleq \{sc' \in SC \mid sc' \leqslant sc\}$.

$sc^\uparrow$ denotes all the possible information flows out of sc, while $sc^\downarrow$ denotes all the possible information flows in to sc, and these are the only permissible flows as per DFM. Thus, the tuple $(sc^\uparrow, sc^\downarrow)$ captures the essence of sc for the purpose of studying information flows and also uniquely identifies sc. The idea is to replace the security class sc with $(sc^\uparrow, sc^\downarrow)$, thereby making the semantics/meaning of the label very explicit without the loss of generality. This transformation of DFM results in the flow model $DFM' = (S, O, SC', \leqslant', \oplus')$, where:

- $SC' = 2^{SC} \times 2^{SC}$; let $(A_1, B_1), (A_2, B_2) \in SC'$. Then
- $(A_1, B_1) \leqslant' (A_2, B_2)$ iff $((A_1 \supseteq A_2) \wedge (B_1 \subseteq B_2))$
- $(A_1, B_1) \oplus' (A_2, B_2) = (A_1 \cap A_2, B_1 \cup B_2)$

The following proposition establishes a very useful connection between the original model and its transformation.

Proposition 1: Given Denning's flow model $DFM = (S, O, SC, \leqslant, \oplus)$, and two elements sc_1 and sc_2 of SC, the following holds:

1. $sc_1 \in sc_1^\uparrow$ and $sc_1 \in sc_1^\downarrow$,
2. $sc_1 \in sc_2^\uparrow$ if and only if $sc_2 \in sc_1^\downarrow$,
3. $sc_1 \in sc_2^\uparrow$ if and only if $sc_1^\uparrow \subseteq sc_2^\uparrow$, and
4. $sc_1 \in sc_2^\downarrow$ if and only if $sc_1^\downarrow \subseteq sc_2^\downarrow$.

Proof of the above proposition is a simple consequence of the reflexivity and transitivity of $\leqslant$. Figure 2 provides the intuition. Interpretation of Fig. 2 is as follows:

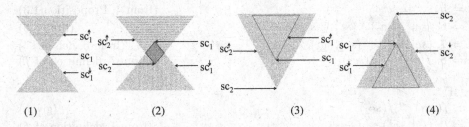

Fig. 2. Intuitive account of the connection between a flow model and its translation.

- Part (1) depicts a lattice point sc_1 together with its outward flows ($sc_1^\uparrow$ - horizontal shaded portion above) and inward flows ($sc_1^\downarrow$ - vertical shaded portion below). Further it also depicts the fact that the two shaded regions intersect exactly at the point sc_1.
- Part (2) depicts a lattice point sc_1 and its inward flows ($sc_1^\downarrow$ - vertical shaded portion below), and a lattice point sc_2 and its outward flows ($sc_2^\uparrow$ - horizontal shaded portion above). From the figure it is easy to observe that sc_1 is in the outward flows of sc_2 if and only if sc_2 is in the inward flows of sc_1.

- Part (3) depicts two lattice points sc_1 and sc_2 and their outward flows, and readily presents the following intuition: sc_1 is in the outward flow of sc_2 if and only if all the outward flows possible from sc_1 are also possible from sc_2.
- Part (4) depicts two lattice points sc_1 and sc_2 and their inward flows, and readily presents the following intuition: sc_1 is in the inward flow of sc_2 if and only if all the inward flows possible to sc_1 are also possible to sc_2.

From Proposition 1, it is easy to verify that the flow models DFM and DFM' are equivalent, in the sense that information flow from a class to another class is permitted in DFM if and only if the flow is permitted between the corresponding classes in DFM'. This is formalized as:

Theorem 1: Given a Denning's flow model $DFM = (S, O, SC, \leqslant, \oplus)$, let $DFM' = (S, O, SC', \leqslant', \oplus')$ where $SC' = 2^{SC} \times 2^{SC}$, $(A_1, B_1) \leqslant' (A_2, B_2) \triangleq ((A_1 \supseteq A_2) \wedge (B_1 \subseteq B_2))$, and $(A_1, B_1) \oplus' (A_2, B_2) \triangleq (A_1 \cap A_2, B_1 \cup B_2)$. The function $f : SC \rightarrow SC'$ defined by $f(sc) = (sc^\uparrow, sc^\downarrow)$ is such that for any two elements sc_1 and sc_2 of SC,

$$sc_1 \leqslant sc_2 \text{ if and only if } f(sc_1) \leqslant' f(sc_2).$$

Proof:
(Only-if)

1. $sc_1 \leqslant sc_2$ (given)
$\Rightarrow$ 2. $sc_2 \in sc_1^\uparrow$ (from 1, definition of $\uparrow$)
$\Rightarrow$ 3. $sc_2^\uparrow \subseteq sc_1^\uparrow$ (from 2, Proposition 1.3)
$\Rightarrow$ 4. $sc_1 \in sc_2^\downarrow$ (from 1, definition of $\downarrow$)
$\Rightarrow$ 5. $sc_1^\downarrow \subseteq sc_2^\downarrow$ (from 4, Proposition 1.3)
$\Rightarrow$ 6. $(sc_1^\uparrow \supseteq sc_2^\uparrow) \wedge (sc_1^\downarrow \subseteq sc_2^\downarrow)$. (from 3,5)
$\Rightarrow$ 7. $(sc_1^\uparrow, sc_1^\downarrow) \leqslant' (sc_2^\uparrow, sc_2^\downarrow)$. (from 6, def. of $\leqslant'$)
$\Rightarrow$ 8. $f(sc_1) \leqslant' f(sc_2)$. (from 7, definition of f)

(If)

1. $f(sc_1) \leqslant' f(sc_2)$ (given)
$\Rightarrow$ 2. $(sc_1^\uparrow, sc_1^\downarrow) \leqslant' (sc_2^\uparrow, sc_2^\downarrow)$. (from 1, definition of f)
$\Rightarrow$ 3. $(sc_1^\uparrow \supseteq sc_2^\uparrow) \wedge (sc_1^\downarrow \subseteq sc_2^\downarrow)$. (from 2, definition of $\leqslant'$)
$\Rightarrow$ 4. $(sc_1^\uparrow \supseteq sc_2^\uparrow)$ (from 3)
$\Rightarrow$ 5. $sc_2 \in sc_2^\uparrow$ (Proposition 1.3)
$\Rightarrow$ 6. $sc_2 \in sc_1^\uparrow$ (from 4,5)
$\Rightarrow$ 7. $sc_1 \leqslant sc_2$ (from 6, definition of $\uparrow$)

where, $\Rightarrow$ denotes logical implication.

STEP (ii): Incorporating the semantics of flow into labels
Next step is to note that information actually flows only because of the actions of subjects (active entities in the information system). Further, note that from the perspective of information flow, actions could be classified into three types:

Type 1: actions that cause information flow from the subject performing the action to the other entity,

Type 2: actions that cause information flow to the subject performing the action from the other entity, and

Type 3: actions that cause no information flow.

Information-flow control defines rules for controlling the first two types of actions. Note that the above interpretation, captures only the flow-relevant aspects of actions of the underlying system and not their specific semantics, thus still retaining generality.

Let $\lambda : S \cup O \rightarrow SC$ be a flow policy on DFM. For a subject $s \in S$ and a class $sc \in SC$, if $\lambda(s) \in sc^{\uparrow}$, then, only a Type 2 action of s on an entity at class sc will cause information to flow from sc to s. Similarly, for a subject $s \in S$ and a class $sc \in SC$, if $\lambda(s) \in sc^{\downarrow}$, then, only a Type 1 action of s on an entity at class sc will cause information to flow from s to sc.

Because of their similarity with familiar operations, we refer to Type 1 actions as WRITE actions and Type 2 actions as READ actions. With these ideas the readers and writers of a security class sc are defined below.

Definition 1 [Readers and Writers]: Given a Denning's flow model $DFM = (S, O, SC, \leqslant, \oplus)$ together with a policy $\lambda : S \cup O \rightarrow SC$, we define the readers, denoted sc^R, and writers, denoted sc^W, of a security class $sc \in SC$ as:

- $sc^R \triangleq \{s \in S \mid \lambda(s) \in sc^{\uparrow}\}$,
- $sc^W \triangleq \{s \in S \mid \lambda(s) \in sc^{\downarrow}\}$.

sc^R denotes the set of those subjects whose actions could result in information flow out of sc, and sc^W denotes the set of those subjects whose actions could result in information flow in to sc. These are the only ways information may flow.

The idea is to replace $sc^{\uparrow}$ with sc^R, and $sc^{\downarrow}$ with sc^W in DFM'. This transformation of DFM' results in the flow model $DFM'' = (S, O, SC'', \leqslant'', \oplus'')$, where:

- $SC'' = 2^S \times 2^S$
- $\leqslant''$ is the same as $\leqslant'$
- $\oplus''$ is the same as $\oplus'$

Define the policy $\lambda'' : S \cup O \rightarrow SC''$ as $\lambda''(e) \triangleq (\lambda(e)^R, \lambda(e)^W)$, where e denotes an entity (subject or object) of the information system. We abuse notion by writing e^R to mean $\lambda(e)^R$ and e^W to mean $\lambda(e)^W$ for an entity e.

The following proposition establishes a very useful connection between the original model and its transformation.

Proposition 2: Given a Denning's flow model $DFM = (S, O, SC, \leqslant, \oplus)$ together with a policy $\lambda : S \cup O \rightarrow SC$, and two subjects s_1 and s_2 in S, and an entity $e \in S \cup O$, the following holds:

1. $s_1 \in s_1^R$ and $s_1 \in s_1^W$,
2. $s_1 \in s_2^R$ if and only if $s_2 \in s_1^W$,
3. $s_1 \in e^R$ if and only if $s_1^R \subseteq e^R$, and
4. $s_1 \in e^W$ if and only if $s_1^W \subseteq e^W$.

Proof of the above proposition is a simple consequence of the definition of the transformation procedure and is omitted for brevity. The intuitions presented in Fig. 2 continue to hold with the following change: instead of collecting the lattice points in a cone, collect the subjects that are mapped (by flow policy) to a lattice point in the cone.

Once again, from Proposition 2, it is easy to see that DFM with policy λ and DFM'' with policy λ'' are equivalent, in the sense that an action is permitted by DFM with λ if and only if the action is permitted by DFM'' with λ''. The property is formally stated below.

Theorem 2: Given a Denning's flow model $DFM = (S, O, SC, \leqslant, \oplus)$ together with a policy $\lambda : S \cup O \rightarrow SC$, let $DFM'' = (S, O, SC'', \leqslant'', \oplus'')$ where $SC'' = 2^S \times 2^S$, $(A_1, B_1) \leqslant'' (A_2, B_2) \triangleq ((A_1 \supseteq A_2) \wedge (B_1 \subseteq B_2))$, and $(A_1, B_1) \oplus'' (A_2, B_2) \triangleq (A_1 \cap A_2, B_1 \cup B_2)$, and $\lambda'' : S \cup O \rightarrow SC''$ be such that $\lambda''(e) \triangleq (\lambda(e)^R, \lambda(e)^W)$, for $e \in S \cup O$. For any subject $s \in S$ and entity $e \in S \cup O$,

1. $\lambda(s) \leqslant \lambda(e)$ if and only if $\lambda''(s) \leqslant'' \lambda''(e)$, and
2. $\lambda(e) \leqslant \lambda(s)$ if and only if $\lambda''(e) \leqslant'' \lambda''(s)$.

The proof of the above theorem is very similar to the proof of Theorem 1 and is omitted for brevity. The above theorem is to be understood in the following way: a Type 1 (WRITE) action by s on e is permitted by DFM with λ only if $\lambda(s) \leqslant \lambda(e)$, which by the above theorem implies $\lambda''(s) \leqslant'' \lambda''(e)$ which in turn implies that the action is permitted by DFM'' with λ'', and vice versa. Similar reasoning applies for Type 2 (READ) actions due to item 2 in the theorem above. In summary, Theorem 2 asserts that any flow causing operation is authorized by DFM with λ if and only if it is authorized by DFM'' with λ''.

Note that in DFM'' security classes are defined only in terms of the active entities of the system being modelled. Further, security classes in DFM'' bring out the semantics of the flow model very explicitly and intuitively. The recasting procedure is summarized in Fig. 3.

3.1   Illustration of the Recasting Procedure Through Examples

In the new label system, we use $R(e)$ and $W(e)$ to denote the first (Readers) and second (Writers) components of the label assigned to an entity e respectively. The output produced by the recasting algorithm in Fig. 4 is referred to as the readers-writers policy.

Example 3: Consider the policy λ_1 given in Example 2. $\lambda_1(s_1) = \lambda_1(o_1) = l_1$ and $\lambda_1(s_2) = \lambda_1(o_2) = l_2$. $s_1 \in R(o_1)$ because $\lambda_1(o_1) \leqslant \lambda_1(s_1)$ reduces to $l_1 \leqslant l_1$ which is true. $s_2 \in R(o_1)$ because $\lambda_1(o_1) \leqslant \lambda_1(s_2)$ reduces to $l_1 \leqslant l_2$ which

Recasting Algorithm

Input	Denning's model $DFM = (S, O, SC, \leqslant, \oplus)$ and policy $\lambda : S \cup O \rightarrow SC$
Output	Flow model $DFM_1 = (S, O, SC_1, \leqslant_1, \oplus_1)$ and policy $\lambda_1 : S \cup O \rightarrow SC_1$
Procedure	
	$SC_1 = 2^S \times 2^S$
	$(A_1, B_1) \leqslant_1 (A_2, B_2) \triangleq [(A_1 \supseteq A_2) \wedge (B_1 \subseteq B_2)]$
	$(A_1, B_1) \oplus_1 (A_2, B_2) \triangleq (A_1 \cap A_2, B_1 \cup B_2)$
	$\lambda_1(e) = (\{s \in S \mid \lambda(e) \leqslant \lambda(s)\}, \{s \in S \mid \lambda(s) \leqslant \lambda(e)\})$, where $e \in S \cup O$

Fig. 3. Algorithm for recasting the Denning's flow policy

is also true. Therefore $R(o_1) = \{s_1, s_2\}$. Similarly, we can derive the following labels on objects: $R(o_2) = \{s_2\}$, $W(o_1) = \{s_1\}$ and $W(o_2) = \{s_1, s_2\}$. The labels for subjects are as below: $R(s_1) = \{s_1, s_2\}$, $R(s_2) = \{s_2\}$, $W(s_1) = \{s_1\}$ and $W(s_2) = \{s_1, s_2\}$.

The original and the inferred policies are depicted in Fig. 4; for simplicity only that portion of the derived lattice is shown where an entity in the system gets mapped.

Example 4: Let us consider a policy defined on the lattice SC_2 of Fig. 1. Let $S = \{s_1, s_2\}$, $O = \{o_1, o_2\}$, and $\lambda_3(s_1) = l_1$, $\lambda_3(s_2) = l_4$, $\lambda_3(o_1) = l_2$ and $\lambda_3(o_2) = l_3$.

In this case, the labelling comes out to be $R(o_1) = R(o_2) = \{s_2\}$, $W(o_1) = W(o_2) = \{s_1\}$, $R(s_1) = S$, $W(s_1) = \{s_1\}$, $W(s_2) = S$, and $R(s_2) = \{s_2\}$.

The original and the inferred policies are depicted in Fig. 5. Note that in Fig. 5 only that portion of the derived lattice where an entity in the system gets mapped is given for simplicity.

At a first glance, the inferred policy in Fig. 5 may seem to be incorrect because, it looks possible that information may flow from o_1 to o_2 in the derived policy as they are assigned the same lattice point, whereas in the original policy they are assigned incomparable lattice points thus preventing any information flows between them. However, note that for information to flow, subjects need to perform actions. The label assigned to o_1 and o_2 is such that s_2 who is capable of reading the objects cannot write to them, and s_1 who is capable of writing to them is unable to read them. This is what prevents any information flow between o_1 and o_2 in our policy.

Note that, in Example 3, the number of useful points in the inferred readers-writers lattice is the same as the original lattice. However, in Example 4, the number of useful points in the lattice resulting from the translation is fewer than the original one.

Examples 3 and 4 clearly illustrate that readers-writers policies are simpler to understand in comparison to policies that are based on syntactic lattices, as the label explicitly provides the influencers of the information as well as the subjects that need access to it.

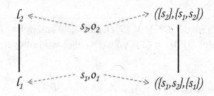

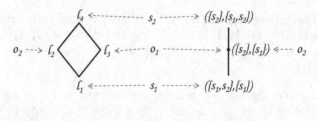

Denning's Policy   Readers-Writers Policy

Fig. 4. Denning's policy and its readers-writers policy inferred in Example 3

Denning's Policy   Readers-Writers Policy

Fig. 5. Denning's policy and its readers-writers policy inferred in Example 4

4   Recasting Readers/Writers Explicitly in Labels

Motivated by the recasting procedure presented in the previous section, we derive a new label structure that explicitly captures the readers and writers of information in a consistent manner.

Basic readers-writers labels, called BRW (Basic Readers and Writers) labels for short, are defined below:

Definition 2 [Basic RW Labels]**:** A BRW label, denoted by (R, W), is a tuple of set of subjects in an information system, i.e., $R \subseteq S$, and $W \subseteq S$, where S is the set of subjects in the system.

In the BRW label (R, W), R denotes the set of principals who are authorized to read this information, and W denotes the set of principals who have influenced this information.

Note: Information may flow between labels only when readers decrease and influencers increase. This is formalized in the definition of permissible flows below.

Definition 3 [Permissible Flows in Basic RW Labels]**:** Given any two BRW labels (R_1, W_1) and (R_2, W_2), information is permitted to flow from (R_1, W_1) to (R_2, W_2), denoted by $(R_1, W_1) \leqslant_B (R_2, W_2)$ only if $R_1 \supseteq R_2$ and $W_1 \subseteq W_2$.

Next, we define the label combining operators: least-upper bound (join) and greatest-lower bound (meet). Intuitively, join defines the least security class to which information from both the input classes is permitted to flow, and meet defines the highest security class from which information is permitted to flow into both the input classes.

Intuitively, when information readable by subjects in R_1 is combined with information readable by subjects in R_2, the resulting information can only be read by subjects in both R_1 and R_2. Similarly, when information influenced by subjects in W_1 is combined with information influenced by subjects in W_2, the resulting information has been influenced by subjects in both W_1 and W_2.

Similarly, when information readable by subjects in R_1 is allowed to flow into information readable by subjects in R_2 and into information readable by subjects in R_3, then it must be the case that every subject in R_2 and R_3 is also in R_1. When information influenced by subjects in W_1 is allowed to flow into information influenced by subjects in W_2 and into information influenced by subjects in W_3, then it must be the case that every subject in W_1 is also in W_2 and W_3.

The above intuitions are formalized below.

Definition 4 [Join and Meet of Basic RW Labels]: Let (R_1, W_1) and (R_2, W_2) be any two BRW labels. Their join ($\oplus_B$) and meet ($\otimes_B$) are defined as

$$(R_1, W_1) \oplus_B (R_2, W_2) = (R_1 \cap R_2, W_1 \cup W_2)$$
$$(R_1, W_1) \otimes_B (R_2, W_2) = (R_1 \cup R_2, W_1 \cap W_2).$$

Definitions 2, 3 and 4 immediately give us the following result:

Theorem 3 [Soundness of Basic RW Labels]: The set of all BRW labels $SC_B = 2^S \times 2^S$, together with the ordering $\leqslant_B$, join ($\oplus_B$) and meet ($\otimes_B$) forms a bounded lattice with minimum element $\perp_B = (S, \emptyset)$ and maximum element $\top_B = (\emptyset, S)$.

Proof: The proof is trivial and follows by observing that it is a product of two power-set lattices, the first one (readers lattice) ordered by reverse inclusion and the second (writers lattice) by inclusion.

Theorem 3 establishes that the basic readers-writers labels satisfy the conditions required by Denning's formulation, and hence, can be used for studying information flow properties.

Combining the above results leads us to the definition of basic readers-writers flow model (B-RWFM) described in the next subsection.

4.1   Basic Readers Writers Flow Model (B-RWFM)

Here, we define the B-RWFM model.

Definition 5 [B-RWFM]: Basic readers-writers flow model B-RWFM is defined as the eight tuple $(S, O, SC_B, \leqslant_B, \oplus_B, \otimes_B, \top_B, \perp_B)$, where

S and O are the set of subjects and objects in the information system,
$SC_B = 2^S \times 2^S$ is the set of labels,
$\leqslant_B = (\supseteq, \subseteq)$ is the permissible flows ordering,
$\oplus_B = (\cap, \cup)$ and $\otimes_B = (\cup, \cap)$ are the join and meet operators respectively, and
$\top_B = (\emptyset, S)$ and $\perp_B = (S, \emptyset)$ are respectively the maximum and minimum elements in the lattice.

The first component of the security class in a B-RWFM is to be interpreted as the set of readers, and the second component as the set of influencers. Note that B-RWFM is fully defined in terms of S, the set of subjects in the information system.

A flow model together with a labelling function defines the access policy. Let $\lambda : S \cup O \rightarrow SC_B$ be a labelling function. For simplicity, we use $R_\lambda(e)$ and $W_\lambda(e)$ to denote the first and second components of the labels assigned to an entity $e \in S \cup O$. Further, the subscript λ is omitted when it is clear from the context. Access rules in the B-RWFM model are defined below.

Definition 6 [Access Rules in B-RWFM]: Given a B-RWFM, and functions R and W describing a labelling,

- a subject s is allowed to read an object o if $R(o) \supseteq R(s)$, $W(o) \subseteq W(s)$, and
- a subject s is allowed to write an object o if $R(s) \supseteq R(o)$ and $W(s) \subseteq W(o)$.

4.2   Characteristic Properties of B-RWFM

In this section, we establish some very useful properties of the basic readers-writers flow model, starting with the completeness result.

Theorem 4 [Completeness of B-RWFM]:   Given a Denning's flow model $DFM = (S, O, SC, \oplus, \leqslant)$ and a policy $\lambda : S \cup O \rightarrow SC$, there exists a labelling, $\lambda_B : S \cup O \rightarrow SC_B$, in the basic readers-writers flow model that enforces the same policy i.e.,

(i) s is permitted to read o by Denning's policy if and only if it is permitted by the basic readers-writers policy.
(ii) s is permitted to write o by Denning's policy if and only if it is permitted by the basic readers-writers policy.

Proof: The proof is constructive. Note that the recasting algorithm presented in Fig. 3 actually produces a B-RWFM and a policy. Further, the policy satisfies Theorem 2, which immediately gives us the desired result.

In any IFC model one looks for capturing "dominance" of certain operations in the model so that either verification or compliance of the operations with respect to policies can be validated. Towards such a goal, we shall discuss the characteristic properties of the model in the following.

Proposition 3: Let DFM with λ be a Denning's flow policy, and let R and W denote the corresponding labelling in B-RWFM. For any subject s, the following holds: $s \in R(s)$ and $s \in W(s)$.

Proposition 4: Let DFM with λ be a Denning's flow policy, and let R and W denote the corresponding labelling in B-RWFM. For any subject s and object o, the following holds:

(i) $R(o) \supseteq R(s) \Rightarrow W(o) \subseteq W(s)$
(ii) $W(s) \subseteq W(o) \Rightarrow R(s) \supseteq R(o)$
    where $\Rightarrow$ denotes logical implication.

Proof is an easy consequence of the construction and is omitted for brevity.

Definition 6 says that, a subject s can be allowed to read an object o if $R(o) \supseteq R(s)$, and $W(o) \subseteq W(s)$ are satisfied. Proposition 4 simplifies this check to $R(o) \supseteq R(s)$. Similar argument holds for writing.

We argued that intuitively $R(o)$ and $W(o)$ capture the set of subjects allowed to read and write o respectively. This is formalized in the proposition below.

Proposition 5: Let DFM with λ be a Denning's flow policy, and let R and W denote the corresponding labelling in B-RWFM. For any subject s and object o, the following holds:

(i) $s \in R(o)$ if and only if $R(o) \supseteq R(s)$
(ii) $s \in W(o)$ if and only if $W(s) \subseteq W(o)$
    where $\Rightarrow$ denotes logical implication.

Proposition 5 further simplifies the access check to $s \in R(o)$ for s to read o, and $s \in W(o)$ for s to write o. Thus, *the model provides for intuitive specifications and also simplifies the algorithm for making access decisions.*

Information Dominance of Subjects

B-RWFM also makes the relations between the subjects in the system explicit. This is formalized below.

Proposition 6: Let DFM with λ be a Denning's flow policy, and let R and W denote the corresponding labelling in B-RWFM. For any two subjects s_1 and s_2, the following holds:

(i) $s_1 \in R(s_2)$ if and only if $R(s_1) \subseteq R(s_2)$.
(ii) $s_1 \in W(s_2)$ if and only if $W(s_1) \subseteq W(s_2)$.

Definition 7 [Read Dominance]: Given subjects s_1 and s_2, we say that s_1 "read dominates" s_2, written $s_2 \preceq_R s_1$, if $s_1 \in R(s_2)$.

Definition 8 [Write Dominance]: Given subjects s_1 and s_2, we say that s_1 "write dominates" s_2, written $s_2 \preceq_W s_1$, if $s_1 \in W(s_2)$.

Definition 9 [Information Dominance]: Given subjects s_1 and s_2, we say that s_1 "information dominates" s_2, written $s_2 \preceq_I s_1$, if $s_2 \preceq_R s_1$ and $s_1 \preceq_W s_2$.

Theorem 5 The dominance relations $\preceq_R$, $\preceq_W$ and $\preceq_I$ on subjects are reflexive and transitive (pre-order).

The above theorem says that the labelling R and W imposes an ordering on the set of subjects of the system. Commonly used notion of principal hierarchy is formulated in terms of $\preceq_R$ and $\preceq_W$ as follows.

Definition 10 [Principal Hierarchy]: Given subjects s_1 and s_2, we say that s_1 "dominates" s_2 in the principal hierarchy, written $s_2 \preceq s_1$, if $s_2 \preceq_R s_1$ and $s_2 \preceq_W s_1$.

Note: Considering the fact that information flows in opposite directions for reading and writing, we advocate that in the context of IFC, information dominance provides a better notion of "superiority" than the classical notion of principal hierarchy. Further, Proposition 6 provides an efficient and intuitive way to compute this relation in B-RWFM. Note that, our notion of information dominance is implicit in the labels and is derived from the underlying flow policy and hence consistent, as opposed to an orthogonally defined principal hierarchy which adversely impacts the flow policy.

5   Encoding Common Security Policies in RWFM

In this section, we demonstrate the expressive power of RWFM by encoding many common security policies in the spectrum of information sharing. At one extreme, we have the total isolation policy which does not permit any sharing, and at the other extreme we have the unrestricted-access policy which permits unconditional sharing.

Total Isolation
Given an information system with n subjects $S = \{s_1, s_2, \ldots, s_n\}$, the total isolation policy is encoded by restricting labels to be of the form $L_i = (\{s_i\}, \{s_i\})$ for $1 \leqslant i \leqslant n$. Note that information labelled L_i is accessible only to the subject s_i, and is unrelated to all other labels L_j, $i \neq j$, and hence this labelling correctly captures the total isolation policy.

Denning, MLS, Bell-LaPadula and Biba
We have already demonstrated in Fig. 3 (cf. Sect. 3) how a Denning's lattice policy is encoded in RWFM. Note that multi-level security policy (MLS), the Bell-LaPadula policy for confidentiality, and the Biba policy for integrity are special cases of Denning's lattice and hence are automatically captured in RWFM.

Chinese-Wall policy
Although the Chinese-Wall policy [3] is also subsumed by the Denning's lattice, it has certain features that make its modelling tricky. In the following, we show how the same can be effectively specified and enforced in RWFM. For simplicity, we assume absence of any sanitized information.

Let $C_1, C_2, \ldots, C_k$ denote the k conflict of interest classes, and $|C_i| = n_i$. The data sets in class C_i are denoted by D_{ij} for $1 \leqslant j \leqslant n_i$. Without loss of generality, we assume that the principal d_{ij} denotes the company whose data set is D_{ij}. $D = \{d_{ij}\}_{1 \leqslant i \leqslant k, 1 \leqslant j \leqslant n_i}$ denotes the set of all the companies.

$P = \{X \subseteq (C_1 \cup C_2 \cup \cdots \cup C_k) \mid \forall 1 \leqslant i \leqslant k, |X \cap C_i| \leqslant 1\}$ denotes the set of all the permissible combinations of data sets on which users may work without violating the conflicts of interest. Note that this definition is similar in spirit to the structure of labels derived by Sandhu [17] for capturing the Chinese Wall policy.

Let E denote the set of all the employees of the consulting firm that sets up the Chinese Wall. $S = E \cup D$ denotes the set of all the subjects, and $O = \{D_{ij}\}_{1 \leqslant i \leqslant k, 1 \leqslant j \leqslant n_i}$ denotes the set of initial objects in the information system. Function $A : S \to P$ defines an allocation of the users to work on various data sets, such that $A(d_{ij}) = \{D_{ij}\}$ i.e., a company can access only its data set.

We define the RWFM labels, $\lambda : S \cup O \to 2^S \times 2^S$, on initial objects as follows:

$$\lambda(D_{ij}) = (\{s \in S \mid D_{ij} \in A(s)\}, \{d_{ij}\})$$

The label tells us that d_{ij} is a permissible reader and also the only influencer of the data set D_{ij}. Further, all those employees that have been assigned to work on D_{ij} are permissible readers.

Properties of the labelling:

- No two data sets in the same conflict class, have a common reader i.e. for $j_1 \neq j_2$, we have $R(D_{ij_1}) \cap R(D_{ij_2}) = \emptyset$. Proof by contradiction: Assume there is a common reader, say s, then $D_{ij_1} \in A(s)$ and $D_{ij_2} \in A(s)$, i.e. $|A(s) \cap C_i| > 1$ which contradicts the definition of P. This fact together with the characteristic properties of RWFM labels guarantee Theorems 1 and 2 of [3].
- Information can never flow from one data set to another. This is a simple consequence of the fact that RWFM requires $W_1 \subseteq W_2$ for information to flow, which is satisfied only when the two data elements are from the same data set in which case $W_1 = W_2$. For data from different data sets $W_1 \cap W_2 = \emptyset$. This accounts for Theorem 3 of [3].

6   Where does RWFM stand in relation to RBAC

RBAC [7] is a very expressive and a policy neutral access control framework, that can be configured to denote either DAC or MAC policies [16]. RBAC is designed considering practical requirements, and has gained wide spread adoption for denoting DAC in commercial organizations due to ease of policy mapping and management. The concept of session in RBAC relates to the notion of subject in traditional systems, and supports the principle of least privilege [7].

Due to the significance of IFC for security, and the necessity of controlling both access and information flow for security of practical systems, researchers have tried to closely understand the relation between RBAC and information flow requirements. Two broad research directions pursued have been:

1. On one hand, approaches to configure RBAC to enforce a given Lattice Based Access Control (LBAC) [18] denoting information flow/multi-level security forms of MAC policy have been proposed [19].

2. On another hand, information flows caused by an RBAC configuration have been studied; it was noted that due to permission inheritance implied by the semantics of role hierarchy, an RBAC configuration may lead to unwanted information flows [4]. Techniques for detection [15] and resolution [20] of information flow conflicts in RBAC configurations have been explored.

In the following, we argue the simplicity of specifying and enforcing LBAC policies in RWFM in comparison to RBAC, and demonstrate RWFM enforcement of the information flows implied by an RBAC configuration.

Completeness of RWFM with respect to Denning's lattice model [5] and the examples presented earlier in the paper clearly highlight the simplicity of RWFM for specifying and enforcing LBAC policies. Although the generality and expressive power of RBAC enables the specification and enforcement of LBAC, the results are quite nonintuitive with many constraints and disjoint lattices for reading and writing. Further, unlike RWFM, RBAC does not permit the creation of new objects because of its inability to compute and automatically assign a security label. It is to be further noted that it has been shown in the information-flow literature that allowing users to selectively activate and deactivate labels in a session lead to covert channels of information-flow.

Consider the following RBAC configuration: users $= \{A, B\}$, roles $= \{R_1, R_2\}$, objects $= \{f_1, f_2\}$, role hierarchy RH $= R_2 > R_1$, user assignment UA $= \{(A, R_2), (B, R_1)\}$, permission assignment (PA),

$$PA = \{(R_1, (f_1, r)), (R_1, (f_1, w)), (R_2, (f_2, r)), (R_2, (f_2, w))\}.$$

The above policy can be interpreted as follows: f_1 can be read and written by both A and B since R_2 is superior to R_1, while f_2 can be read and written by A only. This RBAC configuration is pictorially presented in Fig. 6(a).

Interpreting the above policy from the perspective of information-flow, we get the following security classes for f_1 and f_2. Security class of $f_1 = (\{A, B\}, \{A, B\})$, and security class of $f_2 = (\{A\}, \{A\})$. These two points are incomparable in the lattice of security classes, and therefore no flow of information is allowed between them. Adding the points $(\{A, B\}, \{A\})$ (GLB of the security classes of f_1 and f_2) and $(\{A\}, \{A, B\})$ (LUB of the security classes of f_1 and f_2) completes the lattice. The lattice induced is pictorially presented in Fig. 6(b).

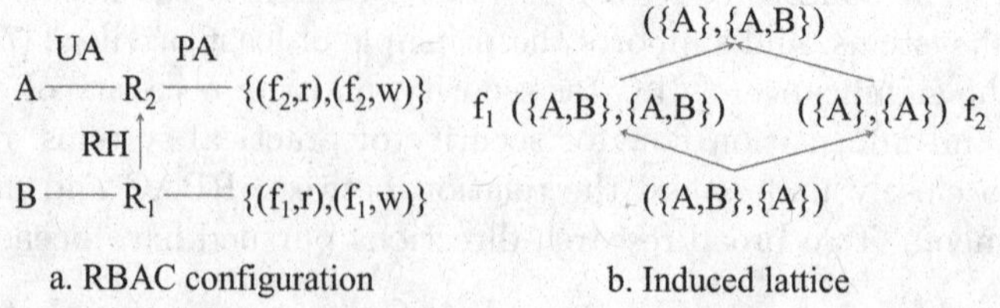

a. RBAC configuration   b. Induced lattice

Fig. 6. An RBAC configuration and the lattice induced by it

It is easy to note that under the RBAC enforcement, A can cause information to flow from f_1 to f_2 and vice versa, thus violating the information flow policy. However, under the RWFM enforcement, A will not be allowed to write f_2 after he has accessed f_1 because A's writers would now consist of both A and B, and B is not permitted to influence f_2. Similarly, under the RWFM enforcement, A will not be allowed to write f_1 after he has accessed f_2 because A's readers become A, and writing to f_1 allows B also to access this information which is not permitted. In the case of RWFM enforcement, the label of the subject succinctly keeps track of the actions of the user, and there is no need/option for users to explicitly choose roles to be activated and deactivated in a session.

For the above RBAC configuration, (i) both RBAC enforcement and RWFM enforcement allow B to perform any action from $[(f_1, r) + (f_1, w)]^*$, and (ii) while RBAC enforcement allows A to perform any action from $[(f_1, r) + (f_1, w) + (f_2, r) + (f_2, w)]^*$, RWFM allows only a strict subset of it $[(f_1, w) + (f_2, w)]^*.[[(f_1, r) + (f_1, w)]^* + [(f_2, r) + (f_2, w)]^*].[(f_1, r) + (f_2, r)]^*$.

7 Conclusions

In this paper, we have arrived at a semantic generative label model for the Denning's lattice model, and established a strong correspondence between syntactic label policies and semantically labelled policies. Using such a correspondence we have derived the basic RWFM model and shown that the RWFM label model provides an application independent concrete generative label model that is sound and complete with respect to Denning's Model. We have demonstrated that reading and writing induce possibly different pre-orders on the set of subjects of the information system and hence, the subject relations become explicit, making it possible to derive the relations from the labels. In fact, such an information can be exploited formally to arrive at correctness of protocols [12]. We further define a notion of information dominance on subjects and show that the notion of principal hierarchy can be naturally defined that is consistent with the IFC model rather than the approach of defining the hierarchy orthogonally that could lead to adverse impact on the flow policy. This enables us to realize RBAC syntactically and also enforce information flow security on RBAC. We demonstrate how the underlying label model succinctly defines various lattice-based access control models like BLP, Biba, Chinese wall model etc. Furthermore, the label model provides a specification of confidentiality and integrity policies (labels) in an integrated way for multi-level security (MLS) rather than the classical approach of taking cross product that could lead to consideration of non-compliable policies. This is very beneficial in MLS, as evidenced in our demonstration of the realization of Chinese wall model via RWFM; additionally, the properties remain invariant both on objects and subjects (or consultants in the context of Chinese wall model) even while they make a transition without the need of additional access control; that is, the RWFM model transitions preserve the properties without additional control.

As the labels are intuitive and capture semantic information, we have found it useful in formally proving the correctness of protocols [12,13]. Further, the underlying dynamic labelling has been extremely useful in our ongoing effort in certifying programs in Python and Java. It must be pointed out that the full RWFMmodel has the capability to do declassifications in a robust manner; these aspects as well comparison of the RWFMlabel model with other label models will be reported elsewhere.

Acknowledgement. The work was done as part of Information Security Research and Development Centre (ISRDC) at IIT Bombay, funded by MEITY, Government of India.

References

1. Bell, D., La Padula, L.: Secure computer systems: Unified exposition and multics interpretation. In: Technical Report ESD-TR-75-306, MTR-2997, MITRE, Bedford, Mass (1975)
2. Blaze, M., Feigenbaum, J., Lacy, J.: Decentralized trust management. In: IEEE SP 1996, pp. 164–173. IEEE Computer Society (1996)
3. Brewer, D., Nash, M.: The Chinese wall security policy. In: 1989 Proceedings of the IEEE Symposium on Security and Privacy, pp. 206–214, May 1989
4. Crampton, J.: On permissions, inheritance and role hierarchies. In: Proceedings of the 10th ACM Conference on Computer and Communications Security, CCS, pp. 85–92 (2003)
5. Denning, D.: A lattice model of secure informatiom flow. Commun. ACM **19**(5), 236–243 (1976)
6. Ellison, C., Frantz, B., Lampson, B., Rivest, R., Thomas, B., Ylonen, T.: RFC 2693: SPKI certificate theory. IETF RFC Publication, September 1999
7. Ferraiolo, D., Kuhn, R.: Role-based access controls. In: 15th NIST-NCSC National Computer Security Conference, pp. 554–563 (1992)
8. Harrison, M.A., Ruzzo, W.L., Ullman, J.D.: Protection in operating systems. Commun. ACM **19**(8), 461–471 (1976)
9. Biba, K.: Integrity considerations for secure computer systems. In: Technical Report ESD-TR-76-372, MITRE, Bedford, Mass (1976)
10. Krishnan, P., Krishna, P.R., Parida, L. (eds.): Distributed Computing and Internet Technology. Lecture Notes in Computer Science, vol. 10109. Springer, Heidelberg (2017). doi:10.1007/978-3-319-50472-8
11. Kumar, N.V.N., Shyamasundar, R.K.: Realizing purpose-based privacy policies succinctly via information-flow labels. In: 2014 IEEE Fourth International Conference on Big Data and Cloud Computing, BDCloud 2014, Sydney, Australia, 3–5 December 2014, pp. 753–760. IEEE Computer Society (2014). https://doi.org/10.1109/BDCloud.2014.89
12. Kumar, N.V.N., Shyamasundar, R.K.: Analyzing protocol security through information-flow control. In: Krishnan et al. [10], pp. 159–171. https://doi.org/10.1007/978-3-319-50472-8_13
13. Kumar, N.V.N., Shyamasundar, R.K.: Dynamic labelling to enforce conformance of cross domain security/privacy policies. In: Krishnan et al. [10], pp. 183–195. https://doi.org/10.1007/978-3-319-50472-8_15
14. Kumar, N.V.N., Shyamasundar, R.: Decentralized information flow securing method and system for multilevel security and privacy domains, 29 November 2016. https://www.google.co.in/patents/US9507929, US Patent 9,507,929

15. Nyanchama, M., Osborn, S.L.: The role graph model and conflict of interest. ACM Trans. Inf. Syst. Secur. **2**(1), 3–33 (1999)
16. Osborn, S., Sandhu, R., Munawer, Q.: Configuring role-based access control to enforce mandatory and discretionary access control policies. ACM Trans. Inf. Syst. Secur. **3**(2), 85–106 (2000). http://doi.acm.org/10.1145/354876.354878
17. Sandhu, R.S.: Lattice-based enforcement of Chinese walls. Comput. Secur. **11**(8), 753–763 (1992)
18. Sandhu, R.S.: Lattice-based access control models. Computer **26**(11), 9–19 (1993)
19. Sandhu, R.S.: Role hierarchies and constraints for lattice-based access controls. In: Bertino, E., Kurth, H., Martella, G., Montolivo, E. (eds.) ESORICS 1996. LNCS, vol. 1146, pp. 65–79. Springer, Heidelberg (1996). doi:10.1007/3-540-61770-1_28
20. Tuval, N., Gudes, E.: Resolving information flow conflicts in RBAC systems. In: Damiani, E., Liu, P. (eds.) DBSec 2006. LNCS, vol. 4127, pp. 148–162. Springer, Heidelberg (2006). doi:10.1007/11805588_11

From Model Checking to a Temporal Proof for Partial Models

Anna Bernasconi[1(✉)], Claudio Menghi[2,3(✉)], Paola Spoletini[4],
Lenore D. Zuck[5], and Carlo Ghezzi[1]

[1] DEIB - Politecnico di Milano, Milan, Italy
{anna.bernasconi,carlo.ghezzi}@polimi.it
[2] Chalmers University of Technology, Gothenburg, Sweden
[3] University of Gothenburg, Gothenburg, Sweden
claudio.menghi@gu.se
[4] Kennesaw State University, Marietta, Georgia
pspoleti@kennesaw.edu
[5] University of Illinois at Chicago, Chicago, USA
lenore@cs.uic.edu

Abstract. Three-valued model checking has been proposed to support verification when some portions of the model are unspecified. Given a formal property, the model checker returns *true* if the property is satisfied, *false* and a violating behavior if it is not, *maybe* and a possibly violating behavior if it is *possibly satisfied*, i.e., its satisfaction may depend on how the unspecified parts are refined. Model checking, however, does not explain the reasons *why* a property holds, or possibly holds. Theorem proving can instead do it by providing a formal proof that explains why a property holds, or possibly holds in a system. Integration of theorem proving with model checking has only been studied for classical two-valued logic – hence, for fully specified models. This paper proposes a unified approach that enriches three-valued model checking with theorem proving to generate proofs which explain why *true* and *maybe* results are returned.

1 Introduction

Multi-valued model checking techniques, such as [5–7, 15, 19], have been proposed to support the verification of models that are *partial*, i.e., their state space is not fully specified. Three-valued model checking is a multi-valued model checking technique that extends classical two-valued model checking by possibly returning an additional *maybe* value. More precisely, it returns *true* if the property definitely holds, *false* if it definitely does not hold, *maybe* otherwise.

In the classical context of two-valued model checking, although a sample violating behavior (a counterexample) is normally returned when the property is violated, no equally useful insight is provided if the property holds. In practice, it would be useful to receive a formal explanation of the reason *why* the system satisfies the property. To achieve this goal, the model checking framework can

© Springer International Publishing AG 2017
A. Cimatti and M. Sirjani (Eds.): SEFM 2017, LNCS 10469, pp. 54–69, 2017.
DOI: 10.1007/978-3-319-66197-1_4

be equipped with a theorem prover that formally justifies why model checking has failed in the search of a counterexample. Theorem proving algorithms have been developed for fully specified models [21, 22], but no known similar approach deals with partial models.

The ability to deal with partial models has a strong practical motivation. Software development often proceeds in an iterative and incremental fashion. Designers may start by providing an initial, high-level version of the model, which is iteratively narrowed down as design progresses and uncertainties are removed. Whenever the result of verification is *true* or *maybe*, the proof can guide the designer throughout the refinement process, and confirm the correctness of the design choices already performed. In some cases, the proof may even implicitly suggest that actually the property does not capture the intended correctness condition, and it should be modified. For this reason, the integration of theorem proving techniques and multi-valued model checking can guide the designer towards the development of a correct model.

This paper proposes THRIVE, a THRee valued Integrated Verification framEwork for partial models. THRIVE enriches model checking for partial models with theorem proving. Theorem proving is used when a *true* or a *maybe* value is returned by the model checker to justify why the verified system *definitely* or *possibly* satisfies the property of interest. In addition to the general framework, we present a specific instance of THRIVE useful for applications, which considers models described as Partial Kripke Structures (PKSs) [5] and properties expressed as Linear Temporal Logic (LTL) [23] formulae. The instance is based on the three-valued LTL semantics [5]. To successfully integrate model checking and theorem proving we customize the theorem proving framework (based on deductive verification) proposed in [22] to support PKSs and LTL formulae.

We consider the applicability of THRIVE w.r.t. *three-valued* [5] and *thorough* [6] LTL semantics. We also discuss its applicability in the case of *self-minimizing* [11] LTL formulae, which are known to represent a practically relevant subset of LTL formulae [2]. We evaluate the benefits of the framework on an example by simulating the design of a medical software critical component [3]. A discussion on the use of THRIVE in real world scenarios concludes the evaluation.

Running example. *We consider a simple grade crossing semaphore. We assume that the designer has identified three simple properties: (1) Red lights up infinitely often – formalized as $\phi_1 = \Box\Diamond red$. (2) Green lights up infinitely often – formalized as $\phi_2 = \Box\Diamond green$. (3) When the light is red, it will always be*

$$
\begin{array}{ccc}
g = \top & g = \bot & g =\,? \\
r = \bot & r = \top & r =\,?
\end{array}
$$

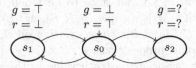

Fig. 1. System model M

green – formalized as $\phi_3 = \Box(red \rightarrow \Box green)$. Note that ϕ_3 is deliberately wrong and will be used later to discuss the application of THRIVE.

Starting from this specification, a designer might initially propose the partially specified model of the semaphore shown in Fig. 1. Each state is associated with the values of the propositions g and r (denoting green and red) holding in that state, which specify whether the green and the red lights are on or off. For example, in state s_0 the red light is on ($r = \top$) while the green is off ($g = \bot$). Instead, s_2 is a state to which the semaphore may be brought, for instance by a manual command. The designer still has to choose whether, in this state, the green and red lights should be on or off. This is indicated by associating the value ? to the propositions g and r. The designer might refine the model by setting g and r to either $\top$ or $\bot$ in s_2.

Related work. Three-valued [5,6,12,13,17] and multi-valued [7,15] model checking supports verification of partial models. Different model checking techniques have been developed depending on the modeling formalisms. For example, several papers focus on Partial Kripke Structures (e.g., [5–7,13,15]), others on Modal Transition Systems (e.g., [12,17]). However, to the best of our knowledge, none of these techniques has been combined with theorem proving.

Theorem proving applies a set of techniques to try to establish the validity of a given formula (see [18]). Some of these techniques (e.g., [20–22,24,25]) exploit the state space generated by the model checker to explain why a property holds. However, to the best of our knowledge, none of these approaches has been applied in a multi-valued context.

Organization. Sect. 2 contains background notations and algorithms. Section 3 describes THRIVE. Section 4 presents an instance of THRIVE, that considers PKSs and LTL formulae. Section 5 evaluates the approach on an example. Section 6 discusses the applicability of THRIVE in real world cases. Section 7 concludes the paper.

2   Background

Checking complete models. Given a Kripke Structure M (KS), the model checking procedure verifies whether a Linear Temporal Logic (LTL) formula ϕ holds or does not hold in M. The procedure works in three steps: (1) generation of a Büchi automaton (BA) $\mathcal{A}_{\neg\phi}$ from the LTL formula $\neg\phi$; (2) generation of the product $\mathcal{G} = M \otimes \mathcal{A}_{\neg\phi}$; (3) emptiness check of $\mathcal{G}$.

Checking partial models. *Partial Kripke Structures* [5] (PKSs) extend KSs by allowing a proposition in a given state to be labelled with ? to represent an unknown value. A PKS M is a tuple $\langle S, R, S_0, AP, L \rangle$, where: S is a set of states; $R \subseteq S \times S$ is a *left-total transition relation* on S; S_0 is a set of initial states; AP is a set of atomic propositions; $L : S \times AP \rightarrow \{\top, ?, \bot\}$ is a *function* that, for each state in S, associates a truth value in the set $\{\top, ?, \bot\}$ to every atomic proposition in AP. The model of the grade crossing semaphore presented in Fig. 1 is an example of a PKS.

A *completion* of a PKS M is a KS M' that completes M by assigning values to the unknown propositions. The set $\mathcal{C}(M)$ contains all the completions of M.
Two kinds of LTL semantics (three valued and thorough) exist for PKSs.

Three-valued LTL semantics $[(M, \pi) \models \phi]$ associates to a model M, a path π of M, and a formula ϕ, a truth value in the set $\{\bot, ?, \top\}$. This semantics specifies that a formula ϕ definitely holds in a PKS M if it is true for all possible values of the unknown propositions in M. Likewise, it is definitely violated if it is false despite the unknown values. According to three-valued semantics [13], given a PKS $M = \langle S, R, S_0, AP, L \rangle$, a path $\pi = s_0, s_1, \ldots$, and a formula ϕ, we inductively define that π satisfies ϕ in the model M as follows:

$$[(M, \pi) \models p] \quad = \quad L(s_0, p)$$
$$[(M, \pi) \models \neg\phi] \quad = \quad \text{comp}([(M, \pi) \models \phi])$$
$$[(M, \pi) \models \phi_1 \wedge \phi_2] \quad = \quad \min([(M, \pi) \models \phi_1], [(M, \pi) \models \phi_2])$$
$$[(M, \pi) \models \bigcirc \phi] \quad = \quad [(M, \pi^1) \models \phi]$$
$$[(M, \pi) \models \phi_1 \mathcal{U} \phi_2] \quad = \quad \max_{j \geq 0}(\min(\{[(M, \pi^i) \models \phi_1] | i < j\} \cup \{[(M, \pi^j) \models \phi_2]\}))$$

where the notation π^i indicates the sub-path $s_i, s_{i+1} \ldots$ of π.

Negation is defined by the function comp (complement), which maps $\top$ to $\bot$, $\bot$ to $\top$, and ? to ?. The conjunction (disjunction) is defined as the minimum (maximum) of its arguments, following the order $\bot < ? < \top$. These functions are extended to sets considering $\min(\emptyset) = \top$ and $\max(\emptyset) = \bot$.

Given a PKS $M = \langle S, R, S_0, AP, L \rangle$, satisfaction of formula ϕ in a state s is defined as $[(M, s) \models \phi] = \min(\{[(M, \pi) \models \phi] | \pi^0 = s\})$. A PKS M *definitely satisfies* a property ϕ $([M \models \phi] = \top)$ iff for all initial states $s_0 \in S_0$ of M, $[(M, s_0) \models \phi] = \top$. A PKS M *does not satisfy* the property ϕ $([M \models \phi] = \bot)$ iff there exists an initial state $s_0 \in S_0$ of M such that $[(M, s_0) \models \phi] = \bot$. A PKS *possibly satisfies* ϕ otherwise.

Three-valued semantics does not behave always in accordance with the natural intuition [6]: there are cases in which ϕ possibly holds for a PKS but all its completions actually satisfy (or do not satisfy) ϕ. For this reason, an alternative semantics, called *thorough LTL semantics* [6] has been proposed. According to it, a formula is possibly satisfied only if there exist two completions $M_1, M_2 \in \mathcal{C}(M)$, such that ϕ is definitely satisfied in one and violated in the other. Thorough semantics defines satisfaction of an LTL formula ϕ by a PKS M as follows:

$$[M \models \phi]_t = \begin{cases} \top & \text{if } M' \models \phi \text{ for all } M' \in \mathcal{C}(M) \\ \bot & \text{if } M' \not\models \phi \text{ for all } M' \in \mathcal{C}(M) \\ ? & \text{otherwise} \end{cases}$$

Given a PKS and an LTL formula ϕ, it has been proved [13] that (1) $[M \models \phi] = \top \Rightarrow [M \models \phi]_t = \top$; (2) $[M \models \phi] = \bot \Rightarrow [M \models \phi]_t = \bot$. That is, a formula which is true (false) under the three-valued semantics is also true (false) under the thorough semantics.

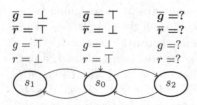

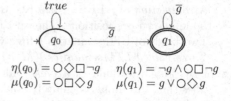

Fig. 2. The PKS of the crossing semaphore.

Fig. 3. The BA associated with ϕ_2.

There exists a subset of LTL formulae, known in the literature as *self-minimizing* [11], such that the two semantics coincide. Formally, given a model M and a self-minimizing LTL property ϕ, then $[M \models \phi] = [M \models \phi]_t$. It has been observed that most practically useful LTL formulae belong to this subset [11].

We present a *model checking* algorithm for PKSs and LTL formulae based on three-valued semantics. This procedure considers a version of M, called *complement-closed* [6], in which for every proposition $p \in AP$, there exists a new proposition $\bar{p}$, called complement-closed proposition, such that $L(s, \bar{p}) = \text{comp}(L(s, p))$, for all $s \in S$. For example, the complement-closed version of the PKS of the semaphore example is presented in Fig. 2.

The model checking procedure for a PKS M is based on an optimistic and pessimistic approximation of M's complement-closure. The optimistic (pessimistic) approximation function L_{opt} (L_{pes}) associates the value $\top$ ($\bot$) to each atomic proposition of the complement-closure of M with value ?. Given a PKS $M = \langle S, R, S_0, L \rangle$, we have $M_{pes} = \langle S, R, S_0, L_{pes} \rangle$ for the pessimistic case, and $M_{opt} = \langle S, R, S_0, L_{opt} \rangle$ for the optimistic one.

The three-valued model checking algorithm assumes that property ϕ is rewritten using complement-closed propositions. The procedure works in two steps. First, the formula is expressed such that negations only appear in front of atomic propositions. Second, each negated proposition is substituted by the corresponding complemented proposition. Let ϕ be an LTL formula obtained using the procedure just discussed, $M = \langle S, R, S_0, L \rangle$ a PKS with $s \in S$, and M_{pes} and M_{opt} the corresponding pessimistic and optimistic cases. Then, [6][1] has defined:

$$[(M, s) \models \phi] = \begin{cases} \top & \text{if } (M_{pes}, s) \models \phi \\ \bot & \text{if } (M_{opt}, s) \not\models \phi \\ ? & otherwise \end{cases}$$

This technique exploits two runs of the classical two-valued model checking performed on a pessimistic and an optimistic completion of M.

Deductive verification. Given a complete KS M and an LTL property ϕ that is satisfied by M, the deductive verification framework produces a proof which

---

[1] In [6] the procedure is presented for PML but is valid also for LTL (see [6,11,13]).

explains why $M \models \phi$ [22] considering the product $\mathcal{G} = M \otimes \mathcal{E}_{\neg\phi}$ where $\mathcal{E}_{\neg\phi}$ is a Generalized Büchi Automaton (GBA [10]) obtained by $\neg\phi$. The approach is based on three considerations. (1) Every state $q \in Q$ of $\mathcal{E}_{\neg\phi}$ is associated with an LTL formula $\eta(q)$ such that, for every accepting run $\sigma = q_0, q_1, \dots$ of $\mathcal{G}$, $\sigma_i \models \eta(q_i)$. The formula $\eta(q)$ is computed during the procedure that converts the LTL formula $\neg\phi$ into $\mathcal{E}_{\neg\phi}$ [10]. For instance, the state q_1 of the automaton presented in Fig. 3 is associated with the formula $\eta(q_1) = \neg g \wedge \bigcirc \Box \neg g$; (2) Each state $\langle s, q \rangle$ which was not created during the computation of $M \otimes \mathcal{E}_{\neg\phi}$, is such that s does not satisfy $\eta(q)$, i.e., $s \models \mu(q)$. Each of these states, called *failed state*, causes a failure in the search of a counterexample and ensures the satisfaction of ϕ in the corresponding state of the system; (3) Given a state $\langle s, q \rangle$ of the automaton $M \otimes \mathcal{E}_{\neg\phi}$, the property $\eta(q)$ associated with the state q of $\mathcal{E}_{\neg\phi}$ is *not* satisfied in s. Indeed, if $\eta(q)$ was satisfied, a counterexample would have been found. Thus, the negation $\mu(q)$ of $\eta(q)$ holds in s.

In the rest of this paper we will use the notation $s_1, s_2 \dots s_n \models \phi$ to indicate that the states $s_1, s_2 \dots s_n$ of a KS satisfy an LTL property ϕ.

The deductive verification framework enriches the product $M \otimes \mathcal{E}_{\neg\phi}$ by considering also failed states as part of it. Since in each failed state $\langle t, p \rangle$ the search of a counterexample has failed, we can write the failure axiom $t \models \mu(p)$. A set of deductive rules is applied to produce the proof. (1) *Successors rule.* Given a state $\langle s, q \rangle$ of the product, if for each of its successors $\langle s_i, q_j \rangle$ the state s_i of M satisfies the formula $\mu(q_j)$, then also s satisfies $\mu(q)$. Intuitively, the rule is based on two observations. First, each successor $\langle s_i, q_j \rangle$ of $\langle s, q \rangle$ does not cause a violation of ϕ, i.e., it ensures that $s_i \models \mu(q_j)$. Second, by moving from $\langle s, q \rangle$ to $\langle s_i, q_j \rangle$ the system does not violate the property of interest, since no counterexample was found. Thus, it must be that s satisfies $\mu(q)$. (2) *Induction rule.* It is a generalization of the successors rule applied on strongly connected components (SCCs). Given a strongly connected component $\mathcal{X}$, let us identify with $Exit(\mathcal{X})$ the set of all states $\langle s_i, q_j \rangle$ that do not belong to $\mathcal{X}$ and have an incoming transition from a source state in $\mathcal{X}$. If every state $\langle s_i, q_j \rangle \in Exit(\mathcal{X})$ is such that $s_i \models \mu(q_j)$, we can conclude that, for every state $\langle s, q \rangle \in \mathcal{X}$, $s \models \mu(q)$ holds. Intuitively, since all the "successors" of $\mathcal{X}$ (the states in $Exit(\mathcal{X})$) ensure the property satisfaction and the states in $\mathcal{X}$ do not violate the property of interest (no counterexample has been found in the product), it must be that each state s satisfies the corresponding property $\mu(q)$. (3) *Conjunction rule.* It connects conclusions made on a given state making temporal logic interferences. The formulae computed for a given state are and-combined.

These rules are applied considering the partial ordering relation $\prec$ between SCCs. The relation $\mathcal{X} \prec \mathcal{X}'$ holds if there exists a transition from some state in $\mathcal{X}$ to some state in $\mathcal{X}'$. If $\mathcal{X} \prec \mathcal{X}'$, before considering the component $\mathcal{X}$, it is necessary to compute the proof of $\mathcal{X}'$.

3 THRIVE

An overview of THRIVE is presented in Fig. 4. THRIVE takes as inputs a partial model M and a property ϕ and produces one of the outputs shown by the grey filled shapes. The outputs are generated by integrating a model checker for partial models and a theorem prover.

The *model checker for partial models* verifies whether the property ϕ of interest is definitely satisfied ($\top$), possibly satisfied (?) or not satisfied ($\bot$) by the current partial model. If the property is *not satisfied* (③), there exist some behaviors which definitively violate the property of interest and do not depend on the unspecified parts of the model. The model checker returns one such behavior, i.e., a definitive counterexample. Whenever a property is *definitely satisfied*, its satisfaction does not depend on the unspecified parts, i.e., on how the incomplete parts are later refined. Finally, if the property is *possibly satisfied* (⑤), the model checker returns a possible counterexample, i.e., a possible violating behavior that the model can exhibit.

The *theorem proving* framework is executed when a $\top$ or ? value is returned by the model checker and computes a proof which specifies why the property ϕ is definitely (possibly) satisfied by M. When a property is *definitely satisfied* (⑥), THRIVE returns a proof that specifies why the search of a definitive and a possible counterexample has failed. Instead, whenever a property is *possibly satisfied* (④), besides providing a possible counterexample, THRIVE returns a proof that specifies why a definitive counterexample has not been found.

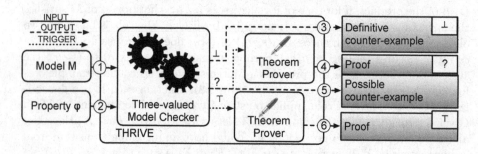

Fig. 4. The THRIVE framework.

4   Using THRIVE with PKS and LTL

This section describes the instance of THRIVE proposed in this paper, using PKSs and and LTL. We first show how we modified the theorem prover framework presented in Sect. 2 to support PKSs and how it is integrated with the three-valued model checker. We further analyze the case of thorough semantics, which is more appealing in practice, and discuss to what extent and how the framework can be used in such a case.

4.1 Adapting the Theorem Prover

The deductive verification framework presented in [22] exploits the product between a state labeled transition system and a GBA $\mathcal{E}_{\neg\phi}$ obtained by $\neg\phi$ to generate the proof. To enable the algorithm to work on KSs and BAs, we describe how to associate LTL formulae with each state of the BA and how to identify failed states of the product automaton.

Identification of the formulae that hold in the states of the BA. We assume that the degeneralization procedure [8], that converts the GBA $\mathcal{E}_{\neg\phi}$ into an equivalent BA $\mathcal{A}_{\neg\phi}$ behaves as follows: when a new state q of $\mathcal{A}_{\neg\phi}$ is created from a state q' of $\mathcal{E}_{\neg\phi}$, the formulae $\eta(q')$ and $\mu(q')$ are also associated to q.

Identification of failed states. Following the procedure mentioned in Sect. 2, the product automaton $M \otimes \mathcal{A}_{\neg\phi}$ between the KS M and the BA $\mathcal{A}_{\neg\phi}$ is modified to also generate *failed states*. Specifically, the product is computed using the rules 1 and 2.

$$\frac{s \to t \wedge q \xrightarrow{L(t)} p}{\langle s, q \rangle \to \langle t, p \rangle} \tag{1}$$

$$\frac{s \to t \wedge q \xrightarrow{L(t)} p}{\langle s, q \rangle \dashrightarrow \langle t, p \rangle} \tag{2}$$

Rule 1 is the classical rule used to compute the product automaton. It specifies that the state of the product $\langle s, q \rangle$ moves to $\langle t, p \rangle$ only if the transition $q \xrightarrow{L(t)} p$ that moves the BA from q to p has the same label of the state t of M. Rule 2 specifies how to compute failed states. It states that the failed state $\langle t, p \rangle$ is generated in the product when a transition that moves the BA $\mathcal{A}_{\neg\phi}$ from q to p is labelled differently with respect to the state t reached by the model $\mathcal{M}$ when the transition $s \to t$ is fired. This is indicated using the notation $q \xrightarrow{L(t)} p$. For this reason, the transition $\langle s, q \rangle \dashrightarrow \langle t, p \rangle$ from $\langle s, q \rangle$ to $\langle t, p \rangle$ is dashed. Let us consider the product presented in Fig. 5 computed from the KS M_{opt} obtained from the PKS in Fig. 2 and the BA of Fig. 3. The transition $\langle s_0, q_0 \rangle$ to $\langle s_1, q_1 \rangle$ of the product presented in Fig. 5 is dashed, since the proposition $\overline{g}$ is false in s_1, while the labeling of the transition from q_0 to q_1 requires $\overline{g}$ to be true for the transition to be performed.

The set $\mathcal{F}(M \otimes \mathcal{A}_{\neg\phi})$ of the *failed states* contains the states $\langle t, p \rangle$ obtained by applying rule 2. Note that, as stated in Sect. 2, each failed state $\langle s, q \rangle$ is such that $s \models \mu(q)$. For example, the state $\langle s_1, q_1 \rangle$ of the product presented in Fig. 5 is a failed state. Indeed, s_1 satisfies the property $\mu(q_1) = g \vee \bigcirc \Diamond g$ associated with the state q_1.

Theorem 1. *The deductive verification procedure is correct.*

Proof. We show that the states identified as *failed* correspond to the ones that would be identified using [22]. In [22], a state $\langle t, p \rangle$ is failed if the propositional

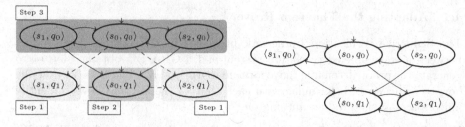

Fig. 5. Product $I_{opt} = M_{opt} \otimes \mathcal{A}_{\neg \phi_2}$ **Fig. 6.** Product $I_{pes} = M_{pes} \otimes \mathcal{A}_{\neg \phi_2}$

assignment of t does not satisfy the conditions specified in the state p. It is well known [8,10], that a GBA $\mathcal{E}_{\neg \phi}$ associated with ϕ is such that (1) all the transitions $(q, \alpha, p) \in \Delta$ that reach a state p of the GBA have the same label α and that (2) a transition $(q, \alpha, p) \in \Delta$ is in the GBA if and only if α satisfies the conjunction of the negated and non negated propositions that hold in the state p. By construction, the latter of these properties also holds in the BA obtained from the GBA by applying the degeneralization procedure [8]. Thus, since all the transitions that reach p are labelled with α, a transition $\langle s, q \rangle \dashrightarrow' \langle t, p \rangle$ is added to the product automaton if and only if the propositional assignment of t does not satisfy the propositional assignment specified in the state p. Furthermore, BAs acceptance condition is a special case of fairness condition used in [22]. Thus, the proposed deductive verification procedure is a special case of [22], with regard to acceptance.

4.2 Integrating the Model Checker and the Theorem Prover

Figure 7 presents an instance of THRIVE obtained as an integration of a model checker for PKSs and LTL based on three-valued semantics and the theorem prover presented in Sect. 4.1. The circled numbers in Fig. 7 indicate how this specific instance is plugged into THRIVE in Fig. 4.

The three-valued model checker presented in Sect. 2 is used by THRIVE to check the satisfaction of the property of interest. Specifically, it runs twice a classical two-valued model checker, considering first the optimistic approximation M_{opt}, then the pessimistic approximation M_{pes} of the PKS M. When M_{opt} is evaluated, if a counterexample is found, this is returned as output of THRIVE. Otherwise, THRIVE verifies M_{pes}. If the property is satisfied, it means that no violating nor possibly violating behaviors have been identified. Thus, THRIVE executes the theorem prover that produces a proof that explains why no counterexample has been found in the pessimistic approximation. Otherwise, the property is possibly satisfied. In this case, THRIVE returns the possible counterexample and runs the theorem prover on M_{opt} to compute a proof that specifies why a definitive counterexample has not be found.

Example. *Properties ϕ_1, ϕ_2 and ϕ_3 of the crossing semaphore example are satisfied, possibly satisfied and not satisfied by the model M of Fig. 2.*

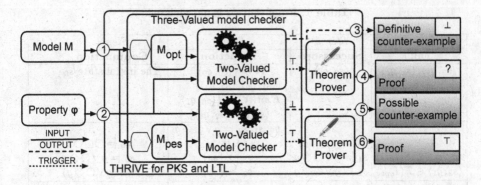

Fig. 7. THRIVE for PKS and LTL.

Property ϕ_2. The products between the optimistic and pessimistic approximation of the model M and the BA automaton $\mathcal{A}_{\neg\phi_2}$ are presented in Figs. 5 and 6. THRIVE explores I_{pes} and returns the possible counterexample $(s_0, s_2)^\omega$. Specifically, by looping an infinite number of times on states s_0 and s_2 the green light is never turned on. Since the property ϕ_2 is possibly satisfied, the search of a definitive counterexample in the product automaton I_{opt} (Fig. 5) fails. THRIVE uses the product automaton I_{opt} to compute a proof (Table 1) that explains the motivation. The states that are analyzed in different steps are circled in Fig. 5 through different grey frames. (Step1). THRIVE analyzes the failed states. Given a failed state $\langle s, q \rangle$, since in this state the search for a counterexample fails, the formula associated with the state q of $\mathcal{A}_{\neg\phi_2}$ holds in s. For example, since the state $\langle s_1, q_1 \rangle$ of I_{opt} is a failed state, the formula green $\vee \bigcirc \Diamond$ green (valid in q_1) is satisfied by the model state s_1. This formula is effectively true in s_1 since the green light is on. (Step2). Since all the successors of $\langle s_0, q_1 \rangle$ satisfy green $\vee \bigcirc \Diamond$ green, it is possible to deduce that this property is also satisfied in s_0. (Step3). The induction rule is applied considering the strongly connected component $\{\langle s_0, q_0 \rangle, \langle s_1, q_0 \rangle, \langle s_2, q_0 \rangle\}$ and allows concluding that s_0 satisfies the property $\bigcirc \square \Diamond$ green. (Step4). THRIVE applies the conjunction rule to s_0. Since s_0 satisfies both $\bigcirc \square \Diamond$ green and green $\vee \bigcirc \Diamond$ green, it is possibly to deduce that s_0 satisfies the property ϕ_2. This provides an interesting insight to the designer: if she/he turns the green light on in s_2 the property becomes satisfied. The proof clearly states why.

Property ϕ_3. THRIVE returns the counterexample $(s_0, s_1)^\omega$. The counterexample specifies that by looping an infinite number of times on states s_0 and s_1 the green light is not permanently on after the red.

Property ϕ_1. THRIVE produces a proof that highlights how and why a definite counterexample is not found in the graph. First, it identifies the states $\langle s_0, q_1 \rangle$ and $\langle s_2, q_1 \rangle$ as failed. The conclusions found on these states are propagated to the state $\langle s_1, q_1 \rangle$. All the successors of the SCC formed by the product states related to the property state q_0 are analyzed. Finally, conclusions are drawn also on this SCC. The proof is omitted for space reasons.

Table 1. Proof that ϕ_2 is not violated.

Step 1	Step 2	Step 3	Step 4
Fail	**Successors**	**Induction**	**Conjunction**
$\langle s_2, q_1\rangle, \langle s_1, q_1\rangle$	$\langle s_0, q_1\rangle$	$\mathcal{X} = \{\langle s_0, q_0\rangle,$ $\langle s_1, q_0\rangle, \langle s_2, q_0\rangle\}$ $Exit(\mathcal{X}) = \{\langle s_0, q_1\rangle,$ $\langle s_1, q_1\rangle, \langle s_2, q_1\rangle\}$	The initial state s_0
$\langle s_1, q_1\rangle \in \mathcal{F}(I_{opt})$ $\langle s_2, q_1\rangle \in \mathcal{F}(I_{opt})$ $s_1, s_2 \models g \vee \bigcirc \Diamond g$	$s_0 \rightarrow \{s_1, s_2\}$ $s_1 \models g \vee \bigcirc \Diamond g$ $s_2 \models g \vee \bigcirc \Diamond g$ $s_0 \models g \vee \bigcirc \Diamond g$	$s_0, s_1, s_2 \models g \vee \bigcirc \Diamond g$ $s_0 \rightarrow \{s_1, s_2\}$ $s_1 \rightarrow \{s_0\}$ $s_2 \rightarrow \{s_0\}$ $s_0, s_1, s_2 \models \bigcirc \Box \Diamond g$	$s_0 \models \bigcirc \Box \Diamond g$ $s_0 \models g \vee \bigcirc \Diamond g$ $\Box \Diamond g \wedge (g \vee \bigcirc \Diamond g) \rightarrow \phi_2$ $s_0 \models \phi_2$

4.3 Thorough Semantics and THRIVE

As stated in Sect. 2, three-valued semantics does not always behave in accordance with the natural intuition [6]. When ϕ possibly holds in M, it is desirable that there exist two completions M' and M'' of M such that M' satisfies ϕ and M'' violates ϕ. This property is not ensured by the three-valued semantics, and is the motivation that leads to introduce thorough LTL semantics. Hereafter, we discuss how the adoption of thorough semantics would affect the use of the THRIVE framework.

Given a PKS M and a property ϕ, THRIVE produces the following outputs:

Property is satisfied. THRIVE works correctly. A property ϕ that evaluates to $\top$ under three-valued semantics is also satisfied under thorough semantics. Thus, the verification result is correct. Also the proof is correct since it shows that any completion of M satisfies ϕ.

Property is not satisfied. THRIVE works correctly. When the model checker returns a $\bot$ value, the counterexample shows a behavior that violates ϕ. A property ϕ that is not satisfied considering the three-valued semantics, is also not satisfied considering the thorough semantics. Thus, the counterexample is correct and proves the existence of a completion of M that violates ϕ.

Property is possibly satisfied. THRIVE does not work correctly for all LTL properties. When the three-valued model checker returns ? the property is possibly satisfied considering the three-valued semantics but no conclusion can be drawn based on thorough semantics. Indeed, there are cases in which a ? is returned, but all the completions of the model either satisfy or do not satisfy ϕ. The computed counterexample and proof can be spurious under the thorough semantics.

Example. *The results obtained for ϕ_1 and ϕ_3 of the crossing semaphore example are correct both considering the three-valued and the thorough semantics. Since ϕ_1 is satisfied, the proof is a correct proof that justifies why all the completions of the model presented in Fig. 1 satisfy ϕ_1. The counterexample returned for ϕ_3*

is correct, i.e., all the completions of the model presented in Fig. 1 exhibit the behavior returned as a counterexample.

Self-minimizing LTL formulae. Self-minimizing LTL formulae are a subset of LTL formulae that present an interesting property: three-valued and thorough semantics are equivalent, i.e., if ϕ is self-minimizing, then $[(M, s) \models \phi] = [(M, s) \models \phi]_t$. Therefore, the three-valued model checking framework presented in Sect. 2 produces a result that is correct also considering the thorough semantics. For this reason, whenever the three-valued model checker returns ?, the proof and the possible counterexample produced by THRIVE are also correct under the thorough semantics. In [11], the authors propose a first grammar for this LTL subset. The grammar does not capture entirely this set. However, it can be used to generate formulae that are self-minimizing by construction, or to check whether a formula is self-minimizing (sufficient condition). Furthermore, the authors argue that the set of self-minimizing LTL formulae contains most property patterns of practical interest, such as absence, universality, existence, response and response chain [9]. For these reasons it is possible in practice to use the version of THRIVE of Fig. 7 also considering the thorough semantics.

Example. *Property ϕ_2 is a special instance of LTL response pattern which, according to [11], is self-minimizing. Thus, the possible counterexample and the proof returned by THRIVE are correct.*

5 Preliminary Evaluation

This section tries to answer the following research question: *how effective is THRIVE w.r.t. incremental development?*

To provide an initial answer, we simulated the design of a critical software system. The system, described in [3], is used by optometrists and ophtalmologists to test visual problems and certify a certain level of stereoacuity. The test requires patients to pass levels with increasing difficulties, in which they have to recognize images. Each time the patient is able to recognize an image the system shifts to a higher level and a more difficult image is shown. When the patient fails, the level is decreased. The test ends in one of these cases: 1. when the patient fails the image recognition and she/he did not pass an easier level; 2. when the top level is reached; 3. if the doctor interrupts the test. The complete model and the obtained results can be found in [4].

Experimental setup. We modelled the system in [3] as a PKS. For simplicity we considered only two levels. We used the atomic propositions *fl*, *sl*, *test*, *edb*, *cert* and *uncert* to specify that the patient is in the first or in the second level of the test, the test is under execution, a mistake has been made by the patient, the patient has been certified and the patient is not certified, respectively. If at some point the doctor quits the test, the patient is not certified. If the patient fails the first level, the patient is not certified. If he/she passes the first level, the second level is entered. If the patient also passes the second level he/she is certified at the second level. Otherwise, we assume that the designer is uncertain on the level in which the component should certify/not-certify the patient (this is formalized by setting $fl =?$, $sl =?$).

We designed a set of properties that the system has to satisfy. Property $\psi_1 = (\neg cert)\mathcal{W} (\neg sl)$ states that a patient is not at the second level before he/she is certified (see [1]). Note that, as observed in the following, this property is wrong. Property $\psi_2 = \Box(test \rightarrow \Diamond(cert \vee uncert))$ specifies that every test must be followed by a certification or a non-certification. Property $\psi_3 = \Box(edb \rightarrow \Diamond(cert \vee fl))$ states that if an error has been made by the patient (edb), she/he cannot be uncertified and be at the second level ($\neg fl$). Indeed, a mistake prevents a patient from increasing the assessed level. Note that these properties are obtained from well-known property patterns [9].

Results. *Property ψ_1.* THRIVE returns the value $\bot$ and returns a definitive counterexample showing that there exists a case in which a patient is assessed at the second level but has not been certified yet. Indeed, the property is wrong; the desired property should have been expressed as $\neg(cert \wedge fl)\mathcal{W}(\neg sl)$, meaning that a patient is not at the second level before he/she is certified at the first level.

Property ψ_2. THRIVE returns the value $\top$, since the property of interest is satisfied. The proof shows that a *test* is always followed by a *cert* or *uncert*.

Property ψ_3. THRIVE returns the value ? and a possible counterexample obtained by assigning $\bot$ to the proposition fl. THRIVE considers the optimistic approximation to produce a proof that no definitive counterexample can be found. The obtained proof is correct since a simple grammar check shows that ψ_3 is self-minimizing. The proof shows why, by assigning $\top$ to the unknown proposition fl, the property of interest is satisfied.

The feedback produced by THRIVE for properties ψ_1, ψ_2 and ψ_3 successfully helps in understanding whether a property of interest is satisfied, possibly satisfied or violated. When the property is satisfied/possibly satisfied, understanding the reason why this is true supports self-confidence.

6   Using THRIVE in Real Cases

This section elaborates on the applicability of THRIVE in real cases.

Three-valued vs thorough semantics. The generalized model checking algorithm [6] (which levies a performance penalty) could be used to check a property under the thorough semantics. In [16], the authors analyze how the generalized model checking really helps. Whenever the model is built using predicate abstraction [14], the thorough check does not provide additional precision. It is also argued that in many practically interesting cases, the thorough semantics is not more precise than the three-valued one. For these reasons, THRIVE can be correctly applied in most of the real world cases.

Temporal patterns of self-minimization. In [2], the authors consider popular syntactic specification patterns, documented at a community-led pattern repository, and check whether formulae compliant with these patterns are self-minimizing.

They show that many such patterns are self-minimizing and the ones that are not can be transformed with linear blowup into a self-minimizing LTL formula. Thus, in most practical cases, the designer will consider a formula that is self-minimizing. A syntactic check can be used to prove self-minimization before running THRIVE.

Checking whether an LTL formula is self-minimizing. Checking whether an LTL formula is self-minimizing is expensive, since it requires to compute an automaton that is exponential in $|\phi|$ [11]. However, if ϕ satisfies some constraints (sufficient conditions) then it is self-minimizing. For example, if it is in its negation normal form and no proposition occurs in mixed polarity, then ϕ is self-minimizing. These checks can be implemented in THRIVE.

Scalability. Three-valued model checking is as expensive as classical model checking [5], which is commonly used to analyze real world problems [26]. Deductive verification has been employed successfully in the verification of digital hardware and software systems [24]. Since THRIVE simply combines multi-valued model checking and theorem proving, its scalability improves as the performance of the employed model checking and deductive verification frameworks enhances.

7 Conclusions and Future Work

This work presented THRIVE, a theoretical framework for a correct integration of existing multi-valued model checkers and theorem provers. Whenever the property of interest is definitely satisfied, or possibly satisfied, THRIVE provides information regarding why a certain result is returned by the model checker. The proof gives intuition on what is working correctly in the current design and insights for the next development rounds. We instantiate THRIVE considering a PKS, to express the model of the system, and LTL, to specify the property of interest. We show that the instantiation is feasible and sound, and requires changing the model checking algorithm to accomodate the execution of the theorem prover. THRIVE has been evaluated considering a safety critical example [3], which showed the effectiveness of the approach. We also discussed the applicability of the approach in real world cases.

As future work, we aim to implement THRIVE by integrating existing model checkers and theorem provers. This will allow us to provide further evidence of the impact of THRIVE in continuous system development and to analyze the challenges of realistic systems. We would like to introduce possible extensions of the currently considered formalisms: other forms of partial systems models and other multi-valued logic options for the properties. Finally, we also wish to investigate thoroughly how the proofs can be written in the most understandable and useful form for the designer.

Acknowledgments. Research partly supported from the EU H2020 Research and Innovation Programme under GA No. 731869 (Co4Robots).

References

1. Alavi, H., Avrunin, G., Corbett, J., Dillon, L., Dwyer, M., Pasareanu, C.: Spec patterns (2017). http://patterns.projects.cs.ksu.edu/documentation/patterns/ltl.shtml
2. Antonik, A., Huth, M.: Efficient patterns for model checking partial state spaces in CTL ∩ LTL. Electron. Notes Theor. Comput. Sci. **158**, 41–57 (2006)
3. Arcaini, P., Bonfanti, S., Gargantini, A., Mashkoor, A., Riccobene, E.: Formal validation and verification of a medical software critical component. In: Formal Methods and Models for Codesign, pp. 80–89. IEEE (2015)
4. Bernasconi, A., Menghi, C., Spoletini, P., Zuck, L., Ghezzi, C.: From model checking to a temporal proof for partial models: preliminary example (2017). arXiv preprint arXiv:1706.02701
5. Bruns, G., Godefroid, P.: Model checking partial state spaces with 3-valued temporal logics. In: Halbwachs, N., Peled, D. (eds.) CAV 1999. LNCS, vol. 1633, pp. 274–287. Springer, Heidelberg (1999). doi:10.1007/3-540-48683-6_25
6. Bruns, G., Godefroid, P.: Generalized model checking: reasoning about partial state spaces. In: Palamidessi, C. (ed.) CONCUR 2000. LNCS, vol. 1877, pp. 168–182. Springer, Heidelberg (2000). doi:10.1007/3-540-44618-4_14
7. Bruns, G., Godefroid, P.: Model checking with multi-valued logics. In: Díaz, J., Karhumäki, J., Lepistö, A., Sannella, D. (eds.) ICALP 2004. LNCS, vol. 3142, pp. 281–293. Springer, Heidelberg (2004). doi:10.1007/978-3-540-27836-8_26
8. Clarke, E.M., Grumberg, O., Peled, D.: Model Checking. MIT press, Cambridge (1999)
9. Dwyer, M.B., Avrunin, G.S., Corbett, J.C.: Property specification patterns for finite-state verification. In: Proceedings of the Second Workshop on Formal Methods in Software Practice, pp. 7–15. ACM (1998)
10. Gerth, R., Peled, D., Vardi, M.Y., Wolper, P.: Simple on-the-fly automatic verification of linear temporal logic. In: Dembiński, P., Średniawa, M. (eds.) Protocol Specification, Testing and Verification, pp. 3–18. Springer, Boston (1996). doi:10.1007/978-0-387-34892-6_1
11. Godefroid, P., Huth, M.: Model checking vs. generalized model checking: semantic minimizations for temporal logics. In: Logic in Computer Science, pp. 158–167. IEEE Computer Society (2005)
12. Godefroid, P., Huth, M., Jagadeesan, R.: Abstraction-based model checking using modal transition systems. In: Larsen, K.G., Nielsen, M. (eds.) CONCUR 2001. LNCS, vol. 2154, pp. 426–440. Springer, Heidelberg (2001). doi:10.1007/3-540-44685-0_29
13. Godefroid, P., Piterman, N.: LTL generalized model checking revisited. Int. J. Softw. Tools Technol. Transfer **13**(6), 571–584 (2011)
14. Graf, S., Saidi, H.: Construction of abstract state graphs with PVS. In: Grumberg, O. (ed.) CAV 1997. LNCS, vol. 1254, pp. 72–83. Springer, Heidelberg (1997). doi:10.1007/3-540-63166-6_10
15. Gurfinkel, A., Chechik, M.: Multi-valued model checking via classical model checking. In: Amadio, R., Lugiez, D. (eds.) CONCUR 2003. LNCS, vol. 2761, pp. 266–280. Springer, Heidelberg (2003). doi:10.1007/978-3-540-45187-7_18
16. Gurfinkel, A., Chechik, M.: How thorough is thorough enough? In: Borrione, D., Paul, W. (eds.) CHARME 2005. LNCS, vol. 3725, pp. 65–80. Springer, Heidelberg (2005). doi:10.1007/11560548_8
17. Larsen, K.G., Thomsen, B.: A modal process logic. In: Logic in Computer Science, pp. 203–210. IEEE (1988)

18. Manna, Z., Pnueli, A.: The Temporal Logic of Reactive and Concurrent Systems: Specification. Springer, New York (1992)
19. Menghi, C., Spoletini, P., Ghezzi, C.: Dealing with incompleteness in automata-based model checking. In: Fitzgerald, J., Heitmeyer, C., Gnesi, S., Philippou, A. (eds.) FM 2016. LNCS, vol. 9995, pp. 531–550. Springer, Cham (2016). doi:10.1007/978-3-319-48989-6_32
20. Namjoshi, K.S.: Certifying model checkers. In: Berry, G., Comon, H., Finkel, A. (eds.) CAV 2001. LNCS, vol. 2102, pp. 2–13. Springer, Heidelberg (2001). doi:10.1007/3-540-44585-4_2
21. Peled, D., Pnueli, A., Zuck, L.: From falsification to verification. In: Hariharan, R., Vinay, V., Mukund, M. (eds.) FSTTCS 2001. LNCS, vol. 2245, pp. 292–304. Springer, Heidelberg (2001). doi:10.1007/3-540-45294-X_25
22. Peled, D., Zuck, L.: From model checking to a temporal proof. In: Dwyer, M. (ed.) SPIN 2001. LNCS, vol. 2057, pp. 1–14. Springer, Heidelberg (2001). doi:10.1007/3-540-45139-0_1
23. Pnueli, A.: The temporal logic of programs. In: Foundations of Computer Science, pp. 46–57. IEEE (1977)
24. Rajan, S., Shankar, N., Srivas, M.K.: An integration of model checking with automated proof checking. In: Wolper, P. (ed.) CAV 1995. LNCS, vol. 939, pp. 84–97. Springer, Heidelberg (1995). doi:10.1007/3-540-60045-0_42
25. Tan, L., Cleaveland, R.: Evidence-based model checking. In: Brinksma, E., Larsen, K.G. (eds.) CAV 2002. LNCS, vol. 2404, pp. 455–470. Springer, Heidelberg (2002). doi:10.1007/3-540-45657-0_37
26. Woodcock, J., Larsen, P.G., Bicarregui, J., Fitzgerald, J.S.: Formal methods: practice and experience. ACM Comput. Surv. **41**(4) (2009)

Modeling and Reasoning on Requirements Evolution with Constrained Goal Models

Chi Mai Nguyen, Roberto Sebastiani[✉], Paolo Giorgini, and John Mylopoulos

DISI, University of Trento, Trento, Italy
roberto.sebastiani@unitn.it

Abstract. We are interested in supporting software evolution caused by changing requirements and/or changes in the operational environment of a software system. For example, users of a system may want new functionality or performance enhancements to cope with growing user population (changing requirements). Alternatively, vendors of a system may want to minimize costs in implementing requirements changes (evolution requirements). We propose to use Constrained Goal Models (CGMs) to represent the requirements of a system, and capture requirements changes in terms of incremental operations on a goal model. Evolution requirements are then represented as optimization goals that minimize implementation costs or customer value. We then exploit reasoning techniques to derive optimal new specifications for an evolving software system. CGMs offer an expressive language for modelling goals that comes with scalable solvers that solve hybrid constraint and optimization problems using a combination of Satisfiability Modulo Theories (SMT) and Optimization Modulo Theories (OMT) techniques. We evaluate our proposal by modeling and reasoning with a goal model for a standard exemplar used in Requirement Engineering.

1   Introduction

We have come to live in a world where the only constant is change. Changes need to be accommodated by any system that lives and operates in that world, biological and/or engineered. For software systems, this is a well-known problem referred to as software evolution. There has been much work and interest on this problem since Lehman's seminal proposal for laws of software evolution [4]. However, the problem of effectively supporting software evolution through suitable concepts, tools and techniques is still largely open. And software evolution still accounts for more than 50% of total costs in a software system's lifecycle.

We are interested in supporting software evolution caused by changing requirements and/or environmental conditions. Specifically, we are interested in models that capture such changes, also in reasoning techniques that derive optimal new specifications for a system whose requirements and/or environment have changed. Moreover, we are interested in discovering new classes of evolution requirements, in the spirit of [10] who proposed such a class for adaptive software systems. We propose to model requirements changes through changes

© Springer International Publishing AG 2017
A. Cimatti and M. Sirjani (Eds.): SEFM 2017, LNCS 10469, pp. 70–86, 2017.
DOI: 10.1007/978-3-319-66197-1_5

to a goal model, and evolution requirements as optimization goals, such as "Minimize costs while implementing new functionality". Our research baseline consists of an expressive framework for modelling and reasoning with goals called Constrained Goal Models (hereafter CGMs) [5]. The CGM framework is founded on and draws much of its power from Satisfiability Modulo Theories (SMT) and Optimization Modulo Theories (OMT) solving techniques [1,8].

The contributions of this paper include a proposal for modelling changing requirements in terms of changes to a CGM model, but also the identification of a new class of evolution requirements, expressed as optimization goals in CGM. In addition, we show how to support reasoning with changed goal models and evolution requirements in order to derive optimal solutions.

The rest of the paper is structured as follows: Sect. 2 introduces the notion of CGM through a working example; Sect. 3 introduces the notion of evolution requirements and requirements evolution through our working example; Sect. 4 formalizes the problem of automatically handling CGM evolutions and evolution requirements for CGMs; Sect. 5 provides a brief overview of our tool implementing the presented approach; in Sect. 6 we draw some conclusions.

Some of the ideas described here were discussed at conceptual level in a non-technical short paper at Conceptual Modeling conference, ER'2016 [6]. A longer and more detailed version of this paper, which includes also a related work section, is available [7].

2   Background: Constrained Goal Models

SMT ($\mathcal{LRA}$) and ($\mathcal{LRA}$). *Satisfiability Modulo the Theory of Linear Rational Arithmetic (SMT ($\mathcal{LRA}$))* [1] is the problem of deciding the satisfiability of arbitrary formulas on atomic propositions and constraints in linear arithmetic over the rationals. *Optimization Modulo the Theory of Linear Rational Arithmetic (OMT ($\mathcal{LRA}$))* [8] extends SMT($\mathcal{LRA}$) by searching solutions which optimize some $\mathcal{LRA}$ objective(s). Efficient OMT($\mathcal{LRA}$) solvers like OPTIMATHSAT [9] allow for handling formulas with thousands of Boolean and rational variables [5,8].

A Working Example. We recall from [5] the main ideas of Constrained Goal Models (CGM's) and the main functionalities of our CGM-Tool through a meeting scheduling example (Fig. 1), a standard exemplar used in Requirements Engineering [3,11].

Notationally, round-corner rectangles (e.g., ScheduleMeeting) are root goals, representing stakeholder *requirements*; ovals (e.g. CollectTimetables) are *intermediate goals*; hexagons (e.g. CharacteriseMeeting) are *tasks*, i.e. non-root leaf goals; rectangles (e.g., ParticipantsUseSystemCalendar) are *domain assumptions*. We call *elements* both goals and domain assumptions. Labeled bullets at the merging point of the edges connecting a group of source elements to a target element are *refinements* (e.g., (GoodParticipation, MinimalConflict) $\xrightarrow{R_{20}}$ GoodQualitySchedule), while the R_is denote their labels. The label of a refinement can be omitted when there is no need to refer to it explicitly.

Intuitively, requirements represent desired states of affairs we want the system-to-be to achieve (either mandatorily or possibly); they are progressively refined into intermediate goals, until the process produces actionable goals (tasks) that need no further decomposition and can be executed; domain assumptions are propositions about the domain that need to hold for a goal refinement to work. Refinements are used to represent the alternatives of how to achieve an element; a refinement of an element is a conjunction of the sub-elements that are necessary to achieve it.

Suppose we want to capture and analyze requirements for a software system that schedules meetings (see [3,11]). The main objective of the CGM in Fig. 1 is to achieve the requirement SionRule ScheduleMeeting, which is *mandatory*. ScheduleMeeting has only one candidate refinement R_1, consisting in five sub-goals: CharacteriseMeeting, CollectTimetables, FindASuitableRoom, ChooseSchedule, and ManageMeeting. Since R_1 is the only refinement of the requirement, all these sub-goals must be satisfied in order to satisfy it. There may be more than one way to refine an element; e.g., CollectTimetables is further refined either by R_{10} into the single goal ByPerson or by R_2 into the single goal BySystem. The subgoals are further refined until they reach the level of domain assumptions and tasks.

Some requirements can be *"nice-to-have"*, like LowCost, MinimalEffort, FastSchedule, and GoodQualitySchedule (in blue in Fig. 1). They are requirements that we would like to fulfill with our solution, provided they do not conflict with other requirements. To this extent, in order to analyze interactively the possible different realizations, one can interactively mark [or unmark] requirements as satisfied, thus making them mandatory (if unmarked, they are nice-to-have ones). Similarly, one can interactively mark/unmark (effortful) tasks as denied, or mark/unmark some domain assumption as satisfied or denied. More generally, one can mark as satisfied or denied every goal or domain assumption. We call these marks *user assertions*. Notice that CGMs can represent both functional requirements (e.g. ScheduleMeeting) and quality requirements (e.g. LowCost).

In a CGM, elements and refinements are enriched by user-defined *constraints*, which can be expressed either graphically as *relation edges* or textually as *Boolean or* SMT($\mathcal{LRA}$) *formulas*. We have three kinds of relation edges. *Contribution edges* "$E_i \xrightarrow{++} E_j$" between elements (in green in Fig. 1), like "ScheduleAutomatically $\xrightarrow{++}$ MinimalConflicts", mean that if the source element E_i is satisfied, then also the target element E_j must be satisfied (but not vice versa). *Conflict edges* "$E_i \xleftrightarrow{--} E_j$" between elements (in red), like "ConfirmOccurrence $\xleftrightarrow{--}$ CancelMeeting", mean that E_i and E_j cannot be both satisfied. *Refinement bindings* "$R_i \longleftrightarrow R_j$" between two refinements (in purple), like "$R_2 \longleftrightarrow R_7$", are used to state that, if the target elements E_i and E_j of the two refinements R_i and R_j, respectively, are both satisfied, then E_i is refined by R_i if and only if E_j is refined by R_j. Intuitively, this means that the two refinements are bound, as if they were two different instances of the same choice.

It is possible to enrich CGMs with logic formulas, representing arbitrary logic constraints on elements and refinements. For example, to require that, as

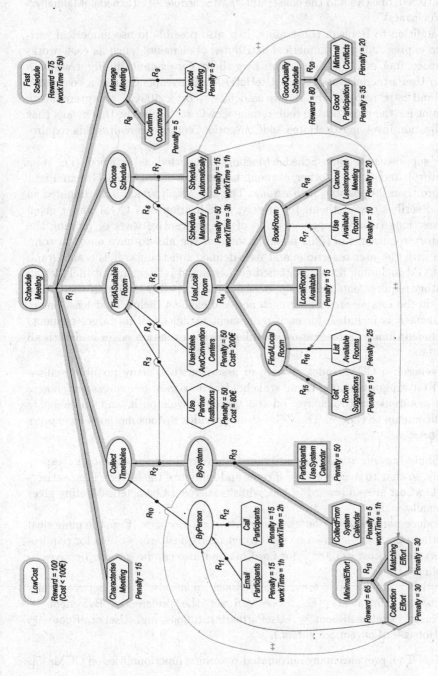

Fig. 1. A CGM $\mathcal{M}_1$, with a realization μ_1 minimizing lexicographically: the difference Penalty-Reward, workTime, and cost. (Color figure online)

a prerequisite for FastSchedule, ScheduleManually and CallParticipants cannot be both satisfied, one can add the constraint "FastSchedule → ¬(ScheduleManually∧ CallParticipants)".

In addition to Boolean constraints, it is also possible to use numerical variables to express different numerical attributes of elements (such as cost, worktime, space, fuel, etc.) and constraints over them. For example, in Fig. 1 we associate to UsePartnerInstitutions and UseHotelsAndConventionCenters a cost value of 80€ and 200€ respectively, and we associate "(cost < 100€)" as a prerequisite constraint for the nice-to-have requirement LowCost. Implicitly, this means that no realization involving UseHotelsAndConventionCenters can realize this requirement.

We suppose now that ScheduleMeeting is asserted as satisfied (i.e. it is mandatory) and that no other element is asserted. Then the CGM in Fig. 1 has more than 20 possible *realizations*. The sub-graph which is highlighted in yellow describes one of them. Intuitively, a realization of a CGM under given user assertions (if any) represents one of the alternative ways of refining the mandatory requirements (plus possibly some of the nice-to-have ones) in compliance with the user assertions and user-defined constraints. It is a sub-graph of the CGM including a set of satisfied elements and refinements: it includes all mandatory requirements, and [resp. does not include] all elements satisfied [resp. denied] in the user assertions; for each non-leaf element included, at least one of its refinement is included; for each refinement included, all its target elements are included; finally, a realization complies with all relation edges and with all constraints.

In general, a CGM under given user assertions has many possible realizations. To distinguish among them, stakeholders may want to express *preferences* on the requirements to achieve, on the tasks to accomplish, and on elements and refinements to choose. The CGM-Tool provides various methods to express preferences:

- attribute *rewards and penalties* to nice-to-have requirements and tasks respectively, so that to maximize the former and minimize the latter; (E.g., satisfying LowCost gives a reward = 100, whilst satisfying CharacteriseMeeting gives a penalty = 15.)
- introduce *numerical attributes*, *constraints* and *objectives*; (E.g., the numerical attribute Cost not only can be used to set prerequisite constraints for requirements, like "(Cost < 100€)" for LowCost, but also can be set as objectives to minimize.)
- introduce a list of *binary preference relations* "⪰" between elements or refinements (E.g., one can set the preferences BySystem ⪰ ByPerson, UseLocalRoom ⪰ UsePartnerInstitutions and UseLocalRoom ⪰ UseHotelsAndConventionCenters.).

The CGM-Tool provides many automated-reasoning functionalities on CGMs [5].

Search/enumerate realizations. One can automatically check the realizability of a CGM – or to enumerate one or more of its possible realizations – under a group of user assertions and of user-defined constraints; (When a CGM is found unrealizable under a group of user assertions and of user-defined constraints, it highlights the subparts of the CGM and the subset of assertions causing the problem.)

Search/enumerate minimum-penalty/maximum reward realizations. One can assert rewards to the desired requirements and set penalties of tasks, then the tool finds automatically the optimal realization(s).

Search/enumerate optimal realizations wrt. pre-defined/user-defined objectives. One can define objective functions $obj_1, ..., obj_k$ over goals, refinements and their numerical attributes; then the tool finds automatically realizations optimizing them.

Search/enumerate optimal realizations wrt. binary preferences. Once the list of binary preference is set, the tool finds automatically realizations maximizing the number of fulfilled preferences.

The above functionalities can be combined in various ways. For instance, the realization of Fig. 1 is the one returned by CGMtool when asked to minimize lexicographically, in order, the difference Penalty-Reward, workTime, and cost.[1] They have been implemented by encoding the CGM and the objectives into an SMT($\mathcal{LRA}$) formula and a set of $\mathcal{LRA}$ objectives, which is fed to the OMT tool OPTIMATHSAT [9]. We refer the reader to [5] for a much more detailed description of CGMs and their automated reasoning functionalities.

3   Requirements Evolution and Evolution Requirements

Here we show how a CGM can evolve, and how we can handle such evolution.

3.1   Requirements Evolution

Constrained goal models may evolve in time: goals, requirements and assumptions can be added, removed, or simply modified; Boolean and SMT constraints may be added, removed, or modified as well; assumptions which were assumed true can be assumed false, or vice versa.

Some modifications *strengthen* the CGMs, in the sense that they reduce the set of candidate realizations. For instance, dropping one of the refinements of an element (if at least one is left) reduces the alternatives in realizations; adding source elements to a refinement makes it harder to satisfy; adding Boolean or SMT constraints, or making some such constraint strictly stronger, restricts the set of candidate solutions; changing the value of an assumption from true to false may drop some alternative solutions. Vice versa, some modifications *weaken* the CGMs, augmenting the set of candidate realizations: for instance, adding one of refinement to an element, dropping source elements to a refinement, dropping

---

[1] A solution *optimizes lexicographically* an ordered list of objectives $\langle obj_1, obj_2, ... \rangle$ if it makes obj_1 optimum and, if more than one such solution exists, it makes also obj_2 optimum, ..., etc.

Boolean or SMT constraints, or making some such constraint strictly weaker, changing the value of an assumption from false to true. In general, however, since in a CGM the goal and/or decomposition graph is a DAG and not a tree, and the and/or decomposition is augmented with relational edges and constraints, modifications may produce combinations of the above effects, possibly propagating unexpected side effects which are sometimes hard to predict.

We consider the CGM of a Schedule Meeting described in Fig. 1 (namely, $\mathcal{M}_1$) as our starting model, and we assume that for some reasons it has been modified into the CGM of Fig. 2 (namely, $\mathcal{M}_2$). $\mathcal{M}_2$ differs from $\mathcal{M}_1$ for the following modifications:

(a) two new tasks, SetSystemCalendar and ParticipantsFillSystemCalendar, are added to the sub-goal sources of the refinement R_{13};
(b) a new source task RegisterMeetingRoom is added to R_{17}, and the binding between R_{16} and R_{17} is removed; the refinement R_{18} of the goal BookRoom and its source task CancelLessImportantMeeting are removed;
(c) the alternative refinements R_8 and R_9 of ManageMeeting are also modified: two new internal goals ByUser and ByAgent are added and become the single source of the two refinements R_8 and R_9 respectively, and the two tasks ConfirmOccurrence and CancelMeeting become respectively the sources of two new refinements R_{21} and R_{22}, which are the alternative refinements of the goal ByUser; the new goal ByAgent is refined by the new refinement R_{23} with source task SendDecision.

3.2   Evolution Requirements

We consider the generic scenario in which a previous version of a CGM $\mathcal{M}_1$ with an available realization μ_1 is modified into a new CGM $\mathcal{M}_2$.

As a consequence of modifying a CGM $\mathcal{M}_1$ into a new version $\mathcal{M}_2$, μ_1 typically is no more a valid realization of $\mathcal{M}_2$.[2] E.g., we notice that μ_1 in Fig. 2 does not represent a valid realization of $\mathcal{M}_2$: not all source tasks of R_{13} are satisfied, BookRoom has no satisfied refinement, and the new goal ByUser and refinement R_{21} are not satisfied. It is thus necessary to produce a new realization μ_2 for $\mathcal{M}_2$.

In general, when one has a sequence $\mathcal{M}_1, \mathcal{M}_2, ..., \mathcal{M}_i, ...$ of CGMs and must produce a corresponding sequence $\mu_1, \mu_2, ..., \mu_i, ...$ of realizations, it is necessary to decide some criteria by which the realizations μ_i evolve in terms of the evolution of the CGMs $\mathcal{M}_i$. We call these criteria, *evolution requirements*. We describe some possible criteria.

Recomputing Realizations. One possible evolution requirement is that of always having the "best" realization μ_i for each $\mathcal{M}_i$, according to some objective

---

[2] More precisely, rather than "μ_1", here we should say "the restriction of μ_1 to the elements and variables which are still in $\mathcal{M}_2$." We will keep this distinction implicit in the rest of the paper.

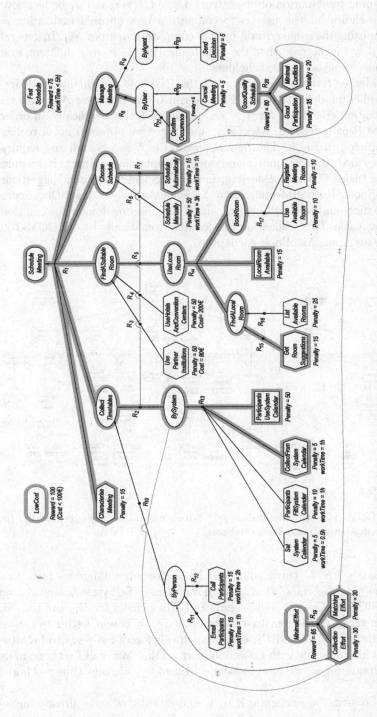

Fig. 2. The novel CGM $\mathcal{M}_2$, with the previous realization μ_1 highlighted for comparison. (Notice that μ_1 is no more a valid realization for $\mathcal{M}_2$.)

(or lexicographic combination of objectives). Let $\mathcal{M}_1$, $\mathcal{M}_2$, and μ_1 be as above. One possible choice for the user is to compute a new optimal realization μ_2 from scratch, using the same criteria used in computing μ_1 from $\mathcal{M}_1$. In general, however, it may be the case that the new realization μ_2 is very different from μ_1, which may displease the stakeholders.

We consider now the realization μ_1 of the CGM $\mathcal{M}_1$ highlighted in Fig. 1 and the modified model $\mathcal{M}_2$ of Fig. 2. If we run CGM-Tool over $\mathcal{M}_2$ with the same optimization criteria as for μ_1 – i.e., minimize lexicographically, in order, the difference Penalty-Reward, workTime, and cost – we obtain a novel realization μ_2^{lex} depicted in Fig. 3. The new realization μ_2^{lex} satisfies all the requirements (both "nice to have" and mandatory) except MinimalEffort. It includes the following tasks: CharateriseMeeting, EmailParticipants, GetRoomSuggestions, UseAvailableRoom, RegisterMeetingRoom, ScheduleManually, ConfirmOccurrence, GoodParticipation, and MinimalConflicts, and it requires one domain assumption: LocalRoomAvailable. This realization was found automatically by our CGM-Tool in 0.059 s on an Apple MacBook Air laptop.

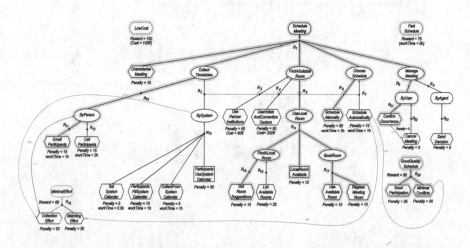

Fig. 3. New CGM $\mathcal{M}_2$, with realization μ_2^{lex} which minimizes lexicographically: the difference Penalty-Reward, workTime, and cost.

Unfortunately, μ_2^{lex} turns out to be extremely different from μ_1. This is due to the fact that the novel tasks SetSystemCalendar and ParticipantsFillSystemCalendar raise significantly the penalty for R_{13} and thus for R_2; hence, in terms of the Penalty-Reward objective, it is now better to choose R_{10} and R_6 instead of R_2 and R_7, even though this forces ByPerson to be satisfied, which is incompatible with CollectionEffort, so that MinimalEffort is no more achieved. Overall, for μ_2 we have Penalty $-$ Reward $= -65$, workTime $= 4$ h and cost $= 0$€.

In many contexts, in particular if μ_1 is well-established or is already implemented, one may want to find a realization μ_2 of the modified CGM $\mathcal{M}_2$ which is as similar as possible to the previous realization $\mathcal{M}_1$. The suitable notion of "similarity", however, may depend on stakeholder's needs. In what follows, we discuss two notions of "similarity" from [2], *familiarity* and *change effort*, adapting and extending them to CGMs.

Maximizing Familiarity. In our approach, in its simplest form, the *familiarity* of μ_2 wrt. μ_1 is given by the number of elements of interest which are common to $\mathcal{M}_1$ and $\mathcal{M}_2$ and which either are in both μ_1 and μ_2 or are out of both of them; this can be augmented also by the number of new elements in $\mathcal{M}_2$ of interest (e.g., tasks) which are denied. In a more sophisticate form, the contribution of each element of interest can be weighted by some numerical value (e.g., Penalty, cost, WorkTime,...). This is formalized in Sect. 4, and a functionality for maximizing familiarity is implemented in CGM-Tool.

For example, if we ask CGM-Tool to find a realization which maximizes our notion of familiarity (see Sect. 4), we obtain the novel realization μ_2^{fam} depicted in Fig. 4. μ_2^{fam} satisfies all the requirements (both "nice to have" and mandatory ones), and includes the following tasks: CharacteriseMeeitng, SetSystemCalendar, ParticipantsFillSystemCalendar, CollectFromSystemCalendar, GetRoomSuggestions, UseAvailableRoom, RegisterMeetingRoom, ScheduleAutomatically, Confirm Occurrence, GoodParticipation, MinimalConflicts, CollectionEffort, and MatchingEffort; μ_2^{fam} also requires two domain assumptions: ParticipantsUseSystemCalendar and LocalRoomAvailable.

Notice that all the tasks which are satisfied in μ_1 are satisfied also in μ_2^{fam}, and only the intermediate goal ByUser, the refinement R_{21} and the four tasks SetSystemCalendar, ParticipantsFillSystemCalendar, UseAvailableRoom, and RegisterMeetingRoom are added to μ_2^{fam}, three of which are newly-added tasks. Thus, on common elements, μ_2^{fam} and μ_1 differ only on the task

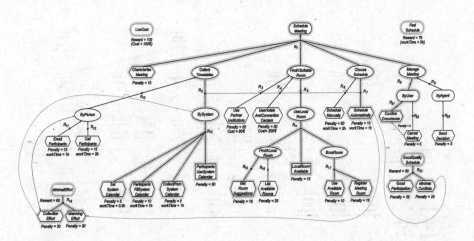

Fig. 4. New CGM $\mathcal{M}_2$, with realization μ_2^{fam} with maximizes the familiarity wrt. μ_1.

UseAvailableRoom, which must be mandatorily be satisfied to complete the realization. Overall, wrt. μ_2^{lex}, we pay familiarity with some loss in the "quality" of the realization, since for μ_2^{fam} we have Penalty−Reward = −50, workTime = 3.5 h and cost = 0€. This realization was found automatically by our CGM-Tool in 0.067 s on an Apple MacBook Air laptop.

Minimizing Change Effort. In our approach, in its simplest form, the *change effort* of μ_2 wrt. μ_1 is given by the number of newly-satisfied tasks, i.e., the amount of the new tasks which are satisfied in μ_2 plus that of common tasks which were not satisfied in μ_1 but are satisfied in μ_2. In a more sophisticate form, the contribution of each task of interest can be weighted by some numerical value (e.g., Penalty, cost, WorkTime,...). Intuitively, since satisfying a task requires effort, this value considers the extra effort required to implement μ_2. (Notice that tasks which pass from satisfied to denied do not reduce the effort, because we assume they have been implemented anyway.) This is formalized in Sect. 4, and a functionality for minimizing change effort is implemented in CGM-Tool.

For example, if we ask CGM-Tool to find a realization which minimizes the number of newly-satisfied tasks, we obtain the realization μ_2^{eff} depicted in Fig. 5. The realization satisfies all the requirements (both "nice to have" and mandatory), and includes the following tasks: CharacteriseMeeitng, SetSystemCalendar, ParticipantsFillSystemCalendar, CollectFromSystemCalendar, UsePartnerInstitutions, ScheduleAutomatically, ConfirmOccurrence, GoodParticipation, MinimalConflicts, CollectionEffort, and MatchingEffort; μ_2^{eff} also requires one domain assumption ParticipantsUse SystemCalendar.

Notice that, in order to minimize the number of new tasks needed to be achieved, in μ_2^{eff}, FindASuitableRoom is refined by R_3 instead of R_5. In fact, in order to achieve R_5, we would need to satisfy two extra tasks (UseAvailableRoom and RegisterMeetingRoom) wrt. μ_1, whilst for satisfying R_3 we only need

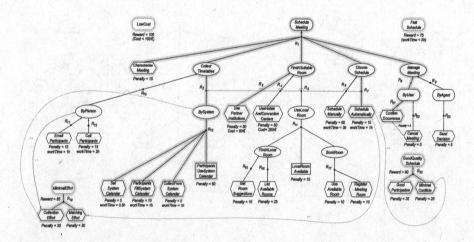

Fig. 5. New CGM $\mathcal{M}_2$, with realization μ_2^{eff} with minimimizes the change effort wrt. μ_1.

to satisfy one task (UsePartnerInstitutions). Besides, two newly added tasks SetSystemCalendar and ParticipantsFillSystemCalendar are also included in μ_2^{eff}. Thus the total effort of evolving from μ_1 to μ_2^{eff} is to implement three new tasks. Overall, for μ_2^{eff} we have Penalty $-$ Reward $= -50$, workTime $= 3.5\,$h and cost $= 80€$. This realization was found automatically by our CGM-Tool in $0.085\,$s on an Apple MacBook Air laptop.

Combining Familiarity or Change Effort with Other Objectives. In our approach, familiarity and change effort are numerical objectives like others, and as such they can be combined lexicographically with other objectives, so that stakeholders can decide which objectives to prioritize.

4   Automated Reasoning with Evolution Requirements

CGMs and Realizations We first recall some formal definitions from [5].

A *Constrained Goal Model (CGM)* is a tuple $\mathcal{M} \overset{\text{def}}{=} \langle \mathcal{B}, \mathcal{N}, \mathcal{D}, \Psi \rangle$, s.t.

- $\mathcal{B} \overset{\text{def}}{=} \mathcal{G} \cup \mathcal{R} \cup \mathcal{A}$ is a set of atomic propositions, where $\mathcal{G} \overset{\text{def}}{=} \{G_1, ..., G_N\}$, $\mathcal{R} \overset{\text{def}}{=} \{R_1, ..., R_K\}$, $\mathcal{A} \overset{\text{def}}{=} \{A_1, ..., A_M\}$ are respectively sets of goal, refinement and domain-assumption labels. We denote with $\mathcal{E}$ the set of element labels: $\mathcal{E} \overset{\text{def}}{=} \mathcal{G} \cup \mathcal{A}$;
- $\mathcal{N}$ is a set of numerical variables in the rationals;
- $\mathcal{D}$ is an and-or directed acyclic graph of *elements* in $\mathcal{E}$ (or nodes) and *refinements* in $\mathcal{R}$ (and nodes);
- Ψ is a SMT($\mathcal{LRA}$) formula on $\mathcal{B}$ and $\mathcal{N}$, representing the conjunction of all relation edges, user-defined constraints and assertions.

The structure of a CGM is an and-or directed acyclic graph (DAG) of *elements*, as nodes, and *refinements*, as (grouped) edges, which are labeled by atomic propositions and can be augmented with arbitrary constraints in form of graphical relations and Boolean or SMT($\mathcal{LRA}$) formulas – typically conjunctions of smaller global and local constraints – on the element and refinement labels and on the numerical variables. Notice that each non-leaf element E is implicitly or-decomposed into the set of its incoming refinements $\{R_i\} \overset{\text{def}}{=}$ RefinementsOf(E) (i.e., $E \leftrightarrow (\bigvee_i R_i)$) and that each refinement R is and-decomposed into the set of its source elements $\{E_j\}$ (i.e., $R \leftrightarrow (\bigwedge_j E_j)$). Intuitively, a CGM describes a (possibly complex) combination of alternative ways of realizing a set of requirements in terms of a set of tasks, under certain domain assumptions.

Let $\mathcal{M} \overset{\text{def}}{=} \langle \mathcal{B}, \mathcal{N}, \mathcal{D}, \Psi \rangle$ be a CGM. A *realization* μ of $\mathcal{M}$ is an assignment of truth values to $\mathcal{B}$ and of rational values to $\mathcal{N}$ (aka, a $\mathcal{LRA}$-interpretation) which:

(a) for each non-leaf element E, μ satisfies $\left(E \leftrightarrow (\bigvee_{R_i \in \text{RefinementsOf(E)}} R_i)\right)$ – i.e., E is part of a realization μ if and only if one of its refinements is in μ;

(b) for each refinement $(E_1, ..., E_n) \overset{R}{\rightarrow} E$, μ satisfies $((\bigwedge_{i=1}^n E_i) \leftrightarrow R)$ – i.e., R is part of μ iff and only if all of its sub-elements E_i are in μ;

(c) μ satisfies Ψ – i.e., the elements and refinements occurring in μ, and the values assigned by μ to the numerical attributes, comply with all the relation edges, the user-defined constraints and user assertions in Ψ.

We say that an element E or refinement R is *satisfied* [resp. *denied*] in μ if it is assigned to $\top$ [resp. $\bot$] by μ. μ is represented graphically as the sub-graph of $\mathcal{M}$ where all the denied element and refinement nodes are eliminated. We say that $\mathcal{M}$, including user assertions, is *realizable* if it has at least one realization, *unrealizable* otherwise.

As described in [5], a CGM $\mathcal{M}$ is encoded into a SMT($\mathcal{LRA}$) formula $\Psi_{\mathcal{M}}$, and the user preferences into *numerical objective functions* $\{obj_1, ..., obj_k\}$, which are fed to the OMT solver OPTIMATHSAT, which returns optimal solutions wrt. $\{obj_1, ..., obj_k\}$, which are then converted back by CGM-tool into optimal realizations.

Evolution Requirements. Here we formalize the notions described in Sect. 3.2. Let $\mathcal{M}_1 \overset{\text{def}}{=} \langle \mathcal{B}_1, \mathcal{N}_1, \mathcal{D}_1, \Psi_1 \rangle$ be the original model, μ_1 be some realization of $\mathcal{M}_1$ and $\mathcal{M}_2 \overset{\text{def}}{=} \langle \mathcal{B}_2, \mathcal{N}_2, \mathcal{D}_2, \Psi_2 \rangle$ be a new version of $\mathcal{M}_1$. We look for a novel realization μ_2 for $\mathcal{M}_2$.

Stakeholders can select a subset of the elements, called *elements of interest*, on which to focus, which can be requirements, tasks, domain assumptions, and intermediate goals. (When not specified otherwise, we will assume by default that all elements are of interest.) Let $\mathcal{E}^* \subseteq \mathcal{E}_1 \cup \mathcal{E}_2$ be the subset of the elements of interest, and let $\mathcal{E}_1^* \overset{\text{def}}{=} \mathcal{E}^* \cap \mathcal{E}_1$ and $\mathcal{E}_2^* \overset{\text{def}}{=} \mathcal{E}^* \cap \mathcal{E}_2$ be the respective subsets of $\mathcal{M}_1$ and $\mathcal{M}_2$. We define $\mathcal{E}_{common}^* \overset{\text{def}}{=} \{E_i \in \mathcal{E}_2^* \cap \mathcal{E}_1^*\}$ as the set of elements of interest occurring in both $\mathcal{M}_1$ and $\mathcal{M}_2$, and $\mathcal{E}_{new}^* \overset{\text{def}}{=} \{E_i \in \mathcal{E}_2^* \setminus \mathcal{E}_1^*\}$ as the set of new elements of interest in $\mathcal{M}_2$.

Familiarity. In its simplest form, the cost of familiarity can be defined as follows:

$$\text{FamiliarityCost}(\mu_2|\mu_1) \overset{\text{def}}{=} |\ \{E_i \in \mathcal{E}_{common}^*\ |\ \mu_2(E_i) \neq \mu_1(E_i)\}\ | \qquad (1)$$
$$+\ |\ \{E_i \in \mathcal{E}_{new}^*\ |\ \mu_2(E_i) = \top\}\ |, \qquad (2)$$

where $|\,S\,|$ denotes the number of elements of a set S. $\text{FamiliarityCost}(\mu_2|\mu_1)$ is the sum of two components:

(1) the number of common elements of interest (e.g., tasks) which were in μ_1 and are no more in μ_2, plus the number of these which were not in μ_1 and now are in μ_2,
(2) the number of new elements of interest which are in μ_2.

In a more sophisticate form, each element of interest E_i can be given some rational weight value $w_i{}^3$, so that the cost of familiarity can be defined as follows:

$$\mathsf{WeightFamiliarityCost}(\mu_2|\mu_1) \stackrel{\text{def}}{=} \sum_{E_i \in \mathcal{E}^*_{common}} w_i \cdot \mathsf{Int}(\mu_2(E_i) \neq \mu_1(E_i)) \quad (3)$$

$$+ \sum_{E_i \in \mathcal{E}^*_{new}} w_i \cdot \mathsf{Int}(\mu_2(E_i) = \top), \quad (4)$$

where $\mathsf{Int}()$ converts true and false into the values 1 and 0 respectively.

Both forms are implemented in CGM-Tool. (Notice that (1) and (2), or even (3) and (4), can also be set as distinct objectives in CGM-Tool.) Consequently, a realization μ_2 maximizing familiarity is produced by invoking the OMT solver on the formula $\Psi_{\mathcal{M}_2}$ and the objective $\mathsf{FamiliarityCost}(\mu_2|\mu_1)$ or $\mathsf{WeightFamiliarityCost}(\mu_2|\mu_1)$ to minimize.

Change effort. We restrict the elements of interest to tasks only. In its simplest form, the change effort can be defined as follows:

$$\mathsf{ChangeEffort}(\mu_2|\mu_1) \stackrel{\text{def}}{=} | \ \{T_i \in \mathcal{E}^*_{common} \ | \ \mu_2(T_i) = \top, \text{ and } \mu_1(T_i) = \bot\} \ | \quad (5)$$

$$+ | \ \{T_i \in \mathcal{E}^*_{new} \ | \ \mu_2(T_i) = \top\} \ | \ . \quad (6)$$

$\mathsf{ChangeEffort}(\mu_2|\mu_1)$ is the sum of two components:

(5) is the number of common tasks which were not in μ_1 and which are now in μ_2,

(6) is the number of new tasks which are in μ_2.

As above, in a more sophisticate form, each task of interest T_i can be given some rational weight value w_i, so that the change effort can be defined as follows:

$$\mathsf{WeightChangeEffort}(\mu_2|\mu_1) \stackrel{\text{def}}{=} \sum_{T_i \in \mathcal{E}^*_{common}} w_i \cdot \mathsf{Int}(\mu_2(T_i) = \top) \cdot \mathsf{Int}(\mu_1(T_i) = \bot)$$

$$+ \sum_{T_i \in \mathcal{E}^*_{new}} w_i \cdot \mathsf{Int}(\mu_2(T_i) = \top).$$

Both forms are implemented in CGM-Tool. Consequently, a novel realization μ_2 minimizing change effort is produced by invoking the OMT solver on the formula $\Psi_{\mathcal{M}_2}$ and the objective $\mathsf{ChangeEffort}(\mu_2|\mu_1)$ or $\mathsf{WeightChangeEffort}(\mu_2|\mu_1)$.

Notice an important difference between (1) and (5), even if the former is restricted to tasks only: a task which is satisfied in μ_1 and is no more in μ_2 worsens the familiarity of μ_2 wrt. μ_1 (1), but it does not affect its change effort (5), because it does not require implementing one more task.

Comparison wrt. Previous Approaches. Importantly, Ernst et al. [2] proposed two similar notion of familiarity and change effort for (un-)constrained goal graphs:

---

[3] Like Penalty, Cost and WorkTime in Fig. 1.

familiarity: maximize (the cardinality of) the set of tasks used in the previous solution;

change effort: (i) minimize (the cardinality of) the set of new tasks in the novel realization – or, alternatively, (ii) minimize also the number of tasks.

We notice remarkable differences of our approach wrt. the one in [2].

First, our notion of familiarity presents the following novelties:

(i) it uses all kinds of elements, on stakeholders' demand, rather than only tasks;
(ii) it is (optionally) enriched also with (2);
(iii) (1) is sensitive also to tasks which were in the previous realization and which are not in the novel one, since we believe that also these elements affect familiarity.

Also, in our approach both familiarity and change effort allow for adding *weights* to tasks/elements, and to combine familiarity and change-effort objectives lexicographically with other user-defined objectives.

Second, unlike with [2], in which the optimization procedure is hardwired, we rely on logical encodings of novel objectives into OMT($\mathcal{LRA}$) objectives, using OPTIMATHSAT as workhorse reasoning engine. Therefore, new objectives require implementing no new reasoning procedure, only new OMT($\mathcal{LRA}$) encodings. For instance, we could easily implement also the notion of familiarity of [2] by asking OPTIMATHSAT to minimize the objective: $| \{T_i \in \mathcal{E}^*_{common} \mid \mu_2(T_i) = \bot, \text{ and } \mu_1(T_i) = \top\} |$.

Third, our approach deals with CGMs, which are very expressive formalisms, are enriched by Boolean and numerical constraints, and are supported by a tool (CGM-Tool) with efficient search functionalities for optimum realizations. These functionalities, which are enabled by state-of-the-art SMT and OMT technologies [8,9], scale very well, up to thousands of elements, as shown in the empirical evaluation of [5]. In this paper we further enrich these functionalities so that to deal also with evolving CGMs and evolution requirements.

Fourth, unlike with [2], where realizations are intrinsically supposed to be *minimal*, in our approach minimality is an objective stakeholders can set and obtain as a byproduct of *minimum* solutions, but it is not mandatory. This fact is relevant when dealing with familiarity evolution requirements, because objective (1) can conflict with minimality, because it may force the presence of tasks from the previous solution which have become redundant in the new model. Thus, sometimes CGM-tool may return a non-minimal model if the stakeholder prioritizes familiarity above all other objectives.

5   Implementation

CGM-Tool provides support for modeling and reasoning on CGMs [5]. Technically, CGM-Tool is a standalone application written in Java and its core is based on

Eclipse RCP engine. Under the hood, it encodes CGMs and invokes the OptiMathSAT[4] OMT solver [9] to support reasoning on CGMs. It is freely distributed for multiple platforms[5]. Currently CGM-Tool supports the functionalities in [5]:

Specification of projects: CGMs are created within the scope of project containers. A project contains a set of CGMs that can be used to generate reasoning sessions with OptiMathSAT (i.e., scenarios);

Diagrammatic modeling: the tool enables the creation of CGMs as diagrams; it provides real-time check for refinement cycles and reports invalid links;

Consistency/well-formedness check: CGM-Tool provides the ability to run consistency analysis and well-formedness checks on the CGMs;

Automated Reasoning: CGM-Tool provides the automated reasoning functionalities mentioned in Sect. 2, and described in detail in [5].

With this work, we have enhanced CGM-Tool with the following functionalities:

Evolution Requirements Modelling and Automated Reasoning: by means of scenarios, stakeholders can generate *evolution sessions*, which allows for (i) defining the first model and finding the first optimal realization, (ii) modifying the model to obtain the new models, and (iii) generating automatically the "similar" realization (as discussed in Sect. 3.2).

As a proof of concept, we have performed various attempts on variants of the CGM of Sect. 3. The automated generation of the realizations always required negligible amounts of CPU time, like those reported in Sect. 3.2.

6 Conclusions

We have proposed to model changing requirements in terms of changes to CGMs. Moreover, we have introduced a new class of requirements (evolution requirements) that impose constraints on allowable evolutions, such as minimizing (implementation) effort or maximizing (user) familiarity. We have demonstrated how to model such requirements in terms of CGMs and how to reason with them in order to find optimal evolutions.

Our future plans for this work include further evaluation with larger case studies, as well as further exploration for new kinds of evolution requirements that can guide software evolution.

---

[4] http://optimathsat.disi.unitn.it.
[5] http://www.cgm-tool.eu/.

86   C.M. Nguyen et al.

References

1. Barrett, C.W., Sebastiani, R., Seshia, S.A., Tinelli, C.: Satisfiability modulo theories. In: Handbook of Satisfiability, pp. 825–885. IOS Press (2009). Chap. 26
2. Ernst, N.A., Borgida, A., Mylopoulos, J., Jureta, I.J.: Agile requirements evolution via paraconsistent reasoning. In: Ralyté, J., Franch, X., Brinkkemper, S., Wrycza, S. (eds.) CAiSE 2012. LNCS, vol. 7328, pp. 382–397. Springer, Heidelberg (2012). doi:10.1007/978-3-642-31095-9_25
3. Feather, M.S., Fickas, S., Finkelsteiin, A., Lamsweerde, A.V.: Requirements and specification exemplars. Automated Software Engineering 4(4), 419–438 (1997)
4. Lehman, M.M.: Programs, life cycles, and laws of software evolution. Proc. IEEE 68(9), 1060–1076 (1980)
5. Nguyen, C.M., Sebastiani, R., Giorgini, P., Mylopoulos, J.: Multi-objective reasoning with constrained goal models. Requir. Eng. J., 1–37 (2016)
6. Nguyen, C.M., Sebastiani, R., Giorgini, P., Mylopoulos, J.: Requirements evolution and evolution requirements with constrained goal models. In: Comyn-Wattiau, I., Tanaka, K., Song, I.-Y., Yamamoto, S., Saeki, M. (eds.) ER 2016. LNCS, vol. 9974, pp. 544–552. Springer, Cham (2016). doi:10.1007/978-3-319-46397-1_42
7. Nguyen, C.M., Sebastiani, R., Giorgini, P., Mylopoulos, J.: Modeling and reasoning on requirements evolution with constrained goal models (2017). Extended version of this paper. http://disi.unitn.it/rseba/papers/sefm17_extended.pdf
8. Sebastiani, R., Tomasi, S.: Optimization modulo theories with linear rational costs. ACM Trans. Comput. Log. 16(2), 12:1–12:43 (2015)
9. Sebastiani, R., Trentin, P.: OptiMathSAT: a tool for optimization modulo theories. In: Kroening, D., Păsăreanu, C.S. (eds.) CAV 2015. LNCS, vol. 9206, pp. 447–454. Springer, Cham (2015). doi:10.1007/978-3-319-21690-4_27
10. Souza, V.E.S.: Requirements-based software system adaptation. Ph.D. thesis, University of Trento (2012)
11. van Lamsweerde, A., Darimont, R., Massonet, P.: Goal-directed elaboration of requirements for a meeting scheduler: problems and lessons learned. In: Proceedings of the RE 1995 - 2nd International Symposium on Requirements Engineering, pp. 194–203. IEEE (1995)

Participatory Verification of Railway Infrastructure by Representing Regulations in RailCNL

Bjørnar Luteberget[1], John J. Camilleri[2], Christian Johansen[3(✉)], and Gerardo Schneider[2]

[1] RailComplete AS, Sandvika, Norway
bjlut@railcomplete.no
[2] Department of Computer Science and Engineering,
Chalmers University of Technology and University of Gothenburg,
Gothenburg, Sweden
{john.j.camilleri,gerardo}@cse.gu.se
[3] Department of Informatics, University of Oslo, Oslo, Norway
cristi@ifi.uio.no

Abstract. Designs of railway infrastructure (tracks, signalling and control systems, etc.) need to comply with comprehensive sets of regulations describing safety requirements, engineering conventions, and design heuristics. We have previously worked on automating the verification of railway designs against such regulations, and integrated a verification tool based on Datalog reasoning into the CAD tools of railway engineers. This was used in a pilot project at Norconsult AS (formerly Anacon AS). In order to allow railway engineers with limited logic programming experience to participate in the verification process, in this work we introduce a controlled natural language, RailCNL, which is designed as a middle ground between informal regulations and Datalog code. Phrases in RailCNL correspond closely to those in the regulation texts, and can be translated automatically into the input language of the verifier. We demonstrate a prototype system which, upon detecting regulation violations, traces back from errors in the design through the CNL to the marked-up original text, allowing domain experts to examine the correctness of each translation step and better identify sources of errors. We also describe our design methodology, based on CNL best practices and previous experience with creating verification front-end languages.

1 Introduction

Automated formal verification techniques have the potential to greatly increase the efficiency of engineering. However, verification engines are not easy to take up in industrial practice. Even if the verification process is fully automated,

Supported by the Norwegian Research Council project *RailCons* – Aut. Methods and Tools for Ensuring Consistency of Railway Designs, and by the Swedish Research Council grant nr. 2012-5746 – Reliable Multilingual Digital Communication: Methods and Applications.

© Springer International Publishing AG 2017
A. Cimatti and M. Sirjani (Eds.): SEFM 2017, LNCS 10469, pp. 87–103, 2017.
DOI: 10.1007/978-3-319-66197-1_6

integrating the tools into the users' workflow and formalizing properties and models requires careful thinking and domain expertise. The gap between automated verification and domain expert users is often caused by the lack of user involvement. The users are usually not experts in verification techniques, i.e. they do not know how to write properties in the verifier's language, nor how to build models for the verifier, nor how to interpret the output of the verifier when violated properties are found. In our case, the users are expert engineers from the railway domain, designing railway infrastructure.

We want to allow the end users to participate in the verification process. Firstly, the domain experts need to understand the verification properties that the tool actually verifies, as well as the model of the system that the tool works with. Secondly, we want to allow the users to actively participate in maintaining the verification properties, i.e. to change and adjust them when needed[1]. Thirdly, we want that the domain experts are able to create their own specifications and feed these into the verification engine, e.g. define specific expert knowledge as verification conditions.[2]

Involving the user in the design of a system is well-studied in the field of participatory design [8,19]. We use the term *participatory verification* when talking about methods for including the end user in the verification process. The goal is to make automated verification techniques accessible to engineers with little programming experience.

We have previously demonstrated [12,13] an efficient verification and troubleshooting tool integrated into the CAD-based program used by railway planning engineers. This tool performs a lightweight type of verification which we call *static infrastructure verification*, and the results are updated continuously as the engineer is modifying the station (see Fig. 1). However, the Prolog-like formal logical specification language that we used for describing railway rules and regulations is not easy for inexperienced programmers to write. Ideally, railway engineers should be able to read the logical specifications to ensure that they correctly represent the engineering domain. Furthermore, engineers should themselves be able to maintain and extend the rule base with limited support from verification experts. When we evaluated with railway engineers from Rail-COMPLETE AS[3] our prototype, they raised yet another concern: how could they trace the violation, which the tool displays graphically, back to the source documents?

These observations have led us to develop a controlled natural language (CNL), which we call RailCNL, meant to be used as an intermediate representation between natural language texts (i.e. the railway regulations) and Datalog [20] logic programs. RailCNL aims to be human-friendly enough for our domain experts to work with to overcome the above challenges, and thus getting them involved in using and improving the automated verification tool. At the same

---

[1] Authorities typically make small adjustments to regulations several times per year, whereas engineering best practices can be revised at any time.

[2] Such expert knowledge is often seen as proprietary valuable assets of the company.

[3] http://railcomplete.no.

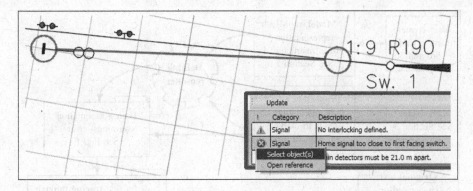

Fig. 1. CAD integrated verification engine, displaying errors and warnings after checking the model extracted from the CAD design against railway regulations on-the-fly.

time, the language is a formal language which can be automatically translated into Datalog.

In our collaboration with Norwegian railway engineers, we have focused on regulations in Norwegian language[4], but our general approach (Sect. 2) is language-independent. In Sect. 3 we present RailCNL, a user-friendly verification front-end language for static railway infrastructure analysis. This comes with an automatic translation into Datalog (Sect. 3.3), and backwards tracing integrated into the CAD program, where marked-up original regulation texts are used together with the CNL text to explain regulatory violations found in the model (Sect. 3.4). In Sect. 4 we extract a design methodology from our experience with RailCNL, and conclude in Sect. 5 by describing the coverage of the defined CNL, and presenting related and future work.

2   Approach to Participatory Verification for Railway Regulations

To promote participatory verification of infrastructure railway designs against regulations, we design a CNL for expressing railway regulations and expert knowledge, integrating it with our previously developed verification engine. Figure 2 presents the overall workflow of using the railway CNL integrated with the engineer's CAD-based environment and our verification engine. Static infrastructure verification requires:

1. *Models:* railway infrastructure plans, typically created by arranging the station layout using CAD-based programs, e.g. extensions of Autodesk Auto-CAD.
2. *Properties:* regulations and expert knowledge, extracted from regulatory and best-practices documents.

---

[4] The examples presented in this text are English translations of originally Norwegian content.

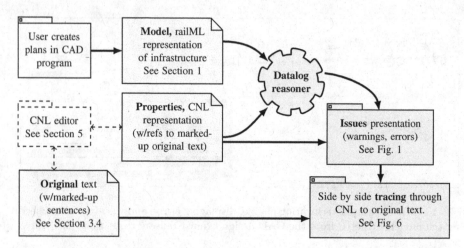

Fig. 2. Verification process overview. *Models* come directly from the CAD program, which engineers are already familiar with. *Properties* come from paraphrasing the regulations using CNL, which in turn are translated into Datalog. The reasoner outputs *issues* (warnings and errors) which are presented to the user in the CAD program by highlighting the objects involved in the violation. Issues are traced back to the original text (i.e. the regulations) though identifiers on the marked-up sentences.

The formalization of these into Datalog is described in our previous work [12] which allows efficient automatic reasoning. Describing verification properties using logical rules in Datalog is not new (along with other logics like temporal [2] or dynamic logics [3,5]), and we expected that the declarative style of Datalog would make it easy for railway engineers to read and write such properties. However, a pilot project with the RailCOMPLETE engineers showed that they were not proficient enough in logic programming to understand our encodings.

To allow the engineers to participate in the verification process, we develop the controlled natural language RailCNL for representing properties on a higher level of abstraction, make them closer to the original text while still retaining the possibility for automatic translation into Datalog. This approach has the following advantages:

- RailCNL is domain-specific, i.e. tailored both to the types of logical statements needed by the verification engine, and to the regulations terminology. This allows concise and readable expressions, increasing naturalness and maintainability.
- The language closely resembles natural language, and can be read by engineers with the required domain knowledge without learning a programming language.
- A separate textual explanation (such as comments used in programming) is not needed for presenting violations textually, as the properties are now directly readable as natural text. Comments could still be used, e.g. to clarify edge cases or to clarify semantics, as is done in the original texts.

– Statements in RailCNL can be linked to statements in the original text, so that reading them side by side reveals to domain experts whether the CNL paraphrasing of the natural text is valid. If not, they can edit the CNL text.

3 RailCNL: A Front-End Language for Railway Verification

A controlled natural languages (CNL) is a constructed language resembling a natural language (such as English) but with added restrictions on its grammar and vocabulary. The restrictions are typically aimed at reducing the ambiguity and complexity of unrestricted natural language. A CNL may or may not also be a formal language, depending on its intended use. Wyner et al. [22] give high-level recommendations on how to design controlled natural languages ranging from informal to formal, general to domain-specific, simple to complex. For a recent survey of CNLs, see Kuhn [9].

Grammatical Framework (GF) is a programming language for multilingual grammar applications [16]. A GF program defines a grammar consisting of an *abstract syntax* and one or more *concrete syntaxes*. The project also features the *resource grammar library* (RGL), which is a comprehensive linguistic model of natural languages with a unified API for forming sentences, and implementations of this API for 32 languages. The RGL encapsulates the linguistic complexity of the underlying natural languages, making the effort needed to map an abstract syntax into another natural language minimal, often reducing to simply providing the domain-specific vocabulary. This makes GF a valuable tool for building CNLs (see [11] for details).

3.1 RailCNL Grammar

With RailCNL, we aim to cover the following content (also see Table 1 on p. 14):

1. Definitions of railway-domain terms from a set of basic terms given by the object types present in the CAD program and the railML exchange format.
2. Regulations (from infrastructure manager technical regulations[5]) which give obligations or recommendations on the design of the railway infrastructure.
3. Expert knowledge given in textual form apart from official regulations, used to gather and formalize engineering practice.

An English version of RailCNL's core grammar is presented in Fig. 3. The full grammar is defined in GF (see [11]), which has some advantages over classical BNF parsers: (i) separation of abstract syntax and concrete syntax; (ii) resource grammar library for natural languages, allowing us to compose sentences in natural language while abstracting away from morphological details; (iii) modularity and extensibility, which we need for evolving a domain-specific language alongside its application; and (iv) tool support for managing text (editors, predictive parsing, visualization).

---

[5] Norwegian infrastructure manager Bane NOR's regulations: https://trv.jbv.no/.

⟨*Statement*⟩ ::= ⟨*OntologyAssertion*⟩
| ⟨*OntologyRestriction*⟩
| ⟨*DistanceRestriction*⟩
| ⟨*PathRestriction*⟩
| ⟨*PlacementRestriction*⟩
| (...) // Partial grammar
⟨*OntologyAssertion*⟩ ::= ⟨*Subject*⟩
⟨*Condition*⟩
⟨*OntologyRestriction*⟩ ::= ⟨*Subject*⟩
⟨*Modality*⟩ ⟨*Condition*⟩
⟨*DistanceRestriction*⟩ ::=
'the distance from' ⟨*Subject*⟩ 'to'
⟨*GoalObject*⟩ ⟨*Modality*⟩ ⟨*Restriction*⟩
⟨*PathRestriction*⟩ ::= ⟨*PathQuantifier*⟩
'from' ⟨*Subject*⟩ 'to' ⟨*GoalObject*⟩
⟨*Modality*⟩ ⟨*PathCondition*⟩
⟨*PlacementRestriction*⟩ ::= ⟨*Subject*⟩
⟨*Modality*⟩ 'be placed in' ⟨*Area*⟩
⟨*Modality*⟩ ::= 'must' | 'shall not'
| 'should' | 'should not'
⟨*PathQuantifier*⟩ ::= 'all paths'
| 'no paths' | (...)
⟨*PathCondition*⟩ ::= 'pass'
⟨*DirectionalObject*⟩
⟨*GoalObject*⟩ ::= ⟨*DirectionalObject*⟩
| 'the first' ⟨*DirectionalObject*⟩
⟨*DirectionalObject*⟩ ::= ⟨*SearchSubject*⟩
| 'a facing switch'
| 'a trailing switch'
| ⟨*SearchSubject*⟩ ⟨*RelativeDirection*⟩

⟨*RelativeDirection*⟩ ::= 'same dir.'
| 'opposite dir.'
⟨*SearchSubject*⟩ ::= 'a' ⟨*Subject*⟩
| 'another'
⟨*Area*⟩ ::= ⟨*BaseArea*⟩
| ⟨*BaseArea*⟩ 'which has'
⟨*PropertyRestriction*⟩
| ⟨*Area*⟩ 'or' ⟨*Area*⟩
| ⟨*Area*⟩ 'and' ⟨*Area*⟩
⟨*BaseArea*⟩ ::= 'tunnel' | 'bridge'
| 'local release area' | ⟨*Identifier*⟩
⟨*Subject*⟩ ::= 'a' ⟨*Class*⟩
| 'a' ⟨*Class*⟩ 'which' ⟨*Condition*⟩
⟨*Condition*⟩ ::= 'is a' ⟨*ClassRestriction*⟩
| 'has' ⟨*PropertyRestriction*⟩
| 'is a' ⟨*ClassRestriction*⟩ 'which has'
⟨*PropertyRestriction*⟩
⟨*PropertyRestriction*⟩ ::= ⟨*Property*⟩
⟨*ValueRestriction*⟩
| (...) // and/or
⟨*ClassRestriction*⟩ ::= ⟨*Class*⟩
| (...) // and/or
⟨*ValueRestriction*⟩ ::= ⟨*Value*⟩
| 'not equal to' ⟨*Value*⟩
| 'less than' ⟨*Value*⟩
| (...) // $\leq, >, \geq$
| (...) // and/or
⟨*Value*⟩ ::= ⟨*Identifier*⟩ | ⟨*Number*⟩ ⟨*Unit*⟩
⟨*Property*⟩ ::= ⟨*Identifier*⟩
⟨*Class*⟩ ::= ⟨*Identifier*⟩

Fig. 3. English version of RailCNL's core grammar in BNF. Some linguistic complexity such as subject-verb agreement is ignored here; the actual grammar is fully specified as GF code, which is ideally suited for handling such cases.

3.2 RailCNL Modules and Examples

RailCNL has a modular design (see Fig. 4) where domain-specific constructs are separated from generic ones. However, CNL modules are not always trivially composable, and care must be taken to retain naturalness while avoiding ambiguity when increasing the complexity of the language. We give a summary of such trade-offs in Sect. 4. We describe below the main modules and constructs of RailCNL, with examples of CNL text and the corresponding abstract syntax tree (AST) obtained from the GF parser (see [11] for more examples).

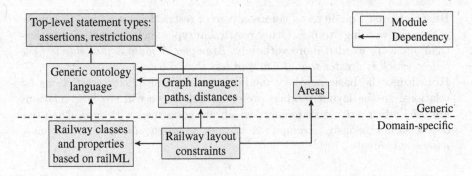

Fig. 4. Modules of the RailCNL (boxes) and their dependencies (arrows). The *generic* modules could be reused when building CNLs for verification in other domains. The *specific* modules are, however, tailored to railway regulations.

Top-Level Statement Types. Most normative sentences in railway regulations are classified into one of the following types, or their negation:

– **Constraint:** logical constraints on the railway infrastructure model. These sentences can be used by the Datalog reasoner to infer new statements.
– **Obligation:** design requirements on the railway infrastructure. The CAD model is checked for compliance, and violations are presented as errors to the user.
– **Recommendation:** design heuristics for railway infrastructure. The CAD model is checked for compliance, but violations are presented as warnings or for information only, which can be dismissed from the view.

Example 1 (Parse tree for an obligation statement.)

CNL: *A vertical segment must have length greater than 20.0m.*
AST: `OntologyRestriction Obligation`
`      (SubjectClass (StringClassAdjective "vertical"`
`          (StringClass "segment")))`
`      (ConditionPropertyRestriction (MkPropertyRestriction`
`          (StringProperty "length")`
`          (Gt (MkValue (StringTerm "20.0m")))))`

Generic Ontology Module. Statements about classes of objects and their properties form a natural basis for knowledge representation. We allow arbitrary string tokens to represent class names, property names and values, and compose these in various ways.

– **Class names:** are arbitrary words, optionally prefixed with another arbitrary word. The reason for allowing this is to give the CNL the power to define new words.
– **Properties and values:** can be arbitrary string tokens. These can be joined by "and" or "or" both on the level of values and of properties.

- **Restrictions:** Equality is a common case of restriction for which we simply choose the wording "to be". Other restriction types such as greater than, less than, etc., are worded more verbosely. *Example: A main signal should have height which is greater than 1.5 m and less than 5.0 m.*
- **Relations:** the basic ontology module contains multiplicity restrictions on relations. In the layout module presented below, we will see how relations are used when writing statements which are concerned with more than one object simultaneously. *Example: A distant signal should have one or more associated signals.*

Layout Module. For writing statements about the topology of the railway track, e.g. about paths as illustrated in Fig. 5c, we use the following language constructs:

- **Goal object:** modifies the `Subject` type defined in the ontology module to add conditions which make sense in a railway graph search, such as the object's orientation (same direction or opposite direction) the search's direction (forwards or backwards) or the termination properties of the search.
- **Path condition:** argument to the search constructors which specifies what restrictions are placed on the paths from source to goal object.
- **Path restrictions:** the combination of the source object, goal object and path conditions. *Example: All paths from a station border to the first facing switch must pass an entry signal.* (See Fig. 5a)
- **Distance restrictions:** See Fig. 5b and Example 2.

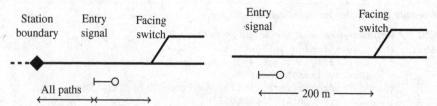

(a) Path restrictions are constructed from a subject, a goal, a quantifier and a condition.

(b) Distance restrictions are constructed from a subject, a goal, and a value restriction.

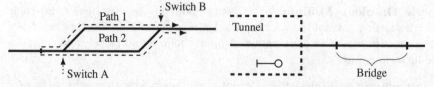

(c) Switches give rise to branching paths, defining a graph of railway tracks.

(d) Area containment can refer to either a planar region or an interval on a track.

Fig. 5. Conditions on railway geographical layout as supported by RailCNL.

Example 2 (Parse tree for a railway layout statement.)

CNL: *Distance from an entry signal to first facing switch must be greater than 200.0 m.*

AST: DistanceRestriction Obligation
    (SubjectClass (StringClassAdjective "entry"
     (StringClass "signal")))
    (FirstFound FacingSwitch)
    (Gt (MkValue (StringTerm "200.0m")))

Area Module. The area module modifies subjects to express whether they are inside a planar area, such as station areas, tunnels or bridges, or belongs to a linear segment of a track, such as being located in a curve or on an incline (see Fig. 5d).

3.3   Translating RailCNL into Datalog

To make use of RailCNL in the verification tool, ASTs obtained by parsing CNL phrases with the GF runtime are transformed into Datalog rules (a description of how this is implemented can be found in Sect. 4.3). Each top-level constructor in the CNL definition has a translation function into the Datalog AST.

Predicate Conventions. We employ the following predicate conventions:

- Class membership as *classname*(*object*).
- Object properties as *propertyname*(*object*, *value*).
- Relation between objects as *relationname*(*object*, *otherobject*).

Explicit Variables. The *Subject* of the sentences of the *Ontology* module defines an arbitrary individual whose definition does not depend on other information. To translate it, we create a new variable denoting the arbitrary individual. The subject makes the starting point for the translation, as other parts of the sentence refer back to the subject.

Ontology Restrictions. For ontology restrictions, such as obligations ("must") and recommendations ("should"), the Datalog rule head contains a predicate which captures any violations of the text. This is achieved by first defining the restrictions themselves (`r1_found` in Example 3 below) and then declaring a rule which uses the negation of these restrictions (`!r1_found`) in order to yield a counter-example.

Example 3 (Datalog translation of an ontology restriction.)

CNL: *A signal must have height 4.0m or 4.5m.*

AST: `OntologyRestriction Obligation`
```
       (SubjectClass
         (StringClassNoAdjective (StringClass "signal")))
       (ConditionPropertyRestriction (MkPropertyRestriction
         (StringProperty "height")
         (OrRestr (Eq (MkValue (StringTerm "4.0m")))
                  (Eq (MkValue (StringTerm "4.5m")))))))
```

Datalog: `r1_found(Subj0) :- signal(Subj0), height(Subj0, 4.0).`
`          r1_found(Subj0) :- signal(Subj0), height(Subj0, 4.5).`
`          r1_obl(Subj0) :- signal(Subj0), !r1_found(Subj0).`

Disjunctive Normal Form. As Datalog does not (necessarily) have an *or* operator, nor negation over complex terms, these must be factored out into separate rules and auxiliary predicates. This transformation can be performed by considering the result of the translation of a sentence to be a *set of rules* (such as the two definitions of `r1_found` in Example 3), and the result of the partial translation (such as adding a class or property constraint to a rule) to be a *set of conjunctions* which are prefixes of the final rules.

Vocabulary Matching. The Norwegian regulations are written in Norwegian and use other terms for class names, properties and relations than the railML representation does. After identifying the class names from the CNL, they will be looked up in a Norwegian/railML dictionary. For example, Norwegian *"akselteller"* is mapped into the railML class *"trainDetector"* with the *"axlecounting"* property.

3.4   Tool Integration

Verification tool usually output a counter-example when the requirements are violated by the model. It is often difficult to understand from the counter-example which of the (possibly several) requirements have been violated, and why. We use the notion of *tracing* to trace such errors from the verification output all the way to the original text regulations. Figure 6 shows our prototype tool (running as a plug-in for the AutoCAD program used by Norwegian railway engineers) presenting a problem in the CAD view, and how it is traced back through the Datalog code, the AST, and the CNL code, to the original regulations text. We mark-up sentences of the original text with an identifier, and create a separate document containing the formalized representation using Rail-CNL, using the identifiers as references back into the original text (Fig. 7). When the verification program finds a violation among the regulations, it outputs the identifier of the rule which has been violated, enabling the tracing.

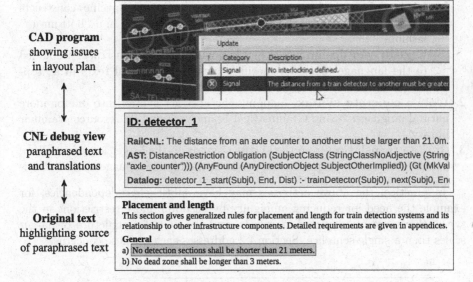

CAD program
showing issues
in layout plan

↕

CNL debug view
paraphrased text
and translations

↕

Original text
highlighting source
of paraphrased text

Fig. 6. Tracing of requirements backwards from CAD program through CNL to markedup original texts. From a regulation violation presented as a warning or error, the user can browse to the corresponding regulatory text, shown side by side with the CNL text.

4 Design Methodology for a Verification Front-End Language

Our methodology is based on CNL and GF best practices; in particular, Ranta et al. [18] describe the construction of a CNL by creating an abstract syntax corresponding to a semantic model, mapping it into natural language, and also how to avoid or handle ambiguity in parsing and translating. In a later report, Ranta et al. [17] give explicit best practices, such as: (i) using a modular structure separating generic and domain-specific parts of the grammar, (ii) letting the AST model the semantics of the text, as opposed to the logic of the underlying formalism, and (iii) trade-offs in modelling language restrictions purely in context-free grammar versus using dependent types. We expand on these best practices in the context of creating intermediate languages for writing diverse natural text in a form which is translatable into formal verification properties.

The main activities for defining a verification front-end language using GF are:

1. Define an **abstract syntax** which is able to represent statements of relevant texts. We suggest two sub-activities to help manage the difficulty and complexity of modelling domain-specific, yet diverse and informally structured, texts:

(a) **Logic-driven design** where basic (often non-domain-specific) constructs which are known from the verification logic are added in a "bottom-up" fashion.

(b) **Text-driven design** where highly domain-specific constructs are added to the language to model specific examples in original texts in a "top-down" fashion.

2. Write a **concrete syntax**, mapping the abstract syntax into one or more natural languages, using Grammatical Framework and its resource grammar library.

3. Create a **translation** from the abstract syntax to the target logic formalism, i.e. the verification properties expressed in the input language of the solver.

In practice, the above activities may have subtle cross-dependencies, for example the need for reducing ambiguity by encoding more restrictions in the types, the usage of restricted keywords, and the need for structure on larger scales than a single sentence. Section 4.2 addresses each of these concerns.

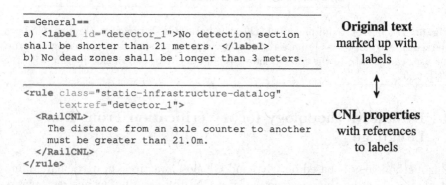

Fig. 7. Excerpt of original text marked-up with sentence identifiers, and properties represented in CNL with references to original text.

4.1 Abstract Syntax

Attempting to formally model a body of informal specifications in its entirety may be neither feasible nor desirable, for a variety of reasons:

1. The text might have some amount of non-normative content intended only to give readers a better understanding of the subject matter.

2. Parts of the normative content might not be suitable for modelling in the target verification tool.

3. The available body of text might be large and complex, and covering all parts of it could require diverse domain knowledge from various disciplines.

Therefore, starting from arbitrary sentences in the natural text and trying to cover them with the CNL will often prove to be a daunting task. Our approach to handling this difficulty is to split the process of designing the abstract syntax into two parts.

We start with a *logic-driven design*, where we define basic concepts in a bottom-up fashion, such as classifying the statement types (*constraints*, *restrictions*, etc.) and describing sets of objects based on their class and their properties. Even when deciding on the basic logic of the language, it might still be wise to abstract away from the details of the underlying verification logic.

Next follows a *text-driven design* phase, where we look for text samples that can be captured in the CNL, and make adjustments and additions to the grammar to cover them. This phase might eventually lead to finding new basic building blocks, such as adding the *graph* module to RailCNL for describing railway layout, or adding *relations* to the ontology module. However, it is easy to get carried away and construct a highly nested language which has too much freedom and therefore becomes difficult to parse. Until the need for more generality is proven, each newly added construct is kept specific.

Alternating between the logic-driven and the text-driven phases can be useful for handling complexity and discovering the middle ground between informal specifications and verification logic. A consequence of this compromise is that the language will seldom be able to cover the exact wordings used in the original texts. We accept this consequence and aim instead to provide a user-friendly comparison of original text and CNL text for traceability (see Sect. 3.4).

4.2   Concrete Syntax

The abstract syntax is mapped into a natural language using the GF resource grammar library (RGL), which is well-covered in the GF documentation and literature (e.g. [17,18]). Each category of the abstract syntax is mapped into a linearization type, often a record data structure. For example, the `Subject` category of RailCNL is assigned the complex noun (`CN`) record type, and `Statement` is assigned to utterance (`Utt`).

A major motivation for formal CNLs is that they can be unambiguously parsed as long as the language is restricted enough. Languages written using GF are often restricted to a pre-compiled vocabulary, to be able to identify structure and handle morphological variation. For our verification application, however, we need users to be able to *define new terms dynamically*, e.g. class names, and afterwards write statements using both built-in and user-defined terms. But allowing arbitrary string tokens can introduce ambiguity, i.e. the parser returning many parse trees for a single statement. We mitigate this problem through several means:

Type-level Restrictions. The railway term "main signal" is the common way to refer to a signal which is of type *main*. Instead of using a recursively defined constructor for this term (e.g. `Adjective : String -> Class -> Class`), we can restrict the number of adjectives to one or two. This restriction is encoded in the type system by separating the adjective-prefixed class name from the non-prefixed one:

```
StringClassAdjective : String -> BaseClass -> Class
StringClassNoAdjective : BaseClass -> Class
```

Reserved Keywords. Using arbitrary names as building blocks of our language resembles the use of identifiers as variables in programming languages. Programming languages have *restricted keywords* which cannot be used as variable names. Similarly, we use the GF parser callbacks system to remove parses which contain function words (such as *"which"*, *"has"*, *"is"*, *"must"*, *"be"*, etc.) as arbitrary names. These are very unlikely to be needed as class or property names.

Weighted Constructors. The GF parser has support for probabilistic grammars, which work by assigning weights (probabilities) to the constructors of the abstract syntax. By assigning a low weight to any constructor which uses the `String` category, we ensure that built-in syntax is always prioritized over arbitrary tokens.

Syntactic Guides. As in programming languages, special symbols and punctuation can be used as guides for the parser if we are willing to compromise on naturalness. Alternatively, we can increase the verbosity of the syntax, to reduce the likelihood of causing ambiguity when embedded in a longer statement.

4.3   Translation into the Target Logic Formalism

If the abstract syntax is made to faithfully model the logic of the verification system, then the translation into the logic formalism can be made by implementing another GF concrete syntax for the target language. However, target logics are often too low-level to represent regulations directly. GF incorporates dependent type features which could allow for a more concise representation of this translation, but this practice has not yet matured to a state in which it can be said to be a recommended practice (see [17]). For RailCNL we have instead written a separate program (in C#, as it is a part of the verification CAD plugin) which translates from the abstract syntax of the CNL into Datalog. Section 3.3 describes the main techniques used.

5   Evaluation and Conclusions

RailCNL formalizes, in a human-readable manner, relevant parts of the technical regulations and expert knowledge used in an on-the-fly verification engine integrated within railway construction design software. This type of verification is limited to static infrastructure analysis, leaving the more heavy-weight analysis, e.g. the implementation of control systems or interlocking specifications, to specialized analysis software such as the products of Prover AB (Sweden) or Systerel (France).

RailCNL is our approach to *participatory verification*, where the end users (railway engineers, in our case) get full access to the verification properties. This allows them to actively participate in the verification by maintaining the rule base and managing their own properties (often based on experience and best practice).

We have collaborated with railway engineers associated with RailCOM-PLETE during the design of the language and the writing of the verification properties. Their feedback on limitations in the coverage of the language and suggestions for simplification will continue to drive the design forwards.

We surveyed the Norwegian railway regulations and counted how much of the relevant regulations our basic RailCNL covers (see results in Table 1, and [11] for methodology and examples). The survey is limited to parts of the regulations covering railway track and signalling, as these are the disciplines that \the RailCOMPLETE software development is currently focusing on.

RailCNL is implemented using the Grammatical Framework and its resource grammar library (RGL). While we have used Norwegian for representing regulations, RailCNL could be easily extended with other languages supported by the RGL. This would allow the system to be used for other authorities' regulations written in other languages. As long as most of the abstract syntax is re-used, the translation into Datalog should also be readily adaptable.

Table 1. Coverage evaluation for a subset of Norwegian regulations. *Phrases* of the original text which could be classified as *normative* (i.e. applying some restriction on design) were evaluated for *relevance* to static infrastructure verification. The *coverage* is the percentage of relevant phrases expressible in RailCNL.

Eng. discipline	Chapter title	Phrases	Normative	Relevant	Covered	Coverage
Track	Planning: general technical	140	74	74	70	95%
Track	Planning: geometry	278	157	152	119	78%
Signalling	Planning: detectors	144	106	35	21	60%
Signalling	Planning: interlocking	376	265	130	81	62%
Total		938	602	391	291	**74%**

Related Work. Johannisson [7] describes a CNL targeting the Object Constraint Language (OCL) for use in reasoning about Java program correctness in the KeY system [3]. The language features dynamic vocabulary based on input UML diagrams where vocabulary updates are achieved by re-compiling the grammar using the GF compiler when needed. Angelov et al. [1] present a conflict detection framework where GF is used to map the contract language $\mathcal{CL}$ [15] into a CNL. Statement modalities, such as obligation, permission and prohibition, are applied to complex actions. The structure of the CNL is modelled after the $\mathcal{CL}$ language. Camilleri et al. [4] take a CNL approach to manipulating contract-oriented diagrams using a visual diagram editor, a CNL with text editor support, and a spreadsheet representation as interfaces to a common model, which can be translated into timed automata for reasoning about system properties.

Other efforts to define domain specific languages for railway verification have typically focused on the implementation of control systems, such as Vu et al. [21], while also considering the verification to be an activity which is separate from design and implementation. James et al. [6] show how to integrate UML modelling of the railway domain with graphical modelling and specification and verification languages, also keeping the focus on verifying the control system implementation of a fixed design.

Future Work. In working with railway engineers, we discovered language features which could be added to increase the coverage of RailCNL:

1. A notion of scopes and exceptions, so that more complex conditional restrictions can be expressed more naturally.
2. Mathematical formulas as a sub-language.
3. Vague or soft requirements represented not for direct use in verification, but for requiring manual checks at some points.

A formal CNL with well-chosen linearizations can be very natural, and often perfectly readable for a non-programmer with the required domain knowledge. However, writing in a formal CNL can potentially be as difficult as writing in a programming language. A solution to this problem is the use of special-purpose editors which guide the user towards structuring their text according to the underlying formal grammar. Different approaches to CNL editors have been explored (see e.g. [4,10,14]). We plan to investigate these further and integrate one such editor for RailCNL in the RailCOMPLETE CAD environment, and carry out a usability study on its efficacy.

We are continuing our collaboration with Norwegian railway engineers to evaluate the usability of our prototype tools, increase the text coverage and extend the language to handle other railway engineering disciplines such as catenary lines and ground works.

Acknowledgements. We thank Martin Steffen and Aarne Ranta for numerous useful interactions, and Claus Feyling (CEO of RailCOMPLETE AS) for allowing us to use the time of his engineers for testing our results and other railway specific interactions.

References

1. Angelov, K., Camilleri, J.J., Schneider, G.: A framework for conflict analysis of normative texts written in controlled natural language. JLAP **82**(5), 216–240 (2013). doi:10.1016/j.jlap.2013.03.002
2. Baier, C., Katoen, J.-P.: Principles of Model Checking. MIT Press, Cambridge (2008)
3. Beckert, B., Hähnle, R., Schmitt, P.H. (eds.): Verification of Object-Oriented Software: The KeY Approach. LNCS (LNAI), vol. 4334. Springer, Heidelberg (2007). doi:10.1007/978-3-540-69061-0
4. Camilleri, J.J., Paganelli, G., Schneider, G.: A CNL for contract-oriented diagrams. In: Davis, B., Kaljurand, K., Kuhn, T. (eds.) CNL 2014. LNCS (LNAI), vol. 8625, pp. 135–146. Springer, Cham (2014). doi:10.1007/978-3-319-10223-8_13
5. Harel, D., Tiuryn, J., Kozen, D.: Dynamic Logic. MIT Press, Cambridge (2000)

6. James, P., Roggenbach, M.: Encapsulating formal methods within domain specific languages: a solution for verifying railway scheme plans. Math. Comput. Sci. **8**(1), 11–38 (2014). doi:10.1007/s11786-014-0174-0

7. Johannisson, K.: Natural language specifications. In: Beckert et al. [3], pp. 317–333. doi:10.1007/978-3-540-69061-0_7

8. Kensing, F., Blomberg, J.: Participatory design: issues and concerns. Comput. Support. Coop. Work (CSCW) **7**(3), 167–185 (1998). doi:10.1023/A:1008689307411

9. Kuhn, T.: A survey and classification of controlled natural languages. Comput. Linguist. **40**(1), 121–170 (2014). doi:10.1162/COLI_a_00168

10. Ljunglöf, P.: Editing syntax trees on the surface. In: NoDaLiDa 2011, pp. 138–145 (2011)

11. Luteberget, B., Camilleri, J.J., Johansen, C., Schneider, G.: Participatory Verification of Railway Infrastructure Regulations using RailCNL (long version). Technical report 465, University of Oslo (2017)

12. Luteberget, B., Johansen, C.: Efficient verification of railway infrastructure designs against standard regulations. Formal Methods Syst. Des., 1–32 (2017). doi:10.1007/s10703-017-0281-z

13. Luteberget, B., Johansen, C., Steffen, M.: Rule-based consistency checking of railway infrastructure designs. In: Ábrahám, E., Huisman, M. (eds.) IFM 2016. LNCS, vol. 9681, pp. 491–507. Springer, Cham (2016). doi:10.1007/978-3-319-33693-0_31

14. Meza Moreno, M.S., Bringert, B.: Interactive multilingual web applications with grammatical framework. In: Nordström, B., Ranta, A. (eds.) GoTAL 2008. LNCS (LNAI), vol. 5221, pp. 336–347. Springer, Heidelberg (2008). doi:10.1007/978-3-540-85287-2_32

15. Prisacariu, C., Schneider, G.: A dynamic deontic logic for complex contracts. J. Logic Algebr. Program. (JLAP) **81**(4), 458–490 (2012). doi:10.1016/j.jlap.2012.03.003

16. Ranta, A.: Grammatical framework. J. Funct. Program. **14**(2), 145–189 (2004). doi:10.1017/S0956796803004738

17. Ranta, A., Camilleri, J., Détrez, G., Enache, R., Hallgren, T.: Grammar tool manual and best practices. Technical report, MOLTO Deliverable D2.3, MOLTO Consortium, Göteborg (2012). http://www.molto-project.eu/biblio/deliverable/grammar-tools-and-best-practices

18. Ranta, A., Enache, R., Détrez, G.: Controlled language for everyday use: the MOLTO phrasebook. In: Rosner, M., Fuchs, N.E. (eds.) CNL 2010. LNCS (LNAI), vol. 7175, pp. 115–136. Springer, Heidelberg (2012). doi:10.1007/978-3-642-31175-8_7

19. Sharp, H., Rogers, Y., Preece, J.: Interaction Design: Beyond Human-Computer Interaction. Wiley, New York (2007)

20. Ullman, J.D.: Principles of Database and Knowledge-Base Systems. CSPP, New York (1988)

21. Vu, L.H., Haxthausen, A.E., Peleska, J.: A domain-specific language for railway interlocking systems. In: FORMS/FORMAT 2014, pp. 200–209. TU Braunschweig (2014)

22. Wyner, A., et al.: On controlled natural languages: properties and prospects. In: Fuchs, N.E. (ed.) CNL 2009. LNCS (LNAI), vol. 5972, pp. 281–289. Springer, Heidelberg (2010). doi:10.1007/978-3-642-14418-9_17

An In-Depth Investigation of Interval Temporal Logic Model Checking with Regular Expressions

Laura Bozzelli[1], Alberto Molinari[2], Angelo Montanari[2(✉)], and Adriano Peron[1]

[1] University of Napoli "Federico II", Napoli, Italy
[2] University of Udine, Udine, Italy
molinari.alberto@gmail.com, angelo.montanari@uniud.it

Abstract. In the last years, the model checking (MC) problem for interval temporal logic (ITL) has received an increasing attention as a viable alternative to the traditional (point-based) temporal logic MC, which can be recovered as a special case. Most results have been obtained by imposing suitable restrictions on interval labeling. In this paper, we overcome such limitations by using regular expressions to define the behavior of proposition letters over intervals in terms of the component states. We first prove that MC for Halpern and Shoham's ITL (HS), extended with regular expressions, is decidable. Then, we show that formulas of a large class of HS fragments, namely, all fragments featuring (a subset of) HS modalities for Allen's relations meets, met-by, starts, and started-by, can be model checked in polynomial working space (MC for all these fragments turns out to be PSPACE-complete).

1 Introduction

Model checking (MC) is commonly recognized as one of the most effective techniques in automatic system verification. It has also been successfully used in databases, e.g., active databases, database-backed web applications, and NoSQL databases, and artificial intelligence, e.g., planning, configuration systems, and multi-agent systems. MC allows one to automatically check whether a model of a given system satisfies a desired property to ensure that it meets the expected behaviour. A good balancing of expressiveness and complexity in the choice of the computational model and the specification formalism is a key factor for the actual exploitation of MC. Systems are usually modeled as finite-state transition graphs (Kripke structures), while properties are commonly expressed by formulas of point-based temporal logics, such as LTL, CTL, and CTL*. Various improvements to the computational model and/or the specification language have been proposed in the literature. As for the former, we mention MC for pushdown systems [7], that feature an infinite state space, and for the latter, the extensions of LTL with promptness [9].

In this paper, we focus on MC with interval temporal logic (ITL) as the specification language. ITL allows one to deal with relevant temporal properties, such as actions with duration, accomplishments, and temporal aggregations, which are inherently "interval-based" and cannot be properly expressed by point-based temporal logics. In the last years, ITL MC has received an increasing attention

© Springer International Publishing AG 2017
A. Cimatti and M. Sirjani (Eds.): SEFM 2017, LNCS 10469, pp. 104–119, 2017.
DOI: 10.1007/978-3-319-66197-1_7

as a viable alternative to the traditional (point-based) temporal logic MC [18], which can be recovered as a special case [4]. ITLs feature intervals, instead of points, as their primitive temporal entities [8,19,21], and they have been fruitfully applied in various areas of computer science, including formal verification, computational linguistics, planning, and multi-agent systems [10,11,19]. Among ITLs, the landmark is Halpern and Shoham's modal logic of time intervals HS [8]. It features one modality for each of the 13 ordering relations between pairs of intervals (the so-called Allen's relations [1]), apart from equality. Its satisfiability problem is undecidable over all relevant classes of linear orders [8], and most of its fragments are undecidable as well [6,13]. Some meaningful exceptions are the logic of temporal neighbourhood $A\overline{A}$ and the logic of sub-intervals D.

The MC problem for HS and its fragments consists in the verification of the correctness of the behaviour of a given system with respect to some relevant interval properties. To make it effective, we need to collect information about states into computation stretches: we interpret each finite computation path as an interval, and we define its labelling on the basis of the labelling of the states that compose it. Most results have been obtained by imposing suitable restrictions on interval labeling: either a proposition letter can be constrained to hold over an interval iff it holds over each component state (homogeneity assumption [20]), or interval labeling can be defined in terms of interval endpoints.

In [14], Molinari et al. deal with MC for full HS over finite Kripke structures, under the homogeneity assumption, according to a state-based semantics that allows branching in the past and in the future. They introduce the fundamental elements of the problem and prove its non-elementary decidability and **PSPACE**-hardness. Since then, the attention was also brought to the fragments of HS, which, similarly to what happens with satisfiability, are often computationally much better [3,5,14–17]. The MC problem for some HS fragments, extended with epistemic operators, has been investigated by Lomuscio and Michaliszyn in [10,11]. Their semantic assumptions differ from those of [14], making it difficult to compare the two approaches. Formulas are interpreted over the unwinding of the Kripke structure (computation-tree-based semantics [4]), and interval labeling takes into account only the endpoints of intervals. The decidability status of MC for full epistemic HS is still unknown. In [12], Lomuscio and Michaliszyn propose to use regular expressions to define the labeling of proposition letters over intervals in terms of the component states. They prove the decidability of MC with regular expressions for some restricted fragments of epistemic HS, giving rough upper bounds to its computational complexity.

In this paper, we prove that MC for full HS with regular expressions is decidable (Sect. 4) and that its complexity, when restricted to system models—that is, if we assume the formula to be constant length—is **P**. Then, by exploiting a small-model theorem (Sect. 5), in Sect. 6, we show that formulas of a large class of HS fragments, i.e., those featuring (any subset of) HS modalities for the Allen's relations *meets, met-by, started-by*, and *starts* ($A\overline{A}B\overline{B}$), can be checked in polynomial working space (MC for all these is **PSPACE**-complete).

Due to lack of space, some proofs are omitted: they can be found in [2].

2 Preliminaries

We first introduce notation and background knowledge, and then the logic HS.

Let $\mathbb{N}$ be the set of natural numbers. For all $i, j \in \mathbb{N}$, we denote by $[i, j]$, with $i \leq j$, the set of naturals h such that $i \leq h \leq j$. Let Σ be an alphabet, w be a non-empty finite word over Σ, and ε be the empty word. We denote by $|w|$ the length of w. For all $1 \leq i \leq j \leq |w|$, $w(i)$ denotes the i-th letter of w (i is called a w-position), while $w(i, j)$ denotes the finite subword of w given by $w(i) \cdots w(j)$. Let $|w| = n$. We define $fst(w) = w(1)$ and $lst(w) = w(n)$. $Pref(w) = \{w(1, i) \mid 1 \leq i \leq n - 1\}$ and $Suff(w) = \{w(i, n) \mid 2 \leq i \leq n\}$ are the sets of all proper prefixes and suffixes of w, respectively. For $i \in [1, n]$, w^i is a shorthand for $w(1, i)$. The concatenation of two words w and w' is denoted as usual by $w \cdot w'$. Moreover, if $lst(w) = fst(w')$, $w \star w'$ represents $w(1, n - 1) \cdot w'$.

For all $h, n \geq 0$, let $\mathsf{Tower}(h, n)$ denote a tower of exponentials of height h and argument n: $\mathsf{Tower}(0, n) = n$ and $\mathsf{Tower}(h + 1, n) = 2^{\mathsf{Tower}(h,n)}$. Moreover, let h-**EXPTIME** denote the class of languages decided by deterministic Turing machines whose number of computation steps is bounded by functions of n in $O(\mathsf{Tower}(h, n^c))$, for some constant $c \geq 1$. Note that 0-**EXPTIME** is **P**.

2.1 Kripke Structures, Regular Expressions, and Finite Automata

Finite state systems are modelled as finite Kripke structures. Let $\mathcal{AP}$ be a finite set of proposition letters, which represent predicates over the states of the system.

Definition 1 (Kripke structure). *A* Kripke structure *is a tuple* $\mathcal{K} = (\mathcal{AP}, S, R, \mu, s_0)$, *where* S *is a set of* states, $R \subseteq S \times S$ *is a* left-total transition relation, $\mu : S \mapsto 2^{\mathcal{AP}}$ *is a total* labelling function *assigning to each state* s *the set of proposition letters that hold over it, and* $s_0 \in S$ *is the* initial state. *For* $s \in S$, *the set* $R(s)$ *of* successors *of* s *is the non-empty set of states* s' *such that* $(s, s') \in R$. *We say that* $\mathcal{K}$ *is* finite *if* S *is finite.*

Let $\mathcal{K} = (\mathcal{AP}, S, R, \mu, s_0)$ be a Kripke structure. A *trace* of $\mathcal{K}$ is a non-empty finite word ρ over S such that $(\rho(i), \rho(i + 1)) \in R$ for $i \in [1, |\rho| - 1]$. A trace is *initial* if it starts from s_0. We denote by $Trc_{\mathcal{K}}$ the *infinite* set of traces of $\mathcal{K}$. A trace ρ induces the finite word $\mu(\rho)$ over $2^{\mathcal{AP}}$ given by $\mu(\rho(1)) \ldots \mu(\rho(n))$, with $n = |\rho|$. We call $\mu(\rho)$ the *labeling sequence* induced by ρ.

Let us now introduce the class of regular expressions over finite words. Since we are interested in expressing requirements over the labeling sequences induced by the traces of Kripke structures, here we consider *proposition-based* regular expressions (RE), where atomic expressions are propositional formulas over $\mathcal{AP}$ instead of letters over an alphabet. Formally, the set of RE r over $\mathcal{AP}$ is defined as $r ::= \varepsilon \mid \phi \mid r \cup r \mid r \cdot r \mid r^*$ where ϕ is a propositional formula over $\mathcal{AP}$. The length $|r|$ of an RE r is the number of subexpressions of r. An RE r denotes a language $\mathcal{L}(r)$ of finite words over $2^{\mathcal{AP}}$ defined as: (i) $\mathcal{L}(\varepsilon) = \{\varepsilon\}$ and $\mathcal{L}(\phi) = \{A \in 2^{\mathcal{AP}} \mid A \text{ satisfies } \phi\}$; (ii) $\mathcal{L}(r_1 \cup r_2) = \mathcal{L}(r_1) \cup \mathcal{L}(r_2)$, $\mathcal{L}(r_1 \cdot r_2) = \mathcal{L}(r_1) \cdot \mathcal{L}(r_2)$, and $\mathcal{L}(r^*) = (\mathcal{L}(r))^*$. By well-known results, the class of RE over $\mathcal{AP}$ captures the class of regular languages of finite words over $2^{\mathcal{AP}}$.

A non-deterministic finite automaton (NFA) is a tuple $\mathcal{A} = (\Sigma, Q, Q_0, \delta, F)$, where Σ is a finite alphabet, Q is a finite set of states, $Q_0 \subseteq Q$ is the set of initial states, $\delta : Q \times \Sigma \mapsto 2^Q$ is the transition function, and $F \subseteq Q$ is the set of accepting states. Given a finite word w over Σ, with $|w| = n$, and two states $q, q' \in Q$, a run (or computation) of $\mathcal{A}$ from q to q' over w is a finite sequence of states $q_1, \ldots, q_{n+1}$ such that $q_1 = q$, $q_{n+1} = q'$, and for all $i \in [1, n]$, $q_{i+1} \in \delta(q_i, w(i))$. The language $\mathcal{L}(\mathcal{A})$ accepted by $\mathcal{A}$ consists of the finite words w over Σ such that there is a run from some initial state to some accepting state over w. A deterministic finite automaton (DFA) is an NFA $\mathcal{D} = (\Sigma, Q, Q_0, \delta, F)$ such that Q_0 is a singleton and for all $(q, c) \in Q \times \Sigma$, $\delta(q, c)$ is a singleton.

Remark 2. By well-known results, given an RE r over $\mathcal{AP}$, one can construct, in a compositional way, an NFA $\mathcal{A}_r$ over $2^{\mathcal{AP}}$, whose number of states is at most $2|r|$, such that $\mathcal{L}(\mathcal{A}_r) = \mathcal{L}(r)$. We call $\mathcal{A}_r$ the *canonical* NFA associated with r. Note that the number of edges of $\mathcal{A}_r$ may be exponential in $|\mathcal{AP}|$ (edges are labelled by assignments $A \in 2^{\mathcal{AP}}$ satisfying propositional formulas ϕ of r); however, we can avoid storing edges, as they can be recovered in polynomial time from r.

2.2   The Interval Temporal Logic HS

An interval algebra to reason about intervals and their relative order was proposed by Allen in [1], while a systematic logical study of interval representation and reasoning was done a few years later by Halpern and Shoham, who introduced the interval temporal logic HS featuring one modality for each Allen relation, but equality [8]. Table 1 depicts 6 of the 13 Allen's relations, together with the corresponding HS (existential) modalities. The other 7 relations are the 6 inverse relations (the inverse $\overline{\mathcal{R}}$ of a binary relation $\mathcal{R}$ is such that $b\overline{\mathcal{R}}a$ iff $a\mathcal{R}b$) and equality. Moreover, if $\langle X \rangle$ is the modality for $\mathcal{R}$, $\langle \overline{X} \rangle$ is the modality for $\overline{\mathcal{R}}$.

Table 1. Allen's relations and corresponding HS modalities.

Allen relation	HS	Definition w.r.t. interval structures	Example
MEETS	$\langle A \rangle$	$[x, y]\mathcal{R}_A[v, z] \iff y = v$	
BEFORE	$\langle L \rangle$	$[x, y]\mathcal{R}_L[v, z] \iff y < v$	
STARTED-BY	$\langle B \rangle$	$[x, y]\mathcal{R}_B[v, z] \iff x = v \wedge z < y$	
FINISHED-BY	$\langle E \rangle$	$[x, y]\mathcal{R}_E[v, z] \iff y = z \wedge x < v$	
CONTAINS	$\langle D \rangle$	$[x, y]\mathcal{R}_D[v, z] \iff x < v \wedge z < y$	
OVERLAPS	$\langle O \rangle$	$[x, y]\mathcal{R}_O[v, z] \iff x < v < y < z$	

Let $\mathcal{P}_u$ be a finite set of *uninterpreted interval properties*. The HS language over $\mathcal{P}_u$ consists of proposition letters from $\mathcal{P}_u$, the Boolean connectives $\neg$ and $\wedge$, and a temporal modality for each of the (non trivial) Allen's relations, i.e., $\langle A \rangle, \langle L \rangle, \langle B \rangle, \langle E \rangle, \langle D \rangle, \langle O \rangle, \langle \overline{A} \rangle, \langle \overline{L} \rangle, \langle \overline{B} \rangle, \langle \overline{E} \rangle, \langle \overline{D} \rangle$, and $\langle \overline{O} \rangle$. HS formulas are defined by the grammar $\psi ::= p_u \mid \neg\psi \mid \psi \wedge \psi \mid \langle X \rangle\psi \mid \langle \overline{X} \rangle\psi$, where $p_u \in \mathcal{P}_u$ and $X \in \{A, L, B, E, D, O\}$. We will also use the standard connectives (disjunction $\vee$

and implication $\rightarrow$). Moreover, for any modality X, the dual universal modalities $[X]\psi$ and $[\overline{X}]\psi$ are defined as $\neg\langle X\rangle\neg\psi$ and $\neg\langle\overline{X}\rangle\neg\psi$, respectively. Given any subset of Allen's relations $\{X_1,\ldots,X_n\}$, we denote by $X_1\cdots X_n$ the HS fragment that features existential (and universal) modalities for $X_1,\ldots,X_n$ only. W.l.o.g., we assume the *non-strict semantics of* HS, which admits intervals consisting of a single point[1]. Under such an assumption, all HS modalities can be expressed in terms of modalities $\langle B\rangle, \langle E\rangle, \langle\overline{B}\rangle$, and $\langle\overline{E}\rangle$ [21]. HS can thus be viewed as a multi-modal logic with 4 primitive modalities. However, since later we will focus on the HS fragments $A\overline{A}E\overline{E}$ and $A\overline{A}B\overline{B}$—which respectively do not feature $\langle B\rangle$, $\langle\overline{B}\rangle$ and $\langle E\rangle, \langle\overline{E}\rangle$—we add both $\langle A\rangle$ and $\langle\overline{A}\rangle$ to the considered set of modalities.

In [14], the authors investigate the MC problem over finite Kripke structures $\mathcal{K}$ for HS formulas where intervals correspond to the traces of $\mathcal{K}$. The approach followed there is subject to two restrictions: (i) the set $\mathcal{P}_u$ of HS-proposition letters and the set $\mathcal{AP}$ of proposition letters for the Kripke structure coincide, and (ii) a proposition letter holds over an interval iff it holds over all its sub-intervals (homogeneity assumption). Here, we adopt a more general and expressive approach according to which an abstract interval proposition letter $p_u \in \mathcal{P}_u$ denotes a regular language of finite words over $2^{\mathcal{AP}}$, that is, every p_u is a (proposition-based) regular expression over $\mathcal{AP}$. Thus, hereafter, an HS formula over $\mathcal{AP}$ is an HS formula whose interval proposition letters (or atomic formulas) are RE r over $\mathcal{AP}$. Given a Kripke structure $\mathcal{K} = (\mathcal{AP}, S, R, \mu, s_0)$, a trace ρ of $\mathcal{K}$, and an HS formula φ over $\mathcal{AP}$, the satisfaction relation $\mathcal{K}, \rho \models \varphi$ is inductively defined as follows (we omit the standard clauses for Boolean connectives):

- $\mathcal{K}, \rho \models r$ iff $\mu(\rho) \in \mathcal{L}(r)$ for each RE r over $\mathcal{AP}$,
- $\mathcal{K}, \rho \models \langle B\rangle\varphi$ iff there exists $\rho' \in Pref(\rho)$ such that $\mathcal{K}, \rho' \models \varphi$,
- $\mathcal{K}, \rho \models \langle E\rangle\varphi$ iff there exists $\rho' \in Suff(\rho)$ such that $\mathcal{K}, \rho' \models \varphi$,
- $\mathcal{K}, \rho \models \langle\overline{B}\rangle\varphi$ iff $\mathcal{K}, \rho' \models \varphi$ for some trace ρ' such that $\rho \in Pref(\rho')$,
- $\mathcal{K}, \rho \models \langle\overline{E}\rangle\varphi$ iff $\mathcal{K}, \rho' \models \varphi$ for some trace ρ' such that $\rho \in Suff(\rho')$.

$\mathcal{K}$ is a *model* of φ, denoted as $\mathcal{K} \models \varphi$, if for all *initial* traces ρ of $\mathcal{K}$, it holds that $\mathcal{K}, \rho \models \varphi$. The *MC problem* for HS is the problem of checking, for a finite Kripke structure $\mathcal{K}$ and an HS formula φ, whether or not $\mathcal{K} \models \varphi$. The problem is not trivially decidable since the set $Trc_{\mathcal{K}}$ of traces of $\mathcal{K}$ is infinite.

3   The General Picture

Here we give a short account of research on MC for HS and its fragments, and we enlighten the original contributions of the present paper (see Table 2).

Let us consider first the MC problem for HS and its fragments, under the homogeneity assumption, according to a state-based semantics [4]. In [14], Molinari et al. provide a MC algorithm for (full) HS, with a non-elementary complexity, that, given a finite Kripke structure $\mathcal{K}$ and a bound k on the nesting depth of $\langle E\rangle$ and $\langle B\rangle$ modalities in the input HS formula, exploits a *finite* and

---

[1] All the results we prove in the paper hold for the strict semantics as well.

Table 2. Complexity of MC for HS and its fragments (†local MC).

	Homogeneity	Regular expressions	Endpoints + KC
Full HS, BE	non-elem. **EXPSPACE**-hard	non-elem. **EXPSPACE**-hard	BE+$KC^\dagger$: **PSPACE** BE†: **P**
$A\overline{A}B\overline{B}E$, $A\overline{A}E\overline{B}E$	**EXPSPACE** **PSPACE**-hard	non-elem. **PSPACE**-hard	
$A\overline{A}BE$	**PSPACE**-complete	non-elem. **PSPACE**-hard	
$A\overline{A}B\overline{B}$, $B\overline{B}$, $\overline{B}$, $A\overline{A}E\overline{E}$, $E\overline{E}$, $\overline{E}$	**PSPACE**-complete	**PSPACE**-complete	$A\overline{B}+KC$: non-elem.
$A\overline{A}B$, $A\overline{A}E$, AB, AE	$\mathbf{P^{NP}}$-complete	**PSPACE**-complete	
$A\overline{A}$, $\overline{A}B$, AE, A, $\overline{A}$	$\mathbf{P^{NP[O(\log^2 n)]}}$ $\mathbf{P^{NP[O(\log n)]}}$-hard	**PSPACE**-complete	
Prop, B, E	**co-NP**-complete	**PSPACE**-complete	

satisfiability-equivalent representation for the infinite set $Trc_\mathcal{K}$, that accounts for $\mathcal{K}$ and k. **EXPSPACE**-hardness of BE, and thus of full HS, has been shown in [3]. An **EXPSPACE** MC algorithm for the fragments $A\overline{A}B\overline{B}E$ and $A\overline{A}E\overline{B}E$ has been devised in [16]. A number of well-behaved HS fragments, whose MC problem has a computational complexity markedly lower than that of full HS, have been identified in [3,5,15,17], where MC has been proved to be (i) **PSPACE**-complete for $A\overline{A}BE$, $A\overline{A}B\overline{B}$, $A\overline{A}E\overline{E}$, $\overline{B}$, and $\overline{E}$, (ii) $\mathbf{P^{NP}}$-complete for AB, $A\overline{A}B$, $\overline{A}E$, and $A\overline{A}E$, (iii) in between $\mathbf{P^{NP[O(\log n)]}}$ and $\mathbf{P^{NP[O(\log^2 n)]}}$ for $A\overline{A}$, A, $\overline{A}$, $\overline{A}B$, and AE, and (iv) **co-NP**-complete for B, E, and Prop (the pure propositional fragment).

In [10,11], Lomuscio and Michaliszyn investigate MC for some HS fragments extended with the epistemic modalities K and C, according to a computation-tree-based semantics [4], under the assumption that interval labeling is defined by interval endpoints only. They prove that *local* MC for BE+KC is **PSPACE**-complete (it is in **P** for BE), and they give a non-elementary upper bound to the complexity of MC for $A\overline{B}+KC$. Later, in [12], they propose an alternative definition of interval labeling for the two fragments, which associates a regular expression over the set of states of the Kripke structure with each proposition letter, that leads to a significant increase in expressiveness, at no extra computational cost. Nothing is said about MC for full HS (with or without K, C).

In this paper, we define interval labeling via regular expressions in a way that can be shown to be equivalent to that of [12]. We first show that MC for (full) HS with regular expressions and state-based semantics is decidable. Then, we prove that relaxing the homogeneity assumption via regular expressions comes at no cost for $A\overline{A}B\overline{B}$, $A\overline{A}E\overline{E}$, $B\overline{B}$, $E\overline{E}$, $\overline{B}$, and $\overline{E}$, that remain in **PSPACE**, while $A\overline{A}B$ and $A\overline{A}E$ and their fragments increase their complexity to **PSPACE**. Since the computation-tree-based semantics and the state-based one behave exactly in the same way when restricted to HS fragments featuring present and future modalities only[2], from the **PSPACE**-completeness of $A\bar{A}B\bar{B}$, it immediately follows the **PSPACE** membership of $A\bar{B}$ with regular expressions, devoid of epistemic operators (in fact, the non-elementary complexity of MC for $A\bar{B}$ in [12] can be hardly ascribed to the addition of epistemic operators). The definitions of interval labeling given in [10,11,14] can be recovered as special cases of the present one as follows. To force homogeneity, all regular expressions in the formula have to be of the form $p \cdot p^*$, for $p \in \mathcal{AP}$, while interval labeling based on endpoints is captured by regular expressions of the form $\bigcup_{(i,j) \in I} (q_i \cdot \top^* \cdot q_j) \cup \bigcup_{i \in I'} q_i$, for some suitable $I \subseteq \{1, \ldots, |S|\}^2$, $I' \subseteq \{1, \ldots, |S|\}$, where $q_i \in \mathcal{AP}$ is a letter labeling the state $s_i \in S$ of $\mathcal{K}$ only.

4   MC for Full HS

In this section, we give an automata-theoretic solution to the MC problem for full HS. Given a finite Kripke structure $\mathcal{K}$ and an HS formula φ over $\mathcal{AP}$, we compositionally construct an NFA over the set of states of $\mathcal{K}$ accepting the set of traces ρ of $\mathcal{K}$ such that $\mathcal{K}, \rho \models \varphi$. The size of the resulting NFA is nonelementary, but it is just *linear in the size of* $\mathcal{K}$. To ensure that the non-elementary blow-up does not depend on the size of $\mathcal{K}$, we introduce a special subclass of NFAs, that we call $\mathcal{K}$-NFA. Let $\mathcal{K} = (\mathcal{AP}, S, R, \mu, s_0)$ be a Kripke structure over $\mathcal{AP}$.

Definition 3. *A $\mathcal{K}$-NFA is an NFA $\mathcal{A} = (S, Q, Q_0, \delta, F)$ over S satisfying: (i) the set Q of states is of the form $M \times S$ (M is called the* main component *or the set of* main states*); (ii) $Q_0 \cap F = \emptyset$, i.e., the empty word ε is not accepted; (iii) for all $(q, s) \in M \times S$ and $s' \in S$, $\delta((q, s), s') = \emptyset$ if $s' \neq s$, and $\delta((q, s), s) \subseteq M \times R(s)$.*

Note that a $\mathcal{K}$-NFA $\mathcal{A}$ accepts only traces of $\mathcal{K}$. Moreover, for all words $\rho \in S^+$, if there is a run of $\mathcal{A}$ over ρ, then ρ is a trace of $\mathcal{K}$.

Proposition 4. *Let $\mathcal{A}$ be an NFA over $2^{\mathcal{AP}}$ with n states. One can construct in polynomial time a $\mathcal{K}$-NFA $\mathcal{A}_\mathcal{K}$ with at most $n + 1$ main states accepting the set of traces ρ of $\mathcal{K}$ such that $\mu(\rho) \in L(\mathcal{A})$.*

Proof. Let $\mathcal{A} = (2^{\mathcal{AP}}, Q, Q_0, \delta, F)$. By using an additional state, we can assume $\varepsilon \notin L(\mathcal{A})$ (i.e., $Q_0 \cap F = \emptyset$). Then, $\mathcal{A}_\mathcal{K} = (S, Q \times S, Q_0 \times S, \delta', F \times S)$, where for all $(q, s) \in Q \times S$ and $s' \in S$, $\delta'((q, s), s') = \emptyset$ if $s' \neq s$, and $\delta'((q, s), s) = \delta(q, \mu(s)) \times R(s)$. Since $R(s) \neq \emptyset$ for all $s \in S$, the thesis follows. $\square$

We now extend the semantics of the HS modalities $\langle B \rangle$, $\langle \bar{B} \rangle$, $\langle E \rangle$, $\langle \bar{E} \rangle$ over $\mathcal{K}$ to languages $\mathcal{L}$ of finite words over S. Given any such language $\mathcal{L}$ over S, let $\langle B \rangle_\mathcal{K}(\mathcal{L})$, $\langle E \rangle_\mathcal{K}(\mathcal{L})$, $\langle \bar{B} \rangle_\mathcal{K}(\mathcal{L})$, $\langle \bar{E} \rangle_\mathcal{K}(\mathcal{L})$ be the languages of traces of $\mathcal{K}$ defined as:

- $\langle B \rangle_\mathcal{K}(\mathcal{L}) = \{\rho \in Trc_\mathcal{K} \mid \exists \rho' \in \mathcal{L} \cap S^+ \text{ and } \rho'' \in S^+ \text{ such that } \rho = \rho' \cdot \rho''\}$,
- $\langle \bar{B} \rangle_\mathcal{K}(\mathcal{L}) = \{\rho \in Trc_\mathcal{K} \mid \exists \rho' \in S^+ \text{ such that } \rho \cdot \rho' \in \mathcal{L} \cap Trc_\mathcal{K}\}$,

---

[2] As shown in [4], this is not the case in general: the computation-tree-based semantics of [10–12] is subsumed by the state-based one of [14] and follow-up papers.

$-\ \langle E\rangle_{\mathcal{K}}(L) = \{\rho \in Trc_{\mathcal{K}} \mid \exists\, \rho'' \in L \cap S^+ \text{ and } \rho' \in S^+ \text{ such that } \rho = \rho' \cdot \rho''\},$
$-\ \langle \overline{E}\rangle_{\mathcal{K}}(L) = \{\rho \in Trc_{\mathcal{K}} \mid \exists\, \rho' \in S^+ \text{ such that } \rho' \cdot \rho \in L \cap Trc_{\mathcal{K}}\}.$

The compositional translation of HS formulas into a $\mathcal{K}$-NFA is based on the following two propositions. First, we show that $\mathcal{K}$-NFAs are closed under the above language operations.

Proposition 5. *Given a $\mathcal{K}$-NFA $\mathcal{A}$ with n main states, one can construct in polynomial time $\mathcal{K}$-NFAs with $n+1$ main states accepting the languages $\langle B\rangle_{\mathcal{K}}(L(\mathcal{A}))$, $\langle E\rangle_{\mathcal{K}}(L(\mathcal{A}))$, $\langle \overline{B}\rangle_{\mathcal{K}}(L(\mathcal{A}))$, and $\langle \overline{E}\rangle_{\mathcal{K}}(L(\mathcal{A}))$, respectively.*

Proof. Let $\mathcal{A} = (S, M \times S, Q_0, \delta, F)$ be the given $\mathcal{K}$-NFA, where M is the set of main states. We omit the constructions for $\langle E\rangle_{\mathcal{K}}(L(\mathcal{A}))$ and $\langle \overline{E}\rangle_{\mathcal{K}}(L(\mathcal{A}))$ (which are symmetric to those for $\langle B\rangle_{\mathcal{K}}(L(\mathcal{A}))$ and $\langle \overline{B}\rangle_{\mathcal{K}}(L(\mathcal{A}))$, respectively): see [2].

Construction for the language $\langle B\rangle_{\mathcal{K}}(L(\mathcal{A}))$. Let us consider the NFA $\mathcal{A}_{\langle B\rangle}$ over S given by $\mathcal{A}_{\langle B\rangle} = (S, (M \cup \{q_{acc}\}) \times S, Q_0, \delta', \{q_{acc}\} \times S)$, where $q_{acc} \notin M$ is a fresh main state, and for all $(q, s) \in (M \cup \{q_{acc}\}) \times S$ and $s' \in S$, $\delta'((q, s), s') = \emptyset$, if $s' \neq s$, and $\delta'((q, s), s)$ is defined as follows:

$$\delta'((q,s),s) = \begin{cases} \delta((q,s),s) & \text{if } (q,s) \in (M \times S) \setminus F \\ \delta((q,s),s) \cup (\{q_{acc}\} \times R(s)) & \text{if } (q,s) \in F \\ \{q_{acc}\} \times R(s) & \text{if } q = q_{acc}. \end{cases}$$

Given an input word ρ, from an initial state (q_0, s) of $\mathcal{A}$, the automaton $\mathcal{A}_{\langle B\rangle}$ simulates the behavior of $\mathcal{A}$ from (q_0, s) over ρ, but when $\mathcal{A}$ is in an accepting state (q_f, s) and the current input symbol is s, $\mathcal{A}_{\langle B\rangle}$ can additionally choose to move to a state in $\{q_{acc}\} \times R(s)$, which is accepting for $\mathcal{A}_{\langle B\rangle}$. From such states, $\mathcal{A}_{\langle B\rangle}$ accepts iff the remaining portion of the input is a trace of $\mathcal{K}$. Formally, by construction, since $\mathcal{A}$ is a $\mathcal{K}$-NFA, $\mathcal{A}_{\langle B\rangle}$ is a $\mathcal{K}$-NFA as well. Moreover, a word ρ over S is accepted by $\mathcal{A}_{\langle B\rangle}$ iff ρ is a trace of $\mathcal{K}$ having some proper prefix ρ' in $L(\mathcal{A})$ (note that $\rho' \neq \varepsilon$ since $\mathcal{A}$ is a $\mathcal{K}$-NFA). Hence, $L(\mathcal{A}_{\langle B\rangle}) = \langle B\rangle_{\mathcal{K}}(L(\mathcal{A}))$.

Construction for the language $\langle \overline{B}\rangle_{\mathcal{K}}(L(\mathcal{A}))$. Let us consider the NFA $\mathcal{A}_{\langle \overline{B}\rangle}$ over S given by $\mathcal{A}_{\langle \overline{B}\rangle} = (S, (M \cup \{q_0'\}) \times S, \{q_0'\} \times S, \delta', F')$, where $q_0' \notin M$ is a fresh main state and δ' and F' are defined as follows: (i) for all $(q, s) \in (M \cup \{q_0'\}) \times S$ and $s' \in S$, $\delta'((q, s), s') = \emptyset$ if $s' \neq s$, and $\delta'((q, s), s)$ is defined as follows:

$$\delta'((q,s),s) = \begin{cases} \displaystyle\bigcup_{(q_0,s)\in Q_0} \delta((q_0,s),s) & \text{if } q = q_0' \\ \delta((q,s),s) & \text{otherwise.} \end{cases}$$

(ii) The set F' of accepting states is the set of states (q, s) of $\mathcal{A}$ such that there is a run of $\mathcal{A}$ from (q, s) to some state in F over some non-empty word. It easily follows by construction that $\mathcal{A}_{\langle \overline{B}\rangle}$ is a $\mathcal{K}$-NFA and $L(\mathcal{A}_{\langle \overline{B}\rangle}) = \langle \overline{B}\rangle_{\mathcal{K}}(L(\mathcal{A}))$. $\square$

We now show that $\mathcal{K}$-NFAs are closed under Boolean operations.

Proposition 6. *Given two $\mathcal{K}$-NFAs $\mathcal{A}$ and $\mathcal{A}'$ with n and n' main states, respectively, one can construct:*

– *in time $O(n + n')$ a $\mathcal{K}$-NFA with $n + n'$ main states accepting $L(\mathcal{A}) \cup L(\mathcal{A}')$;*
– *in time $2^{O(n)}$ a $\mathcal{K}$-NFA with $2^{n+1} + 1$ main states accepting $Trc_{\mathcal{K}} \setminus L(\mathcal{A})$.*

Proof. We omit the construction for union, as it is a natural generalization of the one for NFAs, and focus on complementation. Let $\mathcal{A} = (S, M \times S, Q_0, \delta, F)$. Let n be the number of main states of $\mathcal{A}$. First, we need a preliminary construction. Let us consider the NFA $\mathcal{A}'' = (S, (M \cup \{q_{acc}\}) \times S, Q_0, \delta'', \{q_{acc}\} \times S)$, where $q_{acc} \notin M$ is a fresh main state, and for all $(q, s) \in (M \cup \{q_{acc}\}) \times S$ and $s' \in s$, $\delta''((q, s), s') = \emptyset$ if $s' \neq s$, and

$$\delta''((q, s), s) = \begin{cases} \delta((q, s), s) \cup (\{q_{acc}\} \times S) & \text{if } q \in M \text{ and } \delta((q, s), s) \cap F \neq \emptyset \\ \delta((q, s), s) & \text{if } q \in M \text{ and } \delta((q, s), s) \cap F = \emptyset \\ \emptyset & \text{if } q = q_{acc}. \end{cases}$$

Note that $\mathcal{A}''$ is *not* a $\mathcal{K}$-NFA. However, $L(\mathcal{A}'') = L(\mathcal{A})$.

Next we show that it is possible to construct in time $2^{O(n)}$ a *weak* $\mathcal{K}$-NFA $\mathcal{A}_c$ with 2^{n+1} main states accepting $(Trc_{\mathcal{K}} \setminus L(\mathcal{A}'')) \cup \{\varepsilon\}$, where a *weak* $\mathcal{K}$-NFA is a $\mathcal{K}$-NFA but the requirement that the empty word ε is not accepted is relaxed. Thus, since a weak $\mathcal{K}$-NFA can be easily converted into an equivalent $\mathcal{K}$-NFA by using an additional main state and $L(\mathcal{A}'') = L(\mathcal{A})$, the result follows. Let $\tilde{M} = M \cup \{q_{acc}\}$. Then, the weak $\mathcal{K}$-NFA $\mathcal{A}_c$ is given by $\mathcal{A}_c = (S, 2^{\tilde{M}} \times S, Q_{0,c}, \delta_c, F_c)$, where $Q_{0,c}$, F_c, and δ_c are defined as follows: (*i*) $Q_{0,c} = \{(P, s) \in 2^M \times S \mid P = \{q \in M \mid (q, s) \in Q_0\}\}$; (*ii*) $F_c = \{(P, s) \in 2^M \times S\}$; (*iii*) for all $(P, s) \in 2^{\tilde{M}} \times S$ and $s' \in S$, $\delta_c((P, s), s') = \emptyset$ if $s' \neq s$, and $\delta_c((P, s), s)$ is given by

$$\bigcup_{s' \in R(s)} \left\{ (\{q' \in \tilde{M} \mid (q', s') \in \bigcup_{p \in P} \delta''(p, s)\}, s') \right\}.$$

By construction, $\mathcal{A}_c$ is a weak $\mathcal{K}$-NFA. Hence $\mathcal{A}_c$ does not accept words in $S^+ \setminus Trc_{\mathcal{K}}$. Moreover, by construction, $Q_{0,c} \subseteq F$, thus $\varepsilon \in L(\mathcal{A}_c)$. Finally it is easy to prove that $\rho \in L(\mathcal{A}'')$ if and only if $\rho \notin L(\mathcal{A}_c)$. See [2]. □

Let φ be an HS formula. We can convert φ into an equivalent formula, called *existential form of* φ, that makes use of negations, disjunctions, and the existential modalities $\langle B \rangle$, $\langle \overline{B} \rangle$, $\langle E \rangle$, $\langle \overline{E} \rangle$, only. For all $h \geq 1$, HS_h denotes the syntactical HS fragment consisting only of formulas φ such that the nesting depth of negation in the existential form of φ is at most h. Moreover $\neg\mathsf{HS}_h$ is the set of formulas φ such that $\neg\varphi \in \mathsf{HS}_h$. Given an HS formula φ, checking whether $\mathcal{K} \not\models \varphi$ reduces to checking the existence of an initial trace ρ of $\mathcal{K}$ such that $\mathcal{K}, \rho \models \neg\varphi$.

Theorem 7. *There is a constant c such that, given a finite Kripke structure $\mathcal{K}$ and an HS formula φ, one can construct a $\mathcal{K}$-NFA with $O(|\mathcal{K}| \cdot \mathrm{Tower}(h, |\varphi|^c))$ states accepting the set of traces ρ of $\mathcal{K}$ s.t. $\mathcal{K}, \rho \models \varphi$, where h is the nesting depth of negation in the existential form of φ. For all $h \geq 0$, the MC problem for $\neg\mathsf{HS}_h$ is in h-**EXPTIME** and, for a constant-length formula, it is in **P**.*

5   Exponential Small-Model for $A\overline{A}B\overline{B}$ and $A\overline{A}E\overline{E}$

Here we show an exponential small-model property for the fragments $A\overline{A}B\overline{B}$ and $A\overline{A}E\overline{E}$, that is, if a trace ρ of a finite Kripke structure $\mathcal{K}$ satisfies a formula φ of $A\overline{A}B\overline{B}$ or $A\overline{A}E\overline{E}$, then there exists a trace π, whose length is exponential in the sizes of φ and $\mathcal{K}$, starting from and leading to the same states as ρ, that satisfies φ. We focus on $A\overline{A}B\overline{B}$ (being the case for $A\overline{A}E\overline{E}$ symmetric). Let $\mathcal{K} = (\mathcal{AP}, S, R, \mu, s_0)$ be a finite Kripke structure. We start by introducing the notion of *trace induced* by a trace ρ which is obtained by contracting ρ, concatenating some subtraces of ρ (provided that the resulting sequence is another trace of $\mathcal{K}$).

Definition 8. *Let $\rho \in Trc_{\mathcal{K}}$ be a trace with $|\rho| = n$. A trace induced by ρ is a trace $\pi \in Trc_{\mathcal{K}}$ such that there exists an increasing sequence of ρ-positions $i_1 < \ldots < i_k$, with $i_1 = 1$, $i_k = n$, and $\pi = \rho(i_1) \cdots \rho(i_k)$. Moreover, we say that the π-position j and the ρ-position i_j are corresponding.*

Note that if π is induced by ρ, then $fst(\pi) = fst(\rho)$, $lst(\pi) = lst(\rho)$, and $|\pi| \leq |\rho|$.

Given a DFA $\mathcal{D} = (\Sigma, Q, q_0, \delta, F)$, we denote by $\mathcal{D}(w)$ (resp., $\mathcal{D}_q(w)$) the state reached by the computation of $\mathcal{D}$ from q_0 (resp., $q \in Q$) over the word $w \in \Sigma^*$.

We now consider *well-formedness* of induced traces w.r.t. a set of DFAs: a well formed trace π induced by ρ preserves the states of the computations of the DFAs reached by reading prefixes of ρ and π bounded by corresponding positions.

Definition 9. *Let $\mathcal{K} = (\mathcal{AP}, S, R, \mu, s_0)$ be a finite Kripke structure, $\rho \in Trc_{\mathcal{K}}$ be a trace, and $\mathcal{D}^s = (2^{\mathcal{AP}}, Q^s, q_0^s, \delta^s, F^s)$ with $s = 1, \ldots, k$, be DFAs. A trace $\pi \in Trc_{\mathcal{K}}$ induced by ρ is $(q_{\ell_1}^1, \ldots, q_{\ell_k}^k)$-well-formed w.r.t. ρ, with $q_{\ell_s}^s \in Q^s$ for all $s = 1, \ldots, k$, if and only if for all π-positions j, with corresponding ρ-positions i_j, and all $s = 1, \ldots, k$, it holds that $\mathcal{D}_{q_{\ell_s}^s}^s(\mu(\pi^j)) = \mathcal{D}_{q_{\ell_s}^s}^s(\mu(\rho^{i_j}))$.*

For $q_{\ell_s}^s \in Q^s$, $s = 1, \ldots, k$, the $(q_{\ell_1}^1, \ldots, q_{\ell_k}^k)$-well-formedness relation is *transitive*.

Now it is possible to show that a trace whose length exceeds a suitable exponential threshold, induces a shorter, well-formed trace. Such a contraction pattern represents a "basic step" in a contraction process which allows us to prove the exponential small-model property for $A\overline{A}B\overline{B}$. Let us consider an $A\overline{A}B\overline{B}$ formula φ and let $r_1, \ldots, r_k$ be the RE's over $\mathcal{AP}$ in φ. Let $\mathcal{D}^1, \ldots, \mathcal{D}^k$ be the DFAs such that $L(\mathcal{D}^t) = \mathcal{L}(r_t)$, for $t = 1, \ldots, k$, where $|Q^t| \leq 2^{2|r_t|}$ (see Remark 2). We denote $Q^1 \times \ldots \times Q^k$ by $Q(\varphi)$, and $\mathcal{D}^1, \ldots, \mathcal{D}^k$ by $\mathcal{D}(\varphi)$.

Proposition 10. *Let $\mathcal{K} = (\mathcal{AP}, S, R, \mu, s_0)$ be a finite Kripke structure, φ be an $A\overline{A}B\overline{B}$ formula with RE's $r_1, \ldots, r_k$ over $\mathcal{AP}$, $\rho \in Trc_{\mathcal{K}}$ be a trace, and $(q^1, \ldots, q^k) \in Q(\varphi)$. There exists a trace $\pi \in Trc_{\mathcal{K}}$, which is $(q^1, \ldots, q^k)$-well-formed w.r.t. ρ, such that $|\pi| \leq |S| \cdot 2^{2^{\sum_{\ell=1}^k |r_\ell|}}$.*   *(Proof in [2].)*

The next step is to determine some conditions for contracting traces while preserving the equivalence w.r.t. the satisfiability of a considered $A\overline{A}B\overline{B}$ formula. Hereafter we restrict ourselves to formulas in *negation normal form* (NNF), where negation is applied only to atomic formulas (regular expressions). Any formula in A$\overline{\text{A}}$B$\overline{\text{B}}$ can be converted (in linear time) into an equivalent one in NNF, having at most double length (by using De Morgan's laws and duality of HS modalities). For a trace ρ and a formula φ of A$\overline{\text{A}}$B$\overline{\text{B}}$ in NNF, we fix some special ρ-positions, called *witness positions*, each one corresponding to the minimal prefix of ρ which satisfies a formula ψ occurring in φ as a subformula of the form $\langle B \rangle \psi$ (provided that $\langle B \rangle \psi$ is satisfied by ρ). When a contraction is performed in between a pair of *consecutive* witness positions (thus no witness position is ever removed), we get a trace induced by ρ equivalent w.r.t. satisfiability of φ.

Definition 11 (Witness positions). *Let ρ be a trace of $\mathcal{K}$ and φ be a formula of* A$\overline{\text{A}}$B$\overline{\text{B}}$. *Let us denote by $B(\varphi, \rho)$ the set of subformulas $\langle B \rangle \psi$ of φ such that $\mathcal{K}, \rho \models \langle B \rangle \psi$. The set $Wt(\varphi, \rho)$ of witness positions of ρ for φ is the minimal set of ρ-positions satisfying the following constraint: for each $\langle B \rangle \psi \in B(\varphi, \rho)$, the smallest ρ-position $i < |\rho|$ such that $\mathcal{K}, \rho^i \models \psi$ belongs to $Wt(\varphi, \rho)$.*

Theorem 12 (Exponential small-model for A$\overline{\text{A}}$B$\overline{\text{B}}$). *Let $\mathcal{K} = (\mathcal{AP}, S, R, \mu, s_0)$, $\sigma, \rho \in Trc_{\mathcal{K}}$, and φ be an* A$\overline{\text{A}}B\overline{\text{B}}$ *formula in NNF, with RE's $r_1, \ldots, r_u$ over $\mathcal{AP}$, such that $\mathcal{K}, \sigma \star \rho \models \varphi$. Then, there is $\pi \in Trc_{\mathcal{K}}$, induced by ρ, such that $\mathcal{K}, \sigma \star \pi \models \varphi$ and $|\pi| \leq |S| \cdot (|\varphi| + 1) \cdot 2^{2 \sum_{\ell=1}^{u} |r_\ell|}$.* (Proof in [2].)

Theorem 12 holds in particular if $|\sigma| = 1$, and thus $\sigma \star \rho = \rho$ and $\sigma \star \pi = \pi$. In this case, if $\mathcal{K}, \rho \models \varphi$, then $\mathcal{K}, \pi \models \varphi$, where π is induced by ρ and $|\pi| \leq |S| \cdot (|\varphi| + 1) \cdot 2^{2 \sum_{\ell=1}^{u} |r_\ell|}$. The more general assertion is needed for technical reasons.

We will exploit the small-model for A$\overline{\text{A}}$B$\overline{\text{B}}$ and A$\overline{\text{A}}$E$\overline{\text{E}}$ to prove the **PSPACE**-completeness of the MC problem for the two symmetrical fragments. First, we will provide a **PSPACE** MC algorithm for B$\overline{\text{B}}$ (resp., E$\overline{\text{E}}$); then, we will show that the *meets* and *met-by* modalities A and $\overline{\text{A}}$ can be suitably encoded by using regular expressions, thus they do not increase the complexity of B$\overline{\text{B}}$ (resp., E$\overline{\text{E}}$).

6   PSPACE-Completeness of MC for A$\overline{\text{A}}$B$\overline{\text{B}}$

To start with, we describe a **PSPACE** MC algorithm for B$\overline{\text{B}}$ formulas. W.l.o.g., we assume that the processed formulas do not contain occurrences of the universal modalities $[B]$ and $[\overline{B}]$. Moreover, for a formula ψ, we denote by $\mathsf{Subf}_{\langle B \rangle}(\psi) = \{\varphi \mid \langle B \rangle \varphi \text{ is a subformula of } \psi\}$; Φ represents the overall formula to be checked, while the parametric formula ψ ranges over its subformulas. Due to the result of the previous section, the algorithm can consider only traces having length bounded by the exponential small-model property. Note that an algorithm required to work in polynomial space cannot explicitly store the DFAs for the regular expressions occurring in Φ (their states are *exponentially* many in the length of the associated regular expressions). For this reason, while checking a formula against a trace, the algorithm just stores the *current states* of the computations of the DFAs associated with the regular expressions in Φ, from the respective initial states (in the following such states are denoted—with a little abuse of notation—again by $\mathcal{D}(\Phi)$, and called the "*current configuration*" of the

---

Algorithm 1. Check($\mathcal{K}, \psi, s, G, \mathcal{D}(\Phi)$)

1: **if** $\psi = r$ **then**   ◁ r *is a regular expression*
2:     If the current state of the DFA for r in advance($\mathcal{D}(\Phi), \mu(s)$) is final **return** ⊤
3:     **else return** ⊥
4: **else if** $\psi = \neg\psi'$ (resp., $\psi = \psi_1 \wedge \psi_2$) **then**
5:     Call Check recursively on ψ' (ψ_1, ψ_2) and apply $\neg$ ($\wedge$) to the returned result(s)
6: **else if** $\psi = \langle B \rangle \psi'$ **then**
7:     **If** $\psi' \in G$ **then return** ⊤ **else return** ⊥
8: **else if** $\psi = \langle \overline{B} \rangle \psi'$ **then**
9:     **for each** $b \in \{1, \ldots, |S| \cdot (2|\psi'| + 1) \cdot 2^{2\sum_{\ell=1}^{u} |r_\ell|} - 1\}$
              and each $(G', \mathcal{D}(\Phi)', s') \in \text{Conf}(\mathcal{K}, \psi)$ **do** ◁ $r_1, \ldots, r_u$ *are the reg. expr. of* ψ'
10:        **if** Reach($\mathcal{K}, \psi', (G, \mathcal{D}(\Phi), s), (G', \mathcal{D}(\Phi)', s'), b$) **and** Check($\mathcal{K}, \psi', s', G', \mathcal{D}(\Phi)'$) **then**
11:            **return** ⊤
12:     **return** ⊥

DFAs) and calculates on-the-fly the successor states in the DFAs, once they have read some state of $\mathcal{K}$ used to extend the considered trace (this can be done by exploiting a *succinct* encoding of the NFAs for the reg.expr. of Φ, see Remark 2).

A call to the recursive procedure Check($\mathcal{K}, \psi, s, G, \mathcal{D}(\Phi)$) (Algorithm 1) checks the satisfiability of a subformula ψ of Φ w.r.t. any trace ρ fulfilling the following conditions: (1) $G \subseteq \text{Subf}_{\langle B \rangle}(\psi)$ is the set of formulas that hold true on at least a prefix of ρ; (2) after reading $\mu(\rho(1, |\rho| - 1))$ the current configuration of the DFAs for the regular expressions of Φ is $\mathcal{D}(\Phi)$; (3) the last state of ρ is s. Intuitively, since the algorithm cannot store the already checked portion of a trace (*whose length could be exponential*), the relevant information is *summarized* in a triple $(G, \mathcal{D}(\Phi), s)$. Hereafter the set of all possible summarizing triples $(\overline{G}, \overline{\mathcal{D}(\Phi)}, \overline{s})$, where $\overline{G} \subseteq \text{Subf}_{\langle B \rangle}(\psi)$, $\overline{\mathcal{D}(\Phi)}$ is any current configuration of the DFAs for the regular expressions of Φ, and $\overline{s}$ is a state of $\mathcal{K}$, is denoted by $\text{Conf}(\mathcal{K}, \psi)$.

Let us consider in detail the body of the procedure. First advance($\mathcal{D}(\Phi), \mu(s)$), invoked at line 2, updates the current configuration of the DFAs after reading the symbol $\mu(s)$. If ψ is a regular expression r (lines 1–3), we just check whether the (computation of the) DFA associated with r is in a final state (i.e., the summarized trace is accepted). Boolean connectives are easily dealt with recursively (lines 4–5). If ψ has the form $\langle B \rangle \psi'$ (lines 6–7), then ψ' has to hold over a proper prefix of the summarized trace, namely, ψ' must belong to G.

The only involved case is $\psi = \langle \overline{B} \rangle \psi'$ (lines 8–12): we have to unravel the Kripke structure $\mathcal{K}$ to find an *extension* ρ' of ρ, summarized by the triple $(G', \mathcal{D}(\Phi)', s')$, satisfying ψ'. The idea is checking whether or not there exists a summarized trace $(G', \mathcal{D}(\Phi)', s')$, suitably extending $(G, \mathcal{D}(\Phi), s)$, namely, such that: (1) $\mathcal{D}(\Phi)'$ and s' are *synchronously* reachable from $\mathcal{D}(\Phi)$ and s, resp.; (2) $G' \supseteq G$ contains all the formulas of $\text{Subf}_{\langle B \rangle}(\psi')$ satisfied by some prefixes of the extension; (3) the extension $(G', \mathcal{D}(\Phi)', s')$ satisfies ψ'. In order to check point (1), i.e., synchronous reachability, we can exploit the exponential small-model property and consider only the unravelling of $\mathcal{K}$ starting from s having depth at most $|S| \cdot (2|\psi'| + 1) \cdot 2^{2\sum_{\ell=1}^{u} |r_\ell|} - 1$.[3] The check of (1) and (2) is performed by the procedure Reach (Algorithm 2), which accepts as input two summarized traces

---

[3]   The factor 2 in front of $|\psi'|$ is needed as the small-model requires a formula in NNF.

Algorithm 2. Reach($\mathcal{K}, \psi, (G_1, \mathcal{D}(\Phi)_1, s_1), (G_2, \mathcal{D}(\Phi)_2, s_2), b$)

1: **if** $b = 1$ **then**
2:     **return** Compatible($\mathcal{K}, \psi, (G_1, \mathcal{D}(\Phi)_1, s_1), (G_2, \mathcal{D}(\Phi)_2, s_2)$)
3: **else** $\triangleleft\, b \geq 2$
4:     $b' \leftarrow \lfloor b/2 \rfloor$
5:     **for each** $(G_3, \mathcal{D}(\Phi)_3, s_3) \in$ Conf($\mathcal{K}, \psi$) **do**
6:         **if** Reach($\mathcal{K}, \psi, (G_1, \mathcal{D}(\Phi)_1, s_1), (G_3, \mathcal{D}(\Phi)_3, s_3), b'$) **and** Reach($\mathcal{K}, \psi, (G_3, \mathcal{D}(\Phi)_3, s_3), (G_2, \mathcal{D}(\Phi)_2, s_2), b - b'$) **then**
7:             **return** $\top$
8:     **return** $\bot$

Algorithm 3. Compatible($\mathcal{K}, \psi, (G_1, \mathcal{D}(\Phi)_1, s_1), (G_2, \mathcal{D}(\Phi)_2, s_2)$)

1: **if** $(s_1, s_2) \in R$ **and** advance($\mathcal{D}(\Phi)_1, \mu(s_1)) = \mathcal{D}(\Phi)_2$ **and** $G_1 \subseteq G_2$ **then**
2:     **for each** $\varphi \in (G_2 \setminus G_1)$ **do**
3:         $G \leftarrow G_1 \cap \text{Subf}_{\langle B \rangle}(\varphi)$
4:         **if** Check($\mathcal{K}, \varphi, s_1, G, \mathcal{D}(\Phi)_1) = \bot$ **then**
5:             **return** $\bot$
6:     **for each** $\varphi \in (\text{Subf}_{\langle B \rangle}(\psi) \setminus G_2)$ **do**
7:         $G \leftarrow G_1 \cap \text{Subf}_{\langle B \rangle}(\varphi)$
8:         **if** Check($\mathcal{K}, \varphi, s_1, G, \mathcal{D}(\Phi)_1) = \top$ **then**
9:             **return** $\bot$
10:    **return** $\top$
11: **else**
12:    **return** $\bot$

---

and a bound b on the depth of the unravelling of $\mathcal{K}$. The proposed reachability algorithm is reminiscent of the binary reachability of Savitch's theorem.

Reach proceeds recursively (lines 3–8) by halving at each step the value b of the length bound, until it gets called over two states s_1 and s_2 which are adjacent in a trace. At each halving step, an intermediate summarizing triple is generated to be associated with the split point. At the base of recursion (for $b = 1$, lines 1–2), the auxiliary procedure Compatible (Algorithm 3) is invoked. At line 1, Compatible checks whether there is an edge between s_1 and s_2 ($(s_1, s_2) \in R$), and if, at the considered step, the current configuration of the DFAs $\mathcal{D}(\Phi)_1$ is transformed into the configuration $\mathcal{D}(\Phi)_2$ (i.e., s_2 and $\mathcal{D}(\Phi)_2$ are synchronously reachable from s_1 and $\mathcal{D}(\Phi)_1$). At lines 2–9, Compatible checks that each formula φ in $(G_2 \setminus G_1)$, where $G_2 \supseteq G_1$, is satisfied by a trace summarized by $(G_1, \mathcal{D}(\Phi)_1, s_1)$ (lines 2–5). Intuitively, $(G_1, \mathcal{D}(\Phi)_1, s_1)$ summarizes the maximal prefix of $(G_2, \mathcal{D}(\Phi)_2, s_2)$, and thus a subformula satisfied by a prefix of a trace summarized by $(G_2, \mathcal{D}(\Phi)_2, s_2)$ either belongs to G_1 or it is satisfied by the trace summarized by $(G_1, \mathcal{D}(\Phi)_1, s_1)$. Moreover, (lines 6–9) Compatible checks that G_2 is maximal (i.e., no subformula that must be in G_2 has been forgot).

Note that by exploiting this binary reachability technique, the recursion depth of Reach is *logarithmic in the length of the trace to be visited, hence it can use only polynomial space.* Theorem 13 establishes the soundness of Check.

Theorem 13. *Let Φ be a B$\overline{\text{B}}$ formula, ψ be a subformula of Φ, and $\rho \in Trc_{\mathcal{K}}$ be a trace with $s = lst(\rho)$. Let G be the subset of formulas in $\text{Subf}_{\langle B \rangle}(\psi)$ that hold on some proper prefix of ρ. Let $\mathcal{D}(\Phi)$ be the current configuration of the DFAs*

Algorithm 4. CheckAux($\mathcal{K}, \Phi$)

1: **create**($\mathcal{D}(\Phi)_0$)◁ *Creates the (succinct) NFAs and the initial states of the DFAs for all the regular expressions in Φ*
2: **If** Check($\mathcal{K}, \neg\Phi, s_0, \emptyset, \mathcal{D}(\Phi)_0$) **or** Check($\mathcal{K}, \langle\overline{B}\rangle\neg\Phi, s_0, \emptyset, \mathcal{D}(\Phi)_0$) **then return** $\bot$
3: **else return** $\top$

---

associated with the regular expressions in Φ after reading $\mu(\rho(1, |\rho| - 1))$. Then Check($\mathcal{K}, \psi, s, G, \mathcal{D}(\Phi)$) $= \top \iff \mathcal{K}, \rho \models \psi$.   *(Proof in [2].)*

Finally, the main MC procedure for B$\overline{B}$ is Algorithm 4: CheckAux($\mathcal{K}, \Phi$) starts by constructing the NFAs and the initial states of the DFAs for the regular expressions of Φ. Then CheckAux invokes the procedure Check two times: the first to check the special case of the trace s_0 (i.e., the initial state of $\mathcal{K}$ only), and the second for all right-extensions of s_0 (i.e., initial traces with length ≥ 2).

Theorem 14. *Let $\mathcal{K} = (\mathcal{AP}, S, R, \mu, s_0)$ be a finite Kripke structure, and Φ be a B$\overline{B}$ formula. Then CheckAux($\mathcal{K}, \Phi$) returns $\top$ iff $\mathcal{K} \models \Phi$.*   *(Proof in [2].)*

Corollary 15. *The MC problem for B$\overline{B}$ on Kripke structures is in* **PSPACE**.

Proof. CheckAux decides the problem using *polynomial work space* as: (i) the number of simultaneously active recursive calls of Check is $O(|\Phi|)$ (depending on the depth of Φ); (ii) for any call of Check the used space (in bits) is

$$O\Big(|\Phi| + |S| + \sum_{\ell=1}^{u} |r_\ell| + \log(|S| \cdot |\Phi| \cdot 2^{2\sum_{\ell=1}^{u} |r_\ell|})_{(1)} + (|\Phi| + |S| + \sum_{\ell=1}^{u} |r_\ell|)_{(2)} \cdot$$
$$\log(|S| \cdot |\Phi| \cdot 2^{2\sum_{\ell=1}^{u} |r_\ell|})_{(3)} \Big)$$

where $r_1, \ldots, r_u$ are the reg. expr. of Φ, and S the states of $\mathcal{K}$: (1) $O(\log(|S| \cdot |\Phi| \cdot 2^{2\sum_{\ell=1}^{u} |r_\ell|}))$ bits are used for the bound b on the trace length, (3) for *each subformula* $\langle\overline{B}\rangle\psi'$ of Φ at most $O(\log(|S| \cdot |\Phi| \cdot 2^{2\sum_{\ell=1}^{u} |r_\ell|}))$ calls of Reach may be simultaneously active (the recursion depth of Reach is logarithmic in b), (2) each Reach call uses $O(|\Phi| + |S| + \sum_{\ell=1}^{u} |r_\ell|)$ bits □

Finally, since a Kripke structure can be unravelled against the direction of its edges, and any language $\mathcal{L}$ is regular iff $\mathcal{L}^{\text{Rev}} = \{w(|w|) \cdots w(1) \mid w \in \mathcal{L}\}$ is, the algorithm can be easily modified to deal with the symmetrical fragment E$\overline{E}$.

Let us now focus on A$\overline{A}$B$\overline{B}$. CheckAux can be used iteratively as a basic engine to check formulas Φ of A$\overline{A}$B$\overline{B}$: at each iteration, we select an occurrence of a subformula of Φ, either of the form $\langle A\rangle\psi$ or $\langle\overline{A}\rangle\psi$, without *internal* occurrences of $\langle A\rangle$ and $\langle\overline{A}\rangle$. For such an occurrence, say $\langle A\rangle\psi$ ($\langle\overline{A}\rangle\psi$ is symmetric), we compute the set $S_{\langle A\rangle\psi}$ of states of $\mathcal{K}$ s.t., for any $\rho \in Trc_{\mathcal{K}}$, $\mathcal{K}, \rho \models \langle A\rangle\psi$ iff $lst(\rho) \in S_{\langle A\rangle\psi}$. To this aim we run CheckAux($\mathcal{K}, \neg\psi$) using each $s \in S$ as the initial state (in place of s_0): we have $s \in S_{\langle A\rangle\psi}$ iff the procedure returns $\bot$. Then we replace $\langle A\rangle\psi$ in Φ with a fresh reg. expr. $r_{\langle A\rangle\psi} := \top^* \cdot \big(\bigcup_{s' \in S_{\langle A\rangle\psi}} q_{s'}\big)$—where $q_{s'}$ is an auxiliary letter labeling $s' \in S$ only—obtaining a formula Φ'. If Φ' is in B$\overline{B}$ the conversion is completed, otherwise we proceed with another iteration.

Finally, the pure propositional fragment Prop can be proved **PSPACE**-hard by a reduction from the **PSPACE**-complete *universality problem for regular expressions*: such lower bound immediately propagates to all other HS fragments.

Theorem 16. *The MC problem for formulas of any (proper or improper) sub-fragment of* $A\bar{A}B\bar{B}$ *(and* $A\bar{A}E\bar{E}$*) on finite Kripke structures is***PSPACE***-complete.*

7   Conclusions

In this paper, we have investigated the MC problem for HS and two large frag-ments of it, $A\bar{A}B\bar{B}$ and $A\bar{A}E\bar{E}$, defining interval labelling via regular expres-sions. The approach, stemming from [12], generalizes both the one of [14] (which assumes the homogeneity principle) and of [10,11] (where labeling is endpoint-based). MC turns out to be non-elementarily decidable and **EXPSPACE**-hard for full HS (the hardness follows from that of BE under homogeneity [3]), and **PSPACE**-complete for $A\bar{A}B\bar{B}$, $A\bar{A}E\bar{E}$, and all their sub-fragments. Future work will focus on the fragments $A\bar{A}B\bar{B}\bar{E}$, $A\bar{A}E\bar{B}\bar{E}$, and $A\bar{A}B\bar{E}$, which have been proved to be in **EXPSPACE** (the first two) and **PSPACE**-complete (the third one) under homogeneity [15,16], as well as on the problem of determining the exact complexity of MC for full HS. In addition, we will study the MC problem for HS over *visibly pushdown systems*, in order to deal with infinite state systems.

References

1. Allen, J.F.: Maintaining knowledge about temporal intervals. Commun. ACM **26**(11), 832–843 (1983)
2. Bozzelli, L., Molinari, A., Montanari, A., Peron, A.: An in-depth investigation of ITL MC with regular expressions. Technical report 2, University of Udine, Italy (2017). https://www.dimi.uniud.it/la-ricerca/pubblicazioni/preprints/2.2017/
3. Bozzelli, L., Molinari, A., Montanari, A., Peron, A., Sala, P.: Interval temporal logic model checking: the border between good and bad HS fragments. In: Olivetti, N., Tiwari, A. (eds.) IJCAR 2016. LNCS (LNAI), vol. 9706, pp. 389–405. Springer, Cham (2016). doi:10.1007/978-3-319-40229-1_27
4. Bozzelli, L., Molinari, A., Montanari, A., Peron, A., Sala, P.: Interval vs. point temporal logic model checking: an expressiveness comparison. In: FSTTCS (2016)
5. Bozzelli, L., Molinari, A., Montanari, A., Peron, A., Sala, P.: MC the logic of Allen's relations meets and started-by is $\mathbf{P}^{\mathrm{NP}}$-C. In: GandALF, pp. 76–90 (2016)
6. Bresolin, D., Della Monica, D., Goranko, V., Montanari, A., Sciavicco, G.: The dark side of interval temporal logic: marking the undecidability border. Ann. Math. Artif. Intell. **71**(1–3), 41–83 (2014)
7. Esparza, J., Hansel, D., Rossmanith, P., Schwoon, S.: Efficient algorithms for model checking pushdown systems. In: Emerson, E.A., Sistla, A.P. (eds.) CAV 2000. LNCS, vol. 1855, pp. 232–247. Springer, Heidelberg (2000). doi:10.1007/10722167_20
8. Halpern, J.Y., Shoham, Y.: A propositional modal logic of time intervals. J. ACM **38**(4), 935–962 (1991)
9. Kupferman, O., Piterman, N., Vardi, M.Y.: From liveness to promptness. Formal Methods Syst. Des. **34**(2), 83–103 (2009)
10. Lomuscio, A., Michaliszyn, J.: An epistemic HS logic. In: IJCAI, pp. 1010–1016 (2013)

11. Lomuscio, A., Michaliszyn, J.: Decidability of model checking multi-agent systems against a class of EHS specifications. In: ECAI, pp. 543–548 (2014)
12. Lomuscio, A., Michaliszyn, J.: Model checking multi-agent systems against epistemic HS specifications with regular expressions. In: KR, pp. 298–308 (2016)
13. Marcinkowski, J., Michaliszyn, J.: The undecidability of the logic of subintervals. Fundamenta Informaticae **131**(2), 217–240 (2014)
14. Molinari, A., Montanari, A., Murano, A., Perelli, G., Peron, A.: Checking interval properties of computations. Acta Informatica **53**, 587–619 (2016)
15. Molinari, A., Montanari, A., Peron, A.: Complexity of ITL model checking: some well-behaved fragments of the interval logic HS. In: TIME, pp. 90–100 (2015)
16. Molinari, A., Montanari, A., Peron, A.: A model checking procedure for interval temporal logics based on track representatives. In: CSL, pp. 193–210 (2015)
17. Molinari, A., Montanari, A., Peron, A., Sala, P.: Model checking well-behaved fragments of HS: the (Almost) final picture. In: KR, pp. 473–483 (2016)
18. Montanari, A.: Interval temporal logics model checking. In: TIME, p. 2 (2016)
19. Moszkowski, B.: Reasoning about digital circuits. Ph.D. thesis, Stanford (1983)
20. Roeper, P.: Intervals and tenses. J. Philos. Log. **9**, 451–469 (1980)
21. Venema, Y.: Expressiveness and completeness of an interval tense logic. Notre Dame J. Formal Log. **31**(4), 529–547 (1990)

PARTpw: From Partial Analysis Results to a Proof Witness

Marie-Christine Jakobs[(✉)]

Paderborn University, Paderborn, Germany
marie.christine.jakobs@upb.de

Abstract. Today, verification tools do not only output yes or no, but also provide correctness arguments or counterexamples. While counterexamples help to fix bugs, *correctness arguments* are used to increase the trust in program correctness, e.g., in Proof-Carrying Code (PCC). Correctness arguments are well-studied for single analyses, but not when a *set of analyses* together verifies a program, each of the analyses checking only a particular part. Such a set of partial, complementary analyses is often used when a single analysis would fail or is inefficient on some program parts.

We propose PARTpw, a technique which allows us to automatically construct a proof witness (correctness argument) from the analysis results obtained by a set of partial, complementary analyses. The constructed proof witnesses are proven to be valid correctness arguments and in our experiments we use them seamlessly and efficiently in existing PCC approaches.

1 Introduction

Nowadays, verification tools do not simply output yes (property fulfilled) or no (property violated). Most of them provide a counterexample, when the analysis fails. Additionally, several tools output a correctness argument after a successful verification. Given in a verifier independent format, a correctness argument can be checked by a different verifier to increase the trust in the tool's answer yes. Furthermore, Proof-Carrying Code (PCC) [19] employs correctness arguments to efficiently convince a program executor of the correctness of a program.

A standard approach to build a correctness argument is to start from a representation of the explored state space. For example, PCC approaches like [8,14–16,21,22] construct their correctness arguments from abstract reachability graphs (ARGs), a representation of the explored state space, which is built anyway by many abstract interpretation [9] based tools. However, these PCC approaches typically assume that a single analysis verified the program.

Unfortunately, single analyses do not always succeed, especially when they are restricted to standard abstract domains. For example, consider the program bonus on the left of Fig. 1, which computes a bonus salary of an employee. Predicate abstraction, e.g., [5], can show that executions taking the if-branch do not violate the assertion. Yet, predicate abstraction fails to prove the rest

© Springer International Publishing AG 2017
A. Cimatti and M. Sirjani (Eds.): SEFM 2017, LNCS 10469, pp. 120–135, 2017.
DOI: 10.1007/978-3-319-66197-1_8

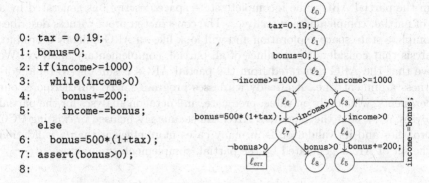

```
0:  tax = 0.19;
1:  bonus=0;
2:  if(income>=1000)
3:      while(income>0)
4:          bonus+=200;
5:          income-=bonus;
        else
6:      bonus=500*(1+tax);
7:  assert(bonus>0);
8:
```

Fig. 1. Example program **bonus** and its control-flow automaton

because it is often restricted to linear integer arithmetic. In contrast, an explicit analysis [18], which tracks concrete variable values, can verify the else-branch, but not the if-branch because it cannot encode the relation between the if- and the while-condition. Also, a standard product analysis combining predicate and explicit analysis is inefficient for program **bonus**. Tracking the concrete value for variable bonus, which changes in each loop iteration, prohibits the analysis to stop the loop exploration after a single iteration as the predicate analysis does.

To get an efficient analysis for program **bonus**, one must either adapt the product analysis to refine and coarsen the components at the right places, apply a different (non-standard) domain, or use a set of partial, complementary analyses, where each analysis is responsible for a specific part of the program. Since non-standard domains might not be supported by a verification tool and it is likely tedious and difficult to adapt the product analysis properly, a set of partial, complementary analyses is the best option. In our example, a predicate analysis analyzes the if-branch and a value analysis the else-branch. Generally, partial, complementary analyses with different strengths and weaknesses should be used.

Instead of a description of the complete state space, a successful verification with a set of partial, complementary analyses results in a set of partial descriptions that together cover the complete state space. To support correctness arguments for partial, complementary analyses, one must thus either extend the existing approaches or unify the incomplete state space descriptions into a single complete one. While one could argue that the first solution offers the advantage to build correctness arguments that are checkable in parallel, existing PCC [15,16] approaches already support parallel validation of the correctness argument. Moreover, the second approach reveals fewer business secrets of the verification tool and allows a seamless integration into existing approaches. Thus, it is much more comfortable.

So far, no approaches exist that describe how to unify partial state space descriptions generated by a set of partial, complementary abstract interpretation based analyses. To overcome this problem, we propose PART_PW, a technique to systematically construct a proof witness, a special form of an ARG, from the partial ARGs, the incomplete state space descriptions generated by a set of partial, complementary analyses. The constructed proof witness describes a complete state space exploration and will look like an ARG built by a product analysis that considers the product of all partial, complementary analyses. We prove that the ARG generated from the partial ARGs is suitable to build correctness arguments, i.e., it already witnesses program safety. Furthermore, our experiments, which rely on value, predicate, and octagon analyses for the partial analyses, show that the generated ARG can seamlessly be used in existing PCC approaches and its validation is in many cases more efficient than a validation of the set of ARGs generated by the partial, complementary analyses.

2   Background

In this section, we introduce our notion of program safety and its analysis. We start with the representation of a program. To simplify our presentation, we assume that the properties of interest are encoded into the program using error locations. While in theory one could model all safety properties as unreachability of error locations [18], our implementation uses observer automata [1], which allow us to directly specify type state (protocol) properties, invariants, etc. Following configurable software verification [3], the underlying concept of the tool in which we integrated our approach, a program is modeled by a *control-flow automaton* (CFA) $P = (L, G_{\mathrm{CFA}}, l_0, L_{\mathrm{err}})$ consisting of a set L of locations, modeling the program counter, a set $G_{\mathrm{CFA}} \subseteq L \times Ops \times L^1$ of control-flow edges defining the follow-up program counter and which operation to execute, an initial location $l_0 \in L$ describing the program entry, and a non-empty set $L_{\mathrm{err}} \subseteq L$ of error locations which are unsafe to reach.

The CFA for our example program bonus is shown in the right of Fig. 1. It contains one location per program counter (the number in front of the statements) plus the error location l_{err}. Assignments are directly translated into control-flow edges. For if- and while-statements, there exist two edges, one per possible outcome of the condition. Finally, the assertion is encoded by two assume statements. When the assertion is valid (*bonus* > 0), control-flow proceeds normally. Otherwise, the violation of the assertion leads to the error location.

The *semantics of a program* P is described by a labeled transition system $T(P) = (C, \rightarrow)$ with a set C of concrete states and a transition relation $\rightarrow \subseteq C \times G_{\mathrm{CFA}} \times C$. From now on, we write $c \xrightarrow{g} c'$ for (c, g, c'). For our approach, we only require that each concrete state $c \in C$ refers to a program location $c(pc) \in L$. Thus, we are able to detect property violations. Standard text book semantics like e.g. [20, pp. 54ff] fulfill this property.

Based on the labeled transition system, we derive the program execution paths, denoted by $paths_P$. A *program execution path* $c_0 \xrightarrow{g_1} \ldots c_{m-1} \xrightarrow{g_m} c_m \in paths_P$ is a

---

[1] We assume *Ops* to be the set of all operations a program may execute. In the implementation we consider C statements.

path in the labeled transition system starting in the initial program location, i.e., $c_0(pc) = l_0$ and $\forall 1 \leq i \leq m : c_{i-1} \overset{g_i}{\to} c_i$. This definition easily leads us to the non-reachability of error locations, our notion of program safety. A *program* $P = (L, G_{\mathrm{CFA}}, l_0, L_{\mathrm{err}})$ *is safe* if no program execution path reaches an error location, i.e., $\forall c_0 \overset{g_1}{\to} \ldots c_{m-1} \overset{g_m}{\to} c_m \in paths_P : c_m(pc) \notin L_{\mathrm{err}}$.

To prove that a program is safe, we rely on an abstract exploration of the reachable state space [9,18]. In principle, we could have used any abstract interpretation alike formalism to specify the analyses. We decided to use the configurable program analysis (CPA) formalism underlying the tool in which we integrated our PART$_\mathrm{PW}$ technique. Next to the abstract domain and the abstract semantics, a CPA defines when and how to combine information or stop exploration of states. Thus, a CPA also configures the state space exploration. Following Beyer et al. [3], a *configurable program analysis* is a four-tuple $\mathbb{A} = (D, \rightsquigarrow, \mathsf{merge}, \mathsf{stop})$ with

Abstract Domain $D = (C, \mathcal{E}, \llbracket \cdot \rrbracket)$ considering lattice $\mathcal{E} = (E, \top, \bot, \sqcup, \sqcap)$ on abstract states E with $\llbracket \top \rrbracket = C$, $\llbracket \bot \rrbracket = \emptyset$, and $\forall e, e' \in E : \llbracket e \rrbracket \cup \llbracket e' \rrbracket \subseteq \llbracket e \sqcup e' \rrbracket \wedge \llbracket e \sqcup e' \rrbracket \subseteq \llbracket e \rrbracket \cap \llbracket e' \rrbracket$,

Transfer Relation $\rightsquigarrow \subseteq E \times G_{\mathrm{CFA}} \times E$ defining the abstract semantics and overapproximating the concrete behavior, i.e., $\forall e \in E, g \in G_{\mathrm{CFA}} : \{c' \mid c \in \llbracket e \rrbracket \wedge c \overset{g}{\to} c'\} \subseteq \bigcup\limits_{(e,g,e') \in \rightsquigarrow} \llbracket e' \rrbracket$,

Merge Operator $\mathsf{merge} : E \times E \to E$, a total function determining when and how to combine abstract information and guaranteeing that no explored information is lost, i.e., $\forall e, e' \in E : \mathsf{merge}(e, e') \sqsupseteq e'$,

Termination Check $\mathsf{stop} : E \times 2^E \to \mathbb{B}$, a total boolean function checking whether to stop the exploration of an abstract state. For soundness, the exploration may only be stopped when an abstract states does not introduce new information, i.e., $\forall e \in E, S \subseteq E : \mathsf{stop}(e, S) \implies \llbracket e \rrbracket \subseteq \bigcup\limits_{e' \in S} \llbracket e' \rrbracket$.

To get a sound combination of different analyses, which we use later, we also require that an abstract state can be covered by a single abstract state, i.e., $\forall e \in E, S \subseteq S : \mathsf{stop}(e, S) \implies \exists e' \in S : \mathsf{stop}(e, \{e'\})$. Furthermore, to build a proof witness from partial, complementary analyses the termination check must detect coverage (1) by the top state and (2) by the same state, i.e., $\forall e \in E, S \subseteq E : e \in S \vee \top \in S \implies \mathsf{stop}(e, S)$.[2]

As done by the software analysis tool CPACHECKER [4], in which we integrate our approach, we assume that each of the (partial) analyses of a program records its explored state space in form of an *abstract reachability graph* (ARG). Nodes in the graph represent explored abstract states. Edges describe successor relations and, thus, document how the state space is explored. The root node marks the entry point of the state space exploration. Formally, an abstract reachability graph is defined as follows.

---

[2] The second requirement also eases the model of the explored state space.

Definition 1. *An abstract reachability graph* $R_{\mathbb{A}}^P = (N, G_{\text{ARG}}, root)$ *for a program* $P = (L, G_{\text{CFA}}, l_0, L_{\text{err}})$ *and CPA* $\mathbb{A}$ *consists of a set* $N \subseteq E_{\mathbb{A}}$ *of nodes, a set* $G_{\text{ARG}} \subseteq N \times G_{\text{CFA}} \times N$ *of edges, and a root node* $root \in N$.

Figure 2 shows two ARGs. These two ARGs could have been obtained when analyzing our example **bonus** with a complementary, partial value [6] and predicate analysis [5][3]. For the sake of readability, we labeled the ARG edges only with the operations of the control-flow edges. Both ARGs start in the initial program location and never reach an error location. The left ARG is the ARG constructed by the value analysis that verified the else-branch and the right ARG shows the ARG generated by the predicate analysis checking the if-branch.

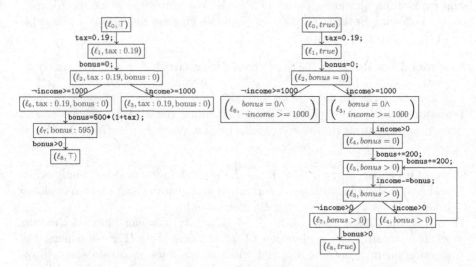

Fig. 2. Partial ARGs obtained by the complementary partial value analysis and partial predicate analysis on example program **bonus**

The definition of an ARG only fixes its syntactical structure, but ARGs in which we are interested must also record a proper (partial) state space exploration. Like programs, analyses must start at the program entry. Hence, the root node must consider all concrete states looking at the initial program location. Additionally, all program executions considered by the analysis must be represented in the ARG. Remembering the inductive definition of program executions and the overapproximation of transfer relations, abstract transfer successors should be covered by ARG successors. However, in partial analyses that did not finish their state space exploration abstract successors of some ARG nodes may not be covered. For example, in the left ARG in Fig. 2 the successors

---

[3] Note that in our example we use single block encoding and, thus, left out the abstraction location, which is identical to the abstract program location, and the path formula which is always true.

of $(\ell_4, \text{tax} : 0.19, \text{bonus} : 0)$ are unexplored. To ease our presentation, we assume that a partial analysis always stops after a complete exploration of a state. This leads us to the notion of partial soundness. All abstract successors of an explored state (ARG node) are either covered by ARG successors or remain all unexplored. Whenever no states remain unexplored, the analysis is not partial, but complete, partial soundness reduces to soundness, i.e., all abstract successors of a node must be covered by the node's successors. So far, the requirements are sufficient to guarantee a proper (partial) state space exploration. Since we plan to use ARGs to assure program safety, additionally none of the explored abstract states should consider an error location. Summing up, we get the following four ARG properties.

Rootedness. The root covers the initial states, $\{c \in C \mid c(pc) = l_0\} \subseteq [\![root]\!]_{\mathbb{A}}$.
Partial soundness. Abstract successors along a control-flow edge are either
 covered by ARG successors or not explored at all, $\forall n \in N, g \in G_{\text{CFA}}$:
 $(n, g, e) \in \leadsto_{\mathbb{A}} \implies (\text{stop}_{\mathbb{A}}(e, \{n' \mid (n, g, n') \in G_{\text{ARG}}\}) \vee \neg \exists (n, g, \cdot) \in G_{\text{ARG}})$.
Soundness. ARG successors cover abstract successors, $\forall n \in N, g \in G_{\text{CFA}}$:
 $(n, g, e) \in \leadsto_{\mathbb{A}} \implies \text{stop}_{\mathbb{A}}(e, \{n' \mid (n, g, n') \in G_{\text{ARG}}\})$.
Safety. Error locations are excluded[4], $\{l \mid c \in [\![N]\!]_{\mathbb{A}} \wedge c(pc) = l\} \cap L_{\text{err}} = \emptyset$.

Given these properties, we define when an ARG is suitable for witnessing program safety. We require that a suitable ARG, which we call *proof witness*, records the state space exploration of a complete and successful analysis of a program.

Definition 2. *An ARG is a* proof witness *if it is rooted, sound, and safe.*

Note that proof witnesses are a common starting point for certificate generation in abstract interpretation based approaches [8, 14–16, 21, 22]. The following theorem states that proof witnesses are indeed well-suited for certificate generation because they already witness program safety.

Theorem 1. *A proof witness ensures program safety.*

Proof (Sketch). Let $R_{\mathbb{A}}^P = (N, G_{\text{ARG}}, root)$ be a proof witness with program $P = (L, G_{\text{CFA}}, l_0, L_{\text{err}})$ and $c_0 \xrightarrow{g_1} \ldots c_{n-1} \xrightarrow{g_m} c_m \in paths_P$ be an arbitrary program execution. First, show by induction that $\forall 0 \leq i \leq m : \exists n \in N : c_i \in [\![n]\!]_{\mathbb{A}}$. By induction, there exists $n \in N$ with $c_m \in [\![n]\!]_{\mathbb{A}}$. We conclude that $c_m(pc) \in \{l \mid c \in [\![N]\!]_{\mathbb{A}} \wedge c(pc) = l\}$. Due to safety, $c_m(pc) \notin L_{\text{err}}$.

In the end, we require a proof witness to apply existing certification techniques. However, partial, complementary analyses, as used to verify our example program **bonus**, do not generate ARGs which are proof witnesses. Each of these partial analyses typically stops successor exploration of some explored states, e.g., because it is not mature enough, it is already too exhaustive for this program part, it timed out, or another partial analysis already explored the corresponding program's concrete successors. While these ARGs are also rooted and safe, they are only partially sound. From now on, we call such ARGs *partial ARGs*.

---

[4] We lifted the concretization to sets of abstract states, i.e., $\forall S \subseteq E_{\mathbb{A}} : [\![S]\!]_{\mathbb{A}} = \bigcup_{e \in S} [\![e]\!]_{\mathbb{A}}$.

Definition 3. *An* ARG *is partial if it is rooted, partially sound, and safe.*

In the following, we want to construct a proof witness from the partial ARGs constructed by the partial, complementary analyses. A proof witness can only be constructed from a set of partial ARGs when the corresponding partial analyses together check program safety. The next section discusses which properties a set of partial ARGs must provide to be suitable for proof witness construction.

3   When Do Partial ARGs Witness Program Safety?

Our goal is to build a proof witness from the ARGs that are constructed by a set of partial, complementary analyses, after the set of partial, complementary analyses together proved program safety. Thus, the successful verification must be reflected by the constructed ARGs. Partial analyses may not finish their exploration, but must not fail to prove safety. Hence, the constructed ARGs are partial ARGs. Furthermore, to witness completeness of the verification, the set of constructed, partial ARGs must capture all possible program execution paths. Summing up, to construct a proof witness we require at least a set of partial ARGs which capture all program execution paths.

The previous characterization of a set of ARGs loses the advantage of abstraction which makes it difficult to check. More importantly, it is improper for proof witness construction. For example, assume that our example **bonus** resets the income to zero when it is larger than 1000 before executing the current program **bonus**. The ARG constructed by a partial value analysis of this modified program is an ARG similar to the left ARG in Fig. 2, but the current root node is preceded by some states of the form $(\ell, \top_V)$. Since the if-branch in the modified version of **bonus** is infeasible, a set only consisting of that ARG for the modified program captures all program execution paths. However, the value analysis cannot detect the infeasibility and still computes a successor for the if-branch, which is not further explored. Therefore, we think it is impossible to construct a proper proof witness from that set without exchanging the abstract domain considered during the analysis. Since we plan to build a proof witness that refers to a product of the partial, complementary analyses, the characterization of a set of ARGs must take those ARG paths into account that are not further explored.

The following definition formally introduces *ARG paths* and so called *incomplete ARG paths* which end in a node that is not fully explored. An ARG path is simply a sequence of ARG nodes that are connected by edges s.t. the first node is the root node. Since we are only interested in partial ARGs, we utilize their partial soundness property and say that an ARG path is incomplete if it ends in a node that has an abstract successor but no leaving ARG edges.

Definition 4. *Let* $R_{\mathbb{A}}^P = (N, G_{\mathrm{ARG}}, root)$ *be an abstract reachability graph for program* $P = (L, G_{\mathrm{CFA}}, l_0, L_{\mathrm{err}})$. *A sequence* $n_0 n_1 \ldots n_m \in N^+$ *is a path in the ARG* $R_{\mathbb{A}}^P$ *if* $n_0 = root$ *and* $\forall 1 \leq i \leq m \exists (n_i, \cdot, n_{i+1}) \in G_{\mathrm{ARG}}$. *An ARG path* $n_0 n_1 \ldots n_m$ *is incomplete if* $\exists (n_m, g, \cdot) \in \leadsto_{\mathbb{A}} : g \in G_{\mathrm{CFA}} \wedge \neg \exists (n_m, g, \cdot) \in G_{\mathrm{ARG}}$.

Incomplete ARG paths indicate that the analysis that generated the ARG may missed program execution paths, namely those having a prefix that considers the same sequence of CFA edges as an incomplete ARG path. To ensure that no program behavior is missed, another ARG must take such program execution paths into account. Avoiding to reason on the concrete level, the idea is to relate ARG paths of different ARGs when they refer to the same sequence of control-flow edges. To account for different maturity in infeasibility detection—another analysis might never explore a related ARG path because it already detects that a subpath of the incomplete path is infeasible—, we introduce the concept of a related, *syntactical subpath*.

Definition 5. *Let* $R_{\mathbb{A}}^P = (N, G_{\text{ARG}}, root)$, $R_{\mathbb{A}'}^P = (N', G'_{\text{ARG}}, root')$ *be two ARGs for program* $P = (L, G_{\text{CFA}}, l_0, L_{\text{err}})$ *and* $p := n_0 n_1 \ldots n_m$ *and* $p' := n'_0 n'_1 \ldots n'_{m'}$ *be two paths in* $R_{\mathbb{A}}^P$ *and* $R_{\mathbb{A}'}^P$, *respectively. ARG path* p' *is a syntactical subpath of ARG path* p *if* $m' = 0$ *or a sequence of control-flow edges* $g_1 g_2 \ldots g_{m'} \in G_{\text{CFA}}^+$ *exists s.t.* $\forall 1 \leq i \leq m' : (n_{i-1}, g_i, n_i) \in G_{\text{ARG}} \wedge (n'_{i-1}, g_i, n'_i) \in G'_{\text{ARG}}$.

The previous definition now let us relate paths in different ARGs. To ensure that a set of partial, complementary analyses does not miss any program execution paths, for incomplete paths there must exist related paths in other ARGs which are not incomplete. We already discussed that sometimes only related subpaths exist. Furthermore, it is not sufficient that for an incomplete path a single related ARG path exists. A transfer relation may use more than one successor to cover the concrete successors. Multiple related ARG (sub)paths might cover the execution paths considered by an incomplete path. Putting all together, we require that for any incomplete ARG path p, there exists another ARG s.t. all ARG paths p' which are syntactical subpaths are not incomplete. Now, the properties of partial ARGs and CPAs should ensure that a set of partial ARGs fulfilling the previous requirement does not miss any program execution. We call a set of partial ARGs fulfilling the previous requirement complete.

Definition 6. *A set* $\mathcal{R}^P = \{R_{\mathbb{A}_1}^P, \ldots, R_{\mathbb{A}_k}^P\}$ *of partial ARGs for program P is complete if for any incomplete path* $p := n_0 n_1 \ldots n_m$ *of a partial ARG* $R_{\mathbb{A}_i}^P \in \mathcal{R}^P$ *there exists an ARG* $R_{\mathbb{A}_j}^P \in \mathcal{R}^P$ *s.t. all paths* $p' := n'_0 n'_1 \ldots n'_{m'}$ *of partial ARG* $R_{\mathbb{A}_j}^P$ *that are syntactical subpaths of p are not incomplete.*

A complete set of partial ARGs is e.g. computed by the software analysis tool CPACHECKER [4] when successfully applying conditional model checking (CMC) [2]. To construct a proof witness from such a complete set of partial ARGS, we need to be sure that this complete set of partial ARGs ensures program safety. The following theorem states this property.

Theorem 2. *A complete set of partial ARGs ensures program safety.*

Proof (Sketch). Let $\mathcal{R}^P = \{R_{\mathbb{A}_1}^P, \ldots, R_{\mathbb{A}_k}^P\}$ be a set of partial ARGs for program $P = (L, G_{\text{CFA}}, l_0, L_{\text{err}})$ and $p := c_0 \xrightarrow{g_1} \ldots c_{n-1} \xrightarrow{g_m} c_m \in paths_P$ be an arbitrary program execution. We need to show that $c_m(pc) \notin L'_{\mathrm{err}}$. First, we define for all $0 \leq i \leq m$ the set $\mathcal{N}_i := \{n_i \mid \exists R_{\mathbb{A}}^P = (N, G_{\mathrm{ARG}}, root) \in \mathcal{R}^P :$ $n_0 \dots n_i$ is an ARG path in $R_{\mathbb{A}}^P \wedge \forall 1 \leq j \leq i : (n_{i-1}, g_i, n_i) \in G_{\mathrm{ARG}}\}$. Now, show by induction that for all $0 \leq i \leq m$ there exists a $n \in \mathcal{N}_i$ with $c_i \in [\![n]\!]$. By induction, there exists $n \in \mathcal{N}_m$ with $c_m \in [\![n]\!]$. By definition, there exists a partial ARG $R_{\mathbb{A}}^P = (N, G_{\mathrm{ARG}}, root) \in \mathcal{R}^P$ with $n \in N$. Due to safety of $R_{\mathbb{A}}^P$, we conclude that $c_m(pc) \notin L_{\mathrm{err}}$.

4   Proof Witnesses from Complete Sets of Partial ARGs

Now, we describe our technique $\mathrm{PART_{PW}}$ and prove it sound. Given a complete set of partial ARGs, we want to construct a proof witness. More concrete, the proof witness should look like as if it was constructed by the product analysis obtained when combining all partial analysis. We start with the definition of the *product CPA* from a set of CPAs. In principle, it is a standard product construction with a product abstract domain and a product transfer relation. The merge is performed element-wise with the help of the respective component CPAs and the termination check returns true if all component stop operators agree that a state is covered by an already explored state.

Definition 7. *Let $\mathcal{A} = \{\mathbb{A}_1, \dots, \mathbb{A}_k\}$ be a set of CPAs. The product CPA $\mathbb{A}_\times = (\mathcal{E}_\times, \leadsto_\times, \mathrm{merge}_\times, \mathrm{stop}_\times)$ from $\mathcal{A}$ is a CPA which consists of*

- *the product abstract domain $D_\times = (C, \mathcal{E}_\times, [\![\cdot]\!])$ with product lattice $\mathcal{E}_\times = (E_\times, \top_\times, \bot_\times, \sqcup_\times, \sqcap_\times)$, element-wise defining $\top_\times, \bot_\times, \sqcup_\times, \sqcap_\times$, and concretization $[\![(e_1, \dots, e_k)]\!] = \bigcap\limits_{1 \leq i \leq k} [\![e_i]\!]_{\mathbb{A}_i}$,*
- *the product transfer relation $\leadsto_\times$, i.e., $((e_1, \dots, e_k), g, (e'_1, \dots, e'_k)) \leadsto_\times \Longleftrightarrow$ $\forall 1 \leq i \leq k : (e_i, g, e'_i) \in \leadsto_{\mathbb{A}_i}$,*
- *$\mathrm{merge}_\times((e_1, \dots, e_k, e'_1, \dots, e'_k) := (\mathrm{merge}_{\mathbb{A}_1}(e_1, e'_1), \dots, \mathrm{merge}_{\mathbb{A}_k}(e_k, e'_k))$, and*
- *$\mathrm{stop}_\times((e_1, \dots, e_k), S) := \exists (e'_1, \dots, e'_k) \in S : \bigwedge\limits_{1 \leq i \leq k} \mathrm{stop}_{\mathbb{A}_i}(e_i, \{e'_i\})$.*

The previous definition describes the CPA considered by the derived proof witness. Next, we explain how to derive the proof witness from a complete set of partial ARGs. The underlying idea of the construction is to combine related ARG paths. However, we stop a combination as soon as one analysis detects infeasibility of the path. Furthermore, during combination incomplete paths are extended with a suffix of top states. Thus, the ARG constructed from a complete set of ARGs starts in the product of the root nodes. The set of ARG nodes is the union of all nodes reachable on combined related paths. The reachability is defined inductively and takes the following two observations on partial ARGs into account: (1) Partial soundness guarantees us that the final node n_m of an incomplete path $n_0 \dots n_m$ has no ARG successors. (2) Safety implies that the top state is no ARG node. Furthermore, an ARG edge labeled with control-flow edge g is introduced between two nodes if in each partial ARG either a respective ARG edge with label g exists or an incomplete path is extended (second case).

Definition 8. *Let* $\mathcal{R}^P = \{R^P_{\mathbb{A}_1}, \ldots, R^P_{\mathbb{A}_k}\}$ *be a complete set of partial ARGs for program P. An ARG from the complete set* $\mathcal{R}^P$ *of partial ARGs is an ARG* $R^P_{\mathbb{A}_\times} = (N, G_{ARG}, root)$ *for program P and product CPA from* $\{\mathbb{A}_1, \ldots, \mathbb{A}_k\}$ *with*

- $root := root_1 \times \cdots \times root_k$
- $N := \bigcup_{i=0}^{\infty} N_i$, *where*
  - $N_0 = \{root\}$ *and*
  - $N_{i+1} = \{(n'_1, \ldots, n'_k) \in N^1 \cup \{\top_1\} \times \cdots \times N^k \cup \{\top_k\} \mid \exists(n_1, \ldots, n_k) \in N_i, g \in G_{CFA} : \forall 0 \leq j \leq k : \exists(n_j, g, \cdot) \in \leadsto_j \wedge ((n_j, g, n'_j) \in G^j_{ARG} \vee \neg\exists(n_j, g, \cdot) \in G^j_{ARG} \wedge n'_j = \top_j)\}$
- $G_{ARG} := \{((n_1, \ldots, n_k), g, (n'_1, \ldots, n'_k)) \in N \times G_{CFA} \times N \mid \forall 1 \leq j \leq m : (n_j, g, n'_j) \in G^j_{ARG} \vee \neg\exists(n_j, g, \cdot) \in G^j_{ARG} \wedge n'_j = \top_j\}$

Figure 3 shows the ARG constructed from the two partial ARGs shown in Fig. 2. Until the beginning of the if- and else-branch, the ARG combines the states of the two partial ARGs. Since the if-branch of program **bonus** is only explored by the predicate analysis, during the if-branch the ARG uses the top state for the value analysis state. Similarly, the else-branch is only explored by the value analysis and in the else-branch the ARG uses the top state for the predicate analysis. We observe that the combined ARG never considers an error state, its root node contains all states considering the initial program location ℓ_0, and for every node the transfer successors are covered by the ARG successors. Thus, the constructed ARG fulfills all properties of a proof witness.

Generally, our goal is to construct proof witnesses. By construction, an ARG from the complete set $\mathcal{R}^P$ of partial ARGs is an ARG for program P and the product CPA. It remains to show the three properties of a proof witness. To prove the safety property, the top state must not be part of the nodes of the constructed ARG. The following lemma claims this property.

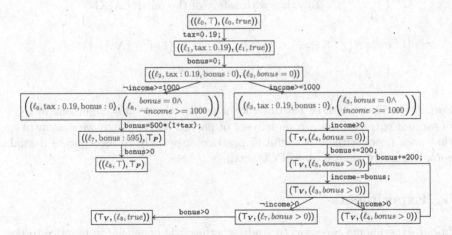

Fig. 3. Combination of the partial ARGs from Fig. 2, which were obtained by complementary partial value analysis and partial predicate analysis on program **bonus**

Lemma 1. *Let $R_{\mathbb{A}_\times}^P = (N, G_{\text{ARG}}, root)$ be an ARG from a complete set of partial ARGs $\{R_{\mathbb{A}_1}^P, \ldots, R_{\mathbb{A}_k}^P\}$. Then, $\top_{\mathbb{A}_\times} \notin N$.*

Proof (Idea). Show by induction that $\forall i \in \mathbb{N}_0 : \neg \exists \top_{\mathbb{A}_\times} = (\top_1, \ldots, \top_k) \in N_i$.

Next, we prove that an ARG from a complete set of partial ARGs is a proof witness. To that end, we show that the constructed ARG fulfills the three proeprties rootedness, soundness, and safety, which mainly follow from the construction of the ARG, the properties of the partial ARGs, and the previous lemma.

Theorem 3. *An ARG from a complete set of partial ARGs is a proof witness.*

Proof. We need to prove rootedness, soundness, and safety.

Rootedness. By definition and rootedness of partial ARGs,

$$\{c \in C \mid c(pc) = l_0\} = \bigcap_{1 \le i \le k} \{c \in C \mid c(pc) = l_0\} \subseteq \bigcap_{1 \le i \le k} [\![root_i]\!]_{\mathbb{A}_i} = [\![root]\!]_{\mathbb{A}_\times}$$

Soundness. Let $n = (n_1, \ldots, n_k) \in N$ and $g \in G_{\text{CFA}}$ be arbitrary s.t. there exists $(n, g, \cdot) \in \leadsto_{\mathbb{A}_\times}$. Consider arbitrary $(n, g, n_s) \in \leadsto_{\mathbb{A}_\times}$ and let $n_s = (n_1^s, \ldots, n_k^s)$. We need to show $\mathsf{stop}_{\mathbb{A}_\times}(n_s, \{(n, g, n') \in G_{\text{ARG}}\})$. By definition of N, G_{ARG}, $\leadsto_{\mathbb{A}_\times}$, requirements on termination check, and partial soundness, there exists $(n, g, (n_1^r, \ldots, n_k^r)) \in G_{\text{ARG}}$ with $n_i^r = \top_i$ or $\mathsf{stop}_{\mathbb{A}_i}(n_i, g, n_i^r)$ for all $1 \le i \le k$. Since $\mathsf{stop}_{\mathbb{A}_i}$ detects coverage by the top state, for all $1 \le i \le k$, we get $\mathsf{stop}_{\mathbb{A}_i}(n^i, g, n_r^i)$. From definition of $\mathsf{stop}_{\mathbb{A}_\times}$, we conclude $\mathsf{stop}_{\mathbb{A}_\times}(n_s, \{(n, g, n') \in G_{\text{ARG}}\})$. Every ARG from a complete set of partial ARGs is sound.

Safety. Due to Lemma 1 and definition of N, for every $(n_1, \ldots, n_k) \in N$ there exists an index $i \in \{1, \ldots, k\}$ s.t. $n_i \in N^i$ and $[\![(n_1, \ldots, n_k)]\!]_{\mathbb{A}_\times} \subseteq [\![n_i]\!]_{\mathbb{A}_i}$. Thus, $[\![N]\!]_{\mathbb{A}_\times} \subseteq \bigcup_{1 \le i \le k} [\![N^i]\!]_{\mathbb{A}_i}$. Together with safety of the partial ARGs,

$$\{l \mid c \in [\![N]\!]_{\mathbb{A}_\times} \wedge c(pc) = l\} \cap L_{\text{err}} \subseteq (\bigcup_{1 \le i \le k} \{l \mid c \in [\![N^i]\!]_{\mathbb{A}_i}\}) \cap L_{\text{err}}$$
$$= \bigcup_{1 \le i \le k} (\{l \mid c \in [\![N^i]\!]_{\mathbb{A}_i}\} \cap L_{\text{err}}) = \bigcup_{1 \le i \le k} \emptyset = \emptyset$$

So far, we discussed how to construct a proper correctness argument in form of a proof witness from a complete set of partial ARGs. Next, we demonstrate that such proof witness is useful in practice, especially to incorporate partial, complementary analyses into PCC settings.

5   Experiments

In our experiments, we want to study whether it is beneficial in practice to use such a generated proof witness. Therefore, we implemented the proof witness generation in CPACHECKER [4] and used it with three different PCC approaches already implemented in CPACHECKER. We consider the ARG approach, which is similar to the approach of Henzinger et al. [14] and checks the three conditions on a proof witness. Furthermore, we use configurable program certification (CC) [16] and its optimization (CC+) [15]. Additionally, we compare PCC with proof witness generation against checking whether a certificate is a complete set of partial ARGs. Our implementation of the latter check, named $c\mathcal{R}$, validates that the certificate consists of partial ARGs and uses the CMC condition to check that an ARG of a subsequent analysis only excludes already checked paths.

In our experiments, we use CMC [2] to compute a complete set of partial ARGs. We use six different combinations of analyses. All start with a value analysis [6]. After a time limit expired[5] or the value analysis gave up, the combined analyses continue either with a predicate [5] or an octagon analysis [17]. The first four combinations use a value and predicate analyses. The value analysis either always tracks all variable values or uses interpolation based refinement [6] to determine which variables to track. The predicate analysis applies adjustable block encoding (ABE) [5] with counterexample-guided abstraction refinement and either abstracts only at loops (standard configuration) or at loops and all locations where control-flow merges (assumed to be simpler for certificate validation). The remaining two combinations incorporate a value with an octagon analysis. One combination always tracks all program variables. The other uses interpolation based refinement to determine which variables to track in the value and octagon analysis, respectively.

For our evaluation, we used a subset of the 2017th SV COMP[6] category ReachSafety. Each combination is evaluated on those programs for which (1) the property is known to be true, (2) the combined analysis succeeded and (3) was more efficient than each of the two analyses alone, i.e., in both cases the combination was faster than the single analysis or the single analysis failed. In total, we got 33 verification tasks. For 19 of them only the combination of analyses is successful within a time limit of 15 min.

We run our experiments within BenchExec [7] on an Intel® Xeon E3-1230 v5 @ 3.40 GHz and OpenJDK 64-Bit Server VM 1.8.0_121 restricting each task to 5 of 33 GB. To re-execute our experiments, start the extension of BenchExec bundled with CPACHECKER[7] with CMC+PCC.xml.

Table 1 shows the result of our experiments. For each task, it provides the time and memory consumption of the verification, the time for generating the proof witness, as well as the time and memory consumption of the validation of the four certificates. Times are given in seconds and memory consumption, used heap plus non-heap, in MB. Programs for which verification only succeeds for the combined analyses are marked with an asterix. Additionally, for each task we highlight the smallest time and memory consumption.

---

[5] We reuse the time limits from the SV-COMP configurations, 10 s when no refinement is used and 60 s in case of refinement.

[6] https://sv-comp.sosy-lab.org/2017/.

[7] https://svn.sosy-lab.org/software/cpachecker/trunk/ rv 24625.

Table 1. For each of the verification tasks, execution time (s) and memory consumption (MB) of the verification and the validation of each PCC approach plus the generation time (s) of the proof witness

Program	V	M	Gen	V_{ARG}	M_{ARG}	V_{CC}	M_{CC}	$V_{\mathrm{CC+}}$	$M_{\mathrm{CC+}}$	$V_{c\mathcal{R}}$	$M_{c\mathcal{R}}$
Value analysis with refinement + predicate analysis (loops)											
nested.i	67.15	1767	0.06	**8.46**	*328*	360.59	2720	357.03	3162	9.82	347
matrix.c	1.53	159	0.01	**0.82**	159	0.88	147	**0.82**	*139*	1.19	154
pals_flood	49.13	1095	0.57	38.71	957	81.86	1258	79.29	1444	**32.42**	*926*
pals_lcr	24.40	721	0.09	7.81	*286*	10.37	324	9.57	332	**7.76**	331
bonus*	0.82	159	0.01	0.16	146	**0.12**	*141*	0.18	156	0.60	156
Value analysis with refinement + predicate analysis (loops & join)											
matrix.c	2.34	160	0.01	**0.91**	148	1.07	156	1.06	*146*	1.25	157
matrix.i	2.40	161	0.01	**0.90**	160	1.08	*147*	1.03	154	1.26	157
bonus*	0.81	158	0.01	0.18	158	**0.16**	158	0.17	*149*	0.59	150
Value analysis + predicate analysis (loops)											
fabs*	1.59	161	0.08	0.57	*156*	0.44	158	**0.41**	161	1.33	162
nested.i	76.13	1470	0.06	**8.77**	*328*	431.31	2873	384.81	1775	9.98	337
pals_START	**5.24**	*293*	0.10	9.15	394	9.93	400	9.80	415	8.23	437
pals_lcr	28.30	944	0.06	8.34	*332*	9.27	500	9.13	458	**8.00**	339
bonus*	0.66	154	0.01	0.17	158	0.17	143	**0.16**	*137*	0.60	156
Value analysis + predicate analysis (loops & join)											
filter2	112.37	954	0.02	31.83	606	50.62	990	57.48	1058	**31.96**	*521*
fabs*	1.40	*149*	0.06	0.55	150	0.47	159	**0.33**	152	1.20	161
matrix.c	5.48	161	0.01	0.96	*149*	1.01	*149*	**0.91**	157	1.29	155
matrix.i	5.36	162	0.01	**0.98**	*152*	1.11	160	0.99	160	1.24	157
bonus*	0.77	156	0.01	**0.16**	*141*	0.21	159	0.22	158	0.59	151
Value analysis + octagon analysis											
soft_float2*	1.10	159	0.07	0.42	159	0.27	159	**0.12**	*158*	1.15	161
soft_float3*	1.23	161	0.06	0.46	160	0.23	159	**0.17**	*157*	1.32	160
soft_float5*	1.27	159	0.11	0.34	159	0.28	160	**0.16**	*158*	1.32	160
rounding1*	1.18	162	0.06	0.45	161	0.16	*156*	**0.13**	159	1.33	161
float21*	1.22	*149*	0.06	0.44	151	0.34	153	**0.14**	160	1.21	158
Value analysis with refinement + octagon analysis with refinement											
soft_float2*	1.98	165	0.12	0.33	160	0.17	160	**0.15**	*156*	1.09	157
soft_float3*	2.19	188	0.17	0.30	160	0.29	157	**0.11**	*155*	1.43	160
Prob16_l59	148.17	4007	8.71	44.89	2608	272.80	2073	**11.10**	*695*	153.86	4139
rounding1*	1.46	162	0.09	0.43	153	0.26	153	**0.12**	*152*	1.26	161
gr2006*	124.76	3525	0.11	0.68	161	0.75	161	**0.28**	*158*	5.22	342
floppy2*	14.72	1247	1.36	3.23	*351*	**3.12**	357	OOM		6.96	666
floppy*	7.99	440	0.55	**1.52**	165	1.57	*161*	227.14	4601	3.67	300
parport*	16.43	1159	0.67	4.13	*315*	**4.12**	*315*	5.29	320	6.59	422
toy*	73.90	4038	0.24	0.28	160	**0.22**	*160*	OOM		51.54	2456

Looking at Table 1, we make the following observations. With less than 10% of the verification time, proof witness generation impose little overhead. Considering the best time and memory, verification is faster in one case and requires less memory in two additional cases. Although the best PCC approach for time and memory consumption depends on the verification task, in all other cases, at least one of the three PCC approaches is faster and requires less memory than verification. Finally, the validation of the complete set of partial ARGs (cR) rarely dominates all other PCC approaches, which use the generated proof witness. In most of the cases, it does not even dominate the ARG approach, which validates the generated proof witness and is closest to the cR idea. In contrast, the cR approach is often already dominated by the ARG approach. A similar observation can be made for the sizes of the certificates, which we omitted due to lack of space. Summing up, it is a good idea to combine our PART$_{PW}$ technique with a standard technique when constructing correctness arguments for partial, complementary analyses.

6   Conclusion

After a successful verification with a set of partial, complementary analyses, our technique PART$_{PW}$ uses the incomplete state space explorations, in form of partial ARGs, to build a proof witness which could have been constructed when using a product of the partial analyses. The underlying idea of the proof witness construction is to combine those paths in the different ARGs that are related. We proved that the constructed proof witness attests program safety. Additionally, our experiments show that PCC should be combined with proof witness generation to get correctness arguments for partial, complementary analyses.

Related Work. Garavel et al. [12] describe a distributive explicit state space construction of a LTS. After distributive construction, the transitions explored by the different compute nodes are united. In contrast, we combine partial abstract state spaces, which may consider different domains, w.r.t. same program paths. Hamid and Shao [13] combine a program certified with the type system XTAL with system code certified in the logic CAP to get a certified machine package. To integrate the different proofs, the XTAL certificate is translated into CAP. The open framework [11] generalizes the previous idea to arbitrary certificate specifications. An interpretation of the specification maps the specification into the logic OCAP. Dong et al. [10] present a logic for intermediate representation with a built-in support for modular certification. It provides two rules to integrate already certified modules in the certification of a program. While these approaches consider logic proofs, we focus on state space descriptions.

Acknowledgements. This work was partially supported by the German Research Foundation (DFG) within the Collaborative Research Centre "On-The-Fly Computing" (SFB 901). The experiments were run in the VerifierCloud hosted by Dirk Beyer and his group.

References

1. Beyer, D., Chlipala, A.J., Henzinger, T.A., Jhala, R., Majumdar, R.: The BLAST query language for software verification. In: Giacobazzi, R. (ed.) SAS 2004. LNCS, vol. 3148, pp. 2–18. Springer, Heidelberg (2004). doi:10.1007/978-3-540-27864-1_2
2. Beyer, D., Henzinger, T.A., Keremoglu, M.E., Wendler, P.: Conditional model checking: A technique to pass information between verifiers. In: FSE, pp. 57:1–57:11. ACM (2012). doi:10.1145/2393596.2393664
3. Beyer, D., Henzinger, T.A., Théoduloz, G.: Configurable software verification: concretizing the convergence of model checking and program analysis. In: Damm, W., Hermanns, H. (eds.) CAV 2007. LNCS, vol. 4590, pp. 504–518. Springer, Heidelberg (2007). doi:10.1007/978-3-540-73368-3_51
4. Beyer, D., Keremoglu, M.E.: CPACHECKER: A tool for configurable software verification. In: Gopalakrishnan, G., Qadeer, S. (eds.) CAV 2011. LNCS, vol. 6806, pp. 184–190. Springer, Heidelberg (2011). doi:10.1007/978-3-642-22110-1_16
5. Beyer, D., Keremoglu, M.E., Wendler, P.: Predicate abstraction with adjustable-block encoding. In: FMCAD, pp. 189–198. FMCAD Inc. (2010)
6. Beyer, D., Löwe, S.: Explicit-state software model checking based on CEGAR and interpolation. In: Cortellessa, V., Varró, D. (eds.) FASE 2013. LNCS, vol. 7793, pp. 146–162. Springer, Heidelberg (2013). doi:10.1007/978-3-642-37057-1_11
7. Beyer, D., Löwe, S., Wendler, P.: Benchmarking and resource measurement. In: Fischer, B., Geldenhuys, J. (eds.) SPIN 2015. LNCS, vol. 9232, pp. 160–178. Springer, Cham (2015). doi:10.1007/978-3-319-23404-5_12
8. Chaieb, A.: Proof-producing program analysis. In: Barkaoui, K., Cavalcanti, A., Cerone, A. (eds.) ICTAC 2006. LNCS, vol. 4281, pp. 287–301. Springer, Heidelberg (2006). doi:10.1007/11921240_20
9. Cousot, P., Cousot, R.: Abstract interpretation: a unified lattice model for static analysis of programs by construction or approximation of fixpoints. In: POPL, pp. 238–252. ACM (1977). doi:10.1145/512950.512973
10. Dong, Y., Wang, S., Zhang, L., Yang, P.: Modular certification of low-level intermediate representation programs. In: COMPSAC, pp. 563–570. IEEE (2009). doi:10.1109/COMPSAC.2009.81
11. Feng, X., Ni, Z., Shao, Z., Guo, Y.: An open framework for foundational proof-carrying code. In: TLDI, pp. 67–78. ACM (2007). doi:10.1145/1190315.1190325
12. Garavel, H., Mateescu, R., Smarandache, I.: Parallel state space construction for model-checking. In: Dwyer, M. (ed.) SPIN 2001. LNCS, vol. 2057, pp. 217–234. Springer, Heidelberg (2001). doi:10.1007/3-540-45139-0_14
13. Hamid, N.A., Shao, Z.: Interfacing hoare logic and type systems for foundational proof-carrying code. In: Slind, K., Bunker, A., Gopalakrishnan, G. (eds.) TPHOLs 2004. LNCS, vol. 3223, pp. 118–135. Springer, Heidelberg (2004). doi:10.1007/978-3-540-30142-4_10
14. Henzinger, T.A., Jhala, R., Majumdar, R., Sanvido, M.A.A.: Extreme model checking. In: Dershowitz, N. (ed.) Verification: Theory and Practice. LNCS, vol. 2772, pp. 332–358. Springer, Heidelberg (2003). doi:10.1007/978-3-540-39910-0_16
15. Jakobs, M.-C.: Speed up configurable certificate validation by certificate reduction and partitioning. In: Calinescu, R., Rumpe, B. (eds.) SEFM 2015. LNCS, vol. 9276, pp. 159–174. Springer, Cham (2015). doi:10.1007/978-3-319-22969-0_12
16. Jakobs, M.C., Wehrheim, H.: Certification for configurable program analysis. In: SPIN, pp. 30–39. ACM (2014). doi:10.1145/2632362.2632372

17. Jeannet, B., Miné, A.: APRON: A library of numerical abstract domains for static analysis. In: Bouajjani, A., Maler, O. (eds.) CAV 2009. LNCS, vol. 5643, pp. 661–667. Springer, Heidelberg (2009). doi:10.1007/978-3-642-02658-4_52
18. Jhala, R., Majumdar, R.: Software model checking. ACM Comput. Surv. **41**(4), 21:1–21:54 (2009). doi:10.1145/1592434.1592438
19. Necula, G.C.: Proof-carrying code. In: POPL, pp. 106–119. ACM (1997). doi:10.1145/263699.263712
20. Nielson, F., Nielson, H.R., Hankin, C.: Principles of Program Analysis, 1st edn. Springer, Heidelberg (2005). Corr. 2. print. edn
21. Rose, E.: Lightweight bytecode verification. J. Autom. Reasoning **31**(3), 303–334 (2003). doi:10.1023/B:JARS.0000021015.15794.82
22. Seo, S., Yang, H., Yi, K.: Automatic construction of hoare proofs from abstract interpretation results. In: Ohori, A. (ed.) APLAS 2003. LNCS, vol. 2895, pp. 230–245. Springer, Heidelberg (2003). doi:10.1007/978-3-540-40018-9_16

Specification and Automated Verification of Dynamic Dataflow Networks

Jonatan Wiik$^{(\boxtimes)}$ and Pontus Boström

Faculty of Science and Engineering, Åbo Akademi University, Turku, Finland
{jonatan.wiik,pontus.bostrom}@abo.fi

Abstract. Dataflow programming has received much recent attention within the signal processing domain as an efficient paradigm for exploiting parallelism. In dataflow programming, systems are modelled as a static network of actors connected through asynchronous order-preserving channels. In this paper we present an approach to contract-based specification and automated verification of dynamic dataflow networks. The verification technique is based on encoding the dataflow networks and contracts in the guarded command language Boogie.

1 Introduction

Modern software systems are increasingly concurrent, as the computing power of modern CPUs is improved mainly by increasing the number of processor cores. At the same time, modern computer platforms are also increasingly parallel, distributed and heterogenous, often involving special processing units, such as GPUs or DSPs for performing specific tasks efficiently. Writing software that effectively exploit the capacity of such platforms is hard. The dataflow paradigm has been proposed as a possible solution to this problem and has received a large amount of attention within the signal processing domain.

A dataflow program consists of a static network of actors. Actors are stateful operators communicating exclusively via asynchronous unidirectional order-preserving channels. Actors evolve concurrently and each actor can execute when the required data is available on the incoming channels. As actors communicate only over channels, computations can easily be mapped to processing units.

In this paper, we present a hierarchical and modular approach to contract-based specification and automated verification of dataflow actors and networks based on assume-guarantee reasoning. We present a novel contract notation for actors and networks. The contracts state functional properties, which the actor or network should adhere to. The goal of the approach is to ensure functional correctness with respect to contracts for actors and networks as well as deadlock freedom for networks. We have also observed that our contracts could be utilised in scheduling. Scheduling methods for dataflow networks, e.g. [4], are based on finding an execution sequence that returns the communication channel

---

The work has been partially funded by the Academy of Finland through the projects Merge (No. 286094) and ADVICeS (No. 266373).

A. Cimatti and M. Sirjani (Eds.): SEFM 2017, LNCS 10469, pp. 136–151, 2017.
DOI: 10.1007/978-3-319-66197-1_9

buffers to the same state. Our contracts explicitly express this state, as well as preconditions on input data, which also could be useful for scheduling.

The verification technique is based on an encoding into the guarded command language Boogie [2]. The Boogie verifier is tightly integrated with the Z3 [6] SMT solver and can thus generate efficient verification conditions. Boogie has also been used as a backend in verifiers for several popular programming languages. Our approach could potentially be integrated in these verifiers to support verification of dataflow actors in other popular languages.

The main contributions of this paper are the following: (1) A method to specify the behaviour of networks based on the reaction of the network to individual tokens. (2) An encoding of actors, networks and their specifications into a guarded command language. (3) A method to automatically generate invariants needed for verification of a common type of actors.

The work presented in this paper acts as a generalisation of previous work [3] by the authors on verification of Simulink models. There, Simulink models are translated to synchronous dataflow (SDF) [10,12] networks for verification. SDF is a subset of the dataflow programs considered here. In dynamic dataflow, as opposed to SDF, the number of tokens produced and/or consumed by an actor can be dynamic and depend on the value of current as well as previously consumed tokens. This significantly complicates the verification task.

The remainder of the paper is structured as follows: We introduce the considered dataflow actors and networks in Sect. 2 and then informally describe our verification technique in Sect. 3. In Sect. 4 we describe the actor and assertion languages. We then describe the encoding of assertions, actors and networks into a guarded command language in Sect. 5. In Sect. 6 we describe our invariant generation method. We then discuss soundness in Sect. 7 before presenting an evaluation of the approach on a number of examples in Sect. 8. We then proceed to related work and conclusions in Sects. 9 and 10.

2   Dataflow Actors and Networks

The dataflow programs considered in this paper consist of static hierarchical networks of actors, which are connected via asynchronous unidirectional order-preserving channels. An actor is a stateful operator consisting of a set of inports, a set of outports, a set of state variables and a set of actions. An actor performs computations by firing enabled actions. An action is enabled or disabled based on the amount and value of input tokens, and the actor state. When an action fires, it consumes tokens on the inports, updates the actor state, and produces tokens on the outports. An action hence describes the reaction of the actor to a sequence of input tokens. The amount of tokens consumed or produced on a port is called rate. An actor that consumes and produces the same amount of tokens each time it fires is considered to have static rate.

We use a language similar to the CAL actor language [7] to describe our actors and networks. More precisely, our language is a subset of the RVC-CAL [14] language, extended with some specification constructs. Some basic examples

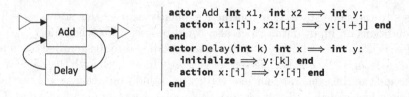

```
actor Add int x1, int x2 ⟹ int y:
  action x1:[i], x2:[j] ⟹ y:[i+j] end
end
actor Delay(int k) int x ⟹ int y:
  initialize ⟹ y:[k] end
  action x:[i] ⟹ y:[i] end
end
```

Fig. 1. Examples of two basic actors and a network formed from these actors.

are given in Fig. 1. The actor Add has two inports, x1 and x2, and one outport y. The actor has one action with the pattern x1:[i], x2:[j] ⟹ y:[i+j], which specifies that the action reads 1 token from each inport and outputs the sum of the read tokens on the outport. The actor Delay in Fig. 1 delays the data on its input channel with one token. The delay is implemented with a special initialisation action, declared with keyword **initialize**, outputting an initial token on the outport. Initialisation actions are only run once, when the actor is initialised and are not allowed to consume input. In the example, the value of the initial token is given as a parameter to the actor.

It is noteworthy that CAL allows non-determinism, as multiple actions can be enabled on the same input. However, in this work we require that actors and networks are deterministic. This is ensured by checking that firing rules are mutually exclusive.

Instances of actors are connected to form networks. The graph in Fig. 1 illustrates a network computing the accumulated sum of its input. It consists of one instance of Add and one instance of Delay. The goal of the work presented in this paper is to specify actors and networks like those given in Fig. 1 and to verify them using contracts. We verify functional correctness with respect to contracts and deadlock freedom of networks. Note that, for instance, the network in Fig. 1 would deadlock without the initialisation action of the Delay actor.

3   Verification Technique

In this section we informally describe our specifications and our verification technique. The channels of a dataflow network can be described as streams of data. A channel c is then a stream $\langle c_0, c_1, \ldots \rangle$, where each c_i is a data token. Actors can then be considered as operators on streams. Our specifications are contracts consisting of preconditions and postconditions for actors and networks. Networks and actors are modularly verified to conform to their contracts.

3.1   Networks

We describe networks using a syntax which resembles the syntax used to describe basic actors. This differs from RVC-CAL, which uses a graphical language to describe networks. The languages are, however, semantically equivalent.

```
network SumNet int in ⟹ int out:
  contract in:1 ⟹ out:1
    requires 0 ≤ in[•]
    ensures out[0] = in[0] ∧ in[•] ≤ out[•]
    ensures 0 < •(out) ⟹ out[•] = out[• − 1] + in[•]
  end
  invariant tokens(b,1)
  chinvariant b[0] = 0 ∧ 0 ≤ b[•]
  entities add = Add(); del = Delay(0); end
  structure
    a: in ⟶ add.in1;   b: del.out ⟶ add.in2;
    c: add.out ⟶ out;  d: add.out ⟶ del.in;
  end
end
```

Fig. 2. The source code with contract of a network for calculating the accumulated sum of the input tokens.

Our network syntax includes an **entities** block, which declares the actor instances in the network, and a **structure** block, which describes the interconnection of the actor instances. For an example, consider the network SumNet given in Fig. 2, which is the source code of the network illustrated in Fig. 1. The **entities** block defines the actor instances add and del. In the **structure** block, the channels interconnecting these actor instances are defined. For instance, the port in1 of actor add is connected to the network inport in. The channels are given labels a, b, c and d, which can be used to refer to the channels in specifications. The instances specified in the **entities** block can themselves be networks. Hence, we allow nested networks.

In addition to the **entities** and **structure** blocks, a network has also several specification constructs. The most central specification construct is the *network contract*, which defines the relationship between input and output tokens of the network. Contracts are similar to actor actions in that they describe the reaction of the network to a finite amount of input tokens. However, contracts are merely used for specification and have no impact on the behaviour.

Definition 1 (Network contract). *A network contract:*

contract $x: n \Longrightarrow y: m$ **guard** G **requires** P **ensures** Q **end**

specifies that, given n input tokens on port x conforming to $G \wedge P$, the network outputs m tokens on port y that conforms to Q.

The difference between guards and preconditions is that a guard determines if the contract is enabled on the input, while a precondition describes valid input. Our verification technique is based on checking that the output streams of the network are composed of finite windows where each window matches a contract. We consider a window of size n for the input stream x, and size m for the output stream y as specified in the contract. For an example, consider the contract of our example SumNet. It specifies that given 1 input token on port in, it will produce 1 output token on port out.

Verifying a network entails checking that the execution of the network satisfies each of the network contracts. A contract as defined in Definition 1 describes the response of the network to a finite input. To ensure that the network does not buffer an infinite amount of tokens on any channel, we require that the amount of tokens on channels between contract windows is fixed. If not explicitly stated otherwise, channels are required to be empty. Essentially, this means that networks are checked to have a periodic behaviour, where the period is described by the contracts.

It is not always desired or possible to have empty channels between contract windows. The network SumNet, for instance, contains a loop and requires that an initial extra token is produced to avoid deadlock. Executing the network for a contract window will then always result in an unread token in this loop. This can be specified in network invariants. Network invariants are declared using the keyword **invariant** and are required to hold between contract windows. In the SumNet example, the invariant **tokens(b,1)** specifies that the network should leave 1 token on the channel b between contract windows. To ensure that other channels are empty, an invariant **tokens(c,0)** is assumed to be defined implicitly for each channel c that is not mentioned explicitly. We have observed that the conditions expressed in our contracts and invariants could be utilised also in scheduling. Scheduling methods for dataflow networks are typically based on finding execution sequences that return the channel buffers to the same state. Such a state is expressed by our **tokens** construct and our contracts specifies an amount of input tokens needed to return buffers to this state.

Network invariants are not required to hold inside contract windows. To track data inside windows we use another type of invariants, which we call channel invariants. The channel invariants, declared with keyword **chinvariant**, need to be preserved by the execution of all actors in the network. For instance, in SumNet, we have a channel invariant $b[0] = 0$, stating that the first token produced on channel b has the value 0. We use indices to refer to stream tokens in assertions. Hence, $c[i]$ refers to the i:th token produced on c.

To write preconditions and postconditions, we want to refer to the tokens produced and consumed during the considered window. This can be done using the function $\bullet(c)$.

Definition 2 (Bullet). $\bullet(c)$ *is the total number of tokens that had been consumed on the channel c before the current contract window.*

Based on the definition of $\bullet$, it is possible to refer to the first token produced on a channel c during the current window using $c[\bullet]$ and to the second token produced using $c[\bullet + 1]$. It is also possible to refer to the last token that was consumed during the previous window using $c[\bullet - 1]$. The offset does not have to be constant. We can also express that a property P holds for the 5 first tokens produced during the action: $\forall$ **int** $i \cdot 0 \leq i \land i < 5 \Rightarrow P(c[\bullet + i])$. The argument to $\bullet$ is left out above, as it is implicit when $\bullet$ is used in the position of an index. Hence, $c[\bullet(c)]$ and $c[\bullet]$ are synonymous.

Consider again the network SumNet. The function $\bullet$ is used in the precondition and postconditions. The precondition $0 \leq in[\bullet]$ states that the input is required to be non-negative. The postcondition $0 < \bullet(\text{out}) \Rightarrow \text{out}[\bullet] = \text{out}[\bullet - 1] + \text{in}[\bullet]$ states that, for any window where $0 < \bullet(\text{out})$, the output should be equal to the previous output plus the current input. The postcondition $\text{out}[0] = \text{in}[0]$ states that the first token produced by the network should be equal to the first input consumed. Additionally, there is also a postcondition stating that the output is always larger than or equal to the input.

Our verification technique is based on an inductive proof. The base step of the inductive proof is checking that the network initialisation establishes the network invariants. The inductive step consists in considering an arbitrary contract window and showing that channels will be returned to the same state, i.e. that the network invariants are preserved. Our approach also guarantees deadlock freedom by ensuring that progress is made from the state described by the network invariants when input specified by the network contract is received.

It should be noted that networks are in practice not executed atomically for a contract window. This means that tokens for the next window can arrive before the preceding window is completed. In Sect. 7 we argue that, despite this, it is sound to verify networks for a contract window in isolation, given that actors are continuous. Essentially, an actor is continuous if it is deterministic.

3.2   Actors

The actors given in Fig. 1 are simple rate-static actors without state and their complete behaviour is described by the action patterns. However, actors can have both state as well as dynamic rates. Consider for instance the actor Sum in Fig. 3. This is a single actor implementing the functionality of the network SumNet in Fig. 2. A state variable sum is used to store the accumulated sum. The action body, starting with keyword **do**, updates the state variable.

For specification, the action of the actor in Fig. 2 has been annotated with a precondition and a postcondition. The precondition requires the input token to be greater than or equal to 0, while the postcondition requires the output, i.e. the state variable sum, to be greater than or equal to the input. To prove that the action satisfies the postcondition, we need to restrict the state variable with an invariant. The invariant $0 \leq \text{sum}$ allows the action to be verified. Actor invariants are required to hold between action firings.

To prove on network level that interconnected actors are compatible, the relationship between input and output of actors can be described using invariants over input and output streams. These invariants can be locally proved and used as assumptions on the network level. In the Sum example, the invariants **tot**$(y) = $ **rd**(x) and $\forall$ **int** j · **every**$(y,j,1) \Rightarrow y[j] = y[j-1] + x[j]$ describe the relationship between tokens on the input stream and the output stream. The functions **tot**(x) and **rd**(x) give the total number of tokens produced and consumed on a stream x at the present moment, respectively. Hence, the first invariant states that the number of tokens produced on stream y is equal to the number of tokens consumed on stream x. In the second invariant, the data

```
actor Sum int x ⟹ int y:
  int sum;
  invariant 0 ≤ sum ∧ tot(y) > 0 ⟹ sum = y[last]
  invariant tot(y) = rd(x) ∧ ∀ int j · every(y,j,1) ⟹ y[j] = y[j−1]+x[j]
  initialize ⟹ do sum := 0; end
  action x:[i] ⟹ y:[sum]
    requires 0 ≤ i
    ensures i ≤ sum
    do sum := sum+i;
  end
end
actor Split int in ⟹ int pos, int neg:
  invariant rd(in) = tot(pos)+tot(neg)
  action in:[i] ⟹ pos:[i] guard 0 ≤ i end
  action in:[i] ⟹ neg:[i] guard i < 0 end
end
```

Fig. 3. The actor Sum is an actor with state. For the actor Split, the number of tokens produced on each output port depends on the value of input tokens.

tokens of the input and output streams are referred to using indices. In the invariant, the construct **every**(y,j,1) is a predicate equal to $1 ≤ j < \mathbf{tot}(y)$. The invariant hence states that every token produced on stream y with an index i of 1 or larger is equal to the previous output plus the input token with index i. The construct y[**last**] denotes the last token produced on the channel y.

Our verification technique can locally check actor invariants and then use them as assumptions in place of channel invariants at the network level. This is possible because every channel in a network has a unique actor reading and a unique actor writing to it. This means that the number of tokens consumed on an input stream x, $\mathbf{rd}(x)$, and the number of tokens produced on an output stream y, $\mathbf{tot}(y)$, can be assumed to not change between actor firings. Note that if an outport is connected to more than one inport, as is the case in Fig. 2, all the connections are considered separate streams. On the other hand, the number of tokens consumed on output streams and the number of tokens produced on input streams is not known locally and cannot be used in assertions that are checked locally. The verifier performs wellformedness checks on assertions to ensure this.

The actor Split in Fig. 3 outputs non-negative input tokens on the outport pos and negative input tokens on the outport neg. When the number of token consumed and/or produced is dependent on the value of input tokens, like in the Split example, it becomes very hard to write invariants that can be locally proved. For actors like this, it is often more feasible to provide the needed properties as channel invariants at the network level instead.

Note that invariants on streams like those described above are also needed for the simple actors in Fig. 1. However, in these cases the verification tool can automatically infer the invariants, as we describe in Sect. 6.

$$
\begin{array}{lll}
Prog & ::= & (ActorDecl \mid NwDecl)^* \\
ActorDecl & ::= & \textbf{actor } id\langle VarDecl^*\rangle \; PortDecl\colon ActorMem^* \textbf{ end} \\
NwDecl & ::= & \textbf{network } id\langle VarDecl^*\rangle \; PortDecl\colon NwMem^* \textbf{ end} \\
PortDecl & ::= & VarDecl^* \Longrightarrow VarDecl^* \\
ActorMem & ::= & VarDecl \mid ActorInv \mid Action \mid InitAction \\
NwMem & ::= & ActorInv \mid ChInv \mid Contract \mid Entities \mid Structure \\
Action & ::= & \textbf{action } (id\colon [id^*])^* \Longrightarrow (id\colon [e^*])^* \; (\textbf{guard } e)^* \; ActSpec \; (\textbf{do } S)^? \textbf{ end} \\
InitAction & ::= & \textbf{initialize } \Longrightarrow (id\colon [e^*])^* \; ActSpec \; (\textbf{do } S)^? \textbf{ end} \\
Contract & ::= & \textbf{contract } (id\colon n)^* \Longrightarrow (id\colon n)^* \; (\textbf{guard } A)^* \; ActSpec \textbf{ end} \\
Entities & ::= & \textbf{entities } (id = id\langle e^*\rangle)^* \textbf{ end} \\
Structure & ::= & \textbf{structure } (id(.id)^? \longrightarrow id(.id)^?)^* \textbf{ end} \\
Inv & ::= & \textbf{invariant } A \\
ChInv & ::= & \textbf{chinvariant } A \\
ActSpec & ::= & (\textbf{requires } A \mid \textbf{ensures } A)^* \\
VarDecl & ::= & type \; id
\end{array}
$$

Fig. 4. Grammar of the actor language.

4 Programming and Assertion Language

In this section we define precisely the language we consider in this paper. The considered language can be split into two parts: the actor language, which is used to describe actors, networks and their interconnection, and the host language, which is used to implement action bodies. The host language we consider is a simple imperative programming language. We also define our assertion language, which is used to express preconditions, postconditions and invariants.

Actor language. The grammar of the actor language is listed in Fig. 4. In the grammar we use $\langle$ and $\rangle$ for concrete parentheses in the language, to differentiate them from the meta-parentheses used to describe the grammar. A program consists of actor and network declarations. In the grammar, S is a statement, A is an assertion, e is an expression, id is an identifier and n is a numeric literal.

Host language. The host language we consider in this paper is a simple imperative programming language without references, which is straight-forward to encode in a verifier. The statement grammar S of the language is given in Fig. 5. Essentially, the language is a small subset of the RVC-CAL host language, consisting of assignments, if statements and while loops. While loops are verified using Hoare logic as in traditional program verification. The expression grammar e is also summarised in Fig. 5. Here $\oplus$ is a binary operator. The host language could easily be extended or substituted with another language which can be encoded in a verifier.

Assertion language. The grammar of the assertion language A is given in Fig. 5. The predicate **tokens** is only allowed as an independent assertion. The reason is that the verifier needs to keep track of channels for which **tokens** has been used; other channels, not mentioned in any **tokens** predicate, are required to be empty between contract windows. Requiring that **tokens** is only used separately

$$S ::= id := e \mid \textbf{if } e \textbf{ then } S_1 \textbf{ else } S_2 \textbf{ end} \mid \textbf{while } e \ (\textbf{invariant } A)^* \textbf{ do } S \textbf{ end}$$
$$A ::= A_1 \wedge A_2 \mid \textbf{tokens}(id, e) \mid e$$
$$e ::= ((\forall \mid \exists) \ (type \ id)^* \cdot e) \mid e_1 \oplus e_2 \mid \neg e \mid -e \mid id\langle e^* \rangle \mid id[e^*] \mid id \mid n \mid \textbf{true} \mid \textbf{false}$$

Fig. 5. Grammar of statements S, assertions A, and expressions e.

means that it will always be required to hold, as it cannot appear in conditions like $v \Rightarrow \textbf{tokens}(x, 1)$. The expressions e in assertions is equivalent to that of the host language. However, a wellformed expression that is not part of an assertion cannot contain the specification constructs $\bullet(c)$, $\textbf{rd}(c)$, $\textbf{tot}(c)$ etc. Although A allows expressions of other types, any wellformed assertion is of Boolean type.

5   Encoding

In this section we present an overview of how the assertions, as well as the proof rules for networks and actors, can be encoded in a guarded command language similar to Boogie [2]. The Boogie verifier carries out the rest of the proof by computing weakest preconditions of the generated code and proving them using an SMT solver. The precise encodings are omitted here due to lack of space, but are provided in a technical report [16].

5.1   Assertions

Our encoding is based on tracking the content of network channels. We do this via a number of global map variables:

$$\mathcal{I}: \textbf{ch} \rightarrow \textbf{int} \qquad \mathcal{R}: \textbf{ch} \rightarrow \textbf{int} \qquad \mathcal{C}: \textbf{ch} \rightarrow \textbf{int} \qquad \mathcal{M}: (\textbf{ch}\langle\beta\rangle, \textbf{int}) \rightarrow \beta$$

The type of $\mathcal{I}$, $\mathcal{R}$ and $\mathcal{C}$ is a map from channels to integers. $\mathcal{I}[c]$ gives the number of tokens read on channel c when the network contract started executing. $\mathcal{R}[c]$ tracks the total number of tokens read on channel c. $\mathcal{C}[c]$ tracks the number of tokens that has been produced on c. $\mathcal{M}$ is a two-dimensional map of type $(\textbf{ch}\langle\beta\rangle, \textbf{int}) \rightarrow \beta$. It is used to track the messages sent on channels. $\mathcal{M}[c, i]$ gives the i:th message produced on channel c. Note that the type of $\mathcal{M}$ is polymorphic and β is the datatype of the messages carried on the channel.

The assertion encoding, denoted with $\|\_\|$, of the most significant constructs of our assertion language is given in Fig. 6. The functions $\bullet(c)$, $\textbf{rd}(c)$ and $\textbf{tot}(c)$ correspond directly to $\mathcal{I}[c]$, $\mathcal{R}[c]$ and $\mathcal{C}[c]$, respectively. The standard logical operators have direct correspondences in Boogie and are not listed here.

5.2   Basic Actors

For a basic actor A, we verify that (1) the output of each actor action $T \in A_{act}$ fulfills its postcondition and (2) that each actor action preserves the actor invariants A_{inv}. To do this we assume that A_{inv} hold when the execution of

$$\|\bullet(c)\| \quad = \mathcal{I}[c] \qquad\qquad \|\mathbf{prev}(c)\| \quad = \mathcal{R}[c] - 1$$
$$\|\mathbf{rd}(c)\| \quad = \mathcal{R}[c] \qquad\qquad \|\mathbf{last}(c)\| \quad = \mathcal{C}[c] - 1$$
$$\|\mathbf{tot}(c)\| \quad = \mathcal{C}[c] \qquad\qquad \|c[i]\| \quad\quad = \mathcal{M}[c, \|i\|]$$
$$\|\mathbf{urd}(c)\| \quad = \mathcal{C}[c] - \mathcal{R}[c] \qquad \|\mathbf{tokens}(c, e)\| = \mathcal{C}[c] - \mathcal{R}[c] = \|e\|$$
$$\|\mathbf{next}(c)\| \quad = \mathcal{R}[c] \qquad\qquad \|\mathbf{every}(c, e)\| \quad = 0 \leq \|e\| \wedge \|e\| < \mathcal{C}[c]$$

Fig. 6. Encoding of assertion constructs.

action T starts and that the input tokens satisfy the precondition T_{pre}. We also assume that the action guard T_{grd} is satisfied, as T would not fire if T_{grd} is not satisfied. The verification technique used is hence analogous to how methods are verified in traditional program verification for object-oriented languages.

Additionally the actor initialisation is also shown to establish A_{inv}. This verification is similar to normal actions, but we do not initially assume the invariants. Instead we assume $\mathcal{R}[x] = 0$ for each inport x, and $\mathcal{C}[y] = 0$ for each outport y and check that the output of the initialisation action I satisfies its postcondition I_{post} and establishes A_{inv}.

5.3 Networks

The goal of the network encoding is to check that the network behaves according to one of its contracts. The verification method is based on checking an arbitrary window for every contract. The verification relies on tracing data on channels using invariants. Below N is a network, $x \in N_{ip}$ is an inport of N and $y \in N_{op}$ is an outport of N. Then N_{nwi} and N_{chi} are the network invariants and channel invariants, respectively. N_{subi} is the locally proven invariants of the sub-actors. N_{frules} is the firing rules of every sub-actor in the network. We further assume that T is a network contract of N, having pattern $x\colon n \Longrightarrow y\colon m$, guard T_{grd}, and precondition T_{pre} and postcondition T_{post}.

- *Initialisation* We check that the network initialisation establishes $N_{nwi} \cup N_{chi}$. This is done by assuming that we start from a state with empty channel histories. We then update the buffers according to the initialisation actions of every sub-actor, assume N_{subi}, and assert $N_{chi} \cup N_{nwi}$. We also assert that no sub-actor action is enabled from the state described by N_{nwi}, i.e. that each $f \in N_{frules}$ is falsified. This ensures that the state described by N_{nwi} is stable in the sense that N cannot make progress from this state without receiving additional input.
- *Compatibility* We check that the interconnected sub-actors are compatible, i.e. that the invariants imply the preconditions of each sub-actor, and that executing any sub-actor preserves N_{chi}. The encoding is as follows for a sub-actor A with action t with pattern $x_t\colon n_t \Longrightarrow y_t\colon m_t$, guard t_{grd}, precondition t_{pre} and postconditon t_{post}: The invariants $N_{chi} \cup N_{subi}$ are assumed. It is then assumed that there are at least n_t tokens on x_t, $n_t \leq \mathcal{C}[x_t] - \mathcal{R}[x_t]$. The input tokens are then assigned to identifiers and the action guard t_{grd} is assumed. We then assert t_{pre}. After this we havoc (non-deterministically

assign any type correct value) to the sub-actor state variables, assume t_{post} and assign the tokens defined in the output pattern to y_t. Finally we assume the invariants A_{inv} of the sub-actor and assert N_{chi}.

- *Network input* We check that N_{chi} is preserved when a new input conforming to $T_{grd} \cup T_{pre}$ is received on port x. This is done by incrementing the value of $\mathcal{C}[x]$. As we consider a finite window, an assumption, $\mathcal{C}[x] - \mathcal{I}[x] < n$, that the amount of input tokens received so far is less than that specified in the action pattern is made.
- *Network output* We check that correct output is produced and that the network is in a state conforming to N_{nwi} if the following conditions hold: (1) On the input x, n tokens satisfying $T_{grd} \cup T_{pre}$ has been received. (2) No sub-actor can be fired, i.e., each $f \in N_{frules}$ is falsified. (3) All sub-actor actions preserve N_{chi}, as checked in *Compatibility*. We assert that these assumptions imply that m tokens satisfying T_{post} has been produced on output y. We then mark the output tokens as read by updating $\mathcal{R}[y]$. The value of $\mathcal{I}$ is then assigned the value of $\mathcal{R}$. This models that the contract window is complete. Finally, we assert $N_{chi} \cup N_{nwi}$.

6   Invariant Generation

To decrease the number of invariants the user needs to provide, we aim to automatically generate actor invariants when possible. This can be done for a common class of actors that can be classified as *rate-static*.

For example, consider the actor Add in Fig. 1. We want to find an invariant expressing the relation between input tokens and output tokens for this actor. The following invariants fulfill this for the actor Add:

$$\mathbf{tot}(out) = \mathbf{rd}(in1) \wedge \mathbf{tot}(out) = \mathbf{rd}(in2)$$
$$\forall\ \mathbf{int}\ j \cdot 0 \leq j < \mathbf{tot}(out) \Rightarrow out[j] = in1[j] + in2[j]$$

In this section we present a general method for generating invariants for all rate-static actors. Essentially, we translate actions into assertions that can be used as invariants. Consider a rate-static actor A with the following two actions:

$$\mathbf{initialize} \implies y\colon [d^r]\ \mathbf{end}$$
$$\mathbf{action}\ x\colon [i^n] \implies y\colon [e^m]\ \mathbf{guard}\ g\ \mathbf{end}$$

Here i^n is a sequence of n input variables and e^m and d^r are sequences of m respectively r functions. Hence A has an input rate n and an output rate m. Additionally it produces r initial tokens. The **initialize** action is only run once when the actor is initialised. We can now relate the number of tokens on the inport to the number of tokens on the outport with the following invariant:

$$(n \times \mathbf{tot}(y)) = (m \times \mathbf{rd}(x)) + r \tag{1}$$

Invariants relating the values of input tokens to the values of output tokens have the following form:

$$\forall\ \mathbf{int}\ j \cdot \mathsf{R} \wedge \mathsf{G} \Rightarrow y[j] = \mathsf{F}(k) \tag{2}$$

where

$$\begin{array}{ll} \mathsf{R} = r \leq j < \mathbf{tot}(y) \land j \,\%\, m = \mathsf{k} & \mathsf{F} = e_k(i_0 \mapsto x[\mathsf{b}(0)], \ldots, i_n \mapsto x[\mathsf{b}(n)]) \\ \mathsf{G} = g(i_0 \mapsto x[\mathsf{b}(0)], \ldots, i_n \mapsto x[\mathsf{b}(n)]) & \mathsf{b}(\mathsf{i}) = (n/m)j + \mathsf{i} - r \end{array}$$

Here the notation $x \mapsto y$ stands for substituting x with y in the expression. A separate invariant is generated for each $\mathsf{k} \in 0..m - 1$. It should be noted that separate invariants are needed for each outport.

Invariants generated according to (1) and (2) can be checked locally, by checking that the actor actions preserve the invariants. However, to verify networks it is often also useful to state properties about the initial amount of tokens on channels. For rate-static actors we can provide the following channel invariant for the network where A is used:

$$(n \times \bullet(y)) = (m \times \bullet(x)) \tag{3}$$

Using invariants in the form described by (1), (2) and (3), it is possible to verify stateless rate-static actors, and networks of such actors, such as Add and Delay in Fig. 1 with only a few user-provided invariants. Typically invariants are then only needed to describe the state between contract windows. For actors with state we have a restriction that state variables cannot be used in output patterns. This can, however, be circumvented by considering the state as a feedback-loop channel. Furthermore, invariants of the form in (1) and (3) can also be generated for networks with static rate. Note also that generated invariants are correct by construction. Hence, it is not necessary to check them during verification, but they can be used as assumptions directly.

7   Soundness

In this section we briefly argue for the soundness of our approach. A more extensive argument is presented in our technical report [16].

Our verification approach is based on an inductive argument. Given a network invariant N_{nwi}, we show that N_{nwi} holds again after an arbitrary contract window. The inductive base step consists in checking that N_{nwi} is established by the network initialisation. Hence, we show that the network has a periodic behaviour, where the period is described by the contract.

In the verification, we assume that the length of the network input is no longer than described by the network contract. In practice this is, however, not necessarily the case, as networks are not executed atomically for a contract window. For the verification to be sound, it is then required that the behaviour of the network cannot change in response to receiving additional input. More formally, assume we have two input sequences x and x', where x is a prefix of x', $x \sqsubseteq x'$. It is then required that the network output for x, $N(x)$, is a prefix of the network output for x', i.e. $x \sqsubseteq x' \Rightarrow N(x) \sqsubseteq N(x')$. This property is called monotonicity and has been defined for Kahn Process Networks [9] along with a stronger property called continuity. Lee and Parks [11] have shown that sufficient conditions for Dataflow Process Networks, which is also what our networks are, to be continuous are that each actor is functional and that the firing rules are sequential. Functional here means that the actor does not have side effects and that the output tokens are a function of the input tokens consumed during that firing. Sequential means that the firing rules can be tested in a predefined order using only blocking reads. Essentially these restrictions mean that actors are required to be deterministic. As we here allow actors with state they do not appear to be functional. However, Lee and Parks [11] note that actor state is just syntactic sugar for having feedback loops in the top-level network. The same conditions hence apply also to actors with state. The condition that firing rules are sequential is in our case ensured by requiring mutually exclusive firing rules.

8   Evaluation

We have implemented our verification approach in a prototype verification tool and successfully verified a number of networks and actors, including both static an dynamic behaviour. The verified networks include, e.g., implementations of digital filters and a ZigBee transmitter. Many of the networks consisted mostly of static actors for which our tool automatically generates invariants. In these cases, most user-provided invariants were used to specify tokens on feedback loops. The tool is written in Scala and is publicly available[1] together with the source code of the evaluated examples.

The results from evaluation of 7 different networks are summarised in Table 1. The table lists the lines of code, the number of actor instances, the number of invariants provided by the user as well as generated by the verifier, the number of assertions in the resulting Boogie encoding, and the total number of lines of code in the Boogie encoding.

In Table 1, SumNet is our running example listed in Fig. 2. The network DataDependent is a network containing the data-dependent actor Split listed in Fig. 3. The network Nested is a network nesting another network. The top-level network nests the network SumNet and also contains the actor Sum given in Fig. 3. The postconditions states that SumNet and Sum produces equivalent output streams.

Table 1. Summary of evaluation

Name	LOC	Instances	User invs.	Gen. invs.	Assertions	Boogie LOC
SumNet	41	2	3	17	31	585
DataDependent	49	2	6	5	61	619
Nested	107	6	15	26	101	1,184
IIR	52	6	2	23	28	1,245
FIR	86	13	5	33	68	4,506
LMS	213	45	9	128	312	46,300
ZigBee	399	6	36	24	288	2,814

---

[1] http://users.abo.fi/jonwiik/actortool/.

The networks IIR, FIR, LMS and ZigBee are based on networks available as part of the Orcc[2] compiler infrastructure for RVC-CAL programs. The networks IIR, FIR and LMS describe digital filters and are essentially SDF networks, except that some of the actors have state. In the IIR and FIR networks we check that the produced output conforms to the difference equations describing the filters. For the LMS filter, we only checked that the network produces one output token for each input token and that the network is deadlock free.

The ZigBee network describes a ZigBee transmitter. It consists of 4 actors, among which two actors have complex dynamic behaviour, where the number of both consumed and produced tokens is data-dependent. Compared to the original Orcc network, we transformed state variables on which firing rules depend into feedback-loops. As the network uses many bitwise operations, we used bit-vectors to represent integers. For verification, we encapsulated the dynamic actors in separate networks. This enabled us to describe several firings of the actor using one network contract, essentially making it appear as a static actor on the network level above. We verified the network to be deadlock free and that the correct number of output tokens is produced for a number of input lengths.

It can be observed in Table 1 that the number of assertions is in many cases roughly proportional to the number of actor instances multiplied by the number of user-provided invariants. This is expected as channel invariants are asserted for each action of every sub-actor. Decomposing networks into hierarchies as well as proving actor invariants locally instead of expressing them as channel invariants at the network level decreases the number of assertions. The evaluated networks, except LMS, were verified within 10 s on a modern laptop. The LMS network took roughly 25 s to verify.

9 Related Work

Chalice [13] is a programming language and verifier for multi-threaded object-based programs. Chalice also supports channels that can be verified to be deadlock free. There, permissions to receive and obligations to send messages on channels are described in assertions. We have opted to not use this method here since it is more complex than needed in our case. We do not need send obligations as the number of tokens to be produced is given statically in actions.

Some automata-based approaches to static analysis of dataflow networks exist. In [8] a method for modular analysis of Dataflow Process Networks based on Interface Automata is presented. Interface Automata are associated with processes to specify the interface behaviour and environmental assumptions. Based on the automata they deduce properties such as deadlock freedom by checking the consistency of components and interface automaton networks. An extension to Interface Automata, named Counting Interface Automata, is presented in [15] and used for checking CAL actor compatibility. The method can capture temporal and quantitative aspects of actor interfaces, as well as token

---

[2] http://orcc.sourceforge.net/.

exchange rates. By composing automata they can prove behavioural type compatibility. However, neither of the approaches [8,15] consider properties given in contracts.

Formal verification of synchronous languages such as Lustre has been studied extensively. One recent approach by Champion et al. is CoCoSpec [5]. They present a mode-aware contract language. This is similar to annotating a network with several contracts in our approach. However, CoCoSpec, as well as other work aimed at synchronous languages, do not consider asynchronous, dynamic actors.

There is a large amount of work, e.g. [1], on verification of asynchronous object programs. Asynchronous objects are similar to our actors, but there are several differences. We consider static networks of actors, while asynchronous objects can be dynamically created. Restricting ourselves to static networks simplifies reasoning and enables us to prove stronger properties fully automatically.

10   Conclusion

We have presented an approach to specification and automated verification of dynamic dataflow networks. Our approach ensures functional correctness with respect to contracts for actors and networks as well as deadlock freedom for networks. The approach is based on checking networks for windows of finite length described by contracts. We have implemented our approach in a prototype tool and successfully verified a number of existing networks and actors.

There are several directions for future work. We plan to investigate more extensively the utilisation of our contracts in the scheduling of dataflow networks, e.g. by integrating them with the approach in [4]. We also plan to investigate extension of our approach to consider networks where actors can be dynamically created. However, we believe that our approach is a good first step towards fully automated contract-based verification of dynamic dataflow actor networks.

References

1. Ahrendt, W., Dylla, M.: A system for compositional verification of asynchronous objects. Sci. Comput. Program. **77**(12), 1289–1309 (2012)
2. Barnett, M., Chang, B.-Y.E., DeLine, R., Jacobs, B., Leino, K.R.M.: Boogie: a modular reusable verifier for object-oriented programs. In: Boer, F.S., Bonsangue, M.M., Graf, S., Roever, W.-P. (eds.) FMCO 2005. LNCS, vol. 4111, pp. 364–387. Springer, Heidelberg (2006). doi:10.1007/11804192_17
3. Boström, P., Wiik, J.: Contract-based verification of discrete-time multi-rate Simulink models. Softw. Syst. Modeling **15**(4), 1141–1161 (2016)
4. Boutellier, J., Ersfolk, J., Lilius, J., Mattavelli, M., Roquier, G., Silvén, O.: Actor merging for dataflow process networks. IEEE Trans. Signal Process. **63**(10), 2496–2508 (2015)
5. Champion, A., Gurfinkel, A., Kahsai, T., Tinelli, C.: CoCoSpec: a mode-aware contract language for reactive systems. In: De Nicola, R., Kühn, E. (eds.) SEFM 2016. LNCS, vol. 9763, pp. 347–366. Springer, Cham (2016). doi:10.1007/978-3-319-41591-8_24

Specification and Automated Verification of Dynamic Dataflow Networks   151

6. de Moura, L., Bjørner, N.: Z3: an efficient SMT solver. In: Ramakrishnan, C.R., Rehof, J. (eds.) TACAS 2008. LNCS, vol. 4963, pp. 337–340. Springer, Heidelberg (2008). doi:10.1007/978-3-540-78800-3_24

7. Eker, J., Janneck, J.W.: CAL language report. Technical report. ERL Technical Memo UCB/ERL M03/48, University of California at Berkeley (2003)

8. Jin, Y., Esser, R., Lakos, C., Janneck, J.W.: Modular analysis of dataflow process networks. In: Pezzè, M. (ed.) FASE 2003. LNCS, vol. 2621, pp. 184–199. Springer, Heidelberg (2003). doi:10.1007/3-540-36578-8_14

9. Kahn, G.: The semantics of a simple language for parallel programming. In: Information Processing 1974 (1974)

10. Lee, E.A., Messerschmitt, D.G.: Synchronous data flow. Proc. IEEE **75**(9), 1235–1245 (1987)

11. Lee, E.A., Parks, T.M.: Dataflow process networks. Proc. IEEE **83**(5), 773–799 (1995)

12. Lee, E.A., Messerschmitt, D.G.: Static scheduling of synchronous data flow programs for digital signal processing. IEEE Trans. Comput. **100**(1), 24–35 (1987)

13. Leino, K.R.M., Müller, P.: A basis for verifying multi-threaded programs. In: Castagna, G. (ed.) ESOP 2009. LNCS, vol. 5502, pp. 378–393. Springer, Heidelberg (2009). doi:10.1007/978-3-642-00590-9_27

14. Mattavelli, M., Amer, I., Raulet, M.: The reconfigurable video coding standard. IEEE Signal Process. Mag. **27**(3), 159–167 (2010)

15. Wandeler, E., Janneck, J.W., Lee, E.A., Thiele, L.: Counting interface automata and their application in static analysis of actor models. In: SEFM 2005. IEEE (2005)

16. Wiik, J., Boström, P.: Specification and automated verification of dynamic dataflow networks. Technical report 1170, TUCS (2016)

Specification Clones: An Empirical Study of the Structure of Event-B Specifications

Marie Farrell[✉], Rosemary Monahan, and James F. Power

Department of Computer Science, Maynooth University, Maynooth, Ireland
mfarrell@cs.nuim.ie

Abstract. In this paper we present an empirical study of formal specifications written in the Event-B language. Our study is exploratory, since it is the first study of its kind, and we formulate metrics for Event-B specifications which quantify the diversity of such specifications in practice. We pay particular attention to refinement as this is one of the most notable features of Event-B. However, Event-B is less well-equipped with other standardised modularisation constructs, and we investigate the impact of this by detecting and analysing specification clones at different levels. We describe our algorithm used to identify clones at the machine, context and event level, and present results from an analysis of a large corpus of Event-B specifications. Our study contributes to furthering research into the area of metrics and modularisation in Event-B.

1 Introduction and Motivation

The Event-B language is a state-based formal method for system-level modelling and verification that combines set theoretic notation and event-driven modelling [3]. Event-B is an industrial-strength tool and examples of its industrial use include train systems, air-traffic control and medical devices. A long term goal of model-driven software development has been to integrate such formalisms with practical software engineering methods and tools. Since the introduction of Event-B, a large number of examples and case studies have been conducted using the formalism, yet there is very little data available on the typical size, scope or structure of Event-B specifications.

In this paper we analyse Event-B specifications essentially as *software artefacts*, and extend software engineering techniques to the Event-B language. We have approached this empirically, by assembling a large corpus of Event-B specifications and developing basic metrics to quantify their size and complexity. Since *refinement* is a key feature of the Event-B approach, we seek to quantify this aspect of Event-B specifications in particular, so we can understand how such refinement is carried out in practice [11].

Apart from refinement, the modularisation constructs in Event-B are not well-developed, and a number of alternatives have been proposed to address this.

M. Farrell—This project is funded by a Government of Ireland Postgraduate Grant from the Irish Research Council.

A. Cimatti and M. Sirjani (Eds.): SEFM 2017, LNCS 10469, pp. 152–167, 2017.
DOI: 10.1007/978-3-319-66197-1_10

As a contribution to the development of modularisation constructs for Event-B, we conduct a study of *clones* in our corpus of Event-B specifications. Studies of this kind already exist for software written in a variety of programming languages, but we believe this is the first time this topic has been addressed at the specification level.

This paper is structured as follows. In Sect. 2 we describe the background and motivation of our work. In Sect. 3 we summarise our exploratory analysis of the corpus of Event-B projects that we have assembled. This allows us to quantify metrics and provide some insight into the refinement process used by developers. Section 4 describes the algorithm that we used to detect specification clones throughout our corpus. In Sect. 5 we summarise the results of this clone detection under the specific headings of context, machine and event clones. We also outline potential ways of reducing the number of clones here. We identify threats to the validity of this work in Sect. 6 and in Sect. 7 we outline our contributions and potential for future work.

2   Background and Related Work

The primary objective of Event-B is to provide a basis for proving the *safety* of a given specification. This is achieved in practice through the Rodin Platform, an Eclipse-based IDE that is the de facto standard for Event-B [2]. Using Rodin, developers can write and type-check Event-B specifications, and use both automatic and interactive theorem proving to discharge *proof obligations* associated with the specification. The Event-B language supports formal refinement enabling the developer to start with a simple, abstract system and gradually add complexity in a verifiable way by means of *refinement steps* [11].

Figure 1 gives an overview of the general structure of Event-B specifications. Event-B models a system using two kinds of components: *contexts* and *machines*. A context is used to model static data using sets, constants and axioms [2], as shown in the leftmost column of Fig. 1. The central column of Fig. 1 shows the general format of a machine definition, which models dynamic behaviour in terms of a set of *events*. Machines can define the state variables and constrain them using variants and invariants.

The rightmost column of Fig. 1 shows the general structure of an event. Here, p is a set of event parameters, $G(x, p)$ formalises a guard predicate over the set of event parameters p and the machine variables x. $W(x, p)$ is a witness predicate and the action $BA(x, p, x')$ is a before-after predicate where x' indicates the after

```
CONTEXT ctx            MACHINE m   refines m0      Event e_i ≙ status
    extends ctx0       SEES ctx                        any p
    SETS S                VARIABLES x                   when G(x,p)
    CONSTANTS c           INVARIANTS I(x)               with W(x,p)
    AXIOMS                VARIANT n(x)                  then BA(x,p,x')
        A(s,c)            EVENTS                     end
                             INITIALISATION, e_1,...,e_n
```

Fig. 1. The general structure of Event-B definitions of contexts, machines and events.

values of the machine variables x. Each event is paired with a status that can be one of ordinary, convergent or anticipated. Events that are labelled as convergent must strictly decrease the variant expression whereas those that are labelled as anticipated must not increase the variant expression. Events that have a status of ordinary do not need to obey any such properties.

There has been some work done on identifying suitable metrics for Event-B developments using the Halstead model [12]. Their objectives were to determine the size of an Event-B specification, the difficulty in constructing it and the effort required in designing and proving. Their case study was limited to just one project with 7 machines, and it is not clear whether the Halstead metrics, dependent on applying formulae to operations and operands, are the most appropriate way of characterising Event-B specifications in general.

2.1   Clones in Code and Specifications

The detection, analysis, management and tool evaluation corresponding to *code clones* represents a growing research area in the field of software engineering [15]. The reuse strategy indicated by code cloning is often beneficial in that it promotes the reuse of reliable code and can save time and effort in development. It is often the case, however, that duplicated code is caused by limitations in the programming paradigm's modularisation mechanisms and thus signals that improvements are required.

Roy et al. identify four different types of code clones [15], based on categorising the nature of the match between different pieces of code:

Type-1: identical code fragments that differ only in variations of white space and comments.

Type-2: structurally/syntactically identical code fragments that differ only in the names of identifiers, literals, types, layout and comments.

Type-3: a more liberal version of Type-2 clones which allow differences such as additions, deletions or modifications of statements.

Type-4: code fragments that exhibit the same functional behaviour but are implemented through very different syntactic structures.

In this paper we extend these definitions to detect clones between Event-B machines, contexts and events. Some work on identifying clones at the specification level has been done as part of the Arís project which retrieves reusable software artefacts using a graph matching approach [13]. However, this approach was based on finding matches in Spec#/C# code, and does not provide any data on the kind of clones found.

2.2   Modularisation of Event-B Specifications

There have been a number of suggested approaches to modularising Event-B specifications. One of the original methods proposed two styles of decomposition, based on the shared variable and shared event approaches [3]. Since then a variety of Rodin plugins have been developed to offer some degree of modularisation for Event-B. We do not have space to discuss them all here, but have listed the relevant plugins for Rodin in Table 1 along with a brief description of the modularisation features they provide. Since these plugins can potentially reduce the number of clones in Event-B specifications, we discuss them, where relevant, in our clone analysis results in Sect. 5.

Table 1. This table summarises the Rodin plugins that we have identified as relevant to our discussion in this paper.

Name	Description	Reference
Feature Composition	Composition of Event-B machines and contexts and aids the user in resolving conflicts	[8]
Generic Instantiation	Instantiate and reuse generic developments within other formal developments	[17]
Model Decomposition	Decomposition of Event-B machines/contexts using the shared variable and shared event styles	[18]
Pattern	Reuse of existing Event-B models including refinement steps within a development in order to save the modelling and proving effort	[7]
Parallel Composition	Composition of Event-B machines using the shared event approach	[14]
Modularisation	Allows the developer to construct modules and prove modular developments	[9]
Renaming refactory	Renames Event-B model elements so that the changes are propagated through the relevant machines, contexts and proof obligations	See footnote[a]
Theory Extension	Extends the Event-B mathematical language (potentially with new data types) and the Rodin proving infrastructure	[5]

[a] http://wiki.event-b.org/index.php/Refactoring_Framework

3 Analysing a Corpus of Event-B Specifications: Metrics and Refinement

Since there has been no previous large scale study in this area, our focus will be on conducting an exploratory data analysis to identify and quantify the main characteristics of Event-B specifications.

In order to carry out this analysis we have assembled a corpus of Event-B specifications. We have obtained the projects in this corpus from a number of publicly-available Event-B resources, including the Event-B Wiki Page, the DEPLOY website and the case study tracks at the ABZ conference (2014 and 2016). Some additional projects were obtained directly from the developers who constructed them. In total we obtained 85 Event-B projects, ranging from smaller textbook-style examples through to large-scale developments.

Table 2. Metrics for the projects that fall into the "smaller" category.

Smaller Projects								
Project	Macs	Cons	Evs	Refs	Sens	Auto	Inter	RP
Bepiv6.4*	2	10	45	1	948	560	370	0
SSF_pilot	4	4	35	3	842	170	2	19
DynStabLSR	7	1	69	6	788	247	140	37
ch8circarbiter	6	2	46	5	764	153	0	31
TreeFilePerm	4	4	33	3	655	107	52	18
RCPert	4	3	53	3	583	199	28	29
RCNorm	4	3	49	3	565	146	32	27
ch912_mobile	6	1	43	5	539	134	19	19
ch917_train	5	3	38	4	539	128	5	23
SignalControl	10	4	106	9	497	135	0	26
ch7_conc	5	1	45	4	484	239	9	22
routing_new	8	4	51	7	479	226	60	47
FloodSet	6	5	27	5	445	209	87	46
ch2_car	4	3	34	3	438	249	4	17
ssf	7	4	51	6	430	48	11	8
seqpattern	5	2	30	3	425	37	1	4
SharedBuffs	4	1	22	3	423	98	5	19
SimpleLyra	4	4	28	3	418	55	0	3
gcd	7	3	32	6	407	91	84	21
ch8circpulser	9	0	52	7	397	93	1	20
ch916_doors	5	3	31	4	380	101	2	14
ch8circroad	5	0	27	4	379	37	0	9
ch8circight	3	0	19	2	370	89	0	25
ch6_brp	6	3	47	5	360	149	0	16
Modes_v2	3	3	30	2	333	108	13	3
aocs_t2	3	2	29	2	297	105	13	18
CtsCtrl	4	3	18	2	274	150	19	21
Rabin	7	7	62	6	262	138	71	2
pomc	5	3	27	4	257	81	27	10
pomcwoterm	5	3	27	4	250	83	13	10
ch913_ieee	6	3	21	4	243	71	21	16
DSAOCSSv3	1	1	9	0	233	82	8	0
AStyleQR	5	1	19	4	226	70	5	14
DSAOCSSv2	1	1	9	0	219	81	8	0
ch4_file_1	5	2	17	4	192	47	5	9
FindP_P1	4	1	21	3	191	27	15	13
aocs_t2_um	2	2	16	1	178	95	8	13
pat9QR	5	0	22	4	161	44	6	8
BinarySearch	3	1	14	2	154	102	6	13
SSF1	1	3	6	0	148	25	0	0
ch911_tree	5	3	15	4	140	81	0	9
SSF_minipilot	1	1	8	0	127	20	4	0
Club-120130	3	4	11	2	105	50	7	5
BoschSwitch	2	1	10	0	102	15	4	0
ch915_sort	3	1	12	2	101	56	11	11
ex-bubblesort	2	1	7	1	98	46	6	7
FindP_D	2	2	8	1	98	47	2	5
FindP_G	1	1	6	0	94	0	0	0
program2	2	2	9	1	88	192	5	3
Zer_ess	0	5	0	0	88	40	15	0
ex-bubbles	2	1	8	1	83	41	1	13
HermanRing	2	3	8	1	82	35	22	2
cae-square	3	3	10	2	78	53	1	2
primrec	2	2	7	1	74	36	0	2
FindP_P2	1	1	4	0	73	0	0	0
ch915_bin	3	1	11	2	68	32	5	7
AStyleQR_2	1	1	5	0	65	10	0	0
TrafficLights	2	1	11	1	58	20	0	0
ch915_inv	2	2	7	1	55	32	0	5
Cowboy	2	1	7	1	53	14	1	1
ch910_ring	2	2	6	1	52	24	4	1
ch915_sqrt	3	1	9	2	44	17	0	5
ch915_rev	2	1	6	1	43	28	3	4
ch915_mini	2	1	6	1	42	24	1	1
DiningCrypt	3	1	6	1	42	21	3	0
AStyleQR_3	1	1	3	0	40	6	0	0
AStyleQR_1	1	1	3	0	37	5	0	0
pat8SynMC	2	0	5	1	34	15	0	0
ch915_search	2	1	6	1	29	17	0	3

Table 3. Metrics for the projects that fall into the "larger" category. Outliers are indicated by an asterisk*.

Legend for column headings:
Macs: # of machines
Cons: # of contexts
Evs: # of events
Refs: # of refinement steps
Sens: # of sentences
Auto: # of automatic proofs
Inter: # of interactive proofs
RP: # of designated refinement proofs

Larger Projects								
Project	Macs	Cons	Evs	Refs	Sens	Auto	Inter	RP
Midas*	43	61	2500	40	26395	2034	3163	2183
FlashFileFS	18	6	320	13	5442	974	531	88
DepSatSpec	14	2	2094	13	4771	1309	549	0
ATM	7	12	129	6	3447	925	37	46
B2Bminip	12	0	228	11	2900	425	73	124
Bepiv3.3	6	6	137	1	2665	153	113	12
TSHHDMac	35	50	1487	18	2661	602	84	15
Bepiv5.0	9	10	329	8	2007	683	317	0
CDIS	7	6	103	6	1894	101	0	3
HDMac	19	25	718	16	1605	448	23	2
Pilot_v3	4	4	98	3	1586	134	9	0
MLLanding	11	2	313	10	1432	286	210	0
FlashFileFL	6	12	109	5	1243	379	13	11
HLanding	11	7	321	9	1213	173	68	17
ch3_press	8	3	144	7	1200	0	0	0
OnbCont	9	3	224	8	1108	438	1	14

Table 4. Summary statistics for the whole data set, and for the two "smaller" and "larger" subdivisions.

All Projects ($n = 85$)								
Project	Macs	Cons	Evs	Refs	Sens	Auto	Inter	RP
Minimum	0	0	0	0	29	0	0	0
Median	4	2	27	3	274	83	5	8
Maximum	43	61	2500	40	26395	2034	3163	2183
MADN	3.0	1.5	28.2	3.0	298.0	86.0	7.4	11.9

Smaller Projects ($n = 69$)								
Project	Macs	Cons	Evs	Refs	Sens	Auto	Inter	RP
Minimum	0	0	0	0	29	0	0	0
Median	3	2	17	2	192	56	5	8
Maximum	10	10	106	9	948	560	70	47
MADN	1.5	1.5	16.3	1.5	206.1	54.9	7.4	11.9

Larger Projects ($n = 16$)								
Project	Macs	Cons	Evs	Refs	Sens	Auto	Inter	RP
Minimum	4	0	98	1	1108	0	0	0
Median	10	6	270	8	1950	431	70	11
Maximum	43	61	2500	40	26395	2034	3163	21.83
MADN	5.2	5.9	203.9	4.4	1076.4	398.1	97.1	17.0

All of the specifications in these 85 projects could be processed using the Rodin platform, and were thus available as a set of XML files in a standardised format. To analyse these projects we developed a suite of Python programs that read in the files in Rodin format, calculated and reported metrics, and searched for occurrences of clones at various levels.

3.1 Quantifying Specification Size

The most obvious measurable entities in an Event-B specification correspond to the major syntactic categories. Just as the size of a software project might be measured using code metrics such as number of classes, methods or lines-of-code, we can get similar information from an Event-B specification in terms of the number of contexts/machines, events and sentences. Specific to a formal approach, we can also measure the number of proof obligations (automatically and interactively proved). The metric values for the 85 projects in the corpus are given in Tables 2 and 3.

In total, for all 85 projects in the corpus there are 359 contexts and 468 machines, which in turn contain 10828 events. One immediate difficulty in analysing the corpus is the overall range of the specifications, from small, textbook-style examples, through to major systems. We chose to divide the corpus based on the *number of sentences* (axioms, invariants, variants, guards, actions and witnesses) per project, since this was the metric closest to lines-of-code, which might best reflect a simple measure of size for a project. Thus the rows of Tables 2 and 3 are ordered based on the total number of sentences in a project. We note that this is a coarse-grained measure as sentences may vary in complexity.

In order to be able to represent this information meaningfully and extract useful information from it, we have split the corpus into two different data sets. We investigated a variety of ways by which to carry out this split, including:

- using the examples from the *Modeling in Event-B* textbook [1] as models of "smaller" projects, and regarding projects with more sentences than these as "larger" projects.
- extracting the outliers using Tukey's test (the median plus 1.5 times the inter-quartile range); all such outliers were larger projects.
- using trimming [10], to identify a fixed proportion at the extreme ends of the data set.

In practice, these three strategies resulted in almost the same set being identified, and we have used Tukey's test to categorise the 16 projects in Table 3 as "larger". This also corresponds to the top 19% of the projects, and excludes all but one of the textbook examples (the exception is the mechanical press controller from Chap. 3). We refer to the 69 remaining projects listed in Table 2 as "smaller". These projects all have 10 contexts or under and 10 machines or under. Some of these are non-trivial projects, however and the number of sentences ranges from just 29 up to 948. Thus we have further divided Table 2 into quartiles based on the number of sentences.

Tables 2 and 3 demonstrate the diversity of Event-B developments and we provide them so that future studies have a measure with which they can gauge the comparative size of Event-B developments.

3.2   Metrics for Event-B Specifications

Figure 2 further illustrates the diversity in size between the projects, showing the distributions of the sentences in the smaller and larger projects. These measurements signal that one should be cautious when choosing a representative Event-B specification as the structures vary so much. In particular, the Midas project is a dramatic outlier of this data set on almost all metrics, as is shown by the rightmost bar in Fig. 2, and thus should be considered quite distinctive as an Event-B specification.

Table 4 summarises the ranges for each of the metrics, giving the minimum, maximum, median and MADN values for the whole data set and its two subdivisions. Due to the uneven distribution we use the median and MADN as robust measures in place of the mean and standard deviation. MADN is the median of the absolute deviations from the median, divided by $z_{0.75}$ [10]. It is notable that in most cases the MADN is close to or exceeds the median, indicating a large spread of values for each of the metrics.

We analysed all of the metrics in Tables 2 and 3 to check for interrelationships, using Spearman's rank correlation coefficient. The most notable very strong correlations (with $p < 0.001$ in all cases) were between the following variables:

- **the number of events and the number of sentences** in the small data set ($\rho = 0.905$), where the median number of sentences per event is 11 (MADN $= 4.4$). However, in the larger project set, this correlation is weak ($\rho = 0.391$). The larger projects contain a greater number of contexts, thus adding sentences to the projects that are not sentences within events.

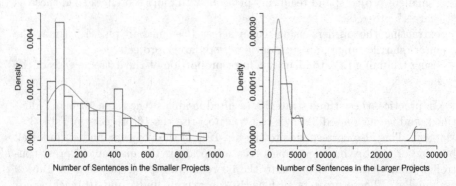

Fig. 2. Histograms showing the distribution of the numbers of sentences per project for the smaller and larger data sets. Note that the vertical axes here are on different scales.

- **the number of machines and the number of events** in both the smaller ($\rho = 0.849$) and larger ($\rho = 0.904$) project sets. The median number of events per machine is 25 (MADN = 9.8) in the larger set and 5 (MADN = 2.7) in the smaller.

There was also a (lower) strong correlation in the smaller projects between the numbers of events/sentences and the number of automatic proofs.

The data in Tables 2 and 3 shows that the number of automatic proofs required dramatically exceeds the number of interactive proofs in general. On average, in the larger projects, 78.6% of the proofs were done automatically with 91.1% of the proofs automatic in the smaller projects. This is important for automated verification, since it is a measure of the relative amount of theorem-proving work imposed on the user, as compared to that done by the underlying prover. It is notable that this percentage is much higher for smaller examples than for the larger ones. This is most likely due to the increased complexity in modelling large-scale systems. As Event-B continues to be used industrially, this metric can be useful in measuring the degree to which automated theorem-proving has increased in effectiveness.

3.3 Quantifying Refinements

Figure 3 contains a histogram with kernel distribution, showing the number of refinement steps for each of the project sets. As can be seen, in the larger project set the Midas project is again a dramatic outlier with 40 refinement steps. The smaller project set does not contain any dramatic outliers, with approximately 50% of these projects containing only one refinement step.

In both the smaller and the larger project sets there is a very strong correlation between the number of machines and the number of refinement steps in a project ($\rho = 0.989$ and $\rho = 0.993$ respectively, $p < 0.001$). In most cases the relationship is almost 1:1, showing that *linear* refinement chains are the most common refinement strategy used. By default, a machine can refine at most one other, so typically a machine will have one 'parent'. These refinement chains bear a striking similarity to the notion of refinement presented in the theory of institutions which is typically a single, linear chain [16]. While the *Feature Composition* plugin for Rodin allows the merging of machines in a refinement step [8], this is clearly not the usual approach taken in these examples.

In Event-B, proof obligations are one indicator of the complexity of the system being modelled. There is a specific set of proof obligations that are generated through the refinement of events (guard strengthening and merging, action simulation, equality of a preserved variable, witness well-definedness and witness feasibility). We list the number of these designated refinement proofs in the rightmost column of Tables 2 and 3. These proofs are only generated for refined events that are labelled as **not extended**. Events that are labelled as **extended** generate no proof obligations that are designated for refinement as they are specific to superposition refinement. This is quite an efficient approach to refinement

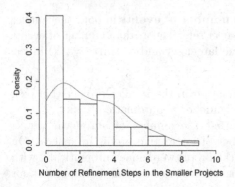
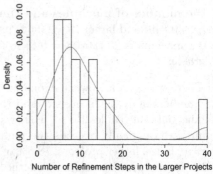

Fig. 3. Histograms with kernel distribution describing the number of refinement steps taken in both the smaller and larger project sets. Note that the vertical axes here are on different scales.

as Rodin avoids the regeneration of these proofs [2], but is only applicable where no data refinement has taken place.

There is a strong correlation between the number of refinement proofs and the number of refinement steps in a project in the smaller project set ($\rho = 0.786$, $p < 0.001$) resulting in the median ratio of 3 refinement proofs to 1 refinement step. However, the correlation is not significant for the larger project set. We found that developers of the larger projects often opted to avoid data refinement and use event extending to streamline their developments. Based on the data in Table 3 we can identify 5 out 16 projects that used this approach.

We had expected that there might be a correlation between the number of refinements and the number of sentences, with machines increasing in size as they became more concrete. However, this correlation is not strong even in the smaller data set ($\rho = 0.695$, $p < 0.001$) and neither strong nor significant in the larger, which, as mentioned earlier, are also influenced by the large number of contexts.

4 Detecting Specification Clones

In this section we describe our strategy for applying the clone types discussed in Sect. 2.1 to Event-B.

In all cases we will be comparing *sentences* from one specification with those in another: this includes axioms in contexts, invariants and variants in machines, and guards, witnesses and actions in events. There are a number of approaches to matching in the literature, including metric, token, text and abstract syntax comparison [4]. Since our sentences are relatively small constructs, we have used these as the smallest unit of matching. All sentences are tokenised to eliminate formatting and white-space, and we compare only sentences of the same kind (thus axioms with axioms, etc.). We have discounted any machines/contexts/events with 2 or less sentences in order to ensure that we are only collecting meaningful clones.

We carry out this matching at three levels: contexts, machines and events. We base our search for clones on the clone types discussed in Sect. 2.1. In all cases, (context, machine and event):

- Type-1 clones correspond to exact matches between the full sentence sequences in each case: that is all sentences in one component must match all those in the other.
- Type-2 clones are matches between the full sentence sequences, but where variable names are anonymised, each variable name being replaced by a positional indicator.
- Type-3 clones are also matches between two sentence sequences (with variable names anonymised or unanonymised), except that now we allow matches between *sub-sequences* of the sentences. We calculate the percentage of type-3 clone similarity using the maximum of the similarity calculated for both the anonymised and unanonymised versions.

We do not explicitly search for type-4 clones (functional equivalence) in what follows. From one perspective, all of our clones could be viewed as type-4, since we are not really comparing code but specifications, and thus identifying a degree of functional equivalence. However, a more robust search for type-4 clones would require us to prove the equivalence of the corresponding generated proof obligations for machines, contexts and events, which we have not attempted. As such, we omit type-4 clones from further discussion here as future work.

We have conducted an automated analysis of our corpus of projects by writing a series of Python scripts that read in the Rodin files, represent the components as an abstract syntax tree, and then perform comparisons at the context, machine and event level. We analyse machines and events both with and without any corresponding variants and invariants included, to distinguish between sentences that are global and local (to events) in the machine. Variants are only included with events that have a status of anticipated or convergent, since, unlike ordinary events, these are required to not increase the variant expression [1].

Our analysis returns pairs corresponding to instances of cloning that have occurred. We refer to these as clone pairs or clonings in what follows.

We have also identified the clones that occur the most frequently throughout our corpus, at the level of machines, contexts and events. As there are no libraries for Event-B specifications and since contexts typically supply custom data types, we were interested to examine whether or not similar contexts have been used in the Event-B projects across our corpus. Thus we also determine whether the clones that we have discovered are *inter*-project (across different projects) or *intra*-project (within the same project) clones.

5   Results of the Clone Analysis

In this section we summarise the results of our clone analysis through the entire corpus. In what follows we regard the three clone types as mutually exclusive: by type-2 we mean all those that are type-2 but not type-1, and by type-3 we mean those that are type-3 but not type-1 or type-2. Table 5 summarises the results of this analysis, providing counts for the number of clonings identified (type-1, type-2 and type-3) and also the number of clones.

5.1   Context Clones

As can be seen in the first row of Table 5, our analysis found 40 clone pairs at the context level in the corpus, consisting of 18 type-1 and 22 type-3 clone pairs. We had expected this, since contexts resemble data types in a programming language. The *theory plugin* offers a potential solution to this problem as it provides a way of adding new data types to Rodin [5].

When we investigated the actual clones that were returned we found 22 context clones, of which 18 occurred on an inter project basis and 6 on an intra project basis. There were 2 which occurred both as inter and intra project clones. The fact that so many of them occurred between different projects supports our claim that they are being re-used in a manner similar to libraries. The inter project clonings occurred mostly between projects that shared a common approach or between projects that were modelling the same kind of system. For example, there were quite a few inter project clonings in the separate developments of a Hemodialysis Machine, the different versions of BepiColombo, and the assortment of file systems being modelled (Flash FS, Flash FL and Tree FS).

Table 5. The occurrence of clone pairs and clones per type throughout the entire corpus. Note that '(+VI)' indicates that the variants (where appropriate) and invariants have been included in the analysis.

Event-B component	Clone Pairs				Actual clones	
	Type-1	Type-2	Type-3	Total	Total	Occur.
Contexts	18	0	22	40	22	51
Machines	13	7	937	957	19	40
Machines (+VI)	9	7	943	959	13	28
Events	276	942	4781	5999	131	417
Events (+VI)	35	158	7229	7422	65	175

5.2   Machine Clones

In Event-B, a machine is generally reused by means of refinement and thus we did not expect to find many type-1 clonings or inter project clones. As can be seen in the second and third data rows of Table 5, we discovered a very small number of type-1 and type-2 machine clonings. We did, however, manage to identify 937 type-3 clone pairs in the analysis without the variants and invariants included.

Since the type-3 clone pairs are identified in terms of their similarity, expressed as percentages, we provide an illustration of the distribution of type-3 clones in Fig. 4. The top two histograms in Fig. 4 show the data for machine-level clone pairs, and the bottom two for event-level clone pairs. As expected, the distributions for machine-level clones skew to the left, as most clones had a low similarity percentage, indicating that there is some basic machine structure being reused over and over again but the part that is being cloned does not contain a large proportion of the sentences. Nonetheless, there is still a significant number of clone pairs that have at lest 50% of their sentences matching.

In total we found 5 inter and 14 intra project full machine clones. This reduced to 3 inter and 10 intra project clones when the variants and invariants were included. Most of these were within the same project and therefore were most likely caused by refinement chains. These numbers are quite small with regards to the size of our corpus, thus we conclude that full machines typically do not incur a huge amount of cloning.

5.3   Event Clones

Since events are the smallest unit of modularisation, we expected a higher level of cloning to be found between pairs at this level. The fourth data row of Table 5 shows that we identified 276 type-1, 942 type-2 and 4781 type-3 clone pairs or instances of event clonings in our corpus. As can be seen from the fifth data row in Table 5, this number decreased for type-1 and type-2 when we included the appropriate variants and invariants (35 and 158) respectively. The number of type-3 clone pairs, however, increased quite dramatically to 7229. This is because the inclusion of variants and invariants increased the size of many small events past our threshold of 2 sentences, thus including events in the analysis that were absent when these variants and invariants were not included.

There were 131 different event clones, of which 30 were inter and 126 were intra project clones. Intra project clonings occurred 382 times and they occur in the scenarios where one event is refined throughout a project and also where there are event clonings within the same machine. We found 210 situations where one event in a machine was a clone of another event in the *same* machine. This accounts for approximately 1.9% of the total events in our corpus and 17.2% of the total type-1 and type-2 event clone pairs. Inter project clonings occurred a total of 37 times.

Based on this analysis, we conclude that there may be a relationship between the number of intra event clones between different machines in the same project and the level of refinement of that project. However, this needs to be examined in more detail.

5.4   Discussion: Dealing with Clones

One way of addressing the large number of type-2 clones at the event level would be through the provision of facilities for event re-use. This could be done either through a renaming feature as a Rodin plugin, or by introducing parameterisation constructs at the Event-B language level.

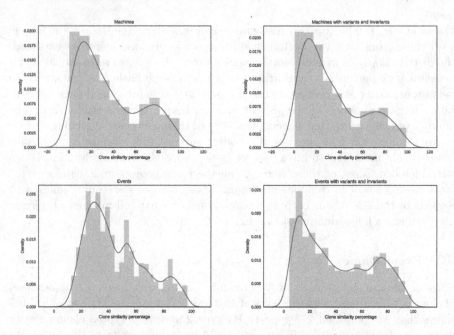

Fig. 4. Histograms describing the distribution of Type-3 clones across the entire corpus of Event-B specifications. Note that we have omitted type-3 *context* clones as there were relatively few of these.

The *renaming refactory* plugin could offer some assistance here as it renames components of an Event-B model with the renamings propagating through to the proof obligation level. However, it does not offer any way of instantiating copies of events. The *Pattern* and the *Generic Instantiation* plugins are also relevant, but these currently work only at the machine level, rather than the event level [7,17].

If more sophisticated modularisation constructs were made available for Event-B, they could potentially alter the development strategy taken by developers and turn what would have been type-3 clones into type-2 clones which could be parametrised and then added to in future refinements. We have proposed the theory of institutions as a mathematically sound framework to incorporate Event-B into and thus provide users of Event-B with access to an array of generic and formalism independent modularisation constructs through the use of specification building operators [6]. These specification building operators could potentially provide a solution to these problems.

6   Threats to Validity

One feature of our work is the creation of a corpus of Event-B projects, and our division of this set into smaller and larger projects. The selection poses a threat to *conclusion validity*, since we are dealing with a heterogeneous group of projects, and there is a risk that the differences in metrics are due to other factors not measured here, such as heterogeneity in terms of the domain of application, e.g. railway, health-care, control systems, algorithms, etc.

Our analysis of the projects is conducted based on the metrics that we have defined and measured. While these metrics corresponded to major syntactic categories in Event-B and have clear analogies with similar constructs in programming languages, there is a threat to *construct validity* here. In particular, further studies would be required to establish the predictive value, if any, of these metrics.

Similarly, in adapting the definition of code clones to Event-B we made a number of decisions on what should be measured and the degree of matching involved; altering these could yield different results. Our measurement of type-3 clones was based on sentence sequences and the in-order anonymisation of variables: a more general technique could produce more clone-pairs, at the cost of a considerable increase in combinatorial matches.

Since our analysis was based on processing the XML files generated by Rodin, we have a high degree of confidence that the measurements are accurate, and do not pose a threat to the *internal validity* of our results. However, in three of the Event-B projects (`ch3_press`, `FindP_G` and `FindP_P2`) the corresponding .bps files, which hold information about the proofs, were empty. Thus these projects have no automatic or interactive proofs recorded even though proof obligations have been generated. We believe that these projects may have used an older version of Rodin or a plugin that we do not have access to. One approach to resolving this would be to remodel them using a current version of the software with no extra plugins installed. We chose not to do this as we wished to remain as impartial as possible with regards to the corpus that we collected.

In total, we have 85 Event-B projects in our corpus, but it is possible that this is not a large enough sample size to study. This causes a threat to *external validity* in terms of the generalisability of our results. We believe that assembling and maintaining a measured corpus of Event-B programs is a worthwhile task in this regard.

7 Summary and Future Work

Our work applies the existing software engineering approaches of calculating metrics and detecting code clones to specifications written using the Event-B formal method. This exploratory study is the first of its kind and has enabled us to provide and analyse the metrics of a corpus of Event-B specifications. In this way, we provide a benchmark against which other Event-B developments can gauge their comparative size and complexity level.

During the evolution of the Event-B formalism from Classical-B, certain facilities for the reuse of machine specifications disappeared such as the modularisation properties supplied by the keywords INCLUDES and USES which facilitated the use of an existing machine in other developments [17]. It is evident not only from experience with industrial projects [9] but also from the sheer abundance of attempts to regain such modularity features for Event-B that there is an underlying requirement for it. Our empirical study supports this claim by evaluating code clones at the specification level.

Future work includes the assessment of *clone genealogies*, particularly in the context of refinement – i.e. how clones evolve throughout successive refinements. This study would show us whether or not clones persist in the specification after it has undergone a (series of) refinement step(s). We are also interested in detecting non-typing invariant clones, this would allow us to analyse data refinement clones using gluing invariants. We did not assess the size of the state (number of variables per machine) in this study but we intend to address this as future work. This will allow us to investigate whether or not the size of the state is indicative of the complexity of the system being modelled.

Acknowledgements. We would like to thank the anonymous reviewers for their feedback and Ruth O'Connor for her work on a preliminary version of our clone detector during her SPUR internship that was funded by Maynooth University.

References

1. Abrial, J.-R.: Modeling in Event-B: System and Software Engineering. Cambridge University Press, New York (2010)
2. Abrial, J.-R., Butler, M., Hallerstede, S., Hoang, T.S., Mehta, F., Voisin, L.: Rodin: an open toolset for modelling and reasoning in Event-B. Int. J. Softw. Tools Technol. Transfer **12**(6), 447–466 (2010)
3. Abrial, J.-R., Hallerstede, S.: Refinement, decomposition, and instantiation of discrete models: application to Event-B. Fundamenta Informaticae **77**(1–2), 1–28 (2007)
4. Baxter, I.D., Yahin, A., Moura, L., Sant'Anna, M., Bier, L.: Clone detection using abstract syntax trees. In: International Conference on Software Maintenance, Maryland, USA, pp. 368–377 (1998)
5. Butler, M., Maamria, I.: Practical theory extension in Event-B. In: Liu, Z., Woodcock, J., Zhu, H. (eds.) Theories of Programming and Formal Methods. LNCS, vol. 8051, pp. 67–81. Springer, Heidelberg (2013). doi:10.1007/978-3-642-39698-4_5
6. Farrell, M., Monahan, R., Power, J.F.: Providing a semantics and modularisation constructs for Event-B using institutions. In: International Workshop on Algebraic Development Techniques, Gregynog, Wales (2016)
7. Fürst, A.: Design patterns in Event-B and their tool support. Master's thesis, Department of Computer Science, ETH Zürich, March 2009
8. Gondal, A., Poppleton, M., Snook, C.: Feature composition-towards product lines of Event-B models. In: International Workshop on Model-Driven Product Line Engineering, Twente, The Netherlands, pp. 18–25 (2009)
9. Iliasov, A., Troubitsyna, E., Laibinis, L., Romanovsky, A., Varpaaniemi, K., Ilic, D., Latvala, T.: Supporting reuse in Event B development: modularisation approach. In: Frappier, M., Glässer, U., Khurshid, S., Laleau, R., Reeves, S. (eds.) ABZ 2010. LNCS, vol. 5977, pp. 174–188. Springer, Heidelberg (2010). doi:10.1007/978-3-642-11811-1_14
10. Kitchenham, B., Madeyski, L., Budgen, D., Keung, J., Brereton, P., Charters, S., Gibbs, S., Pohthong, A.: Robust statistical methods for empirical software engineering. Empir. Softw. Eng. **22**(2), 579–630 (2017)

11. Morgan, C., Robinson, K., Gardiner, P.: On the Refinement Calculus. Springer, London (1988)
12. Olszewska, M., Sere, K.: Specification metrics for Event-B developments. In: International Conference on Quality Engineering in Software Technology, Dresden, Germany (2010)
13. Pitu, M., Grijincu, D., Li, P., Saleem, A., Monahan, R., O'Donoghue, D.P.: Arís: analogical reasoning for reuse of implementation & specification. In: International Workshop on Artificial Intelligence for Formal Methods, Rennes, France, pp. 13–16 (2013)
14. Poppleton, M.: The composition of Event-B models. In: Börger, E., Butler, M., Bowen, J.P., Boca, P. (eds.) ABZ 2008. LNCS, vol. 5238, pp. 209–222. Springer, Heidelberg (2008). doi:10.1007/978-3-540-87603-8_17
15. Roy, C.K., Zibran, M.F., Koschke, R.: The vision of software clone management: past, present, and future. In: Software Maintenance, Reengineering and Reverse Engineering, Antwerp, Belgium, pp. 18–33 (2014)
16. Sanella, D., Tarlecki, A.: Foundations of Algebraic Specification and Formal Software Development. Springer, Heidelberg (2012). doi:10.1007/978-3-642-17336-3
17. Silva, R., Butler, M.: Supporting reuse of Event-B developments through generic instantiation. In: Breitman, K., Cavalcanti, A. (eds.) ICFEM 2009. LNCS, vol. 5885, pp. 466–484. Springer, Heidelberg (2009). doi:10.1007/978-3-642-10373-5_24
18. Silva, R., Pascal, C., Hoang, T.S., Butler, M.: Decomposition tool for event-B. Softw. Practice Exp. 41(2), 199–208 (2011)

User Studies of Principled Model Finder Output

Natasha Danas[1]([⊠]), Tim Nelson[1]([⊠]), Lane Harrison[2],
Shriram Krishnamurthi[1], and Daniel J. Dougherty[2]

[1] Brown University, Providence, USA
{ndanas,tn,sk}@cs.brown.edu
[2] Worcester Polytechnic Institute, Worcester, USA
{lane,dd}@cs.wpi.edu

Abstract. Model-finders such as SAT-solvers are attractive for producing concrete models, either as sample instances or as counterexamples when properties fail. However, the generated model is arbitrary. To
address this, several research efforts have proposed principled forms of
output from model-finders. These include minimal and maximal models,
unsat cores, and proof-based provenance of facts.

While these methods enjoy elegant mathematical foundations, they
have not been subjected to rigorous evaluation on users to assess their
utility. This paper presents user studies of these three forms of output
performed on advanced students. We find that most of the output forms
fail to be effective, and in some cases even actively mislead users. To
make such studies feasible to run frequently and at scale, we also show
how we can pose such studies on the crowdsourcing site Mechanical Turk.

Keywords: Models · User studies · HCI · Minimization · Provenance ·
Unsat core

1 Introduction

Model-finding tools like SAT solvers have seen an explosive growth over the
past two decades. In addition to automation, speed, and a flexible input language, they also produce concrete instances: either instances of the specification
(henceforth, "spec"), or counterexamples. Therefore, they are now used either
directly or indirectly to produce tools in numerous domains such as networking [20,28,33], security [2], and software engineering [21,22]. In particular, the
concrete instances are valuable because they are accessible to users, such as
network operators, who are not usually schooled in formal methods.

The models that these tools produce are, however, arbitrary and reflect internal algorithmic details and sometimes also probabilities. That is, the output does
not follow any particular principle beyond satisfying the given spec. To counter
this, many authors have proposed *principled* forms of output following well-
defined mathematical properties, such as minimality [6,9,17,27,34]. Other principled output forms, like provenance [26] and unsatisfiable (henceforth, "unsat")
cores [36], augment output to aid in understanding.

© Springer International Publishing AG 2017
A. Cimatti and M. Sirjani (Eds.): SEFM 2017, LNCS 10469, pp. 168–184, 2017.
DOI: 10.1007/978-3-319-66197-1_11

These output forms have elegant mathematical properties, making them especially attractive to researchers. However, there has not been any real investigation of whether they are actually effective for users. We therefore present the first effort at evaluating these output forms. We find that they are often misleading to users, with the very properties that make them mathematically attractive causing confusion. Though our efforts are preliminary, they point to a need for the design of principled output forms to be done in conjunction with user studies: merely appealing to elegant mathematical properties for output is insufficient.

Our studies are conducted on students (Sect. 3) and on workers on a crowdsourcing platform (Sect. 4). It would be valuable to also evaluate this work with experts. Unfortunately, experts are difficult to assemble in numbers that yield statistical significance.[1] Nevertheless, as many model finders are integrated into tools (such as those cited) for end-users, advanced students and technology professionals are a reasonable proxy for (or even members of) these audiences.

Space precludes presenting the full details of our study specs; we provide full versions at http://cs.brown.edu/research/plt/dl/model-exploration-studies/, hereafter referred to as the "supplement."

2   Principled Output Methods Being Evaluated

We first describe the formalisms that this paper evaluates. Our studies use Alloy [16], a model-finder popular in the software-engineering community. Alloy searches, up to a user-specified size bound, for models that satisfy an input specification.

2.1   Minimality and Maximality

The choice of which models to present usually depends on the underlying solver algorithms. Users might be shown any models so long as they all satisfy the spec. Several authors (Sect. 5) have proposed the principle of *minimization*—an intuitively appealing notion similar to filing bug reports with only minimal test cases. In a minimal model-finder, users are shown minimal models (first). In this context, minimality is defined in terms of set containment: a model M is said to be smaller than another model M' if M contains a subset of what M' does. Note that there may be more than one minimal model. E.g., there are two different minimal models for the propositional formula $p \vee q$. A "maximal" model finder is the dual: it finds the largest models with respect to user-specified bounds on model size.

---

[1] We tried to conduct a study at the ABZ conference (which has exactly the expertise we need), handing out well over a hundred brief surveys on paper and electronically over several days. Sadly, we received only two responses.

2.2   UNSAT Cores

If the spec is unsatisfiable, no models can be found. A lack of models is often not sufficiently informative. Thus, some model finders return a subset of the spec that is itself unsatisfiable: an *unsat core*. This allows the user to focus on (what is often) a small portion of the spec to localize faults and refine their understanding. When a model search is actually a verification task, an unsat core represents a portion of the spec that suffices to prove the desired property up to the bounds specified. As Torlak, et al. [36] note, an unexpectedly small core can point to problems with the original property or user-specified size bounds.

2.3   Provenance

Even if models are found, each shows only what is *possible*, i.e., an example of what the spec permits. It gives no information about which model elements are necessary rather than only present due to (possibly intentional) under-constraint. Amalgam [26] is an extension of Alloy that fills this explanatory hole. For each component of a model, Amalgam can identify when that component is necessitated by other pieces of the model, along with identifying (as cores do) portions of the spec that serve in the implication.

3   Evaluation with Student Subjects

Attracting student volunteers does not appear to be easy. In a previous year, we had tried to run studies in relevant courses at both our institutions by offering students various rewards for participation. However these yielded unusably low participation rates, and it was difficult to judge the motivation of those students who did participate. Therefore, instead of seeking volunteers, this study was integrated directly into a course. This addressed our enrollment problem: out of about 70 students in the class, over 60 students participated in our studies.

Our students are from an upper-level course entitled "Logic for Systems" at Brown University. The course begins with property-based testing, leading to writing and checking specifications in Alloy. Most students are in the second half of their undergraduate education, having had numerous courses on programming, basic theory, and other topics in computer science; many also have summer internship experience in industry. A handful are graduate students (both master's and PhD). Many of the students will end up at elite companies within a year or two. As a result, though most of the students have not yet graduated, they have extensive computer science experience that is representative of many of the skills and preparation of industrial developers.

The studies were conducted at the ends of course labs; students were allowed to opt out of this part with no impact on their grade. The lab setting is useful in two ways. First, students are motivated to do the material since it is part of their course learning. (The course is not required, so students take it by choice and out of interest.) Second, students are required to attend lab, and are thus likely to stay to perform the study. Integrating the studies into the labs meant we had certain constraints—such as the size of specifications, their placement in the semester, the number of studies, etc.—that were unavoidable. Nevertheless, we do not believe these overly limited our studies.

All the tools have been implemented and were presented as conservative extensions to Alloy. Therefore, students did not need to switch tools, use a new syntax, learn a new visualizer, etc. This eliminates many confounding variables and makes comparisons easier.

3.1   Minimality and Maximality

In this study, we evaluated how counterexample minimization helps students debug satisfiable specifications. By default, Alloy produces arbitrary models: either as concrete instances or counterexamples to help users understand why their assertion about the spec is invalid. As discussed in Sect. 2.1, minimal models are a principled output where only facts *necessary* to satisfy the specification are included (and maximality is the dual).

In lab, students first wrote a reference-counting scheme for garbage collection. Reference-counting is well-known to be sound (it never deallocates reachable memory), but it is incomplete (it can fail to deallocate unreachable memory) when the heap contains cyclic references. Teaching assistants checked that students had completed this before proceeding to the study, in which students explored counterexamples to completeness (models that contain a heap reference cycle) and were asked to propose a constraint to make the algorithm complete— in effect, by banning cycles. (The supplement provides an example spec.)

Study Design. We split the class into two experimental groups: 35 students saw only minimal counterexamples while 25 saw only maximal ones (the imbalance is an artifact of lab section sizes). We did not otherwise modify Alloy's user interface. The first minimal and maximal counterexamples are shown in Fig. 1.

We restricted students to constructing a constraint that fits the template (all s:State | all m:HeapCell | ...). An ideal solution would use transitive closure, which catches cycles of *any* size:

```
all s:State | all m:HeapCell | m not in m.^(s.references)
```

Results. Our first finding was both surprising and disappointing: in both the minimal and maximal model groups, a significant proportion of participants dropped out of the study, switching back to unprincipled output (i.e., regular Alloy). We had 10 students drop out of the maximal group (leaving 15) and 28 students drop out of the minimal group (leaving 7). While we had no official complaints submitted along with the study results, many students in the lab expressed that the principled output frustrated them.

Out of the 7 remaining students in the minimal group, only 3 correctly restricted all reference cycles. 3 students incorrectly restricted self-loops only. The one other student proposed an incorrect and irrelevant edit. In retrospect

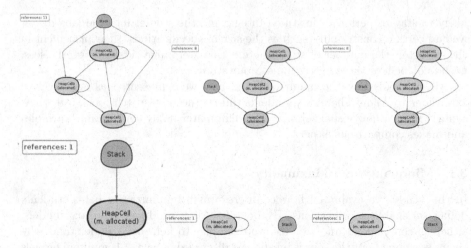

Fig. 1. Maximal (top) and minimal (bottom) counterexamples to GC completeness. Three states are shown from left to right. The transition from left to center updates the current memory references. The transition from center to right applies the specified reference-counting scheme.

this is perhaps unsurprising given the nature of models shown in minimal output, which focus attention entirely on self-loops.

In principle, maximal models do not suffer from this same tunneling of vision. Still, out of the 15 remaining maximal-group students, only 2 correctly restricted all reference cycles. 5 students incorrectly restricted self-loops only. The 8 other students proposed edits that were incorrect and irrelevant to reference cycles. Surprisingly, a higher proportion of the maximal group neglected to restrict reference cycles of any size. We discuss this and other issues in Sect. 3.4.

3.2   UNSAT Cores

In this study, we evaluated how helpful unsat cores are to students debugging unsatisfiable specs. By default, Alloy provides unsat cores to help users understand why their specification is unsatisfiable.

We presented participants with a playful, feline rendition of the "Connections of Kevin Bacon" game, where "Kitty Bacon's" connections are defined as the transitive closure of his friends. Figure 2 gives the specification in full; we explain the colored highlights below. The first group of facts (lines 1–4) define cats and how friendship works; in particular, line 3 states there is NoSelfFriendship allowed. Lines 6–11 define Kitty Bacon and the bounded transitive closure operator ConnectionsOf[Cat]. Lines 13–17 show a comparison between the bounded and unbounded notions of transitive closure. Lines 19–20 create the CoolCatClub, with only the connections of Kitty Bacon as members. The remainder of the specification defines the respective queries for generating cores and provenance

```
/*01*/ sig Cat {friends : set Cat}
/*02*/ fact NoFriendlessCats {no c:Cat | no c.friends}
/*03*/ fact NoSelfFriendship {no c:Cat | c in c.friends}
/*04*/ fact SymmetricFriendship {friends = ~friends}
/*05*/
/*06*/ one sig KittyBacon extends Cat {}
/*07*/ fun F[c:Cat]:set Cat {c.friends}
/*08*/ fun FF[c:Cat]:set Cat {F[F[c]]-F[c]-c}
/*09*/ fun FFF[c:Cat]:set Cat {F[F[F[c]]]-F[F[c]]-F[c]-c}
/*10*/ fun connectionsOf[c:Cat]:set Cat {F[c]+FF[c]+FFF[c]}
/*11*/ pred Connected {Cat-KittyBacon=connectionsOf[KittyBacon]}
/*12*/
/*13*/ pred SConnected {Cat-KittyBacon in KittyBacon.^friends}
/*14*/ assert IsSuperConnected {Connected iff SConnected}
/*15*/ check IsSuperConnected for exactly 3 Cat
/*16*/ check IsSuperConnected for exactly 4 Cat
/*17*/ check IsSuperConnected for exactly 5 Cat
/*18*/
/*19*/ one sig CCC {members : set Cat }
/*20*/ fact CoolCatClub {CCC.members=connectionsOf[KittyBacon]}
/*21*/
/*22*/ // UNSAT CORE QUERY
/*23*/ pred KittyBaconIsCool {KittyBacon in CCC.members}
/*24*/ run KittyBaconIsCool for exactly 4 Cat
/*25*/
/*26*/ // PROV QUERY: why not CCC.members(CCC$0,KittyBacon$0)
/*27*/ run {} for exactly 4 Cat
```

Fig. 2. Kitty Bacon spec with unsat core highlighting why Kitty Bacon is excluded (Color figure online)

(used by Sect. 3.3); here the students ran the **KittyBaconIsCool** predicate and found it was unsatisfiable—i.e., that Kitty Bacon could never be in the club.

The lab asked students to explain why the specification excluded Kitty Bacon from the set. They were shown an unsat core (the red and pink highlights in Fig. 2). We used Alloy's core minimization and granularity settings to reduce the core (i.e., the number of highlights) to its smallest size.

The core highlights the constraints responsible for unsatisfiability. The predicate being run (**KittyBaconIsCool**) fails when Kitty Bacon is excluded from the club, and the rest of the constraints together imply that he is never included. The core highlights three fragments of the specification: forbidding self-friendship (NoSelfFriendship), defining the connections of a cat (ConnectionsOf[Cat]), and the definition of club membership (CoolCatClub). Forbidding self-friendship means Kitty Bacon cannot be his own friend. Because he is not his own friend, Kitty Bacon is excluded from his connections. Since club membership is defined to be equivalent to the connections of Kitty Bacon, Kitty Bacon is never included in the club.

Study Design. To evaluate whether the core helped students debug their spec, we asked students to provide a free-form explanation of why Kitty Bacon was not in the club, and choose the best fix from three candidate edits. The edits were based on the three fragments of the spec highlighted by the unsat core. The correct specification fix is to update the definition of club membership to be equivalent to the union of the connections of Kitty Bacon and Kitty Bacon himself (fixing `CoolCatClub`). This avoids changing the semantics of other predicates, which might have wider-ranging consequences. Two erroneous edits were to allow self-friendship (which violates `NoSelfFriendship`), and to add Kitty Bacon to his own connections, which invalidates the prior portion of the lab (where `ConnectionsOf[Cat]` defined bounded transitive closure). Students could optionally apply no edit if they did not know which one to choose.

Results. We split the pool of students between this study and the study of provenance (Sect. 3.3). For both groups, we code[2] the free-form explanations to match them with the candidate edits related to `NoSelfFriendship`, `ConnectionsOf[Cat]`, and `CoolCatClub`. The 28 students could blame any combination of those three[3], but could choose at most one constraint to edit.

Table 1. Effects of unsat cores on debugging Kitty Bacon spec

Constraint	# Student Blames	# Student Edits	Correct?
`CoolCatClub`	18 (64%)	22 (79%)	Y
`ConnectionsOf[Cat]`	27 (96%)	0 (0%)	N
`NoSelfFriendship`·	14 (50%)	1 (4%)	N
No edit	N/A	5 (18%)	N

Table 1 shows the results. Half of the students exposed to the unsat core blamed disallowing self-friendship, but only one student applied the related (erroneous) edit. This suggests extraneous constraints in the unsat core distract students enough to widen their explanation, but not necessarily enough to cause them to apply the wrong edit. However, we constrained students to make only one change; had we permitted multiple edits, more students may have attempted erroneous ones.

3.3 Provenance

In this study, we evaluated how provenance output helps students debug a satisfiable spec (as opposed to debugging *unsatisfiable* specs aided by unsat cores). As discussed in Sect. 2.3, provenance is an alternative principled output to unsat cores, and highlights facts *necessary* to explain the presence or absence of certain tuples in an output model.

---

[2] Here, "coding" denotes classifying responses, not the colloquial term for programming.

[3] Only one author coded the free-form explanations into the 0–3 possible categories; thus, no inter-coder-reliability is reported. This is reasonable because the objective nature of having students give explanations along the different blame categories suggests a low likelihood of inaccurate coding.

Study Design. We had the other 35 students do the same study as in Sect. 3.2, except using provenances instead of unsat cores. The students looked at the first model returned for the specification, then asked the tool why Kitty Bacon was not in the Cool Cat Club. The tool produces two provenances. Both are subsets of the unsat core in Fig. 2. One is the same as the unsat core, except it excludes `NoSelfFriendship`. The other is the same as the previous provenance, except it excludes `ConnectionsOf[Cat]`.

Results. We code the student explanations in the same way. Again, the students could blame any combination of those three spec fragments but could only choose one edit. We expect the provenance students to blame and edit `NoSelfFriendship` less, as it is not highlighted in either provenance.

Table 2. Effects of provenance on debugging the Kitty Bacon spec

Constraint	# Student Blames	# Student Edits	Correct?
CoolCatClub	20 (57%)	23 (66%)	Y
ConnectionsOf[Cat]	21 (60%)	6 (17%)	N
NoSelfFriendship	9 (26%)	0 (0%)	N
No edit	N/A	6 (17%)	N

Table 2 reports our results. As expected, not highlighting `NoSelfFriendship` resulted in a only a quarter of students mentioning this constraint, and none proposing to remove it. The students who still mentioned self-friendship most likely fixated on the highlighted portions of the `ConnectionsOf[Cat]` definition that removes KittyBacon from his connected group of friends. Almost a fifth of students proposed an edit that invalidates the pedagogic portion of the lab (violating `ConnectionsOf[Cat]`). Considering that no student exposed to the unsat core proposed this erroneous edit, this result was quite surprising. A possible explanation for this surprise is discussed in Sect. 3.4.

3.4 Discussion

We hypothesize some causes for the effects that we have seen. These clearly indicate areas for future study.

Misleading Visualization. Alloy's model-visualization can impact understanding. We see several ways in which this output might have caused more maximal-group students to pick the erroneous edit; these suggest future studies. Figure 1 shows the first maximal model that students saw. Even though this model contains cycles of length 2 and 3, the immediacy and prominence of the 3 self-loops draws the eye. This may have led students in the maximal-model group to jump to the conclusion that self-loops (not cycles in general) were the problem to be fixed. Moreover, Alloy's visualizer represents cycles of length 2 as a single, double-headed arrow. It is easy to not notice that the line represents a *pair* of (cycle-inducing) edges. In addition, the small arrowheads are easy to miss. Furthermore, self-loops and 2-cycles are *explicit*, requiring only one visual object to communicate. In contrast, cycles of size 3 and above are *implicit*; users must follow directed edges through multiple nodes to discover the cycle. This may lead to a tendency to pick out shorter cycles and miss larger ones.

Table 3. Comparing unsat core and provenance on student edits

Constraint	# Unsat Core Edits	# Provenance Edits	Correct?
CoolCatClub	22 (79%)	23 (66%)	Y
ConnectionsOf[Cat]	0 (0%)	6 (17%)	N
NoSelfFriendship	1 (4%)	0 (0%)	N
No edit	5 (18%)	6 (17%)	N

Unnecessary Information is Useful. The provenance output highlighted only the constraints that, *for a current model*, lead to KittyBacon's exclusion. In contrast, the unsat core output highlighted constraints that together imply KittyBacon's exclusion *for all models*. We initially expected provenance to produce higher-quality results since its output was more focused, but almost a fifth of the students exposed to provenance proposed the incorrect ConnectionsOf[Cat] edit—versus zero in the unsat core group (Table 3). This change invalidated bounded transitive closure from the pedagogic portion of the lab. It appears that in directing the students' attention to the extraneous NoSelfFriendship constraint, unsat core output helped them realize the erroneous edit would invalidate the constraint. Thus, we suspect that the "unnecessary" highlight made the students think about the problem more globally, leading to a higher-quality fix.

4   Evaluation with Crowd-Sourced Subjects

While working with classes gives us useful insights, it also imposes several constraints: we have to fit into the time the class can afford, we can run studies only when the course runs, our population size is bounded by the number of enrolled students, and so on. We would prefer larger samples to improve statistical power, and faster responses to efficiently refine our studies. In several domains, crowdsourcing has proven very useful for this purpose.

We have been trying to evaluate principled output using Amazon's Mechanical Turk (MTurk), which provides a virtually limitless population of people who will perform tasks for pay. MTurk happens to attract many technically savvy survey workers [23]; indeed, many of them fit the demographic of users of tools that employ model finders underneath.

We did not reuse the specs of Sect. 3 because we did not want to assume knowledge of garbage collection, and the Kitty Bacon spec is very intricate, making it difficult to develop concise and quick MTurk tasks. (Also, Herman et al. [15] could be read as implying that it is unwise to too directly compare formal and natural language specs, which we use on MTurk.) Instead, we used two others: one based on an address book and the other on a grade book. They are similar (but not isomorphic) in that they contain levels of indirection (the address book has aliases; the grade book has role-based access), and have constraints to prohibit erroneous configurations ("dead end" chains of address redirections; students who can both enroll in and assist grading for a course). Both are understandable to a lay person, and non-trivial while being small.

4.1 Design Decisions

Our MTurk task designs draw on research in both HCI and crowdsourcing.

Ghoniem et al. [12] show that graphs larger than twenty vertices are better represented as a matrix. We therefore avoided showing Alloy graphs. This decision was compounded by Ottley et al.'s work on multiple simultaneous representations for Bayesian reasoning tasks [30], which found the lone textual representation had most impact and, maybe even more counter-intuitively, presenting two representations at once drastically decreases performance. They also suggest presenting the problem and feedback model in a similar language, so users can easily make connections between the two. This inspired the matching syntax between the spec and model in our framework. Simons [35] remarks on participants' difficulty observing changes across sequential images. We therefore switched from multi-page, dynamically changing layouts to a single-page, static layout. We italicized relations across the specification and model because Wills [37] states that linked visualizations increase a user's chances of cognitively linking information. We used Munzner's [25] work on designing user interfaces as a general reference.

We were also inspired by the (rare) non-expert user interfaces for formal methods tools. DeOrio and Bertacco [8] pose SAT problems to humans in a way to optimize performance and engagement. Their use of shapes and highlighting to present logic puzzles to users influenced many of our visualization choices.

Kittur, Chi, and Suh [18] report on the trade-offs of sample sizes, cost, and quality on MTurk. We therefore collected meta-data in our prototypes to assess common Turker misconceptions. We paid our respondents a living wage. We also developed an informal adversarial model to filter out the remaining low quality responses; the specific number of responses removed are in line with Kittur et al.'s results on the rate of uninformative responses on MTurk.

Peer, Vosgerau, and Acquisti [31] investigate MTurk's quality controls and conclude that reputation and productivity do correlate with response quality. Therefore, we restricted our studies to Mechanical Turkers with thousands of completed tasks and high approval rates. Mason et al. [23] evaluate the differences in expert and crowdsourced populations, while also providing a blueprint on how to properly conduct studies on Mechanical Turk. Gould et al. [13] discuss the difficulty of keeping the attention of crowdsourced subjects, finding that without intervention, crowd-workers reach inattention after about 5 min; this influenced our prototypes and final design.

4.2 Training Crowd Workers in Formal Methods

Because we cannot expect workers to know a specific formal language,[4] we systematically translate the specs to English, with a little smoothing of prose. (The full Alloy and translated specs are provided in the supplement.) For instance,

```
fact { all a: Assignment | one a.associated } ⟹
```
"Each assignment is associated with exactly one class."

We present the specs on MTurk as "logic puzzles". This hopefully attracts a more logic-minded audience, but we still want to make sure our workers understand the idea of satisfying models. We therefore include a training phase—which also serves as an assessment of the workers—before we present the actual study. This is also important for weeding out people who don't develop an understanding of the task, people clicking at random (for pay), bots, etc.

We train workers on one of the two specs, and perform the study on the full version of that spec. During training, we present the spec incrementally, adding one constraint at a time. At each step, workers are shown a collection of models and asked to classify them as satisfying or not. The non-satisfying models are not generated at random, since they might be too easy to tell apart. Rather (on steps after the first), we choose models that satisfied all but the last added constraint, and therefore "look about right". This forces workers to actually engage with the spec. (The first task's unsatisfying models are ones with type errors.)

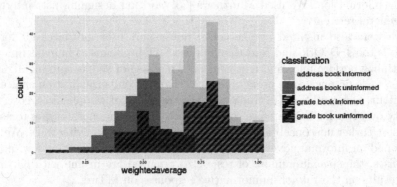

Fig. 3. Classifying crowd workers by understanding

---

[4] We did try to find Alloy users on MTurk. However, in twice the time it took to complete the studies of this section, we received at most 8 valid responses.

At each step, we calculate the percentage of correct classifications. At the end, we compute a weighted average of these percentages. The last step is weighted at 50%, with each previous step halving the next step's weight. This primarily weights their grade by their final classification, but also considers their earlier scores to invalidate workers who happened to guess correctly at the end. Based on the histogram of answers shown in Fig. 3, we found it useful to consider workers with a weighted average of 55% for address book and 70% for grade book. Doing so eliminated 40% and 39% of workers respectively.

We allowed all workers to proceed with the study. However, in the results presented in Sect. 4.3, we only show data from the 60% of workers who were above threshold. We analyzed the results from all workers, and found that those above threshold did perform significantly better than those below. Therefore, including all workers would result in even weaker findings below.

On MTurk, we only studied unsat cores and provenance. We did not study minimality because we presented only minimal models during the training phase. We made this choice to keep the studies small, in keeping with advice for using MTurk. Observe that Sect. 3.1 presents problems with minimality for *debugging*, not *learning*. Nevertheless, studying the use of minimality for learning remains an open question, and may require revisiting these studies.

Our MTurk studies trained 320 workers in total (192 above the threshold). The average response time was less than a minute per constraint. At a "living wage" of 15 cents a minute, grade book (with 9 constraints) would require less than $1.50 to train each respondent. We collected final results in about 6 h between two weekday mornings.

4.3   Effects of Unsat Cores and Provenance

After training, we present workers with the aforementioned erroneous configurations that the spec explicitly forbids. We generate the unsat core and provenance (shown in the supplement) for these situations similarly to the student studies. Workers are asked to blame the constraint responsible for forbidding the situation.

Table 4. Comparing proof output effects on crowd workers

Address book		Grade book	
Proof output type	# Correct	Proof output type	# Correct
Unsat core	9/49 (18%)	Unsat core	23/53 (43%)
Provenance	25/46 (54%)	Provenance	32/44 (73%)

Table 4 shows our results. For both specs, the group of workers exposed to provenance output blamed the truly responsible constraint more than those shown the unsat core. We performed a Chi-square test with Yates' continuity correction on the difference between these two proof outputs. Blaming the proper constraint differed significantly by proof output for the address book spec ($\chi^2(1, N = 95) = 11.85$, p < 0.001, $\phi = 0.375$, the odds ratio is 0.28) and for the grade book spec ($\chi^2(1, N = 97) = 7.27$, p < 0.01, $\phi = 0.295$, the odds ratio is 2.04). As shown by Cramer's V(ϕ), the effect size for both specs is roughly medium (0.3).

4.4 Discussion

It is interesting that provenance is useful for MTurk workers. However, we should note three salient points. First, the specs are (intentionally) much simpler than those given to students. Second, they are working with English translations; these findings may not carry over to formal specs. Finally, these numbers only show a *relative* improvement: they may say more about the difficulty with unsat cores than about the utility of provenance.

To see the latter, we note that in address book, the provenance highlighted only *one* constraint, yet 46% did not select it! In fact, fewer workers correctly chose the single highlighted constraint of address book than between the two in grade book. It is possible that the single highlight led workers to think they were being "tricked" and made them choose a different constraint, though some free-form responses indicate this is not the case: workers genuinely intended to blame a different constraint.

In short, the studies on MTurk are very preliminary and raise many questions. Nevertheless, we believe it is worth continuing to try crowdsourcing studies to understand their limits. In particular, combining a training-and-evaluation phase with an actual evaluation task seems worth considering in future designs. Also, it may be possible, with much more time, to find several qualified Alloy users on MTurk or other platforms.

5   Related Work

Principled Model Finding. Model finders, such as Alloy [16], that rely on SAT/SMT solving techniques after converting specs into boolean logic are known as "MACE-style" model finders [24]. Koshimura et al. [19] compute minimal boolean models to solve job-scheduling problems; Aluminum [27] is a general-purpose variant of Alloy that has a similar approach. Razor [34] is a stand-alone minimal model finder that also enriches models with provenance for facts. Janota [17] generates all minimal models to aid in interactive system configuration. CPSA [9] produces minimal models specifically for the cryptographic-protocol domain. Other approaches to minimal-model generation often rely on tableaux [29] or hyper-resolution [5]. The semantics of non-monotonic reasoning [32] and database updates [10] use a more general definition of minimality. Our work has focused on evaluating Aluminum's definition of minimality; we leave exploring variations for future work. In contrast to minimality, Fu and Malik develop efficient algorithms for generating maximal models [11]. Cunha, et al. [6] implement a target-oriented model finder that generates models based on a user-defined target metric. While general approaches like Cunha's have their own mathematical benefits, we focus on minimality (and its opposite, maximality) as a first step in user evaluation.

User Evaluation of Formal Methods Tools. Much previous work in the intersection of formal methods and HCI (e.g., much of the work appearing at the Workshop on Formal Methods in Human Computer Interaction) centers on using formal methods to improve user interfaces. These works are not significantly related to ours as we focus on the opposite: improving formal tools via user-centric evaluation.

We are not the first to use rigorous human-factors methods to evaluate formal-methods tools. Aitken, et al. [1] perform a user study to validate their hypothesis about the way experts use the HOL theorem prover. Beckert, et al. [3,4] use focus groups to detect gaps between a theorem prover's proof state and a user's internal model of the proof. Hentschel, Hähnle, and Bubel [14] evaluate two different interfaces for a program verifier and find that less experienced users performed significantly better using the interactive debugger interface. These studies all evaluate theorem proving tools, rather than a model finder. The two are fundamentally different, both in their user interfaces and in their essential function: one focuses on finding proofs, the other on constructing concrete examples. These results are therefore not directly applicable to us.

D'Antoni et al. [7] contrast the effectiveness of different feedback styles in an automata-theory tutoring program. Although their tool translates regular-language logic to English, the translation is intrinsic to part of the interface being evaluated. Our translation from Alloy to English (Sect. 4) was created solely for user evaluation and is not a component of Alloy.

All of these works evaluate *interfaces*, whereas we investigate a semantic concept: selecting which models to present. (In the case of D'Antoni et al., although counterexamples feature in the feedback, the choice of which to present is not studied.) Our work also targets a broader range of potential user backgrounds via crowdsourcing in order to obtain larger sample sizes.

6   Conclusion

Though our efforts are preliminary, they point to a need for the design of principled output forms to be done in conjunction with user studies: merely appealing to elegant mathematical properties for output is insufficient. We investigated three forms of principled output and found that, in isolation, these properties often harm user understanding. Our results suggest that minimality (and its maximal dual) can at times be frustrating and misleading, while provenance can lure users into a narrow, local perspective on their spec. While unsat cores do widen the user's vision, their full impact is not clear. User studies can help identify these unforeseen effects.

While evaluating formal methods with crowd-workers requires more effort in study design, our preliminary efforts show that it can be viable, especially when utilizing a "train-classify-evaluate" chain of activity. Crowd-sourced user evaluations have economic, time, and sample size benefits, and hence nicely complement more in-depth, in-person studies. Additionally, effort invested into training crowd-workers may yield techniques that we can also use more broadly to educate both students and laypeople in logic and formal methods.

Acknowledgment. This work is partially supported by the US National Science Foundation.

References

1. Aitken, S., Gray, P., Melham, T., Thomas, M.: Interactive theorem proving: an empirical study of user activity. J. Symb. Comput. **25**(2), 263–284 (1998)
2. Akhawe, D., Barth, A., Lam, P., Mitchell, J., Song, D.: Towards a formal foundation of web security. In: IEEE Computer Security Foundations Symposium (2010)
3. Beckert, B., Grebing, S., Böhl, F.: How to put usability into focus: using focus groups to evaluate the usability of interactive theorem provers. In: Workshop on User Interfaces for Theorem Provers (UITP) (2014)
4. Beckert, B., Grebing, S., Böhl, F.: A usability evaluation of interactive theorem provers using focus groups. In: Workshop on Human Oriented Formal Methods (HOFM) (2014)
5. Bry, F., Yahya, A.: Positive unit hyperresolution tableaux and their application to minimal model generation. J. Autom. Reason. **25**(1), 35–82 (2000)
6. Cunha, A., Macedo, N., Guimarães, T.: Target oriented relational model finding. In: Gnesi, S., Rensink, A. (eds.) FASE 2014. LNCS, vol. 8411, pp. 17–31. Springer, Heidelberg (2014). doi:10.1007/978-3-642-54804-8_2
7. D'Antoni, L., Kini, D., Alur, R., Gulwani, S., Viswanathan, M., Hartmann, B.: How can automatic feedback help students construct automata? Trans. Comput. Hum. Interact. **22**(2), March 2015
8. DeOrio, A., Bertacco, V.: Human computing for EDA. In: Proceedings of the 46th Annual Design Automation Conference, pp. 621–622 (2009)
9. Doghmi, S.F., Guttman, J.D., Thayer, F.J.: Searching for shapes in cryptographic protocols. In: Grumberg, O., Huth, M. (eds.) TACAS 2007. LNCS, vol. 4424, pp. 523–537. Springer, Heidelberg (2007). doi:10.1007/978-3-540-71209-1_41
10. Fagin, R., Ullman, J.D., Vardi, M.Y.: On the semantics of updates in databases. In: Principles of Database Systems (PODS), pp. 352–365. ACM (1983)
11. Fu, Z., Malik, S.: On solving the partial MAX-SAT problem. In: Biere, A., Gomes, C.P. (eds.) SAT 2006. LNCS, vol. 4121, pp. 252–265. Springer, Heidelberg (2006). doi:10.1007/11814948_25
12. Ghoniem, M., Fekete, J.D., Castagliola, P.: A comparison of the readability of graphs using node-link and matrix-based representations. In: Information Visualization (INFOVIS) (2004)
13. Gould, S., Cox, A.L., Brumby, D.P.: Diminished control in crowdsourcing: an investigation of crowdworker multitasking behavior. Trans. Comput. Hum. Interact. **23**, 19:1–19:29 (2016)
14. Hentschel, M., Hähnle, R., Bubel, R.: An empirical evaluation of two user interfaces of an interactive program verifier. In: International Conference on Automated Software Engineering (2016)

15. Herman, G.L., Kaczmarczyk, L.C., Loui, M.C., Zilles, C.B.: Proof by incomplete enumeration and other logical misconceptions. In: International Computing Education Research Workshop, ICER, pp. 59–70 (2008)
16. Jackson, D.: Software Abstractions: Logic, Language, and Analysis. MIT Press, Cambridge (2012)
17. Janota, M.: SAT solving in interactive configuration. Ph.D. thesis, University College Dublin (2010)
18. Kittur, A., Chi, E.H., Suh, B.: Crowdsourcing user studies with Mechanical Turk. In: Conference on Human Factors in Computing Systems (CHI) (2008)
19. Koshimura, M., Nabeshima, H., Fujita, H., Hasegawa, R.: Minimal model generation with respect to an atom set. In: First-Order Theorem Proving (FTP), p. 49 (2009)
20. Maldonado-Lopez, F.A., Chavarriaga, J., Donoso, Y.: Detecting network policy conflicts using Alloy. In: International Conference on Abstract State Machines, Alloy, B, and Z (2014)
21. Maoz, S., Ringert, J.O., Rumpe, B.: CD2Alloy: class diagrams analysis using Alloy revisited. In: Model Driven Engineering Languages and Systems (2011)
22. Maoz, S., Ringert, J.O., Rumpe, B.: CDDiff: semantic differencing for class diagrams. In: European Conference on Object Oriented Programming (2011)
23. Mason, W., Suri, S.: Conducting behavioral research on Amazon's Mechanical Turk. Behav. Res. Methods $44(1)$, 1–23 (2012)
24. McCune, W.: Mace4 reference manual and guide. arXiv preprint cs/0310055 (2003)
25. Munzner, T.: Visualization Analysis and Design. CRC Press (2014)
26. Nelson, T., Danas, N., Dougherty, D.J., Krishnamurthi, S.: The power of "why" and "why not": enriching scenario exploration with provenance. In: Foundations of Software Engineering (2017)
27. Nelson, T., Saghafi, S., Dougherty, D.J., Fisler, K., Krishnamurthi, S.: Aluminum: principled scenario exploration through minimality. In: ICSE, pp. 232–241 (2013)
28. Nelson, T., Barratt, C., Dougherty, D.J., Fisler, K., Krishnamurthi, S.: The Margrave tool for firewall analysis. In: Large Installation System Administration Conference (2010)
29. Niemelä, I.: A tableau calculus for minimal model reasoning. In: Miglioli, P., Moscato, U., Mundici, D., Ornaghi, M. (eds.) TABLEAUX 1996. LNCS, vol. 1071, pp. 278–294. Springer, Heidelberg (1996). doi:10.1007/3-540-61208-4_18
30. Ottley, A., Peck, E.M., Harrison, L.T., Afergan, D., Ziemkiewicz, C., Taylor, H.A., Han, P.K., Chang, R.: Improving Bayesian reasoning: the effects of phrasing, visualization, and spatial ability. Vis. Comput. Graph. $22(1)$, 529–538 (2016)
31. Peer, E., Vosgerau, J., Acquisti, A.: Reputation as a sufficient condition for data quality on Amazon Mechanical Turk. Behav. Res. Methods $46(4)$, 1023–1031 (2014)
32. Robinson, A., Voronkov, A.: Handbook of Automated Reasoning, vol. 1. Elsevier, Amsterdam (2001)
33. Ruchansky, N., Proserpio, D.: A (not) NICE way to verify the OpenFlow switch specification: formal modelling of the OpenFlow switch using Alloy. ACM Comput. Commun. Rev. $43(4)$, 527–528 (2013)
34. Saghafi, S., Danas, R., Dougherty, D.J.: Exploring theories with a model-finding assistant. In: Felty, A.P., Middeldorp, A. (eds.) CADE 2015. LNCS, vol. 9195, pp. 434–449. Springer, Cham (2015). doi:10.1007/978-3-319-21401-6_30

35. Simons, D.J.: Current approaches to change blindness. Vis. Cogn. **7**(1–3), 1–15 (2000)
36. Torlak, E., Chang, F.S.H., Jackson, D.: Finding minimal unsatisfiable cores of declarative specifications. In: International Symposium on Formal Methods (FM) (2008)
37. Wills, G.J.: Visual exploration of large structured datasets. In: Proceedings of New Techniques and Trends in Statistics (NTTS), pp. 237–246 (1997)

Using Shared Memory Abstractions to Design Eager Sequentializations for Weak Memory Models

Ermenegildo Tomasco[1], Truc Lam Nguyen[1(✉)], Bernd Fischer[2],
Salvatore La Torre[3], and Gennaro Parlato[1]

[1] Electronics and Computer Science, University of Southampton, Southampton, UK
tnl2g10@soton.ac.uk
[2] Division of Computer Science, Stellenbosch University, Stellenbosch, South Africa
[3] Dipartimento di Informatica, Università di Salerno,
Fisciano, Italy

Abstract. Sequentialization translates concurrent programs into equivalent nondeterministic sequential programs so that the different concurrent schedules no longer need to be handled explicitly. However, existing sequentializations assume sequential consistency, which modern hardware architectures no longer guarantee. Here we describe a new approach to embed weak memory models within eager sequentializations. Our approach is based on the separation of intra-thread computations from inter-thread communications by means of a shared memory abstraction (SMA). We give details of SMA implementations for the SC, TSO, and PSO memory models that are based on the idea of individual memory unwindings. We use our approach to implement a new, efficient BMC-based bug finding tool for multi-threaded C programs under SC, TSO, or PSO based on these SMAs, and show experimentally that it is competitive to existing tools.

1 Introduction

Developing correct concurrent programs is a complex and difficult task, due to the large number of possible concurrent executions that must be considered. Modern multi-core hardware architectures with *weak memory models* (WMMs) have made this task even harder, because they introduce additional executions that can lead to seemingly counter-intuitive results that confound the developers' reasoning.

Testing remains the most widely used approach to finding bugs; however, it is ineffective for bugs that manifest themselves only rarely and are difficult to reproduce [20]. Such "Heisenbugs" are unfortunately more prevalent with WMMs. Static verification approaches that handle individual executions *explicitly* face the same state space explosion as testing, even with optimizations that

Partially supported by EPSRC EP/M008991/1, and MIUR-FARB 2014-2016 grants.

A. Cimatti and M. Sirjani (Eds.): SEFM 2017, LNCS 10469, pp. 185–202, 2017.
DOI: 10.1007/978-3-319-66197-1_12

eliminate redundant executions. We thus need approaches that can handle multiple concurrent executions *symbolically*.

However, building efficient symbolic verification tools for realistic programming languages like C is hard and extending them for concurrency is harder yet. Tools thus often fold the concurrency handling deep into their general verification approaches (see [1,4,7,9,24,25]), focussing on a specific memory model, typically sequential consistency (SC). This introduces a strong coupling between the two aspects, which makes it hard to reuse existing tools and to generalize solutions to other memory models.

Our goal is to improve on this without losing the efficiency of existing approaches. For this, we separate the computation (i.e., individual threads) and the communication (i.e., shared memory) concerns of concurrent programs as follows. First, we replace all standard concurrency operations in multi-threaded programs (such as shared memory reads, writes, and allocations, thread creation and termination), and synchronization operations (such as thread join and mutex locking and unlocking) by abstract operations over an API called *shared memory abstraction* (SMA). We then provide efficient SMA implementations tailored for the targeted WMM and class of verification algorithms so that we can reuse existing efficient originally designed for SC now for WMMs.

The notion of SMA was originally introduced in [22] where the focus was on *lazy* sequentialization techniques, i.e., based on state-space search algorithms exploring only reachable states. A main achievement of [22] is an efficient SMA implementation based on temporal circular doubly-linked lists. The correctness of such SMAs is only guaranteed when SMA operations are invoked in the program execution order.

Here, we extend the SMA-based design from [22] to *eager* model-checking algorithms (in the style of Lal/Reps sequentialization [17]). In eager approaches, each thread is analysed in isolation thus avoiding the state-space explosion (cross product of the thread-local states) in which lazy approaches may incur. However, eager explorations guess variable valuations when a read operation matches a value written by another thread that has not been explored yet, and maintain auxiliary information to discard infeasible executions resulting from spurious variable valuations. Eager exploration algorithms, implemented through sequentialization, have led to mature symbolic bug-finding tools for SC concurrent C programs (e.g., Smack [10], MU-CSeq [21]).

As our first contribution, we extend the API of the SMA from [22] to achieve a deeper decoupling of the program computation and communication aspects thus making it more suitable for general implementations. We see a program as the composition (synchronized over the SMA API) of a thread control-flow system and an SMA system. We then identify the semantic notions of *thread-wise equivalence* and *thread-asynchronous closure* of transition systems as general properties that allow us to state correctness of a class of methods. Namely, we get that reachability is preserved if we replace in the composed system the thread control-flow part for a thread-wise equivalent one (assuming the SMA part is thread-asynchronous) or the SMA part for its thread-asynchronous closure.

This has two important consequences. First, we can extend existing concurrent verification algorithms that do not reorder statements within each thread (such as the eager ones) to different memory models *simply by implementing* the corresponding SMAs. Second, we get a degree of freedom in designing concurrent verification algorithms, since in executions exploration we can rearrange the order of the statements from different threads. This is implicitly exploited by some algorithms from the literature (e.g., [15,17,21]) which can be recast in our setting and thus extended to WMMs.

As our second contribution, we instantiate our general approach to achieve an efficient BMC-based bug-finding tool. We give efficient SMA-implementations for SC, total store ordering (TSO), and partial store ordering (PSO) that are based on the idea of *individual memory-location unwindings*, where for each variable we keep the (temporally ordered) sequence of all its writes occurring in a computation. We then show through experiments that our prototype tool compares well with existing tools.

2   Weak Memory Models

A *shared memory* is a sequence of memory locations of fixed size. The content of each location can be read or written using an explicit memory operation. The semantics of read and write operations depend upon the adopted memory model. Besides SC, we also consider TSO and PSO, which are implemented in modern computer architectures.

Sequential consistency (SC). SC is the "standard model", where a write into the shared memory is performed directly on the memory location. This has the effect that the newly written value is instantaneously visible to all the other threads.

Total store ordering (TSO). The behaviour of the TSO memory model can be described using a simplified architecture with explicit store buffers [18]. Each thread t is equipped with a local *store buffer* that is used to cache the write operations performed by t according to a FIFO policy. Updates to the shared memory occur nondeterministically along the computation, by selecting a thread, removing the oldest write operation from its store buffer, and then updating the shared memory valuation accordingly. Before updating, the effect of a cached write is visible only to the thread that has performed it. A read by t of a variable y retrieves the value from the shared memory unless there is a cached write to y pending in its store buffer; in that case, the value of the *most recent* write in t's store buffer is returned. A thread can also execute a *fence*-operation to block its execution until its store buffer has been emptied.

Partial store ordering (PSO). The semantics of PSO is the same as for TSO except that each thread is endowed with a store buffer for each shared memory location.

3 Multi-threaded Programs over Shared Memory Abstractions

We consider multi-threaded programs with a standard C-like syntax including pointer arithmetics and dynamic memory allocation. We further consider POSIX-like threads with dynamic thread creation, thread join, and mutex locking and unlocking operations for thread synchronization; threads communicate only via the shared memory. We also assume a `fence` statement that commits all pending write operations of a thread into the shared memory; for TSO and PSO this means it flushes all store buffers of a thread.

Shared Memory Abstractions. The semantics of multi-threaded programs ultimately depends on the underlying memory model. In order to combine existing concurrent verification techniques with different memory models we define a "concurrency interface" or *shared memory abstraction* (SMA) that abstracts away the shared memory operations in the syntax of multi-threaded programs. The intended meaning of the SMA's functions is standard; note that most functions carry the calling thread t as an extra argument to allow the SMA to update its internal state. In detail, the SMA API is:

- `init()` initializes the SMA; this must be the first statement in the program;
- `terminate(t)` ends the execution of t; each thread must explicitly call it;
- `error(t)` flags an assertion failure in t; the computation ends in an *error state*;
- `address(v,t)` returns the memory address of the shared variable v;
- `malloc(n,t)` allocates a continuous block of n memory locations and returns the base address of the block;
- `read(v,t)` (resp. `ind_read(a,t)`) returns the valuation of the shared variable v (resp. memory location with address a) as seen by t;
- `write(v,val,t)` (resp. `ind_write(a,val,t)`) sets the valuation of the shared variable v (resp. memory location with address a) to the value val;
- `fence(t)` commits all pending write operations of t into the shared memory;
- `lock(m,t)` and `unlock(m,t)` are standard thread synchronization primitives that acquire and release a mutex m for t; if m is currently acquired, the `lock` operation is blocking for t, i.e., t is suspended until m is released and then acquired;
- `create(f,t)` spawns a new thread that starts from function f, and returns a fresh thread identifier for this thread;
- `join(t',t)` pauses the execution of t until t' has terminated its execution.

Multi-threaded Programs as Composition of Transition Systems. The formal semantics of multi-threaded programs is given by a transition system that captures the program computations by interleaving the computations of each thread. We exploit the separation between the control flow and the shared memory aspects introduced with the notion of SMA, and give the semantics of a multi-threaded program as the composition $\mathcal{C}|\mathcal{M}$ of the *control-flow transition system* $\mathcal{C}$ that captures the control flow of all threads and the *SMA transition system* $\mathcal{M}$ that implements the behaviours of the SMA. This allows us to keep the semantics of the sequential part and re-interpret it in different ways with different WMMs; it also aligns nicely with different SMA implementations.

The two transition systems are synchronized over the alphabet Σ_{SMA} which contains the calls to the SMA API functions that do not return values, and the calls augmented with a parameter denoting the returned value for the others. For example, read(3,v,t) is the letter corresponding to a call read(v,t) that returns value 3.

Control-flow transition system. The states of the control-flow transition system $\mathcal{C}$ are the tuples of thread configurations. A thread configuration consists of a program counter, an evaluation of the thread-local variables and a call stack. $\mathcal{C}$ has a unique initial state that corresponds to the empty configuration (i.e., no threads are active in the beginning).

The transitions correspond to the execution of any of the statements. Those corresponding to invocations of API functions of SMA are labeled with the corresponding letter from Σ_{SMA}. In particular, transitions from the initial state are labeled with init() and enter a state with the starting configuration of the main thread. No other transitions are labeled with init(). Transitions corresponding to SMA functions that return a value are handled as thread-local assignments with the returned values. On a thread creation the tuple of thread configurations is augmented with the starting configuration of the newly created thread. Similarly, the effect of a transition on terminate(t) is to delete the configuration of the terminated thread and that of a transition on error(t) is to enter an *error state*. Both these kinds of transition disallow further transitions of thread t. The remaining transitions labeled with Σ_{SMA} letters just update the program counter. Transitions corresponding to all other (i.e., sequential) statements are labeled with the empty word ε and update the configuration of the issuing thread as usual.

Shared memory abstraction transition system. With $\mathcal{M}_{sc}$, $\mathcal{M}_{tso}$ and $\mathcal{M}_{pso}$ we denote the *canonical* SMA transitions systems capturing respectively the semantics of SC, TSO and PSO memory models as described in Sect. 2. We observe that each of such systems has an initial state and a state for each possible configuration of the corresponding memory model. In addition, the states of $\mathcal{M}_{tso}$ and $\mathcal{M}_{pso}$ account also for the content of the thread store buffers.

Transitions update the memory configurations to capture the memory model's intended meaning. In particular, from the initial state there are only outgoing transitions labeled with init() that take to any state with: just one thread (which must be active), any number of shared locations (which must all have the value of zero), and any number of mutexes (which must all be unlocked). No other transition have this label. $\mathcal{M}_{sc}$ has no fence-transitions. $\mathcal{M}_{tso}$ and $\mathcal{M}_{pso}$ have instead such transitions on calls to fence by t and also ε-transitions for store buffer updates. Further, in a transition on terminate(t), the three transistion systems enter a state where the status of t is terminated.

Similarly, on error(t), they enter an *error state*. From any of these two kinds of states no other transitions corresponding to invocations of API functions from t are allowed. The final states are error states and all states where all threads are terminated.

4   Verification with Thread-Asynchronous SMAs

Splitting the design of a verification tool into an SMA implementation and a search algorithm for program execution exploration gives a convenient way to extend it to other memory models: one can just replace the SMA implementation. However, obtaining scalable tools would still be an issue. In fact, for correctness, a direct implementation of memory models would require to invoke memory operations as they occur in a run. This may result into a bottleneck for summary based analysis (e.g., BDD-based model checking) due to the state-space explosion caused by the cross product of thread-local states, as well as for bounded model checking where the code of all threads must be included at each possible context-switch point, thus leading to large SAT/SMT formulas.

We thus propose a general framework where we assume the SMA implementation to be *thread-asynchronous* , i.e., insensitive to how the threads are interleaved. This allows us to freely transform the threads as long as we stay within the class of *thread-wise equivalent* programs, i.e., programs where the *intra-thread ordering* of the statements remains the same. Transformations into thread-wise equivalent programs has been already exploited in successful approaches from the literature where program executions are rearranged such that each thread is simulated in turn to completion [15,17,21].

For a thread t, we denote with Σ_{SMA}^t the maximal subset of Σ_{SMA} containing only letters that are issued by t. Clearly, for threads t and t' with $t \neq t'$, Σ_{SMA}^t and $\Sigma_{SMA}^{t'}$ are disjoint. For a thread t and a word α over Σ_{SMA}, let $\alpha_{|t}$ be the projection of α onto Σ_{SMA}^t, i.e., the word obtained from α by deleting all the letters that do not belong to Σ_{SMA}^t. If $t_1, \ldots, t_h$ are all the threads that issue at least a letter in α, we define $\pi(\alpha)$ as the map $\pi(\alpha)(t_i) = \alpha_{|t_i}$ for $i \in [1, h]$.

A language L over Σ_{SMA} is *thread-asynchronous* if for each $\alpha \in L$ and for each α' starting with init() s.t. $\pi(\alpha) = \pi(\alpha')$, also $\alpha' \in L$. The *thread-asynchronous closure* of L, denoted by $L^\#$, is the smallest thread-asynchronous language such that $L \subseteq L^\#$.

Let $\mathcal{A}_1$ and $\mathcal{A}_2$ be two transition systems over the alphabet Σ_{SMA}. We say that $\mathcal{A}_1$ and $\mathcal{A}_2$ are *thread-wise equivalent* if for each word α accepted by one of them there is a word α' that is accepted by the other one such that $\pi(\alpha) = \pi(\alpha')$.

A standard analysis for a multi-threaded program is to search for the reachability of an *error*, often denoted by an error label or a `false`-assertion in the program. In our setting, an error is captured by a transition over label error(t). Since program executions are captured by accepting runs of corresponding transition systems, a program error is reachable if and only if a word containing label error(t) is accepted. We say that an error is reachable in two transition systems

$\mathcal{A}_1$ and $\mathcal{A}_2$, if there are words $\alpha_i \in L(\mathcal{A}_i)$, with $i = 1, 2$, that contain a same label error(t) such that $\pi(\alpha_1) = \pi(\alpha_2)$.

We conclude this section with two theorems stating sufficient conditions under which the reachability of error states is preserved. The first theorem states that if the SMA system is thread-asynchronous, by transforming a program P_1 into a program P_2 such that the corresponding control-flow transitions systems are thread-wise equivalent, an error is reachable in P_1 if and only if it is reachable in P_2. Intuitively, since the SMA transition system is thread-asynchronous, we are guaranteed that the interaction of each thread with the SMA is independent of how threads are interleaved: for any fixed run ρ, the values of the read operations remain the same in all the possible interleavings of the projections of ρ onto each thread. Thus, we get that reachability is preserved.

Theorem 1. *Let $\mathcal{C}_i$ be a control-flow transition system for $i = 1, 2$ and $\mathcal{M}$ be an SMA transition system. If $\mathcal{C}_1$ and $\mathcal{C}_2$ are thread-wise equivalent, and $\mathcal{M}$ is thread-asynchronous, then an error is reachable in $\mathcal{C}_1|\mathcal{M}$ iff it is reachable in $\mathcal{C}_2|\mathcal{M}$.*

Theorem 1 states a crucial property for our approach: we can implement a thread-asynchronous SMA, and combine it with any transformation of the program that rearranges the interleaving among threads and still get a correct verification approach.

The second theorem shows that we can replace an SMA $\mathcal{M}_1$ with another SMA $\mathcal{M}_2$ that captures its thread-asynchronous closure, and still preserve reachability of errors. The interesting case of the proof is when a sequence α is accepted by $\mathcal{M}_2$ but not by $\mathcal{M}_1$. In this case, since the returned values are visible in Σ_{SMA} letters and there must be a sequence α' that is accepted by $\mathcal{M}_1$ such that $\pi(\alpha) = \pi(\alpha')$, we get that the sequence of local states that are visited by any thread of any program P are the same for both sequences α and α'. Therefore, the following theorem holds.

Theorem 2. *Let $\mathcal{C}$ be a control-flow transition system and $\mathcal{M}_i$ be an SMA transition system for $i = 1, 2$. If $L(\mathcal{M}_2) = (L(\mathcal{M}_1))^\#$, then an error is reachable in $\mathcal{C}|\mathcal{M}_1$ iff it is reachable in $\mathcal{C}|\mathcal{M}_2$.*

By the above theorems, we can show the correctness of WMM extensions of correct verification methods that transform programs by keeping the ordering of the operations within each thread, such as the methods from [15–17, 21]. In fact, we just need to provide an SMA that captures the thread-asynchronous closure of the memory model.

5   Individual Memory-Location Unwindings

We now discuss an implementation of thread-asynchronous SMAs for SC, TSO and PSO. The key notion is the *individual memory-location unwinding* (IMU), a set containing exactly one sequence of writes for each shared memory location

(*location unwinding*, LU for short) and such that the unique timestamps associated to each write determine a total order among all the writes of all the LUs (where each timestamp denotes the time of occurrence of a write according to a discrete-time global clock).

Precisely, an LU for a memory location v, denoted by v-LU, is a sequence of triples (t, val, d) where t and val denote the thread identifier and the value of the write and $d > 0$ is the associated timestamp. If Var is the set of location names and μ_v a v-LU for each $v \in Var$, an IMU is a set $\{\mu_v \mid v \in Var\}$ such that: (a) the tuples in each LU are ordered by increasing timestamps, and (b) for each pair of different location names $v_1, v_2 \in Var$ and for each (t_i, val_i, d_i) in μ_{v_i} with $i = 1, 2$, then also $d_1 \neq d_2$ (thus timestamps define a total order among all the writes in the IMU).

IMU-based SMA for SC. A transition system $\mathcal{M}_{sc}^{imu}$ for an IMU-based implementation of SMA first guesses an IMU on the init()-transition and then executes the operations. Namely, it keeps for each thread the current timestamp (i.e., the timestamp of the last executed SMA operation) and for any input sequence α, it ensures that:

- on write(v,val,t) (resp. ind_write(a,val,t)), the next write in the v-LU (resp. the LU identified by the address a) for thread t matches the value val; the current timestamp of t is updated to the timestamp of the matched write in the next state;
- on read(val,v,t) (resp. ind_read(val,a,t)), there must be in the v-LU (resp. the LU identified by the address a) a write with timestamp d that assigns value val to v such that either d is the timestamp of the most recent (before t's current timestamp) write to v or d is between t's current timestamp and the timestamp of t's next write; in the latter case t's current timestamp is updated to d in the next state;
- for each thread, the writes are matched by increasing timestamps.

In order to accept α, create(t,f,t') must occur in α for each thread t with writes guessed in the IMU and the writes in the IMU should be mapped 1-to-1 to the writes in α.

The transition system $\mathcal{M}_{sc}^{imu}$ is thread-wise equivalent to $\mathcal{M}_{sc}$, and additionally, it can execute all computations of $\mathcal{M}_{sc}$ by advancing each involved thread in any order. Moreover, due to the fact that all writes are guessed in advance, the ordering in which we interleave the threads is irrelevant. We thus get the following lemma.

Lemma 1. $L(\mathcal{M}_{sc}^{imu}) = (L(\mathcal{M}_{sc}))^{\#}$.

IMU-based SMA for TSO and PSO. We augment the IMU by adding a second timestamp for each write. In particular, we now make a distinction between the time a write occurs (*occurrence timestamp*) and the time the shared memory is updated with an occurred write (*update timestamp*). For correctness, we also impose on the IMU that for each write the occurrence timestamp should not be greater than the update timestamp.

For TSO, in order to ensure the FIFO policy of the store buffers, we additionally require that for each thread the occurrence and the update timestamps must both order all the writes according to the program order. For PSO, instead it is sufficient to require this only for the writes of a same location.

We will denote with $\mathcal{M}_{tso}^{imu}$ and $\mathcal{M}_{pso}^{imu}$ the IMU-based SMA transition systems corresponding to the TSO and PSO memory models, respectively. $\mathcal{M}_{tso}^{imu}$ can be obtained from $\mathcal{M}_{sc}^{imu}$ with a few changes: on the init()-transition we now guess the IMU with occurrence and update timestamps as observed above; in a read of location v by a thread t the position of the matching write is the last occurred write still in the store buffer of t (i.e., current timestamp of t is between the occurrence timestamp and the update timestamp of the last write of v by t), if any, and the last updated write of v, otherwise (this case works as the read in $\mathcal{M}_{sc}^{imu}$); the current timestamp of a thread t is also updated to the occurrence timestamp of a write when this is executed; a fence(t)-transition updates the current timestamp to the largest update timestamp of the already occurred writes performed by t. Obtaining $\mathcal{M}_{pso}^{imu}$ from $\mathcal{M}_{tso}^{imu}$ is straightforward: the only difference is hidden in the properties that are required on the guessed IMU as observed above.

By the above observations we can derive that $\mathcal{M}_{pso}^{imu}$ and $\mathcal{M}_{tso}^{imu}$ capture the semantics of the corresponding memory models. Moreover, since all the writes are guessed in advance, the ordering in which we interleave the threads is irrelevant. Thus, we get:

Lemma 2. *For* $m \in \{tso, pso\}$, $L(\mathcal{M}_m^{imu}) = (L(\mathcal{M}_m))^\#$.

Verification by eager sequentialization and IMU. We recall that an eager sequentialization, usually implemented through a code-to-code translation that results into a nondeterministic sequential program, is designed such that each thread is simulated in isolation against the shared memory. Thus, eager sequentializations naturally define control-flow transition systems that preserve the ordering in which the statements of each thread are executed, and thus can be combined with thread-asynchronous SMAs by preserving reachability. Here, we take the control-flow transition system defined by the eager sequentialization from [21] and combine it with $\mathcal{M}_{sc}^{imu}$, $\mathcal{M}_{tso}^{imu}$ and $\mathcal{M}_{pso}^{imu}$, thus obtaining new verification methods under SC, TSO and PSO semantics. The correctness of such methods is consequence of the above lemmas, and Theorems 1 and 2.

6   IMU-based SMA Implementations

In this section, we discuss concrete C-implementations of the SMA API from Sect. 3 according to the semantics captured by $\mathcal{M}_{sc}^{imu}$, $\mathcal{M}_{tso}^{imu}$ and $\mathcal{M}_{pso}^{imu}$. We will give some details of the implemented code. Note that our code is optimized for an efficient analysis using BMC tools but implementations for other backends are possible.

IMU Implementation for SC. The implementation is parameterized over several constants. N and U denote the number of *locations with names* (i.e., shared scalar variables) and *locations without names* (i.e., heap locations accessed only through memory addresses), respectively. W denotes the maximum number of write operations for each of these V=N+U tracked memory locations, M and T denote the maximum number of dynamic memory allocations and thread creations, respectively, that may happen during any execution of the input program. *Data structures and invariants.* We use several scalar variables and arrays to maintain the LUs and support the implementation of the SMA operations. We sketch below the main ones that are relevant to the read and write operations; others are used to model thread creation, join, and termination, and the dynamic memory allocation. All are declared global such that they are visible and can be modified in all the functions. For simplicity, we assume that all data is represented by unsigned integers.

The triples (t, val, d) of the LUs are maintained by three different arrays thread, value and tstamp. For every location $v \in [0, V-1]$ and $i \in [0, W-1]$, the triple at position i in the v-LU is stored in thread[v][i], value[v][i] and tstamp[v][i]. We link the writes of a same thread in each LU by an additional array th_next_write. All these arrays are nondeterministically assigned in the function init and never changed in the program execution. init also ensures that:

- timestamps are assigned in increasing order for each LU;
- no two writes in the IMU are assigned the same timestamp;
- for every location $v \in [0, V-1]$, position $i \in [0, W-1]$ and thread identifier $t \in [0, T-1]$, th_next_write[v][i][t] is the first position in the v-LU after i that corresponds to a write by t, if any; otherwise, it is set to W, denoting that no further writes of v by t are expected.

To keep track of the execution of each thread in the IMU, we use the arrays th_pos, last_write and cur_tstamp, and maintain the following invariants for every location $v \in [0, V-1]$ and thread identifier $t \in [0, T-1]$:

- th_pos[v][t] stores the current position of thread t in the v-LU;
- last_write[v] stores the position $i \in [0, W-1]$ of the last executed write operation of location v in the v-LU;
- cur_tstamp[t] stores the current timestamp of thread t during its simulation.

Verification stubs. We only discuss here the implementation of the API functions read and write, which is given in Fig. 1. Both functions first check whether the execution of the simulated thread has been stopped, and return immediately if this is the case; note that in our simulation when calling read on a thread that is indeed terminated the returned value is never used, so here any integer would do (we use 0 in our implementation). For a read operation of thread t from location v, we first jump forward into v-LU by invoking the auxiliary function Jump and then return the value of v at this new position of v-LU. Jump (cf. Fig. 1) works as follows. If the timestamp of the selected write is past the current thread

```
int read(uint v,uint t){                   uint Jump(uint t, uint v){
  if(is_terminated(t)) return 0;             uint jump=*;
  uint jump = Jump(t,v);                     uint j=th_pos[v][t];
  return (value[v][jump]);
}                                            ts_jump = tstamp[v][jump];
                                             assume( (jump <= last_write[v])
void write(uint v,int val,uint t){             && (jump < th_next_write[v][t][j])
  if(is_terminated(t)) return;                 && (tstamp[v][jump+1] > cur_tstamp[t])
  uint i, jump;                              );
  i = th_pos[v][t];
  jump = th_next_write[v][i][t];            cur_tstamp[t] =
  assume( (jump <= last_write[v])              (ts_jump > cur_tstamp[t]) ?
    && (value[v][jump] == val)                       ts_jump : cur_tstamp[t];
    && (tstamp[v][jump] > cur_tstamp[t])     return jump;
  );                                       }
  th_pos[v][t] = jump;
  cur_tstamp[t] = tstamp[v][jump];
}
```

Fig. 1. Read, write, and jump functions.

timestamp, the latter is updated to this value, acknowledging the fact that the corresponding write into the shared memory has occurred. The value of jump is selected nondeterministically within a range of proper values. Namely, jump should not pass the last legal write position for v and must be strictly less than the position of the next write of v by the same thread t (that has not occurred yet). Further, we require that the timestamp at position jump+1 is greater than the current timestamp of t, as we must point to a write of v that is not superseded by already occurred writes.

With the stated invariants we get that Jump identifies a position i in the v-LU that is correct w.r.t. the v-LU (in the sense that it is not jumping over the next write of v by t). However, note that the corresponding timestamp could be still larger then the next write by t (for a different location) but we will catch this while executing the next write of t, when the current timestamp of t will be larger than the one of that write.

In a write operation, we first move forward to the position of the next write by t in the v-LU and block the execution if the value to be written differs from that stored in the v-LU. We also check that the timestamp associated with the new v-LU position for t is greater than the current timestamp of t; if this is not the case, we are then in the error case generated by a wrong update of the thread timestamp in a read, and thus the execution is aborted. If all checks are passed, we update the current position of thread t in the v-LU and the current timestamp accordingly, thus maintaining the invariants.

IMU Implementation for TSO. We give this implementation incrementally on that given for SC; the code of the functions read, fence and write is illustrated in Fig. 2. We use: tstamp[v][i] to store the update timestamp and btstamp[v][i] to store the occurrence timestamp of the write at position i in the v-LU; ts_lastW[t] to store the update timestamp of the write by thread t that occurred last.

For init, we guess the initial values for btstamp[v][i] and then impose that btstamp[v][i] $\leq$ tstamp[v][i] must hold (i.e., the update of the shared memory according to an occurred write may be delayed w.r.t. its occurrence time). Note that here we slightly diverge from the transition system $\mathcal{M}_{tso}^{imu}$ described in Sect. 5. In fact, since we do not require any other condition on the guessed update timestamps, we can carry over an IMU with timestamps that may violate the FIFO policy on the store buffers. We fix this by checking the proper ordering on matching the writes (see below).

```
int read(uint v,uint t){
  if(is_terminated(t)) return 0;
  uint ts_jump, i;
  i = th_pos[v][t];
  uint nxt_write = th_next_write[v][i][t];
  uint fst_write = th_next_write[v][0][t];
  assume (
    (ts_jump >= cur_tstamp[t]) &&
    (ts_jump < btstamp[v][nxt_write])
  );
  cur_tstamp[t] = ts_jump;
  if( fst_write <= i  &&
      tstamp[v][i] > cur_tstamp[t]
  ) return value[v][i];
  return Read_SC(v,t);
}
```

```
void fence(uint t){
  if(ts_lastW[t] > cur_tstamp[t])
    cur_tstamp[t] = ts_lastW[t];
}

void write(uint v,int val,uint t){
  if(is_terminated(t)) return;
  i = th_pos[v][t];
  jump = th_next_write[v][i][t];
  th_pos[v][t] = jump;
  assume(
    btstamp[v][jump] > cur_tstamp[t]
    && value[v][jump] == val
    && tstamp[v][jump] > ts_lastW[t]
  );
  ts_lastW[t] = tstamp[v][jump];
  cur_tstamp[t] = btstamp[v][jump];
}
```

Fig. 2. Functions read, fence and write for TSO.

The fence-operation flushes the store buffer of the executing thread. We thus need to synchronize the current thread timestamp with its last update timestamp, i.e., if ts_lastW[t] is larger than the timestamp of the last occurred write by t, we set ts_lastW[t] to cur_tstamp[t]. Note that if this is not the case then the local store buffer of t is certainly empty, since btstamp[v][i] $\leq$ tstamp[v][i].

The read-function first increases nondeterministically the current timestamp of thread t such that it remains smaller than the occurrence timestamp of the next write of v by t. Now, if at least a write of location v by t has occurred and the last write of v by t is still in the thread buffer, then we return the value of this write. Otherwise, a read from the shared memory is performed by invoking the auxiliary function Read_SC that is exactly the function read from Fig. 1. Note that the update of the current thread timestamp by read can cause this value to be larger than the update timestamp of the last write, which is correct. To avoid that we wrongly move the time back, in fence we make the assignment only when this is not the case.

The write-function first updates the current position in the v-LU of thread t to the next write provided that: the time of occurrence of this write is larger than the current thread timestamp, the value of the write matches the guessed value for it and the update timestamp of the next write is larger than that of the last occurred write (the last one ensures that the thread store buffers are emptied according to a FIFO policy). Note that, in the case of a wrong guess of the update timestamps in init, this condition would not hold and thus the execution would abort. Before returning, the update timestamp of the last write and the current timestamp of thread t are modified consistently.

IMU Implementation for PSO. We just need to slightly modify the implementation for TSO as follows. We use a new array max_tsW instead of ts_lastW to keep for each thread t the maximum update timestamp among all the occurred writes of t. Thus, we replace in write the update of ts_lastW with the assignment of max_tsW[t] with (tstamp[v][jump] > max_tsW[t]) ? tstamp[v][jump] : max_tsW[t].

We further modify function write by removing from the assume-statement the conjunct tstamp[v][jump] > ts_lastW[t] (see Fig. 2). We recall that this conjunct was required in the TSO implementation to ensure the store-buffer FIFO policy for each thread; in PSO, we only need to require this within each LU.

7   Experimental Evaluation

We implemented the approach of Sect. 6 in the IMU-CSeq tool[1] that analyzes C programs over the pthreads API. It uses modules from MU-CSeq [13,21] to transform the original multi-threaded program into a sequential one (sequentialization), then links this against an IMU-based SMA implementation, and finally verifies the resulting program with a BMC tool for sequential programs, in particular CBMC (v5.3). By varying the SMA implementation we thus obtain a tool for verifying multi-threaded programs under SC, TSO, and PSO, respectively. A hybrid tool combining IMU-CSeq and MU-CSeq [23] has won the gold medal in the Concurrency-category of the TACAS Software Verification Competition (SV-COMP16) [8]. We recall that MU-CSeq is based on the notion of *memory unwinding* where all the program writes are kept in a single sequence.

The experiments below were run on a dedicated machine with a Xeon E5-2650 v2 with 2.60 GHz and 132 GB RAM, running Linux 4.2.0-22-generic, using one CPU. We set a 15 GB memory limit and a 900 s time limit. For each tool and benchmark, we set the parameters to the minimum value to expose the error. Verification wall-clock time is reported in seconds.

SC Benchmarks. We first evaluate IMU-CSeq on the Concurrency-benchmarks SV-COMP16 under SC semantics. These cover the core features of the C programming language and the basic concurrency mechanisms. Since we use a BMC tool as a backend, we can only evaluate IMU-CSeq only on files that have a reachable error location. We used the files from the sub-categories shown in Table 1; each row shows the corresponding number of files and lines of code.

---

[1] http://users.ecs.soton.ac.uk/gp4/cseq/files/IMU-2017.zip.

Table 1. Performance comparison among different tools for SC semantics on unsafe instances from the SV-COMP16 *Concurrency category*.

Sub-category	Files	l.o.c.	CBMC svc16			CIVL svc16			Lazy-CSeq svc16			MU-CSeq svc15			IMU-CSeq		
			Pass	Fail	Time	Pass	Fail	Time	Pass	Fail	Time	Pass	Fail	Time	Pass	Fail	Time
pthread	15	2301	14	1	84.23	15	0	33.31	15	0	48.58	15	0	5.42	15	0	**4.88**
pthread-atomic	2	156	2	0	0.59	2	0	17.5	2	0	**1.39**	2	0	1.4	2	0	3.15
pthread-ext	8	616	7	1	154	8	0	13.12	8	0	11.23	8	0	5.45	8	0	**4.88**
pthread-lit	2	73	2	0	0.3	2	0	10.33	2	0	**0.56**	2	0	2.55	2	0	0.88
ldv-races	8	616	3	5	66.96	3	0	14.5	8	0	1.73	-	-	-	8	0	**1.61**

Table 1 shows the results for the SV-COMP16 versions of CBMC [5], CIVL [26], Lazy-CSeq [13,14], the SV-COMP15 version of MU-CSeq [21], [2] and of IMU-CSeq on these benchmarks. We indicate with *pass* the number of correctly found bugs, with *fail* the number of unsuccessful analyses including tool crashes, memory limit hits, and timeouts, and with *time* the average time in seconds to find the bug. The results clearly show that our approach is competitive with existing tools; in particular, the IMU-based SMA-implementation improves over MU-CSeq.

WMM Benchmarks. We then compared IMU-CSeq against three tools with built-in support for WMM, LazySMA [22], CBMC [12], and Nidhugg [1] a bug-finding tool that combines stateless model checking with dynamic partial order reduction.

Simple benchmarks. Table 2 shows the results over a set of (relatively simple) benchmarks collected from the CBMC, Poet, and Nidhugg tools, and the SV-COMP benchmark suite. The unwind parameter was used by all the three tools considered in the comparison, while W, U, and M are used only by IMU-CSeq, as detailed in Sect. 6. The parameter bitwidth gives the size of integers (in bits) used in the sequential analysis.

The first block contains results for some classical mutual exclusions algorithms. The implementations are correct under SC but not under TSO and PSO (as indicated by an entry in the column 'bug?'). All tools find the errors, but because of the problems' small size, Nidhugg outperforms IMU-CSeq, LazySMA and CBMC on these programs.

The second block contains safe and unsafe versions of one of the fibonacci-benchmarks, where two worker threads concurrently increase two shared counters, and a main thread checks whether any of the counters can reach a defined value. A full exploration of the thread interleavings is required to identify the error (or show its absence) in this program and techniques such as partial-order reduction do not apply. Here, IMU-CSeq has substantially a slight edge over both CBMC and LazySMA, while Nidhugg is substantially slower than the other three.

---

[2] Note that the SV-COMP16 version of MU-CSeq is a hybrid tool that already uses IMU for the shown sub-categories. We thus use the SV-COMP15 version here.

Table 2. Analysis runtime under TSO/PSO

	l.o.c.	parameters					TSO runtime (s)					PSO runtime (s)				
		unwind	W	U	M	bitwidth	bug?	files	IMU-CSeq	LazySMA	CBMC	NIDHUGG	bug?	files	IMU-CSeq	LazySMA	CBMC	NIDHUGG
dekker	52	1	2	0	0	5	•	1	0.76	0.77	0.29	**0.04**	•	1	0.76	0.75	0.25	**0.05**
lamport	78	1	2	0	0	5	•	1	0.97	0.88	0.31	**0.05**	•	1	0.97	0.88	0.29	**0.05**
peterson	40	1	3	0	0	5	•	1	0.67	0.66	0.26	**0.04**	•	1	0.68	0.65	0.25	**0.04**
szymanski	57	1	3	0	0	5	•	1	0.84	0.81	0.34	**0.07**	•	1	0.84	0.80	0.32	**0.04**
fib_longer_unsafe	30	6	7	0	0	10	•	1	**2.10**	6.47	8.19	94.84	•	1	2.50	6.51	**1.69**	135.45
fib_longer_safe	30	6	7	0	0	10		1	**4.75**	9.78	22.5	t.o.		1	**3.90**	8.82	31.8	t.o.
pgsql	47	1	2	0	0	5		1	1.92	2.03	**0.03**	0.07	•	1	0.69	0.65	0.22	**0.04**
parker	110	1	2	0	0	5	•	1	1.22	1.68	0.31	**0.05**	•	1	1.21	2.19	0.28	**0.05**
stack_unsafe	110	2	2	1	2	5	•	1	1.46	1.50	0.41	**0.05**	•	1	1.44	1.49	0.35	**0.05**
litmus_safe	-	1	6	1	0	10		5526	1.20	1.26	**0.17**	2.35		4835	1.06	1.22	**0.15**	6.65
litmus_unsafe	-	1	6	1	0	10	•	277	1.67	1.27	**0.16**	3.86	•	968	1.28	1.26	**0.12**	1.58
safestack	83	3	10	7	2	5	•	1	**207.4**	1474.6	t.o.	t.o.	•	1	**1013.3**	1207.3	t.o.	t.o.

The next block contains benchmarks derived from industrial code. pgsql is a well-known SQL bug [4]; it is correct under SC and TSO but not under PSO. parker models a semaphore-like synchronization class that breaks under TSO [1], and stack_unsafe which was taken from SV-COMP [8]. All tools report the expected results; the performance differences between Nidhugg and CBMC are small, while IMU-CSeq's and LazySMA's performance could be improved (each implementation currently parses and unparses each file nearly 20 times).

The fourth block shows the average results for 5803 WMM litmus tests with 297 K lines of code. For TSO, both our tool, LazySMA and CBMC successfully identified the 277 test cases containing a reachable error, while Nidhugg failed to find one of them. For PSO, CBMC claims that there are 971 unsafe instances while Nidhugg, LazySMA and IMU-CSeq find only 968 unsafe ones (we suspect an error in CBMC). Here, symbolic methods are faster, and Nidhugg has two timeouts.

Complex benchmark. Safestack [11] is a lock-free stack implementation designed for WMM. It is written in C++ but we manually translated it into C, providing simulation functions for the C++11 atomic functions, and analyzed this version. It contains a rare bug that is hard to find with automatic bug-finding techniques already under SC (including random testing, Nidhugg, CIVL [26], and other approaches based on BMC) [20]. The only tool we are aware of that can automatically find a genuine counter-example is Lazy-CSeq [13], which requires a minimum of 3 loop unwindings and 4 rounds of computation and more than 7 h to expose a bug. As shown in the last block of Table 2, both Nidhugg and CBMC failed to find the bug, while IMU-CSeq required approx. 3.5 min and 1.5 GB of memory to find it under TSO, and approx. 17 min and 1.8 GB of memory under PSO, and is faster than LazySMA in finding these bugs.

8   Related Work, Conclusions, and Future Work

Related Work. The BMC approach from [5] allows to handle different memory models by adding a conjunct to the formula. The verification algorithm in [3] works on a generic relaxed memory model that can be refined into actual memory models by adding constraints. Our work differs from these both in the scope and the techniques. In particular, we work at the level of source code with code-to-code transformations and give a general approach that allows to combine different verification algorithms with different implementations of memory models, not just a specific algorithm. The development of the two parts can be done independently as long as Theorems 1 and 2 hold.

Another important aspect of our approach is to identify a class of implementations of memory models that allows for a full rearrangement of the thread interleavings in the analysis. As already observed, this is a feature that has been already exploited in verifying concurrent programs [17,21] also with WMM semantics [7].

The axiomatic framework from [6] is introduced to capture the semantics of memory models. Our framework instead aims at a scalable verification approach that encapsulates all differences between the models within the SMA implementation such that the designs of the verification algorithm and of the memory model simulation can be developed independently.

The notion of IMU exactly captures the *coherence* relation that is often used in the description of memory models (see [2,6]). In our setting, we achieve the reordering of the statements that are observed in the relaxed memory models by guessing the timestamps and then checking their consistency with the expected behaviours.

The reachability analysis used in our algorithm [21] is bounded on the number of writes which is orthogonal to bounding the number of context-switches [19].

Conclusions. We have described and evaluated a new verification approach for concurrent programs over different memory models. Our main design goal was to break the coupling between computation (i.e., individual threads) and communication (i.e., shared memory) concerns of multi-threaded programs, without losing the efficiency of existing approaches. We have introduced shared memory abstractions, which capture the standard concurrency operations in multi-threaded programs. We have then shown that reachability is preserved if we exchange a program by a thread-wise equivalent one (assuming the SMA is thread-asynchronous) or an SMA for its thread-asynchronous closure. This allows us to generalize existing concurrent verification approaches to different memory models simply by implementing the corresponding different SMAs. We have described efficient SMA implementations for SC, TSO, and PSO based on the idea of individual memory-location unwindings, which have allowed us to instantiate our approach into an efficient eager-sequentialization-based BMC bug-finding tool. Our experiments show that the resulting prototype tool compares well with existing ones.

Future Work. We plan to extend our approach to other memory models such as POWER. POWER relaxes PSO (and thus TSO) in two key aspects (see [2]): (*i*) the propagation of a write in the shared memory by a thread can be asynchronous, i.e., each thread can see the write at a different time; (*ii*) the order of execution of the statements of a thread can be rearranged liberally (w.r.t. the program order) provided that the dependency relations such as data-flow, address, control and isync are respected. The asynchronous write propagation can be easily captured in the IMU by allowing for each write a different timestamp *per* thread. To capture the dependency relations, a more substantial addition may be required instead. However, on the basis of preliminary empirical experiments, we have evidences that our approach have a potential to scale well to more relaxed memory models. We leave this for future investigations.

References

1. Abdulla, P.A., Aronis, S., Atig, M.F., Jonsson, B., Leonardsson, C., Sagonas, K.: Stateless model checking for TSO and PSO. In: Baier, C., Tinelli, C. (eds.) TACAS 2015. LNCS, vol. 9035, pp. 353–367. Springer, Heidelberg (2015). doi:10.1007/978-3-662-46681-0_28
2. Abdulla, P.A., Atig, M.F., Bouajjani, A., Ngo, T.P.: Context-bounded analysis for POWER. In: Legay, A., Margaria, T. (eds.) TACAS 2017. LNCS, vol. 10206, pp. 56–74. Springer, Heidelberg (2017). doi:10.1007/978-3-662-54580-5_4
3. Abe, T., Maeda, T.: A general model checking framework for various memory consistency models. In: IEEE PDP, pp. 332–341 (2014)
4. Alglave, J., Kroening, D., Nimal, V., Tautschnig, M.: Software verification for weak memory via program transformation. In: Felleisen, M., Gardner, P. (eds.) ESOP 2013. LNCS, vol. 7792, pp. 512–532. Springer, Heidelberg (2013). doi:10.1007/978-3-642-37036-6_28
5. Alglave, J., Kroening, D., Tautschnig, M.: Partial orders for efficient bounded model checking of concurrent software. In: CAV, pp. 141–157 (2013)
6. Alglave, J., Maranget, L., Tautschnig, M.: Herding cats: modelling, simulation, testing, and data mining for weak memory. ACM Trans. Program. Lang. Syst. **36**(2), 7:1–7:74 (2014)
7. Atig, M.F., Bouajjani, A., Parlato, G.: Getting rid of store-buffers in TSO analysis. In: Gopalakrishnan, G., Qadeer, S. (eds.) CAV 2011. LNCS, vol. 6806, pp. 99–115. Springer, Heidelberg (2011). doi:10.1007/978-3-642-22110-1_9
8. Beyer, D.: Reliable and reproducible competition results with BenchExec and witnesses (Report on SV-COMP 2016). In: Chechik, M., Raskin, J.-F. (eds.) TACAS 2016. LNCS, vol. 9636, pp. 887–904. Springer, Heidelberg (2016). doi:10.1007/978-3-662-49674-9_55
9. Bouajjani, A., Calin, G., Derevenetc, E., Meyer, R.: Lazy TSO reachability. In: Egyed, A., Schaefer, I. (eds.) FASE 2015. LNCS, vol. 9033, pp. 267–282. Springer, Heidelberg (2015). doi:10.1007/978-3-662-46675-9_18
10. Carter, M., He, S., Whitaker, J., Rakamaric, Z., Emmi, M.: SMACK software verification toolchain. In: ICSE, pp. 589–592 (2016)
11. Chen, G., Jin, H., Zou, D., Zhou, B.B., Liang, Z., Zheng, W., Shi, X.: Safestack: automatically patching stack-based buffer overflow vulnerabilities. IEEE Trans. Dependable Sec. Comput. **10**(6), 368–379 (2013)

12. Horn, A., Kroening, D.: On partial order semantics for SAT/SMT-based symbolic encodings of weak memory concurrency. In: Graf, S., Viswanathan, M. (eds.) FORTE 2015. LNCS, vol. 9039, pp. 19–34. Springer, Cham (2015). doi:10.1007/978-3-319-19195-9_2

13. Inverso, O., Nguyen, T.L., Fischer, B., La Torre, S., Parlato, G.: Lazy-cseq: a context-bounded model checking tool for multi-threaded c-programs. In: ASE, pp. 807–812 (2015)

14. Inverso, O., Tomasco, E., Fischer, B., La Torre, S., Parlato, G.: Bounded model checking of multi-threaded C programs via lazy sequentialization. In: Biere, A., Bloem, R. (eds.) CAV 2014. LNCS, vol. 8559, pp. 585–602. Springer, Cham (2014). doi:10.1007/978-3-319-08867-9_39

15. La Torre, S., Madhusudan, P., Parlato, G.: Model-checking parameterized concurrent programs using linear interfaces. In: CAV, pp. 629–644 (2010)

16. La Torre, S., Madhusudan, P., Parlato, G.: Sequentializing Parameterized Programs. In: FIT, pp. 34–47 (2012)

17. Lal, A., Reps, T.W.: Reducing concurrent analysis under a context bound to sequential analysis. Formal Methods Syst. Des. 35(1), 73–97 (2009)

18. Owens, S., Sarkar, S., Sewell, P.: A better x86 memory model: x86-TSO. In: Berghofer, S., Nipkow, T., Urban, C., Wenzel, M. (eds.) TPHOLs 2009. LNCS, vol. 5674, pp. 391–407. Springer, Heidelberg (2009). doi:10.1007/978-3-642-03359-9_27

19. Qadeer, S., Rehof, J.: Context-bounded model checking of concurrent software. In: Halbwachs, N., Zuck, L.D. (eds.) TACAS 2005. LNCS, vol. 3440, pp. 93–107. Springer, Heidelberg (2005). doi:10.1007/978-3-540-31980-1_7

20. Thomson, P., Donaldson, A.F., Betts, A.: Concurrency testing using schedule bounding: an empirical study. In: PPopp, pp. 15–28 (2014)

21. Tomasco, E., Inverso, O., Fischer, B., La Torre, S., Parlato, G.: Verifying concurrent programs by memory unwinding. In: Baier, C., Tinelli, C. (eds.) TACAS 2015. LNCS, vol. 9035, pp. 551–565. Springer, Heidelberg (2015). doi:10.1007/978-3-662-46681-0_52

22. Tomasco, E., Nguyen, T.L., Inverso, O., Fischer, B., La Torre, S., Parlato, G.: Lazy sequentialization for TSO and PSO via shared memory abstractions. In: FMCAD, pp. 193–200 (2016)

23. Tomasco, E., Nguyen, T.L., Inverso, O., Fischer, B., La Torre, S., Parlato, G.: MU-CSeq 0.4: individual memory location unwindings. In: Chechik, M., Raskin, J.-F. (eds.) TACAS 2016. LNCS, vol. 9636, pp. 938–941. Springer, Heidelberg (2016). doi:10.1007/978-3-662-49674-9_65

24. Wehrheim, H., Travkin, O.: TSO to SC via symbolic execution. In: Piterman, N. (ed.) HVC 2015. LNCS, vol. 9434, pp. 104–119. Springer, Cham (2015). doi:10.1007/978-3-319-26287-1_7

25. Zhang, N., Kusano, M., Wang, C.: Dynamic partial order reduction for relaxed memory models. In: PLDI, pp. 250–259 (2015)

26. Zheng, M., Rogers, M.S., Luo, Z., Dwyer, M.B., Siegel, S.F.: CIVL: formal verification of parallel programs. In: ASE, pp. 830–835 (2015)

On Run-Time Enforcement of Authorization Constraints in Security-Sensitive Workflows

Daniel Ricardo dos Santos[✉] and Silvio Ranise

Fondazione Bruno Kessler (FBK), Trento, Italy
dossantos@fbk.edu

Abstract. In previous work, we showed how to use an SMT-based model checker to synthesize run-time enforcement mechanisms for business processes augmented with access control policies and authorization constraints, such as Separation of Duties. The synthesized enforcement mechanisms are able to guarantee both termination and compliance to security requirements, i.e. solving the run-time version of the Workflow Satisfiability Problem (WSP). No systematic approach to specify the various constraints considered in the WSP literature has been provided. In this paper, we first propose a classification of these constraints and then show how to encode them in the declarative input language of the SMT-based model checker used for synthesis. This shows the flexibility of the SMT approach to solve the run-time version of the WSP in presence of different authorization constraints.

1 Introduction

A security-sensitive business process (BP) is a structured collection of tasks, defining a workflow, equipped with an authorization policy defining which users are entitled to execute which tasks, and authorization constraints such as Separation or Binding of Duties (SoD or BoD) defining that certain tasks must be executed by different users, or the same user, respectively. The authorization policy and constraints are crucial to comply with regulations and prevent frauds. It is, however, of utmost importance to ensure that business continuity is not endangered, i.e. it must be possible to complete the BP while satisfying the authorization policy and constraints. Finding the best possible trade-off between security and business continuity for BPs is called the Workflow Satisfiability Problem (WSP) [4,6,7,16].

There are business rules, regulations, and policies that either cannot be encoded or are very difficult to encode by using simple SoD/BoD constraints [15]. Some examples are: requiring that a user executes only a certain number of tasks or requiring that users from different (or the same) departments execute a set of tasks. Even more complex policies involving conflicts of interest [26], confidentiality [5], and integrity [8] require data-based constraints. These practical needs have motivated the definition of different types of authorization constraints. In the literature, a variety of authorization constraints have been considered but no

© Springer International Publishing AG 2017
A. Cimatti and M. Sirjani (Eds.): SEFM 2017, LNCS 10469, pp. 203–218, 2017.
DOI: 10.1007/978-3-319-66197-1_13

systematic classification has been given. Additionally, the proposed approaches to solve the WSP only support certain classes of authorization constraints.

Related work. The seminal work of Bertino et al. [6] described the specification and enforcement of authorization constraints in workflow management systems, presenting constraints as clauses in a logic program and an exponential algorithm for assigning users and roles to tasks without violating them, but considering only linear workflows. Tan et al. [29] defined a model for constrained workflow systems that includes constraints such as cardinality, SoD and BoD. They specified a workflow as a partial order on the set of tasks; and a constrained workflow authorization schema, associating roles to tasks. Crampton [14] extended these ideas by defining Type 1 constraints, and developing an algorithm to determine whether there exists an assignment of users to tasks that satisfies the constraints.

Wang and Li. [31] proposed a role-and-relation based access control model to describe the relationships between users and specify complex authorization constraints. The authors reduced the WSP to SAT, showed that it is NP-complete in authorization systems supporting simple constraints and that it is fixed-parameter tractable (FPT) with only BoD and SoD.

Crampton et al. [17] showed that the WSP remains FPT with counting and equivalence constraints. Later [16], they used logical combinations of constraints to support conditional workflows and Type 3 constraints by splitting one instance of the problem into several instances. Cohen et al. [11] solved the WSP using techniques for the Constraint Satisfaction Problem, which allowed the authors to devise a general algorithm that works for several families of constraints. Cohen et al. [12] demonstrated the practicality of the previously designed algorithm by adapting it to the class of user-independent counting constraints and showing its superiority when compared with the classical SAT reduction of the problem. Crampton et al. [15] showed that the WSP remains FPT for class-independent constraints and provided an algorithm to solve it. Crampton et al. [18] used model checking on an NP-complete fragment of LTL to synthesize and validate plans for security-sensitive workflows and argued that this approach is more robust, uniform, and expressive than previous formalizations.

Li and Wang introduced the Separation of Duties Algebra (SoDA) [25] to express and formalize policies based on users' attributes and the number of users executing tasks. The policies are enforced by low-level mechanisms such as static and dynamic SoD in RBAC [27]. Basin et al. [3] generalized SoDA's semantics to workflow traces and refined it for control-flow and role-based authorizations, implementing a SoD enforcement monitor for workflow engines. Later [4], the same authors used Hoare's Communicating Sequential Processes (CSP) to model workflows in two levels: control-flow and task execution, allowing them to synthesize monitors that enforce at run-time obstruction-free, or satisfying, workflow executions.

This work. Our previous approaches to solve the WSP [7,13,21] use an SMT-based model checker to synthesize run-time enforcement mechanisms for business processes augmented with access control policies and SoD/BoD constraints. We focused on these constraints because those works were developed in collaboration

.with SAP. SAP was mainly interested in SoD/BoD because these constraints are the most widely used by their customers. In this paper, we show how to extend our previous encoding of authorization constraints to handle a large number of constraints that we have encountered in the literature and classified. After providing the background concepts on the WSP (Sect. 2), we propose the first classification of authorization constraints (Sect. 3). Then, show how to encode them in the declarative input language of an SMT-based model checker (Sect. 4.3) that is used in a tool called CERBERUS (Sect. 4.2), which is capable of solving the run-time version of the WSP. The tool has been integrated in an industrial framework for workflow management of SAP (Sect. 4.1). We finish by drawing some conclusions and discussing related and future work (Sect. 5).

2   Background

Let T be a finite set of tasks and U a finite set of users. A *scenario* is a finite sequence of pairs of the form (t, u), written as $t(u)$, where $t \in T$ and $u \in U$. The intuitive meaning of a scenario $\eta = t_1(u_1), \ldots, t_n(u_n)$ is that task t_i is executed before task t_j for $1 \leq i < j \leq n$ and that task t_k is executed by user u_k for $k = 1, \ldots, n$. A *workflow* $W(T, U)$ is a set of scenarios. There are various ways to specify security-sensitive workflows. For instance, [17] introduces the notion of "constrained workflow authorization schema," [4] uses CSP, and many works use (extensions of) Petri nets. We adopt the last approach, as it is one of the standard ways to formalize the semantics of workflows specified in BPMN [20]. We illustrate the specification of a security-sensitive workflow in (a variant of) BPMN using an example.

Example 1. The left side of Fig. 1 shows a simple Loan Origination Process, with fours tasks: *Request Loan* ($t1$), *Evaluate External Credit Rating* ($t2$), *Evaluate Internal Credit Rating* ($t3$), and *Approve Loan* ($t4$). Task $t1$ has to be executed first, followed by $t2$ and $t3$ (in any order), followed by $t4$, so the behaviors $t1, t2, t3, t4$ and $t1, t3, t2, t4$ are allowed, whereas, e.g., $t1, t4, t3, t2$ is not (where $t1, \ldots, tn$ represents a sequence of n tasks executed in order, i.e. t_{i+i} is executed after t_i). Now imagine that $t3$ is only executed for loans of more than 10k Euro, then behavior $t1, t2, t4$ becomes allowed, but only for some instances (those where the data object "loan amount" is less than 10k). If the organization running this workflow adopts the authorization policy shown at the center of the Figure and the SoD constraints between $t2$ and $t3$ and between $t3$ and $t4$ (shown as dashed lines labeled by $\neq$ in the Figure), then any behavior containing, e.g., $t2(a)$ and $t3(a)$ is not allowed (where $t(u)$ means that user u executes task t).

The right side of Fig. 1 shows the extended Petri net that can be automatically derived from the BPMN on the left side and that represents its semantics (see, e.g., [7,20]). Tasks are modeled as transitions or events (the boxes in the Figure) whereas places (the circles in the Figure) encode their enabling conditions. At the beginning, there will be just one token in place $p0$ which enables the execution of transition $t1$. This corresponds to the execution constraint that task $t1$ must be performed before all the others. The execution of $t1$ removes the token in $p0$ and puts a token in $p1$ and another in $p2$; this enables the execution of $t2$ and $t3$. Indeed, this corresponds to the causality constraint that $t2$ and $t3$ can be executed in any order after $t1$ and before $t4$. The executions of $t2$ and $t3$ remove the tokens in $p1$ and $p2$ and put a token in $p3$ and one in $p4$, which, in turn, enables the execution of $t4$. This removes the tokén in $p3$ and $p4$ and puts a token in $p5$, which enables no more transitions. This corresponds to the fact that $t4$ is the last task to be executed.   □

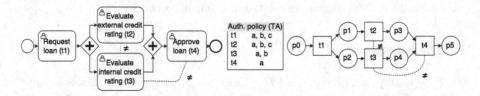

Fig. 1. Loan origination process in BPMN (left) and as a Petri net (right)

Among the scenarios in a workflow, we are interested in those that describe successfully terminating executions in which users execute tasks satisfying the authorization constraints and the authorization policy. Since the notion of successful termination depends on the definition of the workflow (e.g., in case of a conditional choice, we will have two acceptable execution sequences according to the Boolean value of the condition), in the following we focus only on the authorization policy and the authorization constraints while assuming that all the scenarios in the workflow characterize successfully terminating behaviors.

Given a workflow $W(T, U)$, an *authorization relation* TA is a sub-set of $U \times T$. Intuitively, $(u, t) \in TA$ means that u is authorized to execute task t. We say that a scenario η of a workflow $W(T, U)$ is *authorized* according to TA iff (u, t) is in TA for each $t(u)$ in η. An *authorization constraint* over a workflow $W(T, U)$ can be seen as a pair (T', Θ), where $T' \subseteq T$ is called the scope of c and Θ is a set of functions $\theta : T' \to U$ [15]. The functions in Θ specify the assignments of tasks to users that satisfy the constraint. Instead of enumerating every function $\theta \in \Theta$, it is common to define Θ implicitly by using a specification device. A catalog of such devices is presented in Sect. 3 below. Let C be a (finite) set of authorization constraints, a scenario η satisfies C iff η satisfies c, for each c in C. A scenario η of a workflow $W(T, U)$ is *eligible according to a set C of authorization constraints* iff η satisfies C.

The problems raised by the conflicting goals of business compliance and business continuity are further complicated by the interplay between control-flow, data-flow, and authorization. Notice that a common practice in the analysis of workflow satisfiability is to abstract away from parts of a workflow specification. No work besides [7] takes into account the data-flow (some completely disregard it, e.g., [15], and some model it with non-deterministic decisions, e.g., [4]).

It is also common to limit the allowed control-flow constructs and supported authorization constraints. There are different versions of the WSP and one main distinction is whether the order of execution of the tasks is taken into account. Crampton [16] defines a plan $\pi : T \mapsto U$ and a schedule as a tuple $(t_1, \ldots, t_k)$ such that $\{t_1, \ldots, t_k\} = T$ and $t_j \not\leq t_i$ for each $1 \leq i < j \leq k$. The unordered WSP admits as solution a valid plan π, whereas the ordered version admits as solution a plan π with a schedule σ, i.e. the plan must respect the ordering of tasks defined by the control-flow. The two versions of the WSP are only equivalent for well-formed workflows [16], i.e. workflows where for all tasks t_i and t_j that can be executed in any order, $(t_i, t_j, \rho) \in C$ iff $(t_j, t_i, \tilde{\rho}) \in C$ (where $\tilde{\rho}$ is defined as $\{(u, u') \in U \times U : (u', u) \in \rho\}$). We define the (Ordered) WSP as follows.

Definition 1 ((Ordered) Workflow Satisfiability Problem (WSP)). *Given a workflow $W(T, U)$, an authorization relation TA, and a set C of authorization constraints, return (if possible) a scenario η which is authorized according to TA and eligible according to C.*

3   A Catalog of Authorization Constraints

Several classes of authorization constraints for workflows have been identified in the literature. They can all be used, with some ingenuity, to define the functions $\theta \in \Theta$, so they can be recast in the form (T', Θ) shown above [11].

Counting constraints are of the form (t_l, t_r, T'), where $1 \leq t_l \leq t_r \leq k$. A plan satisfies a counting constraint if a user performs either no tasks in T' or between t_l and t_r tasks. One example of counting constraint is $(1, 2, \{t1, t2, t3\})$, which is satisfied if a user $u1$ executes 0, 1 or 2 tasks among those in $\{t1, t2, t3\}$.

Entailment constraints are of the form (T_1, T_2, ρ), where $T_1 \cup T_2 = T'$ and $\rho \subseteq U \times U$. A plan satisfies an entailment constraint iff there exist $t_1 \in T_1$ and $t_2 \in T_2$ such that $(\pi(t_1), \pi(t_2)) \in \rho$. Entailment constraints can be further subdivided in three types. In Type 1 constraints, both sets T_1 and T_2 are singletons. In Type 2 constraints, at least one of the sets must be a singleton, whereas in Type 3 there are no restrictions on the cardinality of sets. Examples of Type 1, 2, and 3 constraints are $(\{t1\}, \{t2\}, \neq)$, $(\{t1, t2\}, \{t3\}, \neq)$, and $(\{t1, t2\}, \{t3, t4\}, \neq)$, respectively. The first constraint is satisfied if a user $u1$ executes $t1$ and $u2$ executes $t2$ (because $u1 \neq u2$). The second and third constraints are satisfied if $u1$ executes $t1$ and $u2$ executes $t3$. Those are examples of SoD constraints, BoD constraints can be similarly defined by using $=$ instead of $\neq$. A special class of Type 1 constraints are equivalence-based constraints, of the form $(t_1, t_2, \sim)$, where $\sim$ is an equivalence relation on U. A plan satisfies this kind of constraint if the user who executes t_1 and the user who executes t_2 belong to the same equivalence class, e.g., same role (or to different classes for $\not\sim$ constraints).

User-independent constraints c are those where given a plan π that satisfies c and any permutation $\phi : U \rightarrow U$, the plan $\pi' = \phi(\pi(s))$ also satisfies c [11].

I.e. user-independent constraints are those whose satisfaction does not depend on the individual identities of users. The SoD constraints presented so far are user-independent, whereas a constraint requiring a specific user to perform at least one task in a set is not user-independent [12].

Class-independent constraints are those whose satisfaction depends only on the equivalence classes that users belong to [15]. Formally, let c be a constraint, $\sim$ be an equivalence relation on U, $U^\sim$ be the set of equivalence classes induced by $\sim$, and $u^\sim \in U^\sim$ be the equivalence class containing u. Then, for any plan π, we can define a function $\pi^\sim : T \to U^\sim$ as $\pi^\sim(t) = (\pi(t))^\sim$. Finally, c is class-independent for $\sim$ if for any function θ, $\theta^\sim \in \Theta$ implies $\theta \in \Theta$, and for any permutation $\phi : U^\sim \to U^\sim$, $\theta^\sim \in \Theta^\sim$ implies $\phi \circ \theta^\sim \in \Theta^\sim$ [15]. One example of class-independent constraint is $(\{t1\}, \{t2\}, \sim)$, where the classes induced by $\sim$ corresponds to departments of a company. This constraint is satisfied if $u(t1) \sim u(t2)$, i.e. the user executing $t1$ and the user executing $t2$ are in the same department. Indeed, every equivalence constraint $(t_1, t_2, \sim)$ (or $(t_1, t_2, \nsim)$) is class-independent and every user-independent constraint is class-independent with respect to the identity relation [15].

3.1   Classification of Constraints

It is not easy to classify authorization constraints in terms of expressiveness, partly because there are many different frameworks to express them. For instance, entailment constraints of Type 3 clearly include those of Types 1 and 2, but counting constraints can also be used to express some forms of SoD [33], so entailment and counting constraints are not disjoint (i.e. in some cases, it is possible to express the same set of behaviors using a counting constraint or an entailment one). Also, clearly user-independent and class-independent constraints subsume parts of the other classes, but it is not clear which parts.

Figure 2 shows an attempt to systematically classify some classes of authorization constraints for workflow systems presented in the literature.

The Figure shows the sets *Ent.* of entailment constraints (the subsets of constraints of Types 1, 2, and 3 are not shown to keep the Figure readable), *Count.* of counting constraints, *Eq.* of equivalence constraints, *CI* of class-independent

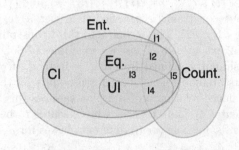

Fig. 2. Relations between constraint classes

constraints and UI of user-independent constraints. Naturally, $Eq. \subset Ent.$ and $CI. \subset Ent.$, since an equivalence relation is an instance of a binary relation. The facts $UI \subset CI$ and $Eq. \subset CI$ were shown by Crampton et al. [15].

The Figure also shows the following intersections: $I1 = Ent. \cap Count.$, $I2 = Eq. \cap Count.$, $I3 = Eq. \cap UI$, $I4 = Count. \cap UI$, $I5 = Count. \cap CI$. We can show that these intersections are non-empty by using SoD and BoD constraints as examples. $I1$ and $I2$ are non-empty because SoD and BoD can be specified using entailment: $(t1, t2, \neq)$ and $(t1, 2, =)$, respectively; counting: $(1, 1, \{t1, t2\})$ and $(2, 2, \{t1, t2\})$, respectively; or equivalence, since $=$ is an equivalence relation. $I3$, $I4$, and $I5$ are non-empty because both constraints are user-independent [12], which also makes them class-independent [15].

To the best of our knowledge, there has never been a comparison between the expressive power of other frameworks, e.g., SoDA and the constraint classes defined by Crampton et al.

3.2 Data-Based Constraints

In business processes, authorization policies and constraints are usually specified and enforced based on the tasks. But policies and constraints can also be defined based on data objects. This allows increased expressiveness (policies such as Chinese Wall [9] cannot be expressed solely on the tasks), as well as simplified specification (at design-time) and enforcement (at run-time), since some policies may require many more task-based constraints than data-based ones. Below, we motivate some well-known classes of data-based policies from the security literature.

Data authorization refers to a user's permission to access a data object in a workflow. An example of the need for data authorization on top of task authorization is to manage conflict of interests (CoI) in contract tender evaluations [2]. In this example, if a user is authorized to perform task *Evaluate Tender*, but they work for one of the companies proposing a tender, they should not be authorized to evaluate the tender of their own company. To perform this task, users should have permission not only to execute the task, but also to access the tender data.

Chinese Wall is used to prevent the CoI that arises when a user has access to the data of two competing organizations. To avoid this kind of conflict, the data is separated into sets representing the classes of conflict and when a user has access to the data of one of the elements of the set, they cannot access the data of the other elements. More examples of CoI policies can be found in [26].

Need to know and privacy constraints can be used to block, for instance, the access to two or more data objects that, taken together, can reveal information that a single object cannot (e.g., a relation of names of patients and time they came in with a relation of medical procedures and time they were performed can be used to identify patients). Need to know means that a user should only know the minimum amount of information required to complete a task. One example is that to approve a loan, financial data is required, but not personal data, so the user who approves the loan should not know the personal data of the applicant. In this example a constraint could be defined between the data objects personal data and financial data, so that any user will only have access to one of them.

Other confidentiality [5] **and integrity** [8] policies can be modeled with data authorization and data constraints, but they require a separation between read access and write access. In the low-water-mark integrity policy [8], for instance, users and data objects have integrity levels $(l[\cdot])$ and whenever a user reads a data object, his/her integrity level is updated $(l[s] \leftarrow l[s] \wedge l[o]$, where $\wedge$ stands for the glb between integrity levels), whereas writing is permitted if $l[o] \leq l[s]$.

4   Encoding Constraints in Cerberus

We have implemented an approach to solve the WSP by synthesizing run-time monitors for security-sensitive workflows in a tool called CERBERUS [13]. Below, we first present a high-level overview of the tool and its integration in an industrial environment. Instead of providing full details, we focus on those aspects that are relevant to model the authorization constraints considered in Sect. 3 and show the termination of monitor synthesis.

4.1   Overview of Cerberus

A reference architecture for Workflow Management (WFM) systems is composed of the five blue elements shown in Fig. 3. *Workflow Modeling* is a user interface for a Process Designer to create workflow models in a modeling language, e.g., BPMN. Models are stored in a *Workflow Model Repository*, while the *Workflow Engine* interprets the models and directs the execution to *Invoked Applications*, in the case of system and script tasks, or to a *Graphical User Interface* (GUI), in the case of user tasks, which are performed by Process Participants.

On top of the WFM components, we add the CERBERUS components shown in red in Fig. 3. The *Monitor Synthesizer* is responsible for interpreting the workflow model and translating it into a transition system format accepted by a *Symbolic Model Checker* (SMC) capable of computing a reachability graph whose paths are all possible executions of the workflow. To solve the WSP, a monitor needs to look to the current state, the past execution history and possible future executions to check if there is any possibility to finish the process. Therefore, we need to be able to pre-compute all possible executions. Notice that precomputing a reachability graph in the presence of data values is infeasible, but, as already mentioned, abstracting away run-time data is standard practice for approaches solving the WSP. Note that only the workflow model (representing the execution constraints) extended with authorization constraints is input to the monitor synthesis. This allows the synthesized monitor to support different authorization policies at run-time. The reachability graph is translated into a language such as Datalog or SQL and stored in the *Monitor Repository*. The *Monitor* itself sits between the GUI and the workflow engine and grants or

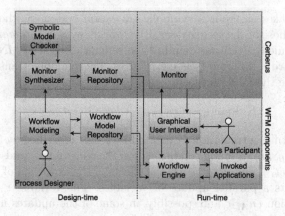

Fig. 3. The architecture of CERBERUS and its interface with a WFM system (Color figure online)

denies user requests to execute tasks (users only access tasks through the GUI and automatic tasks are not part of the authorization policy or constraints).

CERBERUS is implemented on top of the SAP HANA Operational Intelligence platform (OpInt)[1], which offers a BPMN modeling and enactment environment to synthesize, store, combine, and retrieve run-time monitors for security-sensitive workflows therein modeled and enacted. HANA Studio is the IDE that acts as the Workflow Modeling component, while the HANA Repository implements both the Workflow Model Repository and the Monitor repository. We added the constraint specification and monitor synthesis capabilities in the IDE and used MCMT [23] as the SMC (we explain this choice below). The Monitor Synthesizer is written in Python (core algorithms) and JavaScript (IDE and repository integration). The monitors are output in SQL as a view that is queried by the execution engine. The result of this query is used to grant or deny a user's request to execute a task. The OpInt Workflow Engine translates BPMN models to executable JavaScript and SQL code that manage and perform the tasks in the workflows. The invoked applications are handled by SQL procedure calls and the GUI for user tasks is integrated in a web task management dashboard.

The termination of the various modules in CERBERUS is obvious, except for the SMC. Thus, below, we discuss under which hypotheses termination is guaranteed for this module.

4.2   Run-Time Monitor Synthesis

The *Monitor Synthesizer*—by invoking the SMC—solves the WSP by synthesizing run-time monitors capable of ensuring that all executions terminate and authorization constraints in a workflow are satisfied using the approach described in [7]. Here, for lack of space, we focus on the SMC and we discuss the assumptions under which it is guaranteed to terminate.

---

[1] https://help.sap.com/hana-opint.

The SMC takes as input a symbolic transition system S whose executions correspond to those of the security-sensitive workflow. S is *automatically* derived from the (extended) Petri net defining the semantics of a BPMN specification by using standard techniques (see, e.g., [7,28]). The symbolic transitions derived in this way have the following form:

$$t(z) : en_{CF} \wedge en_{Auth} \rightarrow act_{CF} \| act_{Auth} \tag{1}$$

where $t(z)$ identifies a transition t executed by a user identified by the variable z; en_{CF} and en_{Auth} are enabling conditions (on the control-flow and authorization, respectively); act_{CF} and act_{Auth} are the effects of the execution of the transition and $\|$ represents a parallel update of variables. The variable z occurs in the enabling condition en_{Auth} and, possibly, in some of the updates in act_{Auth}.

Example 2. To illustrate, recall Fig. 1 and observe that the fact that there is at most one token per place is an invariant of the Petri net. This allows us to symbolically represent the net as follows: we introduce a Boolean variable per place (named as the places in Fig. 1) together with a Boolean variable representing the fact that a task has already been executed (denoted by d_t and if assigned to true implies that task t has been executed). So, for instance, the enabling condition for the execution constraint on task $t1$ can be expressed as $p0 \wedge \neg d_{t1}$ meaning that the token is in place $p0$ and transition $t1$ has not yet been executed. The effect of executing transition $t1$ is to assign F(alse) to $p0$ and T(rue) to $p1$, $p2$ and d_{t1}; in symbols, we write $p0, p1, p2, d_{t1} := F, T, T, T$. The other transitions are modeled similarly.

Table 1. Workflow as symbolic transition system

event	enabled		action	
	CF	Auth	CF	Auth
$t1(u)$	$p0 \wedge \neg d_{t1}$	$a_{t1}(u)$	$p0, p1, p2, d_{t1} := F, T, T, T$	$h_{t1}(u) := T$
$t2(u)$	$p1 \wedge \neg d_{t2}$	$a_{t2}(u) \wedge \neg h_{t3}(u)$	$p1, p3, d_{t2} := F, T, T$	$h_{t2}(u) := T$
$t3(u)$	$p2 \wedge \neg d_{t3}$	$a_{t3}(u) \wedge \neg h_{t2}(u)$	$p2, p4, d_{t3} := F, T, T$	$h_{t3}(u) := T$
$t4(u)$	$p3 \wedge p4 \wedge \neg d_{t4}$	$a_{t4}(u) \wedge \neg h_{t3}(u)$	$p3, p4, p5, d_{t4} := F, F, T, T$	$h_{t4}(u) := T$

Besides the constraints on the execution of tasks, The Petri net in Fig. 1 shows also the same authorization constraints of the BPMN model. These are obtained by taking into consideration both the access control policy P granting or denying users the right to execute tasks and the SoD constraints between pairs of tasks. To formalize these, we introduce two functions a_t and h_t from users to Boolean, for each task t, which are such that $a_t(u)$ is true iff u has the right to execute t according to the policy P and $h_t(u)$ is true iff u has executed task t. Notice that a_t is a function that behaves as an abstract interface to the policy P whereas h_t is a function that evolves over time and keeps track of which users have executed which tasks. For instance, the enabling condition for the authorization constraint on task $t1$ is simply $a_{t1}(u)$, i.e. it is required that the user u has the right to execute $t1$, and the effect of its execution is to record that u has executed $t1$, i.e. $h_{t1}(u) := T$ (notice that this assignment leaves unchanged the value returned by h_{t1} for any user u' distinct from u). As another example, let us consider the enabling condition for the authorization constraint on $t2$: besides requiring that u has the right to execute $t2$ (i.e. $a_{t2}(u)$), we also need to require the SoD constraints with $t3$ (i.e. $\neg h_{t3}(u)$). The authorization constraints on the other tasks are modeled in a similar way.

Table 1 shows the formalization of all transitions in the extended Petri net of Fig. 1. The first column reports the name of the transition together with the fact that it is dependent on the user u taking the responsibility of its execution. The second column shows the enabling condition divided in two parts: CF, pertaining to the execution constraints, and Auth, to the authorization constraints. The third and last column list the effects of the execution of the transition again divided in two parts: CF, for the workflow, and Auth, for the authorization.

The set of final states can be specified by the following formula:

$$\neg p0 \wedge \neg p1 \wedge \neg p2 \wedge \neg p3 \wedge \neg p4 \wedge p5 \wedge d_{t1} \wedge d_{t2} \wedge d_{t3} \wedge d_{t4}$$

saying that there is just one token in $p5$ and that all tasks have been executed. The set of initial states can be specified, dually, by the formula:

$$p0 \wedge \bigwedge_{i=1,\dots,5} \neg p_i \wedge \bigwedge_{i=1,\dots,4} \neg d_{ti} \wedge \forall u.(\neg h_{t1}(u) \wedge \neg h_{t2}(u) \wedge \neg h_{t3}(u) \wedge \neg h_{t4}(u))$$

saying that there is just one token in $p0$, no task has been executed yet, and no user has executed any task.   □

After building the symbolic transitions and the formulae defining the sets of initial and final states, the SMC computes a symbolic representation of the set of states that are (backward) reachable from the set of final states. In other words, the WSP is reduced to a reachability problem under the assumption that no transition can be enabled infinitely often without being executed. This assumption (called strong fairness in the literature) is considered reasonable in the context of workflow management [30] since decisions to execute tasks are under the responsibility of applications or humans.

To compute the fix-point, MCMT (an SMT-based model checker) computes a directed graph $RG = (N, \lambda, E)$, called reachability graph, whose edges in E are labeled by task-user pairs in which users are symbolically represented by variables and whose nodes in N are labeled—according to the labeling function λ—by a formula of first-order logic. We omit the details of the construction of the full reachability graph and point the interested reader to [7]. Here, it is enough to say that it is built in two steps: a fix-point procedure and a post-processing. The resulting graph is such that its paths describe all possible executions of a transition system that terminate and satisfy the authorization constraints. While the termination of the post-processing step is guaranteed by adopting a suitable semantics for loops, namely the one based on "release-point semantics" of [10] which requires to consider only the user who executed the last iteration of the loop, forgetting all the others), the termination of the fix-point computation for transition systems with a finite but unbounded number of users is non-obvious.

By using MCMT as the SMC, we get the following two advantages. First, MCMT is capable of introducing on-demand new (existential) variables to symbolically represent enough users to satisfy authorization constraints without bounding their number *a priori*. Second, the following theorem is an easy consequence of the results in [22]. Preliminary, generalizing the observations in Example 2, we assume that the formulae describing the transitions as well as the initial and final sets of states are built out of a set V of state predicates (whose values evolve over time) of arity 0 for the places ($p0, p1, \ldots$) and transitions ($d_{t1}, d_{t2}, \ldots$) and of arity 1 for tracking the history of which user has executed a certain task ($h_{t1}, h_{t2}, \ldots$); the set $H \subset A$ contains only the history variables $h_{t1}, \ldots$ We also permit that the static predicates (whose values stay constant over time) of arity 1 from a given finite set A may also occur in such formulae and constitute the interfaces to the authorization policy. Below, a quantifier-free (existentially or universally quantified) formula built out of the predicates in a set $X \in \{H, V, A, V \cup A\}$ is termed X-quantifier-free (existentially or universally quantified, respectively) formula.

Theorem 1. MCMT *terminates when computing the reachability graph of a symbolic transition system in which transitions are of the form (1) where en_{CF} is a V-quantifier-free formula, en_{Auth} is a A-quantifier-free formulae, the final formula is a V-quantifier-free formula, and the initial formula is a conjunction of a V-quantifier-free formula with a H-universally quantified formula.*

Below, we show how Theorem 1 can help showing the termination of SMC on several classes of authorization constraints in Sect. 3.

4.3   Encoding Constraints

We illustrate the main ideas of our symbolic encoding by considering the SoD constraint between $t3$ and $t4$ in Fig. 1. The constraint can be specified as an additional condition that must hold in every state of the executions of the Loan Origination Process (LOP): $\forall w.\neg(h_{t3}(w) \land h_{t4}(w))$ or, equivalently,

$$\forall w.(\neg h_{t3}(w) \lor \neg h_{t4}(w)). \tag{2}$$

To enforce that (2) is satisfied in every state of every possible execution of the LOP, we can conjoin it with the enabling condition en_{Auth} of each transition in S. For instance, transition $t4$ becomes

$$t4(z) : en_{CF} \land a_{t1}(z) \land \forall w.(\neg h_{t3}(w) \lor \neg h_{t4}(w)) \rightarrow act_{CF} || h_{t4}(z) := T$$

where en_{CF} and act_{CF} abbreviate the symbolic representations of the enabling condition and effect, of the control-flow. We can eliminate the universal quantifier by instantiating w with z by using the results in [1], i.e. it is sufficient to consider the following transition:

$$\overline{t4}(z) : en_{CF} \wedge a_{t1}(z) \wedge (\neg h_{t3}(z) \vee \neg h_{t4}(z)) \rightarrow act_{CF} \| h_{t4}(z) := T. \qquad (3)$$

Notice that (3) can be further simplified to

$$\overline{t4}(z) : en_{CF} \wedge a_{t1}(z) \wedge \neg h_{t3}(z) \rightarrow act_{CF} \| h_{t4}(z) := T.$$

since if $t4$ has not yet been executed, then $\neg h_{t4}(z)$ must hold (indeed, the last formula is equivalent to that in the last line of Table 1).

Theorem 2. *Let T be the set of transitions of the form*

$$t(z) : en_{CF} \wedge a_t(z) \wedge \forall w. \neg h_{t'}(w) \rightarrow act_{CF} \| act_{Auth} \qquad (4)$$

for $h_{t'}$ in H and $\overline{T}$ be the set of transitions obtained by instantiating w with z. Under the same assumptions of Theorem 1, the set of possible executions of T and $\overline{T}$ are the same.

This result significantly broadens the scope of applicability of Theorem 1, thereby enabling CERBERUS to cover a large variety of authorization constraints used in security-sensitive workflows.

Interestingly, similar results can be derived for entailment constraints of the form (T_1, T_2, ρ) for T_1 and T_2 sub-sets of the set of tasks and ρ a binary relation over the set of users and for counting constraints (t_l, t_r, T') for $1 \leq t_l \leq t_r$ and T' sub-set of the set of tasks. We omit the details, for lack of space, and just explain how such constraints can be expressed as logical expressions to be conjoined to the enabling condition en_{Auth} in (1). The first type of constraints can be expressed by the formula

$$\forall z_1, z_2. \bigvee_{t_1 \in T_1} \bigvee_{t_2 \in T_2} h_{t1}(z_1) \wedge h_{t2}(z_2) \Rightarrow \rho(z_1, z_2)$$

with ρ a relation that can be specified by sentences that are universally quantified formulae and built out of predicate symbols with equality (no function symbols are allowed). The second type of constraints can be expressed by the formula

$$\forall U_{T'}. \left(\bigwedge_{t' \in T'} h_{t'}(u_{t'}) \Rightarrow \mathsf{AtMost}(U_{T'}, t_r) \wedge \mathsf{AtLeast}(U_{T'}, t_l) \right)$$

where $U_{T'} = \{u_{t'} | t' \in T'\}$, $\mathsf{AtMost}(U_{T'}, t_r)$ abbreviates the disjunction of all formulae of the form $\forall \overline{U_{T'}}. \bigvee_{x \neq y \in U_{T'}} x \neq y$ for $\overline{U_{T'}} \subseteq U_{T'}$ of cardinality t_r and $\mathsf{AtLeast}(U_{T'}, t_l)$ abbreviates the conjunction of all formulae of the form $\exists \overline{U_{T'}}. \bigwedge_{x \neq y \in U_{T'}} x \neq y$ for $\overline{U_{T'}} \subseteq U_{T'}$ of cardinality t_l.

It is also possible to express the data-based authorization constraints of Sect. 3.2 by using logical expressions to define the a_t's in A, even including constraints that are history-dependent in a way similar to the h_t's in H. We omit the details, but emphasize that since the expressions needed to express these policies are quantifier-free, Theorem 1 applies straightforwardly. Thus, CERBERUS is able to synthesize monitors for security-sensitive workflows containing also these constraints.

We conclude by observing that CERBERUS is capable of synthesizing monitors for security-sensitive workflows containing a mixture of the classes of constraints considered above.

5   Conclusion

We have motivated and presented a classification of authorization constraints in security-sensitive workflows, showed how to encode them in the declarative input language of an SMT-based model checker, and described applications of this approach. This work shows the flexibility of the SMT approach to solve the run-time version of the WSP in the presence of different authorization constraints.

Future work. Instance-spanning constraints [24] restrict what users can do across several instances of the same workflow (inter-instance), across several instances of different workflows (inter-process), or across workflows in different organizations (inter-organization). The most usual case is inter-instance authorization constraints, which have been studied in, e.g., [32]. Since we adopt the approach of having one monitor for each instance, support for inter-instance constraints would require a global synchronization of the states of each monitor, possibly using a global execution history. A possibility would be to design a central entity to which selected parts of the state of each monitor are communicated so that it can take the right decision to avoid that some inter-instance constraint is violated. Indeed, each monitor should ask the decision of the central entity before taking a decision. Although the design of this central entity may be challenging, we could take inspiration from cache-coherence protocols (see, e.g., [19]).

References

1. Alberti, F., Ghilardi, S., Pagani, E., Ranise, S., Rossi, G.P.: Universal guards, relativization of quantifiers, and failure models in model checking modulo theories. JSAT **8**, 29–61 (2012)
2. Alhaqbani, B., Adams, M., Fidge, C.J., ter Hofstede, A.H.M.: Privacy-aware workflow management. In: Proceedings of BPM, pp. 111–128. Springer, Heidelberg (2013)
3. Basin, D., Burri, S.J., Karjoth, G.: Dynamic enforcement of abstract separation of duty constraints. TISSEC **15**(3), 13:1–13:30 (2012)
4. Basin, D., Burri, S.J., Karjoth, G.: Obstruction-free authorization enforcement: Aligning security and business objectives. JCS **22**(5), 661–698 (2014)
5. Bell, D.: The bell-lapadula model. JCS **4**(2), 3 (1996)
6. Bertino, E., Ferrari, E., Atluri, V.: The specification and enforcement of authorization constraints in workflow management systems. TISSEC **2**(1), 65–104 (1999)

7. Bertolissi, C., dos Santos, D.R., Ranise, S.: Automated synthesis of run-time monitors to enforce authorization policies in business processes. In: Proceedings of ASIACCS. ACM (2015)
8. Biba, K.: Integrity considerations for secure computer systems. Technical report, DTIC Document (1977)
9. Brewer, D., Nash, M.J.: The Chinese wall security policy. In: Proceedings of S&P. IEEE (1989)
10. Burri, S.J, Karjoth, G.: Flexible scoping of authorization constraints on business processes with loops and parallelism. In: Proceedings of BPMW. Springer (2012)
11. Cohen, D., Crampton, J., Gagarin, A., Gutin, G., Jones, M.: Iterative plan construction for the workflow satisfiability problem. JAIR 51, 555–577 (2014)
12. Cohen, D., Crampton, J., Gagarin, A., Gutin, G., Jones, M.: Algorithms for the workflow satisfiability problem engineered for counting constraints. J. Comb. Optim. 32(1), 3–24 (2016)
13. Compagna, L., dos Santos, D.R., Ponta, S.E., Ranise, S.: Cerberus: Automated synthesis of enforcement mechanisms for security-sensitive business processes. In: Chechik, M., Raskin, J.-F. (eds.) TACAS 2016. LNCS, vol. 9636, pp. 567–572. Springer, Heidelberg (2016). doi:10.1007/978-3-662-49674-9_36
14. Crampton, J.: A reference monitor for workflow systems with constrained task execution. In: Proceedings of SACMAT. ACM (2005)
15. Crampton, J., Gagarin, A., Gutin, G., Jones, M., Wahlström, M.: On the workflow satisfiability problem with class-independent constraints for hierarchical organizations. TOPS 19(3), 81–829 (2016)
16. Crampton, J., Gutin, G.: Constraint expressions and workflow satisfiability. In: Proceedings of SACMAT. ACM (2013)
17. Crampton, J., Gutin, G., Yeo, A.: On the parameterized complexity and kernelization of the workflow satisfiability problem. TISSEC 16(1), 4 (2013)
18. Crampton, J., Huth, M., Kuo, J.: Authorized workflow schemas: deciding realizability through LTL(F) model checking. STTT 16(1), 31–48 (2014)
19. Delzanno, G.: Automatic verification of parameterized cache coherence protocols. In: Emerson, E.A., Sistla, A.P. (eds.) CAV 2000. LNCS, vol. 1855, pp. 53–68. Springer, Heidelberg (2000). doi:10.1007/10722167_8
20. Dijkman, R.M., Dumas, M., Ouyang, C.: Semantics and analysis of business process models in BPMN. Inf. Soft. Tech. 50(12), 1281–1294 (2008)
21. dos Santos, D.R., Ranise, S., Ponta, S.E.: Modular synthesis of enforcement mechanisms for the workflow satisfiability problem: scalability and reusability. In: Proceedings of SACMAT. ACM (2016)
22. Ghilardi, S., Ranise, S.: Backward reachability of array-based systems by SMT solving: Termination and invariant synthesis. LMCS 6(4) (2010)
23. Ghilardi, S., Ranise, S.: MCMT: A model checker modulo theories. In: Giesl, J., Hähnle, R. (eds.) IJCAR 2010. LNCS (LNAI), vol. 6173, pp. 22–29. Springer, Heidelberg (2010). doi:10.1007/978-3-642-14203-1_3
24. Leitner, M., Mangler, J., Rinderle-Ma, S.: Definition and enactment of instance-spanning process constraints. In: Wang, X.S., Cruz, I., Delis, A., Huang, G. (eds.) WISE 2012. LNCS, vol. 7651, pp. 652–658. Springer, Heidelberg (2012). doi:10.1007/978-3-642-35063-4_49
25. Li, N., Wang, Q.: Beyond separation of duty: An algebra for specifying high-level security policies. J. ACM 55(3), 121–1246 (2008)
26. Nassr, N., Steegmans, E.: Mitigating conflicts of interest by authorization policies. In: Proceedings of SIN. ACM (2015)

27. Sandhu, R., Coyne, E., Feinstein, H., Youmann, C.: Role-based access control models. IEEE Comput. **2**(29), 38–47 (1996)
28. Sankaranarayanan, S., Sipma, H., Manna, Z.: Petri net analysis using invariant generation. In: Verification: Theory and Practice. Springer (2003)
29. Tan, K., Crampton, J., Gunter, C.A.: The consistency of task-based authorization constraints in workflow. In Proceedings of CSF. IEEE (2004)
30. van der Aalst, W.M.P., van Hee, K.M., ter Hofstede, A.H.M., Sidorova, N., Verbeek, H.M.W., Voorhoeve, M., Wynn, M.T.: Soundness of workflow nets: classification, decidability, and analysis. Formal Aspects Comp. **23**(3), 333–363 (2011)
31. Wang, Q., Li, N.: Satisfiability and resiliency in workflow authorization systems. TISSEC **13**(4), 401–4035 (2010)
32. Warner, J., Atluri, V.: Inter-instance authorization constraints for secure workflow management. In: Proceedings of SACMAT (2006). ACM
33. Wolter, C., Schaad, A., Meinel, C.: Task-based entailment constraints for basic workflow patterns. ACM, In Proc. of SACMAT (2008)

Trace Partitioning and Local Monitoring
for Asynchronous Components

Duncan Paul Attard[✉] and Adrian Francalanza[✉]

CS, ICT, University of Malta, Msida, Malta
{duncan.attard.01,adrian.francalanza}@um.edu.mt

Abstract. We propose an instrumentation technique for monitoring asynchronous component systems that departs from the traditional runtime verification set-up assuming a single execution trace. The technique generates partitioned traces that better reflect the interleaved execution of the asynchronous components under scrutiny, and lends itself well to local monitoring. We provide argumentation for the qualitative benefits of our approach, demonstrate its implementability for actor-based systems, and justify claims related to the applicability and efficiency gains via an empirical evaluation over a third party component-based system.

1 Introduction

Few systems are constructed in monolithic fashion these days. Rather, a considerable number are architected as *asynchronous components* [2,10,22] that execute independently to one another without recourse to a global clock or shared state; in place of the latter, components interact with one another via well-defined interfaces and non-blocking messaging [20]. Such software organisations encourage code reuse, ease incremental updates, naturally quarantine faults and engender graceful degradation, thus improving time-to-market.

At the same time, component-based systems pose new challenges for ensuring correctness. Their sheer size, dynamic structure, use of third party components, and inherent concurrent execution, complicate the use of traditional pre-deployment verification techniques, at times rendering them ineffective. Runtime Verification (RV) [14,24] is a lightweight post-deployment verification technique that circumvents a number of these obstacles, making it an appealing compromise when ascertaining software correctness. It uses monitors that *incrementally* analyse the behaviour of the running system (exhibited as a sequence of *trace events*) up to the current execution point, in order to determine whether a correctness specification is satisfied or violated.

Recent work [4,8,15,16,28] studies the application of online RV to *general* specification properties describing the branching structure of the system under scrutiny. This is of particular relevance to concurrent (component) systems with multiple executions. Since RV is not as expressive as exhaustive pre-deployment

This work was partly supported by the project "TheoFoMon: Theoretical Foundations for Monitorability" (nr. 163406-051) of the Icelandic Research Fund.

© Springer International Publishing AG 2017
A. Cimatti and M. Sirjani (Eds.): SEFM 2017, LNCS 10469, pp. 219–235, 2017.
DOI: 10.1007/978-3-319-66197-1_14

techniques such as Model Checking, this body of work is concerned with identifying monitorable (*i.e.*, can be verified at runtime) subsets of properties. But even for monitorable properties, the analytical power of the ensuing monitor analysis is still at the mercy of the trace the system decides to exhibit at runtime.

Example 1. Consider the logging system, SYS, consisting of two *independently-executing* components, F and N. Component F handles *file logging* operations, and is permitted actions open (o), close (c) and write (w), whereas component N manages *network logging* activities through send (s) and receive (r) messages. Additionally, both components may signal file or network-related problems by issuing error (e) actions. A possible correctness property is one that *"forbids SYS from sending messages at start-up"*. When SYS exhibits the trace s.o.w.r, the monitor can detect a violation of this property. However, for a different execution interleaving (*e.g.* one producing the witness trace o.s.w.r where s is not the first event) the typical RV analysis would *not* be able to detect the fact that the system is *capable of* performing the initial action s.   ∎

In component architectures, there are instances where *additional* traces can be inferred from an observed trace; whenever these inferred traces are relevant to the correctness specification of interest, they help mitigate the aforementioned *lack of precision* of the technique. In the case of Example 1, we know that (*i*) the system consists of two components F and N whose execution can be arbitrarily interleaved, (*ii*) the trace events o,c and w can be uniquely attributed to F, whereas s and r can be accredited to N. A monitor can use this extra system information to permute the order of events in a witness trace. For example, from trace o.s.w.r, event o (generated by F) can be permuted with s (generated by N) to obtain the trace s.o.w.r which is also a *valid* trace that can be generated by the system and, crucially, provides evidence that SYS violates the property stated in Example 1. Inferring traces may also increase RV's *expressive power*. For instance, the property

$$\text{At start-up, SYS can neither send messages nor can it open files} \qquad (1)$$

is shown *not* to be monitorable in the setting of [15,16]: to detect a violation, it requires at least *two* witness execution traces, one showing that action s can be performed at start-up, another showing that o can be performed at start-up. Monitorability in traditional RV settings typically assumes *one* execution trace. For the case of F and N, from trace o.s.w.r, a monitor can infer the second trace s.o.w.r and *together* these can be used to determine the violation verdict.

Despite the benefits discussed above, trace inference for component-based systems induces additional runtime overheads and may require *unbounded* buffer space to record past trace events. Both aspects afflict the feasibility of the RV analysis, which often requires overheads to be *kept to a minimum*.

Contributions and synopsis. This paper argues that the aforementioned problems stem from the fact that traditional RV set-ups treat component-based systems as one monolithic block, artificially recording executions as one *universal trace*. Instead, we study instrumentation techniques that generate *multiple*

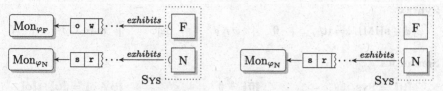

(a) Local monitors analysing the traces for components F and N separately.

(b) Local monitor analysing the trace for component N; no monitor needed for F.

Fig. 1. Local monitors attached to independently executing components.

traces, whereby events are partitioned to better reflect the asynchronous component structure of the system under scrutiny. As depicted in Fig. 1a, our proposed instrumentation technique would report the runtime execution of F and N as the *partitioned traces* o.w and s.r. These may be seen as a more compact representation of a number of universal traces in a traditional RV set-up, denoting both traces o.s.w.r and s.o.w.r mentioned earlier, but also other potentially relevant traces such as o.s.r.w and s.r.o.w.

Partitioned traces are better suited to monitor *decentralisation*. For instance, Property 1 could be evaluated using two submonitors as in Fig. 1a, one analysing whether F starts by issuing event o, and another that checks if N produces s; these would then alert one another accordingly when independent detections are made. In the case of the property from Example 1, partitioning also allows us to *localise monitoring* to the subsystem of interest, as shown in Fig. 1b: this lowers runtime overheads since the local monitor needs to process less events to reach its verdict. Apart from making a case for partitioned traces and localised monitors, our contributions are:

– A unifying account of the types of runtime monitoring approaches that can be applied to generic instantiations of component-based systems, discussing the advantages enjoyed by local monitoring in this setting in Sect. 3;
– An investigation of the implementability of local monitoring in Sect. 4;
– A case study for a third-party component-based system validating our proposed technique from a performance standpoint in Sect. 5.

We conclude by discussing future and related work in Sect. 6.

2 Monitors and Specification

Runtime monitors are typically synthesised from property specifications expressed in a high-level formalism or logic. These specifications *finitely and unambiguously* describe the behaviour of interest for the system under scrutiny.

Monitor *verdicts* are definite *non-retractable* judgements reached after analysing a finite prefix of the system execution trace, and correspond to property satisfactions or violations from which the monitor is synthesised. The monitor may also reach an *inconclusive* verdict whenever, the trace exhibited by

Syntax

$$\varphi, \phi \in \text{sHML} ::= \textbf{tt} \quad | \quad \textbf{ff} \quad | \quad \varphi \wedge \phi \quad | \quad [e]\varphi \quad | \quad \textbf{max}\, X.\varphi \quad | \quad X$$

Semantics

$$[\![\textbf{tt}]\!] \stackrel{\text{def}}{=} \text{Sys} \qquad\qquad [\![\textbf{ff}]\!] \stackrel{\text{def}}{=} \emptyset \qquad\qquad [\![\varphi \wedge \phi]\!] \stackrel{\text{def}}{=} [\![\varphi]\!] \cap [\![\phi]\!]$$

$$[\![[e]\varphi]\!] \stackrel{\text{def}}{=} \left\{ p \mid \forall p', \alpha.\ (p \stackrel{\alpha}{\Longrightarrow} p' \text{ and } \textbf{match}(e, \alpha) = \sigma) \text{ implies } p' \in [\![\varphi\sigma]\!] \right\}$$

$$[\![\textbf{max}\, X.\varphi]\!] \stackrel{\text{def}}{=} \bigcup \{ S \mid S \subseteq [\![\varphi[X \mapsto S]]\!] \}$$

Fig. 2. The syntax and semantics of sHML.

the system does not yield the necessary information for it to reach a definitive judgement.

Following [15,16], this paper uses the *safety* fragment of the branching-time logic μHML [1,23], called sHML (Safety HML), which has been shown to be monitorable and maximally expressive w.r.t. the constraints of runtime monitoring. The sHML syntax, given in Fig. 2, assumes a countable set of logical variables $X, Y \in \text{LVar}$, allowing formulae to recursively express largest fixpoints using the construct $\textbf{max}\, X.\varphi$; this binds free instances of the variable X in φ. In addition to the standard constructs of truth, **tt**, falsehood, **ff**, and conjunction, $\varphi \wedge \phi$, the logic includes a necessity modality construct, $[e]\varphi$, where the term e can contain event *patterns* consisting of free variables that are matched and *bound dynamically* at runtime to specific system events α that carry data.

As in [15,16], the semantics of sHML, defined for *closed* formulae (*i.e.,* without free variables) is interpreted over Labelled Transition Systems (LTSs) — graphs modelling the branching behaviour of systems (see Fig. 3 for examples). Formally, a LTS is comprised of the triple $\langle \text{Sys}, \text{Act}, \longrightarrow \rangle$, consisting of a set of system states $p, q \in \text{Sys}$, a set of actions $\mu \in \text{Act}$ containing a distinguished *silent* action τ (used to represent unobservable actions) and *visible* actions α ranging over $\text{Act} \setminus \{\tau\}$, and finally, a ternary transition relation between states labelled by actions, $p \stackrel{\mu}{\longrightarrow} q$. We use $p \Longrightarrow q$ to denote $p(\stackrel{\tau}{\longrightarrow})^* q$, whereas $p \stackrel{\alpha}{\Longrightarrow} q$ is written in lieu of $p \Longrightarrow \cdot \stackrel{\alpha}{\longrightarrow} \cdot \Longrightarrow q$. Formula **tt** is satisfied by all system states, whereas **ff** is satisfied by none. Conjunctions bear the standard set-theoretic meaning of intersection. Necessity formulae $[e]\varphi$ state that *for all* system executions producing event α (possibly none), pattern e must match α, yielding a set of bindings σ, and the subsequent system state must then satisfy $\varphi\sigma$ (*i.e.,* φ substituted with the bindings in σ). The recursive formula $\textbf{max}\, X.\varphi$ is defined as the union of all the post-fixpoint solutions $S \subseteq \text{Sys}$ of φ; see [1,23] for details. A system state p satisfies formula φ whenever $p \in [\![\varphi]\!]$; conversely, it violates φ whenever $p \notin [\![\varphi]\!]$. In [15,16], the authors show that any sHML formula is monitorable for violations *exclusively* (*i.e.,* the monitor for φ can reach a rejection verdict whenever $p \notin [\![\varphi]\!]$). We note in passing that the full logic μHML contains other logical operators, such as disjunctions, $\varphi \vee \phi$, with the expected

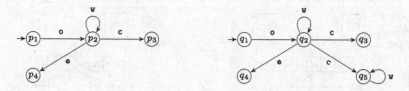

Fig. 3. Two LTSs depicting different behaviours of the file logging component in SYS.

interpretation; [15, 16] show that disjunctions such as $\varphi \vee \phi$ are not monitorable for violations, even when the subformulae φ and ϕ are. Consult [15, 16] for more details.

Example 2. Figure 3 depicts the LTSs of two possible implementations for component F from Example 1. The first one, rooted at state p_1, satisfies property φ_1 below: informally φ_1 describes implementations where, after opening (o) a logfile and performing an arbitrary number of writes (w), do not write to it once closed (c).

$$\varphi_1 = [\mathsf{o}]\big(\mathsf{max}\, X.([\mathsf{w}]X \wedge [\mathsf{c}][\mathsf{w}]\mathsf{ff})\big)$$

Interested readers can indeed check that $p_1 \in [\![\varphi_1]\!]$. The second implementation, rooted at q_1, describes non-deterministic behaviour once the logfile is closed, whereby it can either reach the inert state q_3 or state q_5, which allows further write operations. Although $q_1 \notin [\![\varphi_1]\!]$, the synthesised monitor for φ_1 of [15, 16] depends on the runtime trace exhibited to determine the violation, where: *(i)* it reaches the violation verdict whenever q_1 produces a trace of the form $\mathsf{o.w^*.c.w^+}$, *(ii)* reaches an inconclusive verdict (and stops) if it sees the trace e, and *(iii)* continues monitoring for future events for traces of the form $\mathsf{o.w^*.c}$. ∎

Example 3. The property stated in Example 1 is expressed as $[\mathsf{s}]\mathsf{ff}$ in sHML, whereas Property 1 from Sect. 1 is expressed as $[\mathsf{o}]\mathsf{ff} \vee [\mathsf{s}]\mathsf{ff}$ in the full logic μHML; in [15, 16] this is shown to be non-monitorable. ∎

3 The Approach

Standard RV set-ups consist of the system under scrutiny, the instrumentation extracting and reporting the execution trace, and the monitor analysing this trace. As shown in Fig. 4a, execution events are typically collected as a *single universal* trace that describes the running system in its entirety. We propose an alternative instrumentation approach for asynchronous components whereby the individual execution of the constituent components is reported separately as *partitioned* traces, as depicted in Figs. 4c and d.

A partitioned trace gives an exclusive *localised view* for a subset of the system under scrutiny, delineated by the underlying system structure. Partitioned traces may be analysed individually, whenever this local view suffices, or in conjunction

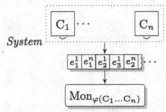

(a) Global monitor analysing the universal trace for components $C_1, \ldots, C_n$.

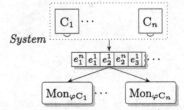

(b) Local monitors analysing the universal trace for components $C_1, \ldots, C_n$.

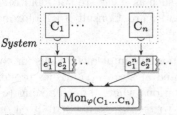

(c) Global monitor analysing the partitioned trace for components $C_1, \ldots, C_n$.

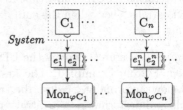

(d) Local monitors analysing the partitioned trace for components $C_1, \ldots, C_n$.

Fig. 4. Four architectural set-ups characterising component-based runtime monitoring.

with other partitioned traces to form a *combined* trace. Note that in asynchronous settings, the merging of all the partitioned traces does *not* yield a unique combined trace, but rather a *set* of possible combined traces. Trace partitioning is advantageous whenever the correctness of a system comprised of asynchronous components is considered from a global view. First off, it does not taint the monitors's view of the system behaviour by reporting artificial orderings, which in turn impinge on the monitor's analytical precision (*e.g.* monitoring for $[s]\mathbf{ff}$ from Example 1). Instead, since the aggregation of partitioned traces (efficiently) encode a set of combined (universal) traces, our proposed instrumentation provides *additional* information about the system's behaviour. This leads to more expressive RV set-ups in terms of the properties that can be monitored for at runtime (*e.g.* $[o]\mathbf{ff} \vee [s]\mathbf{ff}$ from Property 1 can be monitored in set-ups like Figs. 4c and d but *not* in classic set-ups like Fig. 4a); see Sect. 1 for discussion.

Second, trace partitioning yields other benefits in the form of local monitoring. Particularly, it permits the specification of *local properties* that describe the behaviour of a subset of components. *Local monitors* synthesised from these properties need *only* analyse events from single trace partitions in order to reach a verdict relating to the local property being considered. Note that local monitors may also execute w.r.t. a universal trace.

Example 4. Property $[s]\mathbf{ff}$ from Example 1 can be seen as a local property describing the behaviour of component N. In fact, a local monitor can be synthesised from $[s]\mathbf{ff}$ accordingly; this, in turn, is able to reach a rejection verdict just by analysing the partitioned trace for N. Property φ_1 from Example 2 can also be seen as a local property that describes the behaviour of component F from Example 1.   ∎

Executing a local monitor on a universal trace, as shown in Fig. 4b may still lead to detections in cases where the component interleaving prioritises the events of interest (*e.g.* the universal trace s.r.o.w permits a violation detection for the local property [s]**ff**), but extraneous events may affect precision, as discussed in Sect. 1. In practice, one may be able to regain degrees of precision via trace filtering at the monitor level, where conceptually, this equates to converting a local property into a *global* one that accounts for the events of other components.

Example 5. The precision of monitoring for the local property [s]**ff** over a universal trace in Example 1 can be enhanced by converting it into the global property **max** $X.([\text{o}]X \wedge [\text{w}]X \wedge [\text{c}]X \wedge [\text{s}]\textbf{ff})$ that handles extraneous events from F, and reverting to the monitoring set-up of Fig. 4a from that of Fig. 4b. By contrast, monitoring for [s]**ff** on the partitioned trace of N as in Fig. 4d does not require any trace filtering, lowering runtime overheads. Note that the constructed global property **max** $X.([\text{o}]X \wedge [\text{w}]X \wedge [\text{c}]X \wedge [\text{s}]\textbf{ff})$ evaluated over a universal trace still does not attain the precision of [s]**ff** monitored locally, due to the *common* event e that may be generated by *either* of components F or N. Since one cannot infer its provenance at the level of a universal trace, e cannot be filtered out and, correspondingly, an "ignore e" subformula [e]X cannot be added as another conjunction to the global property **max** $X.([\text{o}]X \wedge [\text{w}]X \wedge [\text{c}]X \wedge [\text{s}]\textbf{ff})$ without compromising correctness. Contrastingly, in Fig. 4d, event e is automatically suppressed when exhibited by F, but considered when exhibited by N.   ∎

The benefits of local monitoring over partitioned traces are enjoyed when global properties can be *reformulated* in terms of local properties. Whenever global properties *cannot* be fully localised due to dependencies across the various components, these can still be synthesised in a *decentralised* fashion to exploit the underlying partitioned trace instrumentation set-up. We illustrate this next.

Example 6. Consider the global sHML formula [o]**ff** $\wedge$ [s]**ff** stating that, *"on start-up, the system can never produce an open event, nor can it produce a send event"*. For the set-up in Fig. 1, the property is violated whenever F produces event o *or* N produces event s. Accordingly, [o]**ff** $\wedge$ [s]**ff** can be reformulated as two local properties, [o]**ff** and [s]**ff**, that are runtime verified by two independent local monitors analysing the respective partitioned trace of interest, as in Fig. 4d, and flagging as soon *either* one detects a violation from its local trace.

Moreover, recall the formula [o]**ff** $\vee$ [s]**ff** from Example 3. Although it cannot be synthesised in terms of local monitors (that reach verdicts by *exclusively* analysing their own trace partition), one can still runtime verify the formula in a decentralised fashion using monitors that individually analyse subformulae [o]**ff** and [s]**ff**, and communicate with each other once a detection is made by *both*. Decentralised monitors can *collaboratively* reach a violation verdict only when separate local detections have been made by participating monitors and are *shared* with others. This arrangement constitutes an instance of Fig. 4c.   ∎

A general approach to localising monitoring over partitioned traces begets further advantages. Decomposing global properties into *smaller* local subproperties improves the *maintainability* of specification scripts, since the latter tend to be less complex and more lightweight to instrument. In an effort to increase precision, global properties may be reformulated to account for the potential interleaving due to the underlying asynchronous structure (*e.g.* changing $[o]ff \vee [s]ff$ into $[o][s]ff \wedge [s][o]ff$); this however tends to complicate specifications.

Property decomposition also makes scripts *extensible*, since changes in existing correctness requirements do not necessitate substantial refactoring of global formulae, but merely amendments that are administered to specific local formulae; adding new components into the system carries similar benefits. Segregated monitors over partitioned traces as in Fig. 4d are better equipped to handle *failures* which, in component systems, typically affect only a component subset. For instance in Example 6, the failure of component F does not prevent the monitor at N from making its detections; this renders the whole set-up *fault-tolerant*. By constrast, global monitoring relies on a central trace processing model that can be crippled by the smallest of partial system failures.

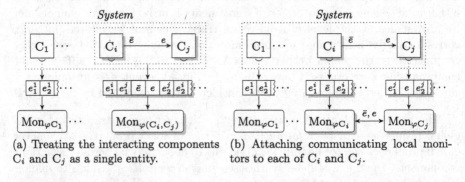

(a) Treating the interacting components C_i and C_j as a single entity.

(b) Attaching communicating local monitors to each of C_i and C_j.

Fig. 5. Local monitoring for interacting components using partitioned traces.

Component interaction synchronises the involved parties, and this interaction is often recorded in the respective traces as an event and its dual (*e.g.* a *write* event in one partitioned trace and a corresponding *written* event in the other). This establishes a partial ordering on events *across* partitioned traces. For instance, Fig. 5a depicts components C_i and C_j generating event sequences $e_1^i, \bar{e}, e_2^i$ and e_1^j, e, e_2^j resp., where event e is the dual of $\bar{e}$. In a combined trace of these partitioned traces, events e_1^i and e_1^j may occur in any order relative to one another; the same applies to events e_2^i and e_2^j. However, event e_1^i must always precede e_2^j, and similarly e_1^j must always precede e_2^i, where the synchronising events $\bar{e}$ and e act as a delimiter for the possible permutations.

In a partitioned trace set-up, the problem of monitoring for properties that span over multiple communicating components can be circumvented by choosing to treat the interacting components as *one* component subset generating a *single* partitioned trace for the respective components. This then allows them to be *locally* monitored, as shown in Fig. 5a with $\mathrm{Mon}_{\varphi(C_i,C_j)}$ monitoring for the local property concerning these components. Alternatively, individual monitors can also be attached to C_i and C_j as shown in Fig. 5b, though these must then *communicate* between themselves in order to determine the relative ordering of the events exhibited by each component in relation to $\bar{e}$ and e. In the sequel, we favour arrangement Fig. 5a since this leads to local monitoring of Fig. 4d.

4   The Implementability of Local Monitoring

We demonstrate the implementability of our local monitoring approach by considering actors in Erlang [3,9] which constitute an instance of asynchronous component systems. Erlang is a general-purpose, concurrent programming language where *actors* are concurrent units of decomposition that do not share any mutable memory. They interact with one another via *asynchronous* messages and change their internal state based on the messages received. Actors are implemented as lightweight processes that are identified via unique process IDs (PIDs). Every actor owns a message queue, called a *mailbox*, to which messages are sent in a non-blocking fashion; subsequently, these messages can be selectively consumed by the recipient actor at any stage.

Our implementation conveniently utilises the tracing mechanism proffered by the Erlang Virtual Machine (EVM) to obtain local trace events. Tracing via the EVM [9] makes it possible to observe actor behaviour *without* modifying the system through commonly used instrumentation techniques such as Aspect-Oriented Programming (AOP). It can be *selectively* applied to specific groups of actors simultaneously, enabling one to independently target different subparts of the system and attain partitioned traces as described in Sect. 3. A *traced* actor generates event messages describing the nature of the trace events (*e.g.* function calls, message sends and receives, *etc.*). These trace messages are directed by the EVM to the mailbox of a specifically designated *tracer* actor. Tracing serves as the basis for a number of utilities, including Erlang's text-based tracing facility dbg [3], and the third-party monitoring tool Recon [18].

The set-up in Fig. 4d can be naturally phrased in terms of Erlang actors. In our tool implementation, actors are used to represent both the system components $C_1, \ldots, C_n$ and their associated monitors $\mathrm{Mon}_{\varphi C_1}, \ldots, \mathrm{Mon}_{\varphi C_n}$: trace event collection is handled by the EVM as explained above, where the role of tracers is assumed by monitor actors. Our tool also handles dynamic reconfiguration of component systems by adjusting the local monitoring set-up of Fig. 4d accordingly. In fact, actor systems typically are not static, since actors may terminate and new actors may be spawned. Our implementation can either terminate or dynamically assign new local monitors to the spawned actors, thereby scaling the monitoring organisation accordingly. A rudimentary implementation of this monitoring mechanism can give rise to race-conditions. Specifically, system (actor) components that require monitoring may spawn and forge ahead executing *before* their associated monitors have been properly attached, potentially leading to a loss of trace events. To avoid this, the tool opts for a *synchronous* monitor instantiation procedure that *pauses* the components that require monitoring until their associated monitors have been created and started correctly. Synchronisation takes place via instrumented source code instructions inside the monitored components which communicate with a special coordinating actor that manages the initialisation sequence of components and their corresponding monitor actors. We have integrated our implementation within the detectEr tool [4] which synthesises monitors from property descriptions expressed as sHML formulae.

We conjecture that such an implementation arrangement does not favour any particular language or property specification formalism, nor is it tied to the unit of decomposition employed by the host language's programming paradigm. In the absence of a tracing mechanism such as that offered by Erlang, one can resort to instrumentation techniques including intermediate code-level (*e.g.* AspectJ) or proxy-based (*e.g.* Spring AOP) weaving [25].

5   Experimental Evaluation

Local monitoring over partitioned traces induces *lower* performance overheads. We substantiate this claim through a series of empirical experiments performed over an Erlang third-party component-based software called Ranch [19]. Ranch is a socket acceptor pool for TCP protocols that can be used to build custom network applications (*e.g.* the Cowboy HTTP web server [19] uses Ranch to manage its client connections). Our evaluation permits us to: *(i)* explore the applicability of local monitoring by identifying cases where it can be used (non-artificially) to monitor third-party software, and also *(ii)* investigate whether it can be *feasibly* applied to real-world scenarios.

5.1   Monitoring for the Ranch Connection Protocol

Performance tests on Ranch were conducted using a number of sHML properties designed to push the application to its limits, the better to assess how local monitoring behaves under usages typical of production environments. The properties target various aspects of Ranch, and focus mainly on communication exchanges, *i.e.*, sends and receives (denoted by ! and ?), that take place between different components inside Ranch.

For instance, the following *recursive* local property describes behaviour for a fragment of the Ranch connection protocol used by acceptor components and the connections supervisor, from the acceptor's point of view:

$$\max X.\big($$
$$[ConnsSup \: ! \: \{\texttt{ranch\_conns\_sup}, \texttt{start\_protocol}, Acpt, Sock\}] \; ❸ \qquad (2)$$
$$([Acpt \: \textbf{stp} \: \texttt{killed}] \, \textbf{ff} \land [Acpt \: ? \: ConnsSup] \, X \, ❺))$$

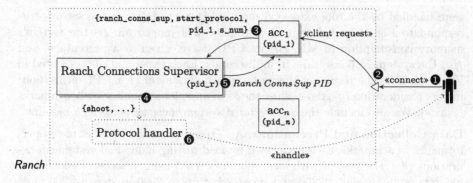

Fig. 6. The Ranch connection protocol used to handle incoming client connections.

In this protocol (see Fig. 6), *acceptors* wait on a port for incoming connections. When a connection is established ❷, the acceptor exchanges its newly acquired client socket information with the *connections supervisor* pid_r ❸. Consequently, a *protocol handler* is spawned by the connections supervisor so that ownership of the client socket is transferred to the handler ❹, permitting it to engage in direct communication with the client from that point onwards ❻. Upon successful creation of the protocol handler, the connections supervisor acknowledges back to the acceptor ❺. Figure 6 shows a Ranch configuration consisting of n acceptors with its first acceptor with PID pid_1 servicing a new client connection.

Property 2 employs pattern matching as explained in Sect. 2 to dynamically bind the formula variables to the process and socket identifiers. Concretely, the pattern [*ConnsSup* ! {ranch_conns_sup, start_protocol, *Acpt, Sock*}] matches the client socket information sent by acceptor pid_1 (encoded as the Erlang tuple {ranch_conns_sup, start_protocol, pid_1, s_num}) to the supervisor pid_r, binding the pattern variables *ConnsSup*, Acpt and *Sock* to the respective values pid_r, pid_1 and s_num ❸. Following this, the acceptor may either crash, thus matching the second necessity subformula [pid_1 **stp** killed] **ff** *violating* Property 2, or receive an acknowledgement message from the connections supervisor, matching the third necessity subformula [pid_1 **?** pid_r] ❺.

5.2 Experiment Set-Up and Design

Our evaluation focusses on global properties that can be cleanly decomposed into a set of local properties which can be verified against a partitioned trace. Each experiment was conducted as a series of performance benchmarks where local properties were monitored over individually executing components, and the results were in turn compared against those yielded by monitoring the original global property over the entire system. Global properties were monitored using the detectEr tool developed in [4], whereas their decomposed local constituents were handled by the tool extension reported in Sect. 4. These two set-ups correspond to Fig. 4a and d resp. Performance was judged on: *(i)* the system's memory consumption in MB, *(ii)* its CPU usage, given as a percentage, and *(iii)* the system response time in milliseconds. Each experiment is presented in Fig. 7, plotting the results of the performance parameter (*e.g.* CPU utilisation) under consideration (*y*-axis) against the local and global monitoring benchmarks (*x*-axis). We also include the *unmonitored* system measurements as a baseline.

Data Collection and Precautions. An *experiment* refers to a set of ten performance benchmarks, each performed by load testing individual system configurations (*e.g.* the system with local monitors, *etc.*) using a series of concurrent requests, commencing at 200 and progressing up to 2000 in steps of 200 (*i.e.,* $200, 400, \ldots, 2000$). Results for repetitions of sets of ten experiments were averaged to obtain the plots shown in Fig. 7. A number of precautions were taken to ensure the accuracy and repeatability of our results: *(i)* ten *repeated readings* for each experiment were taken, after calculating the *coefficient of variation* (*i.e.,* $\frac{\sigma}{\bar{x}} \times 100$) for different sets of experiment repetitions (*e.g.* five, ten, fifteen, *etc.*) showed negligible variability between the data sets obtained with ten repetitions and above, *(ii)* optimisations such as *garbage collection* were switched off so that the readings obtained clearly underscore the differences between local and global monitoring, *(iii)* performance spikes in the initial set of data points due to the lazy start up of the internal VM infrastructure were eliminated by issuing a series of *warm-up requests* before the actual benchmarks tests were performed.

5.3   Results and Analysis

Figure 7 shows the experiment results for monitors synthesised from formulae such as Property 2 using two Ranch configurations: one with a hundred acceptors, and one with four. All experiments were conducted on a 3.1 GHz Intel Core i7 processor with 16 GB of memory.

Realistic Ranch configuration. We first applied local monitoring to the *recommended* Ranch set-up configured with one hundred acceptors [19]. The plots for the unmonitored and locally monitored Ranch set-up in Fig. 7a show that the memory and CPU-related overheads induced by local monitoring are reasonably low and exhibit an analogous rate of change to those of the unmonitored system. This suggests that the resource consumption overheads due to local monitoring follow those of the unmonitored system, and in such cases, one would be able to *forecast* the extra system resource requirements that would be introduced by local monitoring. Response times measure the *observable* impact of monitoring on the behaviour of the system; the plot in Fig. 7a shows that the performance impact of local monitoring is imperceptible for the benchmarks considered. Note that for all three parameters, evaluating global monitoring on this Ranch set-up was not possible because it consistently led to resource exhaustion.

Other configurations. Our attempts at evaluating global monitoring on Ranch configured with one hundred acceptors were stymied by the high amount of overheads. To investigate which settings would permit us to test global monitoring

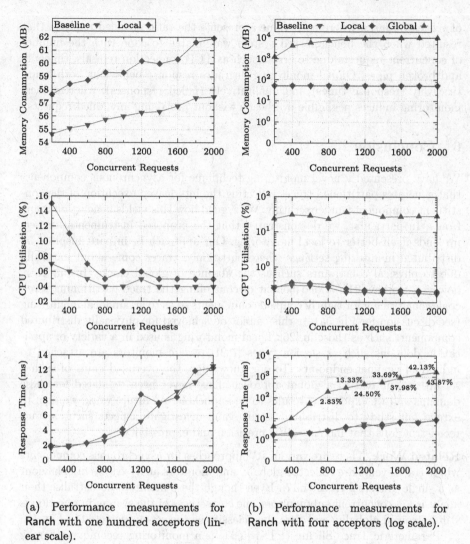

(a) Performance measurements for Ranch with one hundred acceptors (linear scale).

(b) Performance measurements for Ranch with four acceptors (log scale).

Fig. 7. Memory, CPU and response time benchmarks for two Ranch configurations.

suitably, we used various Ranch configurations with different numbers of acceptors. These trials revealed that only Ranch configurations having less than five acceptors could be reliably benchmarked without crashing. Figure 7b shows the memory, CPU and response time plots for Ranch with four acceptors (in log scale). Whereas the overheads induced by global monitoring are infeasibly higher than the baseline, those resulting from local monitoring are decidedly closer to the measurements obtained for the unmonitored system. Specifically, in Fig. 7b we achieved an average memory overhead of 4.54% and an average CPU overhead of 14.22%. The response time plot in Fig. 7b additionally displays the percentage of *request failures*, where each value represents the ratio of failed requests that resulted when the benchmarked system was unable to cope with the number of concurrent requests due to errors such as TCP connection refusals, timeouts and broken pipes. Global monitoring degrades response behaviour both quantitatively (response times) and qualitatively (failed responses), whereas local monitoring induces negligible overheads without provoking any failed requests.

6   Conclusion

We have presented a novel monitoring technique for asynchronous components that generates partitioned traces reflecting the interleaved execution of the constituent components under scrutiny. We argued how this yields benefits on many fronts. In particular, we demonstrated that the proposed instrumentation set-up lends itself better to local monitoring. Our approach is, in part, inspired by distributed monitoring settings where partitioned traces come about naturally due to physical constraints such as the absence of global clocks. In our case, however, we have the added benefit of controlling the trace partitioning level, coalescing tracing for tightly coupled components so as to attain local monitoring (see discussion for Fig. 5a) — this cannot be achieved for physically distributed components such as those in [26]. Local monitoring is used in a variety of application domains such as session types [7,21], where monitors are attached to individual channel endpoints. To our knowledge, the overhead gains of such a set-up, as opposed to a global approach, have never been validated for these domains and we expect our results to be applicable. As future work, we plan to extend our study to distributed settings and investigate aspects such as trace reconstructions that increase RV's precision and expressivity.

Related Work. There are various RV approaches for asynchronous components where trace events are collected globally and monitors analyse system behaviour as a single universal trace [4,17]. Even though these monitors decentralise their analysis via concurrent submonitors, the correctness of the system in question is still perceived globally, and thus they classify as the set-up depicted in Fig. 4a. Parameteric Trace Slicing (PTS) [5,11] is a monitoring technique whereby a universal trace is *projected* into subtraces called *trace slices*, based on parametric specifications, *i.e.*, properties that are specified in terms of *parametrised* symbolic events whose parameters are bound to values from concrete events in the universal trace. Slicing is mainly concerned with filtering events from a universal trace so as to obtain *local* monitors as in Fig. 4b. PTS differs from our work in these respects: *(i)* projection is *not* partitioning since an event may be assigned to multiple subtraces (*i.e.*, their local monitors may overlap w.r.t. events), *(ii)* subtraces are described at the specification level whereas partitioning works at the instrumentation level, *(iii)* parametric specifications typically describe *replicated* component behaviour sharing a common structure, whereas we are able to partition non-replicated components, *(iv)* since PTS works on a universal trace, events that cannot always be attributed to a unique component (*e.g.* event e in F and N of Examples 1 and 5) cannot be filtered as selectively.

ELarva [13] can be seen as an instance of PTS applied to asynchronous components. It also targets Erlang actors and is implemented using the EVM's native tracing mechanism as in Sect. 4. However, ELarva relies on a universal trace, and through an application-level routing mechanism, multiplexes events from the trace to monitors attached to different components. The parametric properties specified per spawned actor facilitate dynamic monitor creation, but the centralised trace processing mechanism induces unnecessary bottlenecks that may hamper gains obtained from monitor parallelism. We are unaware of any PTS used for branching-time specifications of asynchronous components.

The closest work to ours is [6,12] where global LTL formulae are monitored locally over partitioned traces. The authors propose and evaluate a decentralised approach that decomposes a given global LTL specification into smaller subproperties that analyse separate trace partitions and communicate amongst themselves to handle subformula dependencies accordingly, as depicted in Fig. 4c. They also show that local monitoring yields lower monitoring overheads. The work differs from ours w.r.t. the following aspects: *(i)* they consider synchronous systems, governed by a global clock that yields a *unique* combined trace from the respective partitioned traces; asynchronous settings are richer and typically yield multiple combined traces, *(ii)* the logic considered describes execution *traces* whereas we consider a logic describing properties over *programs*; we show how the multiple combined traces inferred in asynchronous settings can be exploited to increase the monitor's precision and monitorability of such properties, *(iii)* they require a complete partitioning of trace events in order to automate formula decentralisation, whereas we allow components to share trace events (*e.g.* components F and N from Example 1 can both exhibit event e), *(iv)* the evaluation in [6,12] focusses on decentralised communicating monitors that still regard correctness from a global perspective (analogous to [o]ff $\vee$ [s]ff from Example 6); our evaluation rather concentrates on properties that can be cleanly decomposed into local ones that fully capitalise on trace partitioning, *(v)* their tool assumes a fixed number of components that remains constant throughout execution as opposed to ours, which can handle dynamic partitioning as well.

Partitioned traces are also used for monitoring shared-state concurrency programs such as [27], where decentralised monitors attached to different executing threads collect and analyse events locally and actively collaborate in order to build a combined representation of the present system state. The data exchange between monitors takes place when shared variables are accessed (for reading or writing) by the executing threads; this can be seen as an instance of the set-up depicted in Fig. 4c. By contrast, our work concentrates on studying local monitors over such partitioned traces, as discussed in Fig. 4d. In particular, we assess the performance impact of local monitoring, whereas performance issues are not a focus of [27]. Instead they study the detection and prediction of particular types of safety properties. As in earlier work by the same authors [26], the investigation is conducted in terms of a linear-time epistemic logic that describes execution traces, whereas we consider a logic describing the branching program behaviour as a computation graph, which gives us scope for inferring other parts of the computation graph from the path observed at runtime.

References

1. Aceto, L., Ingólfsdóttir, A., Larsen, K.G., Srba, J.: Reactive Systems: Modelling, Specification and Verification. Cambridge University Press, New York (2007)
2. Agha, G., Mason, I.A., Smith, S.F., Talcott, C.L.: A foundation for actor computation. J. Funct. Program. **7**, 1–72 (1997)
3. Armstrong, J.: Programming Erlang: Software for a Concurrent World. Pragmatic Bookshelf (2007)
4. Attard, D.P., Francalanza, A.: A monitoring tool for a branching-time logic. In: Falcone, Y., Sánchez, C. (eds.) RV 2016. LNCS, vol. 10012, pp. 473–481. Springer, Cham (2016). doi:10.1007/978-3-319-46982-9_31
5. Barringer, H., Falcone, Y., Havelund, K., Reger, G., Rydeheard, D.: Quantified event automata: towards expressive and efficient runtime monitors. In: Giannakopoulou, D., Méry, D. (eds.) FM 2012. LNCS, vol. 7436, pp. 68–84. Springer, Heidelberg (2012). doi:10.1007/978-3-642-32759-9_9
6. Bauer, A., Falcone, Y.: Decentralised LTL monitoring. In: Giannakopoulou, D., Méry, D. (eds.) FM 2012. LNCS, vol. 7436, pp. 85–100. Springer, Heidelberg (2012). doi:10.1007/978-3-642-32759-9_10
7. Bocchi, L., Chen, T.-C., Demangeon, R., Honda, K., Yoshida, N.: Monitoring networks through multiparty session types. In: Beyer, D., Boreale, M. (eds.) FMOODS/FORTE -2013. LNCS, vol. 7892, pp. 50–65. Springer, Heidelberg (2013). doi:10. 1007/978-3-642-38592-6_5
8. Cassar, I., Francalanza, A.: On implementing a monitor-oriented programming framework for actor systems. In: Ábrahám, E., Huisman, M. (eds.) IFM 2016. LNCS, vol. 9681, pp. 176–192. Springer, Cham (2016). doi:10.1007/ 978-3-319-33693-0_12
9. Cesarini, F., Thompson, S.: Erlang Programming. O'Reilly Media, Sebastopol (2009)
10. Chappell, D.: Enterprise Service Bus: Theory in Practice. O'Reilly Media, Sebastopol (2004)
11. Chen, F., Rosu, G.: Parametric trace slicing and monitoring. In: Kowalewski, S., Philippou, A. (eds.) TACAS 2009. LNCS, vol. 5505, pp. 246–261. Springer, Heidelberg (2009). doi:10.1007/978-3-642-00768-2_23
12. Colombo, C., Falcone, Y.: Organising LTL monitors over distributed systems with a global clock. In: Bonakdarpour, B., Smolka, S.A. (eds.) RV 2014. LNCS, vol. 8734, pp. 140–155. Springer, Cham (2014). doi:10.1007/978-3-319-11164-3_12
13. Colombo, C., Francalanza, A., Gatt, R.: Elarva: a monitoring tool for erlang. In: Khurshid, S., Sen, K. (eds.) RV 2011. LNCS, vol. 7186, pp. 370–374. Springer, Heidelberg (2012). doi:10.1007/978-3-642-29860-8_29
14. Falcone, Y., Fernandez, J., Mounier, L.: What can you verify and enforce at runtime? STTT **14**(3), 349–382 (2012)
15. Francalanza, A., Aceto, L., Ingolfsdottir, A.: On verifying hennessy-milner logic with recursion at runtime. In: Bartocci, E., Majumdar, R. (eds.) RV 2015. LNCS, vol. 9333, pp. 71–86. Springer, Cham (2015). doi:10.1007/978-3-319-23820-3_5
16. Francalanza, A., Aceto, L., Ingólfsdóttir, A.: Monitorability for the Hennessy-Milner Logic with Recursion. Formal Methods Syst. Des., 1–30 (2017)

17. Francalanza, A., Seychell, A.: Synthesising correct concurrent runtime monitors. Formal Methods Syst. Des. **46**(3), 226–261 (2015)
18. Hebert, F.: Recon. http://ferd.github.io/recon. Accessed 13 Mar 2017
19. Hoguin, L.: 99s. http://ninenines.eu. Accessed 13 Mar 2017
20. Hohpe, G., Woolf, B.: Enterprise Integration Patterns: Designing, Building, and Deploying Messaging Solutions. Addison-Wesley Professional, Boston (2003)
21. Jia, L., Gommerstadt, H., Pfenning, F.: Monitors and blame assignment for higher-order session types. In: POPL, pp. 582–594. ACM (2016)
22. Josuttis, N.M.: SOA in Practice: The Art of Distributed System Design: Theory in Practice. O'Reilly Media, Sebastopol (2007)
23. Larsen, K.G.: Proof systems for satisfiability in hennessy-milner logic with recursion. Theor. Comput. Sci. **72**(2&3), 265–288 (1990)
24. Leucker, M., Schallhart, C.: A brief account of runtime verification. J. Log. Algebr. Program. **78**(5), 293–303 (2009)
25. Safonov, V.O.: Using Aspect-Oriented Programming for Trustworthy Software Development. Wiley-Interscience, Hoboken (2008)
26. Sen, K., Vardhan, A., Agha, G., Rosu, G.: Efficient decentralized monitoring of safety in distributed systems. In: ICSE, pp. 418–427 (2004)
27. Sen, K., Vardhan, A., Agha, G., Rosu, G.: Decentralized runtime analysis of multithreaded applications. In: IPPS (2006)
28. Vella, A., Francalanza, A.: Preliminary results towards contract monitorability. In: PrePost@IFM. EPTCS, vol. 208, pp. 54–63 (2016)

Compositional Verification of Interlocking Systems for Large Stations

Alessandro Fantechi[1,2]([⊠]), Anne E. Haxthausen[1], and Hugo D. Macedo[1,3]

[1] DTU Compute, Technical University of Denmark, Lyngby, Denmark
aeha@dtu.dk
[2] DINFO, University of Florence, Firenze, Italy
alessandro.fantechi@unifi.it
[3] Department of Engineering, Aarhus University, Aarhus, Denmark
hdm@eng.au.dk

Abstract. Railway interlocking systems are responsible to grant exclusive access to a route, that is a sequence of track elements, through a station or a network. Formal verification that basic safety rules regarding exclusive access to routes are satisfied by an implementation is still a challenge for networks of large size due to the exponential computation time and resources needed.

Some recent attempts to address this challenge adopt a compositional approach, targeted to track layouts that are easily decomposable into sub-networks such that a route is almost fully contained in a sub-network: in this way granting the access to a route is essentially a decision local to the sub-network, and the interfaces with the rest of the network easily abstract away less interesting details related to the external world.

Following up on previous work, where we defined a compositional verification method that started considering routes that overlap between sub-networks in interlocking systems governing a multi-station line, we attack the verification of large networks, which are typically those in main stations of major cities, and where routes are very intertwined and can hardly be separated into sub-networks that are independent at some degree. At this regard, we study how the division of a complex network into sub-networks, using stub elements to abstract all the routes that are common between sub-networks, may still guarantee compositionality of verification of safety properties.

Keywords: Railway interlocking · Compositional verification · Model checking

1 Introduction

Railway interlocking systems are those systems that are responsible to grant to a train the exclusive access to a *route*: a route is a sequence of track elements

---

A. Fantechi and H.D. Macedo—The authors' research conducted at DTU Compute was funded by Villum Fonden and by the RobustRailS project granted by Innovation Fund Denmark, respectively.

A. Cimatti and M. Sirjani (Eds.): SEFM 2017, LNCS 10469, pp. 236–252, 2017.
DOI: 10.1007/978-3-319-66197-1_15

that are exclusively assigned for the movement of a train through a station or a network. Granting of a route to a train occurs after a reservation request only if the track elements that form the route are not occupied by other trains, and if no conflicting route (that is, no other route that shares track elements with it) has been reserved by another train.

Errors in granting to a train the access to a route can obviously have catastrophic consequences; interlocking systems are therefore ranked as safety-critical systems, and this demands for high standards in the development of the software controlling interlocking systems. The standard CENELEC 50128 [2] labels such software with the highest *safety integrity level* (SIL4), and highly recommends the usage of formal methods and formal verification in its development process.

However, full formal verification of interlocking systems demands heavy if not infeasible computational resources for the phenomenon known as the state explosion problem, that is, the exponential growth of the state space with the number of elements in the controlled track layout. The most recent research in model checking and in applying model checking to the domain of railways [3–6,10,20,21] has developed techniques allowing the verification of models of the interlocking systems controlling quite large and complex networks. For example, abstraction techniques can be applied at the domain modelling level before the model checking is performed [10]. Other very efficient techniques applied to real world railway interlocking systems are bounded model checking [7] and k-induction [20].

However, formal verification that basic safety rules regarding exclusive access to routes are satisfied by an implementation is still a challenge for networks of very large size, due to the exponential computation time and resources needed.

Some recent attempts to address this challenge adopt a *compositional* approach, targeted to track layouts that are easily decomposable into sub-networks such that a route is almost fully contained in a sub-network: in this way granting the access to a route is essentially a decision local to the sub-network, and the interfaces with the rest of the network easily abstract away less interesting details related to the external world. This is the case of [11], where a station layout is divided into two symmetric components that can be separately verified using an assume-guarantee reasoning, and of our previous work [12,13], where we were able to divide a multi-station line into almost independent components by performing cuts in between the stations.

In this paper we extend our previous work [12,13] to provide a new, more complex, way of dividing large networks, such as those typically found in main stations of major cities, where routes are very intertwined and can hardly be separated into sub-networks that are independent. First, in Sect. 2, we give a short introduction to the RobustRails verification tools we are using. Next, in Sect. 3, we elaborate more on the idea of compositional verification and relate our new work to some past, related work. Then, in Sects. 4 and 5 we describe our compositional method with the new cut and make some experiments using it both for a smaller station and a large, real-world station. Finally, in Sect. 6, some conclusions are drawn.

2 Interlocking Systems and Their Verification

In this section we briefly introduce the main notions of interlocking systems: we actually use the terminology and the assumptions of the new Danish ETCS Level 2 resignalling program, and we refer to [13,19] for a more detailed introduction.

In this context, the specification of a given route-based interlocking system consists of two main components: (1) a railway network, and (2) a corresponding interlocking table.

A railway network consists of a number of track and track-side elements of different types[1]: linear sections, points, and marker boards. A *linear section* is a section with up to two neighbours: one in the *up* end, and one in the *down* end. For simplicity, in the examples and figures in the rest of this article, the *up* (*down*) direction is assumed to be the left-to-right (right-to-left) direction. A *point* can have up to three neighbours: one at the *stem*, one at the *plus* end, and one at the *minus* end. The *stem* and *plus* ends form the straight (main) path, and the *stem* and *minus* ends form the branching (siding) path. A point can be switched between two positions: PLUS and MINUS, selecting the main or siding paths, respectively. Linear sections and points are collectively called (train detection) sections, as they are provided with train detection equipment used by the interlocking system to detect the presence of trains. Along each linear section, up to two *marker boards* (one for each direction) can be installed. A marker board can only be seen in one direction and is used as reference location (for the start and end of routes) for trains going in that direction. There are no physical signals in ETCS Level 2, but interlocking systems have a *virtual signal* associated with each marker board. Train drivers do not visually see the aspect of virtual signals (OPEN or CLOSED), that is instead communicated to the onboard computer via a radio network. For simplicity, the terms *virtual signal*, *signal*, and *marker board* are used interchangeably throughout this paper.

A *route* is a path from a *source* signal to a *destination* signal in the given railway network. A route is called an *elementary route* if there are no signals that are located between its source signal and its destination signal, and that are intended for the same direction as the route. In railway signalling terminology, *setting* a route denotes the process of allocating the resources – i.e., sections, points, and signals – for the route, and then *locking* it exclusively for only one train when the resources are allocated.

An *interlocking table* specifies the elementary routes in the given railway network and the conditions for setting these routes. A route is defined by the following attributes:

- src(r) – the source signal of r,
- dst(r) – the destination signal of r,
- path(r) – the list of sections constituting r's path from src(r) to dst(r),
- points(r) – the required position of the points along the route r
- signals(r) – the required settings of signals
- conflicts(r) – a set of conflicting routes which must not be set while r is set.

---

[1] Here we only show types that are relevant for the work presented in this article.

Examples of network layouts and related interlocking tables are deferred to Sect. 4.

Typical safety properties required of an interlocking system are that it always ensures the following safety conditions:

1. **No collisions:** Two trains must never occupy the same track section at the same time.
2. **No derailments:** A point must not be switched, while being occupied by a train.

All required safety properties are expressed as *generic* conditions leading to *specific* conditions for each specific case of a network. Notice that considering such typical safety properties, a route defines the maximal subset of elements whose status affects the safety property, that is, no element outside a route, or, at most, two conflicting routes, can affect a safety property for that route(s).[2]

The RobustRailS verification method [17–20] is a combination of formal methods and a domain-specific language (DSL) to express network diagrams and interlocking tables. A tool is provided by the RobustRailS environment to transform the DSL description into inputs to the model checker, that is, *(i)* a behavioural model of the interlocking system and its environment, and *(ii)* the required safety properties given as linear temporal logic formulae.

The RobustRailS tools can be used to verify the design of an interlocking system in the following steps:

1. A DSL specification of the configuration data (a network layout and its corresponding interlocking table) is constructed in the following order:
   (a) first the network layout,
   (b) and then the interlocking table (this is either done manually or generated automatically from the network layout).
2. The static checker verifies whether the configuration data is statically well-formed according to the static semantics [19] of the DSL.
3. The generators instantiate a generic behavioural model and generic safety properties with the well-formed configuration data to generate the model input of the model checker and the safety properties.
4. The generated model instance is then checked against the generated properties by the bounded model checker performing a k-induction proof.

The static checking in step (2) is intended to catch errors in the network layout and interlocking table, while the model checking in step (4) is intended to catch safety violations in the control algorithm of the instantiated model.

The tool chain associated with the method has been implemented using the RT-tester framework [14, 16].

---

[2] The subset is sometimes extended with overlaps (buffer zones at the end of paths), and points or signals needed for flank protection, since this is sometimes required to protect tracks occupied by a train from another train not succeeding to brake in due space. We do not consider these extra protections in this paper, and we refer to [15, 19] for details and for their modelling.

3   Compositionality

Interlocking systems typically exhibit a high degree of *locality*: if we consider a typical safety property desired for an interlocking system, e.g. that the same track element shall not be reserved by more than one train at a time, it is likely that this property is not influenced by a train moving on a distant, or parallel, track element. Locality of a safety property can be exploited for verification purposes, so limiting the state space on which to verify it. This principle has been exploited in [22] to define domain-oriented optimisation of the variable ordering in a BDD-based verification. Locality can be used also for slicing, as suggested in [1,3,8,9]: the idea is to consider only the portion of the model that has influence on the property to be verified, by a topological selection of interested track elements (therefore closely related to the *cone of influence* of the property): this allows for a much more efficient verification of the single property, but comes at the price of repeating the slicing and the verification for every property, and of separately checking that verifying slices does actually imply the satisfaction of desired properties for the whole system. Nevertheless, it appears that when automated, this process can offer significant time and memory savings.

Compositional verification of interlocking systems also exploits locality: the network layout is divided into two or more sub-networks, so that the separate verification of safety properties on the sub-networks can be used to prove safety properties on the whole network, with a significant advantage in terms of time and memory; moreover, the verification can be run once on the conjunction of all safety properties. Adopting a compositional approach actually needs a proof that the separate verification guarantees the safety properties for the whole network, and this proof depends on the type of division (from now on, *cut*) that is envisaged.

Indeed, in Fig. 1 the dotted light green lines show three different cases of cuts of a network into two small networks:

(a) A line connecting several stations is divided into sub-networks, each including a station; this case has been studied in our previous work [12,13]. We can see that the cut concerns a single track element, that behaves as source and destination of routes from/to one of the stations (A1u-L1u, A2u-L1u, L1d-A1d, L1d-A2d from/to station A, B1d-L1d, B2d-L1d, B3d-L1d, L1u-B1u, L1u-B2u, L1u-B3u from/to station B). Notice that all these routes are almost fully contained in one of the sub-networks: in this way granting the access to a route is essentially a decision local to the sub-network, apart from the single interface track element that is included in both routes of the sub-networks. This allows to consider, in the separate verification, the shared element as an abstraction of all the routes of the Station A when verifying properties related to Station B, and vice versa.

(b) This is the case of a (possibly almost) symmetrical station, that is divided into two halves, as studied in [11]: the verification of one half takes into account assume/guarantee conditions at the interface with the other half. The verification effort is hence repeated for the two halves, with the extra

a)

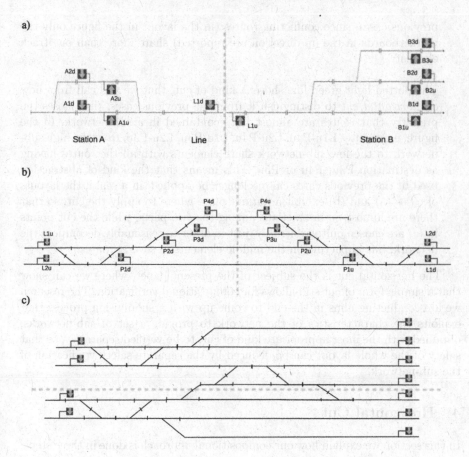

Fig. 1. Three example cuts. (Color figure online)

effort of proving that assume/guarantee conditions do hold at the interface: locality allows such conditions to be rather simple so that they do not add much time to the verification. Again, a route is almost fully contained in one of the two sub-network, and the shared track elements act as an abstraction of the routes of the other sub-network, although there are several shared elements (e.g. routes L1u-P3u and L2u-P3u have a single track element shared with routes L1d-P3d and L2d-P3d).[3]

(c) A more complex case is that of a (terminus) station where more lines (in this case, two double-track lines) converge from one side (in this case from the left side) to the station. The layout has to include paths allowing to go from any input track to any (or almost any) platform, through a sequence of points that in the figure goes from high tracks to low tracks, and vice versa. Notice that it is not possible to operate a cut like the ones of the

---

[3] For simplicity we consider here and in the following only the shortest path routes.

previous cases, since conflicting routes (in the layout in the figure only the markerboards in the up direction are reported) share more than one track element.

The dotted light green line shows a kind of cut, that we will call from now on *horizontal cut* to distinguish it from the previous cases, that looses the property that routes are almost fully contained in a sub-network. In the figure, e.g., routes L1u-P4u, L2u-P4u, L1u-P3u, L2u-P3u, from the high sub-network to the low sub-network share elements with all the routes having as destination P3u, P4u or P5u. This means that the kind of abstraction used in the previous cases can no longer be applied: in a sense, the layouts of cases (a) and (b) exhibit a *natural* place where to apply the cut, so that there are almost no interactions among the two parts, while the cut points in (c) are chosen quite arbitrarily, just in order to reasonably decompose the network, but impacting on the middle elements of several routes.

The horizontal cut is the subject of the present paper, where we can show that a simple form of cut still allows for compositional verification. The research we are conducting aims in the end to come up with a subdivision process that exploits the characteristics of the network to provide a set of sub-networks, obtained with the most appropriate kind of cut, to be verified separately, so that safety of the whole layout can be deduced by the separate safety verification of the sub-network.

4   Horizontal Cut

In this section we explain how our compositional approach is done in three steps:

1. decomposition of the network into sub-networks using the horizontal cut,
2. decomposition of the interlocking table for the network by generation of interlocking tables for the sub-networks, and
3. safety verification for the sub-networks (from step 1) and their associated interlocking tables (from step 2).

Below, we also discuss and analyse the contents of the decomposed interlocking tables achieved in step 2 and examine the soundness of the approach. The explanations are done for an example network called ThreeTracksStation, but can easily be generalised to any network.

4.1   Decomposition of the Network

Figure 2 shows first the layout of the ThreeTracksStation network. In this example we cut this network into two sub-networks by making a horizontal cut (the light green line) at the link between T9 and T10. To each of the two sub-networks (above and below the cut, respectively), two consecutive linear sections (which taken together form a *stub*) are added on the other side of the cut, in order to

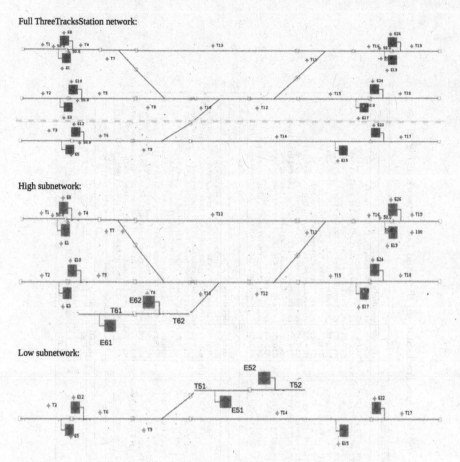

Fig. 2. Layouts of the ThreeTracksStation network and its sub-networks. (Color figure online)

abstract the whole other sub-network. The new sections have proper marker-boards in order to satisfy network conditions about the positioning of marker-boards at borders. The two resulting networks, called High and Low[4], are shown in Fig. 2.

4.2   Decomposition of the Interlocking Table

In the second step, after having decomposed the network into the two sub-networks High and Low, the interlocking tables associated with these sub-networks are generated with the RobustRailS tool. The interlocking tables generated for the full network and for the two sub-networks are shown in Table 1.

---

[4] We reserve the words *up* and *down* for the train travel directions.

Table 1. The interlocking tables for the ThreeTracksStation, High and Low network of Fig. 2.

ThreeTracksStation

id	src	dst	path	points	signals	conflicts
r1	E1	E19	T4;T7;T13;T11;T16	T7:p;T11:p	E26;E8	r12;r13;r1bis;r10;r5;r11;r5bis;r9;r14
r11	E1	E17	T4;T7;T8;T10;T12;T15	T10:p;T7:m;T8:m;T12:p	E24;E8	r1bis;r5;r12;r4;r5bis;r10;r9;r3;r6;r8;r14;r13;r1
r1bis	E1	E19	T4;T7;T8;T10;T12;T11;T16	T10:p;T7:m;T8:m;T11:m;T12:m	E26;E8	r8;r6;r13;r9;r3;r10;r5;r5bis;r14;r4;r12;r11;r1
r3	E22	E12	T14;T9;T6	T9:p	E15;E5	r4;r7;r12;r9;r8
r14	E24	E10	T15;T12;T10;T8;T5	T10:p;T8:p;T12:p	E17;E3	r6;r8;r4;r9;r10;r13;r14;r5bis;r12;r1bis;r11
r4	E24	E8	T15;T12;T10;T8;T7;T4	T10:p;T7:m;T8:m;T12:p	E1;E17	r4;r8;r13;r5bis;r10;r6;r9;r5;r12;r3;r1bis;r1;r11
r5	E26	E12	T15;T12;T10;T9;T6	T10:m;T9:m;T12:p	E17;E5	r6;r7;r10;r5bis;r13;r8;r12;r9;r2;r14;r3;r11;r1bis
r13	E26	E8	T16;T11;T13;T7;T4	T7:p;T11:p	E1;E19	r10;r9;r12;r4;r5bis;r11;r1bis;r14
r5bis	E26	E8	T16;T11;T12;T10;T8;T7;T5	T10:p;T8:p;T11:m;T12:m	E19;E3	r8;r10;r7;r6;r9;r1;r11;r5;r2;r13;r4;r14;r3;r1bis
r12	E3	E19	T16;T11;T12;T10;T8;T7;T4	T10:m;T7:m;T8:m;T11:m;T12:m	E1;E19	r8;r10;r7;r6;r9;r1;r11;r13;r4;r14;r3;r1bis
r6	E3	E12	T5;T8;T10;T12;T15	T10:p;T8:p;T12:p	E19;E24	r8;r9;r10;r3;r5bis;r4;r1bis;r14;r12;r11;r13
r10	E3	E19	T5;T8;T10;T12;T11;T16	T10:p;T8:p;T11:m;T12:m	E10;E24	r9;r8;r10;r3;r5bis;r4;r1bis;r14;r12;r11;r13
r7	E5	E15	T6;T9;T14	T9:p	E10;E26	r8;r9;r2;r4;r12
r8	E5	E17	T6;T9;T10;T12;T15	T10:m;T9:m;T12:p	E12;E22	r9;r14;r6;r7;r3;r5bis;r1bis;r12;r13;r4;r2;r11;r10
r9	E5	E19	T6;T9;T10;T12;T11;T16	T10:m;T9:m;T11:m;T12:m	E12;E24	r5;r6;r3;r8;r7;r1bis;r13;r10;r14;r2;r5bis;r1;r4;r12

High

id	src	dst	path	points	signals	conflicts
r1	E1	E19	T4;T7;T13;T11;T16	T7:p;T11:p	E26;E8	r13;r10;r5;r1bis;r11;r2662;r5bis;r6119;r14
r11	E1	E17	T4;T7;T8;T10;T12;T15	T10:p;T7:m;T8:m;T12:p	E24;E8	r1bis;r6117;r3;r10;r14;r6;r13;r2462;r2662;r5bis;r6119;r5;r1
r1bis	E1	E19	T4;T7;T8;T10;T12;T11;T16	T7:m;T12:p;T8:m;T10:p;T11:m	E26;E8	r10;r14;r6117;r5;r3;r6119;r13;r5bis;r2462;r2662;r6;r11;r1
r3	E24	E8	T15;T12;T10;T8;T5	T12:p;T8:p;T10:p	E17;E3	r10;r2462;r2662;r6117;r5bis;r6119;r13;r5;r3;r1bis;r11;r1
r14	E24	E62	T15;T12;T10;T62	T7:m;T12:p;T8:m;T10:p	E17;E61	r2462;r6117;r14;r10;r2662;r13;r5bis;r6119;r11;r5
r2462	E24	E8	T15;T12;T10;T8;T7;T4	T12:p;T8:m;T10:p	E1;E17	r6119;r13;r5bis;r10;r6;r2662;r1bis;r14;r11
r5	E26	E62	T16;T11;T13;T7;T4	T7:p;T11:p	E19;E3	r2662;r6119;r6;r6117;r5bis;r10;r1;r5;r3;r11;r1bis;r2462;r14
r13	E26	E10	T16;T11;T12;T10;T8;T7;T5	T12:m;T7:p;T8:p;T10:p;T11:m	E1;E19	r6;r10;r6117;r3;r14;r2662;r6119;r5;r2462;r13;r11;r1
r5bis	E26	E62	T16;T11;T12;T10;T8;T7;T4	T7:m;T12:m;T8:m;T10:p;T11:m	E1;E19	r6;r10;r6117;r2662;r6119;r5;r2462;r14;r13;r1bis;r3;r11;r1
r2662	E26	E62	T16;T11;T12;T10;T62	T12:m;T10:m;T11:m	E19;E3	r6;r10;r6117;r13;r14;r3;r1bis;r2462;r5;r11;r5bis;r1bis
r6	E3	E19	T5;T8;T10;T12;T15	T12:p;T8:p;T10:p	E19;E61	r6;r10;r6117;r5;r14;r3;r1bis;r2462;r11;r5bis;r1;r5
r10	E3	E19	T5;T8;T10;T12;T11;T16	T12:m;T8:p;T10:p;T11:m	E10;E24	r6117;r6119;r14;r1bis;r6;r2462;r3;r11;r5bis;r1;r13
r6117	E61	E19	T62;T10;T12;T15	T12:p;T10:m	E10;E26	r5;r6;r13;r11;r2462;r10;r14;r1bis;r3;r5bis;r2662
r6119	E61	E19	T62;T10;T12;T11;T16	T12:m;T10:m;T11:m	E26;E62	r5;r6;r13;r2662;r6117;r14;r10;r2462;r1bis;r3;r11;r5bis;r1

Low

id	src	dst	path	points	signals	conflicts
r2	E22	E12	T14;T9;T6	T9:p	E15;E5	r7;r551;r5212
r7	E5	E15	T6;T9;T14	T9:p	E12;E22	r551;r5212;r2
r551	E5	E51	T6;T9;T51	T9:m	E12;E52	r5212;r7;r2
r5212	E52	E12	T51;T9;T6	T9:m	E5;E51	r7;r551;r2

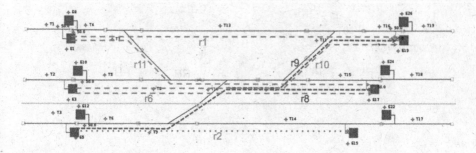

Fig. 3. Up routes of the ThreeTracksStation network (alternative route r1bis is not shown)

Abstraction of Routes. We will now describe the relationship between the routes in the interlocking table for the ThreeTracksStation Network and the routes in the interlocking tables for the High and Low sub-networks. Figure 3 shows the routes of ThreeTracksStation: actually, for readability, it shows only *up* routes, that is, routes that have as source and destination signals in the up direction. These routes are shown in different colour and dotting to distinguish those that are fully contained in one of the two sub-networks, and hence are maintained substantially unchanged in either High (e.g. route r1) or in Low (e.g. route r2), and those that go through the cut, that need to be substituted (*abstracted*) by (often fewer) routes both in High and Low: Fig. 4 shows for example how route r551 in Low abstracts both r8 and r9 in ThreeTracksStation).

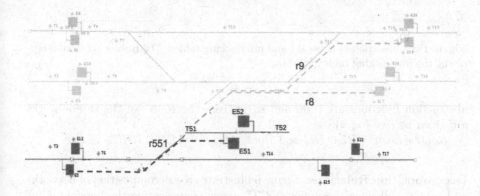

Fig. 4. Abstraction of routes

In general, the set $Routes(N)$ of routes of a network N (in our case ThreeTracksStation) is partitioned in three disjoint sets: RH, RL, Th, which are respectively fully contained in Low, in High and passing through the cut. The cut defines two abstraction functions $\gamma_H : Th \rightarrow RH'$ and $\gamma_L : Th \rightarrow RL'$ that produce the sets of abstract routes for the High and Low networks respectively. The

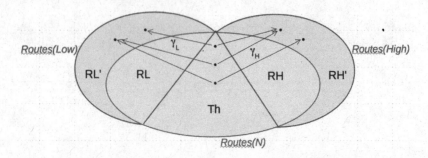

Fig. 5. Relation between the routes of the network and the sub-networks.

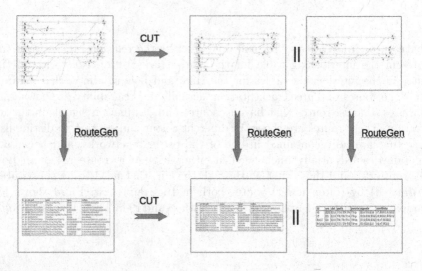

Fig. 6. Decomposition of networks and interlocking tables. The RouteGen arrows represent the interlocking table generator.

abstraction functions are total and surjective. The routes of the sub-networks are given by (see Fig. 5):

$Routes(Low) = RL \cup RL'$ and $Routes(High) = RH \cup RH'$.

Decomposition Relations. Figure 6 illustrates the decomposition of networks and tables. Following the upper "CUT" arrow (representing the horizontal cut operation), the network is decomposed into two sub-networks for which interlocking tables are then generated. These tables provide a decomposition (following the lower "CUT" arrow) of the interlocking table that one would generate from the full network when not using the compositional approach.

The following rules define the relationship between the two sub-networks and the full network, as well the relationship between their associated interlocking tables. Rule 1 defines how the sub-networks are created, rules 2–3 and 4–5 define the route abstractions into sets RL' and RH', and rules 6–10 define the path, required point and signal settings, and route conflicts of the routes in the decomposed interlocking tables, in terms of the corresponding data in the full interlocking table. The rules are instantiated for the ThreeTracksStation example. The different sets of elements have as a suffix the name of the sub-network to which they belong: no suffix means the set belongs to the full network.

1. $Linears_{Low} \cup Linears_{High} = Linears, Linears_{Low} \cap Linears_{High} = \emptyset$
   $Points_{Low} \cup Points_{High} = Points, Points_{Low} \cap Points_{High} = \emptyset$
   $Signals_{Low} \cup Signals_{High} = Signals, Signals_{Low} \cap Signals_{High} = \emptyset$

   The sub-networks Low and High are actually built, respectively, over the sets of elements:

   $(Linears_{Low} \cup \{T51, T52\}, Points_{Low}, Signals_{Low} \cup \{E51, E52\})$
   $(Linears_{High} \cup \{T61, T62\}, Points_{High}, Signals_{High} \cup \{E61, E62\})$
2. all the *up routes* in the ThreeTracksStation starting from $s \in Signals_{Low}$ that incur in the cut (that is, in the path have the pair T9,T10, in our case) are abstracted in the Low sub-network by a route going from s to the stub signal E51;
3. all the *down routes* in the ThreeTracksStation arriving to $s \in Signals_{Low}$ that incur in the cut (that is, in the path have the pair T10,T9) are abstracted in the Low sub-network by a route going from the stub signal E52 to s;
4. all the *down routes* in the ThreeTracksStation starting from $s \in Signals_{High}$ that incur in the cut (that is, in the path have the pair T10,T9) are abstracted in the High sub-network by a route going from s to the stub signal E62;
5. all the *up routes* in the ThreeTracksStation arriving to $s \in Signals_{High}$ that incur in the cut (that is, in the path have the pair T9,T10) are abstracted in the High sub-network by a route going from the stub signal E61 to s;
6. the *path* of the abstract routes contains only the elements to (from) the cut, plus the added stub elements as destination (source); the path of the other routes is unchanged.
7. the *points* of the abstract routes include only the points on the path to (from) the cut; the points of the other routes are unchanged.
8. each abstract route in the Low (High) sub-network abstracting a route r in the full network, keeps as its *signals* that signal of r that was placed in Low (High), while the signal placed on the opposite side of the cut in High (Low) is replaced by the stub signal contrary to the direction of the route. The signals of the other routes are unchanged, except the cases where a signal is placed on the opposite side of the cut, in which case it is replaced by the stub signal in opposite direction of the route.
9. the *conflicts* of an abstract route $r \in RL'$ (RH') in the Low (High) sub-network are given by:
   (a) all the maintained routes of Low (High) that are in conflict in ThreeTracksStation with any of the routes abstracted by r;

(b) all the abstract routes of Low (High) that abstract routes in
ThreeTracksStation in conflict with any of the routes abstracted by r;
10. the *conflicts* of a route $r \in RL$ (RH) in the Low (High) sub-network preserved in the cut are given by:
(a) all the maintained routes of Low (High) that are in conflict in
ThreeTracksStation with r;
(b) all the abstract routes of Low (High) that abstract routes in
ThreeTracksStation that are in conflict with r;

These rules can be easily generalised to the "horizontal" cut of any network,
including the special case of a network where the cut is on up routes that go
from the high part to the low part.

4.3 Safety Verification

In the third step, after having generated the interlocking tables, the safety verification is performed for the sub-networks and their associated interlocking tables,
using the RobustRailS verification tools.[5]

Table 2 shows metrics, for the separate verification of the Low, the High and
the ThreeTracksStation networks, respectively. Furthermore, the row "Low +
High" shows metrics for the combined compositional verification: the execution
time is the sum of the execution times of Low and High, and the memory usage
is the maximum of the memory usages of Low and High. Time is measured in
seconds and memory in MB. As expected, the results show that the compositional approach is advantageous both in terms of the time and memory usage.

Table 2. Verification metrics for the ThreeTracksStation case study.

	Linears	Points	Signals	Routes	$log_{10}(|S|)$	Time	Memory
Low	6	1	6	4	30.50	3.37	93.8
High	11	5	10	12	77.11	187.26	528.1
Low + High						190.63	528.1
ThreeTracksStation	13	6	12	14	91.31	292.68	698.3

4.4 Soundness of the Approach

The soundness of the compositional approach amounts to the following theorem.

Theorem 1. *Given a Network N and its sub-networks H and L obtained by a
horizontal cut, if H and L are separately verified to satisfy safety, then N satisfies
safety too.*

---

[5] The verifications were performed on a machine with an Intel(R) Xeon(R) CPU E5-
2667 0 @ 2.90GHz, 64GB RAM, CentOS 6.6, Linux 2.6.32-504.8.1.el6.x86_64 kernel.

The above considerations on abstracted routes are the ground on which to base a proof. A formal proof can be made in a similar way to the proof presented in [13]: safety properties are expressed as universal quantifications over the sets of linear/point sections, hence, assuming safety is proved for each section of both sub-networks, we need to prove safety for each section in the original network. This can be done by case analysis for three cases: for sections only involved in routes in RL, sections only involved in routes in RH, and sections involved by through routes in Th. The first two cases immediately follows from the assumption. In the third case, the state of some sections (say, in Low) is actually related to the state of the stub added to the Low sub-network, that abstracts the state of sections of High that belong to routes in Th in the full network. We then reason by contradiction, assuming that the state of some of the latter sections violates a safety property for the full network, while their abstraction in the stub of Low does not violate any property in Low. We show that such sections violate safety for High as well, contradicting the initial hypothesis that safety is proved for the High network.

5   A More Complex Example

The next example (called Fismn) is inspired by the layout of the main station of Florence in Italy, and actually refers to a portion roughly of the size of a quarter of the entire station. The layout shown in Fig. 7 has been recovered from Google Maps, so there is no actual relation between this layout and any implemented real interlocking system. Nevertheless, this layout realistically represents a feature that can be found in many large stations, that is a route that traverses all the other routes for connecting the lower incoming track to the upper exiting track. In the real Florence station, the next portion of the layout at the right of this includes the reverse traversing route.

Table 3. Verication metrics for the Fismn case study.

	Linears	Points	Signals	Routes	$log_{10}(|S|)$	Time	Memory
Low	28	13	26	56	243.04	12895.35	12176.6
High	25	10	24	66	239.07	8052.92	9517.9
Low + High						20948.27	12176.6
Fismn	49	23	46	124	472.93	51770.64	42483.7

For the Fismn network, we applied the compositional verification approach. In Fig. 7 the dotted green horizontal line represents the operated cut, between the T30 and T31 points. Note that this cut lies on the low-to-high traversing path. Also in this case the compositional verification is advantageous for the time and memory requirements (see Table 3). Notice that the memory consumption

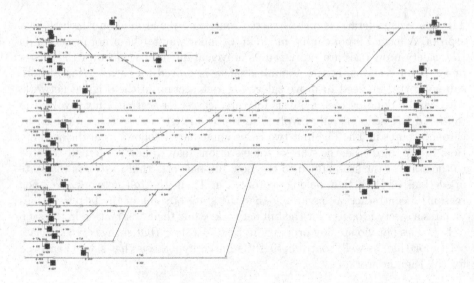

Fig. 7. The Fismn example layout. (Color figure online)

of the Fismn network is actually close to the memory limits (64 GB) so it can be predicted that a bit larger model cannot be treated unless the compositional approach is adopted.

6   Conclusions

We have presented a compositional approach to the problem of model checking interlocking systems of large railway stations. The approach builds up over previous work, by proposing a more general way of decomposing a station layout, that has successfully been applied to a large portion of a real world station. The approach achieves significant improvements in verification time and memory usage, taking into account that the aim of the proposed decomposition is to be able to keep time and memory resources needed for the verification within feasible limits. In fact the idea is to apply multiple cuts, in order to chop a large network in tractable chunks, each to be verified separately. This is the main direction of future work, which will need generalising the decomposition process and automating it by means of a tool supporting the network cutting process. In parallel to this effort to provide an automatic verification method for large networks, some other investigation is still needed, e.g. investigating how counterexamples of a safety verification of the sub-networks carry over to counter examples of the full network, or extending the approach to deal with peculiar interlocking safety functions, such as flank protection, or overlap, that have not yet been considered for the horizontal cut.

Acknowledgement. The authors would like to express their gratitude to Jan Peleska and Linh Hong Vu with whom Anne Haxthausen developed the RobustRailS verification method and tools used in the presented work.

References

1. Bonacchi, A., Fantechi, A., Bacherini, S., Tempestini, M.: Validation process for railway interlocking systems. Sci. Comput. Program. **128**, 2–21 (2016)
2. CENELEC European Committee for Electrotechnical Standardization. EN 50128:2011 - Railway applications - Communications, signalling and processing systems - Software for railway control and protection systems (2011)
3. Ferrari, A., Magnani, G., Grasso, D., Fantechi, A.: Model checking interlocking control tables. In: Schnieder, E., Tarnai, G. (eds.) FORMS/FORMAT 2010, pp. 107–115. Springer, Heidelberg (2010). doi:10.1007/978-3-642-14261-1_11
4. Hvid Hansen, H., Ketema, J., Luttik, B., Mousavi, M.R., Pol, J., Santos, O.M.: Automated verification of executable UML models. In: Aichernig, B.K., Boer, F.S., Bonsangue, M.M. (eds.) FMCO 2010. LNCS, vol. 6957, pp. 225–250. Springer, Heidelberg (2011). doi:10.1007/978-3-642-25271-6_12
5. Haxthausen, A.E., Bliguet, M., Kjær, A.A.: Modelling and verification of relay interlocking systems. In: Choppy, C., Sokolsky, O. (eds.) Monterey Workshop 2008. LNCS, vol. 6028, pp. 141–153. Springer, Heidelberg (2010). doi:10.1007/978-3-642-12566-9_8
6. Haxthausen, A.E., Peleska, J., Kinder, S.: A formal approach for the construction and verification of railway control systems. Formal Aspects Comput. **23**(2), 191–219 (2011)
7. Haxthausen, A.E., Peleska, J., Pinger, R.: Applied bounded model checking for interlocking system designs. In: Counsell, S., Núñez, M. (eds.) SEFM 2013. LNCS, vol. 8368, pp. 205–220. Springer, Cham (2014). doi:10.1007/978-3-319-05032-4_16
8. James, P., Möller, F., Nguyen, H.N., Roggenbach, M., Schneider, S., Treharne, H.: Decomposing scheme plans to manage verification complexity. In: FORMS/FORMAT 2014–10th Symposium on Formal Methods for Automation and Safety in Railway and Automotive Systems, pp. 210–220. Institute for Traffic Safety and Automation Engineering, Technische Universität Braunschweig (2014)
9. James, P., Lawrence, A., Moller, F., Roggenbach, M., Seisenberger, M., Setzer, A., Kanso, K., Chadwick, S.: Verification of solid state interlocking programs. In: Counsell, S., Núñez, M. (eds.) SEFM 2013. LNCS, vol. 8368, pp. 253–268. Springer, Cham (2014). doi:10.1007/978-3-319-05032-4_19
10. James, P., Moller, F., Nguyen, H.N., Roggenbach, M., Schneider, S., Treharne, H.: Techniques for modelling and verifying railway interlockings. Int. J. Softw. Tools Technol. Transf. **16**(6), 685–711 (2014)
11. Limbrée, C., Cappart, Q., Pecheur, C., Tonetta, S.: Verification of railway interlocking - compositional approach with OCRA. In: Lecomte, T., Pinger, R., Romanovsky, A. (eds.) RSSRail 2016. LNCS, vol. 9707, pp. 134–149. Springer, Cham (2016). doi:10.1007/978-3-319-33951-1_10
12. Macedo, H.D., Fantechi, A., Haxthausen, A.E.: Compositional verification of multi-station interlocking systems. In: Margaria, T., Steffen, B. (eds.) ISoLA 2016. LNCS, vol. 9953, pp. 279–293. Springer, Cham (2016). doi:10.1007/978-3-319-47169-3_20

13. Macedo, H.D., Fantechi, A., Haxthausen, A.E.: Compositional model checking of interlocking systems for lines with multiple stations. In: Barrett, C., Davies, M., Kahsai, T. (eds.) NFM 2017. LNCS, vol. 10227, pp. 146–162. Springer, Cham (2017). doi:10.1007/978-3-319-57288-8_11

14. Peleska, J.: Industrial-strength model-based testing - state of the art and current challenges. In: Petrenko, A.K., Schlingloff, H. (eds.) 8th Workshop on Model-Based Testing, Rome, Italy, vol. 111, pp. 3–28. Electronic Proceedings in Theoretical Computer Science, Open Publishing Association (2013)

15. Theeg, G., Vlasenko, S.V., Anders, E.: Railway Signalling & Interlocking: International Compendium. Eurailpress, Germany (2009)

16. Verified Systems International GmbH. RT-Tester Model-Based Test Case and Test Data Generator - RTT-MBT - User Manual (2013). http://www.verified.de

17. Vu, L.H., Haxthausen, A.E., Peleska, J.: A domain-specific language for railway interlocking systems. In: Schnieder, E., Tarnai, G. (eds.) FORMS/FORMAT 2014– 10th Symposium on Formal Methods for Automation and Safety in Railway and Automotive Systems, pp. 200–209. Institute for Traffic Safety and Automation Engineering, Technische Universität Braunschweig (2014)

18. Vu, L.H., Haxthausen, A.E., Peleska, J.: Formal modeling and verification of interlocking systems featuring sequential release. In: Artho, C., Ölveczky, P.C. (eds.) FTSCS 2014. CCIS, vol. 476, pp. 223–238. Springer, Cham (2015). doi:10.1007/978-3-319-17581-2_15

19. Vu, L.H.: Formal development and verification of railway control systems - in the context of ERTMS/ETCS level 2. Ph.D. thesis, Technical University of Denmark, DTU Compute (2015)

20. Vu, L.H., Haxthausen, A.E., Peleska, J.: Formal modelling and verification of interlocking systems featuring sequential release. Sci. Comput. Program. 133(Part 2), 91–115 (2017). doi:10.1016/j.scico.2016.05.010

21. Winter, K.: Symbolic model checking for interlocking systems. In: Flammini, F. (ed.) Railway Safety, Reliability, and Security: Technologies and Systems Engineering. IGI Global (2012)

22. Winter, K.: Optimising ordering strategies for symbolic model checking of railway interlockings. In: Margaria, T., Steffen, B. (eds.) ISoLA 2012. LNCS, vol. 7610, pp. 246–260. Springer, Heidelberg (2012). doi:10.1007/978-3-642-34032-1_24

Formalizing Timing Diagram Requirements in Discrete Duration Calculus

Raj Mohan Matteplackel[1], Paritosh K. Pandya[1(✉)], and Amol Wakankar[2]

[1] Tata Institute of Fundamental Research, Mumbai 400005, India
{raj.matteplackel,pandya}@tifr.res.in
[2] Bhabha Atomic Research Centre, Mumbai, India
amolk@barc.gov.in

Abstract. Several temporal logics have been proposed to formalise *timing diagram* requirements over hardware and embedded controllers. However, succintness and visual structure of a timing diagram are not adequately captured by their formulae [6]. Interval temporal logic QDDC is a highly succint and visual notation for specifying patterns of behaviours [15]. In this paper, we propose a practically useful notation called SeCeNL which enhances the quantifier and negation free fragment of QDDC with features of *nominals* and *limited liveness*. We show that for SeCeNL, the satisfiability and model checking problems have elementary complexity as compared to the non-elementary complexity for the full logic QDDC. Next we show that timing diagrams can be naturally, compositionally and succintly formalized in SeCeNL as compared with PSL-Sugar and MTL. We give a linear time translation from timing diagrams to SeCeNL. As our second main result, we propose a linear time translation of SeCeNL into QDDC. This allows QDDC tools such as DCVALID [15,16] and DCSynth [17] to be used for checking consistency of timing diagram requirements as well as for automatic synthesis of property monitors and controllers. We give an example of a minepump controller to illustrate our tools.

1   Introduction

A *timing diagram* is a collection of binary signals and a set of timing constraints on them. It is a widely used visual formalism in the realm of digital hardware design, communication protocol specification and embedded controller specification. The advantages of timing diagrams in hardware design are twofold, one, since designers can visualize waveforms of signals they are easy to comprehend and two, they are very convenient for specifying ordering and timing constraints between events (see Figs. 1 and 2).

There have been numerous attempts at formalizing timing diagram constraints in the framework of temporal logics such as the *timing diagram logic* [9], with *LTL formulas* [6], and as *synchronous regular timing diagrams* [3]. Moreover, there are industry standard property specification languages such as *PSL-Sugar* and *OVA* for associating temporal assertions to hardware designs [8].

© Springer International Publishing AG 2017
A. Cimatti and M. Sirjani (Eds.): SEFM 2017, LNCS 10469, pp. 253–268, 2017.
DOI: 10.1007/978-3-319-66197-1_16

The main motivation for these attempts was to exploit automatic verification techniques that these formalisms support for validation and automatic circuit synthesis. However, commenting on their success, Fisler *et al.* state that the less than satisfactory adoption of formal methods in timing diagram domain can be partly attributed to the gulf that exists between graphical timing diagrams and textual temporal logic – expressing various timing dependencies that can exist among signals that can be illustrated so naturally in timing diagrams is rather tedious in temporal logics [6]. As a result, hardware designers use timing diagrams informally without any well defined semantics which make them unamenable to automatic design verification techniques.

In this paper, we take a fresh look at formalizing timing diagram requirements with emphasis on the following three features of the formalism that we propose here.

Firstly, we propose the use of an *interval temporal logic* QDDC to specify patterns of behaviours. QDDC is a highly succinct and visual notation for specifying regular patterns of behaviours [12,15,16]. We identify a quantifier and negation-free subset SeCe (for Semi extended Chop expressions) of QDDC which is sufficient for formalizing timing diagram patterns. It includes generalized regular expression like syntax with counting constructs. Constraints imposed by timing diagrams are straightforwardly and compactly stated in this logic. For example, the timing diagram in Fig. 1 stating that P transits from 0 to 1 somewhere in interval u to $u + 3$ cycles is captured by the SeCe formula `[¬P]^<u>^(slen = 3 && [¬P]^[[P]])^[[P]]`. *The main advantage of SeCe is that it has elementary satisfiability as compared to the non-elementary satisfiability of general QDDC.*

P

Fig. 1. Timing diagram with a marked position u and a timing constraint.

Secondly, it is very typical for timing diagrams to have partial ordering and synchronization constraints between distinct events (see Fig. 2). Emphasizing this aspect, formalisms such as two dimensional regular expressions [10] have been proposed for timing diagrams. We find that synchronization in timing diagram may even extend across waveforms. In order to handle such synchronization, we extend our logic SeCe with *nominals* from hybrid temporal logics [11]. Nominals are temporal variables which "freeze" the positions of occurrences of events. They naturally allow synchronization across formulae.

Thirdly, we enhance the timing diagram specifications (as well as the logic SeCe) with *limited liveness operators*. While timing diagrams visually specify patterns of occurrence of signals, they do not make precise the modalities of occurrences of such patterns. We explicitly introduce modalities such as (*a*) initially, a specified pattern must occur, or that (*b*) every occurrence of *pattern1* is necessarily and immediately followed by an occurrence of *pattern2*, or that (*c*) occurrence of a specified pattern is forbidden anywhere within a behaviour. In this, we are inspired by Allen's Interval Algebra relations [1] as well as the LSC operators of Harel for message sequence charts [7]. We confine ourselves to *limited liveness properties* where good things are achieved within specified bounds. For example, in specifying a modulo 6 counter, we can say that the counter will stabilize before completion of first 15 cycles. Astute readers will notice that, technically, our limited liveness operators only give rise to "safety" properties (in the sense of Alpern and Schneider [2]). However, from a designer's perspective they do achieve the practical goal of forcing good things to happen.

Putting all these together, we define a logic SeCeNL which includes quantifier and negation-free fragment of QDDC together with limited liveness operators as well as nominals. The formal syntax and semantics of SeCeNL formulas is given in Sect. 2.3. We claim that SeCeNL provides a natural and convenient formalism for encoding timing diagram requirements. *Substantiating this, we formulate a translation of timing diagrams into SeCeNL formulae in Sect. 3.* (A textual syntax is used for timing diagrams. The textual syntax is inspired by the tool WaveDrom [5], which is also used for graphical rendering of our textual timing diagram specifications.) The translation to SeCeNL is succinct, in fact, linear time computable in the size of the timing diagram. Moreover, the translation is compositional, i.e. it translates each element of the timing diagram as a sub-formula and overall specification is just the conjunction of such constraints. Hence, the translation preserves the structure of the diagram.

With several examples of timing diagrams, we compare its SeCeNL formula with the formulae in logics such as PSL-Sugar and MTL. Logic PSL-Sugar is syntactically a superset of MTL which in turn is a superset of LTL. PSL-Sugar extends LTL with SERE (regular expressions with intersection) and counting which are similar to our SeCe. In spite of this similarity, we show some natural examples where SeCeNL formula is at least one exponent more succinct as compared to PSL-Sugar. This is essentially due to the use of *nominals*.

As the second main contribution of this paper, we consider formal verification and controller synthesis from SeCeNL specifications. In Sect. 3.1, we formulate a reduction from a SeCeNL formula to an equivalent QDDC formula. This allows QDDC tools to be used for SeCeNL. It may be noted that, though expressively no more powerful than QDDC, the logic SeCeNL is considerably more efficient for satisfiability and model checking. We find that these problems have elementary complexity as compared with full QDDC which exhibits non-elementary complexity. Also, the presence of limited liveness and nominals makes it more convenient as compared to QDDC for practical use.

By implementing the above reductions, we have constructed a Python based translator which converts a requirement, consisting of a Boolean combination of timing diagram specifications (augmented with limited liveness) and SeCeNL formulae, into an equivalent QDDC formula. In this sense, we handle heterogenous specification. We can analyze the resulting formula using the QDDC tools DCVALID [15,16] as well as DCSynth [17] for model checking and controller synthesis, respectively. We illustrate the use of our tools by a case study of a minepump controller in Sect. 4. Readers may note that we specify rather rich quantitative requirements not commonly considered, and our tools are able to automatically synthesize monitors and controllers for such specifications.

2 Logic QDDC

Let Σ be a finite non empty set of propositional variables. A *word* σ over Σ is a finite sequence of the form $P_0 \cdots P_n$ where $P_i \subseteq \Sigma$ for each $i \in \{0, \dots, n\}$. Let $len(\sigma) = n + 1$, $dom(\sigma) = \{0, \dots, n\}$ and $\forall i \in dom(\sigma) : \sigma(i) = P_i$.

The syntax of a *propositional formula* over Σ is given by:

$$\varphi := 0 \mid 1 \mid p \in \Sigma \mid \varphi \wedge \varphi \mid \varphi \vee \varphi \mid \neg\varphi,$$

and operators such as $\Rightarrow$ and $\Leftrightarrow$ are defined as usual. Let Ω_Σ be the set of all propositional formulas over Σ.

Let $\sigma = P_0 \cdots P_n$ be a word and $\varphi \in \Omega_\Sigma$. Then, for an $i \in dom(\sigma)$ the satisfaction relation $\sigma, i \models \varphi$ is defined inductively as expected: $\sigma, i \models 1$; $\sigma, i \models p$ iff $p \in \sigma(i)$; $\sigma, i \models \neg p$ iff $\sigma, i \not\models p$, and the satisfaction relation for the rest of the Boolean combinations defined in a natural way.

The syntax of a QDDC formula over Σ is given by:

$$D := \langle\varphi\rangle \mid [\varphi] \mid [[\varphi]] \mid D \,\hat{}\, D \mid \neg D \mid D \vee D \mid D \wedge D \mid D^* \mid$$
$$\exists p.\, D \mid slen \bowtie c \mid scount\ \varphi \bowtie c$$

where $\varphi \in \Omega_\Sigma$, $p \in \Sigma$, $c \in \mathbb{N}$ and $\bowtie \in \{<, \leq, =, \geq, >\}$.

An *interval* over a word σ is of the form $[b, e]$ where $b, e \in dom(\sigma)$ and $b \leq e$. An interval $[b_1, e_1]$ is a sub interval of $[b, e]$ if $b \leq b_1$ and $e_1 \leq e$. Let $Intv(\sigma)$ be the set of all intervals over σ.

Let σ be a word over Σ and let $[b, e] \in Intv(\sigma)$ be an interval. Then the satisfaction relation of a QDDC formula D over Σ, written $\sigma, [b, e] \models D$, is defined inductively as follows:

$$\begin{array}{lll}
\sigma, [b, e] \models \langle\varphi\rangle & \text{iff} & \sigma, b \models \varphi, \\
\sigma, [b, e] \models [\varphi] & \text{iff} & \forall b \leq i < e : \sigma, i \models \varphi, \\
\sigma, [b, e] \models [[\varphi]] & \text{iff} & \forall b \leq i \leq e : \sigma, i \models \varphi, \\
\sigma, [b, e] \models \neg D & \text{iff} & \sigma, [b, e] \not\models D, \\
\sigma, [b, e] \models D_1 \vee D_2 & \text{iff} & \sigma, [b, e] \models D_1 \text{ or } \sigma, [b, e] \models D_2, \\
\sigma, [b, e] \models D_1 \wedge D_2 & \text{iff} & \sigma, [b, e] \models D_1 \text{ and } \sigma, [b, e] \models D_2, \\
\sigma, [b, e] \models D_1 \hat{}\, D_2 & \text{iff} & \exists b \leq i \leq e : \sigma, [b, i] \models D_1 \text{ and } \sigma, [i, e] \models D_2.
\end{array}$$

Operator D^* denotes iterated chop operator. Thus, $\sigma, [b, e] \models D^*$ iff $b = e$ or there exist $n > 0$, $m_0 \leq m_1 \dots \leq m_n$ with $m_0 = b$, $m_n = e$ and $\sigma, [m_i, m_{i+1}] \models D$ for all $0 \leq i < n$. Operator $\exists p.\, D$ denotes existential quantification[1] over a temporal variable p, where $p \in \Sigma$. We call word σ' a p-variant of a word σ if

---

[1] Hence the logic is called QDDC which abbreviates Quantified Discrete Duration Calculus.

$\forall i \in dom(\sigma), \forall q \neq p : \sigma'(i)(q) = \sigma(i)(q)$. Then $\sigma, [b, e] \models \exists p.\, D \Leftrightarrow \sigma', [b, e] \models D$ for some p-variant σ' of σ. We define $\sigma \models D$ iff $\sigma, [0, len(\sigma)] \models D$.

Entities $slen$, and $scount$ are called *terms* in QDDC. The term $slen$ gives the length of the interval in which it is measured, whereas $scount$ φ with $\varphi \in \Omega_\Sigma$ counts the number of positions in the interval under consideration where φ holds. Formally, for $\varphi \in \Omega_\Sigma$ we have $slen(\sigma, [b, e]) = e - b$, and $scount(\sigma, \varphi, [b, e]) = \sum_{i=b}^{i=e} \left\{ \begin{array}{l} 1,\ \text{if } \sigma, i \models \varphi, \\ 0,\ \text{otherwise.} \end{array} \right\}$.

We also use the following derived constructs: $\texttt{pt} = \langle 1 \rangle$, and $\texttt{ext} = [1]$, and $\{\{\varphi\}\} = \langle \varphi \rangle \string^ slen = 1$. Also, $\Diamond D = true \string^ D \string^ true$ and $\Box D = \neg \Diamond \neg D$. Finally, $\forall p.D = \neg \exists p. \neg D$. Moreover, $\Box_{pref} D = \neg((\neg D) \string^ true)$. Hence, $\Box D$ states that D holds for all subintervals where as $\Box_{pref} D$ states that D holds for all prefix intervals. Size of a formula is the number of operators and propositions appearing in it, except that all integer constants are in binary and hence constant c contributes size $log_2(c)$.

Theorem 1 [16]. *For every QDDC formula D over Σ we can construct a DFA $\mathcal{A}(D)$ over alphabet 2^Σ such $\mathcal{L}(D) = \mathcal{L}(\mathcal{A}(D))$. The size of $\mathcal{A}(D)$ is non elementary in the size of D in the worst case.*

2.1 Chop Expressions: Ce and SeCe

Definition 1. *The logic* Semi extended Chop expressions *(SeCe) is a syntactic subset of QDDC in which the operators $\exists p.\, D$, $\forall p.\, D$ and negation $\neg$ are not allowed. The logic* Chop expressions *(Ce) is a sublogic of SeCe in which conjunction $\wedge$ is not allowed.*

Lemma 1. *For any chop expression D of size n we can effectively construct a language equivalent DFA $\mathcal{A}$ of size $\Omega(2^{2^n})$.*

Proof. We observe that for any chop expression D we can construct a language equivalent NFA which is at most exponential in size of D including the constants appearing in it (for a detailed proof see [4] wherein a similar result has been proved). But this implies there exists a DFA of size 2^{2^n} which accepts exactly the set of words σ such that $\sigma \models D$.

Corollary 1. *For any SeCe D of size n we can effectively construct a language equivalent DFA $\mathcal{A}$ of size $\Omega(2^{2^{2^n}})$.*

Proof. Proof follows from the definition of SeCe, Lemma 1 and from the fact that the size of the product of DFA's can be atmost exponential in the size of individual DFA's.

2.2   DCVALID and DCSynth

The reduction from a QDDC formula to its formula automaton has been implemented into the tool *DCVALID* [15,16]. The formula automaton it generates is total, deterministic and minimal automaton for the formula. DCVALID can also translate the formula automaton into Lustre/SCADE, Esterel, SMV and Verilog *observer modules*. By connecting this observer module to run synchronously with a system we can reduce model checking of QDDC property to reachability checking in the observer augmented system. See [15,16] for details. A further use of formula automata can be seen in the tool called *DCSynth* [17] which synthesizes synchronous dataflow controller in SCADE/NuSMV/Verilog from QDDC specification.

2.3   Logic SeCeNL: Syntax and Semantics

We can now introduce our logic SeCeNL which builds upon SeCe (semi extended chop expressions) by augmenting them with *nominals* and *limited liveness operators*.

Syntax: The syntax of SeCeNL atomic formula is as follows. Let D, D_1, D_2 and D_3 range over SeCe formulae and let Θ, Θ_1, Θ_2 and Θ_3 range over subset of propositional variables occurring in SeCe formula. The notation $D : \Theta$, called a *nominated formula*, denotes that Θ is the set of variables used as nominals in the formula D.

> $\mathbf{init}(D_2 : \Theta_2 \ / \ D_3 : \Theta_3) \ | \ \mathbf{anti}(D : \Theta) \ | \ \mathbf{pref}(D : \Theta) \ |$
> $\mathbf{implies}(D_1 : \Theta_1 \rightsquigarrow D_2 : \Theta_2) \ | \ \mathbf{follows}(D_1 : \Theta_1 \rightsquigarrow D_2 : \Theta_2/D_3 : \Theta_3) \ |$
> $\mathbf{triggers}(D_1 : \Theta_1 \rightsquigarrow D_2 : \Theta_2/D_3 : \Theta_3)$

We also assume that $\Theta_2 \cap \Theta_3 \subseteq \Theta_1$, and for $\mathbf{follows}(D_1 : \Theta_1 \rightsquigarrow D_2 : \Theta_2/D_3 : \Theta_3)$, the sets $\Theta_1, \Theta_2, \Theta_3$ are mutually disjoint. *An SeCeNL formula is a Boolean combination of atomic SeCeNL formulae of the form above.* As a convention, $D : \{\}$ is abbreviated as D when the set of nominals Θ is empty.

Limited Liveness Operators: Given an word σ and a position $i \in dom(\sigma)$, we state that $\sigma, i \models D$ iff $\sigma[0, i] \models D$. Thus, the interpretation is that the past of the position i in execution satisfies D. We say $\sigma' \leq_{prefix} \sigma$ if σ' is a prefix of σ, and $\sigma' <_{prefix} \sigma$ if σ' is a proper prefix of σ.

We first explain the semantics of *limited liveness operators* assuming that no nominals are used in the specification, i.e. Θ, Θ_1, Θ_2 and Θ_3 are all empty. A set $S \subseteq \Sigma^*$ is *prefix closed* if $\sigma \in S$ then $\forall \sigma' : \sigma' \leq_{prefix} \sigma \Rightarrow \sigma' \in S$. We observe that each atomic liveness formula denotes a prefix closed subset of $(2^\Sigma)^+$.

- $L(\mathbf{pref}(D)) = \{\sigma \mid \forall \sigma' \leq_{prefix} \sigma : \sigma' \models D\}$. Operator $\mathbf{pref}(D)$ denotes that D holds invariantly throughout the execution.
- $L(\mathbf{init}(D_2/D_3)) = \{\sigma \mid \forall j : \sigma, [0, j] \models D_3 \Rightarrow \exists i \leq j : \sigma, [0, i] \models D_2\}$. Operator $\mathbf{init}(D_2/D_3)$ basically states that if j is the first position which satisfies D_3 in the execution then there exists an $i \leq j$ such that i satisfies D_2. Thus, initially D_2 holds before D_3 unless the execution (is too short and hence) does not satisfy D_3 anywhere.
- $L(\mathbf{anti}(D)) = \{\sigma \mid \forall i, j : \sigma, [i, j] \not\models D\}$. Operator $\mathbf{anti}(D)$ states that there is no observation sub interval of the execution which satisfies D.
- $L(\mathbf{implies}(D_1 \rightsquigarrow D_2)) = \{\sigma \mid \forall i, j : (\sigma, [i, j] \models D_1 \Rightarrow \sigma, [i, j] \models D_2)\}$. Operator $\mathbf{implies}(D_1 \rightsquigarrow D_2)$ states all observation intervals which satisfy D_1 will also satisfy D_2.
- $L(\mathbf{follows}(D_1 \rightsquigarrow D_2/D_3)) = \{\sigma \mid \forall i, j : (\sigma, [i, j] \models D_1 \Rightarrow$
  $(\forall k : \sigma, [j, k] \models \varXi(D_3) \Rightarrow \exists l \leq k : \sigma, [j, l] \models D_2))\}$.
  Operator $\mathbf{follows}(D_1 \rightsquigarrow D_2/D_3)$ states that if any observation interval $[i, j]$ satisfies D_1 and there is a following shortest interval $[j, k]$ which satisfies D_3 then there exists a prefix interval of $[j, k]$ which satisfies D_2.
- $L(\mathbf{triggers}(D_1 \rightsquigarrow D_2/D_3)) = \{\sigma \mid \forall i, j : (\sigma, [i, j] \models D_1 \Rightarrow$
  $(\forall k : \sigma, [i, k] \models \varXi(D_3) \Rightarrow \exists l \leq k : \sigma, [i, l] \models D_2))\}$.
  Operator $\mathbf{triggers}(D_1 \rightsquigarrow D_2/D_3)$ states that if any observation interval $[i, j]$ satisfies D_1 and if $[i, k]$ is the shortest interval which satisfies D_3 then D_2 holds for a prefix interval of $[i, k]$.

Based on this semantics, we can translate an atomic SeCeNL formula ζ without out nominals into equivalent $QDDC$ formula $\aleph(\zeta)$ as follows. Reader may like to recall the $\Box D$ and $\Box_{pref} D$ operators of QDDC. Additionally, for a QDDC formula D let $\varXi(D) = D \wedge \neg(D\hat{}ext)$, which says that if $\sigma, [b, e] \models \varXi(D)$ then $\sigma, [b, e] \models D$ and there exists no proper prefix interval $[b, e_1]$, (i.e. $[b, e_1] \in Intv(\sigma)$ and $b \leq e_1 < e$) such that $\sigma, [b, e_1] \models D$. The translation is as follows.

1. $\aleph(\mathbf{pref}(D)) \stackrel{\text{def}}{=} \Box_{pref} D$.

2. $\aleph(\mathbf{init}(D_2/D_3)) \stackrel{\text{def}}{=} \Box_{pref} (\varXi(D_3) \Rightarrow D_2\hat{}true)$.

3. $\aleph(\mathbf{anti}(D)) \stackrel{\text{def}}{=} \neg(true \hat{} D \hat{} true)$.

4. $\aleph(\mathbf{implies}(D_1 \rightsquigarrow D_2)) \stackrel{\text{def}}{=} \Box(D_1 \Rightarrow D_2)$.

5. $\aleph(\mathbf{follows}(D_1 \rightsquigarrow D_2/D_3)) \stackrel{\text{def}}{=} \Box(\neg(D_1\hat{}(\varXi(D_3) \wedge \neg(D_2\hat{}true))))$.

6. $\aleph(\mathbf{triggers}(D_1 \rightsquigarrow D_2/D_3)) \stackrel{\text{def}}{=} \Box(D_1\hat{}true \Rightarrow (\varXi(D_3) \Rightarrow D_2\hat{}true)) \wedge$
   $\Box(D_1 \Rightarrow \Box_{pref}(\varXi(D_3) \Rightarrow D_2\hat{}true))$.

Lemma 2. *For any $\zeta \in SeCeNL$, if ζ does not use nominals then $\sigma \in L(\zeta)$ iff $\sigma \in L(\aleph(\zeta))$.*

The proof follows from examination of the semantics of ζ and the definition of $\aleph(\zeta)$. We omit the details.

Nominals: Consider a nominated formula $D : \Theta$ where D is a SeCe formula over propositional variables $\Sigma \cup \Theta$. As we shall see later, the propositional variables in Θ are treated as "place holders" - variables which are meant to be true exactly at one point - and we call them *nominals* following [11].

Given an interval $[b, e] \in Intv(\mathbb{N})$ we define a *nominal valuation* over $[b, e]$ to be a map $\nu : \Theta \to \{i \mid b \leq i \leq e\}$. It assigns a unique position within $[b, e]$ to each nominal variable. We can then straightforwardly define $\sigma, [b, e] \models_{\nu} D$ by constructing a word σ_{ν} over $\Sigma \cup \Theta$ such that $\forall p \in \Sigma : p \in \sigma_{\nu}(i) \Leftrightarrow p \in \sigma(i)$ and $\forall u \in \Theta : u \in \sigma_{\nu}(i) \Leftrightarrow \nu(u) = i$. Then $\sigma_{\nu}, [b, e] \models D \Leftrightarrow \sigma, [b, e] \models_{\nu} D$. We state that ν_1 over Θ_1 and ν_2 over Θ_2 are consistent if $\nu_1(u) = \nu_2(u)$ for all $u \in \Theta_1 \cap \Theta_2$. We denote this by $\nu_1 \parallel \nu_2$.

Now we consider formulae where nominals are used and shared between different parts D_1, D_2 and D_3 of an atomic formula such as **implies**$(D_1 : \Theta_1 \rightsquigarrow D_2 : \Theta_2)$.

Example 1 (lags). Let $D_1 : \{u, v\}$ be the formula (`<u> ^ [[P]] && ((slen = n)^ <v> ^ true`) which holds for an interval where P is *true* throughout the interval and v marks the $n + 1$ position from u denoting the start of the interval. Let $D_2 : \{v\}$ be the formula `true ^ <v> ^ [[Q]]`. Then, **implies**$(D_1 : \{u, v\} \rightsquigarrow D_2 : \{v\})$ states that for all observation intervals $[i, j]$ and all nominal valuations ν over $[i, j]$ if $\sigma, [i, j] \models_{\nu} D_1$ then $\sigma, [i, j] \models_{\nu} D_2$. This formula is given by *live timing diagram*[2] in Fig. 4.

Semantics of SeCeNL: In the following v_i denotes nominal valuation over θ_i.

- $L(\textbf{pref}(D_1 : \Theta_1)) = \{\sigma \mid \forall \sigma' \leq_{prefix} \sigma : \exists \nu_1. \ \sigma' \models_{\nu_1} D_1\}$.
- $L(\textbf{init}(D_2 : \Theta_2 \ / \ D_3 : \Theta_3)) = \{\sigma \mid \forall j \forall \nu_3 : \sigma, [0, j] \models_{\nu_3} D_3 \Rightarrow \exists k \leq j \exists \nu_2 : \sigma, [0, k] \models_{\nu_2} D_2\}$.
- $L(\textbf{anti}(D_1 : \Theta_1)) = \{\sigma \mid \forall i, j \forall \nu_1 : \sigma, [i, j] \not\models_{\nu_1} D_1\}$.
- $L(\textbf{implies}(D_1 : \Theta_1 \rightsquigarrow D_2 : \Theta_2)) = \{\sigma \mid \forall i, j \forall \nu_1 : (\sigma, [i, j] \models_{\nu_1} D_1 \Rightarrow \exists \nu_2 : \nu_1 \parallel \nu_2 \wedge \sigma, [i, j] \models_{\nu_2} D_2)\}$.
- $L(\textbf{follows}(D_1 : \Theta_1 \rightsquigarrow D_2 : \Theta_2 / D_3 : \Theta_3)) = \{\sigma \mid \forall i, j \forall \nu_1 : (\sigma, [i, j] \models_{\nu_1} D_1 \Rightarrow (\forall k \forall \nu_3 \parallel \nu_1 : \sigma, [j, k] \models_{\nu_3} \Xi(D_3) \Rightarrow \exists l \leq k \exists \nu_2 : \nu_2 \parallel \nu_1 \wedge \sigma, [j, l] \models_{\nu_2} D_2))\}$.
- $L(\textbf{triggers}(D_1 : \Theta_1 \rightsquigarrow D_2 : \Theta_2 / D_3 : \Theta_3)) = \{\sigma \mid \forall i, j \forall \nu_1 : (\sigma, [i, j] \models_{\nu_1} D_1 \Rightarrow (\forall k \forall \nu_3 \parallel \nu_1 : \sigma, [i, k] \models_{\nu_3} \Xi(D_3) \Rightarrow \exists l \leq k \exists \nu_2 : \nu_2 \parallel \nu_1 \wedge \sigma, [i, l] \models D_2))\}$.

Based on the above semantics, we now formulate a QDDC formula equivalent to a SeCeNL formula. We will make essential use of quantification $\exists p.D$ We first define relativized quantifiers to restrict variables in Θ to singletons. Given $\Theta = \{u_1, \ldots, u_n\}$ let $singleton(\Theta) \overset{\text{def}}{\equiv} (scount \ u_1 = 1 \ \wedge \cdots \wedge \ scount \ u_n = 1)$ which states that in current interval each nominal occurs exactly once. Then, $\forall^1_{\Theta} : D \overset{\text{def}}{\equiv} \forall \Theta. \ (singleton(\Theta) \Rightarrow D)$ and $\exists^1_{\Theta} : D \overset{\text{def}}{\equiv} \exists \Theta. \ (singleton(\Theta) \wedge D)$.

---

[2] The illustration was made with WaveDrom and due to its limitation on naming nominals we were forced to rename the nominals u and v in Q as a and b respectively.

SeCeNL to QDDC : We now define the translation $\aleph$ from SeCeNL to QDDC.

1. $\aleph(\mathbf{pref}(D_1 : \Theta_1)) \stackrel{\text{def}}{=} \square_{pref} (\exists^1_{\Theta_1} : D_1))$.

2. $\aleph(\mathbf{init}(D_2 : \Theta_2 / D_3 : \Theta_3)) \stackrel{\text{def}}{=} \square_{pref} (\forall^1_{\Theta_3} : (D_3 \Rightarrow ((\exists^1_{\Theta_2} : D_2)\hat{\ }true)))$.

3. $\aleph(\mathbf{anti}(D_1 : \Theta_1)) \stackrel{\text{def}}{=} \neg(true \hat{\ }(\exists^1_{\Theta_1} : D_1)\hat{\ }true)$.

4. $\aleph(\mathbf{implies}(D_1 : \Theta_1 \rightsquigarrow D_2 : \Theta_2)) \stackrel{\text{def}}{=} \square(\forall^1_{\Theta_1} : (D_1 \Rightarrow (\exists^1_{\Theta_2 - \Theta_1} : D_2)))$.

5. $\aleph(\mathbf{follows}(D_1 : \Theta_1 \rightsquigarrow D_2 : \Theta_2/D_3 : \Theta_3)) \stackrel{\text{def}}{=}$
   $\square(\neg((\exists^1_{\Theta_1} : D_1)\hat{\ }(\Xi(\exists^1_{\Theta_3} : D_3) \wedge \neg((\exists^1_{\Theta_2} : D_2)\hat{\ }true))))$.

6. $\aleph(\mathbf{triggers}(D_1 : \Theta_1 \rightsquigarrow D_2 : \Theta_2/D_3 : \Theta_3)) \stackrel{\text{def}}{=}$
   $\square(\forall^1_{\Theta_1} : ((D_1 \wedge singeton(\Theta_1))\hat{\ }true \Rightarrow (\Xi(\forall^1_{\Theta_3 - \Theta_1} : D_3) \Rightarrow$
   $$((\exists^1_{\Theta_2 - \Theta_1} : D_2)\hat{\ }true)))) \bigwedge$$
   $\square(\forall^1_{\Theta_1} : (D_1 \Rightarrow \square_{pref}(\Xi(\forall^1_{\Theta_3 - \Theta_1} : D_3) \Rightarrow ((\exists^1_{\Theta_2 - \Theta_1} : D_2)\hat{\ }true))))$

Theorem 2. *For any word σ over Σ and any $\zeta \in SeCeNL$ we have that $\sigma \in L(\zeta)$ iff $\sigma \in L(\aleph(\zeta))$. Moreover, the translation $\aleph(\zeta)$ can be computed in time linear in the size of ζ.*

The proof follows from the semantics of ζ and the definition of $\aleph(\zeta)$.

Lemma 3. *Let $\zeta = \mathbf{implies}(D_1 : \Theta_1 \rightsquigarrow D_2 : \Theta_2)$ and let $|\mathcal{A}(D_i)| = m_i$ for $i \in \{1,2\}$. Then there exists a DFA $\mathcal{A}(\zeta)$ of size at most $2^{2^{m_1 m_2}}$ for ζ.*

Proof. The formula ζ can be written in terms of a negation and two existential quantifiers. Note that each application of existential quantifier will result in an NFA and each time we determinize we get a DFA which is at most exponential in the size of NFA. Since that both $\mathcal{A}(D_1)$ and $\mathcal{A}(D_2)$ are DFA's to start with, this implies we can construct a DFA $\mathcal{A}(\zeta)$ of size at most $2^{2^{m_1 m_2}}$ for ζ.

In an similar way we can show that the size of formula automata for other SeCeNL atomic formulae are also elementary.

Lemma 4. *For any $\zeta \in SeCeNL$ the size of the automaton $\mathcal{A}(\zeta)$ for ζ is elementary in the size of ζ.*

3   Formalizing Timing Diagrams

In this section we give a formal semantics to timing diagrams and formula translation from timing diagrams to SeCeNL. We first give a textual syntax for timing diagrams which is derived from the timing diagram format of WaveDrom [5,18].

The symbols in a *waveform* come from $\Lambda = \{0, 1, 2, \times, 0|, 1|, 2|, \times|\}$ and Θ, an atomic set of nominals. Let $\Gamma = \Theta \cup \Lambda$. The syntax of a *waveform* over Γ is given by the grammar:

$$\pi := \lambda \mid u : \pi \mid \pi_1 \pi_2,$$

where $u \in \Theta$ and $\lambda \in \Lambda$. We call the elements in Θ the *nominals*. As we shall see later, when we convert a waveform to a SeCeNL formula the nominals that appear in the formula are exactly the nominals in the waveform and hence the name. Let Wf be the set of all waveforms over Γ.

An example of a waveform is 01a:2x011xb:x2|220c:00 with $\Theta = \{a,b,c\}$. Intuitively, in a waveform 0 denotes *low*, 1 *high*, 2 and x *don't cares* (there is a subtle difference between 2 and x though) and "|" the *stuttering* operator.

Let Σ be a set of propositional variables. A *timing diagram over* Σ is a tuple $\langle \mathcal{W}, \Sigma, C, \Theta \rangle$ where $\mathcal{W} = \{W_p \in \mathsf{Wf} \mid p \in \Sigma\}$ and $C \subset \Theta \times \Theta \times Intv(\mathbb{N})$ a set of timing constraints.

Figure 2 shows an example timing diagram $T = \langle\{W_p, W_q\}, \{(a, b, [10 : 10]),$ $(a, d, [1 : 8]), (c, d, [20 : 30])\}, \{a, b, c, d, e, f\}\rangle$ along with its rendering in Wave-Drom. As in the case with SeCeNL formulas, nominals act as place holders in timing diagrams which can be shared among multiple waveforms. For example, in the figure W_p and W_q share the nominals a and c. As a result a timing constraint in one timing diagram can implicitly induce a timing constraint in the other. For instance, even though there is no direct timing constraint between a and c in W_p the constraints between a and d, and d and c together impose one on them.

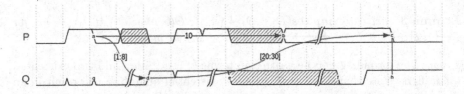

Fig. 2. Timing diagram T and its WaveDrom rendering.

Let $T = \langle \mathcal{W}, \Sigma, C, \Theta \rangle$, $\mathcal{W} = \{W_p \in \mathsf{Wf} \mid p \in \Sigma\}$, be a timing diagram. Let $\nu : \Theta \to [b, e]$ be a nominal valuation. Let $\sigma : [0, n] \to 2^\Sigma$ be a word over Σ and for all $p \in \Sigma$ let $\sigma_p : [0, n] \to \{0, 1\}$ given by $\sigma_p(i) = 1$ iff $p \in \sigma(i)$. Then the satisfaction relation σ_p over a waveform W under the valuation ν is defined as follows.

$$\sigma_p, [b, e] \models_\nu 0 \text{ iff } e = b + 1 \text{ and } \sigma_p(b) = 0,$$
$$\sigma_p, [b, e] \models_\nu 1 \text{ iff } e = b + 1 \text{ and } \sigma_p(b) = 1,$$
$$\sigma_p, [b, e] \models_\nu \lambda \text{ iff } e = b + 1 \text{ and } \lambda \in \{2, \mathsf{x}\},$$
$$\sigma_p, [b, e] \models_\nu 0| \text{ iff } \forall b \leq i < e : \sigma_p(i) = 0,$$
$$\sigma_p, [b, e] \models_\nu 1| \text{ iff } \forall b \leq i < e : \sigma_p(i) = 1,$$
$$\sigma_p, [b, e] \models_\nu 2| \text{ iff } \forall b \leq i < e : \sigma_p(i) \in \{0, 1\},$$
$$\sigma_p, [b, e] \models_\nu \mathsf{x}| \text{ iff } \forall b \leq i < e : \sigma_p(i) = 1 \text{ or } \forall b \leq i < e : \sigma_p(i) = 0,$$
$$\sigma_p, [b, e] \models_\nu u : W \text{ iff } \nu(u) = b \text{ and } \sigma_p, [b, e] \models_\nu W,$$
$$\sigma_p, [b, e] \models_\nu VW \text{ iff } \exists b \leq i < e : \sigma_p, [b, i] \models_{\nu_1} V \text{ and } \sigma_p, [i, e] \models_{\nu_2} W,$$
$$\text{and } \nu_1 || \nu \text{ and } \nu_2 || \nu.$$

We say $\nu \models C$ iff $\forall (a, b, \langle l, r \rangle) \in C : \nu(b) - \nu(a) \in \langle l, r \rangle$. We define $\sigma, [b, e] \models_\nu$ $\langle W, \Sigma, C, \Theta \rangle$ iff $\forall p \in \Sigma : \sigma_p, [b, e] \models_\nu W_p$ and $\nu \models C$.

3.1 Waveform to SeCeNL Translation

We translate a waveform W_p to SeCeNL as follows: every 0 occurring in P is translated to $\{\{\neg P\}\}$, 1 to $\{\{P\}\}$, 2 and x to slen = 1, 0| to ptV[$\neg$ P], 1| to ptV[P], 2| to true, and x| to ptV[P]V[$\neg$ P]. A nominal u that is appearing in W_p is translated to <u>. For instance, the waveform W_p = 01a:2x011xb:x2|220c:00 in T of Fig. 2 will be translated to SeCeNL formula as below.

$$(\{\{\neg P\}\}^\wedge\{\{P\}\}^\wedge<a>^\wedge(\text{slen} = 1)^\wedge(\text{slen} = 1)^\wedge\{\{\neg P\}\}^\wedge\{\{P\}\}^\wedge\{\{P\}\}^\wedge(\text{slen} = 1)^\wedge<b>^\wedge$$
$$(\text{slen} = 1)^\wedge\text{true}^\wedge(\text{slen} = 1)^\wedge(\text{slen} = 1)\ ^\wedge\{\{\neg P\}\}^\wedge<c>^\wedge\{\{\neg P\}\}^\wedge\{\{\neg P\}\}).$$

We denote the translated SeCeNL formula by $\xi(T, W_p)$. Similarly we can translate W_q to get the formula $\xi(T, W_q)$. The timing constraints in C is roughly translated to the SeCeNL formula $\xi(T, C)$ as follows.

$$((\text{true}^\wedge<a>^\wedge((\text{slen} \geq 1) \wedge (\text{slen} \leq 8))^\wedge<d>^\wedge\text{true}) \wedge$$
$$(\text{true}^\wedge<d>^\wedge((\text{slen} \geq 20) \wedge (\text{slen} \leq 30))^\wedge<c>^\wedge\text{true}) \wedge$$
$$(\text{true}^\wedge<a>^\wedge(\text{slen} = 10)^\wedge<b>^\wedge\text{true})).$$

We define $\xi(T) = \xi(T, W_p) \wedge \xi(T, W_q) \wedge \xi(T, C)$. For a timing diagram $T = \langle W, \Sigma, C, \Theta \rangle$, $W = \{W_p \mid p \in \Sigma\}$ we define $\xi(T) = \bigwedge_{p \in \Sigma} \xi(T, W_p) \bigwedge \wedge \xi(T, C)$.

Theorem 3. *Let T be a timing diagram. Then, for all $\sigma \in \Sigma^*$, for all $[b, e] \in Intv(\sigma)$ and for all nominal valuation ν over $[b, e]$, $\sigma, [b, e] \models_\nu T$ iff $\sigma, [b, e] \models_\nu$ $\xi(T) : \Theta$. Also, the translation $\xi(T) : \Theta$ is linear in the size of T.*

Proof. Proof is not difficult and is by induction on the length of the waveform.

Due above theorem we can now use timing diagrams in place of nominated formulas with liveness operators. We call such timing diagrams *live timing diagrams*. For an example of a live timing diagram see Fig. 4.

3.2 Comparision with Other Temporal Logics

In previous section, Theorem 3 showed that timing diagrams can be translated to equivalent SeCeNL formulas with only linear blowup in size. In this section we compare our logic SeCeNL with other relevant logics in the literature viz, LTL, discrete time MTL, and PSL-Sugar. Of these, PSL-Sugar is the most expressive and discrete time MTL and LTL are its syntactic subset. We show by examples that SeCeNL formulae are more succint (smaller in size) than PSL-Sugar and we believe that they capture the diagrams more directly. The full version of this paper [13] gives several more examples.

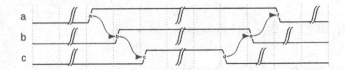

Fig. 3. Example 1.

Example (Ordered Stack). Let us now consider the timing diagram in Fig. 3 adapted from [6]. Rise and fall of successive signals a, b and c follow a stack discipline. The language described by it is given by the SeCeNL formula:

$([\neg a] \; \hat{} <ua> \; \hat{} \; [a] \; \hat{} \; <va> \; \hat{} \; [\neg a]) \land ([\neg b] \; \hat{} <ub> \; \hat{} \; [b] \; \hat{} \; <vb> \; \hat{} \; [\neg b]) \land$
$([\neg c] \; \hat{} <uc> \; \hat{} \; [c] \; \hat{} \; <vc> \; \hat{} \; [\neg c]) \land$
$(ext \hat{} <ua> \; \hat{} \; ext \; \hat{} \; <ub> \; \hat{} \; true) \land (true \hat{} <ub> \; \hat{} \; ext \; \hat{} \; <uc> \; \hat{} \; true) \land$
$(true \hat{} <vc> \; \hat{} \; ext \; \hat{} \; <vb> \; \hat{} \; true) \land (true \hat{} <vb> \; \hat{} \; ext \; \hat{} \; <va> \; \hat{} \; true).$

Note that first three conjuncts exactly correspond to the three waveforms. The next four conjuncts correspond to the four arrows (ordering constraints) between the waveforms. In general, if n signals are stacked, its SeCeNL specification has size $O(n)$.

An equivalent MTL (or LTL) formula is given by:

$$[\neg a \land \neg b \land \neg c] \; \mathbf{UU} \; [a \land \neg b \land \neg c] \; \mathbf{UU} \; [a \land b \land \neg c] \; \mathbf{UU} \; [a \land b \land c] \; \mathbf{UU}$$
$$[a \land b \land \neg c] \; \mathbf{UU} \; [a \land \neg b \land \neg c] \; \mathbf{UU} \; [\neg a \land \neg b \land \neg c]$$

where $a \; \mathbf{UU} \; b$ is the derived modality $a \land \mathbf{X}(aUb)$. For a stack of n signals, the size of the MTL formula is $O(n^2)$. Above formula is also a PSL-Sugar formula. We attempt to specify the pattern as a PSL-Sugar regular expression as follows:

$$((\neg a \land \neg b \land \neg c;)[+]; \; (a \land \neg b \; \& \; \neg c;)[+]; \; (a \land b \land \neg c;)[+]; \; (a \land b \land c;)[+];$$
$$(a \land b \land \neg c;)[+]; \; (a \land \neg b \land \neg c;)[+]; (\neg a \land \neg b \land \neg c;)[+].$$

For a stack of n signals, the size of the PSL-Sugar SERE expression is $O(n^2)$. We believe that there is no formula of size $O(n)$ in PSL-Sugar which can express the above property. Compare this with size $O(n)$ formula of SeCeNL.

Example (Unordered Stack). In ordered stack signal a turns on first and turns off last followed by signals b, c in that order. We consider a variation of the ordered stack example above where signals turn on and off in first-on-last-off order but there is no restriction on which signal becomes high first. This can be compactly specified in SeCeNL as follows.

$([\neg a] \; \hat{} <ua> \; \hat{} \; [a] \; \hat{} \; <va> \; \hat{} \; [\neg a]) \land ([\neg b] \; \hat{} <ub> \; \hat{} \; [b] \; \hat{} \; <vb> \; \hat{} \; [\neg b]) \land$
$([\neg c] \; \hat{} <uc> \; \hat{} \; [c] \; \hat{} \; <vc> \; \hat{} \; [\neg c]) \land$
$(ext \; \hat{} \; <u1> \; \hat{} \; ext \; \hat{} \; <u2> \; \hat{} \; ext \; \hat{} \; <u3> \; \hat{} ext$
$\hat{} \; <v3> \; \hat{} \; ext \; \hat{} \; <v2> \; \hat{} \; ext \; \hat{} \; <v1> \; \hat{} \; ext \;) \land$
$Bijection(ua, ub, uc, va, vb, vc, u1, u2, u3, v1, v2, v3)$

where formula *Bijection* below states that there is one to one correspondence between positions marked by ua, ub, uc, va, vb, vc and positions marked by $u1, u2, u3, v1, v2, v3$. Moreover, if u_a maps to say u_3 than v_a must map to v_3 and so on.

$$[[(u1 \vee u2 \vee u3) \Leftrightarrow (ua \vee ub \vee uc)]] \wedge [[\bigwedge_{1 \leq i,j \leq 3, i \neq j} \neg(u_i \wedge u_j)]]$$
$$[[(v1 \vee v2 \vee v3) \Leftrightarrow (va \vee vb \vee vc)]] \wedge [[\bigwedge_{1 \leq i,j \leq 3, i \neq j} \neg(v_i \wedge v_j)]]$$
$$\bigwedge_{1 \leq i \leq 3, j \in a,b,c} (true \,\hat{}\, <u_i \wedge u_j> \,\hat{}\, true \Leftrightarrow true \,\hat{}\, <v_i \wedge v_j> \,\hat{}\, true).$$

Note that, in general, if n signals are stacked, then the above SeCeNL specification has size $O(n^2)$.

Now we discuss encoding of unordered stack in PSL-Sugar. In absence of nominals, it is difficult to state the above behaviour succinctly in logics PSL-Sugar even using its SERE regular expressions. Each order of occurrence of signals has to be enumerated as a disjunction where each disjunct is as in the example ordered stack (where the order was a, b, c). As there are $n!$ orders possible between n signals, the size of the PSL-Sugar formula is also $O(n!)$. We believe that there is no polynomially sized formula in PSL-Sugar encoding this property. This shows that SeCeNL is exponentially more succint as compared to PSL-Sugar.

In general, presence of nominals distinguishes SeCeNL from logics like PSL-Sugar. In formalizing behaviour of hardware circuits it has been proposed that regular expressions are not enough and operators such as pipelining have been introduced [6]. These are a form of synchronization and they can be easily expressed using nominals. (See [14].)

4   Case Study: Minepump Specification

We first specify some useful generic timing diagram properties.

- **lags**(P, Q, n): *it is defined by Fig. 4*. It specifies that in any observation interval if P holds continuously for $n + 1$ cycles and persists then Q holds from $(n + 1)^{th}$ cycle onwards and persists till P persists.
- **tracks**(P, Q, n): *defined by Fig. 5*. In any observation interval if P becomes true then Q sustains as long as P sustains or upto n cycles whichever is shorter.
- **sep**(P, n): *Fig. 6 defines this property*. Any interval which begins with a falling edge of P and ends with next rising edge of P then the length of the interval should be at least n cycles.
- **ubound**(P, n): *Fig. 7 defines this property*. In any observation interval P can be continuously true for at most n cycles.

Note that we have presented these formulae diagrammatically. The textual version of these live timing diagrams can be found in the full version [13].

We now state the minepump problem. Imagine a minepump which keeps the water level in a mine under control. The pump is driven by a controller which

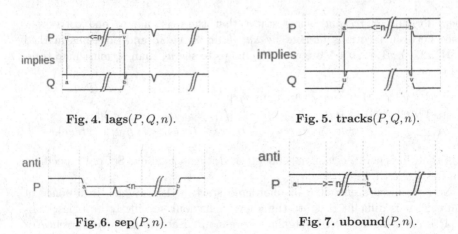

Fig. 4. lags(P, Q, n).   **Fig. 5. tracks**(P, Q, n).

Fig. 6. sep(P, n).   **Fig. 7. ubound**(P, n).

can switch it *on* and *off*. Mines are prone to highly flammable methane leakage trapped underground. So as a safety measure if a methane leakage is detected the controller is not allowed to keep the pump on.

The controller has two input sensors - HH2O which becomes 1 when water level is high, and HCH4 which is 1 when there is a methane leakage. It can generate two output signals - ALARM which is set to 1 to sound/persist the alarm, and PUMPON which is set to 1 to keep the pump on. The objective of the controller is to *safely* operate the pump and the alarm in such a way that the water level is never dangerous, indicated by the indicator variable DH2O, whenever certain assumptions hold. We have the following assumptions on the mine and the pump.

- Sensor reliability assumption: **pref**$([[DH2O \Rightarrow HH2O]])$. If HH2O is false then so is DH2O.
- Water seepage assumptions: **tracks**$(HH2O, DH2O, \kappa_1)$. The minimum no. of cycles for water level to become dangerous once it becomes high is κ_1.
- Pump capacity assumption: **lags**$(PUMPON, \neg HH2O, \kappa_2)$. If pump is kept on for at least $\kappa_2 + 1$ cycles then water level will not be high after κ_2 cycles.
- Methane release assumptions: **sep**$(HCH4, \kappa_3)$ and **ubound**$(HCH4, \kappa_4)$. The minimum separation between the two leaks of methane is κ_3 cycles and the methane leak cannot persist for more than κ_4 cycles.
- Initial condition assumption: **init**$(<\neg HH2O> \wedge <\neg HCH4>, slen = 0)$. Initially neither the water level is high nor there is a methane leakage.

Let the conjunction of these SeCeNL formulas be denoted as MINEASSUME. The commitments are:

- Alarm control: **lags**$(HH2O, ALARM, \kappa_5)$ and **lags**$(HCH4, ALARM, \kappa_6)$ and **lags**$(\neg HH2O \wedge \neg HCH4, \neg ALARM, \kappa_7)$. If the water level is high then alarm will be high after κ_5 cycles and if there is a methane leakage then alarm will be high after κ_6 cycles. If neither the water level is dangerous nor there is a methane leakage then alarm should be off after κ_7 cycle.

– Safety condition: **pref**($[[\neg DH2O \wedge (HCH4 \Rightarrow \neg PUMPON)]]$) . The water level should never become dangerous and whenever there is a methane leakage pump should be off.

Let the conjunction of these commitments be denoted as `MINECOMMIT`. Then, the requirement over the minepump controller is given by the formula `MINEASSUME` $\Rightarrow$ `MINECOMMIT`. Note that the requirement consists of a mixture of timing diagram constraints (such as pump capacity assumption above) as well as SeCeNL formulas (such as safety condition above). Hence the specification is heterogenous.

The tool DCSynth can automatically synthesize a controller for the values, say $\kappa_1 = 10$, $\kappa_2 = 2$, $\kappa_3 = 14$, $\kappa_4 = 2$, and $\kappa_5 = \kappa_6 = \kappa_7 = 1$. For these values, in under 1s it outputs a SCADE/SMV controller with 140 states meeting the specification. If the constants are such that specification is not realizable the tool outputs an explanation. More case studies can be found in the full version of the paper [13].

References

1. Allen, J.F.: Maintaining knowledge about temporal intervals. Comm. ACM **26**(11), 832–843 (1983)
2. Alpern, B., Schneider, F.B.: Recognizing safety and liveness. Distrib. Comput. **2**(3), 117–126 (1987)
3. Amla, N., Emerson, E.A., Kurshan, R.P., Namjoshi, K.S.: Model checking synchronous timing diagrams. In: FMCAD 2000, pp. 283–298 (2000)
4. Babu, A., Pandya, P.K.: Chop expressions and discrete duration calculus. In: Modern Applications of Automata Theory, pp. 229–256 (2012)
5. Chapyzhenka, A., Probell, J.: Wavedrom: rendering beautiful waveforms from plain text. Synopsys User Group (2016). http://wavedrom.com/images/SNUG2016_WaveDrom.pdf
6. Chockler, H., Fisler, K.: Temporal modalities for concisely capturing timing diagrams. In: Borrione, D., Paul, W. (eds.) CHARME 2005. LNCS, vol. 3725, pp. 176–190. Springer, Heidelberg (2005). doi:10.1007/11560548_15
7. Damm, W., Harel, D.: LSCs: breathing life into message sequence charts. Form. Methods Syst. Des. **19**(1), 45–80 (2001)
8. Eisner, C., Fisman, D.: Temporal logic made practical. In: Handbook of Model Checking. Springer (2016, expected). http://www.cis.upenn.edu/~fisman/documents/EF_HBMC14.pdf
9. Fisler, K.: Timing diagrams: formalization and algorithmic verification. J. Logic Lang. Inform. **8**(3), 323–361 (1999)
10. Fisler, K.: Two-dimensional regular expressions for compositional bus protocols. In: FMCAD 2007, pp. 154–157 (2007)
11. Franceschet, M., de Rijke, M., Schlingloff, B.: Hybrid logics on linear structures: expressivity and complexity. In: TIME-ICTL 2003, pp. 166–173 (2003)
12. Kesten, Y., Pnueli, A.: A compositional approach to CTL* verification. Theor. Comp. Sci. **331**(2–3), 397–428 (2005)
13. Matteplackel, R.M., Pandya, P.K., Wakankar, A.: Formalizing timing diagram requirements in discrete duration calulus. CoRR abs/1705.04510 (2017)

14. Pandya, P.K., Ramakrishna, Y.S., Shyamasundar, R.K.: A compositional semantics of esterel in duration calculus. In: AMAST 1995 (1995)
15. Pandya, P.K.: Specifying and deciding quantified discrete-time duration calculus formulae using DCVALID. In: RTTOOLS 2001, Affiliated with CONCUR (2001)
16. Pandya, P.K.: Model checking CTL*[DC]. In: Margaria, T., Yi, W. (eds.) TACAS 2001. LNCS, vol. 2031, pp. 559–573. Springer, Heidelberg (2001). doi:10.1007/3-540-45319-9_38
17. Wakankar, A., Pandya, P.K., Matteplackel, R.M.: DCSynth: guided reactive synthesis with soft requirements and performance measurement. CoRR (2017)
18. WaveDrom: Wavedrom user manual (2016). http://wavedrom.com/tutorial.html

On Approximate Diagnosability
of Metric Systems

Giordano Pola[⊠], Elena De Santis, and Maria Domenica Di Benedetto

Center of Excellence DEWS, University of L'Aquila,
Via G. Gronchi, 67100 L'Aquila, Italy
giordano.pola@univaq.it

Abstract. The increasing complexity in nowadays engineered systems requires great attention to safety hazards and occurrence of faults, which must be readily detected to possibly restore nominal behavior of the system. The notion of diagnosability plays a key role in this regard, since it corresponds to the possibility of detecting within a finite delay if a fault, or in general a hazardous situation, did occur. In this paper the notion of approximate diagnosability is introduced and characterized for the general class of metric systems, that are typically used in the research community working on hybrid systems to study complex heterogeneous processes in cyber–physical systems. The notion of approximate diagnosability proposed captures the possibility of detecting faults on the basis of measurements corrupted by errors, always introduced by non-ideal sensors in a real environment. A characterization of approximate diagnosability in a set membership framework is provided and the computational complexity of the proposed algorithms analyzed. Then, relations are established between approximate diagnosability of a given metric system and approximate diagnosability of a system that approximately simulates the given one. Application of the proposed results to the study of approximate diagnosability for nonlinear systems, presenting an infinite number of states and of inputs, is finally discussed.

1 Introduction

Nowadays engineered systems are becoming more and more complex and therefore detection of safety hazards and faults is of primary importance to possibly restore nominal behavior of the systems. In this regard the notion of diagnosability, corresponding to the possibility of detecting faults within finite delays, plays a key role. Diagnosability has been extensively studied both for Discrete–Event Systems (DES) and continuous control systems. For DES, after the seminal work [21], several results have been achieved, see e.g. [8, 20, 22, 24, 27–29] and the references therein, and the recent survey [31]; see also [10], proposing a unifying framework for the study of observability and diagnosability of DES. For fault–tolerant control of continuous systems, an early review paper was presented in [23]; reconfigurable fault–tolerant control systems are reviewed in [13, 15, 32] and some results on fault–tolerant control for nonlinear systems in [5]; see also the

A. Cimatti and M. Sirjani (Eds.): SEFM 2017, LNCS 10469, pp. 269–283, 2017.
DOI: 10.1007/978-3-319-66197-1_17

recent survey [11]. Extensions to hybrid systems, featuring both discrete and continuous dynamics, have been also explored, see e.g. [3,4,9,16,26]. Apart from differences in the class of systems considered and in the way faults are modeled, to the best of our knowledge, the existing papers, except for [6,7,14], *either assume that the state variables are available, or assume the exact knowledge of output variables.* This is rather limiting in concrete applications where state variables cannot be directly measured, or output variables are measured by sensors that introduce measurement errors. The papers [6,14] investigate diagnosability for quantized systems and model faults as additional inputs to the system: [14] considers continuous–time nonlinear systems and detection is achieved in a stochastic setting, while [6] considers discrete–time linear systems where faults are detected provided that they belong to an appropriate class of functions.

In our recent paper [7] we introduced and investigated the notion of *approximate diagnosability* for nonlinear systems with unknown inputs and quantized output measurements. Given an accuracy $\rho \geq 0$ and a set of faulty states $\mathcal{F}$, approximate diagnosability corresponds to the possibility of distinguishing, within a finite time delay Δ, state trajectories that have reached the set of faulty states $\mathcal{F}$ from state trajectories that have not reached the set $\mathcal{F}+\mathcal{B}_\rho(0)$, obtained by adding to $\mathcal{F}$ a closed ball $\mathcal{B}_\rho(0)$ centered at the origin and with radius ρ. This ambiguity around the set $\mathcal{F}$ represented by the set $\mathcal{B}_\rho(0)$, reflects uncertainties introduced by measurement errors.

In this paper we extend the results reported in [7] from nonlinear systems to the general class of metric systems. Metric systems are typically used in the hybrid systems research community as a unifying mathematical paradigm to properly describe complex heterogeneous processes in cyber–physical systems, which include continuous dynamics, modeling physical processes, and discrete dynamics, modeling software and hardware, see e.g. [25]. We first propose a general definition of approximate diagnosability for metric systems and provide a characterization of this notion in a set membership framework, by extending the algorithms in [10] from exact diagnosability of DES to approximate diagnosability of metric systems; computational complexity of the proposed algorithms is also discussed. We then establish the relation between approximate diagnosability of a given metric system and approximate diagnosability of a system that approximately simulates the given one. As illustrated at the end of the paper, this relation allows, for example, the analysis of approximate diagnosability of systems presenting an infinite number of states and inputs, provided that finite abstractions of such systems are available.

The paper is organized as follows. Section 2 introduces notation and preliminary definitions. Section 3 introduces metric systems. Section 4 introduces the notion of approximate diagnosability and provides a characterization of this notion. Section 5 establishes the relation between approximate simulation and approximate diagnosability. Section 6 proposes an application to nonlinear systems. Section 7 offers some concluding remarks.

2   Notation and Preliminary Definitions

The symbols $\mathbb{N}$, $\mathbb{Z}$, $\mathbb{R}$, $\mathbb{R}^+$ and $\mathbb{R}_0^+$ denote the set of nonnegative integer, integer, real, positive real, and nonnegative real numbers, respectively. The symbol 0_n denotes the origin in $\mathbb{R}^n$. Given $a, b \in \mathbb{Z}$, we denote $[a; b] = [a, b] \cap \mathbb{Z}$. For a finite set X, the symbol $\text{card}(X)$ denotes the cardinality of X. Given a pair of sets X and Y and a relation $\mathcal{R} \subseteq X \times Y$, the symbol $\mathcal{R}^{-1}$ denotes the inverse relation of $\mathcal{R}$, i.e. $\mathcal{R}^{-1} = \{(y, x) \in Y \times X : (x, y) \in \mathcal{R}\}$. Given $X' \subseteq X$ and $Y' \subseteq Y$, we denote $\mathcal{R}(X') = \{y \in Y | \exists x \in X' \text{ s.t. } (x, y) \in \mathcal{R}\}$ and $\mathcal{R}^{-1}(Y') = \{x \in X | \exists y \in Y' \text{ s.t. } (x, y) \in \mathcal{R}\}$. Given a function $f : X \to Y$ and $X' \subseteq X$ the symbol $f(X')$ denotes the image of X' through f, i.e. $f(X') = \{y \in Y | \exists x \in X' \text{ s.t. } y = f(x)\}$. A continuous function $\gamma : \mathbb{R}_0^+ \to \mathbb{R}_0^+$, is said to belong to class $\mathcal{K}$ if it is strictly increasing and $\gamma(0) = 0$; γ is said to belong to class $\mathcal{K}_\infty$ if $\gamma \in \mathcal{K}$ and $\gamma(r) \to \infty$ as $r \to \infty$. Given a vector $x \in \mathbb{R}^n$ we denote by $\|x\|$ the infinity norm of x. Given $a \in \mathbb{R}$ and $X \subseteq \mathbb{R}^n$, the symbol aX denotes the set $\{y \in \mathbb{R}^n | \exists x \in X \text{ s.t. } y = ax\}$.

3   Metric Systems

In this paper we use the mathematical paradigm of metric systems as a unifying framework to describe complex heterogeneous processes in Cyber–Physical Systems (CPS). We start with the definition of system:

Definition 1 [25]. *A system is a tuple*

$$S = (X, X_0, U, \longrightarrow , Y, H),$$

consisting of

- *a set of states X,*
- *a set of initial states $X_0 \subseteq X$,*
- *a set of inputs U,*
- *a transition relation $\longrightarrow \subseteq X \times U \times X$,*
- *a set of outputs Y,*
- *an output function $H : X \to Y$.*

Sets X, U and Y in the definition above do not need to be finite; this is an important aspect of the definition of system since it allows describing finite systems, typically modeling e.g. the cyber part of CPS, but also systems with infinite set of states, typically modeling e.g. the physical part of CPS.

We follow standard practice and denote a transition $(x, u, x') \in \longrightarrow$ of S by $x \xrightarrow{u} x'$. The evolution of systems is captured by the notions of state and output runs. Given a sequence of transitions of S

$$x(0) \xrightarrow{u(0)} x(1) \xrightarrow{u(1)} \ldots \xrightarrow{u(l-1)} x(l) \tag{1}$$

with $x(0) \in X_0$, the sequences

$$x(\cdot) : x(0)\, x(1) \ldots x(l),$$
$$y(\cdot) : H(x(0))\, H(x(1)) \ldots H(x(l)), \tag{2}$$

are called a *state run* and an *output run* of S, respectively. System S is said to be:

- *countable*, if X and U are countable sets;
- *symbolic*, if X and U are finite sets;
- *deterministic*, if for any $x \in X$ and $u \in U$ there exists at most one transition $x \xrightarrow{u} x^+$ and *nondeterministic*, otherwise.

We can now give the following

Definition 2. *A system* $S = (X, X_0, U, \longrightarrow, Y, H)$ *is metric if the set* X *is equipped with a metric* $\mathbf{d}$, *i.e. a function* $\mathbf{d} : X \times X \to \mathbb{R}$, *satisfying for all* $x, x', x'' \in X$:

- $\mathbf{d}(x, x') \geq 0$;
- $\mathbf{d}(x, x') = 0$ *if and only if* $x = x'$;
- $\mathbf{d}(x, x') = \mathbf{d}(x', x)$;
- $\mathbf{d}(x, x') \leq \mathbf{d}(x, x'') + \mathbf{d}(x'', x')$.

4   Approximate Diagnosability

In this section we introduce and characterize the notion of approximate diagnosability for metric systems. We make the following

Assumption 1. *The inputs* u *of metric system* S *are not available to an external observer.*

The assumption above corresponds to the analysis of approximate diagnosability from the point of view of an external observer that cannot have access to the inputs of the system S. However, all definitions and results that will be derived can be applied to the case where inputs of S are available.

We can now present the following

Definition 3 *(Approximate diagnosability of metric systems). Consider a metric system* $S = (X, X_0, U, \longrightarrow, Y, H)$ *with metric* $\mathbf{d}$, *and denote by* $\mathcal{B}_\rho(x)$ *the closed ball induced by metric* $\mathbf{d}$ *centered at* $x \in X$ *and with radius* $\rho \in \mathbb{R}_0^+$, *i.e.*

$$\mathcal{B}_\rho(x) = \{x' \in X | \mathbf{d}(x, x') \leq \rho\}.$$

Given $X' \subseteq X$, *denote by* $\mathcal{B}_\rho(X')$ *the set*

$$\bigcup_{x' \in X'} \mathcal{B}_\rho(x').$$

Consider a set $\mathcal{F} \subseteq X$ *of faulty states of* S *with*

$$\mathcal{F} \cap X_0 = \varnothing.$$

Given a desired accuracy $\rho \in \mathbb{R}_0^+$, system S is $(\rho, \mathcal{F})$-diagnosable if there exists a finite delay $\Delta \in \mathbb{N}$, such that for any pair of state runs x^f, x^s of S for which there exists $t \in \mathbb{N}$ such that

$$x^f(t) \in \mathcal{F}, \text{ and}$$
$$x^f(t') \notin \mathcal{F}, \quad \forall t' \in [0; t-1], \text{ and}$$
$$x^s(t'') \notin \mathcal{B}_\rho(\mathcal{F}), \quad \forall t'' \in [0; t+\Delta],$$

the corresponding output runs y^f, y^s are such that

$$y^f(t') \neq y^s(t'),$$

for some $t' \in [0; t+\Delta]$.

By definition, approximate diagnosability corresponds to the possibility of distinguishing within a finite delay Δ, state runs that have reached the set of faulty states $\mathcal{F}$ from state runs that have not reached the set $\mathcal{B}_\rho(\mathcal{F})$. This ambiguity around the set $\mathcal{F}$ reflects uncertainties introduced by measurement errors in concrete applications. The definition above extends the notion of (exact) diagnosability given in [10] for DES, to metric systems. In particular, when $\rho = 0$, the definition above coincides with the one given in [10], when rewritten for DES. We now proceed with a further step and provide a set membership framework to check approximate diagnosability of metric systems that are assumed in the rest of this section to be symbolic.

Given a metric symbolic system

$$S = (X, X_0, U, \longrightarrow, Y, H), \tag{3}$$

let $\text{Post}(x) = \{x' \in X \mid \exists\, x \overset{u}{\longrightarrow} x'\}$. For a set $X' \subseteq X$, let $\text{Post}(X') = \bigcup_{x \in X'} \text{Post}(x)$. For the sake of simplicity, we assume in the rest of this section that

Assumption 2. *System (3) is nonblocking, i.e. $\text{Post}(x) \neq \varnothing, \forall x \in X$.*

The assumption above can be removed at the expense of a heavier notation. Given the system S in (3) and a set of faulty states $\mathcal{F} \subseteq X$, define the sets

$$\Pi = \{(x, x') \in X \times X : H(x) = H(x')\},$$
$$\Theta = \{(x, x') \in X \times X : x = x'\} \subseteq \Pi.$$

By definition, sets Π and Θ are symmetric, i.e. $(x, x') \in \Pi$ if and only if $(x', x) \in \Pi$ and, $(x, x') \in \Theta$ if and only if $(x', x) \in \Theta$. We recall the following.

Definition 4. *Two state runs of system S in (3) are indistinguishable if their corresponding output runs coincide.*

For a set $X' \subseteq X$ the symbol $\overline{X'}$ denotes the complement of X' in X. The following sets will be useful in characterizing approximate diagnosability:

- $\mathcal{I}^*$, the set of all pairs $(x, x') \in \Pi$ reachable from X_0 with two indistinguishable state runs;
- Λ_ρ^*, the set of all pairs $(x, x') \in \Pi$, with $x \in \mathcal{F}$ and $x' \in \overline{\mathcal{B}_\rho(\mathcal{F})}$ (or vice-versa $x \in \overline{\mathcal{B}_\rho(\mathcal{F})}$ and $x' \in \mathcal{F}$) for which there exist two indistinguishable infinite state runs starting from x and x', respectively, such that the latter is contained in $\overline{\mathcal{B}_\rho(\mathcal{F})}$ (or vice-versa the former is contained in $\overline{\mathcal{B}_\rho(\mathcal{F})}$).

Set $\mathcal{I}^*$ can be computed by using the following recursion:

$$
\begin{aligned}
\mathcal{I}_1 &= (X_0 \times X_0) \cap \Pi, \\
\mathcal{I}_{k+1} &= \{(x, x') \in (\text{Post}(z) \times \text{Post}(z')) \cap \Pi, (z, z') \in \mathcal{I}_k\} \cup \mathcal{I}_k, k \in \mathbb{N}.
\end{aligned}
\tag{4}
$$

Lemma 1

(i) The least fixed point of recursion (4) exists, is unique and is equal to $\mathcal{I}^*$.
(ii) Recursion (4) reaches the fixed point $\mathcal{I}^*$ in at most $\text{card}(X)^2$ steps.

Set Λ_ρ^* can be computed by using the following recursion:

$$
\begin{aligned}
\Psi_1 &= \left(X \times \overline{\mathcal{B}_\rho(\mathcal{F})} \right) \cap \mathcal{I}^*, \\
\Psi_{k+1} &= \{(x, x') \in \Psi_k : (\text{Post}(x) \times \text{Post}(x')) \cap \Psi_k \neq \varnothing\}, k \in \mathbb{N}.
\end{aligned}
\tag{5}
$$

The following result holds where, for a set $\Psi \subseteq X \times X$, the symbol Ψ^- denotes the minimal symmetric subset of $X \times X$ containing Ψ.

Lemma 2. *Consider recursion (5). Then:*

(i) If $\Psi_k \neq \varnothing$, $\forall k \in \mathbb{N}$, then the maximal fixed point Ψ^* of recursion (5), contained in $X \times \overline{\mathcal{B}_\rho(\Omega)}$, is nonempty and unique. Otherwise, $\exists k < \text{card}(X)^2$ such that $\Psi_k = \varnothing$ and $\Psi^* = \varnothing$;
(ii) If $\Psi^* \neq \varnothing$, recursion (5) reaches this maximal fixed point in at most $\text{card}(X)^2$ steps;
(iii) $\Lambda_\rho^* = \left(\Psi^* \cap \left(\mathcal{F} \times \overline{\mathcal{B}_\rho(\Omega)} \right) \right)^-$.

Finally, given the system S in (3), define the metric symbolic system

$$
\widetilde{S} = (X, X_0, U, \underset{\sim}{\longrightarrow}, Y, H),
$$

where $x \overset{u}{\underset{\sim}{\longrightarrow}} x'$ if and only if $x \overset{u}{\longrightarrow} x'$ and $x \notin \mathcal{F}$. Let $\widetilde{\mathcal{I}}^*$ be the set of pairs of states reachable from X_0 with two indistinguishable state runs, computed for $\widetilde{S}$. The set $\widetilde{\mathcal{I}}^* \cap \Lambda_\rho^*$ is the set of pairs (x, x'), where only one of the two states x or x' belongs to $\mathcal{F}$, which are the ending states of a pair of indistinguishable state runs of the system $\widetilde{S}$, with initial state in X_0, such that one of these state runs never reaches the set $\mathcal{F}$, and (x, x') are the initial states of a pair of arbitrarily long indistinguishable state runs of the system S, such that one of them never reaches $\mathcal{B}_\rho(\mathcal{F})$. Then, by definition of $\widetilde{S}$, we can state the following:

Theorem 1. *System S in (3) is $(\rho, \mathcal{F})$–diagnosable if and only if $\widetilde{\mathcal{I}}^* \cap \Lambda_\rho^* = \varnothing$.*

We conclude this section by establishing computational complexity bounds to check $(\rho, \mathcal{F})$–diagnosability of metric symbolic systems:

Proposition 1. *Space and time complexities in computing $\widetilde{\mathcal{I}}^* \cap \Lambda_\rho^*$ are respectively, $O\left(\mathrm{card}(X)^2\right)$ and $O\left(\mathrm{card}(X)^5\right)$.*

The bounds above coincide with the ones derived in [10] to check (exact) diagnosability of DES. The proofs of Lemmas 1, 2, Theorem 1 and Proposition 1 are similar to the corresponding results given in [10] for (exact) diagnosability of DES. They are omitted here for lack of space.

5 Approximate Simulation and Diagnosability

In this section we establish the relation between approximate diagnosability and approximate simulation. We start by introducing the following:

Definition 5. *Consider a pair of metric systems*

$$S_i = (X_i, X_{0,i}, U_i, \xrightarrow[i]{}, Y_i, H_i), \; i = 1, 2, \tag{6}$$

with X_1 and X_2 subsets of some metric set X equipped with metric $\mathbf{d}$, and let $\varepsilon \in \mathbb{R}_0^+$ be a given accuracy. Consider a relation

$$\mathcal{R} \subseteq X_1 \times X_2, \tag{7}$$

satisfying the following conditions:

(i) $\forall x_1 \in X_{0,1} \; \exists x_2 \in X_{0,2}$ such that $(x_1, x_2) \in \mathcal{R}$;
(ii) $\mathbf{d}(x_1, x_2) \leq \varepsilon, \; \forall (x_1, x_2) \in \mathcal{R}$;
(iii) $H_1(x_1) = H_2(x_2), \; \forall (x_1, x_2) \in \mathcal{R}$.

Relation $\mathcal{R}$ is an ε-approximate simulation relation from S_1 to S_2 if it enjoys conditions (i)–(iii) and the following one:

(iv) $\forall (x_1, x_2) \in \mathcal{R}$ if $x_1 \xrightarrow[1]{u_1} x_1'$ then there exists $x_2 \xrightarrow[2]{u_2} x_2'$ with $(x_1', x_2') \in \mathcal{R}$.

System S_1 is ε-simulated by S_2, denoted $S_1 \preceq_\varepsilon S_2$, if there exists an ε-approximate simulation relation from S_1 to S_2.
    Relation $\mathcal{R}$ in (7) is an ε-approximate bisimulation relation between S_1 and S_2 if

– $\mathcal{R}$ is an ε-approximate simulation relation from S_1 to S_2, and
– $\mathcal{R}^{-1}$ is an ε-approximate simulation relation from S_2 to S_1.

Systems S_1 and S_2 are ε-bisimilar, denoted $S_1 \cong_\varepsilon S_2$, if there exists an ε-approximate bisimulation relation between S_1 and S_2.

Remark 1. The definition above extends the classical definition of bisimulation equivalence of [17,18] for concurrent processes, to the class of metric systems in the sense of Definition 2; when condition (ii) is removed, it becomes an adaptation to systems of the one given in [17,18] for concurrent processes. It slightly differs from the one given in [12] where it is assumed that sets $Y_1 = Y_2$ are metric spaces with metric $\mathbf{d}$, and conditions (ii) and (iii) are replaced by

$$\mathbf{d}(H_1(x_1), H_2(x_2)) \leq \varepsilon, \forall (x_1, x_2) \in \mathcal{R}.$$

We can now state the following result.

Theorem 2. *Consider a pair of metric systems* $S_i = (X_i, X_{0,i}, U_i, \underset{i}{\longrightarrow}, Y_i, H_i)$, $i = 1, 2$, *with* X_1 *and* X_2 *subsets of some metric set* X *equipped with metric* $\mathbf{d}$ *and suppose that* $S_1 \preceq_\varepsilon S_2$. *Consider a set* $\mathcal{F}_1 \subseteq X_1$ *of faulty states for* S_1 *and define the set* $\mathcal{F}_2 = \mathcal{B}_\varepsilon(\mathcal{F}_1) \cap X_2$ *of faulty states for system* S_2. *If* S_2 *is* $(\rho_2, \mathcal{F}_2)$–*diagnosable for some accuracy* $\rho_2 \in \mathbb{R}^+$ *then,* S_1 *is* $(\rho_1, \mathcal{F}_1)$–*diagnosable for all* $\rho_1 \geq \rho_2 + 2\varepsilon$.

Before giving the proof we point out that since $S_1 \preceq_\varepsilon S_2$, set $\mathcal{F}_2$ is nonempty.

Proof. Let $\mathcal{R}$ be an ε–approximate simulation from S_1 to S_2 which exists because $S_1 \preceq_\varepsilon S_2$. By contradiction, suppose that S_1 is not $(\rho_1, \mathcal{F}_1)$–diagnosable, with some $\rho_1 \geq \rho_2 + 2\varepsilon$. Then, for any $\Delta \in \mathbb{N}$ there exists a state run

$$x^f(0) \, x^f(1) \, \cdots$$

of S_1 with output run

$$y^f(0) \, y^f(1) \, \cdots \tag{8}$$

such that for some $\mathbf{t} > 0$

$$\left(x^f(\mathbf{t}) \in \mathcal{F}_1 \right) \wedge \left(x^f(t) \notin \mathcal{F}_1, \forall t \in [0; \mathbf{t} - 1] \right), \tag{9}$$

and a state run

$$x^s(0) \, x^s(1) \, \cdots$$

of S_1 with output run

$$y^s(0) \, y^s(1) \, \cdots \tag{10}$$

such that

$$x^s(t) \notin \mathcal{B}_{\rho_1}(\mathcal{F}_1), \forall t \in [0; \mathbf{t} + \Delta], \tag{11}$$

and

$$y^f(t) = y^s(t), \forall t \in [0; \mathbf{t}]. \tag{12}$$

Since $S_1 \preceq_\varepsilon S_2$, by (9) there exists a state run

$$\xi^f(0) \, \xi^f(1) \, \cdots \tag{13}$$

of S_2 and some $\mathbf{t}' \in [0; \mathbf{t}]$ such that

$$\left(\xi^f(\mathbf{t}') \in \mathcal{R}(\mathcal{F}_1) \right) \wedge \left((\mathbf{t} = 0) \vee (\xi^f(t) \notin \mathcal{R}(\mathcal{F}_1), \forall t \in [0; \mathbf{t}' - 1]) \right) \tag{14}$$

with output run

$$\eta^f(0)\,\eta^f(1)\,\ldots$$

coinciding with the corresponding output run (8) of S_1, i.e.

$$\eta^f(t) = y^f(t), \forall t \in [0; \mathbf{t}]. \tag{15}$$

Since by definition of $\mathcal{R}$, see condition (ii) of Definition 5,

$$\mathcal{R}(\mathcal{F}_1) \subseteq \mathcal{B}_\varepsilon(\mathcal{F}_1) \cap X_2,$$

and, since $\mathcal{B}_\varepsilon(\mathcal{F}_1) \cap X_2 = \mathcal{F}_2$ by definition of $\mathcal{F}_2$, condition (14) implies for some $\mathbf{t}'' \in [0; \mathbf{t}']$

$$\left(\xi^f(\mathbf{t}'') \in \mathcal{F}_2\right) \wedge \left((\mathbf{t}' = 0) \vee (\xi^f(t) \notin \mathcal{F}_2, \forall t \in [0; \mathbf{t}'' - 1])\right). \tag{16}$$

Since $S_1 \preceq_\varepsilon S_2$, by (11) there exists a state run

$$\xi^s(0)\,\xi^s(1)\,\ldots \tag{17}$$

of S_2 with output run

$$\eta^s(0)\,\eta^s(1)\,\ldots$$

coinciding with the corresponding output run (10) of S_1, i.e.

$$\eta^s(t) = y^s(t), \forall t \in [0; \mathbf{t}], \tag{18}$$

and such that

$$\xi^s(t) \notin \mathcal{R}(\mathcal{B}_{\rho_1}(\mathcal{F}_1)), \forall t \in [0; \mathbf{t} + \Delta],$$

implying

$$\xi^s(t) \notin \mathcal{B}_{\rho_1 - \varepsilon}(\mathcal{F}_1), \forall t \in [0; \mathbf{t} + \Delta]. \tag{19}$$

Since by assumption, $\rho_1 - 2\varepsilon \geq \rho_2$ we get

$$\mathcal{B}_{\rho_1 - \varepsilon}(\mathcal{F}_1) = \mathcal{B}_{\rho_1 - 2\varepsilon}(\mathcal{B}_\varepsilon(\mathcal{F}_1)) \supseteq \mathcal{B}_{\rho_2}(\mathcal{B}_\varepsilon(\mathcal{F}_1))$$

and hence, condition (19) implies

$$\xi^s(t) \notin \mathcal{B}_{\rho_2}(\mathcal{B}_\varepsilon(\mathcal{F}_1)), \forall t \in [0; \mathbf{t} + \Delta]$$

from which,

$$\xi^s(t) \notin \mathcal{B}_{\rho_2}(\mathcal{B}_\varepsilon(\mathcal{F}_1) \cap X_2) = \mathcal{B}_{\rho_2}(\mathcal{F}_2), \forall t \in [0; \mathbf{t} + \Delta]. \tag{20}$$

Conditions (12), (15) and (18) imply

$$\eta^f(t) = \eta^s(t), \forall t \in [0; \mathbf{t}']. \tag{21}$$

Hence, there exists a pair of state runs (13) and (17) of S_2 such that for any $\Delta \in \mathbb{N}$ conditions (16), (20) and (21) hold, i.e., the output runs corresponding to the state runs (13) and (17) coincide, and ξ^f terminates in a faulty state while ξ^s does not. We then conclude that S_2 is not $(\rho_2, \mathcal{F}_2)$–diagnosable and a contradiction holds.

The result above is important because it allows checking approximate diagnosability of a metric system S_1 on the basis of approximate diagnosability of a metric system S_2 for which $S_1 \preceq_\varepsilon S_2$. Implications of this fact on the analysis of approximate diagnosability for nonlinear systems are discussed in the next section.

6 Application to Diagnosability of Nonlinear Systems

The class of nonlinear systems we consider in this section is described by

$$\Sigma : \begin{cases} x(t+1) = f(x(t), u(t)), \\ y(t) = \begin{bmatrix} I_p & 0 \end{bmatrix} x(t), \\ x(0) \in \mathcal{X}_0, x(t) \in \mathbb{R}^n, u(t) \in U, y(t) \in \mathbb{R}^p, t \in \mathbb{N}, \end{cases} \tag{22}$$

where:

- $x(t)$, $u(t)$ and $y(t)$ denote, respectively, the state, the input and the output, at time $t \in \mathbb{N}$;
- $\mathbb{R}^n$ is the state space;
- $\mathcal{X}_0 \subseteq \mathbb{R}^n$ is the set of initial states;
- $U \subseteq \mathbb{R}^m$ is the input set;
- $\mathbb{R}^p$ is the output space with $p < n$;
- $f : \mathbb{R}^n \times \mathbb{R}^m \to \mathbb{R}^n$ is the vector field;
- I_p is the identity matrix in $\mathbb{R}^p$.

We assume that $\mathcal{X}_0$ is compact, U is compact and contains the origin 0_m and, f is continuous in its arguments and satisfies $f(0_n, 0_m) = 0_n$. We denote by $\mathcal{U}$ the collection of input functions from $\mathbb{N}$ to U. From (22), we are assuming that the output variables of Σ are a selection of the state variables. The general case of nonlinear output functions can be considered at the expense of a heavier notation, as done in our recent work [19]. Moreover, this assumption holds in many concrete applications.

In the sequel we make the following

Assumption 3. *Inputs $u(.) \in \mathcal{U}$ of Σ are not available to an external observer and output $y(t)$ of Σ at time $t \in \mathbb{N}$ is only available through its quantization $[y(t)]_\eta^p$, where $\eta \in \mathbb{R}^+$ is the quantization parameter.*

In the sequel we will reinterpret the results reported in [7] concerning approximate diagnosability of the nonlinear system Σ in the general framework of approximate diagnosability of metric systems. To this purpose we start by providing a representation of Σ in terms of metric systems.

Definition 6. *Given Σ, define the system*

$$S(\Sigma) = (X, X_0, U, \longrightarrow, X_m, Y, H),$$

where

- $X = \mathbb{R}^n$;
- $X_0 = \mathcal{X}_0$;
- U *coincides with the set U in (22)*;
- $x \xrightarrow{u} x^+$, *if* $x^+ = f(x, u)$;
- $Y = \mathbb{R}^p$;
- $H(x) = \begin{bmatrix} I_p & 0 \end{bmatrix} x$, *for all* $x \in X$.

System $S(\Sigma)$ is metric because $X = \mathbb{R}^n$ can be equipped with a metric $\mathbf{d}$; in the sequel we choose

$$\mathbf{d}(x, x') = \|x - x'\|, x, x' \in \mathbb{R}^n. \tag{23}$$

Metric system $S(\Sigma)$ is deterministic and preserves many important properties of Σ such as, for example, reachability properties. Moreover, the following result holds.

Proposition 2. *Nonlinear system Σ is $(\rho, \mathcal{F})$–diagnosable as in Definition 2 of [7] if and only if metric system $S(\Sigma)$ is $(\rho, \mathcal{F})$–diagnosable as in Definition 3.*

Proof. Straightforward consequence of Definition 2 in [7] and of Definition 3.

By the result above, in the sequel we refer without ambiguity to approximate diagnosability of Σ and of $S(\Sigma)$ with the understanding that approximate diagnosability of Σ is given in the sense of Definition 2 in [7], while approximate diagnosability of $S(\Sigma)$ is given in the sense of Definition 3.

The result above allows using the abstract framework of metric systems to study approximate diagnosability of Σ. However, algorithms proposed in Sect. 4 cannot be applied to $S(\Sigma)$ because $S(\Sigma)$ has an infinite number of states and an infinite number of inputs, and hence, it is not symbolic. For this reason, we provide hereafter an approximation of $S(\Sigma)$ that is symbolic.

Given $\theta \in \mathbb{R}^+$ and $x \in \mathbb{R}^n$, we denote

$$\mathcal{B}^n_{[-\theta, \theta[}(x) = \{y \in \mathbb{R}^n | y(i) \in [-\theta + x(i), \theta + x(i)[, i \in [1; n]\}.$$

where here x(i) and y(i) denote the i-th element of vectors x and y, respectively. Note that for any $\theta \in \mathbb{R}^+$, the collection of $\mathcal{B}^n_{[-\theta, \theta[}(x)$ with x ranging in $2\theta \mathbb{Z}^n$ is a partition of $\mathbb{R}^n$. We now define the quantization function. Given a positive $n \in \mathbb{N}$ and a quantization parameter $\theta \in \mathbb{R}^+$, the quantizer in $\mathbb{R}^n$ with accuracy θ is a function

$$[\cdot]^n_\theta : \mathbb{R}^n \to 2\theta \mathbb{Z}^n,$$

associating to any $x \in \mathbb{R}^n$ the unique vector $[x]^n_\theta \in 2\theta \mathbb{Z}^n$ such that $x \in \mathcal{B}^n_{[-\theta, \theta[}([x]^n_\theta)$. Definition of $[\cdot]^n_\theta$ naturally extends to sets $X \subseteq \mathbb{R}^n$ when $[X]^n_\theta$ is interpreted as the image of X through function $[\cdot]^n_\theta$.

We can now give the following

Definition 7. *Given Σ, a state and output quantization parameter $\eta \in \mathbb{R}^+$ and an input quantization parameter $\mu \in \mathbb{R}^+$, define the system*

$$S_{\eta,\mu}(\Sigma) = (X_{\eta,\mu}, X_{\eta,\mu,0}, U_{\eta,\mu}, \xrightarrow[\eta,\mu]{} , Y_{\eta,\mu}, H_{\eta,\mu}),$$

where:

- $X_{\eta,\mu} = [\mathbb{R}^n]_\eta^n$;
- $X_{\eta,\mu,0} = [\mathcal{X}_0]_\eta^n$;
- $U_{\eta,\mu} = [U]_\mu^m$;
- $\xi \xrightarrow[\eta,\mu]{v} \xi^+$, *if* $\xi^+ = [f(\xi,v)]_\eta^n$;
- $Y_{\eta,\mu} = [\mathbb{R}^p]_\eta^p$;
- $H_{\eta,\mu}(\xi) = \begin{bmatrix} I_p & 0 \end{bmatrix} \xi$, *for all* $\xi \in X_{\eta,\mu}$.

The basic idea in the construction above is to replace each state x in Σ by its quantized value $\xi = [x]_\eta^n$ and each input $u \in U$ by its quantized value $v = [u]_\mu^m$ in $S_{\eta,\mu}(\Sigma)$. Accordingly, the evolution of system Σ with initial state x and input v to state $x^+ = f(\xi, v)$, is captured by the transition $\xi \xrightarrow{v}{\eta} \xi^+$ in system $S_{\eta,\mu}(\Sigma)$, where ξ and ξ^+ are the quantized values of x and x^+, respectively, i.e., $\xi = [x]_\eta^n$ and $\xi^+ = [x^+]_\eta^n$. System $S_{\eta,\mu}(\Sigma)$ is metric; in the sequel we use the metric $\mathbf{d}$ in (23); this choice is allowed because $X_{\eta,\mu} \subset X$. Moreover, by definition of the transition relation $\xrightarrow[\eta,\mu]{}$, system $S_{\eta,\mu}(\Sigma)$ is deterministic. By definition of $X_{\eta,\mu}$ and $U_{\eta,\mu}$, system $S_{\eta,\mu}(\Sigma)$ is countable. We now consider the following

Assumption 4. *Given the nonlinear system Σ, there exists a locally Lipschitz function*

$$V : \mathbb{R}^n \times \mathbb{R}^n \to \mathbb{R}_0^+,$$

which satisfies the following inequalities for some $\mathcal{K}_\infty$ functions $\underline{\alpha}$, $\overline{\alpha}$, λ and $\mathcal{K}$ function σ:

(i) $\underline{\alpha}(\|x - x'\|) \leq V(x, x') \leq \overline{\alpha}(\|x - x'\|)$, for any $x, x' \in \mathbb{R}^n$;
(ii) $V(f(x, u), f(x', u')) - V(x, x') \leq -\lambda(V(x, x')) + \sigma(\|u - u'\|)$, for any $x, x' \in \mathbb{R}^n$ and any $u, u' \in U$.

The function V is called an incremental input–to–state stable (δ–ISS) Lyapunov function [1,2] for Σ. Assumption 4 has been shown in [2] to be a sufficient condition for Σ to fulfill the δ–ISS property [1,2].

We now recall two results from our previous work [7], which are instrumental for the subsequent developments.

Proposition 3 [7]. *If the nonlinear system Σ satisfies Assumption 4, then the metric system $S_{\eta,\mu}(\Sigma)$ is symbolic.*

Proposition 4 [7]. *Suppose that Assumption 4 holds and let L be a Lipschitz constant of function V in $\mathbb{R}^n \times \mathbb{R}^n$. Then, for any desired accuracy $\varepsilon \in \mathbb{R}^+$ and for any quantization parameters $\eta, \mu \in \mathbb{R}^+$ satisfying the following inequalities*

$$\begin{aligned} L\eta + \sigma(\mu) &\leq (\lambda \circ \underline{\alpha})(\varepsilon), \\ \overline{\alpha}(\eta) &\leq \underline{\alpha}(\varepsilon), \end{aligned} \tag{24}$$

systems $S(\Sigma)$ and $S_{\eta,\mu}(\Sigma)$ are ε–bisimilar.

We now have all the ingredients to establish connections between approximate diagnosability of $S_{\eta,\mu}(\Sigma)$ and approximate diagnosability of Σ. Given a set $\mathcal{F} \subseteq \mathbb{R}^n$ of faulty states for Σ and an accuracy $\varepsilon \in \mathbb{R}^+$, consider the sets

$$\begin{aligned} \mathcal{F}_\varepsilon &= \mathcal{B}_\varepsilon(\mathcal{F}) \cap [\mathbb{R}^n]_\eta^n, \\ \mathcal{F}_\varepsilon' &= \{x \in \mathcal{F} : \mathcal{B}_\varepsilon(x) \subseteq \mathcal{F}\} \cap [\mathbb{R}^n]_\eta^n. \end{aligned}$$

Corollary 1. *Consider the nonlinear system Σ as in (22) satisfying Assumption 4 and a set $\mathcal{F} \subseteq \mathbb{R}^n$. Consider a triplet $\varepsilon, \eta, \mu \in \mathbb{R}^+$ of parameters satisfying (24). The following statements hold:*

(i) *If $S_{\eta,\mu}(\Sigma)$ is $(k\eta, \mathcal{F}_\varepsilon)$–diagnosable, for some $k \in \mathbb{N}$, then Σ is $(\rho, \mathcal{F})$–diagnosable, for any $\rho > 2\varepsilon + k\eta$.*

(ii) *Suppose that set $\mathcal{F}$ is with interior and parameter $\varepsilon \in \mathbb{R}^+$ is such that[1] $\mathcal{F}_\varepsilon' \neq \varnothing$. If Σ is $(\rho, \mathcal{F})$–diagnosable, for some $\rho \in \mathbb{R}_0^+$, then $S_{\eta,\mu}(\Sigma)$ is $(k'\eta, \mathcal{F}_\varepsilon')$–diagnosable, for any integer $k' > \min\{h \in \mathbb{N} : (\rho + 2\varepsilon) \leq h\eta\}$.*

Proof. Direct application of Theorem 2 and Propositions 2 and 4.

The statement of the corollary above coincides with Theorem 1 of [7]. Here a very simple proof is derived based on the use of metric systems. This result is important because it allows checking approximate diagnosability of Σ presenting an infinite number of states and inputs, for which there are no tools available in the current literature, by checking approximate diagnosability of $S_{\eta,\mu}(\Sigma)$ that is symbolic so that the algorithms presented in Sect. 4 can be applied. In particular, while statement (i) in the result above is useful to check if Σ is $(\rho, \mathcal{F})$–diagnosable, statement (ii) can be used in its logical negation form as a tool to check if Σ is not $(\rho, \mathcal{F})$–diagnosable.

Remark 2. In this section we assumed the existence of a δ–ISS Lyapunov function V for the nonlinear system Σ, see Assumption 4. Under this assumption, by Proposition 4, metric system $S_{\eta,\mu}(\Sigma)$ approximates metric system $S(\Sigma)$ in the sense of approximate bisimulation for any desired accuracy. Since Theorem 2, that is employed in Corollary 1, only requires the existence of an approximate simulation between the metric systems involved, one can in fact construct a symbolic metric system that is an approximate simulation, and not an approximate bisimulation, of the original nonlinear system. To this purpose, one can use the symbolic models proposed in [30] that are in approximate (and *alternating*) simulation with the original system and only require the mild assumption of incremental forward completeness of the nonlinear system.

---

[1] Since $\mathcal{F}$ is with interior there always exists $\varepsilon \in \mathbb{R}^+$ satisfying $\mathcal{F}_\varepsilon' \neq \varnothing$.

7   Conclusions

In this paper, we proposed a new notion of diagnosability, called approximate diagnosability, for the general class of metric systems. We first provided a characterization of approximate diagnosability for metric symbolic systems and analyzed the computational complexity of the proposed algorithms. We then established the relation between approximate diagnosability and approximate simulation. Application of the proposed results to approximate diagnosability of nonlinear systems was finally illustrated and discussed.

Acknowledgments. We would like to thank our Master student Andreu Llabrés for fruitful discussions on the topic of the present paper.

References

1. Angeli, D.: A Lyapunov approach to incremental stability properties. IEEE Trans. Autom. Control **47**(3), 410–421 (2002)
2. Bayer, B., Burger, M., Allgower, F.: Discrete-time incremental ISS: a framework for robust NMPS. In: European Control Conference, Zurick, Switzerland, pp. 2068–2073, July 2013
3. Bayoudh, M., Travé-Massuyes, L., Olive, X.: Hybrid systems diagnosability by abstracting faulty continuous dynamics. In: Proceedings of the 17th International Principles Diagnosis Workshop, pp. 9–15 (2006)
4. Bayoudh, M., Travé-Massuyes, L., Olive, X.: Hybrid systems diagnosis by coupling continuous and discrete event techniques. In: Proceedings of the IFAC World Congress, pp. 7265–7270 (2008)
5. Benosman,M.: A survey of some recent results on nonlinear fault tolerant control. Math. Probl. Eng. **2010** (2010)
6. De Persis, C.: Detecting faults from encoded information. In: Proceedings of the 42nd IEEE Conference on Decision and Control, pp. 947–952 (2013)
7. De Santis, E., Pola, G., Di Benedetto, M.D.: On approximate diagnosability of nonlinear systems (2017). arXiv:1704.02138 [math.OC]
8. Debouk, R., Malik, R., Brandin, B.: A modular architecture for diagnosis of discrete event systems. In: Proceedings of the 41th Conference on Decision and Control, Las Vegas, Nevada, USA, pp. 417–422, December 2002
9. Deng, Y., D'Innocenzo, A., Di Benedetto, M.D., Di Gennaro, S., Julius, A.A.: Verification of hybrid automata diagnosability with measurement uncertainty. IEEE Trans. Autom. Control **61**, 982–993 (2016)
10. De Santis, E., Di Benedetto, M.D.: Observability and diagnosability of finite state systems: a unifying framework. Automatica **81**, 115–122 (2017, to appear). arXiv:1608.03195 [math.OC]
11. Gao, Z., Cecati, C., Ding, S.X.: A survey of fault diagnosis and fault-tolerant techniques-part I: fault diagnosis with model-based and signal-based approaches. IEEE Trans. Industr. Electron. **62**, 3757–3767 (2015)
12. Girard, A., Pappas, G.J.: Approximation metrics for discrete and continuous systems. IEEE Trans. Autom. Control **52**(5), 782–798 (2007)
13. Jiang, J.: Fault-tolerant control systems - an introductory overview. Acta Autom. Sinica **31**, 161–174 (2005)

14. Lunze, J.: Diagnosis of quantized systems based on a timed discrete-event model. IEEE Trans. Man Cybern. Part A Syst. Hum. **30**, 322–335 (2000)
15. Lunze, J., Richter, J.: Reconfigurable fault-tolerant control: a tutorial introduction. Eur. J. Control **144**, 359–386 (2008)
16. Di Benedetto, M.D., Di Gennaro, S., D'Innocenzo, A.: Verification of hybrid automata diagnosability by abstraction. IEEE Trans. Autom. Control **56**, 2050–2061 (2011)
17. Milner, R.: Communication and Concurrency. Prentice Hall, Upper Saddle River (1989)
18. Park, D.: Concurrency and automata on infinite sequences. In: Deussen, P. (ed.) GI-TCS 1981. LNCS, vol. 104, pp. 167–183. Springer, Heidelberg (1981). doi:10.1007/BFb0017309
19. Pola, G., Di Benedetto, M.D.: Approximate supervisory control of nonlinear systems with outputs. In: Proceedings of the 56th IEEE Conference on Decision and Control (2017, to appear)
20. Ricker, S.L., van Schuppen, J.H.: Decentralized failure diagnosis with asynchronous communication between diagnosers. In: Proceedings of the European Control Conference, Porto, Portugal (2001)
21. Sampath, M., Sengupta, R., Lafortune, S., Sinnamohideen, K., Teneketzis, D.: Diagnosability of discrete-event systems. IEEE Trans. Autom. Control **40**(9), 1555–1575 (1995)
22. Schmidt, K.W.: Verification of modular diagnosability with local specifications for discrete-event systems. IEEE Trans. Syst. Man Cybern. **43**(5), 1130–1140 (2013)
23. Stengel, R.: Intelligent failure-tolerant control. IEEE Control Syst. Mag. **11**, 14–23 (1991)
24. Su, R., Wonham, W.M.: Global and local consistencies in distributed fault diagnosis for discrete-event systems. IEEE Trans. Autom. Control **50**(12), 1923–1935 (2005)
25. Tabuada, P.: Verification and Control of Hybrid Systems: A Symbolic Approach. Springer, Dordrecht (2009)
26. Tripakis, S.: Fault diagnosis for timed automata. In: Damm, W., Olderog, E.-R. (eds.) FTRTFT 2002. LNCS, vol. 2469, pp. 205–221. Springer, Heidelberg (2002). doi:10.1007/3-540-45739-9_14
27. Wang, W., Girard, A.R., Lafortune, S., Lin, F.: On codiagnosability and coobservability with dynamic observations. IEEE Trans. Autom. Control **56**(7), 1551–1566 (2011)
28. Wang, W., Lafortune, S., Girard, A.R., Lin, F.: Optimal sensor activation for diagnosing discrete event systems. Automatica **46**, 1165–1175 (2010)
29. Zad, S.H., Kwong, R.H., Wonham, W.M.: Fault diagnosis in discrete-event systems: framework and model reduction. IEEE Trans. Autom. Control **48**(7), 51–65 (2003)
30. Zamani, M., Mazo, M., Pola, G., Tabuada, P.: Symbolic models for nonlinear control systems without stability assumptions. IEEE Trans. Autom. Control **57**(7), 1804–1809 (2012)
31. Zaytoon, J., Lafortune, S.: Overview of fault diagnosis methods for discrete event systems. Annu. Rev. Control **37**(2), 308–320 (2013)
32. Zhang, Y., Jiang, J.: Bibliographical review and reconfigurable fault-tolerant control systems. Annu. Rev. Control **32**, 229–252 (2008)

A Hazard Analysis Method for Systematic Identification of Safety Requirements for User Interface Software in Medical Devices

Paolo Masci[1]([✉]), Yi Zhang[2], Paul Jones[2], and José C. Campos[1]

[1] INESC TEC, Universidade Do Minho, Braga, Portugal
{paolo.masci,jose.c.campos}@inesctec.pt
[2] US Food and Drug Administration, Silver Spring, USA
{yi.zhang2,paul.jones}@fda.hhs.gov

Abstract. Formal methods technologies have the potential to verify the usability and safety of user interface (UI) software design in medical devices, enabling significant reductions in use errors and consequential safety incidents with such devices. This however depends on comprehensive and verifiable safety requirements to leverage these techniques for detecting and preventing flaws in UI software that can induce use errors. This paper presents a hazard analysis method that extends Leveson's System Theoretic Process Analysis (STPA) with a comprehensive set of causal factor categories, so as to provide developers with clear guidelines for systematic identification of use-related hazards associated with medical devices, their causes embedded in UI software design, and safety requirements for mitigating such hazards. The method is evaluated with a case study on the Gantry-2 radiation therapy system, which demonstrates that (1) as compared to standard STPA, our method allowed us to identify more UI software design issues likely to cause use-related hazards; and (2) the identified UI software design issues facilitated the definition of precise, verifiable safety requirements for UI software, which could be readily formalized in verification tools such as Prototype Verification System (PVS).

Keywords: Requirements identification/formalization · User interface software · Medical devices

1 Introduction

Use errors with medical devices are a leading cause of device incidents reported in the healthcare domain (e.g., see [1,15]). Errors in user interface (UI) software in medical devices, including design flaws and implementation mistakes, can disrupt expected device-user interaction and induce use errors. For example, a diabetes management mobile app was recalled in the U.S. because its UI software could erroneously reset the recommended insulin bolus dosage when the user changes the smartphone's orientation, which might cause the user to inadvertently command and receive unsafe insulin therapies [9].

© Springer International Publishing AG (outside the US) 2017
A. Cimatti and M. Sirjani (Eds.): SEFM 2017, LNCS 10469, pp. 284–299, 2017.
DOI: 10.1007/978-3-319-66197-1_18

It is thus crucial to the safety of medical devices to systematically assess their UI software design and ensure that design issues likely inducing use errors are appropriately addressed. Formal methods have the potential to enable such rigorous assessment. For example, our previous research shows that theorem proving can be used to detect latent flaws in data entry software [19]. In fact, the formal methods community has devoted substantial effort on methods and tools for analyzing various aspects of UI software design, including user tasks [3,26], cognitive errors [28,29], and general usability principles [4,6,10,25]. But little attention has been given to tools and methods that can support systematic identification and definition of use-related safety requirements for UI software design, even though the availability of such safety requirements has great impact to the applicability and effectiveness of formal methods in assessing UI software.

Current industrial practices rely on hazard analysis techniques to explore safety hazards associated with a system and formulate requirements to mitigate the identified hazards. However, existing hazard analysis techniques do not provide specialized assistance in analyzing UI software design. For example, Preliminary Hazard Analysis [5] and Root Cause Analysis [13] merely rely on group brainstorming to explore use hazards and their causes in safety-critical systems. Other more systematic methods such as Fault Tree Analysis [16], FMEA [30], and their variants focus on component failures or deviations in physical parameters (as in HAZOP [14]), rather than use hazards and their causes in UI software design. Whilst some variants of HAZOP can be used to analyze use errors (e.g., see [7,12]), their focus is mainly on assessing compatibility with given user tasks.

Leveson's System Theoretic Process Analysis (STPA) [17] is a relatively new hazard analysis method that can be utilized to identify use-related hazards in control systems, and system design issues contributing to these hazards. This method, however, offers limited guidance on formulating hypotheses on what aspects of UI software design could affect the usability and safety of a system under analysis. STPA requires developers to exercise their experience and expertise to find answers to the key question: *What UI software design features could induce the user to operate or interact with a system unsafely?*

In this paper, we extend the standard STPA analysis to provide developers with clear guidelines in finding the answer to this key question. This is done by extending standard STPA with a set of casual factor categories, which are tailored to guide developers in systematically examining UI software design against common use-related safety concerns and widely-accepted design principles. We also refine the standard STPA analysis process such that developers can utilize the casual factor categories to identify UI software design issues and define corresponding safety requirements for realistic medical device systems.

Contribution. This paper makes the following contributions: (i) a novel method that augments STPA to enable a more detailed analysis of UI software in medical devices in terms of safety and usability; (ii) a case study on an experimental medical device demonstrating the applicability and benefits of our method; and (iii) formalization in PVS [24] of natural language safety requirements produced in the case study, which results in the definition of a *safety reference model* [20] that encapsulates the semantics of the requirements against which UI software design must be verified.

2   Background on STPA

STPA focuses on early identification of safety hazards in control systems and their causes in system design. It considers the system under analysis as a *control model*, which in its simplest form includes a control loop with an automated controller and a controlled process. The standard STPA process is carried out in three steps (see the left-hand side of Fig. 1):

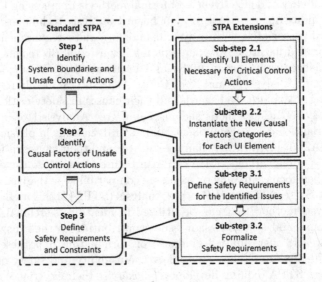

Fig. 1. Enhanced STPA process.

Step 1: Identify system boundaries and unsafe control actions. In this step, developers identify all system elements that could impact, directly or indirectly, system safety. Potential hazards associated with the system are explored in the form of *unsafe control actions* (UCAs) performed by system elements. To identify use-related hazards, a *human operator model* can be introduced to the system's control model to capture hypotheses about the operator's knowledge and understanding of how the system works. STPA guides developers to explore four types of UCAs potentially performed by system elements, including the human operator:

- A control action required for safety is not provided or not followed (e.g., an emergency stop button is not pressed when necessary).
- An unsafe control action is provided that leads to a hazard (e.g., the delivery of a therapy with an excessive dose of radiation).

- A potentially safe control action is provided at the wrong time or in the wrong order (e.g., a button for stopping the delivery of radiation is pressed too late).
- A potentially safe control action is stopped too soon or applied for too long (e.g., a button for decreasing the volume of an alarm is pressed for too long and, as a result, the alarm gets disabled).

Step 2: Identification of causal factors. At this step, developers examine the system's design to identify issues (also called *causal factors*) enabling UCAs. For UCAs from the human operator, STPA recommends to explore three categories of causal factors:

- **Feedback:** feedback provided to the operator is inadequate, missing, or delayed. An example is that the system does not provide an alarm on its UI to inform the operator of abnormal system conditions.
- **Mental Model:** the operator's perception or understanding of how the system works is inconsistent, incomplete, or incorrect. For example, using a non-standard color/symbol to display an alarm on the UI can be easily misunderstood by the operator.
- **External Information:** wrong or missing inputs or external information. This category explores issues related to information communicated to the operator by elements outside the control model. For example, a procedure described in the user manual is wrong, or a prescription used by the operator to setup the therapy contains incorrect information.

Step 3: Define safety requirements and constraints. Developers define testable safety requirements or constraints to address the identified casual factors, and in turn prevent or mitigate UCAs.

3   Enhanced STPA Analysis

We enhanced the standard STPA analysis with the aim of providing developers with additional guidance in systematic identification of UI software issues that likely induce human operators to perform UCAs. The enhancement is realized by refining the standard STPA causal factor categories with 16 new categories that are specialized for identifying UI software issues in medical devices.

3.1   New Causal Factor Categories

The new casual factor categories are derived from usability heuristics [23] and UI design guidelines defined in medical device usability standards (ANSI/AAMI HE75 and ISO 62366-1). For each category, we present a mnemonic name, a definition, and a rationale explaining its relevance to device usability and safety.

Categories Refining STPA Feedback

- **F1: Consistency of feedback.** Feedback for control actions or events that are conceptually similar is not provided using the same modalities (e.g., visual, auditory, haptic) or the same UI elements. *Rationale: Inconsistent feedback leads to confusion and incorrect user actions.*
- **F2: Complexity of feedback:** Feedback for frequent actions or important events (e.g., system failure or patient-related emergencies) requires observing and understanding multiple information resources. *Rationale: In clinical settings, operators may become distracted by other tasks or interrupted during device use. Because of this, they could fail to monitor and analyze feedback from multiple information resources.*
- **F3: Availability of feedback:** Feedback reporting important information (e.g., therapy parameters) or events (e.g., change of device modes) is erroneous, not visible, partially visible, or is visible at the wrong time or for a too short period of time. *Rationale: Operators could lose situation awareness during critical operations if relevant information is not reported on the UI.*
- **F4: Salience of feedback:** Feedback reporting important information or events is not prominent or easy to locate on the UI, or secondary information/events are erroneously more prominent than critical information/events. *Rationale: Feedback on the UI should promote selective attention on information that is important for correct decision-making.*

Categories Refining STPA Mental Model

- **M1: Reversibility of control actions:** Functions for reversing the effect of control actions are not available. *Rationale: UI functions such as undo, stop, cancel, resume should be available to the operator to recover from errors.*
- **M2: Responsiveness to control actions:** The effect of critical control actions is not reported to the operator in a timely manner. *Rationale: If feedback for control actions is delayed, users could fail to realize whether the control actions on the UI have been successfully recognized by the system.*
- **M3: Consistency of controls:** The same UI controls produce different effects in conceptually similar situations, or UI controls that are conceptually similar require different interaction styles. *Rationale: Consistent UI controls facilitate the formation of accurate and complete mental models of how to interact with the system.*
- **M4: Complexity of controls:** Frequently used or critical UI controls require unreasonably complex manipulation or unreasonably long sequence of user actions. *Rationale: Users could fail to perform common or critical actions/tasks if too much time or effort is necessary to complete such actions/tasks with the available UI functions.*
- **M5: Predictability of controls:** The UI does not provide means to help the user anticipate the effects or the consequences of control actions. *Rationale: Predictable UI controls facilitate the formation of an accurate and complete mental model of how to interact with the system.*

- **M6: Forgiveness for erroneous control actions:** Safety interlocks are not available to prevent accidental activation of critical controls or block-/mitigate foreseeable use errors. *Rationale: Lack of built-in safeguards for known/common use errors (e.g., manipulation errors due to variability in human performance or lack of attention) could lead to catastrophic failures.*
- **M7: Availability of controls:** Control widgets necessary for safe operation are partially available or not available on the UI, or they are available at the wrong time or for a too short period of time. *Rationale: UI functions should be provided to allow operators to perform necessary control actions.*
- **M8: Affordance of controls:** The visual appearance (shape, label, etc.), relative position, and behavior of UI controls are not consistent with stereo-typical knowledge about their function. *Rationale: Design features of UI widgets should promote correct understanding of the action-effect relation of the UI function associated with the widget.*
- **M9: Consistency with clinical workflows:** Workflows supported by the UI software are not consistent with best or actual clinical practice. *Rationale: The UI software design should support and enhance existing clinical workflows rather than disrupting them.*

Categories Refining STPA External Information

- **E1: Availability of user manuals:** Information necessary to understand device feedback or operate the device are not available in the user manual. *Rational: User manuals should support the formation of a complete and correct mental model of UI software functions.*
- **E2: Consistency with user manuals:** Workflows described in the user manual are not consistent with the behavior of the device. *Rationale: The software development process should produce user manuals that are correct with respect to the UI software functions.*
- **E3: Complexity of user manuals:** Critical information in the user manual is mixed with non-critical information. *Rationale: Critical information (e.g., recovery procedures) should be readily accessible in the user manual.*

3.2   Process for Using the New Categories

Our method refines the standard STPA process to utilize the new casual factor categories in analyzing specific system designs. As illustrated in Fig. 1, Step 2 of the standard STPA process is decomposed into two sub-steps: Sub-step 2.1 identifies UI elements (displays, controls, etc.) used to perform critical control actions; and Sub-step 2.2 instantiates the new casual factor categories for each identified UI element to explore issues that could induce such UCAs.

Step 3 of the standard STPA process is also decomposed into two sub-steps. Sub-step 3.1 defines a set of natural language safety requirements to address the identified UI software issues. In their simplest form, safety requirements can be formulated as the logical negation of the corresponding design issue. For example, consider the design issue "Changing the smartphone orientation resets the recommended insulin bolus dosage". This issue would have been detected using category *affordance of controls*—stereotypical knowledge associates smartphone orientation changes with view mode changes (landscape/portrait). A safety requirements can therefore be defined as: *"Changing the smartphone orientation shall not reset/change the recommended insulin bolus dosage"*.

Natural language requirements are formalized in Sub-step 3.2, where the method presented in [20] can be adopted for such formalization. The formalization method in [20] identifies key notions and relations in the textual description, and then provides an interpretation to operationalize these notions and relations for a specific design. This process further clarifies the correspondence between requirements and UI software functionalities, and creates a *safety reference model*. Demonstrating equivalence between a UI software design and the safety reference model constitutes evidence that the UI design complies with given requirements.

4   Case Study: The Gantry-2 System

We have evaluated the applicability and potential benefit of our method on the Gantry-2 system, an experimental radiation therapy device for advanced cancer treatment. A team of researchers have applied the standard STPA to analyze the UI design of the Gantry-2 system, based on its preliminary design document [2]. We evaluated the UI software design in the Gantry-2 system and compared our results with [2]. To ensure fair comparison, our study was based on the same set of preliminary design documents, and the same control model and system boundaries, as those considered in [2]. Our study results (illustrated below) demonstrate that our method can help to identify not only all design issues reported in [2] but also new critical UI software issues that were not identified using the standard STPA.

Description of the system. The Gantry-2 system is a radiation therapy device for treatment of tumors attached to mobile organs (e.g., lungs). These tumors require continuous scanning of the patient to ensure correct delivery of radiation to the tumor cells. The operator is responsible for setting up the system for the patient, starting the treatment, monitoring the patient and the device state. These operations are carried out using controls and displays on the Gantry-2 consoles. The specific treatment plan for the patient is loaded by the operator before starting the treatment. The treatment planning software uses the treatment plan to configure automated controllers that will manage the delivery of radiation to the patient. Feedback loops necessary to monitor the patient status and the overall treatment delivery process are realized through beamline sensors and cameras installed in the facility. Full details of STPA control models representing the Gantry-2 system can be found in [2].

Analysis results using the new categories. Due to space limit, we only discuss the analysis of the following UCA: *"Treatment start command is activated even when there is no patient to be treated"*. Identifying UI software issues inducing other UCAs can be carried out similarly.

For this UCA, our analysis identified seven critical issues that were not reported in [2]. To help readers better understand the identified issues and in turn the benefits of our method, we present each of these issues as: a description of the issue, UI elements, and causal factors categories used to identify the issue; a *scenario* describing hazardous situations where the issue potentially induces the operator to perform the UCA under analysis; and *safety requirements* for addressing the issue. Note that the decision of whether it is worth implementing a given safety requirement in the final system depends on the level of risk addressed by the requirement, which can be estimated using standard risk matrices.

- **Issue 1:** UI software does not provide feedback when patient is not ready.
  - UI elements: Display.
  - Causal factor: Availability of feedback.
  - Scenario: Operator erroneously starts the treatment because the alert indicating patient not ready is not available on the UI.
  - **Requirement R1.** *"Patient not ready" alerts shall be displayed on the UI.*
- **Issue 2:** UI software displays patient not ready alerts on the main operator console but not on the remote console.
  - UI elements: Display on the main and remote consoles.
  - Causal factors: Consistency of feedback/Availability of feedback.
  - Scenario: Operator erroneously starts the treatment because inconsistent alerts on two consoles cause incorrect understanding of the patient readiness status.
  - **Requirement R2.** *"Patient not ready" alerts shall be displayed at all consoles.*
- **Issue 3:** UI software fails to display patient not ready alerts in certain system modes when it should.
  - UI elements: Display.
  - Causal factor: Availability of feedback.
  - Scenario: Operator erroneously starts the treatment because the alert "Patient not ready" is not displayed in the "Experimental Mode" (e.g., the patient readiness status is always set as "Ready" in this system mode, which incorrectly disables the alert).
  - **Requirement R3.** *"Patient not ready" alerts shall be displayed when the patient is not ready, regardless of the system's operation mode.*
- **Issue 4:** UI software fails to block the operator's accidental press on the start command (e.g., during system maintenance).
  - UI elements: Start command.
  - Causal factor: Forgiveness for erroneous control actions.
  - Scenario: Operator erroneously starts the treatment because the UI software fails to block the operator's accidental press of the start command when the patient is not ready.
  - **Requirement R4.** *UI software shall not accept a start treatment command when the patient readiness status is not ready.*

- **Issue 5:** If the treatment activation sequence is interrupted (e.g., due to power loss), UI software always resumes the sequence from where it was interrupted, and does not provide the operator means to stop/abort/restart the treatment activation sequence.
  - UI elements: UI commands involved in the treatment activation sequence.
  - Causal factor: Reversibility of control actions.
  - Scenario: Operator erroneously starts the treatment because the treatment activation sequence cannot be canceled.
  - **Requirement R5.** *A control to cancel the treatment activation sequence shall be available on all user interface screens.*
- **Issue 6:** UI software fails to provide timely feedback when the operator presses the start command, which causes the user to press the command multiple times and each press is registered as a legitimate command to deliver the treatment.
  - UI elements: Start command; Displays providing feedback to operator.
  - Causal factor: Responsiveness to control actions.
  - Scenario: Operator erroneously starts the treatment multiple times because the system seems to be not responsive to the first start treatment command. Unbeknownst to the operator, the system registers all start commands and delivers the treatment multiple times, even when the patient is not ready.
  - **Requirement R6.** *When a control action is performed by the operator, the UI should respond within x seconds to indicate whether the action has been recognized.*
- **Issue 7:** A system feature for automatic detection of patient readiness status is disabled when the system is powered on by the operator, and UI software forces the operator to navigate through multiple menus to enable it.
  - UI elements: Widgets for navigating menus and enabling/disabling detection of patient readiness status.
  - Causal factor: Complexity of controls.
  - Scenario: Operator erroneously starts the treatment when the patient is not ready because they fail to, or choose not to, enable the automatic patient detection feature.
  - **Requirement R7.** *Safety interlocks such as the automatic patient readiness detection shall always be enabled when the system is initialized.*
  - **Requirement R8.** *The status (enabled/disabled) of safety interlocks shall always be visible on the UI.*

5   Formalization of Safety Requirements in PVS

Safety requirements R1–R8 are testable in the sense that they prescribe specific properties/design features that the UI software needs to satisfy to ensure safe device-user interaction. Here we demonstrate how to formalize these requirements in the higher order specification language of PVS [24]. The formalization assumes a PVS model structured using the following general pattern [11, 19, 25]:

- The system state is a record of *state attributes*, each characterized by a unique name and a type. A special attribute mode identifies the current mode of operation of the system.
- The system behavior is defined in terms of *actions* initiated either by the operator or by an automated process. For example, action start models the operator's press on the start command.
- Additional aspects of the system such user manuals, workflows, and context of use are modeled using state attributes and system behaviors that capture facts about information resources (see [21,22]).

PVS syntax. A system is modeled as a *theory* and a set of logic expressions describing the system behavior. Requirements are expressed as *theorems*, which can be proved using the PVS theorem prover. PVS supports basic datatypes commonly seen in programming languages. New datatypes (e.g., record or enum types) can be defined using the keyword TYPE. The IMPORTING keyword allows to import definitions from other PVS theories. Functions are in the form of f(x: T1): T2, where f is the function name, x is an argument of type T1, and T2 is the function return type. Arrays are defined as [A -> B], where A is the array index type, and B is the datatype of the array elements.

5.1 Gantry-2 Model in PVS

The specification fragment in Listing 1.1 presents a PVS model of the Gantry-2 system. Its characteristics are defined at a level of abstraction compatible with the safety requirements discussed in Sect. 4. The model has been proved to satisfy all given safety requirements. Thus, it is also called a *safety reference model*, as it encapsulates the semantics of the safety requirements. A systematic comparison against the functionalities of the reference model can be used as a basis to verify a final UI software implementation [20].

```
1  gantry2: THEORY BEGIN IMPORTING gantry2_types
2    Console: TYPE = { main, remote }
3    Modes: TYPE = { off, on, ready, radiation, post }
4    UI: TYPE = [# viz: [Attr -> bool],
5               feedback: [Act -> bool],
6               alerts: [Alert -> bool] #]
7    Controller: TYPE = [# patient: PatientStatus,
8                       interlock: bool, mode: Modes #]
9    State: TYPE = [# console: [ Console -> UI ],
10                   controller: Controller #]
11   %-- actions
12   per_stop(st:State): bool = (controller(st)'mode /= off)
13   stop(c:Console)(st:(per_stop)): State =
14     LET st = action_registered(stop,c)(st)
15       IN st WITH [ controller := controller(st)
16           WITH [ mode := ready ]]
17   %-- ...additional definitions of actions omitted
18 END gantry2
```

Listing 1.1. Fragment of the PVS model of the Gantry-2 system.

The PVS model in Listing 1.1 defines a record type State (lines 9–10) to track the system's operational status, which includes two state attributes for modeling relevant characteristics of the main and remote consoles and the beamline controller. Lines 4–6 in Listing 1.1 model UI consoles using three state attributes. Specifically, attribute viz indicates the visibility of a state attribute on the console. For example, viz(mode) = true means that state attribute mode is visible on the console. Attribute feedback indicates whether feedback is presented on the console for a given command. For example, feedback(start) = true indicates that feedback is presented for the start command. Lastly, attribute alerts indicates whether an alert is displayed on the console. This abstract representation of UI consoles is sufficient for the verification of safety requirements defined in Sect. 4. Similarly, the controller of the Gantry-2 system is represented using three state attributes (lines 7–8 in Listing 1.1): patient, which indicates the patient readiness status; interlock, which indicates whether a safety interlock is enabled to prevent erroneous treatment activation when the patient is not ready; and mode, which indicates the current operation mode of the controller.

The following user actions are defined in the PVS model: start, for starting a treatment; stop, for stopping a treatment; on, for powering on the system; and off, for shutting down the system. An automatic action tick models the advance of time in the system. Further, function init captures the initialization of the system. Lines 13–16 in Listing 1.1 demonstrate how user action stop is formally specified. Specifications for other actions can be defined similarly, but are excluded from Listing 1.1 for brevity. The specification of action stop takes two parameters: c of type Console indicates to which UI console stop is applied; and st indicates the controller's current mode. Note that subtype (per_stop) applied to st indicates that stop can only be applied to system states where the controller's operation mode is not off ((per_stop) is a shorthand for predicate { st: State | per_stop(st) }). The LET-IN construct at lines 14–16 first registers the stop action (line 14), and then returns a new system state with the controller's operation mode set to ready.

5.2   Formalization of the Requirements

Formalization of R1–R3. Safety requirements R1–R3 can be conveniently aggregated into a single requirement *"Patient not ready" alerts shall be presented on both the operator console and remote consoles in all operation modes*, which can be formalized as the PVS theorem patient_alerts_th below.

```
1  patient_alerts_th: THEOREM
2   FORALL (pre, post: State, c: Console):
3    %-- induction base
4    (init?(pre) IMPLIES pt_status_visible?(on(c)(pre))) AND
5    %-- induction step
6     ((pt_status_visible?(pre) AND trans(pre, post))
7         IMPLIES pt_status_visible?(post))
```

Theorem `patient_alerts_th` checks if every possible system state satisfies that the patient readiness status is actually visible, when it should be, on the display of both UI consoles. Predicate `pt_status_visible`, as elaborated below, holds true if the patient readiness status is visible (i.e., `viz(patient)` is true) on the display of both consoles when the patient is not ready and the system is on.

```
1  pt_status_visible?(st: State): bool =
2   (controller(st)'mode /= off AND
3      controller(st)'patient = NOT_READY) IMPLIES
4        (st'console(main)'viz(patient) AND
5            st'console(remote)'viz(patient))
```

Note that theorem `patient_alerts_th` uses *structural induction* to define all possible system states satisfying a property p, i.e., p should be satisfied at the system's initial state (*induction base*); then, if p holds for system state `pre`, it must hold for any successor state `post` reachable from `pre` as the result of executing system actions, as specified by `trans(pre, post)` (*induction step*).

Formalization of R4. Safety requirement R4 prohibits the start of treatment when the patient is not ready. Theorem `patient_not_ready_th` listed below formalizes this requirement, asserting that user action `start` shall not be permitted (i.e., `per_start(st)` returns false) when the patient status is NOT_READY.

```
1  patient_not_ready_th: THEOREM FORALL (st: State):
2   controller(st)'patient = NOT_READY IMPLIES
3     NOT per_start(st)
```

Formalization of R5. This requirement allows the operator to cancel the treatment activation sequence. Its formalization, as listed below as theorem `cancel_activation_th`, asserts that the command is always available when the device is turned on (`controller(st)'mode /= off`), and the system shall go back to mode 'ready' as result of pressing button `stop`.

```
1  cancel_activation_th: THEOREM
2   FORALL (st: State, c: Console):
3     controller(st)'mode /= off IMPLIES
4        controller(stop(c)(st))'mode = ready
```

Formalization of R6. This requirement mandates timely feedback after the operator performs a control action. Theorem `acknowledge_start_th` listed below formalizes this requirement for user action `start`. It is defined based on attribute `feedback(start)`, which is true when feedback is presented on the UI. The attribute is checked immediately after registering user action `start`. This formalization is sufficient for the demonstrative purposes of this paper. An additional condition is also included to ensure that feedback is not displayed persistently (in this case after one `tick`) on the console after pressing `start`. Formalizing R6 for other user actions can be done similarly.

```
1  acknowledge_start_th: THEOREM
2   FORALL (pre, post: State, c: Console):
3    (per_start(pre) AND post = start(c)(pre)) IMPLIES
4    (console(post)(c)'feedback(start) AND
5      NOT console(tick(post))(c)'feedback(start))
```

Formalization of R7. Theorem `interlocks_active_th` formalizes safety requirement R7, which ensures that `interlock` is true (i.e., safety interlocks are enabled) after the system is powered on (modeled by action `on`).

```
1  interlocks_active_th: THEOREM FORALL (st: State):
2   init?(st) AND per_on(st) IMPLIES
3    (FORALL (c: Console): controller(on(c)(st))'interlock)
```

Formalization of R8. Formalization of safety requirement R8 involves defining a predicate `interlock_visible?` that checks whether the status of interlocks (attribute `interlock`) is visible on both UI consoles. Structural induction can then be used to build a theorem, like that used in formalization of R1–R3, to assert that `interlock_visible?` holds true for all reachable system states.

```
1  interlock_visible?(st: State): bool =
2   controller(st)'mode /= off IMPLIES
3    (FORALL (c: Console): st'console(c)'viz(interlock))
```

We have proved that the PVS model in Listing 1.1 satisfies all PVS theorems discussed in this section. The proof was carried out using the predefined PVS proof strategy `grind`, which performs automatic instantiation, rewriting, and expansion of definitions. The full PVS theory and proof can be downloaded from https://goo.gl/7ftTlv.

6   Related Work

STPA extensions dedicated to improving the analysis of use hazards were proposed in [31]. These extensions refine the human controller model in standard STPA using concepts from applied psychology: a detection/interpretation component is introduced to capture the operator's ability of observing and understanding feedback correctly and in a timely manner; and an action identification component is included to model the operator's ability to identify actions suitable to manipulate controls provided on the UI. Whereas this refined model enables developers to identify human cognitive errors that lead to UCAs (e.g., the operator performs an unsafe action because of incorrect interpretation of system feedback), it does not help to explore design issues in the UI software that likely induce such human cognitive errors.

Leveson has introduced an STPA extension designed to validate the assumptions made by developers when defining a control model for the system under analysis [18]. The validation is done using indicators suitable for measuring changes made by developers during the definition of the system's control model. This extension is orthogonal to our method in that it improves the fidelity of control models necessary for the STPA analysis of a system.

Dokas et al. [8] extended the STPA control model to facilitate the analysis of catastrophic failures. The intuition is that detecting early warning signs of catastrophic failures and studying how they propagate in the control model can help improve the overall safety of the system. This extension is suitable to identify management-level causes of use hazards in complex socio-technical systems, rather than UI software design issues.

Procter and Hatcliff used standard STPA to analyze interoperable medical devices and identify safety requirements for mitigating design issues in these systems [27]. They enriched STPA with additional guidelines to support the identification of UCAs and their casual factors in interoperable medical systems, and created AADL extensions for documenting the analysis results and subsequently defined safety requirements. Their focus is on interoperability issues, rather UI software design issues.

7 Conclusion

We have presented an enhanced STPA analysis method to support (i) systematic identification of UI software design issues that could induce use errors with medical devices, and (ii) definition of safety requirements to address such design issues. The benefits of our method has been demonstrated in a case study on an experimental medical system. Our method facilitated the identification of subtle UI software design issues that are difficult to detect with the standard STPA. It also helped us to define testable safety requirements that can be readily formalized to address the identified issues. This might potentially improve the applicability of formal methods in evaluating UI software design in safety-critical systems such as medical devices. Future research includes investigating ways to mechanize the instantiation of the casual factor categories to a specific design, and detailed pragmatic guidelines for formalizing safety requirements identified by our method.

Acknowledgments. Sandy Weininger (FDA), Scott Thiel (Navigant Consulting, Inc.), Michelle Jump (Stryker), Stefania Gnesi (ISTI/CNR) and the CHI+MED team (www.chi-med.ac.uk) provided useful feedback and inputs. Paolo Masci's work is supported by the North Portugal Regional Operational Programme (NORTE 2020) under the PORTUGAL 2020 Partnership Agreement, and by the European Regional Development Fund (ERDF) within Project "NORTE-01-0145-FEDER-000016".

References

1. Association for the Advancement of Medical Instrumentation: Infusing patients safely: Priority issues from the AAMI/FDA Infusion Device Summit. AAMI (2010)
2. Blandine, A.: System Theoretic Hazard Analysis applied to the risk review of complex systems. Ph.D. thesis, MIT (2012)

3. Bolton, M.L., Bass, E.J.: A method for the formal verification of human-interactive systems. In: Proceedings of the Human Factors and Ergonomics Society Annual Meeting, vol. 53(12), pp. 764–768. Sage Publications (2009). doi:10.1177/154193120905301201

4. Bowen, J., Reeves, S.: A simplified Z semantics for presentation interaction models. In: Jones, C., Pihlajasaari, P., Sun, J. (eds.) FM 2014. LNCS, vol. 8442, pp. 148–162. Springer, Cham (2014). doi:10.1007/978-3-319-06410-9_11

5. Ericson, C.: Hazard Analysis Techniques for System Safety. Wiley, New York (2015). doi:10.1002/0471739421.ch1

6. Campos, J.C., Harrison, M.D.: Interaction engineering using the IVY tool. In: EICS 2009, pp. 35–44. ACM (2009). doi:10.1145/1570433.1570442

7. Chudleigh, M., Clare, J.N.: The benefits of SUSI: Safety analysis of user system interaction. In: Górski, J. (ed.) SAFECOMP 1993, pp. 123–132. Springer, London (1993). doi:10.1007/978-1-4471-2061-2_13

8. Dokas, I., Feehan, J., Imran, S.: EWaSAP: an early warning sign identification approach based on a systemic hazard analysis. Saf. Sci. **58**, 11–26 (2013). doi:10.1016/j.ssci.2013.03.013

9. Food and Drug Administration (FDA): Class 2 Device Recall ACCUCHEK Connect Diabetes Management App (2015). https://www.accessdata.fda.gov/scripts/cdrh/cfdocs/cfRES/res.cfm?id=134687

10. Harrison, M.D., Campos, J.C., Masci, P.: Reusing models and properties in the analysis of similar interactive devices. Innov. Syst. Softw. Eng. **11**(2), 95–111 (2015). doi:10.1007/s11334-013-0201-3

11. Harrison, M.D., Masci, P., Campos, J.C., Curzon, P.: Demonstrating that medical devices satisfy user related safety requirements. In: Huhn, M., Williams, L. (eds.) Software Engineering in Health Care: 4th International Symposium, FHIES 2014, and 6th International Workshop, SEHC 2014, Washington, DC, USA, July 17–18, 2014, Revised Selected Papers, pp. 113–128. Springer International Publishing, Cham (2017). doi:10.1007/978-3-319-63194-3_8. ISBN: 978-3-319-63194-3

12. Hussey, A.: HAZOP analysis of formal models of safety-critical interactive systems. In: Koornneef, F., Meulen, M. (eds.) SAFECOMP 2000. LNCS, vol. 1943, pp. 371–381. Springer, Heidelberg (2000). doi:10.1007/3-540-40891-6_32

13. Ishikawa, K., Lu, D.J.: What is Total Quality Control? The Japanese Way. Prentice Hall Business Classics, Prentice-Hall, Englewood Cliffs (1985)

14. Kletz, T.A.: Hazop and hazan: identifying and assessing process industry hazards. Disaster Prev. Manage. Int. J. **10**(1), 30–31 (2001). doi:10.1108/dpm.2001.10.1.30.4

15. Leape, L.L., Berwick, D.M.: Five years after to err is human: what have we learned? JAMA **293**(19) (2005). doi:10.1001/jama.293.19.2384

16. Lee, W.S., Grosh, D.L., Tillman, F.A., Lie, C.H.: Fault tree analysis, methods, and applications: a review. IEEE Trans. Reliab. **34**(3), 194–203 (1985). doi:10.1109/TR.1985.5222114

17. Leveson, N.: Engineering a Safer World. MIT Press, Cambridge (2011)

18. Leveson, N.: A systems approach to risk management through leading safety indicators. Reliab. Eng. Syst. Saf. **136**, 17–34 (2015). doi:10.1016/j.ress.2014.10.008

19. Masci, P., Zhang, Y., Jones, P., Curzon, P., Thimbleby, H.: Formal verification of medical device user interfaces using PVS. In: Gnesi, S., Rensink, A. (eds.) FASE 2014. LNCS, vol. 8411, pp. 200–214. Springer, Heidelberg (2014). doi:10.1007/978-3-642-54804-8_14

20. Masci, P., Ayoub, A., Curzon, P., Harrison, M.D., Lee, I., Thimbleby, H.: Verification of interactive software for medical devices: PCA infusion pumps and FDA Regulation as an example. In: EICS 2013, pp. 81–90. ACM (2013). doi:10.1145/2494603.2480302

21. Masci, P., Curzon, P., Furniss, D., Blandford, A.: Using PVS to support the analysis of distributed cognition systems. Innov. Syst. Softw. Eng. 11(2), 113–130 (2015). doi:10.1007/s11334-013-0202-2

22. Masci, P., Furniss, D., Curzon, P., Harrison, M.D., Blandford, A.: Supporting field investigators with PVS: a case study in the healthcare domain. In: Avgeriou, P. (ed.) SERENE 2012. LNCS, vol. 7527, pp. 150–164. Springer, Heidelberg (2012). doi:10.1007/978-3-642-33176-3_11

23. Nielsen, J.: Usability Engineering. Morgan Kaufmann, San Francisco (1993). doi:10.1016/B978-0-08-052029-2.50001-2

24. Owre, S., Rushby, J.M., Shankar, N.: PVS: a prototype verification system. In: Kapur, D. (ed.) CADE 1992. LNCS, vol. 607, pp. 748–752. Springer, Heidelberg (1992). doi:10.1007/3-540-55602-8_217

25. Masci, P., Rukšėnas, R., Oladimeji, P., Cauchi, A., Gimblett, A., Li, Y., Curzon, P., Thimbleby, H.: The benefits of formalising design guidelines: a case study on the predictability of drug infusion pumps. Innov. Syst. Softw. Eng. 11(2), 73–93 (2015). doi:10.1007/s11334-013-0200-4

26. Paterno, F., Mancini, C., Meniconi, S.: ConcurTaskTrees: a diagrammatic notation for specifying task models. In: Howard, S., Hammond, J., Lindgaard, G. (eds.) Human-Computer Interaction INTERACT '97. ITIFIP, pp. 362–369. Springer, Boston, MA (1997). doi:10.1007/978-0-387-35175-9_58

27. Procter, S., Hatcliff, J.: An architecturally-integrated, systems-based hazard analysis for medical applications. In: MEMOCODE 2014, pp. 124–133. IEEE (2014). doi:10.1109/MEMCOD.2014.6961850

28. Rukšėnas, R., Curzon, P., Back, J., Blandford, A.: Formal modelling of cognitive interpretation. In: Doherty, G., Blandford, A. (eds.) DSV-IS 2006. LNCS, vol. 4323, pp. 123–136. Springer, Heidelberg (2007). doi:10.1007/978-3-540-69554-7_10

29. Rushby, J.: Using model checking to help discover mode confusions and other automation surprises. Reliab. Eng. Syst. Saf. 75(2), 167–177 (2002). doi:10.1016/S0951-8320(01)00092-8

30. Stamatis, D.: Failure Mode And Effect Analysis. ASQ Quality Press, Milwaukee (2003)

31. Thornberry, C.: Extending the human-controller methodology in systems-theoretic process analysis (STPA). Ph.D. thesis, MIT (2014)

Modular Verification of Information Flow Security in Component-Based Systems

Simon Greiner[✉], Martin Mohr, and Bernhard Beckert

Department of Informatics, Karlsruhe Institute of Technology, Karlsruhe, Germany
{Simon.Greiner,Martin.Mohr,beckert}@kit.edu

Abstract. We propose a novel method for the verification of information flow security in component-based systems. The method is (a) modular w.r.t. services and components, i.e., overall security is proved to follow from the security of the individual services provided by the components, and (b) modular w.r.t. attackers, i.e., verified security properties can be re-used to demonstrate security w.r.t. different kinds of attacks.

In a first step, user-provided security specifications for individual services are verified using program analysis techniques. In a second step, first-order formulas are generated expressing that component non-interference follows from service-level properties and in a third step that global system security follows from component non-interference. These first-order proof obligations are discharged with a first-order theorem prover. The overall approach is independent of the programming language used to implement the components. We provide a soundness proof for our method and highlight its advantages, especially in the context of evolving systems.

As a proof of concept and to demonstrate the usability of our method, we present a case study, where we verify the security of a system implemented in Java against two types of attackers. We apply the program verification system KeY and the program analysis tool JOANA for analyzing individual services; modularity of our approach allows us to use them in parallel.

1 Introduction

Information flow (IF) security is a program property ensuring that certain information given as input to a system can only be observed by users of the system who are explicitly allowed to do so (and not by other users). Formal analysis of IF security requires specification of (a) which users shall be able to observe which information and (b) what outputs users can access and read. In practice, there is often more than one type of user – which we consider to be potential

This work was supported by the German Ministry for Education and Research within the framework of the project KASTEL_IoE in the Competence Center for Applied Security Technology (KASTEL) and by the german research foundation in the scope of the priority program "Reliably Secure Software Systems" (grants Sn11/12-1/2/3).

A. Cimatti and M. Sirjani (Eds.): SEFM 2017, LNCS 10469, pp. 300–315, 2017.
DOI: 10.1007/978-3-319-66197-1_19

attackers – each requiring a specification and analysis. Component-based systems, in particular, are designed for re-use and, thus, are deployed in different environments where new user types have to be considered.

Overview of our method. We propose a novel method for the modular verification of IF security properties in component-based systems. Our method uses very expressive IF specifications, where information about arbitrary parts or combinations of input parameters can be declared to be secret as well as information about what service calls other users have initiated. The restricted programming paradigm used for component-based systems provides convenient compositionality properties, that we can use to verify non-interference properties in a modular way.

The first step of our proposed method is the specification (and verification) of service-local IF properties, which are independent of the user/attacker model. These service-local properties are modular and re-usable. We can apply tools with different precision and scalability properties for verification of each service-local specification, which allows us to improve scalability while maintaining precision of verification. Service-local specifications remain valid when other services are changed or new services are added. In the second step, we generate a system-wide specification from the service-local properties and verify that the service-local properties imply the system-wide IF properties. This is done by proving validity of a formula in first-order predicate logic, which is constructed from the specifications in a uniform way. In a third step, we show that the system-wide IF specification implies the required domain-motivated IF property w.r.t. particular user/attacker models.

Our method is tool-independent and allows the combination of different program analysis techniques – to be used in the first step. The second and the third step do not need program analysis but only a first-order theorem prover.

Proof of concept. As a proof of concept, we apply our method to component-based systems implemented in Java, using the program verification tool KeY and the program analysis tool JOANA for verification of service-local IF properties (first step). Further, we use the (Java-independent part of) KeY to prove validity of first-order formulas (second and third step). As an example, we specified and verified IF security of a web shop system consisting of several components w.r.t. two different types of attackers.

Related work. Non-Interference as a program property has its origins in the notion of *strong dependency* by Cohen [7] and the first definition of non-interference by Goguen and Meseguer [10]. The work in this paper is based on a line of work on non-interference for distributed interactive systems (which components can be considered to be) [6,12,25,26]. Work in [28] allows more expressive specifications than our framework, but does not provide compositionality results. Other recent work [2,21,22] discusses compositionality of concurrent threads with a shared state, which however is not present in components.

Approaches for analysis of event-based non-interference notions often use type systems and are limited to toy languages or abstract specification languages (e.g., [20,26,27]). Analysis for batch programs based on type systems (e.g., [3]) is typically limited to syntactical information, and therefore has limited precision. *Dependent types* [24,32] include semantic knowledge into the analysis and use SMT solvers as back ends. JiF [5,23] extends Java with security type systems, which allows analysis of security properties in Java programs at compile time. We assume type-based analysis can be used as an additional technique for the first step of our method.

We use the JOANA tool, for program analysis in this work. Other slicing tools for Java include WALA [15], PIDGIN [16] and Indus [33]. Both WALA and PIDGIN employ program dependency graphs and especially PIDGIN could be a viable alternative in the context of this work, while Indus does not a provide pre-computed PDG, which we require here.

Work on tool combinations for IF analysis includes the RIFL language [9], a specification language for IF policies in programs. It is supported by several tools. However, in contrast to our work, RIFL does not provide a formal semantics for the specifications and does not support secrecy of messages. Küsters et al. propose the *hybrid approach* [18] for the verification of IF properties with declassification in batch programs. Their approach, however, relies on making provably ineffective changes to the program and is limited to the combination of two tools. SHRIFT [19] combines dynamic analysis on the operating system layer and static IF analysis to track information flows through multiple layers of abstraction efficiently and precisely. We limit the presentation here to static analysis tools, while in general, our method would allow dynamic analysis.

Paper outline. Next, we define the formal framework (Sect. 2), i.e., notions of service and component, and non-interference for components and services. Then, in Sect. 3, we introduce our concept of service-local specifications (first step). We show in Sect. 4 how they can be used to generate and verify system-wide properties (second step). And, in Sect. 5, we describe how domain-motivated IF specifications can be derived from system properties (third step). We discuss the proof of concept and the web shop example in Sect. 6. Finally, we conclude.

2   Formal Framework

We present the formalization of components, services, and composition of components, and we formally define non-interference in component-based systems. This formal framework, which we use as a basis for our method, is mainly taken from [12], where also proofs for the theorems can be found.

2.1   Components and Services

Components have a (private) state σ, which is a mapping from a set $\mathcal{V}$ of variables to a set $\mathbb{V}$ of values. A component's functionality is implemented by services, which are sequential, terminating, deterministic programs.

For each service *serv*, a dedicated initial channel *Ini(serv)* and a termination channel *Fin(serv)* is contained in the system's set $\mathbb{C}$ of channels. If the environment wants to call *serv*, it sends a message $m \in \mathbb{M}$, where $\mathbb{M} \subseteq \mathbb{C} \times \mathbb{V}^n$, on the initial channel $Ini(serv) \in \mathbb{C}$ and parameter values from $\mathbb{V}$ to the component. Then, the component executes the service starting in its current state and returns a message on $Fin(serv)$ on completion. While a component executes a service, all other service calls to that component are postponed, making the execution of a component a non-reentrant, sequential composition of service executions.

During execution, a service may call other services *serv'* by sending a message on channel $Ini(serv')$. After the call, the service waits for the termination of *serv'*, making communication synchronous.

This computational model for component-based systems is rather restrictive. It is, nevertheless, consistent with practically used frameworks for implementation of component-based systems. We discuss, for example, how our model applies to the Java Enterprise Edition in Sect. 6. Also, assemblies as used in the .net framework have similar properties. And even relational databases can be considered components according to our definition.

```
Component Shop {                    print(p) {
    int sum, check, payId;              if (check)
    String prods;                           return sum.prods.payId;
                                        else return 0; }
    buy(prodId,price) {             pay(ccnr,pin) {
        sum = sum+price;                check = trans(sum,ccnr,pin);
        prods = prodId.prods;           if (check) payId = ccnr%2;
        return prods; }                 return 0; } }
```

Fig. 1. Shop component as running example (see Example 1)

Example 1. As a running example, we use the simple Shop component shown in Fig. 1. The service buy receives a product id, adds it to the list prods of products in the cart, and increases the variable sum by the product's price. Service pay uses the service trans provided by the environment to perform payment with credit card number ccnr, the given pin and the sum of prices stored in the state. Service print prints the receipt with the paid sum, the products and last bit of the credit card used for paying, if payment was successful.

For messages on a channel α with parameter v, we write $\alpha?v$ (input message), $\alpha!v$ (output message), or $\alpha.v$ (direction irrelevant). The sets of all input messages and all output messages are denoted by $\mathbb{I}$ and $\mathbb{O}$, respectively. The empty trace of messages is denoted by $\langle \rangle$, and $\frown$ is the concatenation operation for traces.

Two components c and d are composed by synchronizing messages on services required by c and provided by d and vice versa. In the trace of the composition, messages resulting from communication between c and d can be observed by the environment as outputs.

2.2   Non-interference

Intuitively, a component is non-interferent, i.e., it has no unwanted information flows, if an environment (or an attacker) observing the public (low) output of a component cannot distinguish between inputs which only differ on (high) secrets. In the following, to distinguish between public (low) and secret (high) inputs and outputs, we use an equivalence relation $\sim \subseteq \mathbb{M} \times \mathbb{M}$. Messages which are equivalent w.r.t. $\sim$ must not be distinguishable by the environment, i.e., it is a secret which of two equivalent messages has been sent. This flexible formalization allows a very precise specification of what-declassification (see [29]).

Example 2. Continuing from Example 1, the relation $\sim$ may be defined for the Shop component by: $Ini(pay)?(ccnr, pin) \sim Ini(pay)?(ccnr', pin')$ iff $ccnr\%2 = ccnr'\%2$, stating that the last bit of the information stored in parameter $ccnr$ is low, while parameter pin is considered to contain high information. The definition $Fin(pay)!r \sim Fin(pay)!r'$ iff $r = r'$ expresses the return value of pay to be low.

Apart from communicated values, the mere existence of communication can contain information. All results provided in the remainder also hold in the case when the specification of high message existence is possible.[1]

Equivalence of messages raises a natural notion of equivalence of message traces, for which we overload $\sim$: Two traces t and t' are equivalent if their projection on the equivalence classes of messages implied by $\sim$ are equal. Then, non-interference for components can be defined as follows:

Definition 1 (Component non-interference). *A component c is non-interferent w.r.t. an equivalent relation $\sim$ on messages if, for all message traces that can be produced by c in some environment, an equivalent trace is produced by c in any environment supplying equivalent inputs.*

In [12], environments are formalized as functions providing for each observation of a component's behavior some input for the component. We omit here this more formal consideration of non-interference and refer to the original work. We do need, however, the following compositionality result:

Theorem 1 (Non-interference compositionality). *If components c and d are non-interferent w.r.t. $\sim$, then the composition of c and d is non-interferent w.r.t. $\sim$.*

We want to verify non-interference of components in a modular way, i.e., by first analyzing individual services. Thus, we need to ensure that one service does not break the non-interference of another service. We must check that no service returns a high value stored in the state by another service. For that purpose, we use an equivalence relation $\approx \subseteq \mathbb{S} \times \mathbb{S}$ over states to define the low part of a state: Two states are equivalent w.r.t. $\approx$ iff they only differ on the secret (high) part of the state. Now, we can define non-interference for services as follows:

---

[1] We omit discussion of high messages here, and refer to [13].

Definition 2 (Service non-interference). *A service serv is non-interferent with respect to* $\sim$ *and* $\approx$ *iff, for all pre-states* σ_1, σ_2, *all post-states* σ_1', σ_2', *and all traces* t_1, t_2 *such that serv started in* σ_i *terminates in* σ_i' *by communicating trace* t_i, *the following holds:*

1. *If* $\sigma_1 \approx \sigma_2$ *and* t_1 *and* t_2 *have equivalent input messages, then* $\sigma_1' \approx \sigma_2'$.
2. *If* $\sigma_1 \approx \sigma_2$ *and* t_1', t_2' *are prefixes of* t_1, t_2 *with equivalent inputs, then there exist longer prefixes* $t_1' \frown t_1''$ *of* t_1 *and* $t_2' \frown t_2''$ *of* t_2 *such that* $t_1' \frown t_1'' \sim t_2' \frown t_2''$.

Condition 1 ensures that the service, when started in equivalent pre-states and provided with equivalent inputs, terminates in equivalent post states, i.e., no high information is written to the low part of the state. Condition 2 ensures that all outputs created by the service are equivalent if the pre-states and all inputs previously provided to the service are equivalent, i.e., no high information is sent as output to the environment.

Non-interference for services as defined above is termination-insensitive. While generally this is a weak non-interference property, that is not relevant here, since we assume every service to terminate. Components, on the other hand, never terminate: After termination of a service, the component continues to offer all its services to the environment.

The following theorem states that non-interference for components can be verified by first proving non-interference for services.

Theorem 2 (Compositionality of Services). *A component c is non-interferent w.r.t.* $\sim$ *(Definition 1) if there exists an equivalence relation* $\approx$ *on states such that all services provided by c are non-interferent w.r.t.* $\sim$ *and* $\approx$ *(Definition 2).*

Note that Theorem 2 requires all services to be non-interferent w.r.t. the *same* relations $(\sim, \approx)$. Moreover, Theorem 1 requires components to be non-interferent w.r.t. the *same* relation $\sim$ to derive non-interference of their composition. In the following sections we describe a method for generating appropriate system-global relations from service-local relations.

3   Service-Local Non-interference Specification

In the first step of our method, we specify and verify information-flow (resp. non-interference) at the level of individual services. We do this in a modular way such that verified properties of services imply properties of the overall system. Modularity is essential as it is very tedious to find and formalize system-wide IF properties for a realistic system and, moreover, properties change whenever a system is modified or deployed in a new context.

As a concept for modular service-local specification, we introduce *dependency clusters*. Whether a dependency cluster is valid, i.e. whether the specification it represents is satisfied by a service, only depends on the service's implementation and not on the environment or other services. Moreover, existence of some information flow does not depend on the system-wide attacker model (but only whether the flow is harmful). We will use dependency clusters as building blocks for system-wide specifications in the second step of our method.

Intuitively, a dependency cluster is a set of message parameters and state variables (resp. more complex expressions) whose values in the post-state of the service only depends on their values in the pre-state. Thus, if the cluster is used to specify which information is public (low), then the service is indeed non-interferent.

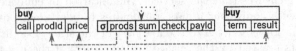

Fig. 2. Two dependency cluster (dashed and dotted arrows) of the service buy. The arrows illustrate dependencies between the state, parameters and the return value.

Example 3. In the Shop component shown in Fig. 1, the return value of service *buy* depends (only) on the value of parameter *prodId* and on the pre-state value of *prods* (the dashed arrows in Fig. 2 illustrate these dependencies). Thus the return value, *prodId*, and *prods* form a valid dependency cluster. A second cluster is formed by the parameter *price* and the state variable *sum* (dotted arrows).

As described in the previous section, we use equivalence relations on messages and states to formalize which information is considered public (low). Thus, more formally, a dependency cluster is a pair $(\sim, \approx)$; it is valid for some service if that service is non-interferent w.r.t. $(\sim, \approx)$:

Definition 3 (Dependency cluster). *A pair $(\sim, \approx)$ of equivalence relations is a* dependency cluster *for a service serv if serv is non-interferent w.r.t. $(\sim, \approx)$.*

For example, the universal relations, defined by $m_1 \sim m_2 \Leftrightarrow true$ and $\sigma_1 \approx \sigma_2 \Leftrightarrow true$, form a trivial dependency cluster for all services. This cluster defines all inputs, outputs and the entire post-state to contain high information (nothing is low). At the other extreme, the dependency cluster defined by $m_1 \sim m_2 \Leftrightarrow m_1 = m_2$ and $\sigma_1 \approx \sigma_2 \Leftrightarrow \sigma_1 = \sigma_2$ is also valid for all services. It declares all inputs, outputs and the entire state to only contain low information. In practice, of course, one needs to find clusters that are valid without being trivial.

Several dependency clusters for the same service *serv* are compositional in the sense that their intersection is again a dependency cluster *serv* (the formal proof, together with all proofs for this paper, can be found in [13]):

Theorem 3 (Compositionality of dependency clusters). *Let $(\sim_1, \approx_1)$ and $(\sim_2, \approx_2)$ be dependency clusters for a service serv. Then the composition $(\sim_1, \approx_1) + (\sim_2, \approx_2) := (\sim_1 \cap \sim_2, \approx_1 \cap \approx_2)$ is a dependency cluster for serv.*

Intuitively, intersecting relations has the effect that equivalence classes become smaller and, thus, more information is considered low. Interestingly, according to Theorem 3, a composition of dependency clusters considers more outputs to be low, i.e., allows less flows than the individual clusters. At the same time, the composition is less restrictive than a mere conjunctive combination of the two individual clusters: Assume, for example, that one dependency cluster allows only flows from state variable a to itself (i.e. if $\sigma_{pre}(a) = \sigma'_{pre}(a)$ then $\sigma_{post}(a) = \sigma'_{post}(a)$), and the other allows only flows b to itself (i.e. if $\sigma_{pre}(b) = \sigma'_{pre}(b)$ then $\sigma_{post}(b) = \sigma'_{post}(b)$). Their intersection (i.e. if $\sigma_{pre}(a) = \sigma'_{pre}(a) \wedge \sigma_{pre}(b) = \sigma'_{pre}(b)$ then $\sigma_{post}(a) = \sigma'_{post}(a) \wedge \sigma_{post}(b) = \sigma'_{post}(b)$) additionally allows flows from a to b and vice versa, for example the program $a = a+b$.

As a formalism for defining dependency clusters and, thus, for specifying information flow properties, we introduce the following notation: Each dependency cluster is given as a pair $(LowIO, LowState)$ of lists, specifying $\sim$ resp. $\approx$. The elements of $LowIO$ are of the form $c.e$, where c is an initial or termination channel and e is an expressions over the parameters or the return values of the service. Two messages on channel c are equivalent iff, for all $c.e \in LowIO$, e evaluates to the same value for the two messages. Similarly, the elements of $LowState$ are expressions over the state variables. Two states are equivalent, if the expressions evaluate to the same values in both states. Intuitively, the two lists $LowIO$ and $LowState$ describe what information is to be considered low. Thus, state variables, parameters, and channels not mentioned in the lists are secret (high).

The above notation can be used to define dependency clusters for services but also to specify global information-flow properties for components and systems.

Example 4. A component-global information-flow specification for the Shop example (Fig. 1) may be given by:

$$LowIO_1 = \langle Ini(buy).(prodId, price), \; Fin(buy).(r), \; Fin(print).(r),$$
$$Ini(pay).(ccnr\%2), \; Fin(pay).(r), \; Fin(trans).(r) \rangle$$
$$LowState_1 = \langle prods, \; sum, \; check, \; payId \rangle$$

We use declassification for the credit card number expressing that (only) the last bit of the contained information is low. We can apply similar expressions for state variables.

The first dependency cluster in Fig. 2 (dashed line) may be defined by $LowIO_2 = \langle Ini(buy).(prodId), \; Fin(buy).(r) \rangle$ and $LowState_2 = \langle prods \rangle$, and the second dependency cluster (dotted line) by $LowIO_3 = \langle Ini(buy).(price) \rangle$ and $LowState_3 = \langle sum \rangle$.

The expressiveness of the list notion depends on the expressions allowed to occur in the lists. We do not define a particular language here but assume computability of the expressions. In practice, the concrete language will depend on the tools for verification of dependency clusters. Heavy-weight methods like theorem provers can deal with more expressive languages while light-weight tools like PDG- or type-based systems may support a limited subset.

Using the list notion, the composition of dependency clusters (see Theorem 3) can be constructed by concatenating the respective lists.

Example 5. The composition of the two dependency clusters from Example 4 can be written as $LowIO_4 = \langle Ini(buy).(prodId, price), Fin(buy).(r) \rangle$ and $LowState_4 = \langle prods, sum \rangle$.

According to Theorem 3, it is sufficient to show for two specifications independently that they are dependency clusters in order to gain a composed, potentially more complicated, specification. Ideally, one uses an analysis method to identify simple dependency clusters which describe information flows inherent to the implementation of a service. More complicated clusters, which are necessary to compare information flow to a security policy, can then be constructed by composing these simple dependency clusters, which may be verified separately by different tools. This makes dependency clusters convenient building blocks for complex information flow specifications for services.

Since we allow declassification to be used in our specifications there are infinitely many potential dependency clusters for each service. The first step of the method proposed in this work is identifying useful dependency clusters for each service. In Sect. 6, we show two concrete approaches for identification. The first approach is to manually specify dependency clusters and verify them using a program verification tool. This is especially useful for declassification, when analysis with high precision is required for analysis. In the second approach, we use an automatic, less precise program analysis tool which directly creates a set of all dependency clusters it can find.

4   Dependency Clusters and Components

In the second step of our method, we compose dependency clusters of all services and thus gain component- and system-wide non-interference specifications. While dependency clusters for the same service are compositional, dependency clusters for different services are not, hence we have to show that composed dependency cluster of different services are consistent.

Since dependency clusters are service-local specifications, each dependency cluster will most likely mention at most the part of the state relevant for the service and the messages sent and received by the service. Consider, for example, the service *buy* in Fig. 1: We have defined several dependency clusters for *buy*; but, none of these clusters mentions the variable *check*.

An approach in program analysis to deal with irrelevant parts of states is *framing* [17]. Framing uses an abstract description of an upper bound of relevant variables for a particular service and of the other services it requires. An *assignable set* describes the variables that a service may at most change. Indirectly, this specifies that the value (and security level) of all variables not in the set remains unchanged. A set $\mathbb{F} \subseteq \mathcal{V}$ is an *assignable set* for a service *serv* iff, for all executions of *serv*, $v \notin \mathbb{F}$ implies $\sigma(v) = \sigma'(v)$ (σ, σ' are the pre- and post-state).

Similar to the assignable sets, a *callable set* is a list of services which can at most be called by a service. $C \subseteq S$ is a *callable set* for service *serv* if all traces produced by execution of *serv* at most contain messages on initial and termination channels of the services in C.

Example 6. In the Shop component, an assignable set for *buy* is $\{sum, prods\}$. And $\{\}$ is an assignable set for *print*. The empty set is a callable set for both *buy* and *print*. A callable set for *pay* is $\{trans\}$.

We can use known dependency clusters, assignable, and callable sets for some service *serv* to check if *serv* is non-interferent w.r.t. a component-global specification as follows:

Theorem 4. *Let C be a callable set for service serv and $\mathbb{F}$ an assignable set for serv. A pair $(\sim_g, \approx_g)$ is a dependency cluster for serv if there is a dependency cluster $(\sim_{serv}, \approx_{serv})$ for serv such that, for all messages m, m' and states $\sigma, \sigma', \sigma_p, \sigma'_p$,*

$$if\ m \sim_g m'\ then\ m \sim_{serv} m', and\ if\ \sigma \approx_g \sigma'\ then\ \sigma \approx_{serv} \sigma' \tag{1}$$

$$if\ m \sim_{serv} m'\ and\ m \in C\ then\ m \sim_g m' \tag{2}$$

$$if\ \sigma \approx_g \sigma'\ and\ \sigma_p \approx_{serv} \sigma'_p\ then\ anon\,(\sigma, \mathbb{F}, \sigma_p) \approx_g anon\,(\sigma', \mathbb{F}, \sigma'_p) \tag{3}$$

where $anon(\sigma, V, \sigma')$ yields a state σ_{anon} such that $\sigma_{anon}(v)$ evaluates to $\sigma'(v)$ if $v \in V$ and to $\sigma(v)$ otherwise.

Condition (1) states that input messages that are equivalent w.r.t. the component-global relation must also be equivalent w.r.t. the service-local relation, and that if two states are equivalent w.r.t. the global state relation, then they must also be equivalent w.r.t. the service-local relation. Indirectly, this ensures that, if all other services provided by a component ensure equivalence w.r.t. the global equivalence relation for their post state, then *serv* is guaranteed to be executed in pre-states which are equivalent w.r.t. the service-local specification.

In Condition (2), we use $m \in C$ as abbreviation for m being an initial or terminating message for a service in C. The condition guarantees that all output messages of a service are equivalent globally if they are service-locally equivalent and the messages can actually be communicated during execution of the service. In a similar fashion, Condition (3) guarantees that the parts of the post-states, which are actually changed by the service, are changed such that they are also equivalent w.r.t. the component-global state-equivalence relation.

Note that the condition to be checked according to Theorem 4 can be formalized in first-order predicate logic, if all expressions in the list notion are first-order. (Which we assume to be sufficiently expressive in practice)

Example 7. Reconsidering Example 4, we can use Theorem 4 to show that $LowIO_1, LowState_1$ is a dependency cluster for the service *buy*, since the service-local specification $LowIO_4, LowState_4$ is a dependency cluster for *buy*, as we have seen in the previous section, the expressions mentioning *prods* and *sum* are identical and *check* and *payId* are not in the assignable set. A similar argument holds for the events and the callable set.

It is not necessary to analyze the actual implementation of *buy* if the service-local specification, the assignable set, and the callable set are given.

The second step of our method creates the global non-interference specifications for a system. We consider identification of assignable and callable sets an orthogonal problem to the framework presented here and assume a useful (i.e., small) assignable set and callable set for each service to be given. (In our proof of concept, we automatically generated them with JOANA.) Further, we assume a set of dependency clusters $\{(\sim_{ij1}, \approx_{ij1}), \ldots, (\sim_{ijk}, \approx_{ijk})\}$ for each service s_j provided by component c_i in the system has been specified and verified in the first step of our method. We create a system-global equivalence relation over messages by intersecting all equivalence relations in the set: $\sim_{sys} = \bigcap_{i,j,k} \sim_{ijk}$. We also create a component-global equivalence relation over states for each component: $\approx_i = \bigcap_{j,k} \sim_{ijk}$. For each service s_j provided by component c_i we prove the first-order formula gained from Theorem 4 with $\sim_g = \sim_{sys}$, $\approx_g = \approx_i$, and $\sim_{serv} = \bigcap_k \sim_{ijk}$, $\approx_{serv} = \bigcap_k \approx_{ijk}$.

The constructed formula is first-order. While each of the formulas is, as we can expect, rather large for a realistic system, big parts trivially evaluate to *true* or *false* because the callable and assignable sets are typically very small compared to the overall system.

Theorem 4 makes dependency clusters very useful for evolving components, since the need for actual program analysis is minimized.

Example 8. Assume that the Shop component from Fig. 1 is re-used in a new context where, due to a changed use case, it is required that the last four digits of the credit card number are low (instead of the last bit). To realize this, the implementation of service *pay* is changed: Line 2 is replaced by "if (check) payId=ccnr-(ccnr/10000)*10000;". Since the code has changed, the dependency clusters for *pay* have to be re-verified. But the dependency clusters for all other services can be re-used without program analysis when the first order proof for step 2 is repeated.

In a second case of evolution, we assume that context remains the same and the implementation is optimized without changing the functionality. Line 2 is now replaced by "if (check) payId = ccnr%10000;". Again, since the code has changed, the dependency clusters for *pay* have to be verified, but since the service's behavior is not changed, no new dependency clusters have to be identified and proofs from step two of our method are still valid.

5   Weakening Specifications

In the third and last step of our method, we show that the system-wide non-interference specification gained from step two implies security of the system against an attacker. The specifications we gain by analyzing dependencies in services do not necessarily match a security policy provided by a domain expert for the system under analysis. While the first two steps of our method provide us with a specification reflecting the actual behavior of the program, the specification from a domain expert is the result of a threat analysis for a system and its context.

In particular, the equivalence relation over messages we gain from the first two steps in our method may be stricter than necessary. We can relax the relation without harm by accepting low input where high input is expected, and we can allow the environment to treat low output of the component as high output.

Definition 4 (Specification weakening). *An equivalence relation $\sim_w$ is a weakening of $\sim$ iff*

- *for $m_1, m_2 \in \mathbb{I}$: $m_1 \sim_w m_2$ implies $m_1 \sim m_2$,*
- *for $m_1, m_2 \in \mathbb{O}$: $m_1 \sim m_2$ implies $m_1 \sim_w m_2$*

Example 9. Consider the simple Shop component from Fig. 1 with the changes discussed in Example 8 in the previous section. When it is deployed, the domain expert may provide a specification expressing that the cashier may know the last five digits of the credit card number. The specification we gained from bottom-up program analysis, however, provides a stricter specification allowing at most the last four digits to be visible to the cashier. In this case, we can nevertheless use our bottom-up specification as an argument for security as the environment-specific IF-property is a weakening of the bottom-up specification.

Theorem 5. *Let serv be a service that is non-interferent w.r.t. $(\sim, \approx)$ and $\sim_w$ a weakening of $\sim$. Then serv is non-interferent w.r.t. $(\sim_w, \approx)$.*

Theorem 5 can easily be extended to components. If all services are non-interferent w.r.t. $(\sim, \approx)$, they also are non-interferent w.r.t. $(\sim_w, \approx)$ and therefore the component is non-interferent w.r.t. $(\sim_w, \approx)$ according to Theorem 2. This implies, for example, that the evolved Shop component from Example 8 is secure in the new environment from Example 9, although the required and the verified IF properties differ.

The third and last step of our method consists of showing that the security policy provided by the domain expert, which represents the actual security requirement, is a weakening of the system-global equivalence relation $\sim_g$ from the second step. Note that the proof obligation implied by Theorem 5 again can be shown using first-order logic and does not require program verification.

On first sight Theorem 5 seems to be a technicality. However, the theorem serves as an important connection between bottom-up specifications, which our method provides, and top-down specifications, gained from context- and attacker-motivated analysis. It frees the systems engineer from finding non-interference specifications for already implemented components which exactly fit the domain-driven idea of secrecy. Thus it serves as a glue which allows flexibility when bringing together domain expertise and context-independent program analysis.

6   Proof of Concept: Verifying JavaEE Implementations

We outline in this section the instantiation of our formal framework for component-based systems (Sect. 2) for a large subset of components implemented in the Java Enterprise Edition (JavaEE) [8], a framework for implementing Component-based Systems in Java. For a full discussion, including all sources and proofs the interested reader is referred to [13].

As a case study, we implemented a simple web-shop consisting of five components. We use the tools KeY and JOANA for verification and analysis of security of the case study against two attackers.

Verification of Dependency Clusters for Services. KeY is a theorem prover designed for the verification of properties in Java programs against specifications formalized in the Java Modeling Language (JML) or Java Dynamic Logic (JavaDL). The KeY system was previously used for verification of non-interference properties in Java batch programs without events [4,30,31]. For a full account of KeY and JavaDL, we refer to [1].

We extend JavaDL by events as part of the domain of the logic. We use a static ghost variable, i.e., a specification-only variable, to record the history of events passed during execution of a service. We formalize the general assumptions ensured by the application container according to JavaEE, e.g. no shared heap between components, as method contracts. We formalize proof obligations from the first step of our method and equivalence relations directly in JavaDL.

Automatically Deriving Service Dependency Clusters. To automatically derive dependency clusters, we use *program dependency graphs* (PDGs), a language-independent graph-representation of the dependencies between the statements and expressions of a program. We use the state-of-the-art information flow analysis tool JOANA [11,14] to build and use PDGs for our purposes.

PDGs guarantee sequential non-interference [34] in the sense that a node n cannot influence a node n' if n cannot reach n' in the PDG. Hence, in order to obtain a dependency cluster, it suffices to perform reachability analysis on the PDG. We applied JOANA to all services in our proof of concept and extracted the majority of all used dependency clusters automatically. Then, we automatically formalized the extracted dependency clusters as JavaDL predicates uniformly to the dependency clusters verified with KeY.

Checking Component-Global Dependency Clusters. In the second step, we re-use formalizations of the equivalence relations from the first step of our method to compose service-local to component-global dependency cluster, formalize Theorem 4 directly in JavaDL and use KeY for the proof. Finally, we used KeY to verify in the third step for each attacker that the attacker-related information-flow specification is a weakening of the specification from step 2, again directly encoded in JavaDL.

Evaluation. We identified 480 dependency clusters in the components of the web shop program with JOANA automatically and manually specified and verified 21 dependency clusters with KeY, for which JOANA was not sufficiently precise.

Verification for the first attacker took about six days, while the main bottlenecks were specification and verification of functional support specifications, as well as manual interaction during verification of proof obligations in steps two and three of our method. Verification for the second attacker only took about one day, since we could make heavy re-use of the specifications for the first attacker.

As a result, we find that KeY is not optimized for proof obligations gained during step 2 and 3 of our method and we assume a high degree of automation if better suited tools are used for this task, for example SMT solvers. Further, we observed that re-using support specifications and dependency clusters for the second attacker made the proof process considerably easier and faster.

7 Conclusion

We introduced dependency clusters as a novel specification approach for information flows caused by a single service in a component-based system. Each specification is independent from other services in the system and the context, which makes dependency cluster very modular and highly re-usable building blocks for system specifications. Further, we introduced a novel method for constructing system-wide security specifications, where verification of dependency clusters at service-level is the only step requiring program analysis. Proof obligations in the second and third step are first-order formulas, which ensure consistency of the constructed specification w.r.t. an attacker-motivated specification.

For each step, we provide a soundness proof. Moreover, in a proof of concept, we show that our method can be instantiated for JavaEE programs and, for example, is usable for a small but realistic system. For verification of dependency clusters we used the KeY tool and JOANA, and verified the proof obligations for step two and three with KeY, re-using dependency cluster formalizations from the first step. The proof of concept especially showed the re-usability of dependency clusters for different types of attackers.

As future work, we plan to implement native JavaEE support for the KeY tool, a specification language for dependency clusters in JML, as well as proof management within the tool. It would also be very interesting if other program analysis methods could be extended to support our notion of non-interference and if some steps in our method could be further automatized.

References

1. Ahrendt, W., Beckert, B., Bubel, R., Hähnle, R., Schmitt, P.H., Ulbrich, M. (eds.): Deductive Software Verification - The KeY Book: From Theory to Practice. Springer, Heidelberg (2016)
2. Askarov, A., Chong, S., Mantel, H.: Hybrid monitors for concurrent noninterference. In: IEEE 28th Computer Security Foundations Symposium, CSF 2015, Verona, Italy, 13–17 July 2015
3. Barthe, G., Pichardie, D., Rezk, T.: A certified lightweight non-interference Java bytecode verifier. In: Nicola, R. (ed.) ESOP 2007. LNCS, vol. 4421, pp. 125–140. Springer, Heidelberg (2007). doi:10.1007/978-3-540-71316-6_10

4. Beckert, B., Bruns, D., Klebanov, V., Scheben, C., Schmitt, P.H., Ulbrich, M.: Information flow in object-oriented software. In: Gupta, G., Peña, R. (eds.) LOP-STR 2013. LNCS, vol. 8901, pp. 19–37. Springer, Heidelberg (2013). doi:10.1007/978-3-319-14125-1_2
5. Chong, S., Vikram, K., Myers, A.C., et al.: SIF: Enforcing confidentiality and integrity in web applications. In: USENIX Security, vol. 7 (2007)
6. Clark, D., Hunt, S.: Non-interference for deterministic interactive programs. In: Degano, P., Guttman, J., Martinelli, F. (eds.) FAST 2008. LNCS, vol. 5491, pp. 50–66. Springer, Heidelberg (2009). doi:10.1007/978-3-642-01465-9_4
7. Cohen, E.: Information transmission in computational systems. SIGOPS Oper. Syst. Rev. **11**, 133–139 (1977)
8. EJB 3.1 Expert Group: JSR 318: Enterprise JavaBeans, Version 3.1. Sun Microsystems (2009). https://jcp.org/en/jsr/detail?id=366. Accessed 31 Aug 2016
9. Ereth, S., Mantel, H., Perner, M.: Towards a common specification language for information-flow security in RS3 and beyond: RIFL 1.0 - the language. Technical Report TUD-CS-2014-0115, TU Darmstadt (2014)
10. Goguen, J.A., Meseguer, J.: Security policies and security models. In: IEEE Security and Privacy (1982)
11. Graf, J., Hecker, M., Mohr, M.: Using Joana for information flow control in Java programs - a practical guide. In: ATPS, February 2013
12. Greiner, S., Grahl, D.: Non-interference with what-declassification in component-based systems. In: CSF (2016)
13. Greiner, S., Mohr, M., Beckert, B.: Modular verification of information flow security in component-based systems - proofs and proof of concept (2017)
14. Hammer, C., Snelting, G.: Flow-sensitive, context-sensitive, and object-sensitive information flow control based on program dependence graphs. Int. J. Inf. Secur. **8**, 399–422 (2009)
15. IBM Research: T.J. Watson Library for Analysis (WALA). http://wala.sf.net
16. Johnson, A., Waye, L., Moore, S., Chong, S.: Exploring and enforcing security guarantees via program dependence graphs. In: PLDI, June 2015
17. Kassios, I.T.: Dynamic frames: support for framing, dependencies and sharing without restrictions. In: Misra, J., Nipkow, T., Sekerinski, E. (eds.) FM 2006. LNCS, vol. 4085, pp. 268–283. Springer, Heidelberg (2006). doi:10.1007/11813040_19
18. Küsters, R., Truderung, T., Beckert, B., Bruns, D., Kirsten, M., Mohr, M.: A hybrid approach for proving noninterference of Java programs. In: CSF, July 2015
19. Lovat, E., Fromm, A., Mohr, M., Pretschner, A.: SHRIFT system-wide hybrid information flow tracking. In: Federrath, H., Gollmann, D. (eds.) SEC 2015. IAICT, vol. 455, pp. 371–385. Springer, Cham (2015). doi:10.1007/978-3-319-18467-8_25
20. Mantel, H.: Possibilistic definitions of security – an assembly kit. In: CSFW (2000)
21. Mantel, H., Sands, D., Sudbrock, H.: Assumptions and guarantees for compositional noninterference. In: CSF (2011)
22. Murray, T.C., Sison, R., Pierzchalski, E., Rizkallah, C.: Compositional verification and refinement of concurrent value-dependent noninterference. In: CSF (2016)
23. Myers, A.C.: JFlow: Practical mostly-static information flow control. In: Proceedings of the 26th ACM SIGPLAN-SIGACT Symposium on Principles of Programming Languages (1999)
24. Nanevski, A., Banerjee, A., Garg, D.: Verification of information flow and access control policies with dependent types. In: IEEE Security and Privacy, May 2011
25. O'Neill, K.R., Clarkson, M.R., Chong, S.: Information-flow security for interactive programs. In: CSFW, Jul 2006

26. Rafnsson, W., Hedin, D., Sabelfeld, A.: Securing interactive programs. In: CSF (2012)
27. Sabelfeld, A., Mantel, H.: Static confidentiality enforcement for distributed programs. In: Hermenegildo, M.V., Puebla, G. (eds.) SAS 2002. LNCS, vol. 2477, pp. 376–394. Springer, Heidelberg (2002). doi:10.1007/3-540-45789-5_27
28. Sabelfeld, A., Sands, D.: A PER model of secure information flow in sequential programs. Higher-Order Symbolic Comput. **14**, 59–91 (2001)
29. Sabelfeld, A., Sands, D.: Declassification: dimensions and principles. J. Comput. Secur. **17**, 517–548 (2009)
30. Scheben, C., Schmitt, P.H.: Verification of information flow properties of JAVA programs without approximations. In: Beckert, B., Damiani, F., Gurov, D. (eds.) FoVeOOS 2011. LNCS, vol. 7421, pp. 232–249. Springer, Heidelberg (2012). doi:10. 1007/978-3-642-31762-0_15
31. Scheben, C., Schmitt, P.H.: Efficient self-composition for weakest precondition calculi. In: Jones, C., Pihlajasaari, P., Sun, J. (eds.) FM 2014. LNCS, vol. 8442, pp. 579–594. Springer, Cham (2014). doi:10.1007/978-3-319-06410-9_39
32. Sheldon, M.A., Gifford, D.K.: Static dependent types for first class modules. In: Proceedings of the 1990 ACM Conference on LISP and Functional Programming. ACM (1990)
33. Ranganath, V.-P., et al.: Indus. http://indus.projects.cs.ksu.edu/. Last visited on 01 Feb 2017
34. Wasserrab, D., Lohner, D.: Proving information flow noninterference by reusing a machine-checked correctness proof for slicing. In: VERIFY (2010)

IJIT: An API for Boolean Program Analysis with Just-in-Time Translation

Peizun Liu[⊠] and Thomas Wahl

Northeastern University, Boston, USA
lpzun@ccs.neu.edu

Abstract. Exploration algorithms for explicit-state transition systems are a core back-end technology in program verification. They can be applied to *programs* by generating the transition system on the fly, avoiding an expensive up-front translation. An on-the-fly strategy requires significant modifications to the implementation, into a form that stores states directly as valuations of program variables. Performed manually on a per-algorithm basis, such modifications are laborious and error-prone.

In this paper we present the IJIT Application Programming Interface (API), which allows users to automatically transform a given transition system exploration algorithm to one that operates on *Boolean* programs. The API converts system states temporarily to program states *just in time* for expansion via image computations, forward or backward. Using our API, we have effortlessly extended various non-trivial (e.g. infinite-state) model checking algorithms to operate on multi-threaded Boolean programs. We demonstrate the ease of use of the API, and present a case study on the impact of the just-in-time translation on these algorithms.

1 Introduction

Boolean programs [4], a finite-data abstraction of general-purpose software obtained by predicate abstraction [13], have proved to be an intermediate notation very useful for verification that factors out the data complexity from programs. State exploration algorithms, however, are typically designed to operate on forms of transition systems. To apply these algorithms to Boolean programs, one can in principle translate the input program into a transition system, before starting the exploration. This input translation incurs, however, a blow-up that is exponential in the number of program variables.

This classic problem in program verification has led to sophisticated algorithms that translate the program into a transition system *on the fly*, as the state space is explored. This idea was pioneered for model checking algorithms by the SPIN tool [14]. In general, to convert an exploration algorithm into an on-the-fly version, the state representation data structure needs to be changed everywhere in the implementation to a tuple over program variable valuations. Consequently, operations on the state representation, notably image computations, need to be re-implemented as well, to reflect the program semantics.

This work is supported by NSF grant no. 1253331.

A. Cimatti and M. Sirjani (Eds.): SEFM 2017, LNCS 10469, pp. 316–331, 2017.
DOI: 10.1007/978-3-319-66197-1_20

Such an algorithm re-implementation avoids the exponential program-to-transition-system translation, but comes with its own cost: due to its low-level nature, it is laborious and error-prone, especially for sophisticated algorithms. In the rest of this paper we describe a way to *automatically* construct on-the-fly program state explorers from implementations operating on transition systems. We leave the system state data structure intact (hence no algorithm re-implementation), and pass the Boolean program as input (hence no input program translation). Our strategy is then as follows: whenever predecessor or successor images need to be computed, the current system state is converted temporarily and *just in time* for the image computation into a Boolean program state. The image is then computed using the program execution semantics, e.g. via pre- or post-conditions. The resulting image states are converted back to, and stored as, system states. This process is repeated for each image computation.

This simple strategy has one crucial advantage: it requires very little change on a per-algorithm basis: once we have provided image operations for Boolean programs (a one-time effort), all we need to do is replace the calls to image functions in the original implementation by new functions that take a system state and (i) convert it to a Boolean program state, (ii) apply the image, and (iii) convert the result back. These steps can be encapsulated into a single operation.

Being largely independent of the underlying algorithm, this strategy can be automated. To this end, we present an Application Programming Interface (API) that provides conversion functions between system and Boolean program states. It further offers implementations of common image operations on Boolean programs, including standard pre- and post-images, as well as more complex image operations for infinite-state system exploration. Our API permits users to transform a wide range of transition system exploration algorithms into Boolean program versions automatically—with little effort and a high degree of reliability—, including sophisticated reachability and coverability algorithms for infinite-state systems such as Petri nets.

For an experimental case study, we have implemented several exploration algorithms in three versions: (a) one that uses the naive **input translate** option, (b) one that implements the manual **algorithm re-implement** option, and (c) one that uses our API to perform **just-in-time translation**. The comparison (c) against (b) demonstrates that the repeated state representation conversion is not harmful: using our API we achieve almost the same efficiency as the gold standard of re-implementation by hand. The comparison (c) against (a) demonstrates that the just-in-time version is vastly more efficient than the version employing up-front input translation.

2 Boolean Programs and Thread-Transition Systems

Our API allows exploration algorithms that operate on transition systems-derived from *Boolean programs* (BP) [4] to be applied directly to such programs, circumventing the blow-up incurred by the input translation. In this section we formalize the language of (possibly threaded) BPs and the transition system model of *thread transition systems*. The latter serve as the input language of exploration algorithms that we later wish to apply directly to BPs.

2.1 Boolean Programs

Boolean programs typically arise from predicate abstractions of application code in system-level languages. All variables are of type `bool`. Control flow constructs are optimized for synthesizability and therefore include "spaghetti statements" like **skip** and **goto**. An overview of the syntax of BPs is given in Fig. 1. A program consists of a **decl**aration of *global* Boolean variables, followed by a list of functions. A function consists of a **decl**aration of *local* Boolean variables, followed by a list of labeled statements.

We illustrate the intuition behind individual statements of BPs. Among the sequential statements (*seqstmt*), **skip** advances the program counter (pc); **goto** *labellist* nondeterministically chooses one of the given labels as the next pc; **assume** terminates executions that do not satisfy the given expression. Statement := assigns, in parallel, each value in the given *exprlist* to the respective variable in the same-length *varlist*, but terminates the execution if the result does not satisfy the **constrain** expression, if any. Statement **assert** indicates assertions for verification and otherwise acts like **skip**. The meaning of function calls (possibly recursive) and return statements is standard and omitted. In all cases, *expr* is a Boolean expression over global and local program variables, the constants 0 and 1, and the choice symbol $\star$; the latter nondeterministically evaluates to 0 or 1.

In the presence of multiple threads, the global variables are *shared* (both read and write) between the threads. The executing thread is called *active*, the others *passive*. All sequential statements have asynchronous semantics, i.e. they change the local variables of only the active thread. The other statements in Fig. 1 intuitively behave as follows:

prog	::=	**decl** *varlist*; *func**	*func*	::=	**void** *name* (*varlist*) **begin**
					decl *varlist*;
					[*label*: *stmt*;]*
stmt	::=	*seqstmt*			**end**
		start_thread *label*			
		end_thread	*seqstmt*	::=	**skip**
		atomic { [*stmt*;]* }			**goto** *labellist*
		wait			**assume** (*expr*)
		signal			*varlist* := *exprlist* [**constrain** *expr*]
		broadcast			**assert** (*expr*)

Fig. 1. Boolean program syntax (partial)

start_thread *label* (i) advances the program counter of the executing thread, and (ii) creates a new thread whose local variables are copied from the executing thread and whose pc is given by *label*;

end_thread terminates the executing thread;

atomic {*stmt**} denotes atomic execution: a thread executing inside an atomic section cannot be preempted;

wait blocks the execution of a thread (see next);

signal advances the pc of the executing thread and nondeterministically wakes up *one* thread blocked at a **wait** statement, if any, i.e. it advances its pc;

broadcast advances the pc of the executing thread and wakes up *all* threads currently blocked at a **wait**.

Wait and release via **signal** or **broadcast** are powerful synchronization mechanisms, allowing many threads to change state at the same time. None of the above six statements change global variables; only **start_thread** and **end_thread** change the number of threads. Fig. 2 (left) shows an example of a BP with an assertion. A precise small-step operational semantics for multi-threaded BPs is given in App. A of [20].

2.2 From Boolean Programs to Thread Transition Systems

Transition systems are the input formalism for many exploration algorithms, such as breadth-first search for reachability analysis, or the Karp-Miller algorithm for deciding *coverability* in infinite-state systems [16]. To apply these to BPs (and thus connect them, via predicate abstraction, to software verification), the programs are typically translated into transition systems.

Let Boolean program $\mathcal{B}$ be defined over sets of global and local variables V_G and V_L, respectively, and let $\{1..pc_{\max}\}$ be the set of program locations.[1] We translate $\mathcal{B}$ into a finite-state *thread transition system* (TTS) $M = (S, R)$, over the state space $S = \{0,1\}^{|V_G|} \times \{1..pc_{\max}\} \times \{0,1\}^{|V_L|}$ and *edges R*.

Individual BP statements are translated into edges, as follows. A given state $s \in S$ determines a (single-threaded) program state $s_\mathcal{B}$ of $\mathcal{B}$ in a straightforward way: s encodes a valuation of all global variables (the $\{0,1\}^{|V_G|}$ part, the *global state*), a program counter, and a valuation of all local variables (the $\{0,1\}^{|V_L|}$ part, the *local state*). Executing $\mathcal{B}$ on $s_\mathcal{B}$ has several effects: first, it generally changes both the global variables, and the local variables of the active thread (including the pc). These changes result in a new state $t \in S$ again in a straightforward way, defining an edge $(s, t) \in R$.

Second, thread creation and termination, as well as signals and broadcasts, typically have "side effects" that alter the thread count, or local variables of passive threads. To capture such effects in the (single-thread) data structure M, each edge comes with a *type*. It is then left to the exploration algorithm, which has access to the current system state, to fully implement transition semantics. As an example, Fig. 2 shows a BP and a translation into a TTS. Symbol $\rightarrowtail$

---

[1] We write $\{l..r\}$ compactly for $\{n \in \mathbb{N} : l \leq n \leq r\}$.

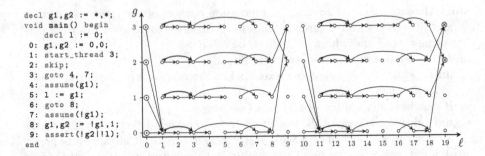

```
decl g1,g2 := *,*;
void main() begin
    decl l := 0;
 0: g1,g2 := 0,0;
 1: start_thread 3;
 2: skip;
 3: goto 4, 7;
 4: assume(g1);
 5: l := g1;
 6: goto 8;
 7: assume(!g1);
 8: g1,g2 := !g1,1;
 9: assert(!g2||l);
end
```

Fig. 2. A Boolean program (left) and a possible translation into a TTS (right). Global variable valuation (g1, g2) is encoded as state $g = 2 \times g2 + g1 \in \{0..3\}$. Similarly, local variable valuation $(pc, 1)$ is encoded as state $\ell = 10 \times 1 + pc \in \{0..19\}$. With this encoding, the four initial program states are shown as $\odot$, the two assertion failure states (satisfying $pc = 9 \wedge g2 = 1 = 1$) as $\otimes$.

marks edge $(0, 1) \rightarrowtail (0, 3)$ as a thread creation edge. The semantics of thread creation (App. A of [20]) prescribes that the active (*creating*) thread moves on (to $pc = 2$); this is reflected by an ordinary edge $(0, 1) \rightarrow (0, 2)$ in the TTS. The *created* thread needs a start location, which is the pc value of the BP state $(g1, g2, pc, 1) = (0, 0, 3, 0)$ encoded by the target TTS state $(0, 3)$ of the edge. Other than above two types of edges shown in Fig. 2, there is one more type, denoted by $\rightsquigarrow$, used in the TTS to characterize broadcasts.

The problem with such a translation from $\mathcal{B}$ to M is of course the potential blow-up: the nominal state space S of M is exponential in the number of global and local variables. This problem has long been known and has led to sophisticated *on-the-fly* temporal-logic model checkers such as SPIN [14], but also to ad-hoc re-implementations of specific exploration algorithms [7,19]. In the rest of this paper we describe an API that automates the construction of on-the-fly program state explorers.

3   BP Analysis with JIT Translation: Overview

We target *exploration algorithms*, i.e. algorithms that operate on a transition system representation of the given program and involve *image computations*: given a system state, they repeatedly compute some notion of successors or predecessors of the state. Figure 3 (left; ignore the boxes for now) shows a schematic version of such algorithms. Input is a transition system M and some target state set T, such as a bad system state whose discovery would indicate a reachable error in the system. The algorithm maintains a worklist W of states to be explored, typically initialized to the initial or bad states of the system, depending on whether the search proceeds forward or backward. It also maintains a set X of explored states, initially empty. The exploration proceeds by extracting an unexplored state w from W and iterating through the set of states w' in w's image, computed by image. If w' is new, we test whether it belongs to the target states T.

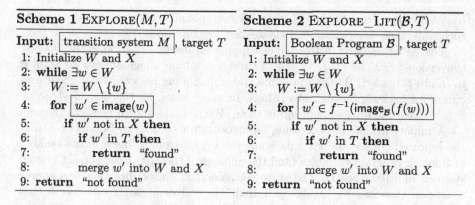

Scheme 1 EXPLORE(M, T)	**Scheme 2** EXPLORE_IJIT$(\mathcal{B}, T)$
Input: transition system M , target T	**Input:** Boolean Program $\mathcal{B}$, target T
1: Initialize W and X	1: Initialize W and X
2: **while** $\exists w \in W$	2: **while** $\exists w \in W$
3: $W := W \setminus \{w\}$	3: $W := W \setminus \{w\}$
4: **for** $w' \in \text{image}(w)$	4: **for** $w' \in f^{-1}(\text{image}_{\mathcal{B}}(f(w)))$
5: **if** w' not in X **then**	5: **if** w' not in X **then**
6: **if** w' in T **then**	6: **if** w' in T **then**
7: **return** "found"	7: **return** "found"
8: merge w' into W and X	8: merge w' into W and X
9: **return** "not found"	9: **return** "not found"

Fig. 3. State exploration over a transition system (left) and a Boolean program (right). Lines 5 and 6 test whether w' has not been explored and w' is a target state, respectively. In a concrete algorithm these tests may involve more than set membership.

If so, we report the success of the search. The search terminates when no more unexplored states exist (in W).

Now suppose the transition system M is actually a translation of a Boolean program $\mathcal{B}$, which we want to explore directly, using the same algorithm scheme. One way to achieve that is to change the data structure that Scheme 1 relies on: instead of storing states to be explored as states of M, we store them as Boolean program states, one entry per program variable. Images are then computed by "executing" $\mathcal{B}$ in accordance with $\mathcal{B}$'s execution model.

However, like with any data structure change in any non-trivial program, the required effort is significant: all of T, W, X must be changed, and therefore virtually every line in a program that implements Scheme 1. Re-implementing image to operate on a Boolean program $\mathcal{B}$ is also involved. The whole change process is not only error-prone; it also creates an entirely new implementation that needs to be maintained independently of the one operating on M.

An alternative to this strategy is shown in Scheme 2 on the right, which is almost identical to that on the left. States are stored as transition system states of M as before, but the input is now the Boolean program $\mathcal{B}$. Since M is no longer available, we cannot apply M's transition relation to compute images. However, since there is a one-to-one correspondence between states of $\mathcal{B}$ and of M, we can compute images by converting, using function f, to $\mathcal{B}$'s state representation *just in time* for the image computation, and reverting the resulting image states back to the system state format of M (Line 4). Note that f^{-1} needs to operate on (and return) *sets* of states.

Operation image$_{\mathcal{B}}$ computes images of an intermediate program state $p :=$ $f(w)$. Its implementation depends on the kind of image computation performed by the algorithm: For standard forward exploration, it can be computed by executing, from p, the statement of $\mathcal{B}$ pointed to by the pc encoded in p. For a backward exploration algorithm, image$_{\mathcal{B}}$ is more complicated: we need to identify statements *leading to* the current pc via $\mathcal{B}$'s control flow graph, and then symbolically execute such statements backwards, e.g. via weakest preconditions [19].

The API presented in this paper supplies an implementation of the $\mathcal{B} \leftrightarrow M$ conversion functions (f, f^{-1}) and of various common image operations applied to (multi-threaded) Boolean program states, including backward statement execution for backward search algorithms. In many cases, all the user needs to do is to replace the image operation in their algorithm, as shown in Fig. 3 (boxes).

A minor runtime cost of using an algorithm according to Scheme 2 is that the repeated conversion will take some time. This time is linear in the number of Boolean program variables (and the number of threads of the current system state, if multi-threaded). The state conversion in either direction is a simple operation that can be highly optimized. We will demonstrate in Sect. 5 that the benefit of avoiding the explicit construction of M often far outweighs the conversion overhead.

We end this section by discussing desirable characteristics of algorithms that will benefit from using our API. We target exploration (search, model checking) algorithms for state transition systems (e.g. TTS) of Boolean programs. The term "exploration" here refers to the reliance of such algorithms on the computation of *standard* pre- and postimages of (sets of) states. The transition systems must relate to the Boolean programs in a way that there is a one-to-one correspondence between program states and system states. In particular, the systems cannot be (lossy) *abstractions* of the Boolean programs; otherwise, a system state may not map to a unique program state, or vice versa.

4   The IJIT Application Programming Interface

In this section we sketch usage and design of our API, named IJIT: **I**nterface for **J**ust-**I**n-**T**ime translation. A detailed tutorial and documentation can be found in [18].

4.1   API Usage

We use a fictitious procedure `explore` to illustrate the use of our API; see Fig. 4 (left). The procedure explores the state space of some transition system given as a TTS. It begins by reading the TTS into a data structure called R (Line 5) and extracts from R sets of initial and final states, respectively (Lines 7 and 8). The procedure then enters some kind of loop to explore the state space represented by R, perhaps until no more unexplored states are available (this is immaterial for our API). Crucial is that the loop body will invoke an image operation on a state `tau` (Line 12), likely at least once in each iteration. We assume R is nondeterministic, so that the call returns a set of states, Tau.

Figure 4 (right) highlights (in gray) the changes the programmer needs to make to have procedure `explore` operate on a Boolean program; we call the resulting procedure `explore_jit`. We explain these changes in the following.

```
// user's headers, namespace, etc.      1    #include "ijit.hh"
                                         2    using namespace ijit;
void explore() {                         3    void explore_jit() {
  // ...                                 4      // ...
  auto R = read_file("filename.tts")1    5      auto P = parser::parse("filename.bp", mode::POST);
                                         6      converter c;
  set<state> I = R.init();               7      set<state> I = c.convert(P.init());
  set<state> F = R.final();              8      set<state> F = c.convert(P.final());
  state tau;                             9      state tau;
  while (...) { // state exploration    10      while (...) {
    tau = ... ; // an unexplored state  11        tau = ... ;
    set<state> Tau = image(tau);        12        set<state> Tau = c.convert(
                                         13                image(c.convert(tau), mode::POST));
    ...                                 14        ...
  } // end while                        15      }
}                                       16    }
```

Fig. 4. An example illustrating the usage of IJIT. Left: a fictitious state space exploration procedure. Right: the just-in-time version obtained using IJIT. Line numbers in the middle; highlighted code shows places that have changed from the original version.

- Instead of reading a TTS, we now read a Boolean program as input (Line 5). This is done using a parser supplied by IJIT. Procedure `parse` has two arguments: the name of input file, and the parser's direction mode: `POST` will cause the parser to generate code for subsequent forward-directed analysis (via postimages). Mode `PREV` does the analogous for backward analysis; a mode of `BOTH` will generate code for both. The parser also offers functionality to return sets `I` and `F` of initial and final program states, extracted from the initial variable declarations and assertions in the BP, respectively.
- The conversion between different state representation formats, explained below, is done via methods of a class `converter`. The user needs to instantiate this class before any conversion methods of the API can be called (Line 6).
- Conversion between state representation formats happens in several places: to convert the initial and final Boolean program state sets into TTS state sets (Lines 7 and 8), and in the image computations. If the algorithm implemented by procedure `explore` operates on TTS as defined in Sect. 2, the JIT version of the procedure can be implemented using conversion functions supplied by the API (Line 12): the current (unexplored) TTS state `tau` is converted into a BP state, followed by a Boolean program image computation using the given direction mode, followed by a back-conversion into a set of TTS states.
  If the API's conversion functions cannot be used, users must supply their own functions. To reduce the programming burden, the API provides an inheritance interface that allows defining conversion functions via specialization. Users are free to define stand-alone conversions.

4.2 API Design

API IJIT is implemented in C++. A schematic overview is shown in Fig. 5.

Parser. The main purpose of the parser is to process the input BP and populate the data structures to be used in image computations. These include the program's control flow graph, and pre- and postcondition expressions for pre- and

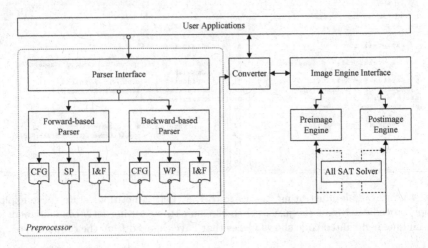

Fig. 5. Schematic overview of IJIT. The preprocessor part is usually called only once. CFG: control flow graph; SP/WP: strongest postcondition/weakest precondition; I/F: the set of initial/final states

postimage computations, respectively. The parser also extracts initial and final state information, the latter by collecting all states violating any of assertions in the Boolean program.

Converter. The converter provides an adapter between system states and program states. In our design, the converter is an abstract C++ class with default implementations of conversion functions. If desired or necessary, users can either inherit the abstract class and override the default implementation, or write a stand-alone converter from scratch.

Image Engine. At the core of our API are the engines to compute the preimage or postimage of a given Boolean program state. These routines make use of the control flow graph obtained by the parser, especially for preimages, in order to determine the set of statements that can lead to the current pc. Once the statement to be executed forward or backward has been determined, the statement's semantics determines the effect on the program data. The semantics is given as a set of first-order predicates expressing strongest post- or weakest preconditions. To perform image computations, the engine instantiates these formulas with the current-state valuations of the program variables. It then invokes an All-SAT solver to obtain the pre- or postimages as satisfiable assignments.

All-SAT Solver. The All-SAT solver used in image computations is not based upon a state-of-the-art SAT solver, which would require CNF conversion. Instead we found it to be more efficient to simply build a custom SAT solver that enumerates solutions. Note that input formulas to the solver formalize Boolean program statements and thus tend to be very short.

5   Case Study: Performance Benefits of IJIT

We evaluate the benefit of our API on a number of diverse benchmark algorithms. All are designed to operate on thread-transition systems (TTS) for either a fixed or an unbounded number of threads; we wish to apply them to multi-threaded Boolean programs directly. For each algorithm, we compare the performance of three versions: (i) the *TTS version*, which is the original version, but prefixed by an input translation from BPs into TTS; (ii) the *BP version*, which is a manual and *optimized* re-implementation where the internal state data structure has been changed to BP states; and finally (iii) the *JIT version*, which employs our API. We expect a performance ranking of the form

$$BPversion \;\; < \;\; JITversion \;\; \ll \;\; TTSversion$$

where "<" ("≪") means "(much) faster". In particular, the hand-crafted BP version makes repeated conversion between state representations unnecessary and can therefore be considered the gold standard for efficiency. We hope the automated JIT version of the algorithm to perform nearly as well.

5.1   Benchmark Algorithms

We sketch the purpose and basic concepts of four diverse algorithms used in our case study; more details are provided in App. B of [20]. The algorithms cover the spectrum of finite- and infinite-state searches, and of forward and backward explorations.

Cutoff Detection via Finite-State Search (Ecut) [15]. ECUT implements *dynamic cutoff detection* for parameterized thread transition systems. A *cutoff* point is a number n_0 of threads that are sufficient to reach all reachable thread states. The core procedure of ECUT is a (multi-threaded but) finite-state search, BFS style. The TTS version of ECUT can be transformed into the JIT version without any programming beyond the few changes discussed in Sect. 4.

Karp-Miller Procedure [16]. We experiment with two variants of this classic procedure; both are in use in unbounded-thread program verification:

(1)   KM decides the reachability of a specific target state t: it stops when a state covering t has been encountered;
(2)   AKM ("All-KM") builds the complete coverability tree, i.e. it runs KM until a fixpoint is reached.

WQOS Backward Search (BWS) [1,2]. This technique is a sound and complete algorithm to decide coverability for *well quasi-ordered systems* (WQOS), a broad family of transition systems that subsumes replicated Boolean programs, Petri nets, VASS, and many more. Note that BWS is a backward exploration. In contrast, the previous three algorithms explore forward.

5.2   Case Study

Experimental Setup. We compare the impact of our API on the efficiency of the four algorithms described in Sect. 5.1. For each algorithm $A \in \{\text{ECUT}, \text{KM}, \text{AKM}, \text{BWS}\}$, we compare three different versions: (1) the TTS version — named A(TTS); (2) the JIT version obtained using our API — named A(JIT); and (3) the hand-implemented Boolean program version — named version A (BP).

We perform the comparison using a collection of Boolean programs obtained via predicate abstraction from 30 concurrent C programs. The C programs are detailed in Table 1. We use SATABS [8] to construct the BPs from these programs. The BPs are also concurrent; threads execute the same Boolean procedure. In most cases, the same C source program generates several BPs (since SATABS goes through several abstract-verify-refine iterations). In the end we obtained 155 BPs for the 30 C programs. For the TTS version of each algorithm, we use SATABS to generate the TTS from the Boolean program (option `--build-tts`; this is where the input format explosion inevitably happens).

For each benchmark, we consider verification of a safety property, specified via an assertion that is pushed, during predicate abstraction, from C to the Boolean program. All experiments are performed on a 2.3 GHz Intel Xeon machine with 64 GB memory, running 64-bit Linux. The timeout is set to 30 min; the memory limit to 4 GB. All benchmarks and implementations are available at [18].

Table 1. Benchmark statistics: $GV/LV/LOC$ = # of global/local C program variables/lines of code; $|V_G|/|V_L|/|PC|/Its.$ = # of global/local Boolean variables/program counters/CEGAR iterations; $|G|/|L|/|R|$ = # of global/local states/transitions in TTS; *Safe?* = ✓: program safe; $|\cdot|$ represents the median of the feature across different BP/TTS resulting from the same C program. Note that often $|G| > 2^{|V_G|}$, due to auxiliary states used by SATABS in the BP $\to$ TTS translation

ID/Program	C Program			BP				TTS			Safe?	ID/Program	C Program			BP				TTS			Safe?
	GV	LV	LOC	$|V_G|$	$|V_L|$	$|PC|$	Its.	$|G|$	$|L|$	$|R|$			GV	LV	LOC	$|V_G|$	$|V_L|$	$|PC|$	Its.	$|G|$	$|L|$	$|R|$	
01/INCREM-L	2	1	46	3	1	40	2	33	71	688	✓	16/TAS-LOCK	2	2	58	3	1	48	2	16385	54	269488	✓
02/INCREM-C	1	3	57	0	4	35	4	5	449	784	✓	17/DBLOCK-1	3	0	70	7	1	79	10	513	151	20928	✓
03/PRNG-L	2	4	63	2	3	45	2	17	265	1488	✓	18/DBLOCK-2	3	0	73	6	1	47	22	33	71	688	✓
04/PRNG-C	1	5	95	0	5	48	2	5	993	1760	✓	19/DBLOCK-3	3	0	66	4	1	73	3	257	67	4976	✓
05/FINDMAX-L	3	3	59	1	0	43	2	9	25	57	✓	20/TICKET-HC	3	1	61	5	1	73	5	257	139	10912	✓
06/FINDMAX-C	2	5	79	0	1	48	2	5	59	76	✓	21/TICKET-LO	3	1	46	5	1	63	5	65	115	2048	✓
07/MAXOPT-L	3	4	69	1	1	48	2	9	63	162	✓	22/BSD-AK	1	7	90	3	1	119	2	33	196	1922	✓
08/MAXOPT-C	2	6	86	0	2	53	2	5	137	196	✓	23/BSD-RA	2	21	87	3	0	138	2	33	107	996	✓
09/STACK-L	4	2	79	1	3	53	3	9	157	360	✓	24/NETBSD	1	28	152	3	1	278	3	33	423	4096	✓
10/STACK-C	3	3	89	3	1	54	2	33	81	740	✓	25/SOLARIS	1	56	122	5	1	182	2	129	283	10847	✓
11/BS-LOOP	0	6	24	0	7	30	1	65	24	448	✗	26/BOOP	5	2	89	5	2	61	4	129	213	8064	✗
12/COND	1	3	56	0	3	29	2	33	25	200	✓	27/QRCU-2	7	6	120	3	0	129	15	33	103	1001	✓
13/FUNC-P	2	1	67	2	6	32	3	5	3969	9728	✓	28/QRCU-4	8	8	182	5	2	275	21	129	873	35024	✓
14/S-LOOP	5	0	60	4	0	37	20	5	209	296	✓	29/UNVER-IF	2	1	25	4	0	53	3	129	95	4096	✓
15/PTHREAD	5	0	85	7	0	60	5	17	3329	20608	✗	30/SPINLOCK	2	0	37	3	0	47	2	129	79	3584	✓

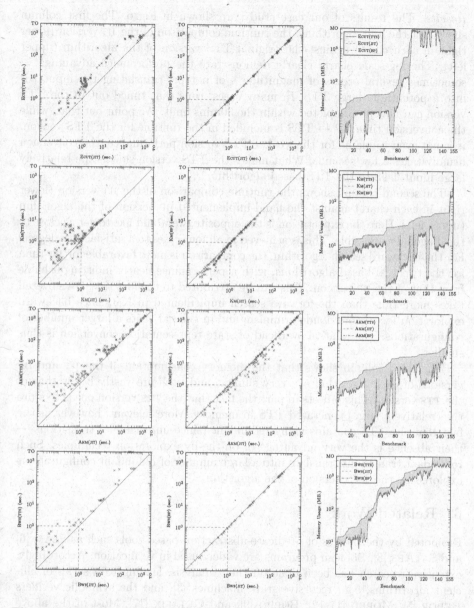

Fig. 6. Performance impact of our API (TO: timeout, MO: memory out). For A ∈ {Ecut, Km, Akm, Bws}:   ▶ runtime comparison: left column: A(TTS) against A(JIT); center: A(BP) against A(JIT). Each dot = execution time on one example. Square in the lower left corner of each chart: runtime of less than 1 second for both algorithms, hence unreliable.   ▶ memory usage comparison: right column: comparing memory usage across the three different versions. The plots are sorted by the memory usage of the TTS version of A. The shadowed areas show the difference. (Color figure online)

Results. The results of our case study are shown in Fig. 6. The first column shows, for the four algorithms, the runtime comparison of the JIT version (lower right in each chart) against the original TTS version of the algorithm (upper left). The log-scale charts clearly demonstrate the performance advantage — sometimes several orders of magnitude – of not pre-translating the input BP into a potentially large TTS. In many cases, runs that timed out in the TTS version can now be completed within the 30mins limit. We point out that, while the conversion time BP → TTS is included in the runtime for the TTS version, it is not even to blame for the weaker TTS version performance: the conversion usually takes a few seconds. What makes the TTS version slow is the relatively large input TTS to the TTS-based algorithm.

The second column shows the runtime comparison of the JIT version (lower right in each chart) against the hand-implemented BP version of the algorithm (upper left). Here the expectation is the opposite: we would like to get as close to the diagonal as possible. This is achieved in all four cases to a satisfactory degree. For the backward search algorithm, the comparison is more favorable for JIT than for the two KM-based algorithms, with a performance nearly indistinguishable from that of the BP version. This can be attributed to the fact that BWS overall takes more time than the forward search implemented in KM, since backward exploration faces more nondeterminism and in general visits a larger number of configurations. The relative overhead of state representation conversion is thus smaller.

The third column shows that the memory consumption of the JIT and BP versions of each algorithm are very similar; and both are vastly below that of the TTS version. This reflects in part the fact that the TTS version needs to store the (relatively large) generated TTS in memory. More relevant, however, is the fact that the TTS contains many redundant (since unreachable) transitions — their absence is the very advantage of on-the-fly exploration techniques. Such redundant transitions translate into a large number of redundant configurations explored by the TTS version of the algorithm.

6   Related Work

Promoted by the success of predicate-abstraction based tools such as SLAM [6] and SATABS [8], Boolean programs are widely used in verification. Accordingly, extensive research has been done on their analysis, leading to a series of efficient algorithms, e.g., recursive state machines [3], and the symbolic verifiers BEBOP [5], MOPED [11,12], BOPPO [9], and GETAFIX [17]. Most of the above approaches use BDDs as symbolic representation, which do not lend themselves to an efficient on-the-fly model construction.

In contrast, explicit-state model checking techniques often construct the state space of the program they are exploring on the fly. A prominent tool that pioneered this strategy is the explicit-state model checker SPIN [14]. Another notable explicit-state on-the-fly model checker is Java PathFinder [21], which takes Java[TM] bytecode and analyses all possible paths through the program, checking for deadlocks, assertion violations, etc.

Solutions addressing the translation blow-up in connection with (more complex) unbounded-thread verification techniques are rare. While these techniques have been applied to program analysis, the application is typically preceded by an up-front translation of the program into an explicit transition system [10,15]. For Boolean programs generated via predicate abstraction, this only works for small local state spaces, for example when the number of predicates is small. When going through several iterations of the predicate abstraction CEGAR loop, in contrast, the number of Boolean program variables quickly becomes large.

On-the-fly techniques for unbounded-thread algorithms applied to Boolean programs are given in tools by Basler et al. [7], and by Liu et al. [19]. Both are re-implementations of the algorithms they are targeting, which is the Karp-Miller procedure for VASS in the former case, and the backward search algorithm for broadcast Petri nets in the latter. Both demonstrate the benefits of exploring BPs directly, but they do not come for free: the re-implementation is low-level work involving tricky data structure changes, affecting the very foundation of the implementation. In fact, the Karp-Miller implementation in [7] generated runtime errors on some of our benchmarks, so we excluded it from our case study.

7 Summary

The problem of the blow-up between programs and transition systems that describe the programs' semantics and are often used in exploration algorithms is well known. Translating a program into an explicit transition system undermines the practical runtime performance of these algorithms, and thus diminishes their value. This problem has been addressed in an ad-hoc way, by re-implementing these algorithms into ones operating on programs. This process is painful and prone to programming errors, to which we attribute the fact the input translation cost is often grudgingly accepted.

In this paper we have introduced an API that largely automates the required transformations. In the best case, programmers mostly need to add calls to an API-provided convert method to (usually few) places in the code where images are computed. In the worst case, programmers have to supply this conversion method. We have demonstrated the huge impact of the use of the API on various algorithms that rely on an up-front BP → TTS translation. We have also compared the performance of the JIT version to the version re-implemented by hand that operates entirely on Boolean programs, and found nearly no performance difference to this gold-standard implementation.

We have presented our API with dedicated support for algorithms that operate on Boolean programs and thread-transition systems, due to their popularity in, and significance for, software verification. Given proper state representation conversion functions, we believe our API to be able to bridge the gap between other types of modeling languages, such as Boolean programs and Petri nets. We leave implementing, and experimenting with, such extensions for the future. Extending the API to support algorithms like partial order reduction that need to perform a nonstandard image computation is another promising research direction and we leave it for the future work too.

References

1. Abdulla, P.A.: Well (and better) quasi-ordered transition systems. Bull. Symbolic Logic **16**(4), 457–515 (2010)
2. Abdulla, P.A., Cerans, K., Jonsson, B., Tsay, Y.K.: General decidability theorems for infinite-state systems. In: LICS, pp. 313–321 (1996)
3. Alur, R., Benedikt, M., Etessami, K., Godefroid, P., Reps, T., Yannakakis, M.: Analysis of recursive state machines. ACM Trans. Program. Lang. Syst. **27**(4), 786–818 (2005)
4. Ball, T., Rajamani, S.: Boolean programs: a model and process for software analysis. Technical report MSR-TR-2000-14, Microsoft Research (2000)
5. Ball, T., Rajamani, S.K.: Bebop: a symbolic model checker for boolean programs. In: Havelund, K., Penix, J., Visser, W. (eds.) SPIN 2000. LNCS, vol. 1885, pp. 113–130. Springer, Heidelberg (2000). doi:10.1007/10722468_7
6. Ball, T., Rajamani, S.K.: The SLAM project: debugging system software via static analysis. In: POPL, pp. 1–3 (2002)
7. Basler, G., Hague, M., Kroening, D., Ong, C.-H.L., Wahl, T., Zhao, H.: BOOM: taking boolean program model checking one step further. In: Esparza, J., Majumdar, R. (eds.) TACAS 2010. LNCS, vol. 6015, pp. 145–149. Springer, Heidelberg (2010). doi:10.1007/978-3-642-12002-2_11
8. Clarke, E., Kroening, D., Sharygina, N., Yorav, K.: SATABS: SAT-based predicate abstraction for ANSI-C. In: Halbwachs, N., Zuck, L.D. (eds.) TACAS 2005. LNCS, vol. 3440, pp. 570–574. Springer, Heidelberg (2005). doi:10.1007/978-3-540-31980-1_40
9. Cook, B., Kroening, D., Sharygina, N.: Symbolic model checking for asynchronous boolean programs. In: Godefroid, P. (ed.) SPIN 2005. LNCS, vol. 3639, pp. 75–90. Springer, Heidelberg (2005). doi:10.1007/11537328_9
10. Delzanno, G., Raskin, J.-F., Begin, L.: Towards the automated verification of multithreaded Java programs. In: Katoen, J.-P., Stevens, P. (eds.) TACAS 2002. LNCS, vol. 2280, pp. 173–187. Springer, Heidelberg (2002). doi:10.1007/3-540-46002-0_13
11. Esparza, J., Hansel, D., Rossmanith, P., Schwoon, S.: Efficient algorithms for model checking pushdown systems. In: Emerson, E.A., Sistla, A.P. (eds.) CAV 2000. LNCS, vol. 1855, pp. 232–247. Springer, Heidelberg (2000). doi:10.1007/10722167_20
12. Esparza, J., Schwoon, S.: A BDD-based model checker for recursive programs. In: Berry, G., Comon, H., Finkel, A. (eds.) CAV 2001. LNCS, vol. 2102, pp. 324–336. Springer, Heidelberg (2001). doi:10.1007/3-540-44585-4_30
13. Graf, S., Saidi, H.: Construction of abstract state graphs with PVS. In: Grumberg, O. (ed.) CAV 1997. LNCS, vol. 1254, pp. 72–83. Springer, Heidelberg (1997). doi:10.1007/3-540-63166-6_10
14. Holzmann, G.J.: The model checker SPIN. IEEE Trans. Softw. Eng. **23**(5), 279–295 (1997)
15. Kaiser, A., Kroening, D., Wahl, T.: Dynamic cutoff detection in parameterized concurrent programs. In: Touili, T., Cook, B., Jackson, P. (eds.) CAV 2010. LNCS, vol. 6174, pp. 645–659. Springer, Heidelberg (2010). doi:10.1007/978-3-642-14295-6_55

16. Karp, R.M., Miller, R.E.: Parallel program schemata. J. Comput. Syst. Sci. **3**(2), 147–195 (1969)
17. La Torre, S., Parthasarathy, M., Parlato, G.: Analyzing recursive programs using a fixed-point calculus. In: PLDI, pp. 211–222 (2009)
18. Liu, P.: http://www.ccs.neu.edu/home/lpzun/ijit/
19. Liu, P., Wahl, T.: Infinite-state backward exploration of Boolean broadcast programs. In: FMCAD, pp. 155–162 (2014)
20. Liu, P., Wahl, T.: IJIT: an API for Boolean program analysis with just-in-time translation (extended technical report) (2017). CoRR arXiv.org/abs/1706.03167
21. Visser, W., Havelund, K., Brat, G., Park, S., Lerda, F.: Model checking programs. Autom. Softw. Eng. **10**(2), 203–232 (2003)

Specification and Semantic Analysis of Embedded Systems Requirements: From Description Logic to Temporal Logic

Nesredin Mahmud[1]([✉]), Cristina Seceleanu[1], and Oscar Ljungkrantz[2]

[1] Mälardalen University, Västerås, Sweden
{nesredin.mahmud,cristina.seceleanu}@mdh.se
[2] Volvo Group Trucks Technology, Gothenburg, Sweden
oscar.ljungkrantz@volvo.com

Abstract. Due to the increasing complexity of embedded systems, early detection of software/hardware errors has become desirable. In this context, effective yet flexible specification methods that support rigorous analysis of embedded systems requirements are needed. Current specification methods such as pattern-based, boilerplates normally lack meta-models for extensibility and flexibility. In contrast, formal specification languages, like temporal logic, Z, etc., enable rigorous analysis, however, they usually are too mathematical and difficult to comprehend by average software engineers. In this paper, we propose a specification representation of requirements, which considers thematic roles and domain knowledge, enabling deep semantic analysis. The specification is complemented by our constrained natural language specification framework, ReSA, which acts as the interface to the representation. The representation that we propose is encoded in description logic, which is a decidable and computationally-tractable ontology language. By employing the ontology reasoner, Hermit, we check for consistency and completeness of requirements. Moreover, we propose an automatic transformation of the ontology-based specifications into Timed Computation Tree Logic formulas, to be used further in model checking embedded systems.

Keywords: Requirements specification · Requirements analysis · Embedded systems · Ontology · Description logic · Timed computation tree logic · Event-based semantics · Thematic roles

1 Introduction

The difficulty of specifying embedded systems requirements has increased due to the high degree of system complexity, and the dependability expected from the solutions, especially for safety-critical systems [1]. Consequently, the development of embedded systems demands stricter approaches of requirements specification and analysis. However, effective specification methods and tools that meet industrial needs, e.g., engineer friendliness, flexibility, fine-grained analysis etc., are lacking. If we consider the automotive industry as the domain of

© Springer International Publishing AG 2017
A. Cimatti and M. Sirjani (Eds.): SEFM 2017, LNCS 10469, pp. 332–348, 2017.
DOI: 10.1007/978-3-319-66197-1_21

focus, current experience tells us that: (i) first, most requirements specification documents are expressed in natural language, therefore it is not uncommon to find inconsistent, ambiguous, vague and imprecise specifications, (ii) second, even if engineers use semi-formal specification methods, such as requirements boilerplates [2] or property specification patters [3,4], as a solution to the aforementioned problems, such methods have fixed sets of templates that frequently limit specification expressiveness, as well as rigid syntactic structures that prevent using different yet equivalent sentences in specification, and (iii) last but not least, the requirements specification methods, as mentioned earlier, do not support computational semantic analysis [5] as used in linguistics, hence rendering the requirements analysis shallow.

Current solutions to the requirements specification and analysis problem involve one or more of the following techniques: domain knowledge, semantics analysis, natural language processing (NLP), logic-based reasoning, conceptual modeling in object-oriented development, property specification patterns, etc. NLP techniques and domain ontologies are used to ease the manual selection of boilerplates [6,7], which is error prone and demanding. However, the approach suffers from inaccurate translations and the lack of a robust meta model that supports scalability and prevents inconsistent definitions of boilerplates. The scalability issue is also shared in property specification patterns [3,4], which define limited sets of patterns that allow the specification of functional and timing requirements of embedded systems. A linguistic approach that uses domain ontology to specify and analyze requirements has already been proposed previously [8]. However, the proposed semantic relations and the thesaurus are very limited, consequently only shallow semantic representations are possible, which limits their application on real-world problems.

To address the above deficiencies and needs, in this paper, we propose a flexible yet rigorous specification of embedded systems requirements. In our previous work [9,10], we have introduced a requirements specification language called *ReSA*, which is a constrained natural language tailored to describing embedded systems requirements. In this paper, we combine *semantic analysis* with *domain ontology* for the semantic representation of ReSA requirements specifications (in brief, ReSA specifications). The semantic analysis enables the consideration of lexical semantics and semantic relations within the analysis of requirements, hence enabling fine-grained analysis. The semantic representation employs an *event-based* approach [11] in conjunction with *thematic roles* [12]. The ontology is encoded in *description logic* (DL) [13], which is a decidable and computationally-tractable part of firs-order logic. Consequently, description logic is a viable solution for the core reasoning of requirements specifications, such as consistency, completeness and entailment. The ontology is also used to automatically generate temporal computation-tree-logic (TCTL) properties from ReSA specifications. The ontology is developed using OWL [14] and the Protégé tool. Our approach is demonstrated on a set of requirements of the *Adjustable Speed Limiter* (ASL) automotive use case, which is an operational and safety-critical automotive system used in Volvo tracks. ASL limits vehicle speed to not exceed a predefined speed, set by the driver.

The rest of the paper is organized as follows. In Sect. 2, we give a brief overview of ReSA, DL, and TCTL. In Sect. 3, we show the semantic representation of ReSA specifications using the event-based approach. We define the equivalence axioms that increase the flexibility of ReSA specifications, in Sect. 4, followed by the proposed approach of analyzing ReSA specifications, in Sect. 5. In Sect. 6, we compare our contributions to related work. Finally, we conclude the paper and outline possible future work in Sect. 7.

2   Preliminaries

In this section, we briefly overview our requirements specification language, ReSA, and its underlying semantic-encoding language, DL. Furthermore, we briefly describe the timed computation tree logic TCTL.

2.1   ReSA

In our previous work [9], we have proposed the requirements specification language ReSA, which closely renders the syntax and semantics of natural language, and allows users to express requirements in a constrained manner. The language targets the embedded systems domain, hence uses concepts such as *System, Para{meter}, Device, Mode, State, Event*, etc. [9]. Further, the language has axioms that guide the specification process, improve the readability, and reduce ambiguity. The concepts and the specification axioms are maintained in a system-level ontology. The ontology is employed for type checking during the specification process in the ReSA Editor [10]. Examples of requirements expressed in ReSA are shown in structured (1-a), tagged (1-b), and plain (1-c) formats, respectively.

(1) (a) If "activation button":inDevice is pressed
           then
                ASL:system shall limit "vehicle speed":para within 500 ms
           endif

     (b) If "activation button":inDevice is pressed, ASL:system shall limit "vehicle speed":para within 500 ms.

     (c) If activation button is pressed, ASL shall limit vehicle speed within 500 ms.

Valid strings of the language include requirements boilerplates, which are sentential forms with dynamic (variable) syntactic elements. In example (1), the boilerplates that are instantiated to construct the requirement are show in Table 1 (the variable elements are enclosed within angle brackets).

At this stage, the language lacks a semantic representation that defines the lexical semantics (semantic roles, quantification, etc.), and semantic relations (synonyms, antonyms, hyponyms and hypernyms, etc.), which are crucial not just to detect non-trivial specification errors, such as inconsistency and incompleteness, but also to discover implicit knowledge of the specifications from explicitly-stated requirements, hence providing better insight into the specifications. In this paper, we give semantics to ReSA in description logic, which enables such functionality.

Table 1. Boilerplates applied in Example (1)

Boilerplate	Type
⟨InDevice⟩ is ⟨Action⟩	Proposition
⟨System⟩ shall ⟨Action⟩ ⟨Parameter⟩	Simple
... within ⟨Time⟩	Prepositional Phrase
if ⟨Antecedent⟩ then ⟨Consequent⟩ endif	Conditional

Table 2. DL constructors

Constructor	Usage	Semantics
⊔ (Union)	$C \sqcup D$	$C^I \cup D^I$
⊓ (Intersection)	$C \sqcap D$	$C^I \cap D^I$
∃ (Existential Qunat.)	$\exists R.C$	$\{x \mid \exists y(x,y) \in R^I \rightarrow y \in C^I\}$
∀ (Value Restriction)	$\forall R.C$	$\{x \mid \forall y(x,y) \in R^I \rightarrow y \in C^I\}$
o (Role Composition)	$R \circ S$	$\{(x,z) \in \Delta^I \times \Delta^I \mid \exists(x,y) \in R^I \wedge \exists(y,z) \in S^I\}$
⊑ (Concept Inclusion)	$C \sqsubseteq D$	$C^I \subseteq D^I$
⊑ (Role Inclusion)	$R \sqsubseteq S$	$S^I \subseteq R^I$
≡ (Equivalence)	$C \equiv D$	$C^I = D^I$
: (Assertion)	x:C	$a^I \in C^I$
	(x,y):R	$(x^I, y^I) \in R^I$
≐ (Definition)	C≐D	$C^I = D^I$

2.2 Description Logic

Description Logic (DL) [13] is a language for knowledge representation, and it is mainly used in fields such as artificial intelligence [15], semantic web [14] and biomedical informatics [16]. DL is designed to contain decidable fragments of first-order logic, for which efficient reasoners exist, e.g., FACT^{++}, HermiT [17].

A DL knowledge base, $K = (T, A)$, contains terminological assertions (a.k.a. TBox, T) and instances (or facts) assertions (a.k.a. ABox, A), and it is built recursively from concepts (unary predicates), roles (binary predicates) and instances (constants) via *Constructors*. DL is inspired by set theory; consequently, the interpretation I of the knowledge-base K is a tuple (Δ^I, F^I), where: Δ^I is the domain, F^I is an interpretation function over the domain, which relates a concept A to a set $A^I \subseteq \Delta^I$, and a role R to a binary set $R^I \subseteq \Delta^I \times \Delta^I$. The knowledge base is consistent if $I \vDash K(or \vDash T \wedge, \vDash A)$ [13]. Table 2 shows the constructors used in this paper, where: (C, D, ⊤ (everything), ⊥ (nothing) are concepts, and R, S are roles).

Besides storing the semantically-consistent specifications, the ontology can be seen as a knowledge base that other systems can use. In this paper, we show how we generate time-bounded response formulas, in TCTL, from the ontology.

2.3   Timed Computation Tree Logic

Timed Computation Tree Logic (TCTL) [18], the timed extension of CTL, is used in this paper as the notation that encodes formalized properties, after the transformation from their ontology-based representation. A well-formed TCTL property is inductively generated based on a production rule (1) that uses a minimal set of operators: $\{true, \neg, \vee, AU, EU\}$, as follows:

$$\phi := true \mid p \mid \neg p \mid \phi \mid \phi \vee \phi \mid \mathsf{E}[\phi \mathsf{U}_{\bowtie t} \phi] \mid \mathsf{A}[\phi \mathsf{U}_{\sim t} \phi], \tag{1}$$

where: p ranges over a set of atomic formulas, A and E are the universal and existential path quantifiers, respectively, U (Until) is a temporal operator, and $\bowtie$ represents one of the relational operators: $\{=, <, \leq\}$. Equivalently, the operators $\square$ and $\Diamond$ are defined as $\neg E[trueU \neg \phi]$ and $A[trueU \phi]$, respectively.

In this paper, we use the following (T)CTL property types (p, q are state properties):

- Invariance: $A \square p$ - The specification evaluates to true if (and only if) every reachable state satisfies p. In this property, A is the universal path quantifier, whereas $\square$ is the path-specific temporal operator.
- Time-bounded Response: $A \square (p \Rightarrow A \Diamond_{\leq t} q)$. This property asserts that, for all paths, it is always the case that once p holds, q eventually holds within t time units ($\Diamond_{\leq t}$ is the "eventually within t" operator).

3   Defining ReSA Semantics in DL

In this section, we describe our framework for semantic analysis, the semantic representation approach and the domain ontology that captures the representations as a knowledge-base system.

3.1   Semantic Analysis Framework

In the context of requirements specification, industrial tools need to support detection and correction of specification errors at both syntactic and semantic levels. Figure 1 illustrates our proposed framework for specifying and analyzing ReSA requirements, using a semantic analysis that takes advantage of open source lexical resources and ontology[1].

The semantic analysis process is described briefly as follows: (i) requirements are specified and syntactically validated in ReSA, (ii) during the parsing of the specifications, the semantic analyzer determines the semantics of each specification, by consulting the *VerbNet, schuler2005verbnet, palmer2009semlink* and the *WordNet* [21] lexical resources through Application Program Interfaces (API), as explained in Sect. 3. VerbNet is a popular open source lexical resource of verbs, which provides verbs semantics, whereas WordNet provides conceptual

---

[1] The *Oval, Rectangular*, and *Cylindrical* shapes represent artifacts, computing functions, and knowledge base, respectively.

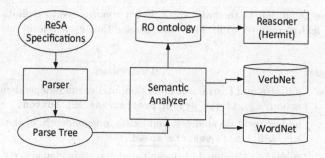

Fig. 1. Semantic analysis framework

semantics and lexical relations of words, e.g., antonyms, synonyms, etc., (iii) the *Semantic Analyzer* asserts the domain types and semantic roles of the lexical elements, and the logical forms of the specifications, into the ontology, also known as *ReSA Ontology* (RO). Each logical form captures the semantic structure of a sentence as opposed to the surface (syntax) of a sentence, and (iv) RO is checked for consistency, completeness and entailment via an ontology reasoner such as Hermit [17].

3.2 Semantic Representation via the Event-Based Approach

The semantics of each specification is computed compositionally from the predicates (i.e., the main verbs), and operators (i.e., the prepositions and conjunctives), via an *event-based semantics* approach [22,23]. In this approach, an event E denotes an occurrence, state or condition. It is expressed using a clause, an adjunct or a statement. The arguments of a predicate or an operator are mapped to an existentially-quantified event, through *thematic roles* [12], which define the semantic roles of arguments with respect to the predicate. In Table 3, we briefly define the commonly used thematic roles, of which some are used in this paper.

To illustrate the event-based approach and thematic roles, let us consider a simple ReSA specification (2-a). The predicate is Limit(args.) and its arguments are ASL and vehicle speed. The argument ASL has an agent role in the predicate, which enables the vehicle speed argument to undergo a state change. Hence, the latter argument has a patient (theme) role. The thematic roles are applied in the event-based semantic representation. Considering the same example, the theme of the specification is about Limiting, hence the event Limiting(e) (or E(e) & Action(e, limit)). The arguments ASL and vehicle speed are related to the event through the Agent and Patient thematic roles, respectively, as shown in (2-b). Further, the thematic roles are restricted to the domain concepts in order to effectively represent the semantics of the specification using *semantic selection* [24], e.g., Agent(e, ASL) & System(ASL).

(2) (a) ASL:system shall limit "vehicle speed":para.

(b) ∃e.[Limiting(e) & Agent(e, ASL) & Patient(e, "vehicle speed") & System(ASL) & Para("vehicle speed")]

Table 3. The Definition of thematic roles. For a comprehensive definition, refer to the VerbNet lexical resource [19]. The word/phrase that each role is referring to, is underlined.

Thematic role	Description
Agent/Cause	initiates and carries out an action, and exists independently of the action, e.g., `If `<u>`the driver`</u>` presses the ASL button, ...`
Patient	undergoes state changes, and exists independently of the action, e.g., `ASL limits `<u>`vehicle speed`</u>`.`
Theme	similar to Patient, but doesn't undergo state changes, e.g., `ASL sends `<u>`notification`</u>` to the driver.`
Destination	a physical entity which indicates the end-point of an action, and exists independently of the action, e.g., `ASL sends notification to `<u>`the driver`</u>`.`
Instrument	used by an agent to cause an action, e.g., `If the driver presses `<u>`the ASL button`</u>`, ...`
Experiencer	a patient that perceives the change of state, e.g., `if `<u>`ASL`</u>` detects a malfunction, ...`
Stimulus	causes an event to occur, e.g., `if ASL detects `<u>`a malfunction`</u>`, ...`

The benefits of our semantic representation are threefold: (i) first, event-based representations are suitable to automate while delivering deep and complex semantic representations through nesting; (ii) second, voice alternations, using active/passive forms, can be represented with almost similar semantic representations, allowing flexibility; and (iii) third, our domain concepts are well-defined in advance, hence the concepts are applied on the thematic roles effectively to restrict the selection of arguments, thereby discarding semantically not sound statements, such as the driver is activated.

The main challenge of applying thematic roles is the lack of a standard definition. Some thematic roles have inconsistent definitions across the relevant literature. In order to mitigate this problem, we opt to apply thematic roles from the VerbNet semantic resource, which defines around 23 thematic roles and over 5200 verb classes [19].

3.3   The ReSA Ontology

The ReSA Ontology (RO) is an upgrade to our previously defined system-level ontology [9] with semantic representations, based on the event-based and thematic roles. Further, RO introduces complex concepts such as *Entity, Attribute, User*, which categorize the embedded systems concepts based on semantic similarities. In this ontology, we also introduce equivalence and definition axioms that realize the flexibility of ReSA, to provide engineers with the choice of equivalent words and phrases, equivalent operators such as prepositions and conjunctives, and sentence alterations (passive and active statements). The ontology can be downloaded from Bitbucket[2].

The RO ontology consists of the TBox and the ABox DL parts. The TBox contains assertions of logical forms, thematic restrictions, classifications of domain concepts and statements. The TBox classification assertions are created once and maintained by ontology experts with domain knowledge. The TBox is also populated with logical forms that conform to various statement types during parsing of the requirements specifications. The logical form can be captured through simple and complex event structures as shown in the next section. The TBox assertions are the meta-language of the ABox, which users employ during specification. In contrast, the ABox contains assertions of concrete instantiations of concepts and roles.

Thematic Role Restrictions. The thematic role restrictions in the TBox detect implausible requirements specifications, such as "a user is activated" ($\exists e.[$ Patient(e, x) & User(x) &... $]$). The given example implies that the user has a *Patient* role, which is considered an illegal assertion since a user cannot change the state upon receiving an action according to our interpretation. In order to apply the restrictions, first, we generalize the domain concepts into complex concepts (*Entity, Attribute* and *User*) based on semantic similarity (3). Next, through expert knowledge and analysis of corpus data, we apply the restrictions following the classification, as shown in (4). The restrictions are defined over the range of roles, so that the roles map to the appropriate concepts, for instance the range of the *Patient* role is restricted to *Entity* and *Attribute* concepts only.

(3)   /* Classification assertions */
         System $\sqsubseteq$ Entity, Device $\sqsubseteq$ Entity

         Para $\sqsubseteq$ Attribute, State $\sqsubseteq$ Attribute, Mode $\sqsubseteq$ Attribute

(4) /* Thematic Roles Restrictions */
         $\top \sqsubseteq \forall$ Patient.(Entity $\sqcup$ Attribute)

         $\top \sqsubseteq \forall$ Agent.(User $\sqcup$ Entity)

         $\top \sqsubseteq \forall$ Instrument.(InDevice)

3.4   Semantics of Clauses and Statements in ReSA

The restricted thematic roles are binary predicates that relate verb and operator arguments to their corresponding events, E. Events can be expressed using a clause (E_{clause}), time phrase (E_{time}), simple (E_{simple}) and complex statements. Further, a simple statement can be timed ($E_{tsimple}$), and a complex statement can be compound complex ($E_{ccomplex}$) or nested complex ($E_{ncomplex}$), as shown in (5).

(5) $\left[E_{clause}, E_{time}, E_{simple}, E_{tsimple}, E_{complex}, E_{ccomplex}, E_{ncomplex} \right] \sqsubseteq E$

---

[2] https://bitbucket.org/nasmdh/ro.

Clause Event E_{clause}. In ReSA, a clause is an atomic proposition (or a simple statement without an adjunct). It expresses an *action* (action clause), or describes a *state* or *condition* (descriptive clause). The predicates of the action clauses are transitive E_{tra} (e.g., activate [object]), intransitive E_{int} (e.g., reboot), or ditransitive E_{dit} (e.g., send[object] to [indirect object]), whereas the descriptive clauses usually assume copula verbs E_{cop} (e.g., is). In the following example, we show how the semantics of a clause, specified in ReSA, is represented via the clause event.

(6) ASL:system shall reboot   /* valid ReSA clause */

(7) Event-based: $\exists e.\big[\, E_{int}(e)$ & Theme(e, ASL) & Action(e, reboot) & System(ASL) & IntV(reboot)$\big]$

(8) (a) TBox: $E \sqcap \exists$Agent.System $\sqcap \exists$Action.IntV $\sqsubseteq E_{int}$

   (b) ABox: $e{:}E_{int}$, (e, ASL):Agent, (e, reboot):Action, ASL:System, reboot:IntVerb

The thematic roles of the "reboot" argument, in (6), are fetched from the VerbNet semantic resource, which are used in the semantic representation (7). In TBox, we assert the logical form of the specification as shown in (8-a), which states that the event is an element of top event E that is related to instances of System and Intransitive Verb (IntVerb) through the Agent and Action thematic roles, respectively, and it belongs to the clause event. In the ABox, we assert the facts (8-b) that are the instances of the clause event, the predicate and its arguments as stated in the specification.

Simple Event. This event type is expressed via a simple statement that makes use of a single clause and an optional adjunct. A *Timed-Simple* event is a simple event extended with an adjunct that states timing information (or uses a prepositional phrase of time). Its event structure is constructed from two events as shown in Fig. 2(a). The timed-simple event e1 has an outer scope over the adjunct event e2, which indicates the extension of e1 with e2, as well as a scope ambiguity resolution, for quantified specifications [25]. The event structure is constructed during parsing according to the input string matches. An example of a timed-simple requirement, which corresponds to Fig. 2(a), is shown in (9), with its representations in the event-based semantics and description logic.

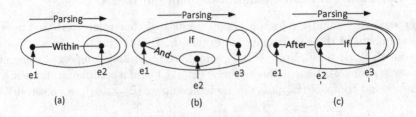

Fig. 2. Event structures

(9) Timed-Simple: $\{$ASL:system shall limit "vehicle speed":para $\{$within 500 ms.$\}_{e2}\}_{e1}$
     Event-Based: $\exists e1.[E_{tsimple}(e1)\&\exists e2.[E_{time}(e2)\&Value(e2,500ms)\&Within(e1,e2)]]$

     TBox: $E \sqcap \exists Value.Time \sqcap \exists Within.E_{time} \sqsubseteq E_{tsimple}$

Complex Event. In contrast to a simple event, a complex event is expressed via a complex statement that uses subordinate conjunctives, e.g., **if, when**, etc. A typical application of this event is in denoting conditionals. Its event structure is similar to the timed-simple event, except in this case we use subordinate conjunctives (10).

(10) Complex: $\{$ if "activation button":inDevice is pressed, $\{$ "ASL":system shall be activated$\}_{.e2}\}_{e1}$

     Event-Based: $\exists e1.[E_{complex}(e1)\&...\exists e2.[E_{simple}(e2)\&...\&If(e1,e2)]]$

     TBox: $E \sqcap \exists If.E_{simple} \sqsubseteq E_{complex}$

A compound-complex contains statements that are connected using the *and/or* conjunctives. Figure 2(a) and (c) show the event structure for compound-complex and nested-complex events, respectively, and examples are shown for each class of complex statements that capture their respective event structure in (11) (12). ***Note:*** *Curly brackets are used to simplify the reading.*

(11)

     Compound-Complex: $\{$ if vehicle:entity is in running:mode and $\{$ "enabling button": inDevice is pressed$\}$, $\{$ASL:system shall be enabled.$\}_{e3}\}_{e2}\}_{e1}$

     Event-Based: $\exists e1.[E_{ccomplex}(e1) \quad \&...\exists e2.[E_{simple}(e2) \quad \&... \quad And(e1,e2)] \quad \& \\ \exists e3.[E_{simple}(e3) \&...If(e1,e3)]]$

     TBox: $E \sqcap \exists And.E_{simple} \sqcap \exists If.E_{simple} \sqsubseteq E_{ccompound}$

(12)

     Nested-complex: $\{$ After "ASL":system is enabled; $\{$if "activation button":inDevice is pressed, $\{$ "ASL":system shall be activated.$\}_{e3}\}_{e2}\}_{e1}$

     Event-Based: $\exists e1.[E_{complex}(e1) \quad \&...\exists e2.[E_{simple}(e2) \quad \&... \quad After(e1,e2) \quad \& \\ \exists e3.[E_{simple}(e3) \&...If(e2,e3)]]$

     TBox: $E \sqcap \exists After.E_{complex} \circ If.E_{simple} \sqsubseteq E_{ncomplex}$

4   Semantic Equivalence in ReSA

ReSA allows the specification of semantically equivalent statements via different syntactic constructions, e.g., by changing the voice of a statement (or diathesis). The advantage of having alternative ways of specifying requirements is that engineers get the choice to select convenient syntactic constructs when expressing requirements, hence increasing the language's usability in practice. However, the task of identifying semantically equivalent constructs is not trivial, as equivalences exist not just at the statements level, but also at syntactic categories level. Besides, a lot of flexibility could contribute to ambiguity and impreciseness of specifications [26], therefore, we consider the trade offs carefully when defining the equivalence axioms. In our context, we define semantic equivalence as follows.

Definition 1 (Semantic equivalence). *The constituents C1 and C2 of ReSA specifications are semantically equivalent if and only if C1 and C2 belong to the same syntactic categories, and C1 is substitutable for C2, and vice versa, in any instances of their usage in requirements specification.*

The notion of semantic equivalence exists at the concept, role and instance levels of the ontology. Equivalent concepts have the same number of instances in the domain, e.g., Parameter $\equiv$ InParameter $\sqcup$ OutParameter. Equivalent roles relate the same domain-range concepts and denote the same properties, e.g., Greaterthan $\equiv$ LessThanorEqTo$^-$. Equivalent instances denote the same value or entity. Since model elements are normally distinct, we consider the N/NPs instances distinct (not equivalent) in the ontology; however, there exist equivalent instances of verbs and description words. For the latter case, the WordNet lexicon resource provides semantic and syntactic relations between lexicons, e.g., synonyms, antonyms, etc. We use the WordNet lexical database [21] and the JWNL library [27] to automate the identification of synonyms and antonyms for the verb and descriptive words of the ReSA syntactic categories.

Table 4 illustrates the various equivalence axioms that exist in RO. The prepositions *within* and *between* are defined in terms of the After$_p$ and Before$_p$ roles, similarly the conjunctive *between*, in terms of the Before$_{sc}$ role. The comparison operators are defined in terms of the Lessthan and Equalto roles. Antonyms and synonyms are defined in terms of the Ant and Syn roles, respectively.

Table 4. Equivalence axioms in ReSA ontology sc-subordinating conjunctive, p-preposition

Subordinate Conj. Equiv.	Synonymous
Before$_{sc}$ $\equiv$ After$_{cc}^-$	(limit, restrict):Syn
Between$_{sc}$ $\doteq$ Before$_{sc}$$\circ$ Before$_{sc}$	(display, expose):Syn
Prepositions of Time Equiv.	**Antonyms**
Between$_p$ $\doteq$ $\exists$After$_p$.Time $\sqcap$ $\exists$Before$_p$.Time	(enable, disable):Ant
$\forall$Within.Time $\equiv$ $\exists$ After$_p$.{Now} $\sqcap$ Before$_p$.Time	(active, inactive):Ant
Comparison Equivalence	
Greaterthan $\equiv$ LessThanorEqTo$^-$	
$\forall$LessThanorEqTo $\equiv$ $\exists$Lessthan$^-$ $\sqcup$ $\exists$ Equalto	
GrThanorEqto$\equiv$Lessthan$^-$	

5 Automated Analysis and Transformation to TCTL Properties

So far, we have presented the semantic representation of ReSA specifications in event-based semantics, encoded in DL. We have also discussed the contributions of the thematic roles and the equivalence axioms for enabling flexible specifications. In this section, we present the various types of analysis of requirements specifications that we can carry out on the RO ontology. Moreover, we show the transformation of the ReSA specifications to TCTL properties, exemplified on the time-bounded properties.

5.1 Consistency Checking

The ontology RO is consistent if there exists an interpretation (or a model) that satisfies the TBox (T) and the ABox(A) assertions, that is, $M \models ax$, where: $ax \in T \cup A$. Inconsistency in the ontology can occur due to inconsistencies at different levels of syntactic categories and statements. For instance, at the lexical syntactic level, the quantifiers of model elements are unique, hence $D \nvDash$ (ASL:System & ASL:Parameter), that is, the stated facts are inconsistent.

At the clause level, if we consider Opposite(active,inactive), the fact that clauses e1 and e2 (13) are contradictory is detected using the assertion in (14), stating a contradictory clause that is related through a reflexive chains of roles.

(13) e1="ASL is active" and e2="ASL is inactive"

(14) $\top \sqsubseteq \exists$ (Theme⁻ o Att o Opposite o Att⁻ o Theme)

5.2 Completeness

The completeness of a requirements specification is checked indirectly from the completeness of the ontology. The ontology is complete if every instance of the syntactic categories has thematic roles (15), and every clause belongs to some statement (16). In the completeness axioms, we assume that the ontology is not empty, since an empty ontology would satisfy universally quantified axioms.

(15) $NP \sqcup VP \sqcup ADJ \sqsubseteq \exists ThematicRole.E$

(16) $Clause \sqsubseteq \exists ThematicRole.E$

5.3 Transformation to TCTL

In the ABox, RO maintains concrete representations of requirements specifications, and such representations can be transformed into different formal logics for further analysis. In this paper, we show the transformation of specifications in the ontology to their counterpart in TCTL, using the Specification Pattern System (SPS) [4,28], which is a collection of recurring patterns of functional and timing requirements. The patterns of SPS have formal semantics in various temporal logics, including TCTL. The benefits of automatically generating (an optimal set of) TCTL properties are: (i) properties are not generated for inconsistent specifications, and (ii) properties are not generated for entailed specifications. Consequently, the effort of subsequent model checking is reduced by optimizing the number of properties to be checked.

Algorithm 1 shows the generation of a time-bounded response formula in TCTL. The input to the algorithm consists of sets of simple and complex events, paired sets of *If* and *Within* roles, and paired sets of thematic roles. For event e in the Complex set, we check if it is related with the *If* role. If it is, we extract its thematic arguments and verbalize the arguments (construct equivalent ReSA syntax), and store them into p. Besides, we get the successor of e, which is represented by $e1$. By using $e1$, we get its arguments verbalized to q. Finally, we get the successor of $e1$, which is represented by $e2$, and from the last event, we get the time argument, t. The output is a time-bounded TCTL formula $A \square (p \Rightarrow A \Diamond_{\leq t} q)$, where p, q are clauses that are expressed in ReSA, and t is a time bound. Other properties can be extracted similarly.

```
input  : A ReSA specification⟨E_tsimple⟩
output : Time-bounded Response
         Formula
while e in Complex do
    arg ⟵ getArguments(e);
    p ⟵ verbalize(arg);
    e1 = getEvent(e,If);
    if e1 is found then
        arg ⟵ getArguments(e1);
        q ⟵ verbalize(arg);
        e2 ⟵ getEvent(e1,Within);
        if e2 is found then
            arg ⟵ getArguments(e2);
            t ⟵ verbalize(arg);
        end
    end
    tctl_boundedResponse[0,1,..i] ⟵
    A □ (p ⇒ A ◊_≤t q).
end
```

```
Complex={e1, e2,...en};
TimedSimple={em, em+1,...
If={<e1,em>,..};
Within={<em,t1>,...};
Agent={<e1, ASL>,...};
Patient={<e2,vehicle

speed>}; ⋮
```

Algorithm 1: Extracts Time-bounded Response from the ReSA Ontology, RO

6   Related Work

The related work discusses the automated support of requirements specification and analysis that mainly uses natural language as initial input language. In the literature, various specification and analysis methods are proposed, and the methods usually employ techniques based on logic, semantic analysis, specification patterns, Natural Language Processing (NLP), etc.

Axel et al. [29] propose a requirements specification method that relies on a goal-oriented approach, where the authors use a requirement model (a.k.a.

KAOS meta model) to capture the possible specification scenarios, and translate the specifications into temporal logic for reasoning. Similarly, Zawgi et al. [30] apply the *Default logic* to the underlying representation of constrained natural language. However, the two approaches face scalability issues that require major changes on the meta-modeling level, especially when new specification patterns are discovered. In a similar logic-based approach, the Requirement Apprentice (RA) [31] has a user-friendly requirements specification interface that makes use of *clitché library* that documents the analysts' experience, but also a general-purpose deduction-based reasoning system (Cake). The reasoning service provides detection of contradiction and completeness in the specification. However, the approach does not handle analysis that requires resolution of complex deduction problems. The approach is domain agnostic and too constraining to be applied in industry.

Haruhiko et al. [8,32] propose a lightweight requirements analysis method, based on ontology, where the ontology is a knowledge base for treasures and inference rules. The authors also define metrics for measuring the quality of the requirements specification, including inconsistency, completeness, correctness and ambiguity. The approach lacks a well-founded formalism of the ontology language. In contrast, we use Description logic, which is decidable and supported by the popular Semantic Web language, OWL. In another study by Stephen et al. [6,33], a boilerplate approach and domain-based ontology are applied in specifying requirements of embedded systems. The tool prototype, DODT, supports matching of requirements to existing boilerplates through the NLP technique, and requires manual work for those requirements that do not match automatically. The boilerplates use concepts with no deep semantic relations, which could potentially lead to implausible boilerplates. In a similar approach, Michael et al. [34] use ontology for semantic analysis of requirements that are first preprocessed through semantic labeling techniques. In the labeling, lexical words and phrases are assigned semantic roles such as *Actor* and *Object*, used for semantic analysis purposes. However, the number of semantic relations is very limited. In contrast, we use the VerbNet and WordNet lexical resources that contain substantial lexical resources.

Template-based specification methods lack flexibility due to the limited set of templates [3,4,6,7,9]. In our approach, we provide a relatively more flexible requirements specification language, and an ontology that captures the semantics of the specifications, providing reasoning support for checking consistency and completeness of requirements.

7   Conclusions

Natural language is intuitive to use for requirements specification of embedded systems. However, it can sometimes lead to inconsistent, vague, ambiguous and imprecise specifications. In order to take advantage of the appeal of natural language, but also reduce the aforementioned problems, template-based methods such as pattern-based systems and boilerplates are often employed in industry, especially for safety-critical applications. However, these methods have limited sets of templates that restrict the engineers' power of expressiveness. The pattern-based templates abstract substantial content into propositional variables, and the boilerplates lack formal specifications and support for rigorous analysis. In this paper, we have applied linguistic techniques to improve specifications and analysis. For this purpose, we have defined a semantic representation to the requirements specification language ReSA, a constrained natural language that is close to the syntax and semantics of English.

We have proposed an event-based semantic representation approach that uses thematic roles and domain concepts from embedded systems, in order to effectively represent the semantics of syntactic elements such that the representations are ready for deep analysis, that is, analysis at various levels of syntactic categories, clauses and statements. The semantics is encoded in a Description-logic-based ontology. We also show how to perform consistency checking and completeness on the ontology. Finally, we have demonstrated the benefit of the ontology by automatically generating optimal sets of property specifications in Timed Computation Tree Logic, which can be further used for model checking embedded systems formal descriptions. In the future, we plan to include temporal reasoning and the implementation of the ontology in the ReSA editor, and validate the approach and its toolchain on large industrial systems.

References

1. Martins, L.E.G., Gorschek, T.: Requirements engineering for safety-critical systems: a systematic literature review. Inf. Softw. Technol. **75**, 71–89 (2016)
2. Hull, E., Jackson, K., Dick, J.: Requirements Engineering. Springer, Heidelberg (2010)
3. Dwyer, M.B., Avrunin, G.S., Corbett, J.C.: Patterns in property specifications for finite-state verification. In: Proceedings of the 1999 International Conference on Software Engineering (IEEE Cat. No.99CB37002), pp. 411–420, May 1999
4. Konrad, S., Cheng, B.H.C.: Real-time specification patterns. In: 27th International Conference on Software Engineering (ICSE), pp. 372–381, May 2005
5. Jacobson, P., Semantics, C.: An Introduction to the Syntax/Semantics Interface. Oxford University Press, Oxford (2014)
6. Farfeleder, S., Moser, T., Krall, A., Stlhane, T., Zojer, H., Panis, C.: DODT: Increasing requirements formalism using domain ontologies for improved embedded systems development. In: 14th IEEE International Symposium on Design and Diagnostics of Electronic Circuits and Systems, pp. 271–274, April 2011
7. Arora, C., Sabetzadeh, M., Briand, L.C., Zimmer, F.: Requirement Boilerplates: Transition from manually-enforced to automatically-verifiable natural language patterns. In: 2014 IEEE 4th International Workshop on Requirements Patterns (RePa), pp. 1–8, August 2014
8. Kaiya, H., Saeki, M.: Ontology based requirements analysis: Lightweight semantic processing approach. In: Fifth International Conference on Quality Software (QSIC 2005), pp. 223–230, September 2005

9. Mahmud, N., Seceleanu, C., Ljungkrantz, O.: ReSA: An ontology-based require-ment specification language tailored to automotive systems. In: 10th IEEE International Symposium on Industrial Embedded Systems (SIES), June 2015

10. Mahmud, N., Seceleanu, C., Ljungkrantz, O.: ReSA tool: Structured requirements specification and SAT-based consistency-checking. In: Proceedings of 2016 Federated Conference on Computer Science and Information Systems (FedCSIS), September 2016

11. Davidson, D.: Essays on Actions and Events: Philosophical Essays. Clarendon Press, Oxford (2001)

12. Parsons, T.: Thematic relations and arguments. Linguist. Inq. **26**(4), 635–662 (1995)

13. The Description Logic Handbook: Theory, Implementation and Applications

14. Bechhofer, S.: OWL: Web ontology language. In: Ling, L., Özsu, T. (eds.) Encyclopedia of Database Systems, pp. 2008–2009. Springer, Heidelberg (2009)

15. Bhatt, M., Freksa, C.: Spatial computing for design an artificial intelligence perspective. In: Studying Visual and Spatial Reasoning for Design Creativity, pp. 109–127. Springer, Heidelberg (2015)

16. Rector, A., Rogers, J.: Ontological and practical issues in using a description logic to represent medical concept systems: experience from GALEN. In: Barahona, P., Bry, F., Franconi, E., Henze, N., Sattler, U. (eds.) Reasoning Web 2006. LNCS, vol. 4126, pp. 197–231. Springer, Heidelberg (2006). doi:10.1007/11837787_9

17. Shearer, R., Motik, B., Horrocks, I.: HermiT: A highly-efficient OWL reasoner. In: OWL: Experiences and Directions, vol. 432, p. 91 (2008)

18. Alur, R., Courcoubetis, C., Dill, D.: Model-checking in dense real-time. Inf. Comput. **104**(1), 2–34 (1993)

19. Schuler, K.K.: VerbNet: A Broad-coverage, Comprehensive Verb Lexicon. Dissertations available from ProQuest. AAI3179808 (2005)

20. Palmer, M.: Semlink: Linking propbank, verbnet and framenet. In: Proceedings of the Generative Lexicon Conference, Italy, pp. 9–15 (2009)

21. Miller, G.A.: WordNet: a lexical database for english. Commun. ACM **38**(11), 39–41 (1995)

22. Parsons, T.: Events in the Semantics of English, vol. 5. MIT Press, Cambridge (1990)

23. Champollion, L.: The Interaction of compositional semantics and event semantics. Linguist. Philos. **38**(1), 31 (2015)

24. Ouhalla, J.: Functional Categories and Parametric Variation. Routledge, London (2003)

25. Kurtzman, H.S., MacDonald, M.C.: Resolution of quantifier scope ambiguities. Cognition **48**(3), 243–279 (1993)

26. Ferreira, V.S., Dell, G.S.: Effect of ambiguity and lexical availability on syntactic and lexical production. Cogn. Psychol. **40**(4), 296–340 (2000)

27. Finlayson, M.A.: Java libraries for accessing the princeton wordnet: comparison and evaluation. In: Proceedings of the 7th Global Wordnet Conference, Tartu, Estonia (2014)

28. Post, A., Menzel, I., Hoenicke, J., Podelski, A.: Automotive behavioral requirements expressed in a specification pattern system: a case study at BOSCH. Requirements Eng. **17**(1), 19–33 (2012)

29. Dardenne, A., Van Lamsweerde, A., Fickas, S.: Goal-directed requirements acquisition. Sci. Comput. Programm. **20**(1–2), 3–50 (1993)

30. Zowghi, D., Gervasi, V., McRae, A.: Using default reasoning to discover inconsistencies in natural language requirements. In: Proceedings Eighth Asia-Pacific Software Engineering Conference, pp. 133–140, December 2001
31. Reubenstein, H.B., Waters, R.C.: The requirements apprentice: automated assistance for requirements acquisition. IEEE Trans. Softw. Eng. **17**(3), 226–240 (1991)
32. Kaiya, H., Saeki, M.: Using domain ontology as domain knowledge for requirements elicitation. In: 14th IEEE International Requirements Engineering Conference (RE 2006), pp. 189–198, September 2006
33. Farfeleder, S., Moser, T., Krall, A., Stålhane, T., Omoronyia, I., Zojer, H.: Ontology-driven guidance for requirements elicitation. In: Antoniou, G., Grobelnik, M., Simperl, E., Parsia, B., Plexousakis, D., Leenheer, P., Pan, J. (eds.) ESWC 2011. LNCS, vol. 6644, pp. 212–226. Springer, Heidelberg (2011). doi:10.1007/978-3-642-21064-8_15
34. Roth, M., Klein, E.: Parsing software requirements with an ontology-based semantic role labeler. In: Language and Ontologies, p. 15 (2015)

Computing Conditional Probabilities: Implementation and Evaluation

Steffen Märcker[(⊠)], Christel Baier, Joachim Klein, and Sascha Klüppelholz

Institute of Theoretical Computer Science,
Technische Universität Dresden, 01062 Dresden, Germany
steffen.maercker@tu-dresden.de

Abstract. Conditional probabilities and expectations are an important concept in the quantitative analysis of stochastic systems, e.g., to analyze the impact and cost of error handling mechanisms in rare failure scenarios or for a utility-analysis assuming an exceptional shortage of resources. This paper reports on the main features of an implementation of computation schemes for conditional probabilities in discrete-time Markov chains and Markov decision processes within the probabilistic model checker PRISM and a comparative experimental evaluation. Our implementation has full support for computing conditional probabilities where both the objective and condition are given as linear temporal logic formulas, as well as specialized algorithms for reachability and other simple types of path properties. In the case of Markov chains we provide implementations for three alternative methods (quotient, scale and reset). We support PRISM's explicit and (semi-)symbolic engines. Besides comparative studies exploring the three dimensions (methods, engines, general vs. special handling), we compare the performance of our implementation and the probabilistic model checker STORM that provides facilities for conditional probabilities of reachability properties.

1 Introduction

Various methods and tools have been developed that support the analysis of systems against reliability and performability requirements. In this paper, we focus on the stochastic setting where finite-state Markovian models are used to carry out the system analysis (see, e.g., [29,35,44]). In the past 25 years, various algorithms to compute the probabilities for safety or liveness properties as well as time- or cost-bounded properties specified in some temporal logic have been proposed and implemented in tools. Most prominent is the probabilistic model checker PRISM [39]. Among others, it provides support for the analysis of discrete- and continuous-time Markov chains as well as Markov decision processes (MDPs) against state properties specified in probabilistic computation tree logic (PCTL) [13,16,28] or ω-regular path properties specified in linear

The authors are supported by the DFG through the collaborative research centre HAEC (SFB 912) and the Excellence Initiative by the German Federal and State Governments (cluster of excellence cfaed) and projects BA 1679/11-1 and 1679/12-1.

A. Cimatti and M. Sirjani (Eds.): SEFM 2017, LNCS 10469, pp. 349–366, 2017.
DOI: 10.1007/978-3-319-66197-1_22

temporal logic (LTL) [18,46]. The focus of PRISM and other probabilistic model checkers, such as MRMC [34], STORM [20], ISCASMC [27] or MARCIE [30], is to provide facilities for the computation of probabilities for temporal path properties, and partly also expected accumulated costs. However, tool support for conditional probabilities, i.e., the probability of an event φ given an event ψ occurs, for temporal properties or conditional expected costs, i.e., the expected costs given an event ψ occurs, in Markovian systems within probabilistic model checkers is rare (see the discussion on related work). This is unfortunate as assertions on conditional probabilities for temporal properties can provide important insights in the reliability of systems or the cost-utility balance. For instance, conditional probabilities and expectations allow to "zoom in" specific error scenarios and to analyze the impact of undetected errors or the cost of repair mechanisms in cases where an error is detected. Conditional probabilities can also serve to formalize the tradeoff between cost and utility functions, e.g., in terms of the conditional probability to achieve a sufficiently high utility level, assuming that a scenario occurs where the available energy is bounded by some constant (see [7]). For another example, forms of anonymity have been formalized by the requirement that the conditional probabilities for on observable o, given a secret s, does not depend on s (see [2]). In the context of the verification of probabilistic programs, conditional probabilities and expectations are used to formalize the semantics of loops under the assumption that the loop terminates [14,17,32].

Contribution. We present an implementation of computation schemes for conditional probabilities in Markov chains and MDPs, where both the objective and condition are LTL formulas, within the probabilistic model checker PRISM [39] (Sect. 3).[1] Our implementation realizes the algorithms of [10], which rely on reductions to unconditional probabilities, and achieves a major speed-up over [10]'s prototype implementation. It uses PRISM's infrastructure to translate LTL formulas into deterministic finite or ω-automata and can be used with all of PRISM's analysis engines, namely explicit, mtbdd, hybrid, and sparse.[2] Besides the automata-based approach for LTL objectives and conditions, our implementation also provides specialized treatment of certain simple formula patterns, e.g., when the condition is a reachability property or an invariant. In the case of Markov chains, our implementation also supports the computation of conditional expected accumulated costs when the condition is an LTL formula.

The second contribution is a report on experiments that have been carried out to evaluate the general feasibility of the algorithms for conditional probabilities of LTL objectives and conditions as well as to compare different methods and

---

[1] In the context of a conditional probability $\Pr(\varphi|\psi)$ we refer to φ as the objective and to ψ as the condition.

[2] PRISM's explicit engine uses sparse matrix representation for the system and carries out all computation in an explicit manner, while the other three engines use multi-terminal binary decision diagrams (MTBDDs) for the model construction. The mtbdd engine is purely MTBDD-based. The hybrid engine uses an MTBDD-representation for the system and an explicit probability vector [38], while the sparse engine uses sparse matrices for the numerical computations.

engines (Sect. 4). For Markov chains, we compare the performance of three methods: the *quotient method* (which computes conditional probabilities according to their definition), the *scale method* proposed in [10] (which transforms the Markov chain into a new one by deleting and copying certain states and rescaling the transition probabilities) and the *reset method* proposed in [10] for MDPs (which "discards" paths that violate the condition by reset transitions returning to the initial state). In the case of MDPs, we compare the running time of the reset method for computing the maximal and minimal condition probability with the running time for computing the unconditional probability for the conjunction of the objective and the condition. For both Markov chains and MDPs, we also compare the running times of our implementation for each of PRISM's engines as well as the general applicable automata-based approach and the specialized treatment of formula patterns. Finally, we also compare the performance of our implementation and that of the new probabilistic model checker STORM, which provides support for reachability objectives and conditions using its explicit engine (Sect. 5). An extended version including an appendix [41], our implementation, all benchmark models and queries as well as the raw data from the measurements are available online[3].

Related Work. For Markov chains (and other purely stochastic models without nondeterminism), the definition $\Pr(\varphi|\psi) = \Pr(\varphi \wedge \psi)/\Pr(\psi)$ of conditional probabilities yields a direct reduction to the unconditional case, called *quotient method*. Thus, all tools with facilities for computing probabilities of conjunctive properties in Markov chains provide an implicit way to compute conditional probabilities. However, this method is not applicable for conditional expectations. Moreover, tools that are restricted to branching-time logics such as PCTL or its continuous-time analogue CSL [5,8] do not support conjunctive path properties. This motivated the work by Gao et al. [24] on conditional probabilities for conditions with nested time-bounded constraints in continuous-time Markov chains. This technique has been implemented in the tool CCMC [23] and adapted in [33] for the discrete-time setting. We are not aware of an implementation of the algorithm proposed in [33]. In our previous work [10], we presented the *scale method* (see. Sect. 2) and reported on a prototypical implemented in PRISM's explicit engine. The scale method has also been implemented in STORM [20] (and its parametric branch PROPhESY [19]) for cases where both the objective φ and the condition ψ are reachability properties. While STORM generally supports both explicit and symbolic computations, the implementation for conditional probabilities and expectations in Markov chains in STORM is limited to the explicit engine using sparse data structures.

In the case of probabilistic models with nondeterminism such as MDPs, the typical task for the system analysis is to carry out a worst- or best-case analysis in terms of the maximal or minimal (unconditional or conditional) probability that can be achieved when ranging over all possible resolutions of the nondeterminism (formalized by schedulers, see Sect. 2). [1,3] proposed a model-checking algorithm for PCTL extended by constraints for conditional probabilities where

---

the objective and the condition are PCTL path formulas. [1,3]'s algorithm for the case where both the objective and the condition are reachability properties has exponential-time complexity, while the *reset method* proposed in [10] is polynomially time-bounded. Both the prototype reported in [10] and the tool STORM [20] realize the reset method for maximal conditional probabilities in MDPs only for reachability objectives and conditions and only non-symbolic, whereas the new implementation presented in this paper covers PRISM's symbolic engines, too. To the best of our knowledge, it is the first implementation providing full support for computing maximal or minimal conditional probabilities in MDPs for LTL objectives and LTL conditions.

2 Preliminaries

We provide an informal overview of the scale and reset methods of [10] underlying our implementation. For the basic principles of Markov chains, Markov decision processes and probabilistic model checking, we refer to [22,44] and Chap. 10 of [9]. We suppose some familiarity with ω-automata (finite automata over infinite words) and linear temporal logic (LTL). See, e.g., [9,25].

Markov decision processes (MDP) can be seen as a finite-state automata model where each state has a nondeterministic choice between finitely many actions. The effect of taking an action in a state is probabilistic and formalized by a probabilistic distribution over the states. By supporting nondeterministic and probabilistic choices, MDPs are a generic model with manyfold applications, e.g., in robotics, operations research and randomized distributed systems. Probabilistic model checking can be used, e.g., to compute the maximal or minimal probability that an ω-regular path property φ holds in state s of an MDP $\mathcal{M}$, denoted $\mathrm{Pr}_{\mathcal{M},s}^{\max}(\varphi)$ resp. $\mathrm{Pr}_{\mathcal{M},s}^{\min}(\varphi)$. The extremum is taken over all resolutions of the nondeterminism in the MDP, formalized as *schedulers* that select for each finite path an action that is enabled in the last state of the path. Thus, $\mathrm{Pr}_{\mathcal{M},s}^{\max}(\varphi) = \max_\sigma \mathrm{Pr}_{\mathcal{M},s}^\sigma(\varphi)$ resp. $\mathrm{Pr}_{\mathcal{M},s}^{\min}(\varphi) = \min_\sigma \mathrm{Pr}_{\mathcal{M},s}^\sigma(\varphi)$ where σ ranges over all schedulers and $\mathrm{Pr}_{\mathcal{M},s}^\sigma$ denotes the probability measure induced by scheduler σ and starting state s. (The maximum and minimum indeed exist.) Discrete-time Markov chains (DTMCs) can be regarded as purely probabilistic MDPs, i.e., each state has at most one enabled action. Thus, DTMCs have a unique scheduler. Given a DTMC $\mathcal{M}$, we write $\mathrm{Pr}_{\mathcal{M},s}(\varphi)$ as $\mathrm{Pr}_{\mathcal{M},s}^{\max}(\varphi) = \mathrm{Pr}_{\mathcal{M},s}^{\min}(\varphi)$.

LTL formulas are built by atomic propositions for the states, the standard Boolean operators (such as $\vee$ "or" and $\wedge$ "and" and $\neg$ "negation") and the unary temporal modalities $\Diamond$ ("eventually"), $\Box$ ("globally"), $\bigcirc$ ("next") as well as the binary temporal modality U ("until"), its dual R ("release") and W ("weak until"). All path properties that are expressible in LTL are ω-regular.

Maximal reachability probabilities $\mathrm{Pr}_{\mathcal{M},s}^{\max}(\Diamond F)$ in MDPs are known to be computable via iterative methods (value or policy iteration) or in polynomial-time via linear programming techniques. To compute the maximal probabilities for LTL formulas, one can use standard algorithms to translate the given LTL formula φ into a deterministic ω-automaton $\mathcal{A}$ and then compute $\mathrm{Pr}_{\mathcal{M},s}^{\max}(\varphi)$ as the maximal probability of a reachability property in the product-MDP $\mathcal{M} \otimes \mathcal{A}$. Minimal probabilities for reachability properties or LTL formulas can be computed in a similar way or using the fact that $\mathrm{Pr}_{\mathcal{M},s}^{\min}(\varphi) = 1 - \mathrm{Pr}_{\mathcal{M},s}^{\max}(\neg\varphi)$.

If $\mathcal{M}$ is a DTMC, the *conditional probability* of objective φ given that condition ψ holds, starting from state s, is given by:

$$\mathrm{Pr}_{\mathcal{M},s}(\varphi \,|\, \psi) \quad \overset{\text{def}}{=} \quad \frac{\mathrm{Pr}_{\mathcal{M},s}(\varphi \wedge \psi)}{\mathrm{Pr}_{\mathcal{M},s}(\psi)} \tag{*}$$

where we suppose that φ and ψ are LTL formulas (or, more generally, ω-regular path properties) such that $\mathrm{Pr}_{\mathcal{M},s}(\psi) > 0$.

Quotient Method. For DTMCs, (*) directly provides a computation scheme for conditional probabilities via the computation of the unconditional probabilities for the conjunction of the objective and condition and for the condition.

Scale Method. [10] presents an alternative method for the computation of the conditional probabilities $\mathrm{Pr}_{\mathcal{M},s}(\varphi \,|\, \psi)$ in DTMCs, which relies on a reduction to unconditional probabilities in a transformed DTMC $\mathcal{M}_\psi$. We sketch the ideas for the case where $\psi = \Diamond C$ is a reachability condition ("eventually some state in C is reached"). In a first step, the probabilities $x_s = \mathrm{Pr}_{\mathcal{M},s}(\Diamond C)$ are computed for all states s in $\mathcal{M}$. Intuitively, the new DTMC $\mathcal{M}_\psi$ simulates $\mathcal{M}$ using in two modes: "before C" and "after C". The structure of $\mathcal{M}_\psi$'s "before C" mode is obtained from $\mathcal{M}$ by removing all states t with $x_t = 0$ and re-scaling the transition probabilities for the remaining states. More precisely, if $x_s > 0$ and $s \notin C$ then the transition probability from s to t in the "before C" mode of $\mathcal{M}_\psi$ is obtained by multiplying the transition probability from s to t in $\mathcal{M}$ with x_t/x_s. If $s \in C$ then $\mathcal{M}_\psi$ switches to the "after C" mode where it behaves exactly as $\mathcal{M}$, i.e., the structure of $\mathcal{M}_\psi$'s "after C" mode is a copy of $\mathcal{M}$. Then, $\mathrm{Pr}_{\mathcal{M},s}(\varphi \,|\, \Diamond C) = \mathrm{Pr}_{\mathcal{M}_\psi,s_b}(\varphi)$ for each measurable path property φ and each state s with $x_s > 0$ where s_b means the copy of s in the "before C" mode. The case where ψ is an arbitrary LTL formula is reducible to the case of a reachability condition using a product construction with a deterministic ω-automaton for ψ. As $\mathcal{M}_\psi$ is independent of the objective, it can also be used to compute conditional expected accumulated costs in $\mathcal{M}$. It is also applicable for continuous-time Markov chains and (time-abstract) LTL conditions.

Reset Method. The reset method has been proposed in [10] to compute maximal conditional probabilities for ω-regular objectives and conditions in MDPs via a reduction to unconditional probabilities. It supposes a fixed initial state s_{init} and relies on a transformation of $\mathcal{M}$ into an MDP $\mathcal{N} = \mathcal{M}_{\varphi | \psi}$ that depends on both the objective and the condition. We first summarize the ideas of the reset method when applied to a DTMC and then sketch the main steps for MDPs.

Let $\mathcal{M}$ be a DTMC. For reachability objectives and conditions, say $\varphi = \Diamond F$ and $\psi = \Diamond C$, where we suppose that C is reachable from the initial state s_{init}, the reset method first performs a reachability analysis to identify all states s that cannot reach C, in which case $\mathrm{Pr}_{\mathcal{M},s}(\psi) = 0$. It then discards the outgoing transitions of all states s with $\Pr_{\mathcal{M},s}(\psi) = 0$ and introduces a reset transition from these states s to s_{init} with transition probability 1. If $\mathcal{N}$ is the resulting DTMC then $\Pr_{\mathcal{M},s_{init}}(\varphi \mid \psi) = \Pr_{\mathcal{N},s_{init}}(\varphi)$. Thus, the reset method provides a reduction of conditional probabilities to unconditional ones. The essential idea of the switch from $\mathcal{M}$ to $\mathcal{N}$ is that via the reset transitions the probability mass of all paths that do not satisfy the condition ψ are transferred to the initial state, where it is distributed over all paths satisfying ψ.

Given an MDP $\mathcal{M}$ with a initial state s_{init}, we address the task to compute:

$$\Pr_{\mathcal{M},s_{init}}^{\max}(\varphi \mid \psi) \overset{\text{def}}{=} \max_{\sigma} \Pr_{\mathcal{M},s_{init}}^{\sigma}(\varphi \mid \psi) = \max_{\sigma} \frac{\Pr_{\mathcal{M},s_{init}}^{\sigma}(\varphi \wedge \psi)}{\Pr_{\mathcal{M},s_{init}}^{\sigma}(\psi)}$$

for given LTL formulas φ and ψ. The maximum ranges over all schedulers σ with $\Pr_{\mathcal{M},s_{init}}^{\sigma}(\psi) > 0$. If there is at least one scheduler where $\Pr_{\mathcal{M},s_{init}}^{\sigma}(\psi) > 0$ then the maximum exists. Minimal conditional probabilities are defined analogously and can be handled using $\Pr_{\mathcal{M},s_{init}}^{\min}(\varphi \mid \psi) = 1 - \Pr_{\mathcal{M},s_{init}}^{\max}(\neg\varphi \mid \psi)$. The quotient and scale methods are not applicable for MDPs, as the task is to maximize the quotient of the probabilities for $\varphi \wedge \psi$ and ψ w.r.t. the same scheduler.

The reset method of [10] for computing $\Pr_{\mathcal{M},s_{init}}^{\max}(\varphi \mid \psi)$, where $\varphi = \Diamond F$ and $\psi = \Diamond C$ are reachability properties, works as follows. It first applies standard algorithms to check whether $\Pr_{\mathcal{M},s_{init}}^{\max}(\psi) > 0$, as otherwise the maximal conditional probability is undefined. If so, $\mathcal{M}$ is transformed into a normal form MDP $\mathcal{M}'$ with $\Pr_{\mathcal{M},s_{init}}^{\max}(\varphi \mid \psi) = \Pr_{\mathcal{M}',s_{init}}^{\max}(\varphi' \mid \psi')$ where $\varphi' = \Diamond F'$ and $\psi' = \Diamond C'$ are reachability properties with $F' \subseteq C'$ and where all states in C' are traps, i.e., they do not have enabled actions. $\mathcal{M}'$ contains a further trap state $fail$ and enjoys the property $\Pr_{\mathcal{M}',s}^{\max}(\Diamond C') > 0$ for all states $s \neq fail$. Having constructed $\mathcal{M}'$, the reset method transforms $\mathcal{M}'$ into another MDP $\mathcal{N}$ that is obtained by adding new transitions, called reset transitions, from $fail$ and from all other states s in $\mathcal{M}'$ with $\Pr_{\mathcal{M}',s}^{\min}(\Diamond C') = 0$ to s_{init}. The reset transitions have a special action name. For the states s in $\mathcal{M}'$ with $s \neq fail$ and $\Pr_{\mathcal{M}',fail}^{\min}(\Diamond C') = 0$, the reset transition is an additional nondeterministic alternative. Then, $\Pr_{\mathcal{M},s_{init}}^{\max}(\varphi \mid \psi) = \Pr_{\mathcal{N},s_{init}}^{\max}(\Diamond F')$. The case where φ, ψ are ω-regular properties is reducible to the base case where the condition and objective are reachability properties using deterministic ω-automata for φ and ψ.

3 Implementation

The foundation of our new implementation is the development branch of PRISM 4.3. We implemented the three methods (quotient, scale and reset) for DTMCs as well as the reset method for DTMCs and MDPs where the objective and the condition are given as LTL formulas. All methods can be employed using PRISM's explicit, mtbdd, hybrid and sparse engine. We rely on PRISM's infrastructure for generating deterministic finite or ω-automata from LTL formulas. To facilitate a more direct and performant implementation of model transformations used in the scale and the reset method, we developed a declarative framework based on atomic operations like *union of models* and *state space restriction*.

Specialized Treatment of Formula Pattern. Besides the automata-based approach of the scale method for DTMCs to treat LTL conditions, our implementation provides direct support for conditions of the form $\Diamond A$ (reachability), $\Box A$ (invariance), $\bigcirc A$ (next), $A \cup B$ (until), $A \, W \, B$ (weak until), and $A \, R \, B$ (release), where A and B are sets of states. The underlying algorithms rely on the same concepts as the treatment of reachability conditions in the scale method for Markov chains presented in [10]. In Sect. 4, we refer to these specialized treatment of the scale method as scale.pattern.

Likewise, for the reset method in DTMCs or MDPs, our implementation provides direct support to treat conditions and/or objectives that are reachability, invariance, (weak) until, or release properties without translating them into deterministic ω-automata. Altogether this yields the following four variants of the reset method. The original method of [10] is denoted by reset.ltl-ltl and uses automata for both the objective and the condition. We shall write reset.pattern-ltl for the reset method that treats the objective directly (assuming the objective is a reachability, invariance, (weak) until, or release property), while the condition is translated to an automaton. reset.ltl-pattern and reset.pattern-pattern have analogous meanings.

Infrastructure Improvements. To increase the efficiency of PRISM's computation of unconditional probabilities, we addressed several weaknesses in PRISM's explicit engine: (i) the replacement of quadratic-time with linear-time algorithms used in a preprocessing step that identifies all states s where a reachability condition holds with probability 1 under all or some schedulers; (ii) techniques to restrict products of models and ω-automata to the product states reachable from the initial states; (iii) the conversion of graph representations of DTMCs into more compact sparse matrices enabling a faster algorithmic treatment.

4 Evaluation and Comparative Studies

4.1 Methodology

We carried out all measurements on a compute server[4] and configured CUDD (the package for manipulating (MT)BDDs used in PRISM) and the JVM to use up to 31 GB RAM each. As recommended in production environments, we fixed the JVM heap size and set the integer cache to hold all boxed integers from 0 to $30 \cdot 10^6$. All experiments timed out after 3600 s. Multiple runs using PRISM's (semi-)symbolic engines yielded the same times and were only negligibly effected by running them in parallel. However, the explicit engine showed deviations, mainly due to JIT warmup effects. Hence, in order to obtain reliable measurements, we ran each property and model instance at least twice, and refrained from running the explicit experiments in parallel. Generally, we consider times ≤ 1 s below the precision of measurements and time differences of a few seconds insignificant.

---

[4] 2 × Intel Xeon E5-2680 (Octa Core, Sandy Bridge) @ 2.70 GHz, 384 GB RAM; Turbo Boost and Hyper Threading enabled; Debian GNU/Linux 8.3.

At the core of probabilistic model checking is the computation of reachability probabilities. PRISM's default methods for this task are different variants of *value iteration*. With the standard termination criterion, the value iteration may abort prematurely and return incorrect results [26]. In [12], we developed a prototype of the *interval iteration* proposed in [26] addressing this issue. However, it is not yet integrated into the current implementation discussed in this paper, but spot tests suggested that our benchmarks do not suffer from that issue.

4.2   Considered Models and Properties

Our experiments aim for an exhaustive examination of the implemented methods and patterns with respect to their performance in comparison to each other. We use established models from the PRISM benchmark suite [40] that allow the formulation of meaningful conditional queries. We included three DTMCs: the *bounded retransmission protocol* [31] (brp), the *crowds protocol for anonymity* [45] (crowds) and the *probabilistic contract signing protocol* [21,43] from Even, Goldreich & Lempel (egl), as well as two MDP models: the *randomized consensus shared coin protocol* [4,36] (consensus) and a model of *CSMA/CA from the IEEE standard 802.11* [37] (wlan). For each model, we combined various temporal path formulas for the objective and condition to cover all the instantiations of the implemented patterns. As we do not want to evaluate the translation from LTL to automata we considered only LTL path formulas of medium complexity that yielded automata with at most 16 states. Our selection includes all models (brp, crowds, wlan) and conditional queries previously used for benchmarking in [10,19]. In total, there are 190 runs required for each instance of a DTMC and 79 runs for each MDP instance. Among the considered properties are the following examples of interest that cannot be computed efficiently without the transformation-based methods. In the case of the *brp* protocol one might be interested in "the expected energy consumption of a successful transfer given the transfer is indeed successful" which has a probability <1. For the *consensus* protocol where multiple processes have to agree on a common date based on coin-flipping, we ask for "the maximal probability that the processes eventually disagree given a defective process always flips coin".

4.3   Results

We present numbers for the explicit and the mtbdd engine in this section and cover the hybrid and sparse engine in [41].

Methods. As the size of the state space and hence the runtimes grow exponentially, we use log-scale for the charts. Figure 1 compares the scale method against the quotient method in DTMCs. It incorporates the results from all DTMC model instances and all properties. The quotient method serves as reference and is plotted on the diagonal. We compare against the minimal time over all patterns of the scale method (scale.min(*)). For the majority of experiments, the scale method is faster than the quotient method. The margin increases with

(a) explicit engine   (b) mtbdd engine

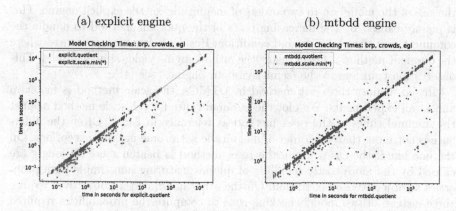

Fig. 1. Runtimes of methods: scale vs quotient (DTMCs)

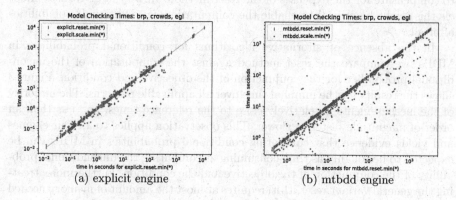

(a) explicit engine   (b) mtbdd engine

Fig. 2. Runtimes of methods: reset vs scale (DTMCs)

(a) explicit engine   (b) mtbdd engine

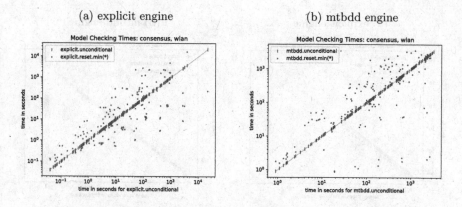

Fig. 3. Runtimes of methods: reset vs objective ∧ condition (MDPs)

the size of the model up to two orders of magnitude for the explicit engine. This is mainly caused by the increasing costs of the quotient method to handle the conjunction of the objective and condition. Besides a few more instances where the quotient method is faster, using the mtbdd engine yields similar results. This observation transfers to the (semi-)symbolic engines, see [41].

Pitted against the reset method in DTMCs, the scale method is faster in almost all experiments. We plot the minimal times for the scale method against the minimal times of the reset method as reference in Fig. 2. Often the difference is not more than one order of magnitude with some notable exceptions. On the one hand, the cases where the reset method is beaten more strikingly are caused by the more costly handling of queries featuring non-simple path properties as objective and condition. On the other hand, certain objectives require three instead of two model-checking runs to compute the probabilities required to construct the normal form MDP $\mathcal{M}'$. However, the transformed model can be very small, e.g., only 6 states and hence, the final computation step fast enough to compensate for the expenses of the reset method. In very large realistic models this might be crucial to enable the computation of conditional probabilities after all.

In the absence of alternative algorithms for conditional probabilities in MDPs, we compare the reset method against the computation of the unconditional probability for the conjunction of the objective and condition. Figure 3 shows the results for the minimal time over all applicable patterns. The majority of the measurements is relatively close to the reference times, i.e., less than an order of magnitude faster or slower. This observation applies to all four engines and yields evidence that computing conditional probabilities in MDPs can be expected to be roughly as time-consuming as computing the unconditional probability of the conjunction of the objective and the condition. Furthermore, treating the general variant reset.ltl-ltl requires at most the amount of memory needed to construct the product of the original model and the automata for the objective and condition, respectively, and less if a specialized pattern applies.

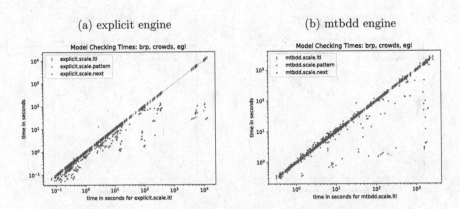

(a) explicit engine   (b) mtbdd engine

Fig. 4. Runtimes of patterns: scale.* vs scale.ltl (DTMCs) (Color figure online)

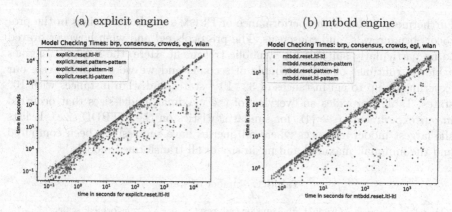

Fig. 5. Runtime of patterns: reset.* vs reset.ltl-ltl (DTMCs & MDPs)

Patterns. Figure 4 compares the runtimes of the specialized treatment of patterns scale.pattern against the general case using scale.ltl (patterns are depicted in different colors). Dots below the diagonale depict runtimes that are better than the general case which is on the diagonale. In general, the specialized methods show significant superiority over the automata-based approach. For the explicit engine (on the left), the special handling gains up to two and a half orders of magnitude. The few exceptions in the lower left are caused by fluctuations below the precision of measurements of about 1 s. Using the mtbdd engine (on the right) the picture is not as clear, since most of the measurements are closer to the general case. The reason for this is that in a purely symbolic approach, the computation time of the probabilities for the scaling step becomes an even more dominating factor. For the semi-symbolic engines hybrid and sparse this effect is not that distinct, and therefore, the results for these engines are similar to the explicit case, see [41]. Though, some cases perform considerably better with an advantage of up to three orders of magnitude (lower right).

Figure 5 considers the specialized patterns of the reset methods for both, DTMCs and MDPs. For all engines, the specialized patterns are clearly faster than the most general pattern reset.ltl-ltl, in larger model instances even up to 3 orders of magnitude. In fact, all specialized methods, e.g., reset.ltl-pattern, outperform the more general patterns, like reset.ltl-ltl, see [41] for details. There are a few, though non-representative, exceptions, most notable using the mtbdd engine. They issue from the wlan protocol and two properties having a certain (simple) until path property as objective. The specialized patterns reset.pattern-pattern and reset.pattern-ltl require the computation of minimal probabilities for the set of states falsifying until objectives, whereas the other patterns don't. As a result, in that MDP this specific computation is more time-consuming than building a product model from a simple automaton.

Engines and Model Sizes. The enhanced explicit engine showed decent performance for model sizes up to a few million states, see, e.g., Sect. 5, Table 2.

Furthermore, it beats the performance of PRISM's symbolic engines in the protocols brp, crowds, and consensus. The protocols egl and wlan however proved to be particularly suitable for symbolic treatment. Here, the symbolic engines achieved runtimes of only a couple of seconds and we were able to scale our experiments up to egl instances of $32 \cdot 10^{12}$ states and wlan instances with 10^9 states. Table 1 provides an overview of the maximal model sizes that occurred in our experiments (see [41] for similar statistics on the MTBDD size). It lists the largest model instances where all queries have successfully been computed and the minimal, maximal and mean size of all transformed models.

Table 1. Number of states

Model		Original #	Transformed: reset			Transformed: scale		
			min	mean	max	min	mean	max
DTMCs	brp	$113 \cdot 10^3$	5	$25 \cdot 10^3$	$119 \cdot 10^3$	$12 \cdot 10^3$	$106 \cdot 10^3$	$223 \cdot 10^3$
	crowds	$189 \cdot 10^6$	6	$5 \cdot 10^6$	$16 \cdot 10^6$	$11 \cdot 10^6$	$86 \cdot 10^6$	$189 \cdot 10^6$
	egl	$32 \cdot 10^{12}$	6	$332 \cdot 10^3$	$2 \cdot 10^6$	$62 \cdot 10^6$	$18 \cdot 10^{12}$	$32 \cdot 10^{12}$
MDPs	consensus	$17 \cdot 10^6$	$1 \cdot 10^6$	$6 \cdot 10^6$	$20 \cdot 10^6$	n.a.	n.a.	n.a.
	wlan	$4 \cdot 10^6$	18	$413 \cdot 10^3$	$12 \cdot 10^6$	n.a.	n.a.	n.a.

Bad Convergence of Reset Method. The reset method's core idea is to redistribute the probability mass of paths not satisfying the condition ψ over the paths satisfying it. This can impose problems in the application of approximation techniques like value iteration. If the model features a rather chain-like topology, it might take a huge number of iteration steps to eventually reach convergence. This phenomenon occurred in the brp protocol, even in a comparably small instance with only about a hundred thousand states. For five properties sharing the same globally condition, the transformation time is only a couple of seconds but the time required to compute the reachability probability in the transformed models is several hundred seconds [41]. However, the other models of our benchmarks are not effected.

5 Comparison Prism vs Storm

In [19], Dehnert et al. report on an experimental evaluation of an early version of their model checker STORM that was included in the PROPhESY tool and our previous prototypical implementation [10] for PRISM's explicit engine. For two benchmark models—brp and crowds—they were able to demonstrate a significant performance advantage of the STORM implementation.

In this section, we provide a comparison of our new implementation with the current, stand-alone release (Version 1.0) of STORM [19]. It supports the computation of conditional probabilities in DTMCs and MDPs but only if both, the objective and the condition, are reachability properties. For MDPs, only maximal probabilities are supported. The computation is based on the algorithms of [10], i.e., the scale method for DTMCs and the reset method for MDPs. Support is limited to STORM's explicit engine (named "sparse" in STORM).

Engines. We compare the performance of PRISM's and STORM's explicit engines and include our measurements for PRISM's symbolic engines as well. Additionally, we provide a comparison against our former prototypical implementation [10] (denoted by explicit'14), as well as a port of that prototype to PRISM 4.3 and the enhanced infrastructure (explicit*). This will allow to distinguish performance improvements due to the general enhancements and those related to the enhanced methods for the computation of condition probabilities.

Solvers. STORM provides a multitude of implementations of solvers for systems of linear equations (SLE), partially relying on highly-efficient external libraries. We provide a comparison (i) using the *default solvers* of both PRISM and STORM, as well as (ii) using the *same solvers* for both model checkers. This allows to determine the impact of solvers on the performance. For *default solvers*, PRISM uses the Jacobi method in the symbolic engines and the Gauss-Seidel method in the explicit engine in combination with value iteration in the case of MDPs. For DTMCs, STORM defaults to the *generalized minimal residual method* (GMRES) and preconditioning with *incomplete LU decomposition* (ILU). For MDPs, STORM uses value iteration with the power method. For the comparison using the *same solvers* for SLEs and linear programs (LP), we changed the settings for PRISM to use value iteration with the power method for MDPs, and for STORM to use the Gauss-Seidel method for DTMCs.

Table 2. Sum of model-checking times, default solvers

Model		PRISM						STORM
		hybrid	mtbdd	sparse	explicit	explicit*	explicit'14	explicit
DTMCs	brp	349 s	18,413 s	334 s	45 s	44 s	3515 s	4 s
	crowds	309 s	409 s	322 s	148 s	124 s	1933 s	55 s
	egl	242 s	13 s	299 s	242 s	412 s	2117 s	74 s
MDPs	consensus	319 s	2518 s	106 s	41 s	68 s	116 s	120 s
	wlan	70 s	16 s	46 s	45 s	264 s	241 s	26 s

Results. We present an aggregated comparison, one for the *default settings* (Table 2) and one with the *same solvers* (Table 3). Comprehensive tables can be found in [41]. Comparing the performance of explicit'14 and explicit*, the significant impact of the infrastructure improvements is apparent. In our observation this is mostly due to the computations of the state sets having probability 0 or 1 and the use of sparse data structures for DTMCs. Comparing explicit and explicit*, we see a considerable performance improvement for some of the models due the special handling of formula patterns and further enhancements in the computation of conditional probabilities (see Sect. 3), especially in MDPs. The new implementation employs additional graph analysis to reduce the size of the transformed models which does not pay off in the crowds protocol.

Comparing PRISM's and STORM's explicit engines using the *default settings* (Table 2), we see that STORM has better performance for the considered DTMC instances. Comparing this to STORM's performance when forcing the *same solvers* (Table 3), we can see that this advantage is due to the integration of the highly optimized linear equation solvers in STORM. For the egl protocol, STORM is still faster in this setting. But we suspect this is mainly due to the size of the model, which causes PRISM to operate close to the memory limit. This has a considerable performance impact caused by excessive garbage collection.

For MDPs, we achieve better performance using the explicit engine for the consensus case study, while STORM achieves better performance in the wlan protocol. Switching to the *same solvers*, i.e., value iteration using the power method, only has an impact on the consensus results for PRISM's explicit engine.

Taking both scenarios into account, we conclude that efficient solution methods for SLEs and LPs are a dominating factor besides sophisticated methods for the computation of conditional probabilities. Offering a variety of efficient solvers the user can choose between, STORM excels in this respect [20]. This is illustrated by the observation that STORM's internal value iteration is much slower for certain protocols, e.g., wlan, than the default, external implementation. However, the experiments also suggest that for the implementation of model-checking algorithms, choosing Java must not be a disadvantage performance-wise. Further optimized implementations can be expected to approach the performance of implementations in the C programming language [15,42]. A comparison of the build times of PRISM and STORM is presented in [41]. Furthermore, experiments on another computer resulted in surprisingly huge time differences, although the general trend does not change, see [41].

Table 3. Sum of model-checking times, same solvers

Model		PRISM						STORM
		hybrid	mtbdd	sparse	explicit	explicit*	explicit'14	explicit
DTMCs	brp	349 s	18,413 s	334 s	45 s	44 s	3515 s	228 s
	crowds	309 s	409 s	322 s	148 s	124 s	1933 s	192 s
	egl	242 s	13 s	299 s	242 s	412 s	2117 s	89 s
MDPs	consensus	310 s	2684 s	109 s	79 s	128 s	177 s	120 s
	wlan	78 s	16 s	47 s	48 s	262 s	229 s	26 s

6   Conclusion

Despite the significance of conditional probabilities and the numerous tools for computing unconditional probabilities for temporal properties in Markovian models, tool support for conditional probabilities was very limited. To the best of our knowledge, our implementation is the first that supports the computation of conditional probabilities in Markovian models where the objective and the condition are temporal properties specified as LTL formulas. We evaluated different methods (quotient, scale and reset for DTMCs) and explicit and (semi-)symbolic engines. The experiments indicate a superiority of the scale method over the reset method, which again performs better than the naive quotient method in most cases. Further performance improvements are obtained by using specialized (automata-less) treatments of simple path properties rather than the generic automata-based reduction to reachability properties. In many cases, the performance of the reset method for maximal conditional probabilities in MDPs was fairly in the same order as the computation of unconditional probabilities for conjunctive events. As an overhead compared to the unconditional case is unavoidable, this can be taken as evidence for the general feasibility of reasoning about extremal conditional probabilities for temporal properties in MDPs.

Our implementation allows to compute conditional expected accumulated costs in Markov chains using the scale method. In future work we plan to mature and integrate the prototypical implementation of the algorithm [11] for the computation of maximal expected accumulated costs in MDPs. Other future directions include the integration of our implementation in the public version of PRISM to ease links to other facilities, such as the interval iteration [12,26] or the Hanoi framework [6] to provide support for the full class of ω-regular objectives and conditions.

References

1. Andrés, M.: Quantitative analysis of information leakage in probabilistic and non-deterministic systems. Ph.D. thesis, UB Nijmegen (2011)
2. Andrés, M.E., Palamidessi, C., van Rossum, P., Sokolova, A.: Information hiding in probabilistic concurrent systems. Theor. Comput. Sci. **412**(28), 3072–3089 (2011)
3. Andrés, M.E., van Rossum, P.: Conditional probabilities over probabilistic and nondeterministic systems. In: Ramakrishnan, C.R., Rehof, J. (eds.) TACAS 2008. LNCS, vol. 4963, pp. 157–172. Springer, Heidelberg (2008). doi:10.1007/978-3-540-78800-3_12
4. Aspnes, J., Herlihy, M.: Fast randomized consensus using shared memory. J. Algorithms **11**(3), 441–461 (1990)
5. Aziz, A., Sanwal, K., Singhal, V., Brayton, R.K.: Model-checking continous-time Markov chains. ACM Trans. Comput. Logic **1**(1), 162–170 (2000)
6. Babiak, T., Blahoudek, F., Duret-Lutz, A., Klein, J., Křetínský, J., Müller, D., Parker, D., Strejček, J.: The Hanoi omega-automata format. In: Kroening, D., Păsăreanu, C.S. (eds.) CAV 2015. LNCS, vol. 9206, pp. 479–486. Springer, Cham (2015). doi:10.1007/978-3-319-21690-4_31
7. Baier, C., Dubslaff, C., Klein, J., Klüppelholz, S., Wunderlich, S.: Probabilistic model checking for energy-utility analysis. In: Breugel, F., Kashefi, E., Palamidessi, C., Rutten, J. (eds.) Horizons of the Mind. A Tribute to Prakash Panangaden. LNCS, vol. 8464, pp. 96–123. Springer, Cham (2014). doi:10.1007/978-3-319-06880-0_5
8. Baier, C., Haverkort, B.R., Hermanns, H., Katoen, J.: Model-checking algorithms for continuous-time Markov chains. IEEE Trans. Softw. Eng. **29**(6), 524–541 (2003)
9. Baier, C., Katoen, J.-P.: Principles of Model Checking. MIT Press, Cambridge (2008)

10. Baier, C., Klein, J., Klüppelholz, S., Märcker, S.: Computing conditional probabilities in Markovian models efficiently. In: Ábrahám, E., Havelund, K. (eds.) TACAS 2014. LNCS, vol. 8413, pp. 515–530. Springer, Heidelberg (2014). doi:10. 1007/978-3-642-54862-8_43

11. Baier, C., Klein, J., Klüppelholz, S., Wunderlich, S.: Maximizing the conditional expected reward for reaching the goal. In: Legay, A., Margaria, T. (eds.) TACAS 2017. LNCS, vol. 10206, pp. 269–285. Springer, Heidelberg (2017). doi:10.1007/ 978-3-662-54580-5_16

12. Baier, C., Klein, J., Leuschner, L., Parker, D., Wunderlich, S.: Ensuring the reliability of your model checker: interval iteration for Markov decision processes. In: Majumdar, R., Kunčak, V. (eds.) CAV 2017. LNCS, vol. 10426, pp. 160–180. Springer, Cham (2017). doi:10.1007/978-3-319-63387-9_8

13. Baier, C., Kwiatkowska, M.Z.: Model checking for a probabilistic branching time logic with fairness. Distrib. Comput. 11(3), 125–155 (1998)

14. Barthe, G., Espitau, T., Ferrer Fioriti, L.M., Hsu, J.: Synthesizing probabilistic invariants via Doop's decomposition. In: Chaudhuri, S., Farzan, A. (eds.) CAV 2016. LNCS, vol. 9779, pp. 43–61. Springer, Cham (2016). doi:10.1007/ 978-3-319-41528-4_3

15. Besset, D.H.: Object-Oriented Implementation of Numerical Methods: An Introduction with Java and Smalltalk. Morgan Kaufmann Publishers Inc., Burlington (2000)

16. Bianco, A., de Alfaro, L.: Model checking of probabilistic and nondeterministic systems. In: Thiagarajan, P.S. (ed.) FSTTCS 1995. LNCS, vol. 1026, pp. 499–513. Springer, Heidelberg (1995). doi:10.1007/3-540-60692-0_70

17. Chatterjee, K., Fu, H., Goharshady, A.K.: Termination analysis of probabilistic programs through Positivstellensatz's. In: Chaudhuri, S., Farzan, A. (eds.) CAV 2016. LNCS, vol. 9779, pp. 3–22. Springer, Cham (2016). doi:10.1007/ 978-3-319-41528-4_1

18. Courcoubetis, C., Yannakakis, M.: The complexity of probabilistic verification. J. ACM 42(4), 857–907 (1995)

19. Dehnert, C., Junges, S., Jansen, N., Corzilius, F., Volk, M., Bruintjes, H., Katoen, J.-P., Ábrahám, E.: PROPhESY: a PRObabilistic ParamEter SYnthesis tool. In: Kroening, D., Păsăreanu, C.S. (eds.) CAV 2015. LNCS, vol. 9206, pp. 214–231. Springer, Cham (2015). doi:10.1007/978-3-319-21690-4_13

20. Dehnert, C., Junges, S., Katoen, J.P., Volk, M.: A storm is coming: a modern probabilistic model checker. In: Majumdar, R., Kunčak, V. (eds.) CAV 2017. LNCS, vol. 10427, pp. 592–600. Springer, Cham (2017). doi:10.1007/978-3-319-63390-9_31

21. Even, S., Goldreich, O., Lempel, A.: A randomized protocol for signing contracts. Commun. ACM 28(6), 637–647 (1985)

22. Forejt, V., Kwiatkowska, M.Z., Norman, G., Parker, D.: Automated verification techniques for probabilistic systems. In: Bernardo, M., Issarny, V. (eds.) SFM 2011. LNCS, vol. 6659, pp. 53–113. Springer, Heidelberg (2011). doi:10.1007/ 978-3-642-21455-4_3

23. Gao, Y., Hahn, E.M., Zhan, N., Zhang, L.: CCMC: a conditional CSL model checker for continuous-time Markov chains. In: Hung, D., Ogawa, M. (eds.) ATVA 2013. LNCS, vol. 8172, pp. 464–468. Springer, Cham (2013). doi:10.1007/ 978-3-319-02444-8_36

24. Gao, Y., Xu, M., Zhan, N., Zhang, L.: Model checking conditional CSL for continuous-time Markov chains. Inf. Process. Lett. 113(1–2), 44–50 (2013)

25. Grädel, E., Thomas, W., Wilke, T. (eds.): Automata Logics, and Infinite Games. LNCS, vol. 2500. Springer, Heidelberg (2002). doi:10.1007/3-540-36387-4

26. Haddad, S., Monmege, B.: Reachability in MDPs: refining convergence of value iteration. In: Ouaknine, J., Potapov, I., Worrell, J. (eds.) RP 2014. LNCS, vol. 8762, pp. 125–137. Springer, Cham (2014). doi:10.1007/978-3-319-11439-2_10

27. Hahn, E.M., Li, Y., Schewe, S., Turrini, A., Zhang, L.: ISCASMC: a web-based probabilistic model checker. In: Jones, C., Pihlajasaari, P., Sun, J. (eds.) FM 2014. LNCS, vol. 8442, pp. 312–317. Springer, Cham (2014). doi:10.1007/978-3-319-06410-9_22

28. Hansson, H., Jonsson, B.: A logic for reasoning about time and reliability. Formal Aspects Comput. **6**, 512–535 (1994)

29. Haverkort, B.R.: Performance of Computer Communication Systems: A Model-Based Approach. Wiley, Hoboken (1998)

30. Heiner, M., Rohr, C., Schwarick, M.: MARCIE – model checking and reachability analysis done efficiently. In: Colom, J.-M., Desel, J. (eds.) PETRI NETS 2013. LNCS, vol. 7927, pp. 389–399. Springer, Heidelberg (2013). doi:10.1007/978-3-642-38697-8_21

31. Helmink, L., Sellink, M.P.A., Vaandrager, F.W.: Proof-checking a data link protocol. In: Barendregt, H., Nipkow, T. (eds.) TYPES 1993. LNCS, vol. 806, pp. 127–165. Springer, Heidelberg (1994). doi:10.1007/3-540-58085-9_75

32. Jansen, N., Kaminski, B.L., Katoen, J., Olmedo, F., Gretz, F., McIver, A.: Conditioning in probabilistic programming. In: Mathematical Foundations of Programming Semantics (MFPS), ENTCS, vol. 319, pp. 199–216 (2015)

33. Ji, M., Wu, D., Chen, Z.: Verification method of conditional probability based on automaton. J. Netw. **8**(6), 1329–1335 (2013)

34. Katoen, J.-P., Zapreev, I.S., Hahn, E.M., Hermanns, H., Jansen, D.N.: The ins and outs of the probabilistic model checker MRMC. Perform. Eval. **68**(2), 90–104 (2011)

35. Kulkarni, V.G.: Modeling and Analysis of Stochastic Systems. Chapman & Hall, Boca Raton (1995)

36. Kwiatkowska, M., Norman, G., Segala, R.: Automated verification of a randomized distributed consensus protocol using cadence SMV and PRISM? In: Berry, G., Comon, H., Finkel, A. (eds.) CAV 2001. LNCS, vol. 2102, pp. 194–206. Springer, Heidelberg (2001). doi:10.1007/3-540-44585-4_17

37. Kwiatkowska, M., Norman, G., Sproston, J.: Probabilistic model checking of the IEEE 802.11 wireless local area network protocol. In: Hermanns, H., Segala, R. (eds.) PAPM-PROBMIV 2002. LNCS, vol. 2399, pp. 169–187. Springer, Heidelberg (2002). doi:10.1007/3-540-45605-8_11

38. Kwiatkowska, M.Z., Norman, G., Parker, D.: Probabilistic symbolic model checking with PRISM: a hybrid approach. Int. J. Softw. Tools Technol. Transf. (STTT) **6**(2), 128–142 (2004)

39. Kwiatkowska, M.Z., Norman, G., Parker, D.: PRISM 4.0: verification of probabilistic real-time systems. In: Gopalakrishnan, G., Qadeer, S. (eds.) CAV 2011. LNCS, vol. 6806, pp. 585–591. Springer, Heidelberg (2011). doi:10.1007/978-3-642-22110-1_47

40. Kwiatkowska, M.Z., Norman, G., Parker, D.: The PRISM benchmark suite. In: 9th International Conference on Quantitative Evaluation of SysTems (QEST), pp. 203–204. IEEE Computer Society (2012)

41. Märcker, S., Baier, C., Klein, J., Klüppelholz, S.: Computing conditional probabilities: implementation and evaluation (extended version) (2017). http://wwwtcs.inf.tu-dresden.de/ALGI/PUB/SEFM17/

42. Nikishkov, G.P.: Programming Finite Elements in Java^{TM}, 1st edn. Springer, London (2010)

43. Norman, G., Shmatikov, V.: Analysis of probabilistic contract signing. In: Abdallah, A.E., Ryan, P., Schneider, S. (eds.) FASec 2002. LNCS, vol. 2629, pp. 81–96. Springer, Heidelberg (2003). doi:10.1007/978-3-540-40981-6_9
44. Puterman, M.L., Processes, M.D.: Discrete Stochastic Dynamic Programming. Wiley, Hoboken (1994)
45. Reiter, M.K., Rubin, A.D.: Crowds: anonymity for web transactions. ACM Trans. Inf. Syst. Secur. (TISSEC) **1**(1), 66–92 (1998)
46. Vardi, M.Y.: Automatic verification of probabilistic concurrent finite-state programs. In: 26th IEEE Symposium on Foundations of Computer Science (FOCS), pp. 327–338. IEEE Computer Society (1985)

Validating the Meta-Theory
of Programming Languages
(Short Paper)

Guglielmo Fachini[1]($\boxtimes$) and Alberto Momigliano[2]

[1] INRIA Prosecco, Paris, France
guglielmo.fachini@inria.fr
[2] Dipartimento di Informatica, Università degli Studi di Milano, Milan, Italy
momigliano@di.unimi.it

Abstract. We report on work in progress in building an environment
for the validation of the meta-theory of programming languages artifacts, for example the correctness of compiler translations; the basic idea
is to couple *property-based testing* with *binders*-aware functional programming as the meta-language for specification and testing. Treating
binding signatures and related notions, such as new names generation,
α-equivalence and capture-avoiding substitution correctly and effectively
is crucial in the verification and validation of programming language
(meta)theory. We use *Haskell* as our meta-language, since it offers various libraries for both random and exhaustive generation of tests, as well
as for binders. We validate our approach on benchmarks of mutations
presented in the literature and some examples of code "in the wild". In
the former case, not only did we very quickly (re)discover all the planted
bugs, but we achieved that with very little configuration effort with comparison to the competition. In the second case we located several simple
bugs that had survived for years in publicly available (academic) code.
We believe that our approach adds to the increasing evidence of the usefulness of property-based testing for semantic engineering of programming languages, in alternative or prior to full verification.

1 Introduction

Recent years have seen major advances in what we could call the *meta-
correctness* of programming, that is the (formal) verification of the trustworthiness of the *tools* with which we write programs: from static analyzers to
compilers, including parsers, pretty-printers all the way down to run time systems, see projects such as *CakeML* (http://cakeml.org) and *VST* (http://vst.
cs.princeton.edu).

More specifically, we are (and in pretty good company too [8,11], to cite only
two projects such as Spoofax and PLT-Redex) interested in providing support

---

This is a short paper accepted in the new ideas and work-in-progress section of
SEFM 2017.

A. Cimatti and M. Sirjani (Eds.): SEFM 2017, LNCS 10469, pp. 367–374, 2017.
DOI: 10.1007/978-3-319-66197-1_23

to the "working semanticist" while designing and prototyping programming languages and related artifacts. To date, very few programming languages (PL) are based on rigorous models, Standard ML being the shining example. On the other corner, infamous is the case of PHP:

> "There was never any intent to write a programming language (...) I have absolutely no idea how to write a programming language, I just kept adding the next logical step on the way". (Rasmus Lerdorf, see http://itc. conversationsnetwork.org/shows/detail58.html)

In the middle we find lengthy prose documents such as the *Java Language Specification*, whose internal consistency is but a dream, as a very recent paper shows [1]. The properties that PL artifacts should satisfy span from type soundness as in the above case, to compiler correctness (e.g., projects as *CompCert*), to more intensional guarantees related to security (*SECOMP*). Further, although the average programmer is not likely to write her own programming language, she may try her hands on a *Domain Specific Language*, and this design may incorporate flaws that will trickle down and produce hard-to-find bugs in the final product. In this sense "every programmer is a language designer at some point" (Pierce, from the introduction to *Software Foundations*, available at www. cis.upenn.edu/~bcpierce/sf).

This is all good, but the formal verification of PL metatheory is still a very labor-intensive task, even (or more so) with a proof-assistant, so much that there are perhaps only a few dozen people in the world able and willing to carry out such an endeavor. A lighter alternative is *validation*, in the form of *property-based testing* (PBT) as pioneered by QuickCheck [6]: here, we try to *refute*, rather than prove, the properties of the calculus underlying our software artifacts, via *random* or *exhaustive* generation of test cases. For many classes of (typically) shallow bugs, a tool that automatically finds counterexamples can be surprisingly effective and can complement formal proof attempts by warning when the property we wish to prove has easily-found counterexamples. The beauty of this form of meta-theory model checking is that the properties that should hold are already given by means of the theorems that the calculus under study is supposed to satisfy. Of course, those need to be fine tuned for testing to be effective, but we are free of the thorny issue of specification generation.

A particular dimension in validation in this domain is the handling of *binding signatures*, by which we mean the encoding of PL constructs sensitive to naming and scoping: declarations, closures, α-equivalence of method/function arguments, capture-avoiding substitutions, generation of fresh names, nonces, etc. These are ubiquitous in the specification of high-level programming languages, surprisingly easy to get wrong, often callously ignored or so awkwardly supported that they may constitute a unnecessary stumbling block for validation and verification.

This paper describes work in progress in building an environment where one can validate PL meta-theoretical properties with a combination of automated testing tools and an appropriate treatment of binders. We use *Haskell* as our meta-language, since it offers not only a very expressive type system, but various libraries for both random and exhaustive generation of tests [6,7,9] as well as for binders [12]. The idea is to allow the user to specify her semantic model(s) with a human-friendly notion of binders and validate them with a cascade of testing tools with the least amount of configuration effort. This is contrast with the competition where either the testing strategy is fixed [3,4] or binding issues are totally ignored (or both) [8]. We validate our approach on benchmarks of mutations presented in the literature and some examples of code "in the wild". In the former case, not only did we very quickly (re)discover all the planted bugs, but we achieved that with very little configuration effort. In the second, case we located several simple bugs that had survived for years in publicly available (academic) code. As a side effect, we have gained some new insights about which testing tool is better suited to the various domains and facets of PL meta-theory.

2   Binders-Aware Property-Based Testing

We offer a PBT environment integrating several Haskell libraries, composed, as expected, with a thin layer of monadic code. There are several (non-orthogonal) dimensions around which we can arrange test data generation in a PBT setting:

- *random* vs. *exhaustive* test generation;
- *automatic* vs. *hand-written* configuration of generators;
- For exhaustive enumeration, whether we define upper bounds for generation in terms of *size*, that is, number of constructors in a term or *depth* — depth of the tree representation (AST) of a constructor.

We assume that the reader is familiar with QuickCheck [6] (random enumeration, hand-written generators, minimization of counterexamples (*shrinking*) left to the user) and we briefly describe the others libraries we have integrated. SmallCheck [9] is essentially an exhaustive enumeration version of QuickCheck, where the upper bound is defined as term depth. LazySmallCheck [9] is a variant of SmallCheck that leverages Haskell's laziness to get around the limits of SmallCheck's brute enumeration of values: the idea is to use *partially-defined* expressions (in logical terms, non-ground ones) to stand for the set of all their instantiations; e.g. lazy evaluation will realize that a list such as (1 : 0 : undefined) is not, say, *ordered* without generating any concrete list (1 : 0 : xs) for any further instantiation of xs. Feat [7] is built on the concept of functional enumerations, that is, efficiently computable bijections from natural numbers to values, which are partitioned with respect to their size. This fact combined with specific implementation techniques (i.e. memoisation, memory sharing) allows the enumeration process to be performed for a specific size or, more interestingly, from an arbitrary index, without incurring in the cost of enumerating the preceding smaller values. All the above tools supports the automatic derivation of generators out of the grammar rules of the language under study; however, it is also possible to fine tune them manually, to a different degree in each tool, e.g., adjusting the weights of certain constructors.

The next ingredient is how to best represent binders, a long standing issue in the context of meta-theory verification. Using a naive named syntax is out of the question, for its inadequacy and prone-ness to mistakes; one choice is the locally nameless representation [2]: this couples the use of raw names for free variables with de Bruijn indexes for bound variables; the latter are basically pointers linking a bound variable to its binding site, thus collapsing all α-equivalent terms into a unique canonical representation. E.g., Java 8 anonymous functions (int x) -> x and (int y) -> y would both be mapped to the same AST L(int, 1), for L a putative constructor for lambdas.

While this technique is handy and widespread, it is very hard to read for humans and furthermore it needs to be re-implemented for every binding operator in every case study one wants to validate. Unbound [12] is a Haskell library that provides a DSL for the nameless representation, while offering to the user a named surface syntax. The library ensures that we cannot encode illegal values (i.e. a bound variable without a surrounding binder) and at the same time it implements useful operations such as capture-avoiding substitutions, fresh name generations etc. Since Unbound sits on top of several other Haskell libraries, its coexistence with PBT tools is not immediate.

3   Experiments

We validate our approach with two sets of experiments, the first showing that we easily handle some of the benchmarks of mutations presented in the literature [8], the second hunting for bugs "in the wild". We give some details of the first case, while we refer to the first author's thesis for much more.

Functional programming with lists. This comes from the PLT-Redex benchmark suite http://docs.racket-lang.org/redex/benchmark.html and concerns the type soundness of a prototypical λ-calculus with lists and related operations, whose BNF includes the following:

$$\begin{array}{lll} \text{Types} & \sigma & ::= int \mid ilist \mid \sigma \rightarrow \sigma' \\ \text{Terms} & M & ::= x \mid \lambda x{:}\sigma.\ M \mid M_1\ M_2 \mid c \\ \text{Constants}\ c & ::= n \mid nil \mid cons \mid hd \mid tl \mid plus \\ \text{Values} & V & ::= c \mid \lambda x{:}\sigma.\ M \mid cons\ V \mid cons\ V_1\ V_2 \mid plus\ V \end{array}$$

Given rules for typing $(\Gamma \vdash M : \tau)$ and small step reduction $(M \rightsquigarrow M')$, and a judgment *error* identifying expressions that may produce run-time errors such as taking the head of an empty list, the properties we wish to validate are:

$$M : \tau \wedge M \rightsquigarrow M' \implies M' : \tau \hspace{3cm} \text{(Preservation)}$$

$$M : \tau \wedge \neg(M \text{ is a value}) \wedge \neg(M \text{ error}) \implies \exists M'.M \rightsquigarrow M' \hspace{0.5cm} \text{(Progress)}$$

To give a feel of what using Unbound entails we report the encoding of *Terms* in which **Constant** and **Type** are the data-types for the eponymous grammar rules, whereas **Bind** comes from Unbound's DSL, signaling that the constructor

Lam has a binding occurrence of a variable Name, which can be substituted for an Exp; this provides for free α-equivalence of terms with binders and automatically derives functions for substitutions, free names etc.

```
data Exp = Const Constant
         | Var (Name Exp)
         | Lam Type (Bind (Name Exp) Exp)
         | App Exp Exp
```

For example, we encode the identity function on integers as Lam TyInt (bind x) (Var x), where x = s2n"x", using a built-in that converts strings to Unbound names; the above term is actually syntactic sugar for the nameless one we saw in Sect. 2.

The benchmark introduces nine mutations to be spotted as a violation of either or both properties. E.g., the first mutation introduces a bug in the typing rule for application, matching the range of the function type to the type of the argument (on the right, the correct rule):

$$\frac{\Gamma \vdash M : \sigma \to \tau \quad \Gamma \vdash N : \tau}{\Gamma \vdash M\,N : \tau} \; \text{T} - \text{APP} - \text{B1} \qquad \frac{\Gamma \vdash M : \sigma \to \tau \quad \Gamma \vdash N : \sigma}{\Gamma \vdash M\,N : \tau} \; \text{T} - \text{APP} - \text{OK}$$

We show in Table 1 some experimental results, taken on a machine with an Intel Core 2 Duo CPU 2.4 GHz and 4 GB of RAM. The measurements are reported in milliseconds and were collected by averaging the execution times of ten runs. The cells marked with '✗' indicate that no counterexamples have been produced within the time limit, which we set to 300 s. Cl reports Redex's classification of the hardness of bugs (shallow, medium, unnatural); hw and au stand for the hand-written and automatically derived generators, whereas F, SC, LSC and QC are respectively Feat, SmallCheck, LazySmallCheck and QuickCheck.

Table 1. Performances on the functional programming with lists benchmark

Bug	Cl	F (au)	F (hw)	SC (au)	SC (hw)	LSC (hw)	QC (hw)
B#1 (prog.)	S	10.2	1.5	1.0	2.8	0.1	18.0
B#1 (pres.)	S	35.4	61.1	✗	✗	18007.7	341.4
B#2 (prog.)	M	618.2	65.6	3960.7	13269.2	0.8	4010.8
B#3 (prog.)	S	9.7	1.6	1.0	2.8	0.1	16.4
B#3 (pres.)	S	10.8	9.4	7.2	68.7	2.7	7.3
B#4 (prog.)	S	✗	✗	✗	✗	10.1	✗
B#5 (pres.)	S	37134.8	4191.7	✗	✗	2.9	✗
B#6 (prog.)	M	36453.6	4158.8	✗	✗	2.5	✗
B#7 (prog.)	S	124.1	445.7	4.7	3792.1	2.4	510.4
B#8 (pres.)	U	2.8	9.5	✗	759.7	5.6	100.4
B#9 (pres.)	S	35.5	58.6	✗	✗	17297.1	243.2

QuickCheck missed three bugs and, as usual, it required a hand-written generator whose development can be tricky, especially if one also wants shrinking. SmallCheck was the worst of the five and it found its bugs only when invoked with the exact specific depth of the bug, which of course is an unrealistic assumption. Using partially defined AST seems to really help in quickly discarding a whole classes of non-well typed terms; indeed, LazySmallCheck was the only tool that was able to find all the bugs. Feat's performances are encouraging, considering it does not use laziness as LazySmallCheck does, which, as admitted in [9], may not always be a successful strategy. Feat was able to find all but one counterexamples in less than five seconds without incurring in the exponential explosion brought by enumeration by depth. The hand-written generators performed better than the automated ones, but only in two cases this would have been discernible by the user. By construction Feat exhibits size-minimal counter-examples, while (Lazy)SmallCheck produces depth-minimal ones. In this benchmark, however, they essentially reported very similar terms.

Code "in the wild". While it is reassuring to be able to find mutations listed in the literature, the proof of the pudding is exercising code whose validity is not known, save for having stood some unit testing. This also eliminates any bias in the definition of hand-written generators, which can be skewed by the foreknowledge of the existence of a bug. Of course, we are limited to testing Haskell implementation of PL artifacts available on the net and we selected some whose soundness properties were immediate. We adopted a feedback-loop strategy by which we searched for bugs, corrected the spec and then restarted. Once we reached what seemed like a fixed point, we collected coverage statistics about the main functions and declared "victory". We set the system to use Feat first and it paid off immediately — the other strategies did not contribute any further bug. Among several experiments, here we mention taking on a Haskell porting (http://code.google.com/archive/p/tapl-haskell) of the code coming with Pierce's textbook "Types and Programming Languages", in particular *fullsimple*, a model of the core of Standard ML. We found nine fairly shallow bugs falsifying the progress property, which we do not have the space here to discuss. We impute them to lack of attention to the interaction of different language features, such as type ascription, variant types, etc. However trivial, they had survived some pretty extensive, at least for academic standards, unit testing.

4   Conclusions and Future Work

Although at an early stage of development, we believe our approach adds to the increasing evidence of the usefulness of property-based testing for semantic engineering of programming languages, in alternative or prior to full verification, and should be added to the work flow of PL design and verification: spec'n'check in this context is dirt simple, quick and effective in locating shallow but irritating bugs; it also doubles as a compelling way to do *regression* testing.

The success of our approach can be attributed to two factors: first, the integration with a tool such as Unbound, which handles binders almost as easily as we had named syntax; this without incurring in any significant run-time penalties or, more importantly in this setting, false positives stemming from incorrect implementation of basic notions such as substitutions etc. Secondly, the possibility of leveraging different cascading testing strategies: in each benchmark, at least one strategy was successful in catching the required bug. Contrary to common expectations, we found random testing to be in this domain labour intensive without providing the ability to go "deep" in any meaningful way. Exhaustive enumeration, by contrast, revealed to be an excellent choice: easy to use, predictable and reasonably effective in bug finding. Recent improvements [5] in the generate-and-test approach for properties with hard to satisfy conditions will make it scale even further.

We envision our testing environment to be the target of even more declarative semantic engineering tools such as *Ott* [10], which offers the possibility of specifying PL theory as high-level informal texts (grammars and proof rules in ASCII) and then converting it to executable specs in a variety of proof assistants — one strong point in common with us being the use of the locally nameless style for binders. The framework would benefit from an extension with a source language for specifying and automatically deriving custom generators. We also plan to tackle bigger case studies, such as validating existing programming languages directly implemented in Haskell: Idris (http://www.idris-lang.org/) comes to mind, a functional programming language with dependent types for whose implementation features several conjectured soundness properties ready to be validated.

References

1. Amin, N., Tate, R.: Java and Scala's type systems are unsound: the existential crisis of null pointers. In: OOPSLA 2016, pp. 838–848 (2016)
2. Charguéraud, A.: The locally nameless representation. J. Autom. Reason. **49**(3), 363–408 (2012)
3. Cheney, J., Momigliano, A.: αCheck: a mechanized metatheory model checker. Theory Pract. Log. Program. **17**(3), 311–352 (2017)
4. Cheney, J., Momigliano, A., Pessina, M.: Advances in property-based testing for αProlog. In: Aichernig, B.K.K., Furia, C.A.A. (eds.) TAP 2016. LNCS, vol. 9762, pp. 37–56. Springer, Cham (2016). doi:10.1007/978-3-319-41135-4_3
5. Claessen, K., Duregård, J., Pałka, M.H.: Generating constrained random data with uniform distribution. In: Codish, M., Sumii, E. (eds.) FLOPS 2014. LNCS, vol. 8475, pp. 18–34. Springer, Cham (2014). doi:10.1007/978-3-319-07151-0_2
6. Claessen, K., Hughes, J.: QuickCheck: a lightweight tool for random testing of Haskell programs. In: ICFP 2000, pp. 268–279. ACM (2000)
7. Duregård, J., Jansson, P., Wang, M.: Feat: functional enumeration of algebraic types. In: Voigtländer, J. (ed.) Haskell Workshop, pp. 61–72. ACM (2012)
8. Felleisen, M., Findler, R.B., Flatt, M.: Semantics Engineering with PLT Redex. MIT Press, Cambridge (2009)
9. Runciman, C., Naylor, M., Lindblad, F.: Smallcheck and lazy SmallCheck: automatic exhaustive testing for small values. In: Haskell Workshop, pp. 37–48 (2008)

10. Sewell, P., Nardelli, F.Z., Owens, S., Peskine, G., Ridge, T., Sarkar, S., Strnisa, R.: Ott: effective tool support for the working semanticist. J. Funct. Program. **20**(1), 71–122 (2010)
11. Visser, E., et al.: A language designer's workbench: a one-stop-shop for implementation and verification of language designs. In: Onward! 2014, SPLASH 2014, pp. 95–111 (2014)
12. Weirich, S., Yorgey, B.A., Sheard, T.: Binders unbound. In: Chakravarty, M.M.T., Hu, Z., Danvy, O. (eds.) ICFP 2011, pp. 333–345. ACM (2011)

Towards Inverse Uncertainty Quantification in Software Development (Short Paper)

Matteo Camilli[1]([⊠]), Angelo Gargantini[2], Patrizia Scandurra[2],
and Carlo Bellettini[1]

[1] Department of Computer Science, Università degli Studi di Milano, Milan, Italy
{camilli,bellettini}@di.unimi.it
[2] Department of Management, Information and Production Engineering (DIGIP),
Università degli Studi di Bergamo, Bergamo, Italy
{angelo.gargantini,patrizia.scandurra}@unibg.it

Abstract. With the purpose of delivering more robust systems, this paper revisits the problem of *Inverse Uncertainty Quantification* that is related to the discrepancy between the measured data at runtime (while the system executes) and the formal specification (i.e., a mathematical model) of the system under consideration, and the value calibration of unknown parameters in the model. We foster an approach to quantify and mitigate system uncertainty during the development cycle by combining Bayesian reasoning and online Model-based testing.

1 Introduction

The problem of *uncertainty quantification* is recently gaining attention in the software engineering community since it has a significant impact on the ability of a software system to satisfy its objectives [1,2]. Preliminary works towards this direction aim at establishing a common vocabulary and taxonomy of uncertainty from the perspective of a software system (see works [2,3] to name a few).

Sources of uncertainty can occur either at requirements, design, or execution phase, and propagate throughout all phases [3]. At each of these phases, uncertainty can be introduced into the system by the system itself (i.e., *system uncertainty*) or its execution environment (i.e., *environmental uncertainty*). Examples of sources of uncertainty include: parameter uncertainty (due to uncertain input values given to the mathematical model), structural uncertainty (due to approximations in the mathematical model), algorithmic uncertainty (coming from numerical approximations per implementation of the computer model), experimental uncertainty (due to the inherent variability of experimental measurements), etc. From a different perspective uncertainty can be classified taking into account the *nature* [2]. The nature concerns the uncertainty due to

---

This is a short paper accepted in the new ideas and work-in-progress section of SEFM 2017.

A. Cimatti and M. Sirjani (Eds.): SEFM 2017, LNCS 10469, pp. 375–381, 2017.
DOI: 10.1007/978-3-319-66197-1_24

the lack of knowledge (i.e., *epistemic*) or because of inherent randomness of the observed phenomenon (i.e., *aleatory*). Both kinds of uncertainties often come up in practice, during the development of real world applications.

Uncertainty quantification, in this context, has two major problems: *Forward Uncertainty Propagation* (FUQ) and *Inverse Uncertainty Quantification* (IUQ) [4]. The first problem focuses on studying the quantification of uncertainties in system output(s) propagated from uncertain inputs. This is useful in reliability engineering and to assess the complete probability distribution of the outputs in order to calculate and optimize the utility function. The latter one is essentially the inverse problem. Given some experimental measurements of a system and some simulation outputs from its mathematical model, inverse uncertainty quantification estimates the discrepancy between the measured data at runtime and the mathematical model (i.e., *bias correction*) and estimates the values of unknown parameters in the model if there are any (i.e., *parameter calibration*). FUQ is easier and more studied [5], while IUQ is recently drawing increasing attention in the engineering design community, since uncertainty quantification of a model and its inference from the true system response(s) are of great interest in designing robust systems.

In this paper, we revisit the IUQ problem in software development and propose an approach for quantifying system uncertainty [4] before the deployment of a release build. We depart from the unrealistic assumption that the outputs as well as specific properties are known for a given system before accounting for evidence during the actual system's execution. In fact, mathematical models are often imperfect and measured data from a running system is subject to noise. Therefore, it is of extreme importance to quantify and reduce the uncertainty to determine how likely certain outcomes are if some aspects of the system are not exactly known at design-time. To this purpose, we propose an exploration methodology to quantify and mitigate uncertainty during system development by combining Bayesian reasoning [6] and online *Model-based testing* (MBT) techniques [7]. The intuition behind our envisioned approach is to leverage the capability of online MBT to explore the state space in a controlled way, while the given system is up and running. At the same time, we gather information about the uncertain aspects of the system to perform inference activity.

As specification formalisms, we adopt Markov models, such as Discrete/Continuous Time Markov Chains (D/CTMCs) [8], that are a widely accepted stochastic formalisms able to support modeling of randomly changing systems (or probabilistic systems), as well as quantitative verification of requirements using probabilistic temporal logic (e.g., PCTL, or CSL) model checking [9].

This paper is organized as follows. In Sect. 2, we introduce our approach to IUQ based on Bayesian reasoning applied through online MBT. We discuss related work in Sect. 3, and conclude and discuss challenges ahead in Sect. 4.

2 Overview of the Approach

Our approach to IUQ aims at estimating the discrepancy between the measured data y^e at runtime and the model response $y^m(\Theta)$ that depends on different uncertain parameters Θ of the Markov model m. Starting from the approximation $y^m(\Theta) \simeq y^e$, we perform a sequence of observations in orderto infer a probability distribution of Θ^* describing the best knowledge of the true parameter values, such that $y^m(\Theta^*) = y^e$.

The Bayesian methodology [6] provides a viable technique to incrementally update our *prior* uncertain knowledge (hypothesis) on a given phenomenon by observing its own behavior. The general formula is: $p(\Theta|y^e) \propto p(y^e|\Theta) \cdot p(\Theta)$, where $p(\Theta)$ represents the set of prior distributions for parameter set Θ and uses probability to express uncertainty about Θ before the data (i.e., the current evidence) is observed, $p(y^e|\Theta)$ is the likelihood function that expresses the compatibility of the evidence with the given hypothesis, and $p(\Theta|y^e)$ is the joint *posterior* distribution of the parameters after taking both the prior and the evidence into account. This formula basically links the degree of belief in the prior knowledge before and after accounting for evidence.

The inherent uncertainty of the system is explicitly modelled by means of *Prior* distributions of the parameters of interest of the Markov model. Observations to enable Bayesian reasoning are made at runtime during online MBT, where test strategies are created dynamically as testing goes on, taking advantage of the knowledge gained by exploring the model and by observing the evidence. A high-level overview of our methodology is shown in Fig. 1. It relies on the iteration of two different phases, which are described below.

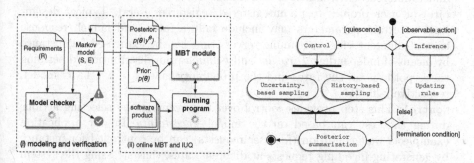

Fig. 1. IUQ methodology.   **Fig. 2.** Online MBT activity diagram.

Design-time modeling and verification – This phase concerns the development of the mathematical model of the system under development. The model includes a formal representation of both the specification (S) and the environment (E). This separation is explicitly represented by disjointly partitioning the state transitions into *controllable* and *observable* ones. This choice is motivated by our problem domain of MBT. Thus, we follow the notation introduced in [7] to distinguish between full *controllable* behavior from the tester (i.e., the environment, such as user requests) and only *observable* behavior from the running software system (i.e., the specification, such as inter-components interaction). Markov models allow both the controllable and the observable behavior of system under development to be described in probabilistic terms from different perspectives, such as the architecture of the application, the response time of the components, or even the energy consumption (using for instance costs/rewards model extensions [10]).

Design-time model checking serves as a means to verify the desired requirements against the model of the system that contains our assumptions.

Online MBT and IUQ – This phase concerns the validation of the system and the inverse uncertainty quantification during testing activity. Figure 2 shows the activity diagram of the main operations performed by our online MBT algorithm. Besides the *observation* until *termination* paradigm [7], usually applied in MBT and runtime verification, our approach relies on two additional steps: incremental inference and test scenarios control based on the design-time *uncertainty*.

- Inference: Given the natural conjugate priors for the uncertain parameters Θ of the Markov model, inference following the Bayesian approach reduces to the application of incremental updating rules [6,8] for the posterior distributions based on the evidence that can be efficiently computed while the system is observed (i.e., foreach occurring *observable* action) at runtime. As an example, consider a video streaming web application, accessed from clients through HTTP requests via mobile application. Different components (e.g., data manager, cache, payment system, etc.) interact to satisfy users requests under different environmental conditions, such as workload (e.g., request rate) or user profiles (e.g., unregistered/registered users). Typical design-time uncertain parameters may include failure rates, and launch/response time of different video streaming servers that can be expressed for instance by means of independent *Dirichlet* and *Gamma* prior distributions describing the hypothesis on the rates and the probability matrix of a CTMC model, respectively [6,8].
- Control: This step provides control over test scenarios by selecting actions during the test run based on the model *uncertainty*. In our application example, a wait condition (for user requests) can be controlled for instance by generating incoming requests at different rates, thus stressing the system in different workload conditions. In particular, if the running system is in a state of *quiescence* [11], the MBT algorithm chooses a legal *controllable* action such that the probability of this choice in the current state is governed by two weighted sampling methods.

The uncertainty-based sampling method is related to the likelihood of exploring uncertain regions of the model, choosing different controllable actions from the current state. It is grounded on the computation of the *maximum likelihood* trajectories [12] connecting the current state to states containing uncertain parameters of the Markov model.

The `history-based sampling` method takes advantage of the knowledge gained by exploring the model, thus allows the strategy to be configured based on the test run history. In particular *decrementing weights* [7] can be adopted to call particular controllable actions a specific number of times in the test runs, in favor of unexplored regions.

Once termination has been reached, each uncertain parameter of interest can be described by summarizing the posterior distribution (i.e., the `summarization` activity) through the posterior *mode* and the *highest posterior density* (HPD) intervals [8]. Thus, the uncertainty can be numerically quantified by evaluating the discrepancy between the initial design-time parameter values and the mode values after accounting for evidence.

Estimated parameter values represent the basis of new verification phases and the prior knowledge for future evolutions of the software system.

3   Related Work

In the community of self-adaptive systems, there have been several efforts focusing on studying the FUQ problem and on dealing with changing requirements and unpredictable environment (see [2,3,13,14], to name a few), some by employing Markov models. Our approach revisits the IUQ problem and focus mainly on the system uncertainty [4] in software development.

An interesting effort has been shown in [15]. It focuses primarily on design-time verification aspects to assure quality-of-service (QoS) properties of systems that exhibit stochastic behavior. The presented technique and toolchain aim at establishing confidence intervals for the QoS properties of a software system modeled as a Markov chain with uncertain transition probabilities.

Concerning testing techniques, a promising *Active Learning* query strategy to black-box test generation has been proposed in [16]. It aims at overcoming the problem of intractability in MBT and generating test cases which the inferred model is "least certain" about. The usage of machine learning algorithms and Bayesian reasoning represents an attractive approach to achieve reliable and efficient software testing and program analysis [17]. Despite the inherent potential of these methods, their employment in software testing and program analysis, to tackle the IUQ problem, is still in its early stages.

4   Conclusion

We proposed an approach to quantify and mitigate system uncertainty during system development life cycle, by combining Bayesian reasoning [6,18] and online *Model-based testing* (MBT) [7]. The key idea is to explicitly model the inherent uncertainty and provide a means to stress and observe the software product in order to quantify the design-time uncertainty before the deployment of a release build. In order to validate our current prototypal implementation, we are going to conduct several experiments with case studies of different size and complexity. Our experience in this context has been very positive. A great advantage of the underlying probabilistic representation and our incremental update scheme of the posterior knowledge is the robustness to unreliable/spurious observations (difficult to achieve with non-probabilistic techniques).

There are also challenges to be faced. A very critical issue, for example, is that stochastic techniques and Bayesian reasoning are computationally expensive, thus often unsuitable for use at run-time. However, in our approach, expensive probabilistic model checking is used only at design-time, while very efficient incremental inference steps are carried out at run-time during testing activity.

References

1. Garlan, D.: Software engineering in an uncertain world. In: Proceedings of the FSE/SDP Workshop on Future of Software Engineering Research, pp. 125–128 (2010)
2. Esfahani, N., Malek, S.: Uncertainty in self-adaptive software systems. In: Lemos, R., Giese, H., Müller, H.A., Shaw, M. (eds.) Software Engineering for Self-Adaptive Systems II. LNCS, vol. 7475, pp. 214–238. Springer, Heidelberg (2013). doi:10. 1007/978-3-642-35813-5_9
3. Ramirez, A.J., Jensen, A.C., Cheng, B.H.C.: A taxonomy of uncertainty for dynamically adaptive systems. In: Proceedings of the 7th International Symposium on Software Engineering for Adaptive and Self-Managing Systems (SEAMS), pp. 99–108 (2012)
4. Arendt, P.D., Apley, D.W., Chen, W.: Quantification of model uncertainty: calibration, model discrepancy, and identifiability. J. Mech. Des. 134(10) (2012)
5. Lee, S.H., Chen, W.: A comparative study of uncertainty propagation methods for black-box-type problems. Struct. Multi. Optim. 37(3), 239 (2008)
6. Berger, J.: Statistical Decision Theory and Bayesian Analysis, Springer Series in Statistics. Springer, New York (1985)
7. Broy, M., Jonsson, B., Katoen, J.-P., Leucker, M., Pretschner, A.: Model-Based Testing of Reactive Systems: Advanced Lectures (Lecture Notes in Computer Science). Springer, New York (2005)
8. Insua, D., Ruggeri, F., Wiper, M.: Bayesian Analysis of Stochastic Process Models, Wiley Series in Probability and Statistics. Wiley, Hoboken (2012)
9. Kwiatkowska, M., Norman, G., Parker, D.: PRISM 4.0: verification of probabilistic real-time systems. In: Gopalakrishnan, G., Qadeer, S. (eds.) CAV 2011. LNCS, vol. 6806, pp. 585–591. Springer, Heidelberg (2011). doi:10.1007/978-3-642-22110-1_47
10. Kwiatkowska, M., Norman, G., Pacheco, A.: Model checking expected time and expected reward formulae with random time bounds. Comput. Mathe. Appl. 51(2), 305–316 (2006)
11. Tretmans, J., Belinfante, A.: Automatic testing with formal methods. In: 7th European International Conference on Software Testing, Analysis & Review, pp. 8–12 (1999)
12. Perkins, T.J.: Maximum likelihood trajectories for continuous-time markov chains. In: Proceedings of the 22nd International Conference on Neural Information Processing Systems, pp. 1437–1445 (2009)
13. Perez-Palacin, D., Mirandola, R.: Uncertainties in the modeling of self-adaptive systems: a taxonomy and an example of availability evaluation. In: Proceedings of the 5th ACM/SPEC International Conference on Performance Engineering, pp. 3–14 (2014)

14. Epifani, I., Ghezzi, C., Mirandola, R., Tamburrelli, G.: Model evolution by run-time parameter adaptation. In: 2009 IEEE 31st International Conference on Software Engineering, pp. 111–121, May 2009
15. Calinescu, R., Ghezzi, C., Johnson, K., Pezzè, M., Rafiq, Y., Tamburrelli, G.: Formal verification with confidence intervals to establish quality of service properties of software systems. IEEE Trans. Reliab. **65**(1), 107–125 (2016)
16. Walkinshaw, N., Fraser, G.: Uncertainty-driven black-box test data generation. In: IEEE International Conference on Software Testing, Verification and Validation (2017)
17. Namin, A.S., Sridharan, M.: Bayesian reasoning for software testing. In: Proceedings of the FSE/SDP Workshop on Future of Software Engineering Research, pp. 349–354 (2010)
18. Bernardo, J., Smith, A.: Bayesian Theory, Wiley Series in Probability and Statistics. Wiley, Hoboken (2006)

Interpolation-Based Learning as a Mean to Speed-Up Bounded Model Checking (Short Paper)

Gianpiero Cabodi, Paolo Camurati, Marco Palena[✉], Paolo Pasini,
and Danilo Vendraminetto

Dipartimento di Automatica Ed Informatica, Politecnico di Torino, Turin, Italy
marco.palena@polito.it

Abstract. In this paper (This is a short paper accepted in the new ideas and work-in-progress section of SEFM 2017.) we introduce a technique to improve the efficiency of SAT calls in Bounded Model Checking (BMC) problems. The proposed technique is based on exploiting interpolation-based invariants as redundant constraints for BMC.

Previous research addressed the issue using over-approximated state sets generated by BDD-based traversals. While a BDD engine could be considered as an external tool, interpolants are directly related to BMC problems, as they come from SAT-generated refutation proofs, so their role as a SAT-based learning is potentially higher. Our work aims at understanding whether and how interpolants could speed up BMC checks, as they represent constraints on forward and backward reachable states at given unrolling boundaries.

Being this work preliminary, we do not address a tight integration between interpolant generation and exploitation. We thus clearly distinguish an interpolant generation (learning) phase and a subsequent interpolant exploitation phase in a BMC run. We experimentally evaluate costs, benefits, as well as invariant selection options, on a set of publicly available model checking problems.

1 Introduction

Bounded Model Checking (BMC) [2] is a state-of-the-art formal verification technology with widespread industry-level application in various domains. Though the approach is incomplete, as it is just able to produce bounded proofs, it is considered a successful debugging technique, due to its simple and scalable SAT-based approach. Complete SAT-based verification approaches based on BMC have been studied in order to address the completeness issue: inductive techniques and Craig interpolation based model checking [5] are among the most notable and successful ones. Recently, IC3 has emerged as an approach unrelated to BMC, as it does not require transition relation unfoldings.

This paper focuses on Craig interpolation as an operator able to provide a form of redundant learning, derived from a BMC-like problem, to be exploited

A. Cimatti and M. Sirjani (Eds.): SEFM 2017, LNCS 10469, pp. 382–387, 2017.
DOI: 10.1007/978-3-319-66197-1_25

in order to speed-up subsequent BMC queries. So our target is to accelerate SAT-based BMC with the help of ITP-based learning.

From a Model Checking perspective, Craig interpolation is an operator able to compute over-approximated images. The approach can be viewed as an iterative refinement of proof-based abstractions, to narrow down a proof to relevant facts. Over-approximations of the reachable states are computed from refutation proofs of unsatisfied BMC formulas.

The paper is organized as follows. Section 2 introduces some preliminary concepts on notation, SAT techniques for verification, and reachability analysis. Section 3 outlines our approach, in terms of strategies and top-level algorithm. Section 4 presents our experimental results. Section 5 concludes the paper.

2   Background

2.1   Model, Notation and Property Definition

We address systems modelled by labelled state transition structures and represented implicitly by Boolean formulas. From our standpoint, a system M is a triplet $M = (S, S_0, T)$, where S is a finite set of states, $S_0 \subseteq S$ is the set of initial states, and $T \subseteq S \times S$ is a total transition relation. The system state space is encoded through an indexed set of Boolean variables $X = \{x_1, \ldots, x_n\}$, such that a state $s \in S$ corresponds to a valuation of the variables in X and a set of states can be implicitly represented through a Boolean formula over X.

Given a system M, a state path of length k is a sequence of states $\pi = (s_0, \ldots, s_k)$ such that $T(s_i, s_{i+1})$ is true for all $0 \leq i < k$. A state set R is said to be reachable if there exists a path of any length connecting a state in S_0 to another state in R. An over-approximation R^+ of a set of states R is any state set including $R : R \subseteq R^+$. Given a system M, we assume that p is an invariant property to be verified over M.

2.2   Bounded Model Checking

Given a sequential system M and an invariant property p, SAT-based BMC [2] is an iterative process to check the validity of p up to a given bound. To perform this task, the system transition relation T is unrolled k times

$$T^k(X^{0..k}) = \bigwedge_{i=0}^{k-1} T(X^i, X^{i+1}) \tag{1}$$

to implicitly represent all state paths of length k. After that, BMC tools may implement variants of SAT checks, such as:

$$bmc^k(X^{0..k}) = S_0(X^0) \wedge T^k(X^{0..k}) \wedge \neg p(X^k)$$

looking for counterexamples of length k[1], starting from set of the initial states S_0.

---

[1] For sake of simplicity we refer here to the so called *exact bound* BMC problem, that look for counteraxamples of an exact length. Other forms of BMC problems exists, checking for lengths $\leq k$.

SAT solvers generally operate on propositional formulas bmc^k specified in Conjunctive Normal Form (CNF).

In [3] the authors propose a method to improve standard BMC using BDDs representing over-approximations of reachable states. The overestimated reachable state sets are used to restrict the search space of a SAT-based BMC. Such an information can thus be seen as an explicit constraint for the SAT solver.

2.3   Craig Interpolants

A Craig interpolant I for two Boolean formulas A, B is a formula such that:
(1) $A \Rightarrow I$, (2) $I \wedge B \equiv \bot$, and (3) I is expressed over the shared alphabet of A and B

We use ITP to denote the interpolation operation. An interpolant $I = \text{ITP}(A, B)$ can be derived, as an AND-OR circuit, from the refutation proof of $A \wedge B$, as described in [5].

In the context of this work, we take into account interpolation sequences [6]. Given an inconsistent BMC problem $bmc^k_{eb}(X^{0..k})$, an interpolation sequence for bmc^k_{eb} is a set of interpolants $I = \{I_0, I_1, \ldots, I_k\}$ such that: (1) $I_0 \equiv S_0$, (2) for each $0 < j < k$ it holds that $I_j \wedge T \Rightarrow I_{j+1}$.

Such a sequence, for the purposes of this work, is obtained as by-product of IGR [4] runs.

3   Combining SAT-based BMC and Interpolation

In this section we briefly overview our methodology that, in its present form, can be viewed s a way to partition a verification task between an ITP and a SAT engine, and as an optimization of a SAT-based BMC, by means of redundant information learned in the form of interpolants.

We perform a preliminary effort with interpolation in order to determine an ITP sequence to be used alongside BMC. Ideally, one would like to be able to leverage interpolants generated from a concurrent model checking engine running alongside BMC.

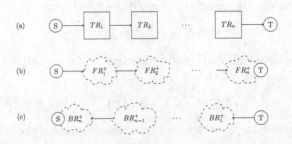

Fig. 1. (a) Standard combinational unrolling for SAT-based BMC; (b) approximate forward traversal from S to T; (c) approximate backward traversal from T to S.

Figure 1 shows the main flow of our methodology. Figure 1(a) shows a graphical representation of standard SAT-based BMC. As introduced in Sect. 2, the goal is to find a path of length k between the start state S and the target state T on the CNF representation of the problem.

Our basic idea is to help the SAT solver with information coming from an ITP-based model checking engine, in the shape of an interpolation sequence. Those ITPs contain redundant information representing constraints on the input space of each time frame in the combinational unrolling. More specifically, a constraint for the i–th time frame is already (and implicitly) present in the original formulation of the BMC problem, but it is represented in terms of all variables in all time frames of the combinational unrolling. A state set provides constraints as a function of local state variables of time frame i, thus the effect is an expected enhanced ability to early detect invalid variable assignments at a given time frame, in order to better guide the search for a satisfying solution.

Let us considered a BMC problem f bound k, $bmc_{eb}^{k}(X^{0..k})$, and an interpolation sequence of length $h < k$.

Considering an interpolant at bound i, it is possible to provide at the same time an overapproximation for both the forward (from S to T) and backward (from T to S) reachable state set. On the one hand, using notation FR_j for states reachable at time frame j, it is known that $FR_j \rightarrow I_j$ holds (an interpolant is an over-approximation of reachable states). On the other hand, one could see the complement of an interpolant as an over-approximation of backward reachable states. Let BR_i represent states backward reachable from the target $\neg p$ in i steps. Given an interpolation sequence of bound k, then $\neg I_j \leftarrow BR_j$ holds, for all $j < h - i$.

So for each time frame boundary one could use interpolants as extra constraints for both forward and backward reachability.

For a generic j time frame, we could consider a redundant forward constraint $FC_j = I_j$ and a backward constraint $BC_j = \neg I_{h-j}$. Forward and backward constraints can be considered as a form of (redundant) learning inherited from ITP problems. The expected benefit stems from the fact that ITPS are expressed in terms of local state variables at given time frames.

Using forward and backward constraints at all time frames would result in highly redundant formulas, where the expected overhead would overweight possible benefits for the SAT solver.

We thus need heuristics, and a thorough experimental work, in order to find good cost-benefit trade-offs. In this preliminary work we empirically (by limited experimentation) selected two forward constraints at timeframes $h/2$ and $2h/3$, and one backward constraint $\neg I_{h/2}$ applied at all even time frames $j > k - h/2$.

4   Experimental Results

Our prototype software package has been implemented on top of our verification tool PDTRAV. Experiments were run on an Intel Core i7-3770, with 8 CPUs running at 3.40 GHz, 16 GBytes of main memory DDR III 1333, and hosting a

Ubuntu 12.04 LTS Linux distribution. All the experiment were run taking into account a time limit and a memory limit of 1800 seconds and 8 GB respectively.

The benchmarks set considered was derived from a subset of past HWMCC suites [1], focusing primarily on instances belonging to the deep bound track (as considered hard to solve instances). The set includes hardware as well as software verification problems. We focused on problems characterized by increasingly expeisive BMC bounds. We thus discarded (as unmeaningful for the proposed optimization) problems characterized by a single hard-to-solve bound following a sequence of very easy-to-check bounds. We also omitted problems showing a SAT cost linearly increasing with bounds.

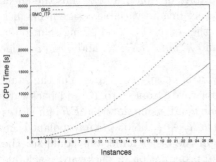 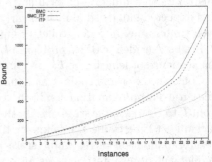

(a) Cumulative distribution of execution times for the base technique (BMC) and the proposed variation (BMC ITP) sampled at deepest common bound.

(b) Cumulative distribution of reached bound for the base technique (BMC), the proposed variation (BMC ITP) and depth of provided interpolants (ITP).

Fig. 2. (a) Cumulative distribution of execution times for the base technique (BMC) and the proposed variation (BMC_ITP) sampled at deepest common bound. (b) cumulative distribution of reached bound for the base technique (BMC), the proposed variation (BMC_ITP) and depth of provided interpolants (ITP)

Figures 2a and b provide a summary of the experimental results, as a dispersion of cumulative execution times and reached bounds, respectively. Figure 2a shows that the overall execution times of the proposed technique is significantly lower w.r.t. to standard BMC. Figure 2b illustrates the gap, in terms of depth reached, between the two techniques, as well as the depth for the provided interpolants. Though the gap between the two is rather limited, this is mainly related to the high computational cost for each of the deep bounds in the selected (hard-to-solve) instances. We deem a difference of few bounds is relevant in such a scenario.

Due to the preliminary steps of our work, we also show in Fig. 3, as a motivating example, a more detailed representation of the run associated with 6s376r, a benchmark where the proposed technique gets a relevant improvement also in terms of BMC bound. The time vs. bound plot clearly shows the advantage attained by the extra learning starting around bound 120.

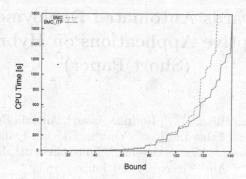

Fig. 3. Bound-per-bound run comparison between the base technique (BMC) and the proposed variation (BMC_ITP) for **6s376r**.

5   Conclusions

In this paper we proposed to leverage ITP-based learning to constrain the overall search space of a SAT solver engine during BMC runs. We develop specific strategies to appropriately mix interpolation and SAT efforts. We showed experimentally the potential of using ITP-based constraining to improve the performance of standard bounded model checking approaches. Though the work is clearly preliminary amd requiring more effort on heuristics, automation, tool engineering, some promising data already come form the initial experimentation done.

References

1. Biere, A., Jussila, T.: The Model Checking Competition Web Page. http://fmv.jku.at/hwmcc
2. Biere, A., Cimatti, A., Clarke, E., Zhu, Y.: Symbolic model checking without BDDs. In: Cleaveland, W.R. (ed.) TACAS 1999. LNCS, vol. 1579, pp. 193–207. Springer, Heidelberg (1999). doi:10.1007/3-540-49059-0_14
3. Cabodi, G., Nocco, S., Quer, S.: Improving SAT-based bounded model checking by means of BDD-based approximate traversals. J. Universal Comput. Sci. (JUCS) (2004). Special issue on SAT for Formal Verification and Testing
4. Cabodi, G., Palena, M., Pasini, P.: Interpolation with guided refinement: revisiting incrementality in sat-based unbounded model checking, pp. 43–50. FMCAD 2014 (2014)
5. McMillan, K.L.: Interpolation and SAT-based model checking. In: Hunt, W.A., Somenzi, F. (eds.) CAV 2003. LNCS, vol. 2725, pp. 1–13. Springer, Heidelberg (2003). doi:10.1007/978-3-540-45069-6_1
6. Vizel, Y., Grumberg, O.: Interpolation-sequence based model checking. In: 2009 Formal Methods in Computer-Aided Design, pp. 1–8, November 2009

Towards Automated Deployment
of Self-adaptive Applications on Hybrid Clouds
(Short Paper)

Lom Messan Hillah[1,2]([✉]), Rodrigo Assad[3], Antonia Bertolino[4],
Marcio Delamaro[5], Fabio De Rosa[6], Vinicius Garcia[7], Francesca Lonetti[4],
Ariele-Paolo Maesano[6], Libero Maesano[6], Eda Marchetti[4], Breno Miranda[7],
Auri Vincenzi[8], and Juliano Iyoda[7]

[1] Univ. Paris Nanterre, 92000 Nanterre, France
[2] Sorbonne Universités, UPMC, CNRS, LIP6 UMR7606, 75005 Paris, France
lom-messan.hillah@lip6.fr
[3] Ustore, Recife, Brazil
assad@usto.re
[4] ISTI-CNR, 56124 Pisa, Italy
{antonia.bertolino,francesca.lonetti,eda.marchetti}@isti.cnr.it
[5] Universidade de São Paulo, São Carlos, Brazil
delamaro@icmc.usp.br
[6] Simple Engineering, 75011 Paris, France
{fabio.de-rosa,ariele.maesano,libero.maesano}@simple-eng.com
[7] Universidade Federal de Pernambuco, Recife, Brazil
{vcg,bafm,jmi}@cin.ufpe.br
[8] Universidade Federal de São Carlos, São Carlos, Brazil
auri@dc.ufscar.br

Abstract. Cloud computing promises high dynamism, flexibility, and elasticity of applications at lower infrastructure costs. However, resource management, portability, and interoperability remain a challenge for cloud application users, since the current major cloud application providers have not converged to a standard interface, and the deployment supporting tools are highly heterogeneous. Besides, by their very nature, cloud applications bring serious traceability, security and privacy issues. This position paper describes a research thread on an extensible Domain Specific Language (DSL), a platform for the automated deployment, and a generic architecture of an ops application manager for self-adaptive distributed applications on hybrid cloud infrastructures. The idea is to overcome the cited limitations by empowering the cloud applications with self-configuration, self-healing, and self-protection capabilities. Such autonomous governance can be achieved by letting cloud users define their policies concerning security, data protection, dependability and functional compliance behavior using the proposed DSL. Real world trials in different application domains are discussed.

This is a short paper accepted in the new ideas and work-in-progress section of SEFM 2017.

A. Cimatti and M. Sirjani (Eds.): SEFM 2017, LNCS 10469, pp. 388–393, 2017.
DOI: 10.1007/978-3-319-66197-1_26

1 Introduction

Cloud computing is used to provision the physical resources (servers, storage, network) of the digital ecosystem, allowing a substantial optimization of the operating costs. However, cloud computing is more than a cost-optimizing technology. It bears to users significant features - virtualization, job scheduling, and programmability - allowing the sustainable implementation of robust scalability, availability, and serviceability requirements on commodity hardware.

However, the most notable features of cloud computing, such as virtualization, come at the price of increased security and data protection risks. Moving to a virtualized environment does not free from the security risks already faced in the physical environment, but rather introduces new ones, related to virtual machine and network management, resource exhaustion, hypervisor vulnerabilities, multi-tenancy handling, and cloud access control.

DevOps is an emerging paradigm of integration of the development process within the production stage. To adopt DevOps effectively, cloud application developers have yet to find solutions to tough problems: (i) how to design, develop, deploy, and operate efficiently applications that fulfill, on one side, stringent scalability, availability and serviceability needs, and, on the other side, strict security and data protection obligations; (ii) how to cope with the heterogeneity and lack of interoperability of cloud infrastructures and the consequent lack of portability of cloud applications; (iii) how to combine the advantages of agile, flexible, and continuous integration, testing, delivery, and deployment, and of mission-critical quality assurance, test, and verification.

The main solution of the aforementioned problems is the automation of DevOps jobs, in particular test, configuration, deployment, and ops management. This position paper introduces an ongoing research on automating installation, configuration, startup, and operation management of self-adaptive distributed applications on hybrid cloud infrastructures. In particular, it presents an envisaged solution based on three correlated research topics: (i) a declarative, cloud agnostic, and extensible Domain Specific Language (DSL) for structural and behavioral modeling and policy definition for automated deployment and self-management; (ii) a generic and instantiated architecture of an autonomic ops application manager enabling self-configuration, self-healing, and self-protection; (iii) a DSL workbench as a service, equipped with editors, wizards, consoles, and dashboards for deployment and monitoring of self-adaptive cloud applications.

2 Related Work and Background

Self-aware management is becoming commonplace to address the scale, growth, and reliability of cloud applications. The authors of [IZM+17] propose a conceptual framework for analyzing the state-of-the-art and comparing practical characteristics, benefits, and drawbacks of self-awareness approaches used for cloud applications in different domains. A big challenge of self-aware and adaptive distributed systems on cloud is achieving self-protection as well as guaranteeing self-configuration, self-healing, and self-optimization. Aceto et al. [ABdDP13] examine current platforms and services for cloud monitoring pointing out their issues and challenges whereas the authors of [KA12] investigate testing models, recent research works, and commercial tools for cloud testing. However, the main open issues emerging from the analysis of the literature related to the management of elasticity, dependability, and security of cloud applications are mainly about the limitations of flexibility and portability in a multi-cloud environment.

The OASIS TOSCA [OAS16] standard covers the cloud-portable automation of installation, configuration, and startup of conventional cloud applications. TOSCA is a declarative language that let model the distributed application topology independently from the particular target cloud infrastructure. It uses the following concepts: (i) **Nodes** - nodes represent components of an application or service and their properties; example nodes are computer, network, storage (i.e. infrastructure-oriented), OS, VM, DB, Web Server (i.e. platform-oriented), functional libraries, or modules (i.e. applicative); (ii) **Relationships** - they represent the logical relations between nodes (e.g. hosted on, connects to), and describe the valid source and target nodes they link together; (iii) **Artifacts** - they describe installable and executable objects required to instantiate and manage a service; (iv) **Service Templates** - they group the nodes and relationships that make up a service's topology. In summary, TOSCA DSL allows describing a distributed cloud application at the infrastructure level in a portable way. Current TOSCA implementations target the main cloud provider infrastructures.

3   Outline of the Solution

A DSL for self-adaptive cloud applications. We plan to overcome the limitations sketched in the section above by extending the TOSCA standard and implementations. The planned extensions of the TOSCA standard are about: (i) language traits for the installation, configuration, and setup of security and data protection provisions; (ii) language traits for structural and behavioral modeling of distributed applications, beyond the infrastructure level, at the application/service level; (iii) a policy description language that enables the definition of self-configuration, self-healing, and self-protection policies to be fulfilled at runtime. Security and data protection provisions to be automatically installed, configured and setup with the DSL deal with standard authentication, confidentiality, and integrity. Besides the DSL language traits to efficiently and conveniently express these security requirements, the implementation shall take into account security matters that are particular to cloud deployment. These concerns are about multi-sites communication, different hypervisors (code which manages the virtual machines), different hypervisor provided services that could have various security issues or expose security loopholes, different CPU/memory/storage. The TOSCA standard already provides a rich and flexible language for structural modeling (topology) at the infrastructure level. We plan to enrich the language with traits for structural modeling at the applicative level, by describing a distributed application as a graph of logical components connected by service dependency wires. At deployment time, this structure shall be installed, configured and setup at the applicative level too. This structural model is referenced by the self-configuration, self-healing and self-protection policies. Behavioral modeling shall leverage an existing standardized notation, such as the State Chart XML (SCXML) [W3C14]. SCXML provides a powerful, general-purpose and declarative modeling language to describe the behavior of timed, event-driven, state-based systems. Therefore, in our context, state machines shall describe the external interactions between service components, explicitly showing the states of the conversation of each component with its wired interlocutors. Behavioral modeling will enable runtime checks and adaptation thanks to monitoring. The runtime policy language extension shall enable: (i) non-intrusive logging of events at the infrastructure and the applicative levels; (ii) non-intrusive monitoring (analysis of the logging stream) with slightly delayed evaluation of infrastructure events and distributed application behavior (asynchronous passive testing); (iii) non-intrusive active testing of the deployed application in a concurrent staging environment; (iv) intrusive active testing in the production environment to check application robustness and fault tolerance; (v) runtime installation, configuration and setup of components without service interruption, including new version deployment and version backtracking; (vi) automatic elasticity (scalability up and down); (vii) server failover (self-recovery); (viii) masking of transient network failures; (ix) circuit breaking at the application level; (x) generalized timeout management. An autonomic ops application manager shall implement and enforce these policies at run time.

The autonomic ops application manager. The classical autonomic architecture combines the managed application and an autonomic manager that oversees it. The abstract (platform independent) architecture of our ops manager includes (i) a supervisor, and (ii) a collection of concurrent feedback loops. Each feedback loop monitors and analyses a particular aspect of the managed application and its cloud environment and, if needed, plans and executes an adaptation process, driven by DSL policies, which brings the managed system to a new state. The abstract (platform independent) model of the feedback loop is the original MAPE-K generic architecture [IW15]. The supervisor controls the concurrent feedback loops and handles the interaction with the user, through the monitoring facility of the DSL workbench. There are no interferences between the managed application and the Ops manager, except for those performed by the adaptation processes. Significant concerns for the supervisor are the stability, accuracy, short settling-time, robustness, termination (no deadlock), consistency, scalability, and security of the adaptation processes. Important research questions are (i) the coordination of autonomous ops manager within cross-organizational distributed applications, and (ii) the DSL policy change at run time.

The DSL workbench. The DSL workbench (WB) is a Platform as a Service deployed on the cloud. It shall be accessible by the user via (i) the Web-based Graphical User Interface, and (ii) the WB API, a REST interface. The workbench is composed of three main layers: GUI, Processing, and Storage. The GUI Edit wizard allows: (i) easy graphical drafting of the DSL artifacts (models, policies), (ii) reverse engineering of existing legacy artifacts into the DSL ones, and (iii) straightforward building of the DSL archives (sets of models and policies for an application to be deployed) and self-adaptive application releases (AR). The GUI Deploy wizard lets initiate and supervise the deployment of a AR on the target cloud infrastructure. When deployed, the application ops manager interacts with the user through the GUI Monitoring wizard. The Processing layer is composed of three main components: the DSL Compiler, the Application Deployer, and the Application Monitor. The compiler builds the AR. The deployer installs, configures, and startups the application with the AR on the target (multi-)cloud infrastructure. The monitor implements the interaction with the deployed Ops Manager. The Storage layer contains: (i) the Legacy Artifact Base, that stores the existing legacy artifacts such as Juju Charms, Kubernetes, Chef cookbooks; (ii) the DSL Artifact Base that stores the DSL artifacts; (iii) the Code Base that stores the codes of the Managed Application and of the Ops Manager. The general architecture is sketched in Fig. 1.

Limitations of the approach. The main limitations of the proposed approach relate to: (i) the fact that the proposed DSL is based on TOSCA and could collide or overlap with other emerging standards; (ii) the inability or difficulty to integrate the proposed solution within all the available cloud provider infrastructures

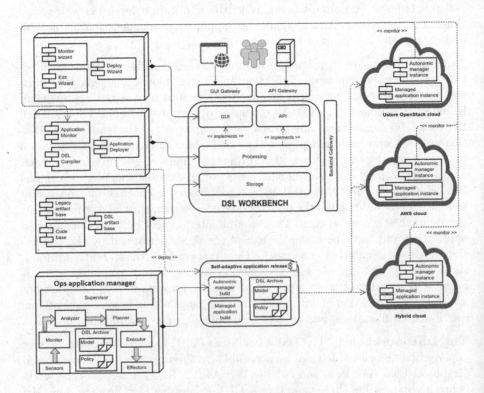

Fig. 1. General architecture

(i.e. Microsoft Azure, Google Cloud, etc.); (iii) the lack of optimization methods for self-adaptive applications on cloud, except for the automatic scaling up and down - the current project focuses on security, dependability, and fault-tolerance, not on self-optimization.

4 Real-World Trials

We plan to try our solution with real-world applications and systems, in particular in the logistics and high-tech industries. In the logistics domain, decision making is distributed. All stakeholders make decisions locally and autonomously, so the most important challenge is to achieve collaborative decision-making in practice. The proposed solution can be adopted in the logistic domain for building a cloud-based logistics information platform, as a general exchange platform, where cloud services are composed to collect, classify, store, analyze, evaluate, publish (release), manage and control relevant information on interorganizational logistics operations, processes, and management.

The proposed solution shall be applied to simplyTestify [sim], which is a geo-distributed, multi-instance and multi-tenant PaaS offering self-provisioning and pay-as-you-go test automation services. Even if simplyTestify core modules have been designed and implemented for cloud portability, the implementation of strong elasticity, dependability, security, and performance requirements is IaaS-dependent (the current version of simplyTestify runs on the Amazon Web Services public cloud). The DSL, the autonomic ops application manager, and the workbench shall allow the automatic installation, configuration, and startup of the PaaS and the policy-driven implementation of the mentioned requirements in a hybrid cloud including private and other public clouds, such as Microsoft Azure, Google Cloud, IBM Cloud, etc.

References

[ABdDP13] Aceto, G., Botta, A., de Donato, E., Pescap, A.: Cloud monitoring: a survey. Comput. Netw. **57**(9), 2093–2115 (2013)

[IW15] De La Iglesia, D.G., Weyns, D.: MAPE-K formal templates to rigorously design behaviors for self-adaptive systems. ACM Trans. Auton. Adapt. Syst. **10**(3), 15:1–15:31 (2015)

[IZM+17] Iosup, A., Zhu, X., Merchant, A., Kalyvianaki, E., Maggio, M., Spinner, S., Abdelzaher, T., Mengshoel, O., Bouchenak, S.: Self-awareness of cloud applications. In: Kounev, S., Kephart, J.O., Milenkoski, A., Zhu, X. (eds.) Self-Aware Computing Systems, pp. 575–610. Springer, Cham (2017). doi:10.1007/978-3-319-47474-8_20

[KA12] Katherine, A.V., Alagarsamy, K.: Software testing in cloud platform: a survey. Int. J. Comput. Appl. **46**(6), 21–25 (2012)

[OAS16] OASIS. TOSCA Simple Profile in YAML Version 1.0. OASIS Committee Specification 01, June 2016

[sim] simplyTestify. http://simplytestify.com/pages/simplyTestify

[W3C14] W3C. State Chart XML (SCXML): State Machine Notation for Control Abstraction, May 2014. http://www.w3.org/TR/scxml/

A Diagnosis Framework for Critical Systems Verification (Short Paper)

Vincent Leildé[1]([✉]), Vincent Ribaud[2], Ciprian Teodorov[1],
and Philippe Dhaussy[1]

[1] Lab-STICC, Team MOCS, ENSTA-Bretagne, rue Fran çois Verny, Brest, France
{vincent.leilde,ciprian.teodorov,philippe.dhaussy}@ensta-bretagne.fr
[2] Lab-STICC, Team MOCS, Université de Bretagne Occidentale,
Avenue le Gorgeu, Brest, France
Vincent.Ribaud@univ-brest.fr

Abstract. For critical systems design, the verification tasks play a crucial role. If abnormalities are detected, a diagnostic process must be started to find and understand the root causes before corrective actions are applied. Detection and diagnosis are notions that overlap in common speech. Detection basically means to identify something as unusual, diagnosis means to investigate its root cause. The meaning of diagnosis is also fuzzy, because diagnosis is either an activity - an investigation - or an output result - the nature or the type of a problem. This paper proposes an organizational framework for structuring diagnoses around three principles: that propositional data (including detection) are the inputs of the diagnostic system; that activities are made of methods and techniques; and that associations specialize that relationships between the two preceding categories.

Keywords: Diagnosis · Verification · Critical systems · Framework

1 Introduction

Critical systems are concerned by *dependability*, i.e. the ability of an entity to perform as and when required [3], that requires the *means* of improving the quality of systems design. This should be realized in three cyclical phases: verification, diagnosis and correction. Verification aims to demonstrate whether a system meets specification properties. This may be achieved using various techniques such as static analysis, simulation or model checking. Model checking is an automated technique that, given a finite-state model of a system and a formal property, systematically checks whether this property holds for that model [4]. If a property is violated, a counter-example is produced as a trace from the initial state to the state in which the error was detected. This triggers a diagnosis process (generally carried out through detection, localization and identification

---

This is a short paper accepted in the new ideas and work-in-progress section of SEFM 2017.

A. Cimatti and M. Sirjani (Eds.): SEFM 2017, LNCS 10469, pp. 394–400, 2017.
DOI: 10.1007/978-3-319-66197-1_27

tasks) that aims to outline the violation root causes. Consequently, the system is corrected and the design cycle repeated.

There are many frameworks and approaches for performing a diagnosis [2,5,6,11,13], all of which face the following two issues. First, poor management and control [19] of the verification process produces a profusion of heterogeneous interrelated models that makes it more difficult to understand errors, for instance, localizing the relevant parts in a detailed source-level trace to identify why a verification run failed [10]. Second, diagnosis is also loosely formalized. As a result, models produced during the design and verification process are not well adapted to diagnosis tasks. Therewith, diagnosis is weakly integrated with other activities and interoperability between tools and processes is not easily achieved.

For the above reasons, understanding and formalizing the diagnosis is intended to foster the definition of diagnosis tools and methodologies, and reduce the set of diagnoses. If diagnosis is applicable in different fields (medicine, plant and process supervision), frameworks differ, and cannot be fully applied to trace-based diagnosis. We propose an organizational framework for diagnosis systems, based on three concepts: *activity*, *propositional object* and *association*.

2 Background

If model checking is often dedicated to faults detection, some frameworks also employ it for faults localization. For instance, slicing-based approaches [21] use dependency analysis to retrieve the set of elements which contains the fault. State space reduction [13] aims at reducing the state space size by exploiting the concurrent transitions commutativity. Ball et al. [5] introduced an approach to compare the counter-examples with successful traces and thus isolate faulty state transitions. In [6], the authors propose a Symbolic Model Checking framework for safety analysis diagnosis. These approaches focus on trace processing, and the identification task, i.e. identifying the specific nature of faults, is not considered. Consequently, a semantic gap between design models and traces still holds.

Some approaches allow for a complete diagnostic. For instance in [11], the authors define a framework that combines an abductive model-based diagnosis approach with a Labelled Transition System. This kind of method is also experienced by [2], who associated logic learning with trace-based diagnosis and error correction using positive and negative traces. These approaches are restricted to one diagnosis technique, model-based, that imposes the presence of either a fault or a well-functioning model, which is not always available.

Venkatasubramanian [20] has broadly classified fault diagnosis methods into quantitative model-based methods, qualitative model-based methods, and process history-based methods. This classification provides a large spectrum of methods and techniques, but focuses on industrial processes, and put aside important techniques for trace-based diagnosis like interaction-based techniques.

To the best of our knowledge, there are no frameworks for characterizing diagnosis systems, unrestricted to any diagnosis techniques, activities or application domains. Therefore, we focus on understanding diagnosis in order to identify a core set of concepts that can be applied for any diagnoses systems.

3   Conceptual Framework

We propose a framework for characterizing diagnosis systems, not restricted to a diagnosis technique or method. We start from a general definition of diagnosis given by Merriam Webster [1]: *"diagnosis is an investigation or analysis of the cause or nature of a condition, situation, or problem"*. This framework is based on three concepts: - *Activity*, a set of mechanisms or tasks used to perform the diagnosis; - *Propositional object*, tangible or immaterial, produced or consumed by activities; - *Association* between propositional objects and activities.

3.1   Activities

The foremost part of the diagnosis definition refers to an *activity*, whether *an investigation or an analysis*. An *activity* is a set of cohesive *tasks*. Activities and tasks use *mechanisms* as means to achieve their outcomes.

Diagnosis tasks. According to the literature, diagnosis systems support three main tasks, *fault detection, isolation*, and *causal analysis* [20].

Fault detection establishes that a system run raises so-called abnormal event. In the particular case of verification by model checking, detection is done by model checking itself.

When a diagnosis is required, the ensuing step consists in *isolating* the subset of elements, part of models, that needs to be corrected [9]. *Isolation* is performed through various techniques, such as slicing-based approaches [21], state space reduction techniques [13] or counter-example comparisons [5].

Once suspicious elements are localized, the *causal analysis* task, associates causes to the observed abnormalities. This is generally a reasoning process, either deductive, inductive or abductive. Deduction is concerned by deducting knowledge from already learned knowledge, induction identifies general rules from observations, and abductive reasoning discovers causes from facts by elaborating hypothesis. Each type of reasoning fits with a different situation, abduction produces ideas and concepts to be explained, then induction contributes to the construction of the abductive hypothesis by giving it consistency, finally deduction formulates a predictive explanation from this construction [8].

Mechanisms. Activities and tasks are supported by a set of mechanisms, including tools and methods, that can be organized in *model-based* or *process history-based* category. We complete the list with an *interaction-based* category, relevant for trace-based diagnosis.

Model-based mechanisms assume that a model of the system is available, representing its correct (consistency-based) [18] or abnormal (abductive-based) [22] behavior. In consistency-based, the reasoning consists in rejecting a set of assumptions using the correct behaviour, to restore consistency with (abnormal) observations [7]. In the opposite, abductive-based reasoning works with causes and effects models, for instance using Inductive Logic Programming to provide automated support for correcting the errors identified by model checking [2].

Process-history based mechanisms relies on the availability of large amount of historical process data. Mechanisms may use knowledge extraction techniques, like data mining or statistical analysis. Liu [15] uses statistical models to remove false positive counterexamples. Probabilities can also be applied, using decision trees or Bayesian networks. In machine learning approach, neural networks and case-based reasoning try to reproduce the human way of reasoning. When a strong expertise is available, one can simply use expert systems gathering problems set, rules and an inference engine.

Interactions-based mechanisms allow for observing, controlling, understanding and altering the system execution. By storing the execution traces, omniscient debuggers enable back-in-time navigation features, postmortem query processing, trace-analysis and reduction facilities, and execution replay [17]. Besides, a large number of visualization tools exists [12], including diagram structures ranging from waveforms, finite state machines and business representations.

3.2 Propositional Objects

Activities handle different kinds of information [1], whether "situation or problem". As information may be tangible or immaterial, we define any information items as *propositional objects* that are, or represent sets of propositions about real or imaginary things.

Set of circumstances. Situation or problem are related to propositional objects. A *situation* is a way in which something is positioned with respect to its surroundings [1]. Regarding model checking, propositional objects comprises design models, properties, exploration graphs or model checker configurations. A *problem* is a difficulty that has to be resolved or dealt with [1]. Thus situation and problem are generalized in a concept called *set of circumstances*.

Observations. Problems are revealed by *symptoms*, a special case of *observations*, which are effects or visible consequences of the passage of the system into an abnormal state. Regarding model checking it includes counterexamples. As stated by [18], "real world diagnostic settings involve observations, and without observations, have no way determining whether something is wrong and hence whether a diagnosis is called for".

3.3 Associations

"Cause or nature" are both *diagnoses*, i.e. statements or conclusions from diagnosis analysis [1]. A diagnosis specializes an *association* between activities and propositional objects. Following a systemic triangulation, we organize *diagnoses* in three viewpoints, *causality*, concerned with functional aspects, *nature*, concerned with structural aspects, and *evolution*, concerned with historical aspects.

Causality is defined by [16] as a sequence of linked events. Consider for instance a car with flat tires that suddenly slips on a water poll, resulting to an accident. The accident is a succession of related events. Closed to our concerns, a *Fault,* an *Error* and a *Failure* are considered for [3] as causal events, a *fault* may produce an *error,* which may lead to a *failure.*

Nature consists in determining the type, the characteristics or the essence of something, "what the object is". By taking up the example of a car, the owner inspects each tires and finds that some are more damaged than others, and classifies one tire in the category "too flat". The *nature* association itself can be refined in more specific relations, like generalization or specialization.

Evolution represents the historical, that is linked to the evolutionary nature of the system, "what the system was or is becoming". For instance, a man is driving when an impact happen closed to the car wheels. He remembers he found one flat tire during his last car inspection, and supposes the tire is scratched.

4   Framework by Example

We present different kind of diagnosis systems using our framework, each pursuing a different objective (see Table 1). We refer to the classical example of a one bit adder, see in Fig. 1 an illustration from wikimedia commons *Full-adder.svg.* A full adder is composed of two AND gates, two XOR gates, and one OR gate.

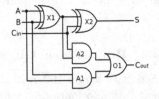

Fig. 1. Full adder

An analysis of the nature of a situation pursues a *pedagogical* objective. If we are not aware of the purpose of a digital circuit, we might build the truth table which sets out the output values for each combination of input values. The truth table is a diagnosis that helps to understand how the circuit works (assuming the circuit behavior is normal). The analysis associates outputs (observations) to inputs (facts) and tries to figure out the nature of the circuit. Regarding verification, simulation activity helps to understand the way the system behaves, or ensure it behaves correctly.

An investigation of the cause of a problem pursues a *curative* objective. Consider we expect from the circuit a full adder behavior, and thus one expected property is *P1: "for the set of entries A=1, B=1 and C=1, the result is S=1 and Cout=1".* Assume that the XOR gate X1 was inadvertently replaced by an OR gate. Then the output of the circuit conflicts with the property P1, i.e. *"S=0 and Cout= 1",* and we must investigate the cause of the failure. Regarding

Table 1. Diagnosis systems examples

(**Analysis** ∨ *Investigation*) of the (*Cause* ∨ **Nature** ∨ *Evolution*) of a (**Situation** ∨ *Problem*) ⇒ **Pedagogical objective**	(*Analysis* ∨ **Investigation**) of the (**Cause** ∨ *Nature* ∨ *Evolution*) of a (*Situation* ∨ **Problem**) ⇒ **Curative objective**	(**Analysis** ∨ *Investigation*) of the (*Cause* ∨ *Nature* ∨ **Evolution**) of a (**Situation** ∨ *Problem*) ⇒ **Prognosis objective**

model checking, if a violation of functional specifications is discovered by a model checker. One has to correct the design or model accordingly.

An analysis of the evolution of a situation pursues a *prognosis* objective. Given a set of properties (probably non-exhaustive), running the model checker over the set without any errors yields an indication that the circuit, as far we know, behaves correctly. The underlying diagnosis is used as a prognosis of circuit major dysfunctions. In software, design patterns, like security patterns, are prevention mechanisms. Regarding model checking of system design, if we consider a set of historical state spaces, one could apply design prognosis by using statistical and probability analysis.

5   Conclusion

In this paper we presented core concepts of a framework for understanding diagnosis. We believe that this set of concepts will enable the exploration of the possible and constrained compositions of diagnostic systems, reducing the minimal set of diagnoses. This work paves the way for the construction of an organizing system, an ongoing work [14], for storing system data (propositional objects), interpreting them (association), and diagnosing critical systems (activities).

References

1. Dictionary—Merriam-Webster. https://www.merriam-webster.com
2. Alrajeh, D., Kramer, J., Russo, A., Uchitel, S.: Automated support for iagnosis and repair. Commu. ACM **58**(2), 65–72 (2015)
3. Aviienis, A., Laprie, J.C., Randell, B., Landwehr, C.: Basic concepts and axonomy of dependable and secure computing. IEEE Trans. Dependable Secure Comput. **1**(1), 11–33 (2004)
4. Baier, C., Katoen, J.P.: Principles of Model Checking. MIT Press, Cambridge (2008)
5. Ball, T., Naik, M., Rajamani, S.K.: From symptom to cause: localizing errors in counterexample traces. In: ACM SIGPLAN, vol. 38. ACM (2003)
6. Bertoli, P., Bozzano, M., Cimatti, A.: A symbolic model checking framework for safety analysis, diagnosis, and synthesis. In: Edelkamp, S., Lomuscio, A. (eds.) MoChArt 2006. LNCS, vol. 4428, pp. 1–18. Springer, Heidelberg (2007). doi:10. 1007/978-3-540-74128-2_1
7. Bourahla, M.: Model-based diagnostic using model checking. In: 2009 Fourth International Conference on Dependability of Computer Systems, Brunow, pp. 229–236 (2009). doi:10.1109/DepCoS-RELCOMEX.2009.33
8. Buccafurri, F., Eiter, T., Gottlob, G., Leone, N.: Enhancing model checking in verification by AI techniques. Artif. Intell. **112**(1), 57–104 (1999)
9. Cleve, H., Zeller, A.: Locating causes of program failures, p. 342. ACM Press (2005)
10. Groce, A., Visser, W.: What went wrong: explaining counterexamples. In: Ball, T., Rajamani, S.K. (eds.) SPIN 2003. LNCS, vol. 2648, pp. 121–136. Springer, Heidelberg (2003). doi:10.1007/3-540-44829-2_8

11. Gromov, M., Willemse, T.A.C.: Testing and model-checking techniques for diagnosis. In: Petrenko, A., Veanes, M., Tretmans, J., Grieskamp, W. (eds.) FATES/TestCom -2007. LNCS, vol. 4581, pp. 138–154. Springer, Heidelberg (2007). doi:10.1007/978-3-540-73066-8_10

12. Hamou-Lhadj, A., Lethbridge, T.C.: A survey of trace exploration tools and techniques. In: CASCON 2004, pp. 42–55. IBM Press (2004)

13. Holzmann, G.J.: The theory and practice of a formal method: NewCoRe. In: IFIP Congress (1), pp. 35–44 (1994)

14. Leilde, V., Ribaud, V., Dhaussy, P.: An organizing system to perform and enable verification and diagnosis activities. In: Yin, H., Gao, Y., Li, B., Zhang, D., Yang, M., Li, Y., Klawonn, F., Tallón-Ballesteros, A.J. (eds.) IDEAL 2016. LNCS, vol. 9937, pp. 576–587. Springer, Cham (2016). doi:10.1007/978-3-319-46257-8_62

15. Liu, Y., Xu, C., Cheung, S.: AFChecker: effective model checking for context-aware adaptive applications. J. Syst. Softw. **86**(3), 854–867 (2013)

16. Mackie, J.L.: The Cement of the Universe: A study of causation. Clarendon Library of Logic and Philosophy, 5. dr. edn. Clarendon Press, Oxford (1990). oCLC: 258760915

17. Pothier, G., Tanter, É., Piquer, J.: Scalable omniscient debugging. ACM SIGPLAN Not. **42**(10), 535–552 (2007)

18. Reiter, R.: A theory of diagnosis from first principles. Artif. Intell. **32**, 57–95 (1987)

19. Ruys, T.C., Brinksma, E.: Managing the verification trajectory. Int. J. Softw. Tools Technol. Transf. (STTT) **4**(2), 246–259 (2003)

20. Venkatasubramanian, V., Rengaswamy, R., Kavuri, S.N.: A review of process fault detection and diagnosis. Comput. Chem. Eng. **27**(3), 293–311 (2003)

21. Visser, W., Havelund, K., Brat, G., Park, S., Lerda, F.: Model checking programs. Autom. Softw. Eng. **10**(2), 203–232 (2003)

22. Wotawa, F., Rodriguez-Roda, I., Comas, J.: Abductive reasoning in environmental decision support systems. In: AIAI workshops, pp. 270–279. Citeseer (2009)

Design of Embedded Systems with Complex Task Dependencies and Shared Resource Interference (Short Paper)

Fotios Gioulekas[1,5P], Peter Poplavko[2], Rany Kahil[2], Panagiotis Katsaros[1,4(✉)],
Marius Bozga[2], Saddek Bensalem[2], and Pedro Palomo[3]

[1] Information Technology Institute, CERTH, Thessaloniki, Greece
gioulekas@teemail.gr
[2] Universite Joseph Fourier - Verimag, Grenoble, France
{petro.poplavko,rany.kahil,marius.bozga,saddek.bensalem}@imag.fr
[3] Deimos-Space S.L.U, Madrid, Spain
pedro.palomo@deimos-space.com
[4] Aristotle University of Thessaloniki, Thessaloniki, Greece
katsaros@csd.auth.gr
[5] University General Hospital of Larissa, Larissa, Greece

Abstract. Languages for embedded systems ensure predictable timing behavior by specifying constraints based on either data streaming or reactive control models of computation. Moreover, various toolsets facilitate the incremental integration of application functionalities and the system design by evolutionary refinement and model-based code generation. Modern embedded systems involve various sources of interference in shared resources (e.g. multicores) and advanced real-time constraints, such as mixed-criticality levels. A sufficiently expressive modeling approach for complex dependency patterns between real-time tasks is needed along with a formal analysis of models for runtime resource managers with timing constraints. Our approach utilizes a model of computation, called Fixed-Priority Process Networks, which ensures functional determinism by unifying streaming and reactive control within a timed automata framework. The tool flow extends the open source TASTE tool-suite with model transformations to the BIP language and code generation tools. We outline the use of our flow on the design of a spacecraft on-board application running on a quad-core LEON4FT processor.

Keywords: Model-based design · Embedded systems · Model of computation · Code generation · Multicores

---

This work was supported by ESA under contract No. 4000111814/14/NL/MH. This is a short paper accepted in the new ideas and work-in-progress section of SEFM 2017.

A. Cimatti and M. Sirjani (Eds.): SEFM 2017, LNCS 10469, pp. 401–407, 2017.
DOI: 10.1007/978-3-319-66197-1_28

1   Introduction

The model-based design philosophy for embedded systems is grounded on the evolutionary design using models [4], which support the analysis, the gradual refinement and the setting of real-time attributes that ensure predictable timing behavior. For being able to analyze the models, they are specified with languages based on formal models of computation [1], which allow the synthesis and the optimization of behavior into an implementation solution. Such models provide syntax for describing dependencies between the runtime entities of a design and rules for computation of the behavior, given the syntax. The well-known streaming models of computation are suitable for describing complicated data transfer functions, whereas the reactive control models used in synchronous languages are suitable for complex control dependencies, which are compiled to sequential code as tasks, and classical schedulability methods can then be applied.

However, in modern embedded systems the task dependencies are further complicated, due to various sources of interference in shared software and hardware resources (e.g. buses, DMAs, I/Os in multicores) and additional constraints, such as mixed-criticality levels, dynamic voltage and frequency scaling. Thus, the design should ensure predictable timing behavior, while allowing adaptation to unexpected overload cases by dynamically reallocating resources.

To this end, we present a rigorous design approach that integrates a recently introduced model of computation, the Fixed Priority Process Networks (FPPNs) [3], with the TASTE toolset [5] and a timed automata analysis framework with "resource managers" [6], i.e. software functions that monitor utilization of compute resources and adapt the schedule in cases of shortage [2]. The FPPN model of computation combines the expressiveness of streaming and reactive control, retains the efficiency potential of parallel processing and ensures functional determinism, i.e. the program's outputs are neither dependent on the tasks' execution times, nor on their scheduling. TASTE is an open source toolset based on a system-level architecture description language, the AADL. It supports the incremental model-based integration (through ASN.1) of application functionalities using various languages (C/C++, SDL, VHDL, Ada, Python) and tools (SCADA, Simulink). We utilized TASTE's extensibility support towards enabling the design of FPPN programs. Moreover, a model transformation was implemented to a timed automata modeling framework in BIP, a language with formal operational semantics and code generation tools, for execution engines ported to various embedded platforms. Our approach allows scheduling the program's tasks, while taking into account their dependencies and the various sources of interference, through explicit interference models and resource managers. A resource manager is an integral part of an online scheduler that implements a customized online scheduling policy.

We present the scheduling of a Guidance, Navigation and Control (GNC) application on the quad-core LEON4FT in ESA's Next Generation Microprocessor platform (NGMP) [7]. Section 2 summarizes background knowledge on the FPPN model of computation. Section 3 introduces the TASTE toolset extensions to support FPPNs, the TASTE2BIP model transformations and task graph extraction, which enable the application's scheduling based on appropriate interference models. Section 4 presents the scheduling of the GNC application and the paper concludes with an overview of the exposed contributions.

2   Fixed Priority Process Networks

The FPPN [3] extends the reactive control models of computation by introducing synchronization and pipelined execution for a set of processes (tasks), which communicate data through channels. It allows the specification of time dependent, yet deterministic, behavior and real time task properties (sporadic or periodic activations with deadlines), and can be scheduled on single or multiple processors with or without priorities. The determinism is ensured by a *functional priority* relation between the tasks that are executed in an order, which is determined first by the task release times, i.e. when the tasks are invoked, and secondly by the task priorities.

An FPPN consists of *processes*, *data channels* and *event generators*. The processes represent subroutines with *functional code* featuring internal variables and ports connected to their input/output channels. A subroutine invocation is defined as a job with bounded execution time, which is subject to worst-case execution time (WCET) analysis. Every process is associated with an event generator, which can be either periodic or sporadic. The data channels support non-blocking read and write operations, which means that reading from an empty channel does not block the reader. The returned data value is accompanied by a validity flag, i.e. a boolean indicator of whether the data is valid. There are inter-process and external (environment) channels of two possible types, FIFO or blackboard. The blackboard remembers the last written value, which can be read multiple times.

Every process p has a deadline d_p. An event generator's sequence of timestamps τ_k determines when the kth job of process p is "activated". The periodic processes are activated with period T_p, whereas for sporadic processes T_p denotes the minimum inter-arrival time. Each job's execution has to be completed by $D_k = \tau_k + d_p$. We assume that all simultaneous process activations are signaled synchronously and we consider two variants of FPPN semantics. According to the *zero-delay* semantics the processes' execution takes zero time and since all deadlines can be met without exploiting parallelism, we assume for simplicity that it takes place sequentially. The deterministic ordering of non-blocking accesses to the shared variables between the processes is ensured by a set of rules detailed in [3]. The zero-delay semantics allows the functional simulation of the FPPN through its sequential execution. The real time semantics defines how the FPPN is executed on embedded platforms, which is a relaxed version of the zero-delay semantics, since it allows jobs to have any execution time, as well as to start concurrently at any time after their invocation.

For certain subclasses of FPPNs it is possible to statically derive a *task graph*, which then serves as input to a scheduling algorithm. A task graph is a directed acyclic graph $TG(J, \mathcal{E})$ with nodes representing jobs $J = \{J_i\}$ and edges $\mathcal{E}$ that are called *precedence edges*, which constrain the job execution order. A job is characterized by a tuple $J_i = (p_i, k_i, A_i, D_i, C_i)$ where p_i is the process to which the job belongs, k_i is the job's invocation count, $A_i \in Q_{\geq 0}$ is the arrival time, $D_i \in Q_+$ is the required time (absolute deadline) and $C_i \in Q_+$ is the WCET.

3   Design and Scheduling for FPPNs in TASTE

Figure 1 delineates our model based design flow that integrates FPPNs within TASTE [5], along with a timed automata modeling framework in BIP [3] (parts in grey color depict our contribution) and its associated scheduling and code generation tools. The latter ensure predictable timing behavior, when executing the application on a multithreaded BIP Runtime Environment (BIB RTE). Specifically, a representation of the software is provided through the TASTE front-end tools (Interface View, Data View, Deployment View), which were amended to capture FPPN-compliant models. The TASTE functions can be assigned attributes that characterize the FPPN node (e.g. blackboard, periodic process). Each process is associated with a unique integer (larger numbers imply lower priorities) and a criticality level (only HI and LO are supported), for scheduling the application with multiple criticality levels [6]. Additionally, functional C/C++ code primitives are inserted in TASTE including also ASN.1 based data types.

The next step is the TASTE2BIP model transformation, where (i) the TASTE FPPN is transformed to a BIP FPPN model and (ii) the TASTE attributes are used to generate the task graph through graph rewriting. At this stage, we take into account the interference on shared software and hardware resources, which invalidates the canonical WCET and schedulability analysis,

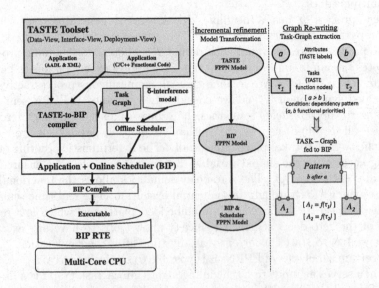

Fig. 1. Model-based design and tool flow for FPPNs in TASTE.

due to a feedback influence. This step involves the design of an interference model, as detailed in [6]. The schedule obtained from the static scheduler together with the interference model are then translated into parameters of the online-scheduler model in BIP. The joint application and scheduler representation is compiled into an executable, which is linked with the resource manager BIP RTE and executed on the target platform on top of the real time operating system.

4 Case-Study: Guidance Navigation Control Application

The described approach was applied on the design and scheduling of a GNC application ported onto ESA's NGMP with the aim to utilize multiple cores of the quad-core LEON4FT processor [7]. The main objective of a GNC application is to affect the movement of the vehicle and provide the corresponding sensor and controller with the necessary data. It comprises the Guidance Navigation Task (Functional Priority = 4, Period = 500 ms, Deadline = 500 ms, WCET = 22 ms), the Control Output Task (Functional Priority = 3, Period = 50 ms, Deadline = 50 ms, WCET = 3 ms) that sends the outputs to the appropriate spacecraft unit, the Control FM Task (Functional Priority = 2, Period = 50 ms, Deadline = 50 ms, WCET = 8 ms) which runs the control and flight management algorithms, and the Data Input Dispatcher Task (Functional Priority = 1, Period = 50 ms, Deadline = 50 ms, WCET = 6 ms), which reads, decodes and dispatches data to the right destination whenever new data from the spacecraft's sensors are available.

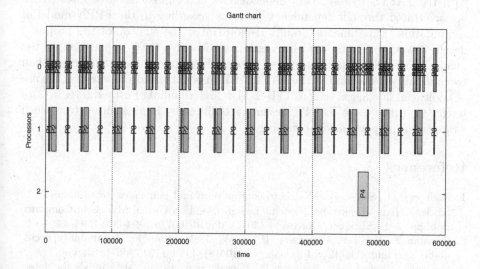

Fig. 2. Execution of the GNC application on LEON4FT (in microseconds).

The TASTE2BIP tool transformed the TASTE Interface View models (XML and C language) to an equivalent FPPN BIP model. The calculated hyper-period (least common multiple of periods) was $H = 500$ ms. The Guidance Navigation and Control Output Tasks start with time offsets 450 ms and 30 ms, respectively. This information was inserted into the BIP model by manually modifying the default design flow script. The task graph data was then passed to the BIP offline scheduler tool, which estimated the load (utilization) to be 112% (thus requiring two compute cores) and provided the time-triggered scheduling tables. This computation took into account the interference of the BIP engine and the precedence constraints. The last step was to compile the BIP model, to link it with the BIP RTE and to execute it on the quad-core LEON4FT processor. The executables were subsequently loaded and executed on the LEON4FT board. Figure 2 depicts the execution of the GNC model on the NGMP, within a time frame equal to the hyper-period of 500 ms plus another 50 ms. The GNC application utilizes one core for the resource manager P20 (BIP RTE and BIP controllers) and two computing cores for the application's tasks. Process P1 corresponds to the Data Input Dispatcher Task, P2 to the Control FM Task, P3 to the Control Output Task and P4 to the Guidance Navigation Task. Minor time shifts to the jobs execution time are noticed and this is due to the P20 overhead. However, runtime overhead is present in every execution environment.

5   Conclusion

A rigorous model-based design flow was introduced for embedded systems with complex task dependencies and shared resource interference, which is integrated with the TASTE toolset. Task dependencies and shared resource interference are arbitrated through dependency patterns according to the FPPN model of computation. Experimental results demonstrated the efficacy of the proposed design flow through the modeling and execution of a GNC application on the quad-core LEON4FT processor. As future work, we intend to support more than two criticality levels, and at the TASTE2BIP model transformation level the use of additional languages such as ITU-T SDL and Simulink. Furthermore, we also intend to utilize more TASTE design capabilities by implementing test-bench wrappers using python test-benching.

References

1. Radojevic, I., Salcic, Z.: Models of computation and languages. In: Radojevic, I., Salcic, Z. (eds.) Embedded Systems Design Based on Formal Models of Computation, pp. 7–41. Springer, Dordrecht (2011). doi:10.1007/978-94-007-1594-3_2
2. Fersman, E., Krcal, P., Pettersson, P., Yi, W.: Task automata: schedulability, decidability and undecidability. Inf. Comput. **205**(8), 1149–1172 (2007). Elsevier
3. Poplavko, P., Socci, D., Bourgos, P., Bensalem, S., Bozga, M.: Models for deterministic execution of real-time multiprocessor applications. In: Design, Automation and Test in Europe Conference and Exhibition, DATE 2015, Grenoble, France, pp. 1665–1670 (2015)

4. Hugues, J., Zalila, B., Pautet, L., Kordon, F.: From the prototype to the final embedded system using the ocarina AADL tool suite. ACM Trans. Embed. Comput. Syst. **7**(4), 42:1–42:25 (2008)
5. Perrotin, M., Conquet, E., Delange, J., Schiele, A., Tsiodras, T.: TASTE: a real-time software engineering tool-chain overview, status, and future. In: Ober, I., Ober, I. (eds.) SDL 2011. LNCS, vol. 7083, pp. 26–37. Springer, Heidelberg (2011). doi:10. 1007/978-3-642-25264-8_4
6. Poplavko, P., Kahil, R., Socci, D., Bensalem, S., Bozga, M.: Mixed-critical systems design with coarse-grained multi-core interference. In: Margaria, T., Steffen, B. (eds.) ISoLA 2016. LNCS, vol. 9952, pp. 605–621. Springer, Cham (2016). doi:10. 1007/978-3-319-47166-2_42
7. GR-CPCI-LEON4-N2X: Quad-Core LEON4 Next Generation Microprocessor Evaluation Board. http://www.gaisler.com/index.php/products/boards/gr-cpci-leon4-n2x

Author Index

Printed in the United States
By Bookmasters